AWARDS AND RECOGNITION FOR *BONHOEFFER*
PASTOR, MARTYR, PROPHET, SPY

The Canterbury Medal by the Becket Fund for Religious Liberty

The Christopher Award

Kirkus Reviews—Top 25 Non-Fiction Books of the Year

Kirkus Reviews—Pleasant Surprise of the Year

Barnes & Noble—Top 10 Non-Fiction Books of the Year

Evangelical Christian Publishing Association's
2011 Christian Book of the Year

Evangelical Christian Publishing Association's
2011 Non-Fiction Book of the Year

Preaching Today—Feeding
the Preacher's Soul Book of the Year Award

John Pollock Award for Christian Biography

Relevant—Top 10 Books of the Year

Townhall.com—Top 10 Gifts for Men

Christian Retailing—2011 Readers Choice Award

PRAISE FOR *BONHOEFFER*
PASTOR, MARTYR, PROPHET, SPY

"This is an important book and I hope many people will read it."
—PRESIDENT GEORGE W. BUSH

"Eric Metaxas has created a biography of uncommon power—intelligent, moving, well researched, vividly written, and rich in implication for our own lives. Or to put it another way: Buy this book. Read it. Then buy another copy and give it to a person you love. It's that good. . . . Eric Metaxas has written the kind of extraordinary book that not only brings Dietrich Bonhoeffer, his times and his witness vividly alive, but also leaves us yearning to find the same moral character in ourselves. No biographer can achieve anything higher."
—ARCHBISHOP CHARLES CHAPUT, *FIRST THINGS*

"[A] beautifully constructed biography. . . . Throughout his book, but especially toward the end, Metaxas turns this erudite and at times abstruse theologian into a living and tragic human being."
—ALAN WOLFE, *THE NEW REPUBLIC*

"Eric Metaxas clears up many misconceptions, giving priority to Bonhoeffer's own words and actions, in a massive and masterful new biography, *Bonhoeffer: Pastor, Martyr, Prophet, Spy*. During a harrowing time when many churches adopted Nazi ideology and others buckled under government pressure, Bonhoeffer stood strong, if sometimes alone. Metaxas presents Bonhoeffer as a clear-headed, deeply convicted Christian who submitted to no one and nothing except God and his Word."
—CHRISTIANITY TODAY

"In *Bonhoeffer: Pastor, Martyr, Prophet, Spy*, Eric Metaxas tells Bonhoeffer's story with passion and theological sophistication, often challenging revisionist accounts that make Bonhoeffer out to be a 'humanist' or ethicist for whom religious doctrine was easily disposable. . . . His was a radical obedience to God, a frame of mind widely viewed today with fear and loathing, even among the faithful. In *Bonhoeffer*, Mr. Metaxas reminds us that there are forms of religion—respectable, domesticated, timid—that may end up doing the devil's work for him."
—WALL STREET JOURNAL

"In the finest treatment of the man since Eberhard Bethge's *Dietrich Bonhoeffer: Man of Vision, Man of Courage* (1970), Metaxas presents a complete, accessible picture of this important figure, whose story is inspiring, instructive and international in scope. Metaxas . . . bring[s] Bonhoeffer and other characters to vivid life. A definitive Bonhoeffer biography for the 21st century."
—KIRKUS REVIEWS

"[U]ntil now, American readers have lacked an account of Bonhoeffer's life that is both thorough *and* engagingly readable, a book that captures the full sweep of his remarkable story and highlights its meaning for us today. In *Bonhoeffer: Pastor, Martyr, Prophet, Spy*, Eric Metaxas has given us just such a book. . . . [T]his new biography is a welcome and significant contribution. Metaxas keeps a firm grasp on the scholarly consensus while holding the reader's attention from the first page to the last, and his book will serve as a gateway for many people to a much fuller understanding of Bonhoeffer."

—BOOKS & CULTURE

"In this weighty, riveting analysis of the life of Dietrich Bonhoeffer, Metaxas . . . offers a comprehensive review of one of history's darkest eras, along with a fascinating exploration of the familial, cultural, and religious influences that formed one of the world's greatest contemporary theologians. A passionate narrative voice combines with meticulous research to unpack the confluence of circumstances and personalities that led Germany from the defeat of WWI to the atrocities of WWII. . . . Insightful and illuminating, this tome makes a powerful contribution to biography, history and theology."

—PUBLISHER'S WEEKLY

"For anyone whose faith has been strengthened by the life and witness of Dietrich Bonhoeffer, this is the biography you have always wanted. Eric Metaxas has written a rich, detailed, and beautiful account of the great pastor and theologian who gave us *The Cost of Discipleship* and sacrificed his life for opposing Hitler. Metaxas' Bonhoeffer is a monumental achievement and a deeply important work."

—GREG THORNBURY, PH.D., DEAN, SCHOOL OF CHRISTIAN STUDIES AT UNION UNIVERSITY

"Dietrich Bonhoeffer's great gift is that his understanding of faith in times of conflict speaks to generation after generation. Eric Metaxas' *Bonhoeffer* is the biography for this generation—a masterpiece that reads like a great novel and weaves together in one opus an understanding of Bonhoeffer's theology, the complex and tragic history of twentieth-century Germany, and the human struggle of a true Christian hero. Eric Metaxas is claiming his place as the preeminent biographer of Christianity's most courageous figures."

—MARTIN DOBLMEIER, FILMMAKER, BONHOEFFER

"With great skill, energy, and warmth, Eric Metaxas reminds us why the life of Dietrich Bonhoeffer stands as a rebuke both to believers and skeptics. Rarely has the story of a Christian martyr been told with such realism and depth. It's a gem of a book."

—JOSEPH LOCONTE, LECTURER IN POLITICS, THE KING'S COLLEGE, NEW YORK CITY;
EDITOR, THE END OF ILLUSIONS: RELIGIOUS LEADERS CONFRONT HITLER'S GATHERING STORM

"Moving, comprehensive, and engaging . . . Metaxas tells a compelling story . . . Recommended."

—LIBRARY JOURNAL

"The first major biography of Bonhoeffer in more than 40 years, bringing together newly available documents and a fresh outlook into the many facets of Bonhoeffer's life. Both theologian and spy, Bonhoeffer's life is brilliantly documented and aspects of his faith in the light of great struggle are examined. An invigorating and informative book, Eric Metaxas writes an incredible biography of a massively influential character that is sure to impress and enlighten readers."

—THE CHURCH OF ENGLAND NEWSPAPER

"Metaxas examines the life of a man caught in a heart-rending dilemma: stand up to the Nazis and Hitler himself, necessitating deceit and complicity in an assassination; or remain silent, allowing the murder of thousands. . . . Christians interested in Bonhoeffer's theology will find it illuminated in the fuller context of his life. Believers seeking inspiration for living a bold life of faith will receive it in abundance. Readers fascinated with this era in history will discover revealing glimpses behind the scenes of the anti-Hitler movement. . . . [H]istorians will find this a solid academic work."

—DIANE GARDNER, FOREWORD REVIEWS

"A stunning achievement recounting Bonhoeffer's life with lucidity, historical detail, and a concretely contextualized handling of [his] often misunderstood theological legacy. . . . Metaxas masterfully distills Bonhoeffer's eventful and complex life into a true narrative biography that is comprehensive and vivid without being overwhelming."

—CHRISTIANBOOK.COM

"Dietrich Bonhoeffer has at last found the writer he deserves. Eric Metaxas has written a book that adds a new dimension to World War II, a new understanding of how evil can seize the soul of a nation and a man of faith can confront it— and transform defeat into victory, lies into transcendent truth. No one who cares about the history of the modern world can afford to ignore this book."

—THOMAS FLEMING, AUTHOR, THE NEW DEALERS' WAR: FDR AND THE WAR WITHIN WORLD WAR II

"A powerful story beautifully told about a man who didn't just write about the cost of discipleship but lived it. Deeply moving."

—MEROLD WESTPHAL, PH.D., DISTINGUISHED PROFESS OR OF PHILOSOPHY, FORDHAM UNIVERSITY

"Clearly the definitive work [on Bonhoeffer] . . . One of the great biographies I've ever read."

—CHARLES COLSON, FOUNDER, PRISON FELLOWSHIP; FOUNDER AND CHAIRMAN, THE WILBERFORCE FORUM

"[D]efinitive and incredibly detailed . . . a powerful, powerful book . . . Highly recommended!"

—MIKE HUCKABEE, THE HUCKABEE REPORT

"One of the finest and most moving biographies I have ever read. Eric Metaxas responds to a great life with a great book."

—CAL THOMAS, AMERICA'S NO. 1 NATIONALLY SYNDICATED COLUMNIST

"Riveting. . . ."

—JOHN ORTBERG JR., SENIOR PASTOR, MENLO PARK PRESBYTERIAN CHURCH

"[M]onumental, authoritative, humbling and inspirational . . . "

—KATHERINE JEAN LOPEZ, *NATIONAL REVIEW ONLINE*

"Crammed with insight, outrage, and urgency, this book positions Bonhoeffer where he belongs, in the ranks of the great Christian humanists who have struggled against the prevailing winds of culture to faithfully and bravely interpret Christianity for their historical moment.

"This is also a deeply humanizing book, full of vignettes that reveal Bonhoeffer as a son, as a lover, a pastor, a friend, all in the context of the deadly work for which he is most remembered: resistance to the growing menace of Nazism."

—CALEB J. D. MASKELL, ASSOCIATE DIRECTOR, JONATHAN EDWARDS CENTER, YALE UNIVERSITY (2004-2007); DEPARTMENT OF RELIGION, PRINCETON UNIVERSITY

"As in his previous biography, *Amazing Grace: William Wilberforce and the Heroic Campaign to End Slavery*, Metaxas in *Bonhoeffer* brings to life the extraordinary and selfless accomplishments of a true hero. Metaxas has the rare skill of taking the mundane but crucial details of life and weaving them into a history that flows like a novel. For anyone interested in what the strength of belief and conviction can accomplish, *Bonhoeffer* is an essential read.

—GERALD SCHROEDER, PH.D., ISRAELI PHYSICIST AND TEACHER AT THE AISH HA TORAH COLLEGE OF JEWISH STUDIES IN JERUSALEM; AUTHOR, *GENESIS AND THE BIG BANG* AND *THE SCIENCE OF GOD*.

"A captivating and inspiring read from start to finish. Sets the record straight on Bonhoeffer's commitment to Scripture and his unyielding passion for truth that led him to give up his life in the battle to save the Jews of Europe. Buy it. This book could change your life."

—JAMES N. LANE, FOUNDER, NEW CANAAN SOCIETY; FORMER GENERAL PARTNER, GOLDMAN, SACHS & CO.

"Eric Metaxas has delivered a masterwork of compelling literary and historical proportions. This extraordinary biography exposes the formative impressions in Bonhoeffer's life that reveal him as a gifted, complex, humanely sensitive twentieth-century figure responding to the call of God and his unfolding spiritual understanding of his times. This book begs to be read and discussed widely today."

—GORDON RIDDLE PENNINGTON, CEO, BURNING MEDIA GROUP

"Metaxas' *Bonhoeffer* will be regarded as one of the best books of the year. There are a few books that, years after I have read them, I realize have had a great influence on me. This is sure to be one of them. You can't go wrong with this book; I give it my highest recommendation."

—WhileWeSojourn.com

"Get this book if you can!"

—NewsDissector.org

"Metaxas is a graceful writer with a sure grasp of his subject matter."

—The Internet Review of Books

"Metaxas's *Bonhoeffer: Pastor, Martyr, Prophet, Spy* is a modern-day classic that should be on 'best of' lists for the decade. . . ."

—Relevant

"[A]n electrifying account of one man's stand against tyranny."

—Human Events

"Who is Dietrich Bonhoeffer? He's a guy that you should know. This is a book that you should read."

—Glenn Beck

"If ever there was an "Evil Empire" it was Hitler's Germany. If ever there were a reluctant hero it was Dietrich Bonhoeffer. Eric Metaxas has written a splendid biography in a gripping story of a man who took God seriously."

—Haddon Robinson, Harold John Ockenga Professor of Preaching, Gordon-Conwell Theological Seminary

"As a faithful, reformist Muslim, I'm inspired by Dietrich Bonhoeffer. Now more than ever. This is a gloriously humanizing biography of a hero for people of conscience—in all faiths, for all times."

—Prof. Irshad Manji, Director of the Moral Courage Project, New York University

BONHOEFFER

BONHOEFFER

PASTOR, MARTYR, PROPHET, SPY

A RIGHTEOUS GENTILE VS. THE THIRD REICH

ERIC METAXAS

THOMAS NELSON
Since 1798

NASHVILLE   DALLAS   MEXICO CITY   RIO DE JANEIRO

Published in Nashville, Tennessee, by Thomas Nelson. Thomas Nelson is a registered trademark of Thomas Nelson, Inc.

Thomas Nelson, Inc., titles may be purchased in bulk for educational, business, fund-raising, or sales promotional use. For information, please e-mail SpecialMarkets@ThomasNelson.com.

Unless otherwise noted, Scripture quotations are taken from THE KING JAMES VERSION.

Scripture quotations marked NIV are from HOLY BIBLE: NEW INTERNATIONAL VERSION®. © 1973, 1978, 1984 by International Bible Society. Used by permission of Zondervan Publishing House. All rights reserved.

Scripture quotations marked NKJV are from THE NEW KING JAMES VERSION. © 1982 by Thomas Nelson, Inc. Used by permission. All rights reserved.

Scripture quotations marked ESV are from the ENGLISH STANDARD VERSION. © 2001 by Crossway Bibles, a division of Good News Publishers.

Scripture quotations marked RSV are from REVISED STANDARD VERSION of the Bible. © 1946, 1952, 1971, 1973 by the Division of Christian Education of the National Council of the Churches of Christ in the U.S.A. Used by permission.

Library of Congress Control Number: 2010922204

ISBN: 978-1-59555-138-2
ISBN: 978-1-59555-318-8 (IE)
ISBN: 978-1-59555-246-4 (TP)

2010922204

Printed in the United States of America
16 RRD 18

Zum Andenken an meinen Großvater
Erich Kraegen (1912 – 1944)
"Denn das ist der Wille des, der mich gesandt hat, daß,
wer den Sohn sieht und glaubt an ihn, habe das ewige Leben;
und ich werde ihn auferwecken am Jüngsten Tage."

CONTENTS

Foreword xv

Prologue 1

CHAPTER 1: Family and Childhood 5

CHAPTER 2: Tübingen, 1923 41

CHAPTER 3: Roman Holiday, 1924 49

CHAPTER 4: Student in Berlin, 1924–27 58

CHAPTER 5: Barcelona, 1928 69

CHAPTER 6: Berlin, 1929 88

CHAPTER 7: Bonhoeffer in America, 1930–31 99

CHAPTER 8: Berlin, 1931–32 119

CHAPTER 9: The Führer Principle, 1933 138

CHAPTER 10: The Church and the Jewish Question 150

CHAPTER 11: Nazi Theology 165

CHAPTER 12: The Church Struggle Begins 176

CHAPTER 13: The Bethel Confession 183

CHAPTER 14: Bonhoeffer in London, 1934–35 195

CHAPTER 15: The Church Battle Heats Up 204

CHAPTER 16: The Conference at Fanø 234

CHAPTER 17: The Road to Zingst and Finkenwalde 246

CHAPTER 18: Zingst and Finkenwalde 261

CHAPTER 19: Scylla and Charybdis, 1935–36 278

CHAPTER 20: Mars Ascending, 1938 302

CHAPTER 21: The Great Decision, 1939 321

CHAPTER 22: The End of Germany 347

CHAPTER 23: From Confession to Conspiracy 358

CHAPTER 24: Plotting Against Hitler 380

CHAPTER 25: Bonhoeffer Scores a Victory 394

CHAPTER 26: Bonhoeffer in Love 405

CHAPTER 27: Killing Adolf Hitler 423

CHAPTER 28: Cell 92 at Tegel Prison 432

CHAPTER 29: Valkyrie and the Stauffenberg Plot 475

CHAPTER 30: Buchenwald 504

CHAPTER 31: On the Road to Freedom 517

Notes 545

Bibliography 567

Epilogue and Errata 571

About the Author 573

Acknowledgments 577

Index 579

Reading Group Guide 593

FOREWORD

I'm delighted that my friend Eric Metaxas has penned this volume on Dietrich Bonhoeffer. The English-speaking public needs to know far more than it does about his thought as well as his life. When I became a Christian in college, Bonhoeffer's *Cost of Discipleship* was one of the first books I read, followed not long after by his *Life Together*. Though this second book is perhaps the finest single volume I have ever read on the character of Christian community, it was the first book that set me on a lifelong journey to understand the meaning of grace.

It is impossible to understand Bonhoeffer's *Nachfolge* without becoming acquainted with the shocking capitulation of the German church to Hitler in the 1930s. How could the "church of Luther," that great teacher of the gospel, have ever come to such a place? The answer is that the true gospel, summed up by Bonhoeffer as *costly grace*, had been lost. On the one hand, the church had become marked by formalism. That meant going to church and hearing that God just loves and forgives everyone, so it doesn't really matter much how you live. Bonhoeffer called this *cheap* grace. On the other hand, there was legalism, or salvation by law and good works. Legalism meant that God loves you because you have pulled yourself together and are trying to live a good, disciplined life.

Both of these impulses made it possible for Hitler to come to power. The formalists in Germany may have seen things that bothered them, but saw no need to sacrifice their safety to stand up to them. Legalists responded by having pharisaical attitudes toward other nations and races that approved of Hitler's policies. But as one, Germany lost hold of the brilliant balance of the gospel that Luther so persistently expounded—"We are saved by faith alone, but not by faith which is alone." That is, we are saved, not by anything we do, but by grace. Yet if we have truly understood and believed the gospel, it will *change* what we do and how we live.

By the time of Hitler's ascension, much of the German church understood grace only as abstract acceptance—"God forgives; that's his job." But we know that true grace comes to us by costly sacrifice. And if God was willing to go to the cross and endure such pain and absorb such a cost in order to save us, then *we* must live sacrificially as we serve others. Anyone who truly understands how God's grace comes to us will have a changed life. That's the gospel, not salvation by law, or by cheap grace, but by costly grace. Costly grace changes you from the inside out. Neither law nor cheap grace can do that.

This lapse couldn't happen to us, today, surely, could it? Certainly it could. We still have a lot of legalism and moralism in our churches. In reaction to that, many Christians want to talk only about God's love and acceptance. They don't like talking about Jesus' death on the cross to satisfy divine wrath and justice. Some even call it "divine child abuse." Yet if they are not careful, they run the risk of falling into the belief in "cheap grace"—a noncostly love from a non-holy God who just loves and accepts us as we are. That will never change anyone's life.

So it looks like we still need to listen to Bonhoeffer and others who go deep in discussing the nature of the gospel.

Timothy J. Keller

New York Times best-selling author of *The Reason for God*

PROLOGUE

27 JULY 1945, LONDON

We are troubled on every side, yet not distressed; we are perplexed, but not in despair; persecuted, but not forsaken; cast down, but not destroyed; always bearing about in the body the dying of the Lord Jesus, that the life also of Jesus might be made manifest in our body. For we which live are always delivered unto death for Jesus' sake, that the life also of Jesus might be made manifest in our mortal flesh. So then death worketh in us, but life in you.

—2 CORINTHIANS 4:8–12

Peace had at last returned to Europe. Her familiar face—once evilly contorted and frightening—was again at rest, noble and fresh. What she had been through would take years to understand. It was as though she had undergone a terribly protracted exorcism, one that had extracted from her the last farthing. But in the very end, protesting with shrieks as they went, the legions of demons were driven out.

The war had been over for two months. The tyrant took his own life in a gray bunker beneath his shattered capital, and the Allies declared victory.

Slowly, slowly, life in Britain turned to the task of restoring itself. Then, as if on cue, summer arrived. It was the first summer of peace in six years. But as if to prove that the whole thing hadn't been a dream or a nightmare, there were constant fresh reminders of what had happened. And they were as awful as anything that had gone before. Often they were worse. In the early part of this summer, the ghastly news of the death camps emerged along with the unfathomable atrocities that the Nazis had visited upon their victims in the hellish outposts of their short-lived empire.

Rumors of such things circulated throughout the war, but now the reality was confirmed by photographs, newsreel footage, and eyewitness accounts from the soldiers who liberated the camps in April during the last days of the war. The depth of these horrors had not been known or imagined, and it was almost too much for the war-fatigued British public to absorb. Their hatred of the Germans was confirmed and reconfirmed afresh with every nauseating detail. The public reeled at the very evilness of the evil.

At the beginning of the war, it was possible to separate the Nazis from the Germans and recognize that not all Germans were Nazis. As the clash between the two nations wore on, and as more and more English fathers and sons and brothers died, distinguishing the difference became more difficult. Eventually the difference vanished altogether. Realizing he needed to fuel the British war effort, Prime Minister Winston Churchill fused the Germans and the Nazis into a single hated enemy, the better to defeat it swiftly and end the unrelenting nightmare.

When Germans working to defeat Hitler and the Nazis contacted Churchill and the British government, hoping for assistance to defeat their common enemy from the inside—hoping to tell the world that some Germans trapped inside the Reich felt much as they did—they were rebuffed. No one was interested in their overtures. It was too late. They couldn't participate in such evils and, when it was convenient, try to settle for a separate peace. For the purposes of the war effort, Churchill maintained the fiction that there were no good Germans. It would even be said that the only good German—if one needed to use the phrase—was a dead German. That lack of nuance was also part of the hellishness of war.

But now the war was over. And even as the full, unspeakable evil of the Third Reich was coming to light, the other side of things had to be seen too. Part of the restoration to peacetime thinking was the ability to again see beyond the blacks and whites of the war, to again discern nuance and shades, shadows and colors.

And so today in Holy Trinity Church—just off the Brompton Road in

London—a service was taking place that was incomprehensible to some. To many others it was distasteful and disturbing, especially to those who had lost loved ones during the war. The memorial service being held today on British soil and being broadcast on the BBC was for a German who had died three months earlier. The word of his demise so slowly staggered out of the war's fog and rubble that only recently had any of his friends and family learned of it. Most of them still knew nothing about it. But here in London were gathered those few who did.

In the pews were the man's thirty-nine-year-old twin sister, her half-Jewish husband, and their two girls. They had slipped out of Germany before the war, driving at night across the border into Switzerland. The dead man took part in arranging their illegal flight—although that was among the most negligible of his departures from National Socialist orthodoxy—and he helped establish them in London, where they settled.

The man counted among his friends a number of prominent persons, including George Bell, the bishop of Chichester. Bell arranged the service, for he had known and loved the man being honored. The bishop met him years before the war when the two were engaged in ecumenical efforts, trying to warn Europe against the designs of the Nazis, then trying to rescue Jews, and finally trying to bring news of the German resistance to the attention of the British government. Just hours before his execution in Flossenbürg concentration camp, the man directed his last words to this bishop. That Sunday he spoke them to a British officer, who was imprisoned with him, after he performed his last service and preached his last sermon. This officer was liberated and brought those last words and the news of the man's death across Europe with him.

Across the English Channel, across France, and across Germany, in the Charlottenburg district of Berlin, in a three-story house at 43 Marienburger Allee, an elderly couple sat by their radio. In her time the wife had given birth to eight children, four boys and four girls. The second son had been killed in the First War, and for a whole year his young mother had been unable to function. Twenty-seven years later, a second war would take two more boys from her. The husband was the most prominent psychiatrist in Germany. They had both opposed Hitler from the beginning and were proud of their sons and sons-in-law who had been involved in the conspiracy against him. They all knew the dangers. But when the war at last ended, news of their two sons was slow to arrive in Berlin. A month earlier they had finally heard of the death of their third son, Klaus. But about their youngest son, Dietrich, they had heard nothing. Someone claimed to have seen him alive. Then a neighbor told them that the BBC would the next day broadcast a memorial service in London. It was for Dietrich.

At the appointed hour, the old couple turned on their radio. Soon enough the service was announced for their son. That was how they came to know of his death.

As the couple took in the hard news that the good man who was their son was now dead, so too, many English took in the hard news that the dead man who was a German was good. Thus did the world again begin to reconcile itself to itself.

The man who died was engaged to be married. He was a pastor and a theologian. And he was executed for his role in the plot to assassinate Hitler.

This is his story.

CHAPTER 1

FAMILY AND CHILDHOOD

*The rich world of his ancestors set the standards for Dietrich
Bonhoeffer's own life. It gave him a certainty of judgment and
manner that cannot be acquired in a single generation. He grew up
in a family that believed the essence of learning lay not in a formal
education but in the deeply rooted obligation to be guardians of a
great historical heritage and intellectual tradition.*

—EBERHARD BETHGE

In the winter of 1896, before the aforementioned older couple had met,
they were invited to attend an "open evening" at the house of the physicist Oscar Meyer. "There," wrote Karl Bonhoeffer years later, "I met a
young, fair, blue-eyed girl whose bearing was so free and natural, and
whose expression was so open and confident, that as soon as she entered
the room she took me captive. This moment when I first laid eyes upon my
future wife remains in my memory with an almost mystical force."

Karl Bonhoeffer had come to Breslau—today Wroclaw in Poland—three
years earlier, to work as the assistant to Karl Wernicke, the internationally
renowned professor of psychiatry. Life consisted of working at the clinic and
socializing with a few friends from Tübingen, the charming university town
where he had grown up. But after that memorable winter evening, his life
would change dramatically: for one thing, he immediately began ice-skating
on the canals in the mornings, hoping to meet—and often meeting—the
captivating blue-eyed girl he had first beheld that evening. She was a teacher,

and her name was Paula von Hase. They married on March 5, 1898, three weeks shy of the groom's thirtieth birthday. The bride was twenty-two.

Both of them—doctor and teacher—came from fabulously illustrious backgrounds. Paula Bonhoeffer's parents and family were closely connected to the emperor's court at Potsdam. Her aunt Pauline became a lady-in-waiting to Crown Princess Victoria, wife of Frederick III. Her father, Karl Alfred von Hase, had been a military chaplain, and in 1889 he became chaplain to Kaiser Wilhelm II but resigned after criticizing the kaiser's description of the proletariat as a "pack of dogs."

Paula's grandfather, Karl August von Hase, loomed large in the family and had been a famous theologian in Jena, where he taught for sixty years and where his statue still stands today. He had been called to his post by Goethe himself—then a minister under the Duke of Weimar—and met privately with the eighty-year-old national treasure, who was composing his *Faust, Part Two*. Karl August's textbook on the history of dogma was still used by theological students in the twentieth century. Toward the end of his life, he was awarded a hereditary peerage by the Grand Duke of Weimar and a personal peerage by the king of Württemberg.

The maternal side of Paula's family included artists and musicians. Her mother, Clara von Hase, née Countess Kalkreuth (1851–1903), took piano lessons from Franz Liszt and Clara Schumann, wife of the composer. She bequeathed her love of music and singing to her daughter, and these would play a vital role in the Bonhoeffers' lives. Clara's father, Count Stanislaus Kalkreuth (1820–94), was a painter known for his large Alpine landscapes. Although from a family of military aristocrats and landed gentry, this count married into the Cauer family of sculptors and became director of the Grand Duke's School of Arts in Weimar. His son, Count Leopold Kalkreuth, improved upon his father's success as a painter; his works of poetical realism today hang in museums throughout Germany. The von Hases were also related to the socially and intellectually prominent Yorck von Wartenburgs, and they spent much time in their society. Count Hans Ludwig Yorck von Wartenburg* was a philosopher whose famous correspondence with Wilhelm Dilthey developed a hermeneutical philosophy of history, which influenced Martin Heidegger.

---

* His grandson Peter Yorck von Wartenburg (1904–44) was a cousin of Colonel Claus von Stauffenberg and played a key role in the July 20, 1944, assassination plot against Hitler.

The lineage of Karl Bonhoeffer was no less impressive. The family traced itself to 1403 in the annals of Nymwegen on the Waal River in the Netherlands, near the German border. In 1513, Caspar van den Boenhoff left the Netherlands to settle in the German city of Schwäbisch Hall. The family was afterward called Bonhöffer, retaining the umlaut until about 1800. *Bonhöffer* means "bean farmer," and the Bonhöffer coat of arms, still prominent on buildings around Schwäbisch Hall,* pictures a lion holding a beanstalk on a blue background. Eberhard Bethge tells us that Dietrich Bonhoeffer sometimes wore a signet ring bearing this family crest.

The Bonhoeffers were among the first families of Schwäbisch Hall for three centuries. The earliest generations were goldsmiths; later generations included doctors, pastors, judges, professors, and lawyers. Through the centuries, seventy-eight council members and three mayors in Schwäbisch Hall were Bonhöffers. Their importance and influence may also be seen in the *Michaelskirche* (St. Michael's Church), where Bonhöffers are marmoreally and otherwise memorialized in baroque and rococo sculptures and epitaphs. In 1797, Karl's grandfather, Sophonias Bonhöffer, was the last of the family born there. Napoleon's invasion in 1806 ended the free city status of Schwäbisch Hall and scattered the family, though it remained a shrine to which subsequent umlautless generations repaired. Karl Bonhoeffer's father took his son to the medieval town many times and schooled his son in the details of their patrician history, down to the "famous black oak staircase in the Bonhoeffer house in the Herrengasse" and the portrait of the "lovely Bonhoeffer woman" that hung in the church, with a copy in the Bonhoeffers' home during Dietrich's childhood. Karl Bonhoeffer did the same for his own sons.

Karl Bonhoeffer's father, Friedrich Ernst Philipp Tobias Bonhoeffer (1828–1907), was a high-ranking judiciary official throughout Württemberg, and he ended his career as president of the Provincial Court in Ulm. When he retired to Tübingen, the king awarded him a personal peerage. *His* father had been "a fine hearty parson, who drove about the district in his own carriage." Karl Bonhoeffer's mother, Julie Bonhoeffer, neé Tafel (1842–1936), came from a Swabian family that played a lead role in the democratic movement of the nineteenth century and was devotedly liberal. Of his mother's father, Karl Bonhoeffer later wrote, "My grandfather and his three brothers

---

* One may be seen on 7 Klosterstrasse there.

were plainly no average men. Each had his special trait, but common to them all was an idealistic streak, with a fearless readiness to act on their convictions." Two of them were temporarily banished from Württemberg for their democratic leanings, and in a telling coincidence, one of them, Karl's great-uncle Gottlob Tafel, was imprisoned in the Hohenasperg fortress. He was there at the same time as Dietrich's great-grandfather Karl August von Hase, who before embarking on his theological career went through a period of youthful political activity. These two forebears of Dietrich Bonhoeffer came to know each other during their mutual imprisonment. Karl Bonhoeffer's mother lived to be ninety-three, and had a close relationship with her grandson Dietrich, who spoke the eulogy at her funeral in 1936 and treasured her as a living link to the greatness of her generation.

The family trees of Karl and Paula Bonhoeffer are everywhere so laden with figures of accomplishment that one might expect future generations to be burdened by it all. But the welter of wonderfulness that was their heritage seems to have been a boon, one that buoyed them up so that each child seems not only to have stood on the shoulders of giants but also to have danced on them.

And so in 1898 these two extraordinary lines intermingled in the marriage of Karl and Paula Bonhoeffer, who brought eight children into the world within a decade. Their first two sons came into the world in the space of a year: Karl-Friedrich was born on January 13, 1899, and Walter—two months premature—on December 10. Their third son, Klaus, was born in 1901, followed by two daughters, Ursula in 1902 and Christine in 1903. On February 4, 1906, their fourth and youngest son, Dietrich, was born ten minutes before his twin sister, Sabine, and he teased her about this advantage throughout their lives. The twins were baptized by the kaiser's former chaplain, their grandfather Karl Alfred von Hase, who lived a seven-minute walk away. Susanne, the last child, was born in 1909.

All of the Bonhoeffer children were born in Breslau, where Karl Bonhoeffer held the chair in psychiatry and neurology at the university, and was director of the hospital for nervous diseases. On New Year's Eve the year Susanne was born, he wrote in his diary, "Despite having eight children—which seems an enormous number in times like these—we have the impression that there are not too many of them! The house is big, the children develop normally, we parents are not too old, and so we endeavor not to spoil them, and to make their young years enjoyable."

Their house—at 7 Birkenwäldchen—was near the clinic. It was a gigantic, rambling three-story affair with gabled roofs, numerous chimneys, a screened porch, and a large balcony overlooking the spacious garden where the children played. They dug caves and climbed trees and put up tents. There was much visiting between the Bonhoeffer children and Grandfather Hase, who lived across the river, a branch of the Oder. His wife died in 1903, after which his other daughter, Elisabeth, looked after him. She, too, became an important part of the children's lives.

Despite his busy schedule, Karl Bonhoeffer took much joy in his children. "In winter," he wrote, "we poured water on an old tennis court with an asphalt surface, so that the two oldest children could try skating for the first time. We had a big outbuilding meant to hold a carriage. We didn't have a carriage or horses, but we did use this outbuilding to keep all kinds of animals." There were animals in the house proper as well. One room in the house became a zoo for the children's pets, which included rabbits, guinea pigs, turtledoves, squirrels, lizards, and snakes, and a natural history museum for their collections of birds' eggs and mounted beetles and butterflies. The two eldest girls had another room set up as a dolls' house, and on the first floor the three eldest boys had a workshop, complete with carpenter's bench.

Their mother presided over the well-appointed home; the staff included a governess, a nursemaid, a housemaid, a parlor maid, and a cook. Upstairs was the schoolroom, with desks where Paula taught the children their lessons. It was somewhat shocking when Paula Bonhoeffer chose to take the teacher's examination as a single woman,* but as a married woman, she used what she learned to great effect. She was openly distrustful of the German public schools and their Prussian educational methods. She subscribed to the maxim that Germans had their backs broken twice, once at school and once in the military; she wasn't about to entrust her children to the care of others less sensitive than she during their earliest years. When they were a bit older, she sent them to the local public schools, where they invariably excelled. But until each was seven or eight, she was the sole educator.

---

* She received her diploma in April 1896 from the Royal Provincial School College in Breslau.

Paula Bonhoeffer had memorized an impressive repertoire of poems, hymns, and folk songs, which she taught her children, who remembered them into their old age. The children enjoyed dressing up and performing plays for each other and for the adults. There was also a family puppet theater, and every year on December 30—her birthday—Paula Bonhoeffer put on a performance of "Little Red Riding Hood." This continued into her old age, when she did it for her grandchildren. One of them, Renate Bethge, said, "She was the soul and spirit of the house."

In 1910 the Bonhoeffers decided to look for a place to spend their holidays and chose a remote idyll in the woods of the Glatz Mountains near the Bohemian border. It was a two-hour train ride south of Breslau. Karl Bonhoeffer described it as being "in a little valley at the foot of Mount Urnitz, right at the edge of the wood, with a meadow, a little brook, an old barn, and a fruit-tree which had a raised seat with a little bench for the children built into its wide branches." The name of this rustic paradise was Wolfesgründ. It was so far off the beaten track that the family never saw another soul, save for a single odd character: a "bigoted forestry official" who wandered through now and again. Bonhoeffer later memorialized him in a fictionalized account as the character *Gelbstiefel* (Yellow Boots).

We get our first glimpses of Dietrich during this time, when he was four and five years old. They come to us from his twin, Sabine:

> My first memories go back to 1910. I see Dietrich in his party frock, stroking with his small hand the blue silk underskirt; later I see him beside our grandfather, who is sitting by the window with our baby sister Susanne on his knee, while the afternoon sun pours in in the golden light. Here the outlines blur, and only one more scene will form in my mind: first games in the garden in 1911, Dietrich with a mass of ash-blond hair around his sunburnt face, hot from romping, driving away the midges and looking for a shady corner, and yet only obeying very unwillingly the nursemaid's call to come in, because the immensely energetic game is not yet finished. Heat and thirst were forgotten in the intensity of his play.

Dietrich was the only child to inherit his mother's fair complexion and flaxen-colored hair. The three elder brothers were dark like their father. Klaus, the youngest of Dietrich's brothers, was five years older than Dietrich. So his three brothers and two older sisters formed a natural quintet, while Dietrich found himself grouped with Sabine and their little sister, Susi, as the "three little ones." In this trio, Dietrich enjoyed his role as the strong and chivalrous protector. "I shall never forget Dietrich's sweetness of character," Sabine later wrote, "which showed when we gathered berries on the hot summer slopes. He would fill my little pitcher with the raspberries he had toiled to collect, so that I would not have less than he, or share his drink with me." When they read together, "he pushed the book in front of me . . . though this made his own reading difficult, and was always kind and helpful if asked for anything."

His chivalrous bent went beyond his sisters. He adored Fräulein Käthe van Horn, their governess from infancy, and "of his own free will he assumed the role of her good spirit who helped and served her, and when her favourite dish was on the table he cried: 'I have had enough,' and forced her to eat his portion too. He told her: 'When I am grown up I shall marry you, then you will always be with us.'"

Sabine also remembered when, at about age six, her brother marveled at the sight of a dragonfly hovering above a stream. Wide-eyed, he whispered to his mother: "Look! There is a creature over the water! But don't be afraid, I will protect you!"

When Dietrich and Sabine were old enough to be schooled, their mother turned the duty over to Fräulein Käthe, though she still presided over the children's religious instruction. Dietrich's earliest recorded theological inquiries occurred when he was about four. He asked his mother: "Does the good God love the chimney sweep too?" and "Does God, too, sit down to lunch?"

Sisters Käthe and Maria van Horn came to the Bonhoeffers six months after the twins were born, and for two decades they formed a vital part of the family's life. Fräulein Käthe was usually in charge of the three little ones. Both van Horn sisters were devout Christians schooled at the community of Herrnhut, which means "the Lord's watch tower," and they had a decided spiritual influence on the Bonhoeffer children. Founded by Count

Zinzendorf in the eighteenth century, Herrnhut continued in the pietist tradition of the Moravian Brethren. As a girl, Paula Bonhoeffer had attended Herrnhut for a time.

Count Zinzendorf advocated the idea of a personal relationship with God, rather than the formal churchgoing Lutheranism of the day. Zinzendorf used the term *living faith*, which he contrasted unfavorably with the prevailing nominalism of dull Protestant orthodoxy. For him, faith was less about an intellectual assent to doctrines than about a personal, transforming encounter with God, so the Herrnhüter emphasized Bible reading and home devotions. His ideas influenced John Wesley, who visited Herrnhut in 1738, the year of his famous conversion.

The place of religion in the Bonhoeffer home was far from pietist, but followed some Herrnhut traditions. For one thing, the Bonhoeffers rarely went to church; for baptisms and funerals, they usually turned to Paula's father or brother. The family was not anticlerical—indeed, the children loved to "play" at baptizing each other—but their Christianity was mostly of the homegrown variety. Daily life was filled with Bible reading and hymn singing, all of it led by Frau Bonhoeffer. Her reverence for the Scriptures was such that she read Bible stories to her children from the actual Bible text and not from a children's retelling. Still, she sometimes used an illustrated Bible, explaining the pictures as she went.*

Paula Bonhoeffer's faith was most evident in the values that she and her husband taught their children. Exhibiting selflessness, expressing generosity, and helping others were central to the family culture. Fräulein Käthe remembered that the three children liked to surprise her by doing nice things for her: "For instance they would lay the table for supper, before I could do it. Whether Dietrich encouraged his sisters to do this I don't know, but I should suspect it." The van Horn sisters described all the children as "high-spirited" but as absolutely never "rude or ill-mannered." Still, their good behavior did not always come naturally. Fräulein Käthe remembered:

---

* Bonhoeffer well knew the dangers of pietism, but he drew on the conservative theological tradition of the Herrnhüter throughout his life, always using the Moravian's daily Bible texts for private devotions. Each day there was a verse from the Old Testament and a verse from the New Testament. Published yearly since Zinzendorf's time, they were known to Bonhoeffer as *Losungen* (watch words), although he sometimes just called them "the texts." These *Losungen* figured prominently in his decision to return to Germany in 1939. He continued these devotions to the end of his life and introduced the practice to his fiancée and many others.

Dietrich was often mischievous and got up to various pranks, not always at the appropriate time. I remember that Dietrich specially liked to do this when the children were supposed to get washed and dressed quickly because we had been invited to go out. So one such day he was dancing round the room, singing and being a thorough nuisance. Suddenly the door opened, his mother descended upon him, boxed his ears right and left, and was gone. Then the nonsense was over. Without shedding a tear, he now did what he ought.

The Move to Berlin, 1912

In 1912, Dietrich's father accepted an appointment to the chair of psychiatry and neurology in Berlin. This put him at the head of his field in Germany, a position he retained until his death in 1948. It's hard to overstate Karl Bonhoeffer's influence. Bethge said that his mere presence in Berlin "turned the city into a bastion against the invasion of Freud's and Jung's psycho-analysis. Not that he had a closed mind to unorthodox theories, or denied on principle the validity of efforts to investigate unexplored areas of the mind." Karl Bonhoeffer never publicly dismissed Freud, Jung, or Adler and their theories, but he held them at arm's length with a measured skepticism borne of his devotion to empirical science. As a medical doctor and scientist, he took a dim view of excessive speculation into the unknown realm of the so-called psyche. Bethge quoted Karl Bonhoeffer's friend, Robert Gaupp, a Heidelberg psychiatrist:

> In intuitive psychology and scrupulous observation Bonhoeffer had no superior. But he came from the school of Wernicke, which was solely concerned with the brain, and permitted no departure from thinking in terms of cerebral pathology. . . . [He] had no urge to advance into the realm of dark, undemonstrable, bold and imaginative interpretation, where so much has to be assumed and so little can be proved. . . . [He] remained within the borders of the empirical world that was accessible to him.

Karl Bonhoeffer was wary of anything beyond what one might observe with one's senses or deduce from those observations. Concerning both psychoanalysis and religion, he might be termed an agnostic.

There was a strong atmosphere in his home against fuzzy thinking, which included a prejudice against certain kinds of religious expressions. But there was no conflict between the father's realm and the mother's. By all accounts, the two complemented each other beautifully. That these two people loved and respected each other was evident to all. Eberhard Bethge described theirs as "a happy relationship in which each partner adroitly supplemented the strength of the other. At their golden wedding anniversary it was said that they had not spent a total of one month apart during their fifty years of marriage, even counting single days."

Karl Bonhoeffer would not have called himself a Christian, but he respected his wife's tutelage of the children in this and lent his tacit approval to it, even if only by participating as an observer. He was not the sort of scientist who ruled out the existence of a realm beyond the physical and seemed to have had a genuine respect for the limits of reason. With the values that his wife taught the children, he was entirely in agreement. Among those values was a serious respect for the feelings and opinions of others, including his wife's. She was the granddaughter, daughter, and sister of men whose lives were given to theology, and he knew she was serious about her faith and had hired governesses who were serious about it. He was present at family religious activities and at the holiday celebrations his wife orchestrated, which invariably included hymns, Bible readings, and prayers. "In all that pertained to our education," Sabine remembered, "our parents stood united as a wall. There was no question of one saying one thing and the other something else." It was an excellent environment for the budding theologian in their midst.

The faith that Paula Bonhoeffer evinced spoke for itself; it lived in actions and was evident in the way that she put others before herself and taught her children to do the same. "There was no place for false piety or any kind of bogus religiosity in our home," Sabine said. "Mama expected us to show great resolution." Mere churchgoing held little charm for her. The concept of cheap grace that Dietrich would later make so famous might have had its origins in his mother; perhaps not the term, but the idea behind it, that faith without works is not faith at all, but a simple lack of obedience to God. During the rise of the Nazis, she respectfully but firmly prodded her son to make the church live out what it claimed to believe by speaking publicly against Hitler and the Nazis, and taking actions against them.

The family seemed to have the best of what we today might think of as conservative and liberal values, of traditional and progressive ones. Emmi Bonhoeffer, who had known the family long before she married Dietrich's brother, Klaus, recalled, "Without any doubt the mother ruled the house, its spirit and its affairs, but she would never have arranged or organized anything which the father would not have wanted her to do, and which would not have pleased him. According to Kierkegaard, man belongs either to the moral or the artistic type. He did not know this house which formed a harmony of both."

Sabine observed that her father possessed

great tolerance that left no room for narrow-mindedness and broad-ened the horizons of our home. He took it for granted that we would try to do what was right and expected much from us, but we could always count on his kindness and the fairness of his judgement. He had a great sense of humour and often helped us to overcome inhibitions with a timely joke. He had too firm a grip upon his own emotions to allow himself ever to speak a word to us which was not wholly suitable. His dislike of clichés did at times make some of us inarticulate and uncertain of ourselves. But it has the effect that as adults we no longer had any taste for catchwords, gossip, commonplaces or loquacity. He, himself, would never have used a catchword or a "trendy" phrase.

Karl Bonhoeffer taught his children to speak only when they had some-thing to say. He did not tolerate sloppiness of expression any more than he tolerated self-pity or selfishness or boastful pride. His children loved and respected him in a way that made them eager to gain his approval; he hardly had to say anything to communicate his feelings on a subject. Often a cocked eyebrow was all it took.

Professor Scheller, a colleague, once said, "Just as he utterly disliked all that is immoderate, exaggerated or undisciplined, so too, in his own per-son everything was completely controlled." The Bonhoeffer children were taught to be in firm control of their emotions. Emotionalism, like sloppy communication, was thought to be self-indulgent. When his father died, Karl Bonhoeffer wrote, "Of his qualities, I would wish that our children inherit his simplicity and truthfulness. I never heard a cliché from him, he spoke little and was a firm enemy of everything faddish and unnatural."

The family's move from Breslau to Berlin must have felt like a leap. For many, Berlin was the center of the universe. Its university was one of the best in the world, the city was an intellectual and cultural center, and it was the seat of an empire.

Their new house—on the Brückenallee, near the northwest part of the Tiergarten—was less spacious than their Breslau house and situated on smaller grounds. But it had the special distinction of sharing a wall with Bellevue Park, where the royal children played. One of the Bonhoeffers' governesses—probably Fräulein Lenchen—was something of a monarchist, who ran excitedly with her charges to catch a glimpse of the kaiser or crown prince as they drove past. The Bonhoeffers valued humility and simplicity, and would not abide anything like gawking at royals. When Sabine boasted that one of the little princes had come close to her and tried to poke her with a stick, the response was disapproving silence.

In Berlin the older children were no longer taught at home, but went to the school nearby. Breakfasts were on the veranda: rye bread, butter and jam, with hot milk and sometimes cocoa. Classes began at eight. Lunch was small sandwiches—butter and cheese or sausage—wrapped in grease-proof paper, which they carried to school in their satchels. There was no such thing as lunch in Germany in those days, so this meal was called a second breakfast.

In 1913, seven-year-old Dietrich began school outside the home. For the next six years he attended the Friedrich-Werder Gymnasium. Sabine said he was expected to walk to school by himself:

> He feared walking there alone, which involved crossing a long bridge.
> So he had to be taken at first, and his companion walked on the other
> side of the street so that he need not be ashamed in front of the other
> children. He eventually overcame this fear. He was also very frightened
> of Santa Claus, and showed a certain fear of the water when we twins
> learned to swim. The first few times he raised a terrific outcry. . . . Later
> he was an excellent swimmer.

Dietrich did well in school, but was not beyond needing discipline, which his parents didn't hesitate to provide. When he was eight, his father wrote, "Dietrich does his work naturally and tidily. He likes fighting, and does a great deal of it." Once he attacked a schoolmate, whose mother suspected an atmosphere of anti-Semitism at home. Paula Bonhoeffer was horrified at the thought and made sure the woman knew that nothing of the kind was tolerated in her house.

Friedrichsbrunn

With the move to Berlin their Wölfesgrund house was too far away, so they sold it and found a country home in Friedrichsbrunn in the Harz Mountains. It had once been a forester's lodge, and they retained its feeling of simplicity. They didn't install electricity for thirty years. Sabine described traveling there:

> The journey, in two specially reserved compartments under the supervision of Fräulein Horn, was a joy in itself. At Thale two carriages and pairs would already be waiting for us, one for the smallest members of the party and the adults and one for the luggage. Most of the heavy luggage would have been sent on ahead and two housemaids would have travelled on in advance a few days earlier to clean and warm the house.

Sometimes the boys sent the carriage ahead at Thale and walked the remaining four miles through the woods. The caretakers, Herr and Frau Sanderhoff, lived in a cottage on the property. Herr Sanderhoff kept the meadow scythed, and Frau Sanderhoff made sure there were vegetables from the garden and firewood.

The van Horn sisters usually went to Friedrichsbrunn ahead of the Bonhoeffer parents, taking the children with them. There was always great excitement over the parents' arrival. Sabine and Dietrich sometimes rode in the carriage down to the train station at Thale to greet them. "In the meantime . . . we would have lit up the house with little cup candles which we used to place in all the windows," Sabine recalled. "Thus even from afar the house would be aglow to greet the new arrivals."

In the thirtysomething years they visited Friedrichsbrunn, Dietrich had only one nightmarish memory. It happened in 1913, their first summer. One sweltering July day Fräulein Maria decided to take the three little ones and Ursula to a nearby mountain lake. Fräulein Lenchen went along too. Fräulein Maria warned them to cool off before they went in, but Fräulein Lenchen ignored the warning and quickly swam toward the middle of the lake, where she promptly sank. Sabine remembered:

> Dietrich was the first to notice it and uttered a piercing cry. At one glance Fräulein Horn took in what had happened. I can still see her throw her watch-chain aside and, in her long woollen skirt, swim out with strong, swift strokes, shouting back to us over her shoulder, "Stay on the shore everyone!"
>
> We were seven years old and could not yet swim. We cried and trembled and held on very firmly to little Susie. We could hear our dear Fräulein Horn crying out to the drowning woman, "Keep swimming! Keep swimming!" We saw how difficult it was for Fräulein Horn to save Lenchen and bring her back. At first Lenchen hung onto her neck, but soon became unconscious, and we heard Fräulein Horn exclaiming, "Help me dear God, help me!" as she swam back with Fräulein Lenchen on her back. Fräulein Lenchen, still unconscious, was laid down on her side. Fräulein Horn put her finger down her throat so as to let out the water. Dietrich gently patted her on the back and we all crouched round Fräulein Lenchen. Soon she recovered consciousness and Fräulein Horn said a long prayer of thanksgiving.

The Bonhoeffer children brought friends to Friedrichsbrunn, although throughout Dietrich's childhood, his circle of friends was limited to family. His cousin Hans-Christoph von Hase visited for long stretches, and together they dug trenches and went for hikes in the vast pine woods to search for wild strawberries, onions, and mushrooms.

Dietrich spent much time reading too.

> Under the rowan-trees on our meadow Dietrich loved to sit and read his favourite books, like *Rulamann*,* the story of a man of the stone age, and *Pinocchio* which made him roar with laughter and whose funniest passages he read out to us again and again. He was about ten years old at that time, but he retained his sense of high-spirited comedy. The

---

* A popular book for boys that purported to relate the prehistoric adventures of a caveman in the Schwabian Alps.

book *Heroes of Everyday** moved him very much. They were stories of young people who by their courage, presence of mind and selflessness saved others' lives, and these stories often ended sadly. *Uncle Tom's Cabin* kept him busy for a long time. Here in Friedrichsbrunn he also read the great classic poets for the first time, and in the evenings we did play-reading with different parts.

Sometimes in the evenings they played ball games with the village children in the meadow. Inside they played guessing games and sang folk songs. They "watched the mists from the meadows waft and rise along the fir-trees," Sabine noted, and they watched dusk fall. When the moon appeared, they sang "Der Mond ist Aufgegangen":

> Der Mond ist aufgegangen,
> die goldnen Sternlein prangen
> am Himmel hell und klar!
> Der Wald steht schwarz und schweiget
> und aus den Wiesen steiget
> der weiße Nebel wunderbar.**

The worlds of folklore and religion were so mingled in early twentieth-century German culture that even families who didn't go to church were often deeply Christian. This folk song is typical, beginning as a paean to the beauty of the natural world, but soon turning into a meditation on mankind's need for God and finally into a prayer, asking God to help us "poor and prideful sinners" to see his salvation when we die—and in the meantime here on earth to help us to be "like little children, cheerful and faithful."

German culture was inescapably Christian. This was a result of the legacy of Martin Luther, the Catholic monk who invented Protestantism. Looming over the German culture and nation like both a father and a mother, Luther was to Germany something like what Moses was to Israel; in his lusty, cranky person were the German nation and the Lutheran faith wonderfully and

---

* One of the last books he read was *Plutarch's Lives*. He parted with it hours before his execution. (See page 526)

** The moon has climbed into the sky, where golden stars shine bright and clear. The woods are dark and silent; and from the meadows like a dream, the white fog rises in the air.

terribly combined. Luther's influence cannot be overestimated. His translation of the Bible into German was cataclysmic. Like a medieval John Bunyan,
Luther in a single blow shattered the edifice of European Catholicism and in
the bargain created the modern German language, which in turn effectively
created the German people. Christendom was cleft in twain, and out of the
earth beside it sprang the *Deutsche Volk*.

The Luther Bible was to the modern German language what the works
of Shakespeare and the King James Bible were to the modern English language. Before Luther's Bible, there was no unified German language. It
existed only in a hodgepodge of dialects. And Germany as a nation was an
idea far in the future, a gleam in Luther's eye. But when Luther translated
the Bible into German, he created a single language in a single book that
everyone could read and did read. Indeed, there was nothing else *to* read.
Soon everyone spoke German the way Luther's translation did. As television
has had a homogenizing effect on the accents and dialects of Americans,
watering down accents and sanding down sharp twangs, Luther's Bible created a single German tongue. Suddenly millers from München could communicate with bakers from Bremen. Out of this grew a sense of a common
heritage and culture.

But Luther brought Germans to a fuller engagement with their faith
through singing too. He wrote many hymns—the most well-known being
"A Mighty Fortress Is Our God"—and introduced the idea of congregational
singing. Before Luther, no one outside the choir sang in church.

"Hurrah, There's a War!"

The Bonhoeffers spent the summer of 1914 at Friedrichsbrunn. But on the
first day of August, while the three younger children and their governess
were in the village enjoying themselves, the world changed. Flitting here
and there through the crowd, until it reached them, was the stunning news
that Germany had declared war on Russia. Dietrich and Sabine were eight
and a half, and she recalled the scene:

> The village was celebrating its local shooting festival. Our governess
> suddenly dragged us away from the pretty, enticing market stalls and
> the merry-go-round which was being pulled by a poor white horse, so

as to bring us back as quickly as possible to our parents in Berlin. Sadly I looked at the now emptying scene of the festivities, where the stall-holders were hastily pulling down their tents. In the late evening we could hear through the window the songs and shouts of the soldiers in their farewell celebrations. Next day, after the adults had hastily done the packing, we found ourselves sitting in the train to Berlin.

When they arrived back home, one of the girls ran into the house and exclaimed, "Hurrah! There's a war!" She was promptly slapped. The Bonhoeffers were not opposed to war, but neither would they celebrate it.

They were in the minority on that point, however, and a general tone of giddiness prevailed in those first days. But on August 4, the first discordant note was sounded: Britain declared war on Germany. Suddenly what lay ahead might not be as wonderful as everyone thought. That day, Karl Bonhoeffer was walking along Unter den Linden with the three eldest boys:

> The elation of the crowds outside the palace and the government build-ings which has been mounting during the last days had now given place to a dreary silence, which had an extraordinarily oppressive effect. The severity of the conflict which lay ahead was now evidently manifest even to the masses, and the hope for a speedy end to the war was extin-guished for those who had insight, by Britain's entry into the ranks of our enemies.

For the most part, however, the boys were thrilled and remained so for some time, though they were careful in expressing it. War, as a concept, had not yet fallen out of favor across Europe; that would take the next four years. At this early stage of the conflict, the schoolboy's motto "Dulce Et Decorum Est Pro Patria Mori"* had not yet been spoken with bitterness or irony. To inhabit the world of one's lead soldiers—to put on a uniform and march off to war as the heroes of the past had done—was a romantic thrill.

Dietrich's brothers wouldn't be eligible to enlist until 1917, and no one dreamed the war could last that long. But they could at least get caught up in the whole thing and talk about it knowledgeably, as the grown-ups did.

---

* It is a sweet and noble thing to die for one's country.

Dietrich often played at soldiers with his cousin Hans-Christoph, and the next summer at Friedrichsbrunn, he wrote his parents asking them to send newspaper articles about events at the front. Like many boys, he made a map and stuck colored pins into it, marking the Germans' advancement.

The Bonhoeffers were sincerely patriotic, but they never exhibited the nationalistic passion of most other Germans. They maintained a sense of perspective and a coolness, which they taught their children to cultivate. Once, Fräulein Lenchen bought Sabine a small brooch that had on it "Now We'll Thrash Them!" "I was very proud to have it glittering on my white collar," Sabine recalled, "but at midday when I showed myself to my parents with it on my father said, 'Hallo, what have you got there? just give it to me,' and it disappeared into his pocket." Her mother asked where she'd gotten it and promised to find her a prettier brooch to replace it.

In time the realities of war came home. A cousin was killed. Then another. Another cousin lost a leg. Their cousin Lothar had an eye shot out and a leg severely crushed. Another cousin died. Until they were ten, the twins slept in the same bedroom. After their prayers and hymns, they lay in the dark, and their conversation turned to death and eternity. They wondered what it would be like to be dead and to live in eternity; somehow they got the idea that they could touch eternity by focusing exclusively on the word itself, *Ewigkeit*. The key was banishing all other thoughts. "After concentrating intensely for a long time," Sabine said, "our heads often used to swim. We staunchly kept up this self-imposed exercise for a long time."

Food grew scarce too. Even for the relatively well-to-do Bonhoeffers, hunger became an issue. Dietrich distinguished himself as especially resourceful in procuring food. He got very involved in tracking down food supplies, so much so that his father praised him for his skill as a "messenger and food scout." He even saved his own money to buy a hen. He was eager to do his part. Some of that had to do with his sense of competition with his older brothers. They were five, six, and seven years older than he, and brilliant, as were his sisters. But the one area in which he would outstrip them all was in musical ability.

When Dietrich turned eight, he began piano lessons. All the children had music lessons, but none showed such promise. His ability to sight-read was remarkable. He became so accomplished that he seriously thought of taking it up as a career. At ten he was playing Mozart's sonatas. The opportunities for exposure to great music in Berlin were endless. When he was eleven, he heard Beethoven's Ninth Symphony performed by the Berlin Philharmonic, under the direction of Arthur Nikisch, and he wrote to his grandmother about it. Eventually, he even arranged and composed. He loved the Schubert song "Gute Ruh'"* and, when he was about fourteen, arranged it as a trio. That same year he composed a cantata on the sixth verse of Psalm 42, "My soul is cast down within me." Although he eventually chose theology over music, music remained a deep passion throughout his life. It became a vital part of his expression of faith, and he taught his students to appreciate it and make it a central aspect of their expressions of faith.

The Bonhoeffers were a deeply musical family, so most of Dietrich's earliest musical experiences came in the context of the family's musical evenings each Saturday night. His sister Susanne remembered,

> We had supper at half-past seven and then we went into the drawing room. Usually, the boys began with a trio: Karl-Friedrich played the piano, Walter the violin, and Klaus the cello. Then "Hörnchen"** accompanied my mother as she sang. Each one who had had teaching that week had to present something that evening. Sabine learned the violin, and the two big sisters sang duets as well as Lieder by Schubert, Brahms, and Beethoven. Dietrich was far better at the piano than Karl-Friedrich.

According to Sabine, Dietrich was especially sensitive and generous as an accompanist, "always anxious to cover over the mistakes of the other players and to spare them any embarrassment." His future sister-in-law Emmi Delbrück was often there too:

> While we were playing, Dietrich at the piano kept us all in order. I do not remember a moment when he did not know where each of us was. He never just played his own part: from the beginning he heard the whole of it. If the cello took a long time tuning beforehand, or between movements, he sank his head and didn't betray the slightest impatience. He was courteous by nature.

---

* "Lullabye of the Stream" from *Die Schöne Müllerin*.

** It was the term they sometimes used for their governess, Maria van Horn.

Dietrich particularly enjoyed accompanying his mother when she sang the Gellert-Beethoven psalms, and every Christmas Eve he accompanied her singing of the Cornelius *Lieder*. The family's Saturday musical evenings were held for many years and continued to include new friends. Their circle always seemed to be expanding. They also gave special performances and concerts for birthdays and other special occasions, culminating in their last performance together in late March 1943, for Karl Bonhoeffer's seventy-fifth birthday, when the much-increased family performed Walcha's cantata "Lobe den Herrn" ("Praise the Lord"), which Dietrich directed and in which he played piano.

Grunewald

In March 1916, while the war raged on, the family moved from the Brückenallee to a house in Berlin's Grunewald district. It was another prestigious neighborhood, where many of Berlin's distinguished professors lived. The Bonhoeffers became close to many of them, and their children spent so much time together that they eventually began marrying each other.

Like most homes in Grunewald, the Bonhoeffer home at 14 Wangenheimstrasse was huge, with a full acre of gardens and grounds. It's quite likely their choice had to do with its large yard; during wartime, with a brood of eight children, including three teenage boys, they never had enough food. So they planted considerable vegetable gardens and even kept chickens and goats.

Their home was filled with artistic treasures and family heirlooms. In the parlor were oil portraits of Bonhoeffer ancestors, side by side with etchings by the eighteenth-century Italian artist Piranesi. Huge landscapes by their great-grandfather, Count Stanislaus von Kalkreuth, were displayed as well. He had designed the imposing sideboard that commanded the dining room. It stood eight feet tall and evoked a Greek temple, with friezes and other carvings, and two pillars supporting a crenellated pediment. Dietrich would somehow scale this heirloom and from its lonely ramparts spy upon the comings and goings in the large dining room far below, whose table could seat twenty, and whose parquet floors were polished daily. In one corner—supported by an intricately carved pedestal that opened to reveal the cruet—was a bust of their illustrious forebear, the theologian Karl August von Hase. Since he was their mother's grandfather, the pedestal cabinet was called *Grossvater*.

Bonhoeffer's childhood seems something from a turn-of-the-century illustration by the Swedish artist Carl Larsson or from Ingmar Bergman's *Fanny and Alexander*, without the undertones of angst and foreboding. The Bonhoeffers were that terribly rare thing: a genuinely happy family, and their ordered life continued along through the weeks and months and years as it always had, with musical evenings every Saturday, and with many birthday and holiday celebrations too. In 1917 Dietrich suffered appendicitis and a subsequent appendectomy, but the interruption was slight and not unwelcome. As always, Paula Bonhoeffer's annual orchestrations of the Christmas holidays were especially beautiful, incorporating Bible reading and hymns in such a way that even those who were not particularly religious felt included. Sabine remembered,

> On the Sundays of Advent we all assembled with her round the long dinner table to sing Christmas carols; Papa joined us too and read from the fairy tales of Andersen. . . . Christmas Eve began with the Christmas story. The whole family sat in a circle, including the maids in their white aprons, all solemn and full of expectation, till our mother began to read. . . . She read the Christmas story with a firm, full voice, and after that she always intoned the hymn, "This is the day that God has made." . . . The lights were now extinguished and we sang Christmas carols in the dark, until our father, who had slipped out unnoticed, had lit the candles at the manger and the tree. Now the bell sounded, and we three small ones were allowed to go first into the Christmas room, to the candles at the tree, and there we stood and sang happily: "The Christmas tree is the loveliest tree." Only then did we look at our Christmas presents.

The War Comes Home

As the war continued, the Bonhoeffers heard of more deaths and injuries among their wide circle. In 1917 their two eldest, Karl-Friedrich and Walter, would be called up. Both were born in 1899; now they would go to war. Though they might easily have done so, their parents didn't pull any strings to help them avoid serving on the front lines. Germany's greatest need was in the infantry, and there both boys enlisted. In a way their bravery foreshadowed what lay twenty years ahead in the next war. The Bonhoeffers raised their children to do the right thing, so when they behaved selflessly and bravely, it was difficult to argue. The extraordinary words that Karl Bonhoeffer would write to a colleague in 1945 after learning of the deaths of his sons Dietrich and Klaus—as well as the deaths of two sons-in-law—capture the Bonhoeffers' attitude during both wars: "We are sad, but also proud."

Following basic training, the two young Bonhoeffers would be sent to the front. Karl-Friedrich actually took along his physics textbook. Walter had been preparing for this moment since the war broke out, strengthening himself by taking long hikes with extra weights in his backpack. Things were still looking very well for Germany that year. In fact, the Germans were so confident that on March 24, 1918, the kaiser declared a national holiday.

In April 1918 it was Walter's turn to go. As they had always done and would do for their grandchildren's generation twenty-five years hence, they gave Walter a festive send-off dinner. The large family gathered around the large table, gave handmade presents, and recited poems and sang songs composed for the occasion. Dietrich, then twelve, composed an arrangement for "Now, at the last, we say Godspeed on your journey" and, accompanying himself on the piano, sang it to his brother. They took Walter to the station the next morning, and as the train was pulling away, Paula Bonhoeffer ran alongside it, telling her fresh-faced boy: "It's only space that separates us." Two weeks later, in France, he died of a shrapnel wound. Walter's death changed everything.

"I can still remember that bright morning in May," Sabine wrote,

and the terrible shadow which suddenly blotted it out for us. My father was just in the act of leaving the house to drive to his clinic, and I was on the point of going through the door on my way to school. But when a messenger brought us two telegrams I remained standing in the hall. I saw my father hastily open the envelopes, turn terribly white, go into his study and sink into the chair at his desk where he sat bowed over it with his head resting on both his arms, his face hidden in his hands. . . . A few moments later I saw my father through the half-open door holding onto the banisters as he went up the broad easy stairway which

at other times he mounted so lightly to go to the bedroom where my
mother was. There he remained for many hours.

Walter was injured by an exploding shell on April 23. The doctors hadn't
thought the wounds serious and wrote the family, assuaging their concerns.
But an inflammation developed, and his condition worsened. Three hours
before his death, Walter dictated a letter to his parents:

My dears,
Today I had the second operation, and I must admit that it went far
less pleasantly than the first because the splinters that were removed
were deeper. Afterwards I had to have two camphor injections with
an interval between them, but I hope that this is the end of the matter. I am using my technique of thinking of other things so as not to
think of the pain. There are more interesting things in the world just
now than my wounds. Mount Kemmel and its possible consequences,
and today's news of the taking of Ypres, give us great cause for hope.
I dare not think about my poor regiment, so severely did it suffer in
the last few days. How are things going with the other officer cadets?
I think of you with longing, my dears, every minute of the long days
and nights.
From so far away,
your Walter.

Later, the family received other letters that Walter had written in the few
days before his death, indicating how he had hoped they might visit. "Even
today," his father wrote many years later, "I cannot think of this without
reproaching myself for not going to him straightaway in spite of previous
reassuring telegrams which explicitly stated it was unnecessary." They later
learned that Walter's commanding officer was very inexperienced and had
foolishly taken all of his soldiers to the front lines together.

In early May a cousin on the general staff escorted Walter's body home.
Sabine recalled the spring funeral, and "the hearse with the horses decked
out in black and all the wreaths, my mother deathly pale and shrouded in
a great black mourning veil . . . my father, my relatives, and all the many
silent people dressed in black on the way to the chapel." Dietrich's cousin

Hans-Christoph von Hase remembered "the young boys and girls weeping, weeping. His mother, I had never seen her weep so much."

Walter's death was a turning point for Dietrich. The first hymn at the service was "Jerusalem, du Hochgebaute Stadt."* Dietrich sang loudly and clearly, as his mother always wished the family to do. And she did, too, drawing strength from its words, which spoke of the heart's longing for the heavenly city, where God waited for us and would comfort us and "wipe away every tear." For Dietrich, it had to seem heroic and filled with meaning:

> The patriarchs' and prophets' noble train,
> With all Christ's followers true,
> Who bore the cross and could the worst disdain
> That tyrants dared to do,
> I see them shine forever,
> All-glorious as the sun,
> Midst light that fadeth never,
> Their perfect freedom won.

Dietrich's uncle Hans von Hase preached the sermon. Recalling a Paul Erhardt hymn, he spoke of how this world of pain and sorrow was but a moment when compared with the joyous eternity with God. At the end of the service, Walter's comrades bore the coffin down the aisle as trumpeters played the hymn that Paula Bonhoeffer had chosen: "Was Gott tut, das ist Wohlgetan." Sabine remembered the trumpets playing the familiar cantata and later marveled at the lyrics her mother had chosen:

> What God has done, it is well done.
> His will is always just.
> Whatever He will do to me,
> In Him I'll ever place my trust.

Paula Bonhoeffer took such sentiments seriously. Yet the death of her dear Walter was devastating. During this bitter season, Karl-Friedrich remained in the infantry, and the unspeakable but real possibility that

---

* "Jerusalem, Thou City Fair and High."

they might lose him too compounded her agony. Then seventeen-year-old Klaus was called up. It was too much. She collapsed. For several weeks, unable to get out of bed, she stayed with close neighbors, the Schönes. Even when she returned home, this extremely capable and strong woman could not resume her normal duties for a year. It was several years before she seemed herself again. Throughout this time, Karl Bonhoeffer was the strength of the family, but it was ten years before he could write his annual new year's diary again.

The earliest recorded words we have from Dietrich Bonhoeffer appeared in a letter he wrote a few months before Walter's death. It was a few days before his—and Sabine's—twelfth birthday. Walter had not yet gone to the front, but was away at military training.

> Dear Grandmama,
> Please come on February 1, so you'll already be here on our birthday. It would really be a lot nicer if you were here. Please decide at once and come on the 1st. . . . Karl-Friedrich is writing to us more often. Recently he wrote that he won the first prize in a race in which all of the junior officers of his company competed. The prize is 5 marks. Walter will return on Sunday. Today we were given seventeen fine flounder from Boltenhagen on the Baltic Sea, which we will eat this evening.

Boltenhagen is a seaside resort on the Baltic Sea. Dietrich, Sabine, and Susanne sometimes went there with the van Horn sisters. Their neighbors, the Schönes, had a holiday home there.

Dietrich was sent there with the van Horn sisters in June 1918, a few weeks after Walter's death. There he could escape the heaviness of Wangenheimstrasse for a little while; he could play and be a boy. Our second letter from him was written to his elder sister Ursula during this time:

> On Sunday, we got up at 7:30. First we ate breakfast. . . . After this we ran to the beach and built our own wonderful sand castle. Next, we made a rampart around the wicker beach chair. Then we worked on the fortress. While we left it alone for 4–5 hours for dinner and tea, it was

completely washed away by the sea. But we had taken our flag with us. After tea we went back down and dug canals. . . . Then it began to rain, and we watched Mr. Qualmann's cows being milked.

In another letter to his grandmother (postmarked July 3) he chattered excitedly in a similar vein, but even in this childhood world of sand castles and imaginary battles, the outside world of death intruded. He described two seaplanes performing maneuvers until one of them suddenly went into a dive:

> Soon we saw a thick black pillar of smoke rising above the ground, and we knew this meant that the plane had crashed! . . . [S]omebody said that the pilot had completely burned up but the other had jumped out and had sustained only a hand injury. Afterwards he came over and we saw that his entire eyebrows were singed. . . . In the afternoon a few days ago (Sunday), we slept in our sand castle and all got very sunburned. . . . We have to take a nap every afternoon. Two other boys are also here. One is 10 years old and the other 14. A little Jewish boy is also here. . . . Everything was lit up with spotlights again yesterday evening, certainly because of the pilots. . . . Tomorrow, the last day, we also plan to make a garland out of oak leaves for Walter's grave.

In September Dietrich joined his von Hase cousins in Waldau, about forty miles east of Breslau. Uncle Hans, Paula Bonhoeffer's brother, was the superintendent of the Liegnitz church district there and lived in a parsonage. Dietrich's visits formed part of his connection with his mother's side of the family, for whom being a pastor or theologian was as normal as being a scientist was for the Bonhoeffer side. Dietrich spent many vacations with his cousin Hans-Christoph, who was called Hänschen and was a year younger than Dietrich. They remained close into adulthood, and Hans-Christoph would follow in his cousin's footsteps as a Sloane Fellow at Union Theological Seminary in 1933, three years after Dietrich. That September in Waldau the boys took Latin lessons together. But in a letter to his siblings, Dietrich was more excited about other things:

I don't know if I already wrote you that we found partridge eggs, and that four have already hatched. We had to help two because they couldn't get out. The hen under which we placed them is not showing them how they should eat, and we don't know how to teach them. I now help Hänschen more often when he brings in the animals. I always go first. That means I steer the animals to the hay bales that need to be loaded, and recently I even drove the wagon a good piece around quite a few turns. Yesterday Klärchen and I rode horses. It was very nice. We glean here often and successfully, and so gather quite a lot. Today I want to thresh again and let it go through the separator. . . . Regrettably the fruit harvest is not particularly good. . . . This afternoon we want to go boating on the lake.

His boyish zeal for fun was never far away—not even as an adult when the threat of danger was great—but he always had a noticeably intense and serious side. Walter's death and the increasing possibility that Germany would lose the war brought that out now. It was around this time that he began to think about studying theology. And at the end of the war, as Germany staggered under the weight of a devastated economy, he continued to take the lead in procuring food. At the end of the month he wrote his parents:

Yesterday we took my gleanings to be ground up. There will even be 10–15 pounds more than I had thought, depending on how fine it will be ground. . . . The weather here is magnificent, with sunshine almost the whole time. In the next few days we will harvest the potatoes. . . . I work every day here with Hänschen and Uncle Hans translating Latin. Will you come to Breslau, this time, dear mama, since Karl-Friedrich is not on active duty?

Germany Loses the War

If 1918 can be seen as the year that Dietrich Bonhoeffer left childhood, it can be seen as the year that Germany did too. Sabine called the era before the war a time "in which a different order prevailed, an order which seemed to us then firmly established enough to last for ever, an order imbued with Christian meaning, in which we could pass a sheltered and secure childhood." In 1918 all that changed. The kaiser, who represented the authority of both church and state, and who, as a figurehead, represented Germany and the German way of life, would abdicate. It was devastating.

Things began to unravel in August when the final German offensive failed. After this, things began to fall apart in ways no one could imagine. Many German soldiers grew disaffected and turned against their leaders. Weary, hungry, and increasingly angry at the powers that be who had led them to their miserable state, they began to warm to ideas that had been whispered among them. Communism was still bright and brand-new—the horrors of Stalin and the Gulag Archipelago were decades in the future—and it gave them hope again and someone to blame. Copies of Rosa Luxemburg's *Spartacus Letters** were circulated, further stirring discontent among the soldiers, who thought that if anything could be salvaged from the chaos, perhaps they must take the lead. Hadn't the Russian troops revolted against their commanders? Before long, German soldiers elected their own councils and spoke openly of their mistrust of the old regime and the kaiser.

Finally, in November, the nightmare came true: Germany lost the war. The turmoil that followed was unprecedented. Just a few months earlier they had been on the bright verge of victory. What had happened? Many blamed the Communists for sowing seeds of discontent among the troops at a crucial time. This was where the famous *Dolchstoss* (stab-in-the-back) legend came about. It maintained that the real enemy in the war was not the Allied powers, but those pro-Communist, pro-Bolshevist Germans who had destroyed Germany's chances of victory from within, who had "stabbed it in the back." Their treachery was far worse than any enemies Germany had faced across the battlefields, and they were the ones who must be punished. This *Dolchstoss* idea grew after the war, and was especially beloved by the rising National Socialists and their leader, Hitler, who lived to rail against the Communist traitors who had done this. With great success he fanned the flames of this idea, and increasingly harped on the idea that Bolshevism was really international Jewry, that the Jews and the Communists had destroyed Germany.

The threat of a Communist coup was palpable at the end of 1918. The events in Russia the previous year were fresh in every German's mind. The government leaders must prevent the same horror from overtaking Germany,

---

*   An illegal, pro-Communist newspaper.

at all costs, and firmly believed that by throwing the old kaiser to the wolves, Germany could survive, albeit in another form, as a democratic government. It was a high price to pay, but there was no alternative: the kaiser must abdicate. The people clamored for it, and the Allied powers demanded it.

So in November it fell to the beloved Field Marshal von Hindenburg to do the dirtiest work of all. He must go to Supreme Headquarters and persuade Kaiser Wilhelm that monarchy in Germany had come to an end.

It was a grotesque and painful task, since Hindenburg was a monarchist. But for the sake of the nation, he went to the Belgian city Spa and delivered the epochal ultimatum to his kaiser. When Hindenburg left the conference room after that meeting, a seventeen-year-old orderly from Grunewald was standing in the hallway. Klaus Bonhoeffer never forgot the moment when the stout Hindenburg brushed past him. After the death of Walter, with Karl-Friedrich still in the infantry, it's no wonder the Bonhoeffer parents wanted to find their youngest soldier a position out of harm's way. As a result, he was stationed at Spa, and that day witnessed history. He later described the exiting Hindenburg as being "rigid as a statue both in countenance and bearing."

On November 9 the kaiser saw no alternative and abdicated the throne. In a moment, the Germany of the last fifty years vanished. But the mobs milling around Berlin weren't satisfied. Revolution was in the air. The ultraleft Spartacists, led by Rosa Luxemburg and Karl Liebknecht, had taken over the kaiser's palace and were on the verge of declaring a Soviet republic. The Social Democrats had a majority in the Reichstag, but any moment it could all vanish. Just outside the window on the Koenigsplatz the angry crowds clamored for change, demanding something, *anything*—and that's precisely what they got. Throwing political caution to the winds and a cheap sop to the crowd below, Philipp Scheidemann* opened the gigantic window, and without any particular authority to do so, he declared a German republic! That was that.

But it was not that simple. This impetuous declaration of the Weimar Republic was as imperfect a beginning of a democratic regime as one could imagine. It was a compromise to which no one had really agreed. Rather than pull together the deep fissures in the German body politic, it papered over them, inviting future troubles. The right-wing monarchists and the military

---

* Philipp Scheidemann (1865–1939) was a German politician.

pledged to support the new government, but never did. Instead they would distance themselves from it and blame the loss of the war on it, and on all other leftist elements, especially Communists and Jews.

Meanwhile, less than a mile down the street, the Communists, having taken over the kaiser's *Stadtschloss* (palace), were not ready to surrender. They still wanted a full-blown Soviet republic, and two hours after Scheidemann had declared "the German republic" from the Reichstag window, Liebknecht followed suit, throwing open a window in the *Stadtschloss* and declaring a "free Socialist republic"! It was in this childish way, with two windows flung open in two historic buildings, that the great troubles began. The four-month-long civil war, called the German Revolution, now started.

The army eventually restored order by defeating the Communists and murdering Luxemburg and Liebknecht. In January 1919 an election was held, but no one gained a majority and there was no consensus. These forces would keep fighting for years, and Germany would remain divided and confused until 1933, when a wild-eyed vagabond from Austria would end the confusion by outlawing all dissent, and then the real troubles would begin.

But as the spring of 1919 wore on, just as everyone thought things were being restored to something they could live with, the most humiliating and crushing blow of all came. That May, the Allies published the full terms of peace that they demanded and that they had signed in the fabled Hall of Mirrors at Versailles. The Germans were astonished. They had thought the worst was over. Hadn't they done all the Allies had asked? Hadn't they chased the kaiser from his throne? And then hadn't they crushed the Communists? And after they'd dealt with the right and the left, hadn't they set up a decently centrist democratic government that possessed elements of the U.S., English, French, and Swiss governments? What more could be decently expected from them? As it turned out, much more.

The treaty required Germany to give up territory in France, Belgium, and Denmark, as well as all of her Asian and African colonies. It also required her to pay exorbitant reparations in gold, ships, lumber, coal, and livestock. But there were three demands that were particularly unbear-able: first, Germany must give up most of Poland, thus cutting off East Prussia from the rest of the nation; second, she must officially accept sole responsibility for the war; and third, she must eviscerate her military. These demands were individually heinous, but taken together, they were something beyond comprehension.

The outcry from all quarters was great. It was intolerable. It amounted to a death sentence for the nation, and that it would prove to be. But at the moment there was no recourse but to accept it and the deep humiliation that came with it. Scheidemann, the man who had thrown open the Reichstag window and fatuously proclaimed the German republic, now pronounced a curse: "May the hand wither that signs this treaty!" It was signed nonetheless.

A year earlier, when the Germans still expected overall victory in the war and had just defeated Russia, hadn't they forced the Russians to sign a treaty that was almost certainly worse than what they were being forced to sign now? Hadn't they shown less mercy then than they were being shown? The worm had turned, and these tit-for-tat troubles, now being sown like wind, would grow and grow.

The Bonhoeffer family, like all German families, followed the action closely. Living a few miles from the center of Berlin, they could not avoid it. One day a battle between the Communists and government troops broke out a half mile from the Bonhoeffer home, at the Halensee train station. Dietrich, in the tone of a typical thirteen-year-old boy thrilled to be close to "the action," wrote his grandmother:

> It wasn't too dangerous, but we could hear it quite clearly because it happened at night. The whole thing lasted about an hour. Then these fellows were pushed back. When they tried it again around 6 o'clock in the morning, they only got bloody heads. This morning we heard artillery fire. We don't know yet where it came from. At the moment it is thumping again, but it seems to be only in the distance.

But Dietrich had concerns even closer to home. His mother was still reeling from Walter's death. In December 1918, he wrote his grandmother: "Mama is doing much better now. In the morning she still feels very weak, but in the afternoon she feels quite steady again. Sadly, she still eats hardly anything." A month later: "So far mama is feeling pretty good again. . . . For a while she lived with the Schönes across the street. Since then, she has been doing significantly better."

That year Dietrich finished at the Friedrich-Werder school and enrolled at the exclusive Grunewald Gymnasium. He had already decided he would become a theologian, but he was not ready to announce it. Turning thirteen was an important transition from childhood to adulthood, and his parents acknowledged it by enrolling him and Sabine in dancing lessons. They also let him and Sabine stay up with the adults that New Year's Eve:

> About eleven o'clock the lights were extinguished, we drank hot punch and the candles on the Christmas tree were lit once again. All this was a tradition in our family. Now that we were all sitting together, our mother read the ninetieth psalm: "Lord, thou hast been our dwelling-place in all generations." The candles grew shorter and the shadows of the tree longer and longer, and while the year was fading out, we sang Paul Gerhardt's New Year's Eve hymn: "Now let us go singing and praying, and stand before our Lord, who has given our life strength until now." When the last stanza had died away, the church bells were already ringing in the new year.

The social world of Grunewald was especially rich for the children, who ranged from Susanne, now eleven years old, to Karl-Friedrich, now twenty-one. No one had married yet, but there was a circle of friends who did everything together. Emmi Delbrück, who later married Klaus, remembered:

> We had our parties and dances where wit and imagination triumphed, and skating on the lakes till it was dark; both the brothers performed waltzes and figures on the ice with a simply entrancing elegance. Then, on summer evenings, we had strolls in the Grunewald, four or five couples of the Dohnanyis, the Delbrücks and the Bonhoeffers. Of course there was occasional gossip and vexation but such things were quickly swept away: there was so much style, such a clear standard of taste, such an intense interest in different fields of knowledge, that this period of our youth now seems to me like a gift which at the same time carried an immense obligation, and probably we all felt that way more or less consciously.

Bonhoeffer Chooses Theology

It wasn't until 1920, when Dietrich turned fourteen, that he was ready to tell anyone he had decided to become a theologian. It took a bold and courageous person to announce such a thing in the Bonhoeffer family. His father might treat it with respect and cordiality, even if he disagreed with it, but his brothers and sisters and their friends would not. They were a formidable group, all highly intelligent, and most of them openly and often mockingly opposed their cocky young brother's ideas. They always teased him and gave him a hard time over many things much less important than his choice of profession. When he was about eleven, he mispronounced the name of a play by Friedrich Schiller to roars of laughter. That he should be reading Schiller at that age was taken for granted.

Emmi Bonhoeffer remembered the atmosphere then:

> To keep a distance in manners and spirit, without being cool, to be interested without curiosity—that was about [Dietrich's] line. . . . He could not stand empty talk. He sensed unfailingly whether the other person meant what he said. All the Bonhoeffers reacted with extreme sensitivity against every mannerism and affectation of thought; I think it was in their nature, and sharpened by their education. They were allergic to even the slightest touch of this, it made them intolerant, even unjust. Whereas we Delbrücks shrank from saying anything banal, the Bonhoeffers shrank from saying anything interesting for fear it might turn out to be not so interesting after all, and the inherent claim might be ironically smiled at. Such an ironical smile from their father may often have hurt the gentle natures, but it did sharpen the strong ones. . . . In the Bonhoeffer family one learnt to think before asking a question or making a remark. It was embarrassing to see their father raise his left eyebrow inquiringly. It was a relief when this was accompanied by a kindly smile, but absolutely devastating when his expression remained serious. But he never really wanted to devastate, and everybody knew it.

Emmi also recalled that once Dietrich announced his choice to study theology, they peppered him with questions:

We liked to ask him questions that haunted us, e.g. was evil really overcome by good, or did Jesus want us to offer the other cheek to the insolent person too, and hundreds of other problems which drive young people into a deadlock when they face real life. He often countered with another question which took us further than a concise answer might have done, e.g. "Do you think Jesus wanted anarchy? Did he not go into the temple with a whip to throw out the money-changers?" He himself was one who asked questions.

Dietrich's brother Klaus had chosen a career in law and would become the top lawyer at the German airline Lufthansa. In a dispute about Dietrich's choice of theology, Klaus homed in on the problem of the church itself, calling it a "poor, feeble, boring, petty bourgeois institution." "In that case," said Dietrich, "I shall have to reform it!" The statement was mainly meant as a defiant rebuff to his brother's attack, and perhaps even as a joke, since this was not a family in which one made boastful statements. On the other hand, his future work would lean more in that direction than anyone could have guessed.

His brother Karl-Friedrich was the least pleased with Dietrich's decision. Karl-Friedrich had already distinguished himself as a brilliant scientist. He felt Dietrich was turning his back on scientifically verifiable reality and escaping into the fog of metaphysics. In one of their arguments on this subject, Dietrich said, "Dass es einen Gott gibt, dafür lass ich mir den Kopf abschlagen," which means something like, "Even if you were to knock my head off, God would still exist."

Gerhard von Rad, a friend who knew Bonhoeffer from his visits to his grandmother's home in Tübingen, recalled that "it was very rare for a young man of this academic elite to decide in favor of the study of theology. The study of theology, and the profession of theologian, were not highly respected in those circles. In a society whose ranks were still clearly discernible, the university theologians stood rather apart, academically and socially."

Although the Bonhoeffers weren't churchgoers, all their children were confirmed. At fourteen, Dietrich and Sabine were enrolled in Paster Hermann Priebe's confirmation class at the Grunewald church. When he was confirmed in March 1921, Paula Bonhoeffer gave Dietrich his brother Walter's Bible. For the rest of his life he used it for daily devotions.

Dietrich's decision to become a theologian was firm, but his parents weren't quite convinced this was the best path for him. He was so talented as a musician, they thought he still might want to turn in that direction. The famed pianist Leonid Kreutzer was teaching at the Berliner Hochschule für Musik, and the Bonhoeffers arranged for Dietrich to play for him and hear his opinion.* Kreutzer's verdict was inconclusive. In any case, later that year Dietrich chose to take Hebrew as his elective in school. That might have been when his choice of theology became irrevocable.

In November 1921, at age fifteen, Bonhoeffer went to the first evangelistic meeting of his life. General Bramwell Booth of the Salvation Army had conducted ministry in Germany before the war, and in 1919, greatly moved by reports of the suffering there, especially the hunger among children, he found a way around the official channels and was able to have milk distributed. He also gave five thousand pounds to relief efforts.

Two years later, Booth came to Berlin to lead a series of evangelistic meetings. Thousands showed up, including many soldiers, broken by the war. Sabine recalled that "Dietrich was eager to take part in it. He was the youngest person there, but he was very interested. He was impressed by the joy he had seen on Booth's face, and he told us of the people carried away by Booth, and of the conversions." A part of him was powerfully attracted to this sort of thing, but he wouldn't see anything like it again for ten years, when he attended the Abyssinian Baptist Church in New York City.

The turmoil of the early Weimar Republic was never far away, especially in Berlin. When Bonhoeffer was sixteen, it came especially close. On June 25, 1922, he wrote Sabine, "I went to school and arrived after the third period. I just arrived when one heard a peculiar crack in the courtyard. Rathenau had been assassinated—barely 300 meters away from us! What a pack of right-wing Bolshevik scoundrels! . . . People are responding with crazed excitement and rage here in Berlin. They are having fist-fights in the Reichstag."

---

* Kreutzer was a German Jew later targeted by the Nazis (Alfred Rosenberg in particular) as a "cultural enemy," forcing him to immigrate to America in 1933.

Walther Rathenau, a politically moderate Jew, had been the German foreign minister, and he felt Germany should pay its war debts as stipulated by the Treaty of Versailles while simultaneously trying to renegotiate them. For these views, and for his Jewishness, he was despised by the right wing, who that day dispatched a carful of thugs with machine guns to murder him on his way to his offices in the Wilhelmstrasse, near Bonhoeffer's school. Eleven years later, when Hitler rose to power, these murderers were declared German national heroes. June 24 was made a national day of celebration to commemorate their deed.

Peter Olden, a classmate of Bonhoeffer, recalled that they heard the shots during class: "I still recall my friend Bonhoeffer's passionate indignation, his deep and spontaneous anger. . . . I remember his asking what would become of Germany if its best leaders were killed. I remember it because I was surprised at the time that someone could know so exactly where he stood."

Bonhoeffer had been raised in an elite community where many of his family's friends were Jewish. In his class that morning were several children of prominent Jewish families. One of them was Rathenau's niece.

A few weeks later he wrote his parents about a train ride to Tübingen: "One man actually began to talk about politics as soon as he had entered the railway compartment. He was really very narrow-mindedly right-wing. . . . The only thing he had forgotten was his swastika."

CHAPTER 2

TÜBINGEN

1923

From the time I was thirteen years old it was clear to me that I would study theology.

—Dietrich Bonhoeffer

Significant changes came in 1923 for the Bonhoeffers, including the first marriage among the children. Ursula, the eldest daughter, married Rüdiger Schleicher, a brilliant lawyer. His father had been a friend and classmate of Karl Bonhoeffer at Tübingen. Rüdiger studied there, too, and had joined the Igel fraternity, of which Karl Bonhoeffer was a distinguished past member. When he paid a visit to this famous alumnus in Berlin, he met his future wife.

In 1923 Maria van Horn also married: Richard Czeppan was a beloved classics teacher at the Grunewald Gymnasium, and had been part of the life at 14 Wangenheimstrasse for years. He had been Klaus's tutor, often played the piano at family musical gatherings, and in 1922 took a hiking trip in Pomerania with Dietrich.

Also that year, Karl-Friedrich landed a prestigious research position at the Kaiser Wilhelm Institute, where he would soon split the atom, absurdly raising the already high bar of accomplishment for his intelligent and ambitious siblings. His success as a physicist brought invitations from top universities around the world, including the United States, which he would visit, paving the way for Dietrich a few years hence.

And in 1923 Dietrich would leave home, although no one in this close-knit family ever really left. Within a few years, Christel and her husband would move in across the street; and in the thirties, Ursula and Rüdiger would move next door to her parents in Charlottenburg, their homes being almost extensions of each other. Family members visited so often, and were visited so often, and talked on the phone so often that Dietrich's friends teased him about it. The next year, Dietrich would return from Tübingen to study at Berlin University and would live at home again. He would live under his parents' roof for much of the next twenty years, until the day he was arrested in 1943. Still, for the family his departure for Tübingen was a significant moment.

He left at the end of April for the summer term and traveled with Christel, who was also studying there. Their grandmother Julie Bonhoeffer lived in Tübingen at 38 Neckarhalde, on the Neckar River, and they stayed with her for most of their time there. Their parents visited often. Bethge wrote that Bonhoeffer "remained far more rooted in his home than was customary among his fellow students" and "did little without first consulting his parents." Indeed, it was family tradition that all Bonhoeffers begin their university studies with a year in Tübingen. Karl-Friedrich had done so in 1919; Klaus and Sabine had followed. Christel was already there, and of course their father had begun the tradition.

Dietrich also followed in his father's footsteps by joining the Igel fraternity. The Igels had come into existence in 1871, the same year as the German Reich. It was then, following France's defeat in the Franco-Prussian War, that Prussia had led the way in uniting the twenty-five states of Germany. They became a federation called the German Empire, and for the nearly fifty years of its existence this Reich was led by Prussia and the Hohenzollern dynasty. The first German emperor was Wilhelm I, king of Prussia. He served as *primus inter pares* (first among equals) with the heads of the other twenty-four states. Kaiser Wilhelm appointed the Prussian prince Otto von Bismarck as his prime minister. Bismarck took the title of chancellor and came to be known as the Iron Chancellor. Although the Igels were patriotically devoted to Reich and kaiser, they were not as nationalistic or militaristic as other fraternities of their day. Their values were more in keeping with those of the politically moderate Bonhoeffer family, so it wasn't difficult for Dietrich to feel comfortable joining. Still, he was the only one of his brothers to do so.

The German word *Igel*—pronounced "eagle"—means "hedgehog." Members wore hats made from hedgehog pelts. For their official colors they cheekily chose light, medium, and dark gray, monochromatically thumbing their noses at the other fraternities, all of whom had outsized affections for brightly colored hats and ghastly dueling scars. It was a great distinction in German society of the nineteenth and early twentieth centuries to have had one's face manfully disfigured in a fraternity duel.*

The Bonhoeffers were far too secure to fall for such highfalutin buffoonery; they were neither ultranationalists nor monarchists. But they were generally patriotic, so the national pride that characterized the Igels was not unappealing. Karl Bonhoeffer always recalled his time there favorably, but disapproved of the peer pressure to drink. Most Igel members in his day had middle-of-the-road political convictions, being champions of the kaiser and of the policies of Bismarck. Their castlelike headquarters sat on the brow of the hill overlooking the city.

Years later a fellow member recalled Dietrich as extremely secure and self-confident, not vain, but "able to tolerate criticism." He was also "a companionable, physically agile and tough young man" who possessed a "sharp nose for essentials and a determination to get to the bottom of things" and who was also "capable of subtly teasing people and [who] had a great deal of humor."

For Germany, 1923 was disastrous. The German mark, which had begun to slide two years earlier, went into free fall. In 1921 it dropped to 75 marks to the dollar; the next year to 400; and by early 1923 it plunged to 7,000. But this was only the beginning of sorrows. Germany was buckling under the pressure of meeting the payments stipulated by the Versailles Treaty.

---

* A scar earned this way was called a *Schmiss*, or *Renommierschmiss* (literally, bragging scar). Such duels were less duels than baroquely orchestrated poking contests with swords in which participants stood within sword's reach of each other at all times. Bodies and arms were well protected, but as the whole point of this rigmarole was to get a scar and prove one's bravery, faces were not. A hideously gouged cheek or bisected nose would for a lifetime shriek its disfigured bearer's bravery to all and croak his fitness to stand in the noble circle of German elites. So coveted were these ghastly badges of hypertrophic or keloided scar tissue that undergraduates unable to earn them in duels sometimes resorted to other, less approved methods.

In 1922, unable to bear up any longer, the German government asked for a moratorium. The savvy French wouldn't be taken in by this ruse and staunchly refused. But it was no ruse, and Germany soon defaulted. The French promptly dispatched troops to occupy the Ruhr region, Germany's center of industry. The resultant economic turmoil would make the bleak conditions of a few months earlier look like the good old days: by August a dollar was worth one million marks; and by September, August seemed like the good old days. By November 1923 a dollar was worth about four billion German marks.

On November 8 Hitler, sensing his moment, led his famous Munich *Bierhall Putsch*. But he sensed it prematurely and was trundled off to jail for high treason. There, in the peace and quiet of Lansberg am Lech, like an exiled emperor, he met with cronies, dictated his crackpot manifesto *Mein Kampf*, and planned his next move.

Toward the end of 1923 a life-insurance policy of Karl Bonhoeffer's matured, paying him 100,000 marks. He had made the payments for decades, and now, because of inflation, the reward was only enough to purchase a bottle of wine and some strawberries. When the money arrived, it was worth even less and covered only the berries. It was a boon that Karl Bonhoeffer saw many patients from around Europe because they paid him in their own country's currency. Nonetheless, by the end of 1923, things had become impossible. In October Dietrich wrote that every meal cost one billion marks. He wanted to pay for two or three weeks of meals in advance, but needed the family to send him funds. "I don't have that much money on hand," he explained. "I had to spend 6 billion for bread."

A new member of the Igels was a *Fuchs* (Fox), alluding to the ancient Greek poet Archilochus, who famously declared that "the fox knows many little things, but the hedgehog knows one big thing." Each Fuchs had to pen a short curriculum vitae about himself in the fraternity's *Fuchsbuch*, as Bonhoeffer did:

> In Breslau on February 4, 1906, I, with my twin sister, saw the light of day as the son of the university professor *der alter Herr* Karl Bonhoeffer and my mother, née von Hase. I left Silesia when I was six years old, and we moved to Berlin where I entered the Friedrich-Werder Gymnasium. Due to our move to Grunewald, I entered the school

there, where I passed my Abitur at Easter 1923. From the time I was thirteen years old it was clear to me that I would study theology. Only music caused me to waver during the past two years. I am now studying here in Tübingen for my first semester, where I took the customary step for every dutiful son and became a Hedgehog. I have chosen Fritz Schmid to be my personal bodyguard. I have nothing else to share about myself.

Dietrich Bonhoeffer.

"Today I Am a Soldier"

Among the harshest conditions of Versailles was the prohibition against military conscription: Germany was allowed only a 100,000-man army. This meant flirting with national suicide, since the Russians, just over the border in Poland, might at any time have marched in and subdued them. Or an internal group—there were several candidates—could have militarily taken over the country without much difficulty. That nearly happened on November 8, with Hitler's attempted putsch. Such political turmoil called for a level of military readiness that the Allies were unwilling to grant, so the Germans invented ways around it to avoid the interference of the Allied Control Commission. One was for university students to receive covert training during the semesters. These troops were referred to as the Black Reichswehr. In November 1923 it was Dietrich's turn.

His training would take two weeks and would be overseen by the Ulm Rifles Troop in Ulm, not far from Tübingen. Many of his Igel brethren would join him, and all of the other fraternities participated. Bonhoeffer felt no great hesitation, seeing it as a part of his most basic patriotic duty. But he knew he must have his parents' approval and wrote them on the eve of his departure:

The sole purpose is to train as many people as possible before the Control Commission is put in place. . . . There is a one-day notice period and every member of the [Igel] fraternity who has studied at the university for 7 semesters or less is going. . . . I said I would go until approximately Tuesday when I expected to hear what you had to say about this situation. If you had any specific objections I would then return to Tübingen. At first I thought that I could do this at another time and that it would be better not to interrupt the semester. I now think, however, that the sooner one gets this over with the better; then one can have the secure feeling that one can help in crises. Grandmama is sad that she will be alone for 14 days, but says I should go ahead and go.

Two days later he wrote, "Today I am a soldier. Yesterday, as soon as we arrived, we were invested with a uniform and were given our equipment. Today we were given grenades and weapons. Until now, to be sure, we have done nothing but assemble and disassemble our beds."

A few days later he wrote again:

The exercises have not been very taxing at all. There are approximately 5 hours of marching, shooting, and gymnastics daily, and 3 instruction periods, as well as other things. The rest of the time is free. We live 14 to a room. . . . The only thing that the examination found amiss were my eyes. I'll probably have to wear glasses when I fire a weapon. The Lance Corporal who trains us is very good-natured and nice.

He even found the food decent. The second week he wrote Sabine:

We practiced ground maneuvers with assaults and such. It is especially horrible to throw oneself down on the frozen field with a rifle and a knapsack. Tomorrow we have a big marching exercise with all our equipment, and on Wednesday we have a battalion maneuver. After that the fortnight will soon be over. The oily spots on this paper do not, it happens, come from the pancakes we had at noon but from cleaning a rifle.

By December 1, it was all over. He informed his parents in another letter: "Dear Parents, Today I am a civilian."

Perchance to Rome

That winter while Dietrich was living with his grandmother, they discussed the idea of his visiting Gandhi in India. His grandmother encouraged it.

What her interest in Gandhi was we cannot know for sure. During the previous century, she was active in the budding field of women's rights: she built a home for elderly women and founded a domestic school for girls in Stuttgart. For her efforts she was awarded a medal of the Order of Olga, presented to her by the queen of Württemberg. It's possible the Indian leader's strong support of women's rights attracted her attention. In any case, she thought the experience advisable for Dietrich and offered to pay for it. But something else took him abroad in another direction entirely.

The seventeen-year-old Dietrich often skated on the Neckar River that winter, but in late January 1924, he slipped and fell on the ice, striking his head so hard that he lay unconscious for some time. When his father, the brain expert, learned the details of the accident and of how long his son was unconscious, he and his wife immediately traveled to Tübingen. Dietrich had suffered a concussion, nothing more, and what began as an unpleasant journey turned into a pleasant visit. For Dietrich it was extremely pleasant because it was during this time of convalescence, in which he celebrated his eighteenth birthday, that the utterly capital idea of a semester in Rome presented itself. Dietrich seemed almost to have lost his mind for joy at the prospect.

The day after their birthday, he wrote Sabine. Their silly competitive teasing knew no bounds:

I received all sorts of fabulous and magnificent things for my birthday. Surely you know about the books. I received something else that you won't even be able to guess at, a splendid guitar. I'm sure you'll be jealous because it has a wonderful tone. Papa had given me 50 marks for anything else I wanted, so I bought a guitar and am very happy about it. And just so you won't get over your astonishment, I'll tell you about the next completely unbelievable occurrence. Just think, it is possible that next semester—I will be studying in Rome!! Of course, nothing is at all certain yet, but it would be absolutely the most fabulous thing that could happen to me. I can't even begin to imagine how great that would be! . . . [Y]ou can certainly shower me with advice; but don't be too envious while you are doing it. I'm already making inquiries everywhere around here. Everyone is telling me that it is very inexpensive. Papa still thinks that I really should postpone it. Nevertheless after thinking

about it, I want to do it so much that I can't imagine ever wanting to
do it more than I do now. . . . Talk about it a lot at home; it can only
help things. Keep your ears open as well. . . . Best wishes, and don't be
too envious.

Yours, Dietrich

In a series of letters quickly following, Dietrich tried to wheedle his parents' approval for the trip—presenting reasons for its sensibleness and trying
to hide his giddy excitement. To his tremendous satisfaction, and probably
because his brother Klaus would accompany him, they lent their approval.
The date for his departure was set. On the evening of April 3, half-wild with
expectation, he and Klaus would board the night train for Rome. What he
would experience in the glorious and fabled city would be more important
to his future than even he had expected.

The weeks before departure would be the last of his time in Tübingen.
After his summer in Rome, he would not return there, but would complete
his studies in Berlin. In a few years the zeitgeist would blow the Igel fraternity to the right and when, in 1935, they officially adopted the terrible
Aryan Paragraph, Bonhoeffer and his brother-in-law Walter Dress would dis-
gustedly and publicly resign their memberships.

CHAPTER 3

ROMAN HOLIDAY

1924

The universality of the church was illustrated in a marvelously
effective manner. White, black, yellow members of religious orders—
everyone was in clerical robes united under the church. It truly seems
ideal.

—DIETRICH BONHOEFFER

Because of the distaste for France and England engendered by the war and Versailles, traveling to Italy became especially popular among Germans. But for Klaus and Dietrich Bonhoeffer it was the cultural and ancestral pilgrimage of a lifetime.

Like many of their generation, both received educations that sang the glories of Rome, and both knew well its language, art, literature, and history. At sixteen, Dietrich chose to write his lengthy graduation paper on the lyric poetry of Horace and Catullus. At the Grunewald Gymnasium, pictures of the Roman forum decorated the classroom walls. Richard Czeppan was a veritable "walking lexicon of ancient Rome," who had visited innumerable times and had thrilled them with his memories. There was a family connection too. Their great-grandfather, Karl August von Hase, the famous theologian, had visited Rome twenty times and had strong ties there. Over the years, this ancestor's influence increased as Dietrich became interested in following in his theological footsteps.

The eighteen-year-old pilgrim kept a detailed journal. On the train, just beyond the Brenner Pass, he wrote, "It feels strange when one first crosses the Italian border. Fantasy begins to transform itself into reality. Will it really be nice to have all one's wishes fulfilled? Or might I return home completely disillusioned after all?"

The answer was not long in coming: he was bowled over in Bologna, which he described as "extremely and astoundingly beautiful." And then at last, Rome! "However," he wrote, introducing a discordant note, "the knavery already began at the train station." An Italian boy who shared a cab with them and led them to their destination demanded they pay his fare and give him a tip to boot. (They paid his fare, but not the tip.) Upon arriving at their accommodations, they learned that their rooms had been ready for two days, and those days must be paid for!

Bonhoeffer spun through Rome like a cyclone, absorbing as much of its culture as possible. Unsurprisingly he revealed himself as impressively knowledgeable in art history. On the Colosseum: "This building has such power and beauty that, from the moment one sees it, one knows one has never seen nor been able to imagine anything like it. Antiquity is not completely dead. . . . It becomes very clear after only a few moments how false is the statement *Pan o megas tethniken*.* The Colosseum is overgrown, entwined with the most luxurious vegetation, palm trees, cypress, pine, herbs, and all sorts of grasses. I sat there for almost an hour." On the *Laocöon*: "When I saw the *Laocoön* for the first time, I actually shuddered; it is incredible." On the Sistine Chapel: "Terribly full. Only foreigners. Nonetheless the impression is indescribable." On Trajan's Forum: "The column is magnificent, but the rest looks like a harvested vegetable garden." On the choir at St. Peter's: "The *'Christus Factus*,' *'Benedictus'* (Luke 1–2) and *'Miserere'* (Psalm 50) by the choir were simply indescribable." On the eunuch who sang the alto solos that day: "There is something about the way they sing that is thoroughly inhuman, English, dispassionate, and united with a peculiar rapturous ecstasy." On Reni and Michelangelo: "One thing that is enchantingly beautiful is the *Concert of Angels* by Reni. No one should be allowed to leave Rome without having seen this work. It is absolutely perfect in its design and, without a doubt, ranks among the premier artworks of Rome. But the busts begun by Michelangelo

---

* The great god Pan is dead!

leave one cold, especially the one of the pope, which is, I think, devoid of any complexity in artistic style or expression."

At the Vatican he was enraptured with the Sistine Chapel:

I was hardly able to move beyond Adam. There is an inexhaustible abundance of ideas in the picture. The figure of God reverberates with colossal power and tender love, or rather with the divine attributes that supersede these two human attributes that are often far removed from each other. Man is about to awake to life for the first time. The meadow sends out shoots in front of unending mountain ranges, thereby fore- shadowing man's later fate. The painting is very worldly and yet very pure. In short, one can't express it.

His favorite figure in Michelangelo's masterpiece was Jonah. As if to burnish his aesthetic credentials, he raved to his diary about its "perspectival shortening."

The eighteen-year-old's precocity in these observations was outdone only in his self-confident thoughts on the subject of interpretation and observation itself:

At the moment it gives me great pleasure to try to guess the schools and the individual artists. I believe that gradually I am better able to understand something about the subject than I was before. However, it might be better for a layperson to be completely silent and to leave everything to the artists, because the current art historians really are the worst guides. Even the better ones are awful. This includes Scheffler and Worringer, who arbitrarily interpret, interpret, and further interpret the artworks. There is no criterion for their interpretation and its correct- ness. Interpreting is generally one of the most difficult problems. Yet, our whole thinking process is regulated by it. We have to interpret and give meaning to things so that we can live and think. All of this is very difficult. When one doesn't have to interpret, one should just leave it alone. I believe that interpretation is not necessary in art. One doesn't need to know whether it is "Gothic" or "primitive," etc., persons who express themselves in their art. A work of art viewed with clear intel- lect and comprehension has its own effect on the unconscious. More interpretation won't lead to a better understanding of the art. One either intuitively sees the right thing or one doesn't. This is what I call an understanding of art. One should work diligently to try to understand the work while looking at it. After that one gets the absolutely certain feeling, "I have grasped the essence of this work." Intuitive certainty arises on the basis of some unknown procedure. To attempt to put this conclusion into words and thereby to interpret the work is meaningless for anyone else. It doesn't help one person, other people won't need it, and the subject itself gains nothing by it.

Bonhoeffer's letters home touched on less noble subjects. In an April 21 letter to his parents, he described their arrival in Naples: "After a long search for a trattoria I was directed to a 'buona trattoria' that was to be sure, as unbelievably filthy as the nastiest farmhouse in Germany. Hens, cats, dirty children, and unpleasant aromas surrounded us. Drying clothes fluttered all around us. But hunger, fatigue, and ignorance of the countryside induced us to sit down."

Not long after their foul repast, the two brothers boarded a ship for Sicily. Klaus's stomach and sea travel were irreconcilable under even the best circumstances; now they became bitter enemies. "The sea made great demands on him," Bonhoeffer wrote, "and he was able to hold out against it only for a short time. It invited me to perform my duty only at first sight of the magnificent sunny mountainous cliffs." Even expressing an emetic plural, Dietrich maintained decorum. As ever, his travels spawned further travels. The brothers decided to visit North Africa and boarded a ship for Tripoli: "The voyage was quiet. Klaus, as always, did his duty." They visited Pompeii: "Vesuvius was in good working order, and now and again it spewed out a bit of lava. There, at the summit, one believes one has been transported back to the time before the creation of the world." Commenting on a visit to St. Stefano Rotondo and St. Maria Navicella, he noted, "A disagreement with the sexton's thieving wife couldn't take away the idyllic atmosphere of the whole."

So it went for months. Yet the real significance of this trip for Dietrich Bonhoeffer lay not in its culture-broadening aspect as a mini–grand tour or in its academic aspect as a semester abroad, but in its prompting his thoughts on the question that he would ask and answer for the rest of his life: *What is the church?*

What Is the Church?

In his diary Bonhoeffer recorded that Palm Sunday was "the first day that something of the reality of Catholicism dawned on me, nothing romantic or the like, but rather that I am beginning, I believe, to understand the concept 'church.'" This new idea forming in the eighteen-year-old's mind that day in Rome would end up having profoundly significant ramifications.

The occasion for his epiphany that day was a Mass at St. Peter's performed by a cardinal, with a boys' choir whose singing took his breath away. A host of other clergy, including seminarians and monks, was at the altar: "The universality of the church was illustrated in a marvelously effective manner. White, black, yellow members of religious orders—everyone was in clerical robes united under the church. It truly seems ideal." He had likely been to a Catholic service in Germany, but now, in Rome, in the Eternal City, the city of Peter and Paul, he saw a vivid illustration of the church's transcendence of race and national identity. It obviously affected him. During the Mass, he stood next to a woman with a missal and was able to follow along and enjoy it all the more. He gushed over the choir's singing of the *Credo*.

To think of the church as something universal would change everything and would set in motion the entire course of Bonhoeffer's remaining life, because if the church was something that actually existed, then it existed not just in Germany or Rome, but beyond both. This glimpse of the church as something beyond the Lutheran Protestant Church of Germany, as a universal Christian community, was a revelation and an invitation to further thinking: *What is the church?* It was the question he would attack in his doctoral dissertation, *Sanctorum Communio*, and in his post-doctoral work, *Act and Being*.

But Bonhoeffer was no mere academic. For him, ideas and beliefs were nothing if they did not relate to the world of reality outside one's mind. Indeed, his thoughts on the nature of the church would lead him into the ecumenical movement in Europe, causing him to link hands with Christians outside Germany, and therefore to see instantly the lie at the heart of the so-called orders of creation theology, which linked the idea of the church with the German *Volk*. This idea of a church defined by racial identity and blood—which the Nazis would violently push and so many Germans tragically embrace—was anathema to the idea of the universal church. So it was on this Palm Sunday in Rome that Bonhoeffer's course was set in motion.

Ideas had consequences, and this idea, now just budding, would flower in his opposition to the National Socialists and bear fruit in his involvement in the conspiracy to kill a human being.

The openness that Bonhoeffer brought to this idea of the church—and to the Roman Catholic Church—was hardly typical of German Lutherans. Several things account for it, the first being his upbringing. He had been reared to guard against parochialism and to assiduously avoid relying on feelings or anything unsupported by sound reasoning. To his father's scientist's mind, any actions and attitudes based on anything like tribal affiliations were wrong, and he had trained his children to think the same way. For Dietrich the theologian to hold a prejudice in favor of Lutheranism or Protestantism, or even Christianity, would be wrong. One must consider every possibility and avoid predisposing oneself to where it would all lead. During his lifetime, Bonhoeffer brought this critical and "scientific" attitude to all questions of faith and theology.

But another reason he was so open to the Catholic church now had to do with Rome itself, where the best of the classical pagan world he so loved met and coexisted harmoniously with the world of Christendom. Here in Rome it was all part of some continuum. For him, it was difficult to be closed to a church that somehow partook of the splendor of classical antiquity, that seemed to see the best in it and even to redeem some of it. The Lutheran and Protestant traditions were less connected to the great classical past and could therefore veer toward the heresies of Gnostic dualism, of denial of the body and of the goodness of this world. But here in Rome the mingling of these two worlds was everywhere. It was in the Vatican, for example, that he beheld the *Laocoön*, probably his favorite sculpture; and in a letter to Eberhard Bethge years later, he remarked that the face of this pagan priest on a Hellenistic sculpture with a classical Greek theme might have been a model for subsequent artistic depictions of Christ. Somehow Rome plausibly brought everything together. In his diary he wrote, "It is Rome as a whole that came to be epitomized most clearly by St. Peter's. It is the Rome of antiquity, the Rome of the Middle Ages, and equally the Rome of the present. Simply stated, it is the fulcrum of European culture and European life. My heart beat perceptibly when I saw the old water conduits accompanying us to the walls of the city for the second time."

A third reason for his openness to Catholicism was encouraged by his tenure under Adolf Schlatter, the teacher at Tübingen who had the greatest influence on him. Schlatter often used theological texts that were traditionally used only by Catholic theologians. Bonhoeffer had felt an innate desire to ecumenically draw these "Catholic" texts back into the larger Christian theological conversation.

That Palm Sunday Bonhoeffer attended Evensong too. At six o'clock he was at the Trinità dei Monti and found it "almost indescribable." He wrote of the "forty young girls who wanted to become nuns entered in a solemn procession wearing nun's habits with blue or green sashes. . . . With unbelievable simplicity, grace, and great seriousness they sang Evensong while a priest officiated at the altar. . . . The ritual was truly no longer merely ritual. Instead, it was worship in the true sense. The whole thing gave one an unparalleled impression of profound, guileless piety."

During Holy Week, he wondered about the Reformation and whether it went wrong when it officially became a church rather than simply remaining a "sect." In a few years this would become crucially important to him. When the Nazis were taking over the German Lutheran Church, he would lead the charge to break away and start the Confessing Church. That, too, was first considered a movement—the Confessional Movement—but then it became an official church. He would have much to do with its taking that direction. Bonhoeffer was already laying the intellectual groundwork for what he would face in the Germany of the Third Reich, ten years ahead.

At this stage, though, he seemed to be in favor of the idea of a movement that did not become an organized church. In his diary, he wrote,

> If Protestantism had never become an established church the situation would be completely different . . . [it] would represent an unusual phenomenon of religious life and serious thoughtful piety. It would therefore be the ideal form of religion. . . . [The church] must completely separate herself from the state. . . . It wouldn't be long before the people return because they must have something. They would have rediscovered their need for piety. Could this be a solution? Or not?

Bonhoeffer typically took complete advantage of being in a new place, and while in Rome that Holy Week, he attended morning and afternoon

Masses from Wednesday through Saturday at St. Peter's or at the Basilica of St. John Lateran. At every service he used the missal, studying it carefully. He wrote his parents, "The generally dreadful recitation of these texts by the priest and the choir at home leads one to believe that the quality of the texts themselves is equally poor. This is completely wrong. For the most part the texts are wonderfully poetic and lucid."

He attended one Armenian-Catholic service that seemed "stiff and devoid of new life." He felt that Roman Catholicism was moving in that direction but observed that there were "many religious establishments where a vital religious life still plays a part. The confessional is an example of this." He exulted in much of what he saw. But he did not feel led to embrace Catholicism as a convert. An acquaintance he met in Rome tried to convince him, but Bonhoeffer was unmoved: "He would really like to convert me and is quite honestly convinced of his method. . . . Following these discussions, I find I am once again much less sympathetic to Catholicism. Catholic dogma veils every ideal thing in Catholicism without knowing that this is what it is doing. There is a huge difference between confession and dogmatic teachings about confession—unfortunately also between 'church' and the 'church' in dogmatics." He considered the union of both churches: "The unification of Catholicism and Protestantism is probably impossible, although it would do both parties much good." In a few years he would incorporate the best of both into his Christian communities at Zingst and Finkenwalde—and be roundly criticized for it by many German Lutherans.

Somehow, before the semester was over, Bonhoeffer got an audience with the pope: "*Saturday*, audience with the Pope. Great expectations dashed. It was fairly impersonal and coolly [celebratory]. The pope made a fairly indifferent impression on me. He lacked everything indicative of a pope. All grandeur and anything extraordinary was missing. Sad that it had that effect!"

Before he knew it, his glorious time in Rome was at an end: "When I looked at St. Peter's for the last time, there was a pain around my heart, and I quickly got on the trolleycar and left."

Three years later, Bonhoeffer led a discussion group called the Thursday Circle. It consisted of bright young men around sixteen or seventeen years of age. They covered many topics, and one week they discussed the Catholic church, prompting Bonhoeffer to summarize his thoughts in the following short paper:

It is hard to overestimate the importance of the Catholic church's value for European culture and for the whole world. It Christianized and civilized barbaric peoples and for a long time was the only guardian of science and art. Here the church's cloisters were preeminent. The Catholic church developed a spiritual power unequaled anywhere, and today we still admire the way it combined the principle of catholicism with the principle of one sanctifying church, as well as tolerance with intolerance. It is a world in itself. Infinite diversity flows together, and this colorful picture gives it its irresistible charm (*Complexio oppositorum*). A country has seldom produced so many different kinds of people as has the Catholic church. With admirable power, it has understood how to maintain unity in diversity, to gain the love and respect of the masses, and to foster a strong sense of community. . . . But it is exactly because of this greatness that we have serious reservations. Has this world [of the Catholic church] really remained the church of Christ? Has it not perhaps become an obstruction blocking the path to God instead of a road sign on the path to God? Has it not blocked the only path to salvation? Yet no one can ever obstruct the way to God. The church still has the Bible, and as long as she has it we can still believe in the holy Christian church. God's word will never be denied (Isa. 55:11), whether it be preached by us or by our sister church. We adhere to the same confession of faith, we pray the same Lord's Prayer, and we share some of the same ancient rites. This binds us together, and as far as we are concerned we would like to live in peace with our disparate sister. We do not, however, want to deny anything that we have recognized as God's word. The designation Catholic or Protestant is unimportant. The important thing is God's word. Conversely, we will never violate anyone else's faith. God does not desire reluctant service, and God has given everyone a conscience. We can and should desire that our sister church search its soul and concentrate on nothing but the word [1 Cor. 2:12–13]. Until that time, we must have patience. We will have to endure it when, in false darkness, the "only holy church" pronounces upon our church the "anathema" (condemnation). She doesn't know any better, and she doesn't hate the heretic, only the heresy. As long as we let the word be our only armor we can look confidently into the future.

 CHAPTER 4

STUDENT IN BERLIN

1924–27

It was hard for any group of people to live up to the standards expected and maintained in the Wangenheimstrasse. Bonhoeffer himself admitted that newcomers to his home were put under the microscope. With that background it was easy for him to create the impression of being superior and stand-offish.

—Eberhard Bethge

Bonhoeffer returned from Rome in mid-June, enrolling in the summer semester at Berlin University. Switching colleges after a year or two was common in Germany. He'd never planned to stay in Tübingen more than a year. He would study in Berlin seven semesters, earning his doctorate in 1927, at age twenty-one.

Bonhoeffer again lived at home, but since he'd left, something important had changed: Sabine was now studying in Breslau, and she was engaged to a young lawyer named Gerhard Leibholz, who was Jewish. Through Sabine and her future family, the Bonhoeffers would experience the difficulties of the years ahead in an especially personal way.

Dietrich's decision to study at Berlin University was not difficult. For one thing it was in Berlin, which for someone addicted to cultural stimulation made it ideal. Hardly a week passed that he didn't go to a museum,

opera, or concert. And Berlin was home, with all that entailed. A more stimu-
lating environment cannot be imagined. Karl-Friedrich was working with
Albert Einstein and Max Planck. According to Bethge, "It was hard for any
group of people to live up to the standards expected and maintained in the
Wangenheimstrasse. Bonhoeffer himself admitted that newcomers to this
home were put under the microscope. With that background it was easy
for him to create the impression of being superior and stand-offish." But
Bonhoeffer's principal reason for choosing Berlin University was its theological faculty, which was world-renowned and had included the famous
Friedrich Schleiermacher, whose presence still hovered palpably.

In 1924 the theological faculty was headed by Adolf von Harnack, then
seventy-three and a living legend. He was a disciple of Schleiermacher,
which is to say staunchly theologically liberal, and one of the leaders of the
historical-critical method of the nineteenth and early twentieth centuries.
His approach to the Bible was limited to textual and historical-critical analysis, and had led him to conclude that the miracles it described never happened, and that the gospel of John was not canonical. Harnack lived in the
Grunewald neighborhood, as did most distinguished academics then, and the
young Bonhoeffer would often walk with him to the Halensee train station
and ride with him into Berlin. He attended Harnack's prestigious seminar for
three semesters and esteemed the venerable scholar greatly, though he rarely
agreed with his theological conclusions. A fellow student in Harnack's seminar, Helmuth Goes, recalled feeling a "secret enthusiasm" for Bonhoeffer's
"free, critical and independent" theological thinking:

> What really impressed me was not just the fact that he surpassed
> almost all of us in theological knowledge and capacity; but what pas-
> sionately attracted me to Bonhoeffer was the perception that here
> was a man who did not only learn and gather in the *verba* and *scripta*
> of some master, but one who thought independently and already
> knew what he wanted and wanted what he knew. I had the experi-
> ence (for me it was something alarming and magnificently new!) of
> hearing a young fair-haired student contradict the revered historian,
> his Excellency von Harnack, contradict him politely but clearly on
> positive theological grounds. Harnack answered, but the student con-
> tradicted again and again.

Bonhoeffer was a remarkably independent thinker, especially for one so young. Some professors regarded him as arrogant, especially because he refused to come too directly under the influence of any one of them, always preferring to maintain some distance. But someone who grew up dining with Karl Bonhoeffer, and who was allowed to speak only when he could justify every syllable, had probably developed a certain intellectual confidence and may be somewhat excused if he was not intimidated by other great minds.

Besides Harnack, three other Berlin professors had a decided influence on Bonhoeffer. They were Karl Holl, who was perhaps the greatest Luther scholar of that generation; Reinhold Seeberg, who specialized in systematic theology, and under whom Bonhoeffer wrote his doctoral thesis; and Adolf Deissman, who was Bonhoeffer's introduction to the ecumenical movement, which would play such an important role in his life and provide the means by which he became involved in the conspiracy against Hitler. But there was another theologian who had a greater influence on Bonhoeffer than any of these, and whom he would revere and respect as much as anyone in his lifetime, who would even become a mentor and a friend. This was Karl Barth of Göttingen.

Barth was Swiss by birth and was almost certainly the most important theologian of the century; many would say of the last five centuries. Bonhoeffer's cousin Hans-Christoph was studying physics at Göttingen in 1924, but after hearing Barth, he promptly switched to theology and stayed there. Like most theological students in the late nineteenth century, Barth absorbed the regnant liberal theology of his time, but he grew to reject it, quickly becoming its most formidable opponent. His groundbreaking 1922 commentary, *The Epistle to the Romans*, fell like a smart bomb into the ivory tower of scholars like Adolf von Harnack, who could hardly believe their historical-critical fortress pregnable, and who were scandalized by Barth's approach to the Bible, which came to be called neo-orthodoxy, and which asserted the idea, particularly controversial in German theological circles, that God actually exists, and that all theology and biblical scholarship must be undergirded by this basic assumption, and that's that. Barth was the principal figure in challenging and overturning the influence of the German historical-critical approach pioneered at Berlin University by Schleiermacher—and furthered there by the current *éminence grise* Harnack. Barth stressed the transcendence of God, describing him as "wholly other," and therefore completely unknowable by man, except via revelation. Fortunately he believed in revelation, which was further scandalous to theological liberals like Harnack. For refusing to swear his allegiance to Hitler, Barth would be kicked out of Germany in 1934, and he would become the principal author of the Barmen Declaration, in which the Confessing Church trumpeted its rejection of the Nazis' attempts to bring their philosophy into the German church.

Harnack's theology was something like Archilochus's proverbial fox, knowing many little things, while Barth's theology was like a hedgehog, knowing one big thing. Bonhoeffer would side with the hedgehog, but he was in the fox's seminar, and through his family and the Grunewald community, he had many ties with the fox. As a result of his intellectual openness, Bonhoeffer learned how to think like a fox and respect the way foxes thought, even though he was in the camp of the hedgehogs. He could appreciate the value in something, even if he ultimately rejected that something—and could see the errors and flaws in something, even if he ultimately accepted that something. This attitude figured into his creation of the illegal seminaries of Zingst and Finkenwalde, which incorporated the best of both Protestant and Catholic traditions. Because of this self-critical intellectual integrity, Bonhoeffer sometimes had such confidence in his conclusions that he could seem arrogant.

The debate during Bonhoeffer's time between the neo-orthodox Barthians and the historical-critical liberals was similar to the contemporary one between strict Darwinian evolutionists and advocates of so-called Intelligent Design. The latter allow the possible involvement of something "outside the system"—some Intelligent Creator, whether divine or other—while the former reject this by definition. Theological liberals like Harnack felt it was "unscientific" to speculate on who God was; the theologian must simply study what is here, which is to say the texts and the history of those texts. But the Barthians said no: the God on the other side of the fence had revealed himself *through* these texts, and the only reason for these texts was to know him.

Bonhoeffer agreed with Barth, seeing the texts as "not just historical sources, but [as] agents of revelation," not merely "specimens of writing, but sacred canon." Bonhoeffer was not against doing historical and critical work on biblical texts; indeed he had learned from Harnack how to do it and could do it brilliantly. Harnack powerfully flattered the eighteen-year-old when, after reading the fifty-seven-page essay Bonhoeffer wrote for his seminar, he suggested Bonhoeffer might someday do his dissertation in the field. Harnack obviously hoped to convince him to follow in his footsteps by choosing the field of church history.

As ever, Bonhoeffer cagily maintained a certain distance. He wished to learn from the old master, but would preserve his intellectual independence. In the end he would not choose church history. He respected that field, as he demonstrated by mastering it, to Harnack's delight, but he disagreed with Harnack that one must stop there. He believed that picking over the texts as they did, and going no further, left behind "rubble and fragments." It was the God beyond the texts, the God who was their author and who spoke to mankind through them, that fired his interest.

For his doctoral dissertation Bonhoeffer was drawn to dogmatics, the study of the beliefs of the church. Dogmatics was closer to philosophy, and Bonhoeffer was at heart more philosopher than textual critic. He didn't want to disappoint his friendly old neighbor, Harnack, who continued to woo him, but now Bonhoeffer had another eminent professor to deal with. Reinhold Seeberg's field was dogmatics, so it seemed Bonhoeffer might write his dissertation under him. This presented not one, but two difficulties. First, Seeberg was a bitter rival of Harnack, and the two of them were competing for the theological affections of the same young theological genius. And second, Seeberg was deeply opposed to Barthian theology.

In his essay for Seeberg's seminar, Bonhoeffer expressed the Barthian idea that in order to know anything at all about God, one had to rely on revelation *from* God. In other words, God could speak into this world, but man could not reach out of this world to examine God. It was a one-way street, and of course this was directly related to the especially Lutheran doctrine of grace. Man could not earn his way up to heaven, but God could reach down and graciously lift man toward him.

Seeberg disagreed, and after reading Bonhoeffer's essay, he became agitated: it was as though a cocky Barthian rooster had sneaked into his chicken coop. He thought he might talk sense into the brash young genius's head by appealing to a higher authority, and that summer, at a meeting of distinguished Berlin academics, he had a conversation with Karl Bonhoeffer. Perhaps this eminent scientist could reach his son. Karl Bonhoeffer was intellectually closer to Seeberg's views than to his son's, but his respect for Dietrich's mind and intellectual integrity was such that he did not try to influence him.

That August, Dietrich was hiking along the Baltic coast. From the house of an Igel brother near Bremen he wrote his father, asking what Seeberg had said and how to proceed. The answer was inconclusive. Then his mother weighed in, suggesting that perhaps he should study under Holl, the Luther expert, and write his dissertation on dogmatics after Seeberg was out of the picture. As the daughter of a respected theologian and the granddaughter of a world-famous one, she likely had more to say on this subject than any mother in Germany. The intellect of both Bonhoeffer parents and their interest in their son's academic progress are remarkable, and we can hardly wonder at his closeness to them. They were an unwavering and unflagging resource of wisdom and love for him to the very end.

By September he made his decision: he would write his doctoral dissertation under Seeberg after all, but it would be on a subject dogmatic *and* historical. He would write about the subject he had begun puzzling over in Rome, namely, *What is the church?* It was eventually titled *Sanctorum Communio: A Dogmatic Inquiry into the Sociology of the Church*. Bonhoeffer would identify the church as neither a historical entity nor an institution, but as "Christ existing as church-community." It was a stunning debut.

During these three years in Berlin, Bonhoeffer had a staggering workload, yet he completed his doctoral dissertation in eighteen months. But somehow he had a very full life beyond the world of academics too. He was endlessly attending operas, concerts, art exhibitions, and plays; he maintained a copious correspondence with friends, colleagues, and family; and he was perpetually traveling, whether on shorter trips to Friedrichsbrunn or on longer trips to the Baltic seashore. In August 1925 he hiked on the Schleswig-Holstein peninsula and sailed in the North Sea. In August 1926 he and Karl-Friedrich visited the Dolomites and Venice. In April 1927, Dietrich and his sister Susi took a trip through the German countryside with another brother-and-sister pair, Walter and Ilse Dress. Like many of the children who grew up in the Grunewald neighborhood together, Susi and Walter soon paired off and were married.

Bonhoeffer spent much time at home too: 14 Wangenheimstrasse was a proverbial hive of activity, with friends, relatives, and colleagues forever coming and going. Karl and Paula Bonhoeffer's children had been getting married and having children, and these families visited. Everyone managed to stay in touch with everyone else, even as their numbers expanded. When Grandmother Bonhoeffer left Tübingen and moved in with them, there were sometimes four generations in the house. The tradition of Saturday night musical evenings also continued, and almost every week someone was having a birthday or anniversary.

As a theological candidate, Bonhoeffer had an obligation of parish work as well. He could have gotten permission to do a minimal amount, since his superiors knew how much academic work he was carrying, but characteristically Bonhoeffer did the opposite, ambitiously taking on a Sunday school class at the Grunewald parish church with vigor and vision. He worked under a youth pastor, Rev. Karl Meumann, and every Friday at Meumann's house he and the other teachers prepared their Sunday lessons. Bonhoeffer became deeply involved in this class, and it took up many hours each week. In addition to the lessons, he often preached sermons in which he used dramatic stories to communicate the gospel, sometimes inventing fairy tales or parables. With Sabine gone, Bonhoeffer became closer to his youngest sister, Susanne. He persuaded her to help him run the class, and soon they were inviting these children home to play games or taking them on outings around Berlin.

Bonhoeffer had an obvious gift for communicating with children. He was greatly taken with them and would work with children at three significant points in the near future: during his year in Barcelona; during his year in New York; and then back in Berlin, when he taught a memorable confirmation class in a tough, working-class neighborhood. What happened in each instance happened now at Grunewald. He became involved with the children beyond the classroom, devoting significant time and energy to them. He was so popular that children from other classes left to join his, causing some embarrassment. Bonhoeffer began to wonder whether he ought to pursue the life of a pastor rather than that of an academic. His father and brothers thought that would be a waste of his great intellect, but he often said that if one couldn't communicate the most profound ideas about God and the Bible to children, something was amiss. There was more to life than academia.

Out of this Sunday school class grew something else: the Thursday Circle, a weekly reading and discussion group of young men he personally selected, which met at his home and which he taught. He issued invitations to this group, which began in April 1927. The invitations stated that the group would meet "Every Thursday 5:25–7:00 p.m." Bonhoeffer did it of his own accord; it had no connection to his church obligations. But he felt it vitally important to train up the next generation of young men. The participants tended to be bright and mature for their ages, and some came from prominent Jewish families in Grunewald.

The Thursday Circle covered a multitude of topics, including religion, ethics, politics, and culture. Part of the requirement for the group entailed attending cultural events. One week Bonhoeffer gave a talk on Wagner's *Parsifal* and then took the group to see the opera itself. There were questions of Christian apologetics: "Did God create the world? . . . What is the purpose of prayer? . . . Who is Jesus Christ?" There were ethical questions: "Is there such a thing as a necessary lie?" They discussed the Christian perspective on Jews, on rich and poor, and on political parties. One week the topic was "the gods of the ancient Germans," and another week it was "the gods of the Negro tribes." One week the topic was "famous poets and their God (Goethe, Schiller)," and another it was "famous painters and their God (Grünewald, Dürer, Rembrandt)." They discussed mystery cults, the Muslim faith, music, Luther, and the Catholic church.*

After he left for Barcelona, Bonhoeffer continued to stay in touch with a number of these young men. One of them, Goetz Grosch, took over after Bonhoeffer left, and seven years later he became a seminary candidate at Finkenwalde. Tragically Grosch and most of the young men from the Thursday Circle died during the war, either on the field of battle or in concentration camps.

First Love

Many who knew him have described Bonhoeffer as having a bit of distance between him and others, as though he had his guard up, or as though for sheer diffidence he didn't wish to intrude on other people's dignity. Others simply described him as aloof. He was unquestionably intense and always measured in his dealings with others. He never took others lightly, even if they took themselves lightly. Apart from his family—who provided as much intellectual and social stimulation as anyone might have required—he didn't seem to have close friends until later in his life. During these three years in Berlin, he was something of a loner. But at the end of this period and through most of his twenties, there was a woman in Dietrich Bonhoeffer's life.

---

* See pages 56–57.

She has been rarely mentioned in biographies, and in those cases her name has not been given. They spent much time together and, by all accounts, were in love and perhaps had even been engaged. The relationship began in 1927 when he was twenty-one, and she, twenty. Like Dietrich, she was a theological student at Berlin University. He took her to concerts and museums and operas, and they certainly had many deep theological conversations. For nearly eight years they remained close. She was actually a distant cousin and was said to resemble his sister Sabine. Her name was Elizabeth Zinn.

Elizabeth wrote her doctoral dissertation on the theosophist Friedrich Christoph Oetinger, and one of Bonhoeffer's favorite quotations came from him, by way of her: "Embodiment is the end of God's path." When Bonhoeffer's post-doctoral thesis was published in 1930, he inscribed a copy to her; and when her dissertation was published in 1932, she inscribed a copy to him. During his pastorate in London from late 1933 until early 1935, Bonhoeffer sent all of his sermons to her, which is how they have been preserved.

In 1944, when Bonhoeffer was imprisoned at Tegel, he was engaged to Maria von Wedemeyer. The book *Love Letters from Cell 92* contains the moving correspondence between them. They were sure he would be released from prison soon and were making plans for their upcoming wedding. In one letter Bonhoeffer told Maria about his early love affair with Elizabeth Zinn:

I was once in love with a girl; she became a theologian, and our paths ran parallel for many years; she was almost my age. I was 21 when it began. We didn't realize we loved each other. More than eight years went by. Then we discovered the truth from a third person, who thought he was helping us. We then discussed the matter frankly, but it was too late. We had evaded and misunderstood each other for too long. We could never be entirely in sympathy again, and I told her so. Two years later she married, and the weight on my mind gradually lessened. We never saw or wrote to each other again. I sensed at the time that, if I ever did get married, it could only be to a much younger girl, but I thought that impossible, both then and thereafter. Being totally committed to my work for the Church in the ensuing years, I thought it not only inevitable but right that I should forgo marriage altogether.

From this letter and from other clues we can ascertain that Bonhoeffer's relationship with Elizabeth Zinn was an important part of his life from 1927 until 1936, although he spent a year in Barcelona, nine months in New York, and eighteen months in London. Even when living in Berlin, he was often traveling on behalf of the ecumenical movement. After his year in Barcelona, things seem to have cooled somewhat, but the relationship survived that separation. It was after his return from London in late 1935 that a well-meaning third party told them of their feelings for each other. But as he explained in his letter, it was then too late. Bonhoeffer had changed greatly over the years, and by then he had dedicated his heart and soul to the battle to save the church from the Nazis. He was running the Confessing Church's seminary at Finkenwalde. It wasn't until the beginning of 1936 that he made things clear to Elizabeth, and the chapter between them was closed. He wrote her a letter, telling her of the change in him and dramatically explaining that God had called him to devote himself completely to the work of the church: "My calling is quite clear to me. What God will make of it I do not know. . . . I must follow the path. Perhaps it will not be such a long one. . . . Sometimes we wish that it were so (Philippians 1:23). But it is a fine thing to have realized my calling. . . . I believe that the nobility of this calling will become plain to us only in the times and events to come. If only we can hold out."

It's extraordinary that in 1936 he quoted the verse in Philippians where Paul expressed his desire to "depart, and to be with Christ." If Elizabeth Zinn ever doubted his sincerity, surely that put the matter to rest. But she knew him better than almost anyone, so it's doubtful that she ever could have doubted his sincerity. In 1938 she married the New Testament theologian Günther Bornkamm.

At the end of 1927, Bonhoeffer passed his doctoral examination and publicly defended his dissertation against three of his fellow students. One was his future brother-in-law Walter Dress; another was his friend Helmut Rössler. All went very well, and of the twelve doctoral graduates in theology from Berlin University that year, only Bonhoeffer received the distinction of summa cum laude. With his doctorate, he was eligible for ministry training by his regional church, but he was still deciding whether to enter the ministry or remain in academia. His family hoped for the latter, but he leaned toward the former.

That November Bonhoeffer was offered a position as vicar of a German congregation in Barcelona, Spain. It was for one year, and he decided to take it.

"This offer," he wrote, "seemed to bring to fruition a wish that had grown stronger and stronger over the past few years and months, namely, to stand on my own feet for a longer period completely outside my previous circle of acquaintances."

 CHAPTER 5

BARCELONA

1928

*Where a people prays, there is the church; and where the church is,
there is never loneliness.*

*It is much easier for me to imagine a praying murderer, a praying
prostitute, than a vain person praying. Nothing is so at odds with
prayer as vanity.*

*The religion of Christ is not a tidbit after one's bread; on the contrary,
it is the bread or it is nothing. People should at least understand and
concede this if they call themselves Christian.*

Christianity conceals within itself a germ hostile to the church.

—DIETRICH BONHOEFFER

n his diary early in 1928, Bonhoeffer wrote about how he decided to
go to Barcelona. It provides an early window into his decision-making
process and into the self-consciousness he brought to it:

I myself find the way such a decision comes about to be problematic. One thing is clear to me, however, that one personally—that is, consciously—has very little control over the ultimate yes or no, but rather that time decides everything. Maybe not with everybody, but in any event with me. Recently I have noticed again and again that all the decisions I had to make were not really my own decisions. Whenever there was a dilemma, I just left it in abeyance and—without really consciously dealing with it intensively—let it grow toward the clarity of a decision. But this clarity is not so much intellectual as it is instinctive. The decision is made; whether one can adequately justify it retrospectively is another question. "Thus" it happened that I went.

Bonhoeffer was always thinking about thinking. He meant to see things through to the bottom, to bring as much clarity as possible. The influence of his father, the scientist, is unmistakable. But the difference between his thinking now and in the future was that now, despite his being a theologian and pastor, he didn't mention God's role in the process or God's will. Still, what he said here in his diary curiously and clearly presaged the famously difficult decision he would make in 1939, trying to determine whether he should remain safely in America or sail back to the terrible *Terra Incognita* of his homeland. In both cases, he sensed that there was a right decision, but that ultimately it wasn't his. Later on he would say it explicitly: that he had been "grasped" by God; that God was leading him, and sometimes where he preferred not to go.

There were many farewells before he left Berlin. On January 18 he met with his Thursday Circle for the last time. They discussed a theme to which Bonhoeffer often returned: the difference between man-made "religion" and what he called "the real essence of Christianity." On January 22, he presided over his last children's service at the Grunewald church:

I spoke about the man with palsy and especially about the assertion that your sins are forgiven, and tried once more to disclose to the children the core of our gospel; they were attentive and perhaps a bit moved, for I spoke, I think, with some emotion. Then came the farewell. . . .

The congregational prayer has long sent shivers down my spine, and it did so incomparably more when the group of children, with whom I have spent two years, prayed for me. Where a people prays, there is the church; and where the church is; there is never loneliness.

There were other farewell events, and on February 4 everyone cele-brated his twenty-second birthday. His departure was set for February 8. He booked a ticket on the night train to Paris, where he planned to rendez-vous with his Grunewald classmate Peter Olden. They would spend a week together before he continued on to Barcelona.

On the evening of his departure there was a grand farewell dinner with the whole family. Everyone was there to mark the occasion: his parents, his grandmother, all his siblings, and by chance, Uncle Otto. When the family festivities neared an end, two cabs were called. With some difficulty he said good-bye to his grandmother, and then at 10:00 p.m. the rest of them piled into the taxis and the party drove to the train station. At eleven o'clock the whistle blew and the train pulled away. For the first time, Dietrich Bonhoeffer was on his own. For the next year he would be away from family, and for the first time since he could remember, he would not be a student. Dietrich had set off into the wide world.

As with so many young men, the wide world began with Paris. And, in a way, with prostitutes, though hardly in the conventional sense. The train had an hour layover in Liege, Belgium. Never one to squander an oppor-tunity to see something new, Bonhoeffer hired a cab and drove around in the rain. Peter Olden had already booked a room for Bonhoeffer at the Hotel Beausejour, next to the Ranelagh Gardens. When he arrived in Paris, he immediately went there. The two friends would spend the next week sightseeing, mostly in bad weather. They visited the Louvre a number of times and twice went to the opera, seeing *Rigoletto* and *Carmen*. It was in church that Bonhoeffer saw the prostitutes, and God used them to give him a picture of grace:

On Sunday afternoon I attended an extremely festive high mass in Sacré Coeur. The people in the church were almost exclusively from Montmartre; prostitutes and their men went to mass, submitted to all the ceremonies; it was an enormously impressive picture, and once again one could see quite clearly how close, precisely through their fate and guilt, these most heavily burdened people are to the heart of the gospel. I have long thought that the Tauentzienstrasse [Berlin's red-light district] would be an extremely fruitful field for church work. It's much easier for me to imagine a praying murderer, a praying prostitute, than a vain person praying. Nothing is so at odds with prayer as vanity.

On Tuesday he bid Paris adieu, taking a late afternoon train from the Quai d'Orsay. At dawn the next morning he opened his eyes someplace along the coast. He was outside Narbonne, an hour from the Spanish border. "The sun," he wrote, "which I had not seen for fourteen days, was just rising and illuminated a pre-spring landscape that looked as if it came from a fairy tale." During the night, while he slept, he had been transported to another realm: the gray chill and rain of Paris had given way to a world of bright color: "The meadows were green; the almond and mimosa trees were blooming. . . . Soon I saw the snowy peaks of the Pyrenees shining in the sun and the blue sea to the left." When they got to the border, at Port Bou, he was put aboard a luxury coach for the rest of the southward journey, and at 12:55 he arrived in Barcelona.

Bonhoeffer was met at the station by Pastor Friedrich Olbricht, a "large, dark-haired, and apparently very cordial man who speaks quickly and indistinctly," and who "looks quite unlike a pastor, but is not elegant." Olbricht ushered his new assistant to the creaky boardinghouse that would be his home. It was near the parsonage and quite primitive by Bonhoeffer's exacting standards. The only place to wash up was the toilet, which his brother Karl-Friedrich, who visited later, described as "very like a third-class lavatory on a train, except that it doesn't shake." The three women who ran the boardinghouse spoke only Spanish and that day made an impressive effort to pronounce "Dietrich." They failed. Two other Germans were residents: Herr Haack, a businessman, and Herr Thumm, an elementary schoolteacher. Both had lived there for some time, and they took an instant liking to Bonhoeffer, immediately inviting him to join them for lunch.

After lunch Bonhoeffer reconvened with Pastor Olbricht. They discussed Bonhoeffer's responsibilities, which included running a children's service and sharing Olbricht's pastoral duties. He would also preach whenever Olbricht traveled, which was much. Olbricht looked forward to leaving his congregation in capable hands while he took a long-needed vacation. He would visit his parents in Germany that summer, staying three months.

In Barcelona, Bonhoeffer discovered a world strikingly different from Berlin. The German expatriate community was staid and conservative. It seemed untouched by the dramatic events of the last decade in Germany and was nothing like the intellectual, sophisticated, and liberal-minded world of Berlin. For Bonhoeffer it must have seemed a bit like leaving the intellectual and social ferment of Greenwich Village for a community of prosperous, self-satisfied, and intellectually incurious Connecticut suburbanites. The transition was not easy; at the end of the month he wrote, "I have not had a single conversation in the Berlin-Grunewald style." A few weeks later he wrote Sabine: "I notice more and more that the émigrés, adventurers, and entrepreneurs who leave Germany are damned materialistic and have not received any sort of intellectual lift from their stay abroad; the same applies to the teachers."

The materialism was evident among the younger generation, too, who had not lived through the war and its privations. The influential German Youth Movement of the previous decades was unknown in Barcelona; its romantic notions had never flown so far south. Most young men hardly gave a thought to the possibilities open to them; they simply expected to follow their fathers into the family business.

The intellectual dullness and the overwhelmingly languorous atmosphere of Barcelona pushed hard against Bonhoeffer's hyperactive mind and personality. He was amazed at how people of all ages seemed to while away the hours sitting at cafés in the middle of the day, chattering about little of any real substance. He observed that besides coffee, vermouth-and-sodas were particularly popular, usually served with half a dozen oysters. Though Bonhoeffer was taken aback at what he now experienced, he may be given credit for not merely kicking against the goads: he adapted to the local lifestyle. He might have complained privately to those nearest and dearest to him, but he didn't let himself become gloomy or stymied by any of it. He wanted to be effective in his role as pastor, and he knew he must enter the lives and, to some extent, the lifestyles of the people he was charged with serving.

As in Rome, he was interested in the Catholic expressions of faith there. In a letter to his grandmother he described a surprising scene:

> Recently I saw something splendid. There was a large group of cars lined up one after the other on the main street here, all pressing to get through two narrow, specially erected gates under which priests were standing and sprinkling the cars with consecrated water as they drove through; there was also a band playing marches and dances, with clowning around and yelling—what was going on?—it was the day of the saint for cars and tires!

Bonhoeffer was zealous about experiencing and understanding as much as possible about his new circumstances. He gamely joined the Barcelona German Club, which held dances and other gala events—there was a masked ball coming up soon—and where everyone played *Skat*.* He also joined the German Tennis Club and German Chorale Society, where he instantly became the piano accompanist. In all these places he developed social relationships that opened pastoral doors, and he lost little time in walking through them whenever he could.

Perhaps the most difficult thing for him, but a vital part of this new community, was relaxing. But he did his best in this too. Twelve days after he arrived, he spent an entire Tuesday afternoon at the movies. On February 28 he and his new schoolteacher friend Hermann Thumm saw the 1926 silent feature version of *Don Quixote*, starring the then-popular Danish comic team of Pat and Patachon. This was the famous fat-and-skinny comedy team *before* Laurel and Hardy. It ran three hours nineteen minutes and did not strike Bonhoeffer's fancy, but he allowed this might be because of his unfamiliarity with the story. So he decided to read Cervantes' novel in the original tongue. It was an opportunity to improve his already good Spanish.

Bonhoeffer liked Barcelona in general. In a letter to his superintendent, Max Diestel, he described it as "an unusually lively metropolis caught in an economic upsurge in grand style, in which one can live quite pleasantly in every respect." He found the landscape of the area and the city itself to be "unusually charming." The harbor—called the Mole—was beautiful, and there were "good concerts" and "a good—though very old-fashioned—theater." Still, something was lacking: "namely intellectual discussion which one does not find when one looks for it, even in Spanish academic circles." When he finally

---

* It was a popular German card game, developed in the early nineteenth century in the city of Altenburg.

found a Spanish professor with whom he might have a more elevated level of conversation, the man turned out to be bitterly "anti-clerical." Bonhoeffer read contemporary Spanish writers and found them similarly disposed.

There was one activity that Bonhoeffer would enjoy in Barcelona, but could never enjoy in Berlin. That was the *arte taurina* (bull fighting). Though an aesthete and an intellectual, Bonhoeffer was neither effete nor squeamish. His brother Klaus arrived for a visit on Easter Saturday, and on Easter afternoon—Bonhoeffer preached that morning—they were "dragged" by a German teacher, presumably Thumm, to the "great Easter corrida." He wrote his parents about it:

> I had already seen one and cannot really say that it shocked me all that much, that is, the way many people think they owe it to their central European civilization to be shocked. It is, after all, a great spectacle to see wild, unrestrained power and blind rage fight against and ultimately succumb to disciplined courage, presence of mind, and skill. The gruesome element plays only a small role, especially since in this last bullfight the horses had stomach protectors for the first time so that the horrible images from my first corrida were absent. What is interesting is that it took a long struggle before they were permitted to start using these stomach protectors for the horses. Probably the majority of spectators do indeed just want to see blood and cruelty. Overall, the people vent all these powerful emotions, and you get drawn into it yourself.

In a letter to Sabine, who blanched at the thought of such spectacles, he said he conceded being astonished at "how much more cold-bloodedly I viewed the whole thing the second time than the first, and I must say that I can indeed sense from a distance that there is an allure to the whole thing that allows it to become a passion for some."

Ever the theologian, he expressed to her something else that had been going on in his mind:

> I have never seen the swing from "Hosanna!" to "Crucify!" more graphically evoked than in the virtually insane way the crowd goes berserk when the toreador makes an adroit turn, and they immediately follow this with an equally insane howling and whistling when some mishap

occurs. The momentary character of this mass mood goes so far that they applaud for the bull and against the toreador if, for example, the latter proves to be cowardly and—quite understandably—his courage fails him for a moment.

But he was not always profound. In October Bonhoeffer sent a novelty postcard to Rüdiger Schleicher. It pictured him behind a life-sized cardboard picture of a matador and a bull so that his head was on the matador's body: "The quiet hours in which I cultivated the *Arte taurina*, have, as you can see, led to tremendous success in the arena. . . . Greetings from the matador. Dietrich."

Bonhoeffer loved wandering the antique and secondhand shops and one day bought a huge eighteenth-century brazier made of carved chestnut wood, with a monstrously large brass bowl. It later became a fixture at Finkenwalde. When Klaus was visiting, they traveled to Madrid where Klaus bought an oil painting that seemed to be a Picasso. In a letter to their parents, Klaus described it as depicting "a degenerate woman drinking an aperitif (absinthe?)." When he took it back to Berlin, an American dealer offered him twenty thousand marks for it, and several others expressed interest. Then one of them contacted Herr Picasso directly. Picasso said his work had often been forged by a Madrid friend. No one was willing to decide firmly one way or the other, and Klaus kept the painting. It and the brazier were destroyed by Allied bombs in 1945.

In Madrid, Bonhoeffer developed an appreciation for the work of El Greco. He and Karl went on to Toledo, Cordoba, and Granada together, and then as far south as Algeciras, near Gibraltar. Every place he visited seemed to be a launching pad for further excursions. His grandmother sent him money to travel to the Canary Islands, but he had to return to Berlin before it was possible. He told her he would use the money toward his trip to India to visit Gandhi, which he still planned to do.

Assistant Pastor

Bonhoeffer had gone to Barcelona mainly to serve the church. While there he preached nineteen sermons and ran a children's service, though this did not begin with the bang he had hoped.

Before Bonhoeffer's arrival, Olbricht had issued invitations for the new children's service led by the new young pastor from Berlin. But on Bonhoeffer's first Sunday, the children's congregation consisted of one girl. In his diary, Bonhoeffer wrote, "That will have to improve." It did. His winning personality made a good impression, and the next week fifteen students came. He visited the homes of all fifteen that week, and the next Sunday there were thirty. From then on, there were always thirty or more in every service. Bonhoeffer loved his work with the children. He was stunned at their theological ignorance, but also found it wonderful: "They have not yet been tainted in any respect by the church."

The number of Germans in Barcelona then was about six thousand, but only a fraction of them were part of the church, and of them, only about forty showed up each Sunday. In the summers this number dropped farther. Bonhoeffer would be all alone that summer, with Olbricht away in Germany.

Bonhoeffer's sermons challenged the congregations both spiritually and intellectually. In his first sermon he leaped into his favorite subject, the difference between a faith based on our own moral efforts and one based on God's grace. Along the line he mentioned Plato, Hegel, and Kant, and quoted Augustine. One can only imagine some of the Barcelona businessmen puzzling over this earnest twenty-two-year-old, freshly descended from the ivory tower. And yet there was an undeniable vitality to what he was saying; he rarely lost their attention.

On Easter, with Olbricht away, Bonhoeffer preached again and the next week too. Each time he challenged his hearers and somehow won them over. It soon happened that whenever Bonhoeffer was scheduled to preach, the congregation grew noticeably. Olbricht noticed and promptly discontinued announcing the preaching schedule.

Although Olbricht was generally pleased with Bonhoeffer, there can be no doubt of issues between them. In letters home, Bonhoeffer mentioned that Olbricht was "not exactly a dynamic pulpit presence," nor did he fail to notice other failings. In another letter he wrote that Olbricht "has apparently hitherto done nothing in the way of addressing the younger generation in his parish." For example, Bonhoeffer saw that religious instruction at the German school where Thumm taught only went as far as the fourth year. So he brightly proposed starting classes for the older children. Every time

Olbricht turned around, Bonhoeffer was initiating something that would make more work for him when Bonhoeffer left. Olbricht scotched the idea.

Bonhoeffer was sensitive to the situation and properly deferential; he did nothing to exacerbate tensions. So Olbricht generally appreciated him and his efforts. Bonhoeffer's ability to keep his eyes on his own temptation to pride is a testimony to his upbringing, where selfishness and pride weren't tolerated. But Bonhoeffer was aware of the temptation of pride from a Christian perspective too. In a letter to his friend Helmut Rössler, also a pastor, Bonhoeffer talked about his satisfaction with his work and about the double nature of that satisfaction:

> This summer, in which I am on my own for three months, I have to preach every fortnight . . . and I am thankful that I have success in it. It is a mixture of subjective pleasure, let us call it self-satisfaction, and objective gratitude—but that is the judgement upon all religion, this mixture of the subjective and the objective, which one may possibly ennoble, but which one can never fundamentally uproot, and the theologian suffers doubly from this—but again, should one not rejoice at a full church, or that people are coming who had not come for years, and on the other hand, who dare analyse this pleasure, and be quite certain that it is free from the seeds of darkness?

The most dramatic departure from anything he had done before was Bonhoeffer's work with the Deutsche Hilfsverein, a German charitable organization with offices in the parsonage. Bonhoeffer ran this office in the mornings, and here stepped far beyond the privileged world of his Grunewald youth. He would see how the so-called other half lived, meeting and spending time with people whose businesses had failed, with victims of poverty and crime, and with truly desperate individuals, as well as with bona fide criminals. Writing Karl-Friedrich, he painted a vivid picture:

> One has to deal with the strangest persons, with whom one would otherwise scarcely have exchanged a word: bums, vagabonds, criminals on the run, many foreign legionaries, lion and other animal tamers

who have run away from the Krone Circus on its Spanish tour, German dancers from the music-halls here, German murderers on the run—all of whom tell one their life-story in detail. . . . Yesterday for the first time I had a man here who behaved so impudently—he claimed that the minister had forged his signature—that I practically shouted at him and threw him out. . . . While taking a hurried departure he cursed and swore, and said something that I have now often heard: "We shall see each other again, just come down to the harbor!" . . . Afterwards I found out at the consulate that he is a well-known swindler who has been hanging about here for a long time.

Through such experiences, Bonhoeffer's heart for the first time awoke to the plight of the poor and the outcast, which soon became an important theme in his life and theology. In the letter to Rössler, he touched upon this too:

Every day I am getting to know people, at any rate their circumstances, and sometimes one is able to see through their stories into themselves— and at the same time one thing continues to impress me: here I meet people as they are, far from the masquerade of "the Christian world"; people with passions, criminal types, small people with small aims, small wages and small sins—all in all they are people who feel homeless in both senses, and who begin to thaw when one speaks to them with kindness—real people; I can only say that I have gained the impression that it is just these people who are much more under grace than under wrath, and that it is the Christian world which is more under wrath than grace.

At the end of June, the German population in Barcelona plummeted. Many left for three months, to return in October. Pastor Olbricht was one of them. Most of the teachers Bonhoeffer knew would be gone too. But he seemed to enjoy himself and to be typically productive. Every morning till ten he ran the Hilfsverein office and then worked on his sermons or on his dissertation, *Sanctorum Communio*, which he was preparing for publication.

He also read and thought about subjects for his postdoctoral dissertation, *Act and Being*. At one o'clock he would walk back to the boardinghouse for lunch, after which he would write letters, practice piano, visit parishioners in the hospital or at home, work on his various writings, or escape into the city to drink coffee and meet acquaintances. Sometimes, more often than he wished, he succumbed to the withering heat and spent the afternoon the way many Barcelonians did, sleeping. That summer he conducted his children's services every Sunday, but preached only every other week. "That suffices for me," he wrote Karl-Friedrich, "since preaching in this heat is not necessarily very pleasant, especially since the sun shines on the pulpit at this time of year."

Bonhoeffer had an undeniably rare ability to communicate difficult theological ideas to ordinary churchgoers, but some passages in his Barcelona sermons must have been a bit much in the withering heat. He sometimes soared over the heads of his hearers to such theological altitudes as would suggest them shielding their eyes and squinting in frustration as they tried to follow him, a dot vanishing into the blueness of the sky itself. *Where is the tame old crow who used to preach here, whom we and our children could afterward pet and feed bits of apple and crackers? Won't good old Olbricht come back to us?*

Still, Bonhoeffer's solo flight as pastor was an undeniable success: every summer church attendance dropped significantly, but that summer the numbers actually increased. In August Bonhoeffer told a friend: "It is quite a remarkable experience for one to see work and life really coming together—a synthesis which we all looked for in our student days, but hardly managed to find. . . . It gives the work value and the worker an objectivity, a recognition of his own limitations, such as can only be gained in real life."

Bonhoeffer's parents visited in September. The three of them used the occasion for further travel, journeying north along the coast into France, visiting Arles, Avignon, and Nîmes; and south along the coast to Montserrat. On September 23 the parents heard their son preach on a theme central to him throughout his life, supporting the accurately earthly, incarnational aspect of the Christian faith against the Gnostic or dualistic idea that the body is inferior to the soul or spirit. "God wants to see human beings," he said, "not ghosts who shun the world." He said that in "the whole of world history there is always only one really significant hour—the present. . . . [I]f you want to find eternity, you must serve the times." His words presaged what he would write to his fiancée from his prison cell years later: "Our marriage must be a 'yes' to God's earth. It must strengthen our resolve to do and accomplish something on earth. I fear that Christians who venture to stand on earth on only one leg will stand in heaven on only one leg too." In another letter to her he wrote that "human beings were taken from the earth and don't just consist of thin air and thoughts."

Another theme that worked itself into many sermons then and into the future was the Barthian idea of God as initiator, as the one who must reveal himself to us, since we can do nothing to reach him. Several times Bonhoeffer used Barth's image of the Tower of Babel as a picture of "religion," of man trying to reach heaven through his own efforts, which always failed. But in a letter to Rössler, Bonhoeffer pushed the idea further:

> I have long thought that sermons had a center that, if you hit it, would move anyone or confront them with a decision. I no longer believe that. First of all, a sermon can never grasp the center, but can only itself *be grasped* by it, by Christ. And then Christ becomes flesh as much in the word of the pietists as in that of the clerics or of the religious socialists, and these empirical connections actually pose difficulties for preaching that are absolute, not merely relative.

This was a very radical and dramatic thing to say, but it is the perfectly logical conclusion to the idea that apart from God's grace, one can do nothing worthwhile. Anything good must come from God, so even in a sermon that was poorly written and delivered, God might manifest himself and touch the congregation. Conversely in a sermon wonderfully written and delivered, God might refuse to manifest himself. The "success" of the sermon is utterly dependent on the God who breaks through and "grasps" us, or we cannot be "grasped."

There was a foreshadowing of Bonhoeffer's famous "Jeremiah" sermon a few years hence, and of his attitude toward his fate under the Nazis. What did it mean to be "grasped" by God? And why did Bonhoeffer already begin to have a deep sense that God had "grasped him," had chosen him for something?

Three Early Lectures

In the fall of 1928 Bonhoeffer decided that in addition to his other duties, he would give three lectures, each delivered on a Tuesday evening: one in November, one in December, and one in February, just before he was scheduled to leave. No one expected him to do that, and one wonders what Olbricht thought of the new initiative. The lectures were extraordinarily ambitious in scope. Bonhoeffer was obviously motivated by his concern for the young men in the sixth form of the German school, who were about the age of those in his Thursday Circle. The church wasn't reaching them, and he wanted to do what he could.

The three lectures are impressive, especially for someone only a few years out of high school, and touch on most of the themes for which he would become famous in future years. The first lecture was "The Tragedy of the Prophetic and Its Lasting Meaning"; the second, "Jesus Christ and the Essence of Christianity"; and the third, "Basic Questions of a Christian Ethic."

The second lecture, delivered on December 11, is probably the best. As with most of his sermons, Bonhoeffer began provocatively, putting forth the notion that Christ had been exiled from the lives of most Christians. "Of course," he said, "we build him a temple, but we live in our own houses." Religion had been exiled to Sunday morning, to a place "into which one gladly withdraws for a couple of hours, but only to get back to one's place of work immediately afterward." He said that one cannot give him only a "small compartment in our spiritual life," but must give him everything or nothing. "The religion of Christ," he said, "is not a tidbit after one's bread; on the contrary, it is the bread or it is nothing. People should at least understand and concede this if they call themselves Christian."

In a typically well-turned passage reminiscent of C. S. Lewis's *Mere Christianity*, Bonhoeffer talked about the exclusiveness of Christ:

One admires Christ according to aesthetic categories as an aesthetic genius, calls him the greatest ethicist; one admires his going to his death as a heroic sacrifice for his ideas. Only one thing one doesn't do: one doesn't take him seriously. That is, one doesn't bring the center of his or her own life into contact with the claim of Christ to speak the revelation of God and to be that revelation. One maintains a distance between himself or herself and the word of Christ, and allows no serious encounter to take place. I can doubtless live with or without Jesus as a religious genius, as an ethicist, as a gentleman— just as, after all, I can also live without Plato and Kant. . . . Should, however, there be something in Christ that claims my life entirely with the full seriousness that here God himself speaks and if the word of God once became present only in Christ, then Christ has not only relative but absolute, urgent significance for me. . . . Understanding Christ means taking Christ seriously. Understanding this claim means taking seriously his absolute claim on our commitment. And it is now of importance for us to clarify the seriousness of this matter and to extricate Christ from the secularization process in which he has been incorporated since the Enlightenment.

We may assume Olbricht had not recently mentioned the Enlightenment to his congregation. In this lecture, Bonhoeffer tipped one sacred cow after the other. Having dealt with the idea of Christ as no mere great ethicist, he proceeded to explain the similarity of the Christian religion to other religions. Then he came to his main point: the essence of Christianity is not about religion at all, but about the person of Christ. He expanded on the theme learned from Karl Barth that would occupy so much of his thinking and writing in the years to come: religion was a dead, man-made thing, and at the heart of Christianity was something else entirely—God himself, alive. "Factually speaking," he said, "Christ has given scarcely any ethical prescriptions that were not to be found already with the contemporary Jewish rabbis or in pagan literature." Christianity was not about a new and better set of behavioral rules or about moral accomplishment. He must have shocked some of his listeners, but his logic was undeniably compelling. He then aggressively attacked the idea of "religion" and moral performance as the very enemies of Christianity and of Christ because they present the false idea that somehow we can reach God through our moral efforts. This led to hubris and spiritual pride, the sworn enemies of Christianity. "Thus," he said, "the Christian message is basically amoral and irreligious, paradoxical as that may sound."

It's startling that Bonhoeffer put it that way in 1928, sixteen years before he famously wrote to Eberhard Bethge about "religionless Christianity" in those letters that Bethge buried in the Schleichers' backyard in a gas-mask canister. But it's more startling that those exhumed ruminations have sometimes been described as marking a profound and new turn in his theology. Nearly all that Bonhoeffer would say and write later in life marked a deepening and expansion of what he had earlier said and believed, but never any kind of significant theological change. He was building on what had been established, like a scientist or mathematician. However high and far one built from the foundation, one could never disown or float free of that foundation. In fact, the higher one went, the more one confirmed the solidity and integrity of the foundation and the previous stories. Bonhoeffer did go high and far, and those who focus overmuch on these latter heights may be somewhat excused for failing to know that somewhere below the clouds, there was an orthodox theological foundation to which they were solidly connected.

In this same lecture, Bonhoeffer made another bold and provocative point:

> With that we have articulated a basic criticism of the most grandiose of all human attempts to advance toward the divine—by way of the church. Christianity conceals within itself a germ hostile to the church. It is far too easy for us to base our claims to God on our own Christian religiosity and our church commitment, and in so doing utterly to misunderstand and distort the Christian idea.

Here, in the lecture of the twenty-two-year-old to a handful of high schoolers, one sees something close to his most mature thinking in the future. He differentiated between Christianity as a religion like all the others—which attempt but fail to make an ethical way for man to climb to heaven of his own accord—and following Christ, who demands everything, including our very lives.

In the lectures he sometimes chose language that must have been difficult for those present, as when he said that the essence of Christianity "is the message of the eternally other, the one who is far above the world, yet who from the depth of his being has mercy on the person who gives glory to him alone." It's unlikely that many listening knew of Karl Barth or had heard the word *other* used as an abstract philosophical concept.

Bonhoeffer's sentences could be impressive. "The message of grace," he said, ". . . pronounces upon the death of people and nations its eternal: I have loved you from eternity; stay with me, and you will live." There are Chestertonian aphorisms too: "Christianity preaches the infinite worth of that which is seemingly worthless and the infinite worthlessness of that which is seemingly so valued."

Before he was finished, he made a third provocative point. He identified "the Greek spirit" or "humanism" as "the most severe enemy" that Christianity ever had. He then masterfully linked the idea of "religion" and moral accomplishment as a false way to God with dualism, the idea that the body is at war with the soul. Dualism was a Greek notion, not a Hebrew or biblical notion. The biblical affirmation of the body and the material world was another theme to which he would return again and again in his life:

> Humanism and mysticism, the seemingly most beautiful blossoms put forth by the Christian religion, extolled today as the highest ideals of the human spirit, indeed often as the crown itself of the Christian idea—[but] it is precisely the Christian idea itself that must reject them as an apotheosis of the creature and as such as a challenge to the honor belonging to God alone. The deity of humanism, of the idea of God presented by Christianity orients those human wishes to itself rather than the reverse.

"Herr Wolf Ist Tot!"

One reason Bonhoeffer wished to spend a year as a pastor in Barcelona was that he believed communicating what he knew theologically—whether to indifferent businessmen, teenagers, or younger children—was as important as the theology itself. His success in children's ministry shows this, and this letter to his future brother-in-law Walter Dress gives us a glimpse into this aspect of his year in Barcelona:

> Today I encountered a completely unique case in my pastoral counseling, which I'd like to recount to you briefly and which despite its simplicity really made me think. At 11:00 a.m. there was a knock at my door and a ten-year-old boy came into my room with something I had

requested from his parents. I noticed that something was amiss with the boy, who is usually cheerfulness personified. And soon it came out: he broke down in tears, completely beside himself, and I could hear only the words: "*Herr Wolf ist tot*" [Mr. Wolf is dead.], and then he cried and cried. "But who is Herr Wolf?" As it turns out, it is a young German shepherd dog that was sick for eight days and had just died a half-hour ago. So the boy, inconsolable, sat down on my knee and could hardly regain his composure; he told me how the dog died and how everything is lost now. He played only with the dog, each morning the dog came to the boy's bed and awakened him—and now the dog was dead. What could I say? So he talked to me about it for quite a while. Then suddenly his wrenching crying became very quiet and he said: "But I know he's not dead at all." "What do you mean?" "His spirit is now in heaven, where it is happy. Once in class a boy asked the religion teacher what heaven was like, and she said she had not been there yet; but tell me now, will I see Herr Wolf again? He's certainly in heaven." So there I stood and was supposed to answer him yes or no. If I said "no, we don't know" that would have meant "no." . . . So I quickly made up my mind and said to him: "Look, God created human beings and also animals, and I'm sure he also loves animals. And I believe that with God it is such that all who loved each other on earth—genuinely loved each other—will remain together with God, for to love is part of God. Just how that happens, though, we admittedly don't know." You should have seen the happy face on this boy; he had completely stopped crying. "So then I'll see Herr Wolf again when I am dead; then we can play together again"—in a word, he was ecstatic. I repeated to him a couple of times that we don't really know how this happens. He, however, *knew*, and knew it quite definitely in thought. After a few minutes, he said: "Today I really scolded Adam and Eve; if they had not eaten the apple, Herr Wolf would not have died." This whole affair was as important to the young boy as things are for one of us when something really bad happens. But I am almost surprised—moved, by the naïveté of the piety that awakens at such a moment in an otherwise completely wild young boy who is thinking of nothing. And there I stood—I who was supposed to "know the answer"—feeling quite small next to him; and I cannot forget the confident expression he had on his face when he left.

In November Bonhoeffer was asked to stay in Barcelona, but he wanted to complete his postdoctoral degree, or *Habilitation*. On February 15, a year after leaving, he returned to Berlin.

CHAPTER 6

BERLIN

1929

*It is a question of the freedom of God, which finds its strongest evidence
precisely in that God freely chose to be bound to historical human
beings and to be placed at the disposal of human beings. God is free not
from human beings but for them. Christ is the word of God's freedom.*

—DIETRICH BONHOEFFER

*If I had been a Jew and had seen such dolts and blockheads govern and
teach the Christian faith, I would sooner have become a hog than a
Christian.*

—MARTIN LUTHER

When Bonhoeffer returned from Barcelona, he found
a Germany increasingly impatient with the Weimar
Republic. Many thought it an unpleasant political hash
forced on them by their enemies, who knew nothing of
German history and culture, and who wanted Germany to be weak anyway.
Parliamentary government—where no party had the power to lead—was a
drastic change from the days of the kaiser, whose leadership was unquestioned and respected. For many, the rudderless squabbling of the current
system was simply un-German. Many Germans longed for a return to some

kind of leadership and were increasingly less fussy about what kind of leadership it should be. They wanted leadership itself, and a leader who would lead! There was just such a leader, but his party's showing in the 1928 elections had been disappointing. He began working toward the next elections, focusing mainly on winning votes in rural areas. He would return at a more opportune time.

Bonhoeffer wasn't quite sure what he wanted to do with himself. He had enjoyed his year in Barcelona and was considering leaving academia for the ministry. But at twenty-three, he was two years too young for ordination. Since he didn't want to close off the possibility of a future in academia, he decided to finish his second postdoctoral thesis—what was called a *Habilitation*—in order to qualify as a lecturer at Berlin University.

In wrestling with an answer to the question, *What is the church?* his thesis, titled *Act and Being (Akt und Sein)*, was very much a continuation of *Sanctorum Communio*. In *Act and Being*, he used philosophical language to show that theology is not merely another branch of philosophy, but something else entirely. For him, philosophy was man's search for truth apart from God. It was a type of Barth's "religion," in which man himself tried to reach heaven or truth or God. But theology begins and ends with faith in Christ, who reveals himself to man; apart from such revelation, there could be no such thing as truth. Thus the philosopher—and the theologian who operates on a philosopher's assumptions—chases his own tail and gazes at his own navel. He cannot break out of that cycle, but God, via revelation, can break *in*.

Bonhoeffer finished *Act and Being* that year, submitting it in February 1930. Eberhard Bethge reckoned the following its "classic passage":

In revelation it is not so much a question of the freedom of God—eternally remaining with the divine self, aseity—on the other side of revelation, as it is of God's coming out of God's own self in revelation. It is a matter of God's *given* Word, the covenant in which God is bound by God's own action. It is a question of the freedom of God, which finds its strongest evidence precisely in that God freely chose to be bound to historical human beings and to be placed at the disposal of human beings. God is free not from human beings but for them. Christ is the word of God's freedom. God *is* present, that is, not in eternal non-objectivity but—to put it quite provisionally for now—"haveable," graspable in the Word within the church. Here the formal understanding of God's freedom is countered by a substantial one.

In the year after Barcelona, Bonhoeffer returned to the vast social and intellectual swirl of friends and family members in the larger Grunewald circle. Much was happening among them. That year, his sister Susanne married his friend Walter Dress. His eldest sibling, Karl-Friedrich, married Grete von Dohnanyi. And two days before Bonhoeffer sailed for America, his brother Klaus married Emmi Delbrück, who along with her brothers, Max and Justus, had been a part of their family life since they were children together. Bonhoeffer was not quite so close to marriage, but he continued to spend time with Elizabeth Zinn, who was studying for her doctorate from Berlin University.

Hans Dohnanyi had gotten a job as the personal assistant to the Reich minister of justice in Berlin, so he and Christel returned from Hamburg, moving in right across the street from 14 Wangenheimstrasse. They lived with the Schönes, who were somehow related to the Bonhoeffers.*

When *Act and Being* was completed, submitted, and officially accepted, Bonhoeffer would be eligible to become a university lecturer. But until then, he would have to be satisfied with something much less prestigious. In April 1929, at the beginning of the summer term, he took the post of "voluntary assistant university lecturer" in the university's systematic theology seminar. It entailed performing all the duties beneath the dignity of a full professor. For Bonhoeffer this included "handing out and securing the return of keys, supervising the seminar library, and recommending new book purchases."

In the summer of 1929 Bonhoeffer was invited to attend the final seminar taught by Adolf von Harnack, then eighty-seven. Bonhoeffer had obviously turned in a different theological direction from Harnack, but he knew that he owed much of what he had learned to Harnack. Asked to speak at Harnack's farewell ceremony, he graciously said, "That you were our teacher for many sessions is a thing of the past; but that we may call ourselves your

---

* This was the family with whom Paula Bonhoeffer stayed during the worst of her time after Walter's death in 1918 and who had a vacation home in Boltenhagen.

pupils remains still."

One significant aspect of this year after Barcelona was his friendship with a wisecracking theology student named Franz Hildebrandt. They had met on December 16, 1927, outside Reinhold Seeberg's seminar, the day before Bonhoeffer publicly defended his dissertation. According to Hildebrandt, "within five minutes we were in an argument with each other—and we never stopped arguing from that day until we were separated by exile and war." Hildebrandt said they argued every day they were together: "You could not be a friend of Dietrich's if you did not argue with him."

So now, with Bonhoeffer back in Berlin, they resumed their argument. Hildebrandt became Bonhoeffer's best friend, his first close friend outside the family. In a few years Hildebrandt would also become Bonhoeffer's closest ally in the church struggle. Hildebrandt was three years Bonhoeffer's junior and, like Bonhoeffer, had grown up in the Grunewald district of Berlin. His father was a renowned historian, and his mother was Jewish. By the German standards of the time, Franz Hildebrandt was considered Jewish, which brings us to the thorny issue of Jewishness in Germany.

Luther and the Jews

Many Jews in Germany, like Sabine's husband, Gerhard, and like Franz Hildebrandt, were not merely culturally assimilated Germans, but were baptized Christians too. And many of them, like Franz Hildebrandt, were devout Christians who chose to enter the Christian ministry as their life's work. But in a few years, as part of their effort to push Jews out of German public life, the Nazis would attempt to push them out of the German church too. That these "non-Aryans" had publicly converted to the Christian faith meant nothing, since the lens through which the Nazis saw the world was purely racial. One's genetic makeup and ancestral bloodline were all that mattered; one's most deeply held beliefs counted for nothing.

To understand the relationship between Germans, Jews, and Christians, one has to go back again to Martin Luther, the man in whom Germanness and Christianity were effectively united. His authority as the man who defined what it was to be a German Christian was unquestioned, and it would be used by the Nazis to deceive many. But when it came to the Jews, Luther's legacy is confusing, not to say deeply disturbing.

At the very end of his life, after becoming a parody of his former cranky self, Luther said and wrote some things about the Jews that, taken on their own, make him out to be a vicious anti-Semite. The Nazis exploited these last writings to the utmost, as though they represented Luther's definitive take on the matter, which is impossible, given what he'd said earlier in life.

In the beginning of his career, Luther's attitude toward the Jews was exemplary, especially for his day. He was sickened at how Christians had treated Jews. In 1519 he asked why Jews would ever want to become converted to Christianity given the "cruelty and enmity we wreak on them—that in our behavior towards them we less resemble Christians than beasts?" Four years later in the essay "That Jesus Christ Was Born a Jew," he wrote, "If I had been a Jew and had seen such dolts and blockheads govern and teach the Christian faith, I would sooner have become a hog than a Christian. They have dealt with the Jews as if they were dogs rather than human beings; they have done little else than deride them and seize their property." There is no question that Luther believed Jews could convert to the Christian faith and wished they would do so—and therefore never thought being a Jew and being a Christian mutually exclusive, as the Nazis did. On the contrary, like the apostle Paul, Luther hoped to give them the inheritance meant for them in the first place, before it was meant for Gentiles. Paul declared that Jesus came "for the Jews first."

But this initial cheeriness and optimism would not last long. For much of his adult life Luther suffered from constipation, hemorrhoids, a cataract in one eye, and a condition of the inner ear called Ménière's disease, which results in dizziness, fainting spells, and tinnitus. He also suffered mood swings and depression. As his health declined, everything seemed to set him off. When a congregation sang anemically, he called them "tone-deaf sluggards" and stormed out. He attacked King Henry VIII as "effeminate" and blasted his theological opponents as "agents of the devil" and "whore-mongers." His language waxed fouler and fouler. He called the pope "the Anti-christ" and "a brothel-keeper above all brothel-keepers and all lewdness, including that which is not to be named." He blasted the Catholic church's regulation of marriage and accused the church of being "a merchant selling vulvas, genitals, and pudenda." Expressing his contempt for the devil, he said that he would give him "a fart for a staff." He viciously mocked Pope Clement III's writings: "Such a great horrid flatus did the papal arse let go here! He certainly pressed with great might to let out such a thunderous flatus—it is a wonder that it did not tear his hole and belly apart!" Luther seemed to have an absolutely torrid love affair with all things scatological. Not only were his linguistic flourishes styled along such lines, but his doctors seem to have followed suit: for one of his ailments, they persuaded him to take a draught of "garlic and horse manure," and he infamously received an enema—in vain—moments after he had departed this world. So it is in this larger context that one has to take his attitude toward the Jews, which, like everything else in his life, unraveled along with his health.

The troubles started in 1528 when, after a large meal of kosher food, he suffered a shattering attack of diarrhea. He concluded that the Jews had tried to poison him. By that time he was making enemies everywhere. In his last decade, his list of ailments ballooned to include gallstones, kidney stones, arthritis, abscesses on his legs, and uremic poisoning. Now his nastiness would hit its stride. He wrote the vile treatise "Von den Jüden und Iren Lügen" ("On the Jews and Their Lies"), and the man who once described the Jews as "God's chosen people" now called them "a base and whoring people." What he wrote during this time would rightly haunt his legacy for centuries and would in four centuries become the justification for such evils as Luther in even his most constipated mood could not have dreamed. To be fair, he was an equal opportunity insulter, the Don Rickles of Wittenberg, attacking everyone with equal fury, including Jews, Muslims, Catholics, and fellow Protestants. As the lights began to dim, he became convinced that the Apocalypse was imminent, and his thoughts toward everyone took on darker and darker tones. The thought of reasoned persuasion went out the window; at one point he called reason "the devil's whore."

But the tragicomedy became purest tragedy when, three years before his death, Luther advocated actions against the Jews that included, among other things, setting fire to their synagogues and schools, destroying their houses, confiscating their prayer books, taking their money, and putting them into forced labor. One may only imagine what Luther's younger self would have thought of such statements. But Goebbels and the other Nazis rejoiced that Luther's ugliest ravings existed in writing, and they published them and used them with glee, and to great success, giving the imprimatur of this great German Christian to the most un-Christian and—one can only assume—demented ravings. The hundreds of thousands of sane words he had written were of little interest to the men in brown.

It's noteworthy that Luther's foulest condemnations of the Jews were never racial, but were stirred because of the Jews' indifference to his earlier offers to convert them. The Nazis, on the other hand, wished adamantly to prevent Jews from converting. But when one considers how large the figure of Luther loomed over Germany, one can imagine how confusing it all was. The constant repetition of Luther's ugliest statements served the Nazis' purposes and convinced most Germans that being a German and being a Christian were a racial inheritance, and that neither was compatible with being Jewish. The Nazis were anti-Christian, but they would pretend to be Christians as long as it served their purposes of getting theologically ignorant Germans on their side against the Jews.

Years later, Eberhard Bethge said that most people, including him and Bonhoeffer, were unaware of the anti-Semitic ravings of Luther. It was only when the arch-anti-Semite propagandist Julius Streicher began to publish and publicize them that they became generally known. It must have been shocking and confusing for devout Lutherans like Bonhoeffer to learn of these writings. But because he was so intimately familiar with all else Luther had written, he most likely dismissed the anti-Semitic writings as the ravings of a madman, unmoored from his own past beliefs.

Given all that was about to happen in Germany, Bonhoeffer's friendship with Franz Hildebrandt began at an opportune time. Bethge told us that Hildebrandt and Bonhoeffer "saw eye-to-eye" in all practical matters and that Hildebrandt "influenced Bonhoeffer's imminent conversion to a stronger biblicism." Hildebrandt was also an excellent piano player and became the official accompanist at Bonhoeffer family concerts that Bonhoeffer could not attend.

In April 1930 Bonhoeffer went back to Barcelona for the wedding of his teacher friend, Hermann Thumm. Soon afterward he began thinking about going to America for a year of study. His superintendent, Max Diestel, recommended it since it was impossible for Bonhoeffer to be ordained until he turned twenty-five, a year away. Bonhoeffer's brother Karl-Friedrich had been invited to lecture in America in 1929 and could give him the lay of the land. Bonhoeffer didn't have much interest in an American trip until the possibility of a Sloane Fellowship at Union Theological Seminary in New York City presented itself.

In June, Adolf von Harnack died. The Kaiser Wilhelm Society would hold a memorial service for him on June 15, and the list of speakers was impressive, as befitted the legendary figure. One of them was twenty-four-year-old Dietrich Bonhoeffer, speaking on behalf of Harnack's former students. Bethge stated that what he said "compared favorably with the older and eminent speakers who preceded him." These included the nation's culture minister, the minister of state, the interior minister, and other such luminaries. "Many were astonished," Bethge wrote, "at the breadth of vision and sympathy he showed for his former teacher, since it was clear that his own path had taken a different direction." Bonhoeffer declared:

> It became clear to us through him that truth is born only of freedom. We saw in him the champion of the free expression of a truth once recognized, who formed his free judgment afresh time and time again, and went on to express it clearly despite the fear-ridden restraint of the majority. This made him . . . the friend of all young people who spoke their opinions freely, as he asked of them. And if he sometimes expressed concern or warned about recent developments of our scholarship, this was motivated exclusively by his fear that the others' opinion might be in danger of confusing irrelevant issues with the pure search for truth. Because we knew that with him we were in good and solicitous hands, we saw him as the bulwark against all trivialization and stagnation, against all the fossilization of intellectual life.

Bonhoeffer's words reveal that he was never what one might today term a *culture warrior*, nor could he easily be labeled *conservative* or *liberal*. He disagreed with Harnack's liberal theological conclusions but agreed profoundly with the underlying assumptions that guided Harnack, and he rightly saw that these were more important than the conclusions to which they led. Anyone on the side of truth, wherever it led, was a compatriot to be lauded. This virtue had come to Bonhoeffer, in part, from Harnack and the liberal Grunewald tradition in which he had flourished, and Bonhoeffer was generous enough to see it and state it publicly. Bonhoeffer's father was his primary mentor in this way of thinking. Karl Bonhoeffer's conclusions may have been different from his son's, but his respect for truth and for other human beings of different opinions formed the foundation of a civil society in which one might disagree graciously and might reason together civilly and productively. In the years ahead this would be seriously attacked, and the Nazis would stoke the fires of the culture wars (*Kulturkampf*) to play their enemies against each other. They would brilliantly co-opt the conservatives and the Christian churches, and when they had the power to do so, they would turn on them too.

Bonhoeffer took his second theological examination on July 8. *Act and Being* was accepted on July 18, qualifying him as a university lecturer, and he gave his inaugural lecture on July 31. The decision to go to America that fall was not easy. Bonhoeffer didn't think much of what America had to offer theologically. American seminaries seemed to him more like vocational schools than actual seminaries. But in the end, it made sense enough to go. The decision would change his life.

To get ready, Bonhoeffer prepared a notebook of American idioms. He also wrote out an argument against the idea that Germany had been solely to blame for the war. He was going, after all, to a country where most people would not share his views, and he didn't want to be unprepared. Bonhoeffer felt Germany had been treated unfairly and poorly by the Allies after the war, so he began his trip being a bit defensive on the subject. During his time in America, he bravely gave public talks on this subject, explaining the German point of view. But the Americans would turn out to be more sympathetic to this position than he had guessed.

Bonhoeffer planned to sail for America on September 6. On the fourth, his brother Klaus married Emmi Delbrück. The day after the wedding, he traveled with his parents to Bremerhaven, and at eight thirty on the morning of the sixth, they escorted him onto the ship *Columbus*. They explored the vast ship together for two hours and then said their good-byes. They snapped a final picture from the dock as he waved down at them from the ship's railing. At eleven thirty, the ship weighed anchor.

The *Columbus* was a splendidly appointed thirty-three-ton ship, Germany's fastest and largest, and the very image of her bright, imagined future. Her brochure boasted that there was no other ship "in which modern scientific attainment and artistic merit has dealt so lavish a hand in beautifying interiors and developing seagoing luxury." Nine years later, on December 19, 1939, the *Columbus* was scuttled off the coast of Delaware to avoid capture by a British man-of-war. Her breathtaking interiors would fill with seawater and she would sink three miles down into the darkness. But all that was far in the future. Today she steamed confidently westward at the amazing speed of twenty-two knots.

Bonhoeffer spent that evening in the ship's "writing salon" and wrote his grandmother:

> My cabin seems not unfavorably located. It lies deep in the belly of the ship. I actually haven't seen my cabin companion yet. I've tried to get a picture of him from the items he has left about. The hat, the walking cane, and a novel . . . suggest an educated young American to me. I hope he doesn't turn out to be an old German prole. I have eaten two enormous meals with a healthy appetite; in a word, I'm enjoying the ship as long as it can be enjoyed. I've also gotten to know several nice people, so the time is going by quickly. I'll soon be going to bed since I'd like to see as much of England as possible early tomorrow morning. Just now we are traveling along the Belgian coast. You can see lights way off in the distance.

Bonhoeffer's cabin mate turned out to be Dr. Edmund De Long Lucas, a prosperous forty-eight-year-old American who was the principal of Forman Christian College in Lahore, India. Lucas had gotten his doctorate at Columbia, just across the street from Union, where Bonhoeffer was headed. Bonhoeffer eagerly shared his plans of traveling to India, and Dr. Lucas invited him to visit in Lahore. They even planned that Bonhoeffer should see Lahore on an eastward trip across northern India to Benares.

Two more people Bonhoeffer befriended were a German-American woman named Mrs. Ern and her eleven-year-old son, Richard. They had been in Switzerland visiting the boy's younger sister, who was being treated for meningitis at a homeopathic spa. Bonhoeffer grew close to them and during this year sometimes took the train out to the suburb of Scarsdale for a weekend visit.

On his first morning aboard the ship, Bonhoeffer awoke early. Around 7:00 a.m., for the first time in his life, he saw England. The chalky cliffs of Dover were visible off the *Columbus's* starboard side. Bonhoeffer had little idea how much time he would end up spending in England or how particularly important England and the friends he made there would become.

While he was sailing westward across the sea, the first copies of *Sanctorum Communio* arrived at his parents' house, just in time to miss him. He finished the book three years earlier, and its publication was so anticlimactic that he was unaware of it. The books even arrived with a bill for additional printing costs. Bonhoeffer was obviously in no position to help publicize it or give copies to friends. According to Bethge, "the book sank unnoticed in the general debate of the time. The dialecticians did not discuss it, as Bonhoeffer had expected, and professors did not use it as a text."

 CHAPTER 7

BONHOEFFER IN AMERICA

1930–31

[The Union students] talk a blue streak without the slightest
substantive foundation and with no evidence of any criteria
. . . They are unfamiliar with even the most basic questions. They
become intoxicated with liberal and humanistic phrases, laugh at the
fundamentalists, and yet basically are not even up to their level.

In New York they preach about virtually everything; only one thing
is not addressed, or is addressed so rarely that I have as yet been
unable to hear it, namely, the gospel of Jesus Christ, the cross, sin and
forgiveness, death and life.

—DIETRICH BONHOEFFER

When Bonhoeffer's ship steamed past the Statue of Liberty
and toward the fabled island of Manhattan, the city overwhelmed him. Manhattan at the end of the Jazz Age was
a dizzying place for any visitor, even one as cosmopoli-
tan as Dietrich Bonhoeffer. If Berlin exemplified the Old World–weary
sophistication of the actress just past her prime, New York City seemed

to exhibit the crazy, boundless energy of a bright-eyed adolescent in full growth spurt: the whole island seemed to be bursting at the seams in every direction, grinning as it did so. The tallest building on the planet, the Bank of Manhattan Trust building, had just three months earlier been topped by the silver spire of the newest leader, the Chrysler Building. But the Empire State Building, which would in a few months surpass them all—and hold the lead for forty years—was that very minute growing at the unprecedented rate of four and a half stories per week. The nineteen-building Art Deco masterpiece that would become Rockefeller Center was under construction, too, and far uptown, also under construction, was the George Washington Bridge—soon to be the longest bridge in the world, almost doubling the previous record.

Despite all this activity, the stock market crash of the previous year had taken its toll, and Bonhoeffer would soon see its effects. But before he had a chance to see anything of the urban landscape of Manhattan, he would see the suburbs of Philadelphia. Bonhoeffer was greeted at the dock by his Tafel relatives, Harold and Irma Boericke, who whisked him to Pennsylvania, where he spent the next week with them and their very American children, Ray, Betty, and Binkie. Karl-Friedrich had visited the Boerickes the year before, and Bonhoeffer wrote him now: "We travel around a lot by car. Today I'm supposed to learn how to play golf; in the evenings we're often invited out, or we stay at home and play games. You can hardly believe you're so far away from Europe here, so much is so similar."

The irony of his words becomes evident only when we realize what he could not at the time: while he was working on his golf swing in the City of Brotherly Love, lightning had struck at home. On September 14, two days after his arrival in America, a Reichstag election had been held, and the results were shocking: the Nazis had entered the lists as the ninth and smallest of Germany's political parties, with a pitiful twelve members in the Reichstag—Hitler hoped to quadruple that number—but by day's end they would have exceeded even his own febrile expectations, amassing 107 seats, and in a single bounding *alley-oop* had vaulted into being the second largest political party in the land. History lurched forward clumsily, but decisively. And Bonhoeffer was horsing around with Ray, Betty, and Binkie in Philadelphia; he knew nothing about it.

"There Is No Theology Here"

Bonhoeffer went to Union with a bit of a chip on his shoulder and not without reason. German theologians were unsurpassed in the world; Bonhoeffer had studied with the best of them—and ridden the trolley with them. Not many Union students could lay claim to commuting with Adolf von Harnack. Bonhoeffer had a doctorate from Berlin University and could almost as easily have been lecturing at Union as studying there. So while all of the other exchange students worked toward earning a master's degree, Bonhoeffer saw this as unnecessary or perhaps simply beneath his dignity. By not entering a degree program, he had much more freedom to study what he liked and do as he pleased, and as it turned out, it was his extracurricular activities in New York that would have the greatest influence on his future.

When Bonhoeffer experienced things firsthand at Union, he found the theological situation worse than he'd feared. To his superintendent, Max Diestel, he wrote:

> There is no theology here. . . . They talk a blue streak without the slightest substantive foundation and with no evidence of any criteria. The students—on the average twenty-five to thirty years old—are completely clueless with respect to what dogmatics is really about. They are unfamiliar with even the most basic questions. They become intoxicated with liberal and humanistic phrases, laugh at the fundamentalists, and yet basically are not even up to their level.

Bonhoeffer had no idea what he was walking into at Union, but the bloody battle royale between the liberals and fundamentalists was in full swing in 1930. Union students had a front-row seat. In one corner, weighing in on the side of theological liberalism and occupying the pulpit of Riverside Church—a pebble's toss from Union and built just for him by John D. Rockefeller—was the most famous liberal preacher in America, Harry Emerson Fosdick. In the other corner, weighing in on the side of the historic faith and descried as a fundamentalist, stood Dr. Walter Duncan Buchanan, who occupied the pulpit of Broadway Presbyterian Church six blocks south of Union and built with no help from Mr. Rockefeller, thank you.

Fosdick had been the pastor at New York's First Presbyterian Church when in 1922 he preached an infamous sermon titled "Shall the Fundamentalists Win?" In it he laid out a kind of Apostate's Creed in which he expressed his serious doubts about most of the historic assertions of the Christian faith, including the virgin birth, the resurrection, the divinity of Christ, the atonement, miracles, and the Bible as the Word of God. This sermon was the opening salvo in a battle that would rage particularly hotly through the 1920s and 1930s. The local presbytery immediately conducted an investigation, but as a son of the moneyed East Coast WASP establishment, Fosdick had little to fear. His defense was conducted by another establishment scion, John Foster Dulles, who would serve as Eisenhower's secretary of state, and whose father was a well-known liberal Presbyterian minister. Fosdick resigned before they could censure him, and he was given the pastorate of the fashionably progressive Park Avenue Baptist Church, where John D. Rockefeller was a prominent member, and whose foundation's philanthropic arm was run by Fosdick's own brother.

Seeing an opportunity to knock out fundamentalism in New York, the Rockefeller Foundation promptly funded the construction of a church for Fosdick, one that would serve as a proper platform for his "progressive" modernist views. Bonhoeffer had just begun his studies at Union when it opened—and it opened to such pomp and circumstance that no one could have failed to know about it. It was a major cultural event.

But this church was no mere church. It was a spare-no-expenses cathedral to modernism and progress that had quite literally been modeled on Chartres Cathedral. It had a 392-foot tower and the world's largest carillon, with 72 bells, among them the world's largest. It had a commanding view of the mighty Hudson and was strategically adjacent to Union Theological Seminary, from which Fosdick had graduated and where he would teach courses on homiletics, and where his theology was generally welcomed and disseminated. It was intended to influence the impressionable students of Union, Columbia, and Barnard along its theological lines. It continues to do so eight decades later.

Time magazine, run by another son of the East Coast establishment, Henry Luce, would lead the cheering when Riverside opened that October. It put Fosdick's face on the cover and ran a glowing cover story on him and the church written in the kind of cooing tone usually reserved for something like a *Town and Country* feature titled "Myrna Loy at Home":

Dr. Fosdick proposes to give this educated community a place of greatest beauty for worship. He also proposes to serve the social needs of
the somewhat lonely metropolite. Hence on a vast scale he has built all
the accessories of a community church—gymnasium, assembly room
for theatricals, dining rooms, etc., etc. He will have two assistant pastors besides many a staff worker. In ten stories of the 22-story belltower
are classrooms for the religious and social training of the young, from
nurslings to college scholars. One floor is for the Women's Society's
sewing room, another for the Women's Bible Class. Dr. Fosdick's study
and conference rooms are on the 18th floor, richly decorated. Simple,
but more massive in furniture is the floor above where the board of
trustees meet. . . . Not all of them rich, not all of them powerful, but all
of them sociologically minded.

The flattering portrait painted of Fosdick suggested the son of Galileo
and Joan of Arc, and the article managed to take a few potshots at the
unwashed fundamentalist hordes whom the ruddy shepherd boy Fosdick was
bravely fighting with his slingshot and Rockefeller's millions.

Bonhoeffer observed that Union was on the side of Fosdick, Rockefeller,
and Luce. In an attempt to be more sophisticated than the fundamentalists, whom they hated, they had jettisoned serious scholarship altogether.
They seemed to know what the answer was supposed to be and weren't
much concerned with how to get there. They knew only that whatever
answer the fundamentalists came up with must be wrong. For Bonhoeffer,
this was scandalous. He did not agree with Harnack's liberal conclusions,
but he appreciated and respected Harnack's respect for the truth and for
academic inquiry. At Union he found people who would have agreed with
Harnack's liberal conclusions, but who were unworthy to tie the thongs
of his sandals. They had no real idea how he came to his conclusions, nor
seemed to care.

The following summer Bonhoeffer reported on his experiences at Union
for the German church authorities. "To understand the American student,"
he wrote, "it is important to have experienced life in a hostel." He was genuinely taken with the importance and openness of community that he saw at
Union and in American life generally. In many ways it provided the key to
everything else that he observed:

Living together day by day produces a strong spirit of comradeship, of a mutual readiness to help. The thousandfold "hullo" which sounds through the corridors of the hostel in the course of the day and which is not omitted even when someone is rushing past is not as meaningless as one might suppose. . . . No one remains alone in the dormitory. The unreservedness of life together makes one person open to another; in the conflict between determination for truth with all of its consequences and the will for community, the latter prevails. This is characteristic of all American thought, particularly as I have observed it in theology and the church; they do not see the radical claim of truth on the shaping of their lives. Community is therefore founded less on truth than on the spirit of "fairness." One says nothing against another member of the dormitory as long as he is a "good fellow."

Bonhoeffer's famous experiment in communal Christian living at Zingst and Finkenwalde, five years hence, was informed by his year of semi-communal living in the dorm at Union. But he saw the downside too:

Not only quietness is lacking, but also the characteristic impulse towards the development of individual thought which is brought about in German universities by the more secluded life of the individual. Thus there is little intellectual competition and little intellectual ambition. This gives work in seminar lecture or discussion a very innocuous character. It cripples any radical, pertinent criticism. It is more a friendly exchange of opinion than a study in comprehension.

He conceded that American theological students knew more about "everyday matters" than their German counterparts and were more concerned with the practical outworkings of their theology, but "a predominant group [at Union] sees it in exclusively social needs." He said that "the intellectual preparation for the ministry is extraordinarily thin."

He believed that students fell into several basic groups, but

without doubt the most vigorous . . . have turned their back on all genuine theology and study many economic and political problems. Here, they feel, is the renewal of the Gospel for our time. . . . At the instigation of this group, the student body of Union Theological seminary has, over the winter, continually provided food and lodging for thirty unemployed—among them three Germans—and has advised them as well as possible. This has led to considerable personal sacrifice of time and money. It must not, however, be left unmentioned that the theological education of this group is virtually nil, and the self-assurance which lightly makes mock of any specifically theological question is unwarranted and naïve.

Another group was mostly interested in the philosophy of religion and gathered around a certain Dr. Lyman, whom Bonhoeffer admired, although in "his courses the students find an opportunity of expressing the crassest heresy." Bonhoeffer said that

the lack of seriousness with which the students here speak of God and the world is, to say the least, extremely surprising. . . . Over here one can hardly imagine the innocence with which people on the brink of their ministry, or some of them already in it, ask questions in the seminar for practical theology—for example, whether one should really preach of Christ. In the end, with some idealism and a bit of cunning, we will be finished even with this—that is their sort of mood.

The theological atmosphere of the Union Theological Seminary is accelerating the process of the secularization of Christianity in America. Its criticism is directed essentially against the fundamentalists and to a certain extent also against the radical humanists in Chicago; it is healthy and necessary. But there is no sound basis on which one can rebuild after demolition. It is carried away with the general collapse. A seminary in which it can come about that a large number of students laugh out loud in a public lecture at the quoting of a passage from Luther's *De servo arbitrio* on sin and forgiveness because it seems to them to be comic has evidently completely forgotten what Christian theology by its very nature stands for.

His conclusion was withering: "I am in fact of the opinion that one can learn extraordinarily little over there . . . but it seems to me that one also gains quiet insights . . . where one sees chiefly the threat which America signifies for us."

Bonhoeffer's professor John Baillie reckoned Bonhoeffer "the most convinced disciple of Dr. Barth that had appeared among us up to that time, and withal as stout an opponent of liberalism as had ever come my way."

Bonhoeffer's observations on American churches, especially in New York City, were closely related to his views on Union:

Things are not much different in the church. The sermon has been reduced to parenthetical church remarks about newspaper events. As long as I've been here, I have heard only *one* sermon in which you could hear something like a genuine proclamation, and that was delivered by a negro (indeed, in general I'm increasingly discovering greater religious power and originality in Negroes). One big question continually attracting my attention in view of these facts is whether one here really can still speak about Christianity, . . . There's no sense to expect the fruits where the Word really is no longer being preached. But then what becomes of Christianity per se?

The enlightened American, rather than viewing all this with skepticism, instead welcomes it as an example of progress. The fundamentalist sermon that occupies such a prominent place in the southern states has only one prominent Baptist representative in New York, one who preaches the resurrection of the flesh and the virgin birth before believers and the curious alike.

In New York they preach about virtually everything; only one thing is not addressed, or is addressed so rarely that I have as yet been unable to hear it, namely, the gospel of Jesus Christ, the cross, sin and forgiveness, death and life.

In a homiletics seminar at Union taught by Fosdick, Fosdick gave out sermon topics. A few of them were on what he condescendingly called "traditional themes." Bonhoeffer was stunned that in this category was a sermon "on the forgiveness of sins and on the cross!" The heart of the gospel had been marginalized and quaintly labeled "traditional." He said:

This is quite characteristic of most of the churches I saw. So what stands in place of the Christian message? An ethical and social idealism borne by a faith in progress that—who knows how—claims the right to call itself "Christian." And in the place of the church as the congregation of believers in Christ there stands the church as a social corporation. Anyone who has seen the weekly program of one of the large New York churches, with their daily, indeed almost hourly events, teas, lectures, concerts, charity events, opportunities for sports, games, bowling, dancing for every age group, anyone who has heard how they try to persuade a new resident to join the church, insisting that you'll get into society quite differently by doing so, anyone who has become acquainted with the embarrassing nervousness with which the pastor lobbies for membership—that person can well assess the character of such a church. All these things, of course, take place with varying degrees of tactfulness, taste, and seriousness; some churches are basically "charitable" churches; others have primarily a social identity. One cannot avoid the impression, however, that in both cases they have forgotten what the real point is.

The one, notable exception, Bonhoeffer again observed, was in the "negro churches." If his year in New York had value, it was mainly because of his experiences in the "negro churches."

As always, Bonhoeffer did much more than focus on academic pursuits. He wasted no time in exploring the city and all it had to offer, and he did most of it with four fellow Union students: Jean Lasserre was French; Erwin Sutz was Swiss; Paul Lehmann was American; and Albert Franklin "Frank" Fisher was African American. Bonhoeffer's experiences with each of them formed an important part of his year at Union. But it was probably his friendship with Fisher, who grew up in Alabama, that would have the greatest influence.

When Fisher came to Union in 1930, his social work assignment was the Abyssinian Baptist Church in Harlem. Bonhoeffer quickly grew weary of the sermons in places like Riverside, so when Fisher invited him to a service at Abyssinian, he was thrilled to go along. There, in the socially downtrodden

African American community, Bonhoeffer would finally hear the gospel preached and see its power manifested. The preacher at Abyssinian was a powerful figure named Dr. Adam Clayton Powell Sr.

Powell was the son of slaves; his mother was a full-blooded Cherokee and his father, an African American. Born three weeks after Lee surrendered at Appomattox, Powell spent his early years caught up in the stuff that conversion stories are made of: heavy drinking, violence, gambling, and the like. But during a weeklong series of revival meetings in Rendville, Ohio, he came to faith in Christ and never looked back. In 1908 he became the senior pastor at the already historic Abyssinian Baptist Church, which was started exactly one hundred years earlier, during the presidency of Thomas Jefferson, when a group of African Americans left the First Baptist Church of New York City over its segregated seating policy. Powell brought an outsized vision and faith to the pulpit. In 1920 he fought and won a contentious battle to move the church to Harlem, where he built a huge new building on 138th Street, as well as one of the first community recreation centers in Harlem. "Not a ticket or a dish of ice cream was sold to pay for the erection of Abyssinian Baptist Church and Community House," he said. "Every dollar of the money was brought in through tithes and offerings, and God fulfilled His promise by pouring out a blessing upon us that our souls were not able to contain." By the mid-1930s, Abyssinian boasted fourteen thousand members and was arguably the largest Protestant church of any kind in the whole United States. When Bonhoeffer saw it all, he was staggered.

Starving from the skim milk at Union, Bonhoeffer found a theological feast that spared nothing. Powell combined the fire of a revivalist preacher with great intellect and social vision. He was active in combating racism and minced no words about the saving power of Jesus Christ. He didn't fall for the Hobson's choice of one or the other; he believed that without both, one had neither, but with both, one had everything and more. When the two were combined, and only then, God came into the equation. Then and only then was life poured out. For the first time Bonhoeffer saw the gospel preached and lived out in obedience to God's commands. He was entirely captivated, and for the rest of his time in New York, he was there every Sunday to worship and to teach a Sunday school class of boys; he was active in a number of groups in the church; and he gained the trust of many members and was invited to their homes. Bonhoeffer realized that the older people at Abyssinian had been born when slavery was legal in the United States. Surely some of them were born into the horrid institution.

The music at Abyssinian formed an important part of his experience. Bonhoeffer searched New York record shops to find recordings of the "negro spirituals" that had so come to transfix him every Sunday in Harlem. The joyous and transformative power of this music solidified his thinking on the importance of music to worship. He would take these recordings back to Germany and play them for his students in Berlin, and later in the sandy Baltic outposts of Zingst and Finkenwalde. They were some of his most treasured possessions, and for many of his students, they seemed as exotic as moon rocks.

Bonhoeffer also read a great deal of "negro literature," and during the Thanksgiving holiday, he accompanied Fisher to Washington, D.C. To his parents, he wrote that he "traveled to Washington by car with a white person and two Negro students." Bonhoeffer expressed awe over the design of the Mall and the way the Capitol Building, the Washington Monument, and the Lincoln Memorial "all lined up, separated only by broad expanses of grass." The Lincoln Memorial was "enormously imposing, portraying Lincoln himself ten or twenty times larger than life, brightly illuminated at night, in a mighty hall . . . the more I hear about Lincoln the more he interests me."

The trip to Washington with Fisher gave him an intimate view of the racial situation in America, one that few whites had seen:

> In Washington I lived completely among the Negroes and through the students was able to become acquainted with all the leading figures of the negro movement, was in their homes, and had extraordinarily interesting discussions with them. . . . The conditions are really rather unbelievable. Not just separate railway cars, tramways, and buses south of Washington, but also, for example, when I wanted to eat in a small restaurant with a Negro, I was refused service.

They visited Fisher's alma mater, the all-black Howard University, where a young man named Thurgood Marshall was then a law student. Bonhoeffer became deeply interested in the racial issue in America, and that March, when news of the Scottsboro case gripped the nation, he followed it closely. To Karl-Friedrich, he wrote:

I want to have a look at church conditions in the South, which alleg-
edly can still be quite peculiar, and get to know the situation of the
Negroes in a bit more detail. I don't quite know whether I have not
perhaps spent too much time on this question here, especially since we
don't really have an analogous situation in Germany, but I've just found
it enormously interesting, and I've never for a moment found it boring.
And it really does seem to me that there is a real movement forming,
and I do believe that the negroes will still give the whites here considerably more than merely their folk-songs.

His belief that there was no "analogous situation in Germany" would
change soon enough. Karl-Friedrich wrote back: "I had the impression when
I was over there that it is really *the* problem." And he revealed that the racism
he had seen in America caused him to decline an appointment at Harvard:
he feared living permanently in America could somehow taint him and his
future children as part of "that legacy." Like his younger brother, he didn't see
an analogous situation in Germany at that time, and he even ventured that
"our Jewish question is a joke by comparison; there won't be many people
who claim they are oppressed here."

It's easy to snicker at the lack of foresight, but the Bonhoeffers had
grown up in Grunewald, a neighborhood of academic and cultural elites, a
third of whom were Jewish. They had never seen or heard of anything comparable to what they discovered in America, where blacks were treated like
second-class citizens and had an existence wholly separated from their white
contemporaries. What Bonhoeffer soon saw in the South was more grievous still. The comparison was more difficult because in Germany, Jews had
economic parity, while in America, blacks certainly did not. In terms of influence, German Jews held top positions in every sphere of society, something
far from the situation among blacks in America. And in 1931, no one could
imagine how the German situation would deteriorate within a few years.

Bonhoeffer's experiences with the African American community underscored an idea that was developing in his mind: the only real piety and power
that he had seen in the American church seemed to be in the churches where
there were a present reality and a past history of suffering. Somehow he had
seen something more in those churches and in those Christians, something
that the world of academic theology—even when it was at its best, as in

Berlin—did not touch very much. His friendship with the Frenchman Jean Lasserre spoke to him in a similar way.

Bonhoeffer respected Lasserre as a theologian but did not agree with his strongly pacifist views. But because Bonhoeffer respected his theology, and perhaps because both were Europeans, he was open to exploring what Lasserre had to say. Lasserre got Bonhoeffer thinking along lines that would lead him to become involved in the ecumenical movement: "Do we believe in the Holy Catholic Church, the Communion of Saints, or do we believe in the eternal mission of France? One can't be a Christian and a nationalist at the same time."

Yet it was not a conversation, but a movie that most powerfully brought Lasserre's views home for Bonhoeffer.

The Power of Film

The now-classic antiwar novel *All Quiet on the Western Front* exploded across Germany and Europe in 1929. Its publication was a phenomenon that had a hugely significant effect on Dietrich Bonhoeffer's view of war, which in turn determined the very course of his life and ultimately led to his death. It was written by Erich Maria Remarque, who had served as a German soldier during the war. The book sold nearly a million copies instantly, and within eighteen months was translated into twenty-five languages, making it the best-selling novel of the young century. Bonhoeffer likely read the book for Reinhold Niebuhr's class at Union in 1930, if not earlier, but it was the movie more than the book that would change Bonhoeffer's life.

With a rawness and power unheard of at the time, the film pulled no punches in portraying the graphic horrors of the war. It won Oscars for Best Picture and Best Director, but for its aggressively antiwar stance it caused a firestorm of outrage across Europe. In the opening scene, a wild-eyed old teacher exhorts his young charges to defend the fatherland. Behind him, on the chalkboard, are the Greek words from the *Odyssey* invoking the Muse to sing the praises of the great soldier-hero who sacked Troy. From the old teacher's lips comes Horace's famous line, "Dulce et decorum est pro patria mori" (It is a sweet and fitting thing to die for one's country). The glories of war were for these young men a part of the great Western tradition in which they were being schooled, and en masse they marched off to the mud and death of the trenches. Most of them died, and nearly all of them cowered in fear or lost their minds before doing so.

The film is antiheroic and disturbing, and to anyone harboring nationalist sympathies, it must have been at times embarrassing and enraging. It's no surprise that for the budding National Socialists, the film seemed vile internationalist propaganda, coming from the same places—principally Jewish—that had led to the defeat of Germany in the very war being depicted. In 1933, when they came to power, the Nazis burned copies of Remarque's book and spread the canard that Remarque was a Jew whose real surname was Kramer—Remark spelled backward. But now, in 1930, they attacked the film.

Their newly minted minister of propaganda, Joseph Goebbels, leaped into action. He marshaled the juvenile arm of the party, the *Hitlerjugend* (Hitler Youth), to release sneezing powder, stink bombs, and mice inside theaters during screenings of the film. Outside the theaters the black-uniformed *Schutzstaffel*, later known as the SS, instigated riots. The resultant bedlam was an early example of Nazi intimidation tactics. As a result, the film was soon banned across Germany and remained so until 1945.

In the United States, however, it was on screens everywhere, and one Saturday afternoon in New York City Bonhoeffer saw it with Jean Lasserre. It was a searing indictment of the war in which their countries were bitter enemies, and here they sat, side by side, watching German and French boys and men butchering one another. In perhaps the most moving scene of the film, the hero, a young German soldier, stabs a French soldier, who eventually dies. But before dying, as he lies in the trench, alone with his killer, he writhes and moans for hours. The German soldier is forced to face the horror of what he has done. Eventually he caresses the dying man's face, trying to comfort him, offering him water for his parched lips. And after the Frenchman dies, the German lies at the corpse's feet and begs his forgiveness. He vows to write to the man's family, and then he finds and opens the man's wallet. He sees the man's name and a picture of his wife and daughter.

The sadness of the violence and suffering on the screen brought Bonhoeffer and Lasserre to tears, but even worse to them was the reaction in the theater. Lasserre remembered American children in the audience laughing and cheering when the Germans, from whose point of view the story

The eight Bonhoeffer children (circa 1910) and their governess at the holiday home in Wölfelsgrund in the Glatz Mountains. Karl and Paula Bonhoeffer stand in the background. Dietrich is just to the right of the governess, who holds Susanne, the youngest. Karl Bonhoeffer described Wölfelsgrund as lying "in a little valley at the foot of Mount Urnitz, right at the edge of the wood, with a meadow, a little brook, an old barn, and a fruit-tree which had a raised seat with a little bench for the children built into its wide branches."
(Art Resource, NY)

Karl Bonhoeffer with his four boys, circa 1911. In ascending order: Karl-Friedrich (1899–1957), Walter (1899–1918), Klaus (1901–1945), and Dietrich (1906–1945).

2008 photo of 14 Wangenheimstrasse in Berlin's Grunewald district. The Bonhoeffer family moved here in 1916. Today the vast house is divided into eight apartments. *(Eric Metaxas photo)*

Bonhoeffer in 1928. *(Art Resource, NY)*

Bonhoeffer in his class at Grunewald High School in Berlin, 1920–21. Left to right: Elizabeth Caspari, Felix Prentzel, Ursula Andeae (niece of Walter Rathenau), Ellen-Marion Winter (Later Countess Peter Yorck), Maria Weigert, teacher Willibald Heininger, Hans-Robert Pfeil, Georg Seligsohn, Dietrich Bonhoeffer, Erdmann Niekisch von Rosenegk, Kurt Mähne, Herbert Mankiewitz. It was during class the following year that Bonhoeffer heard the shot that assassinated Rathenau, a politically moderate Jew. *(Art Resource, NY)*

During Easter in 1932 Bonhoeffer took some of his rowdy Zionskirche confirmands to the family holiday home at Friedrichsbrunn. "Apart from a broken windowpane," he wrote, "everything is as it was. . . . Only Frau S. [the housekeeper] is somewhat indignant at the proletarian invasion."

(Art Resource, NY)

The seminarians at Sigurdshof in 1938. Bonhoeffer stands far left in the third row. Eberhard Bethge stands far right in the fourth row. *(Art Resource, NY)*

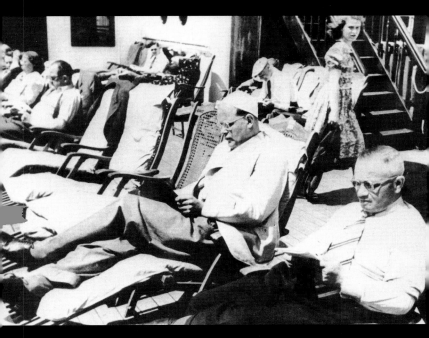

Bonhoeffer bound for New York aboard the *Bremen* during the second week of June 1939.

Ettal Monastery in the Bavarian Alps, where Bonhoeffer worked on his *Ethics* during the winter of 1940–41. He wrote Bethge: "I eat in the refectory, sleep in the hotel, can use the library, have my own key to the cloister, and yesterday had a long and good conversation with the abbot." *(Eric Metaxas photos)*

Um CHRISTI willen
im Widerstand gegen das Naziregime verfolgt
weilten in Ettal

P. Rupert MAYER SJ *1876 †1945
Aug. 1940 – Mai 1945

Pastor Dietrich BONHOEFFER *1906 †1945
Nov. 1940 ~ Febr. 1941

Herr, wann Du willst, dann ist es Zeit,
und wann Du willst, bin ich bereit,
genug, daß ich Dein Eigen bin.

Von guten Mächten wunderbar geborgen,
erwarten wir getrost, was kommen mag.
Gott ist mit uns am Abend und am Morgen
und ganz gewiß an jedem neuen Tag.

Plaque at Ettal Monastery *(Eric Metaxas photo)*

uly 1939. Dietrich with his twin sister Sabine in London, just after his return from America nd before his final return to Germany. *(Art Resource, NY)*

2008 photo of the Bonhoeffer home at 43 Marienburgerallee. Today it is a museum.

Bonhoeffer's parents, Karl and Paula Bonhoeffer. Eberhard Bethge described their marriage as "a happy relationship in which each partner adroitly supplemented the strength of the other. At their golden wedding anniversary it was said that they had not spent a total of one was told, were killing the French. For Bonhoeffer, it was unbearable. Lasserre later said he could barely console Bonhoeffer afterward. Lasserre believed that on that afternoon Bonhoeffer became a pacifist.

Lasserre spoke often about the Sermon on the Mount and how it informed his theology. From that point forward it became a central part of Bonhoeffer's life and theology, too, which eventually led him to write his most famous book, *The Cost of Discipleship*.* Just as important, though, was that as a result of his friendship with Lasserre, Bonhoeffer became involved in the ecumenical movement, which eventually led him to become involved in the Resistance against Hitler and the Nazis.

Bonhoeffer's voracious appetite for culture almost met its match in New York. To Max Diestel, he wrote, "If you really try to experience New York completely, it almost does you in." For someone who loved new experiences, America gave him a hatful. When he wasn't wringing another drop of culture from Manhattan, he was on a train or in a car traveling someplace else. Several times he visited his Tafel relatives in Philadelphia, and a number of times he took the train to Scarsdale to visit the Ern family. In December he and Erwin Sutz traveled south via train as far as possible, and when they ran out of land in Florida, they took a boat to Cuba.

In Cuba, Bonhoeffer met up with his childhood governess Käthe van Horn, then a teacher at a German school in Havana. Bonhoeffer celebrated Christmas there and preached at the German congregation, taking as his text the story of Moses' death on Mount Nebo. This story haunted Bonhoeffer for much of life. Thirteen years in the future, he would write to his fiancée about his Cuban experience:

> The sun has always attracted me, and I've often been reminded by it that human beings were taken from the earth and don't just consist of thin air and thoughts. So much so that once, when I went to Cuba to preach there at Christmas, and exchanged the ice of North America for its luxuriant tropical vegetation, I almost succumbed to sun-worship

---

* The German title of the book is *Nachfolge*, so the English translation should simply be *Discipleship*, which will be used in subsequent references in this book.

and could hardly remember what I was really supposed to preach. It was a genuine crisis, and a hint of it assails me every summer when I get to feel the sun.

Before and after Cuba, Bonhoeffer spent time in the American South, where he continued to puzzle over race relations:

The separation of whites from blacks in the southern states really does make a rather shameful impression. In railways that separation extends to even the tiniest details. I found that the cars of the negroes generally look cleaner than the others. It also pleased me when the whites had to crowd into their railway cars while often only a single person was sitting in the entire railway car for negroes. The way the southerners talk about the negroes is simply repugnant, and in this regard the pastors are no better than the others. I still believe that the spiritual songs of the southern negroes represent some of the greatest artistic achievements in America. It is a bit unnerving that in a country with so inordinately many slogans about brotherhood, peace, and so on, such things still continue completely uncorrected.

That January—two weeks before their twenty-fifth birthday—Bonhoeffer wrote Sabine. Twenty-five was a milestone for him. Having earned his doctorate at twenty-one, he expected great things of himself. Somehow things seemed a bit stalled:

It's so unnerving for me that we really are going to be twenty-five now. . . . [I]f I were to imagine I had already been married for over five years, had two children, my own house, well, then I could feel fully justified turning twenty-five. . . . How I shall spend the day I do not quite know yet. Several people have learned of the date and are demanding we have a birthday party, which I would then give at the house of one of the married students. But perhaps I'll also find something nice at the theater. Unfortunately I can't even toast you with a glass of wine at this occasion, since it's forbidden by federal law; how frightfully tedious, this Prohibition in which no one believes.

Bonhoeffer ended up celebrating with Paul and Marion Lehmann at their apartment in Greenwich Village. He had written Sabine that he hoped to travel to India in May, to reconnect with Dr. Lucas and see Mahatma Gandhi. He hoped to circumnavigate the globe westward to Germany. But the expense of going to India from New York was prohibitive. He and Lehmann made the rounds of the New York docks, looking for a freighter captain who might let Bonhoeffer hitch a cheap ride, but in vain. He decided to postpone his trip for another time.

The Lehmanns were as close to a family as Bonhoeffer had in New York. He felt comfortable in their company, and they in his. Many years later, in an address on the BBC, Paul Lehmann said:

> [Bonhoeffer] was German in his passion for perfection, whether of manners or performance, or of all that is connoted by the word *Kultur*. Here in short was an aristocracy of the spirit at its best. But at the same time Bonhoeffer was the most un-German of Germans. His aristocracy was unmistakable yet not obtrusive, chiefly, I think, owing to his boundless curiosity about every new environment in which he found himself, and his irresistible and unfailing sense of humour.

When the Lehmanns visited Bonhoeffer in Germany two years later, he and Paul wrote to the American rabbi Stephen Wise, telling him of the deteriorating situation among the Jews of Germany. Bonhoeffer's initial introduction to Wise was on Easter 1931. Bonhoeffer hoped to attend services in an American church, but in a letter to his grandmother he explained that it hadn't worked out because one had to

> get entry tickets for the larger churches far ahead of time. Because I didn't know that, nothing remained but to go hear a famous rabbi here who preaches every Sunday morning in the largest concert hall before a full audience; he delivered an enormously effective sermon on corruption in New York and challenged the Jews, who make up a third of the city, to build from this city the City of God, to which the Messiah would then truly be able to come.

It's remarkable that on the only Easter he spent in New York, Bonhoeffer attended services in a synagogue.

Road Trip

Bonhoeffer's trip to India was not coming together, but as his academic year at Union drew to a close, he made plans for another trip. He would drive to Mexico via Chicago.

Bonhoeffer and Lasserre had a notion of exploring Mexico's Catholic culture and decided to make the trip together. The trip involved four thousand miles of driving at speeds considerably slower than fifty-five. The Ern family generously offered to lend Bonhoeffer their 1928 Oldsmobile for the journey. He visited them twice that March, and they gave him driving lessons. But he failed the driver's test several times. The Lehmanns were convinced he should relax his German pride and slip the instructor five dollars. Bonhoeffer refused.

Eventually it was decided Paul Lehmann could come along and drive them as far as Chicago. Bonhoeffer thought by that time, he would feel comfortable driving. Then Erwin Sutz decided to join them. But Sutz was part of a chorus scheduled to sing at Carnegie Hall, so the trip was delayed until May 5. Sutz, like Bonhoeffer, was a pianist, and their love of music took them to many concerts together that year, including a Toscanini concert.

On May 5, the four theologians left the island of the Manhattoes in the borrowed Olds. The plan was to drive a thousand or so miles due west, to St. Louis. When they got to St. Louis, Sutz decided he had had enough and hopped a train back east. Lehmann and Lasserre would motor ahead with Bonhoeffer. Most of the time they camped out like hoboes.

Lasserre recalled:

Once at night, we had pitched our tent in a quiet grove of trees, without suspecting that we were taking over the dormitory of a herd of pigs. We had a hard time driving them away and discouraging these angry and noisy animals from reclaiming their bedrooms. After finally settling the matter we were worn out with fatigue and Dietrich fell quickly asleep. I was not so sure and I slept badly. At dawn I awoke with a start, because of a regular but ferocious snoring quite near to me. Thinking Dietrich quite ill, I threw myself towards him, only to find that he was sleeping peacefully as a child. The snoring which had terrified me was that of a huge pig who had stretched out against the whole side of the tent. . . . Dietrich was undisturbed, apparently quite unflappable, whatever happened. He had an extraordinarily even temperament, capable of ignoring anger, anxiety and discouragement. He seemed unable to despise anyone.

Finally Lasserre and Bonhoeffer reached the Mexican border in Laredo, Texas. But they discovered that if they wished to reenter the United States, they must obtain authorization to do so before they entered Mexico. So they found themselves stuck in Laredo at the St. Paul Hotel, trying to get the proper authorization. They sent a telegram to Paul Lehmann, now back in New York, asking him to try to sort it out. They also sent a telegram to the German ambassador in Mexico. They needed to prove that when they returned from Mexico, they had tickets in New York for their return trip to Bremen. The U.S. was in no economic condition to support Europeans trying to slip into the country via Mexico. Eventually Lehmann replied with instructions: "Proceed to Mexico City Stop When returning apply American consul for transit visa Stop Commissioner General assures no trouble Stop."

They left the Oldsmobile in Laredo and entered Mexico. The two traveled twelve hundred miles on Mexican trains. In Victoria City there was a teachers' training college where Lasserre had arranged through a Quaker friend for him and Bonhoeffer to give a joint address. The novelty of these eternal enemies—a Frenchman and a German—appearing together can hardly be overstated. That they spoke on the subject of peace was inconceivable. South of Mexico City, north of Cuernavaca, Bonhoeffer visited Aztec ruins. On a postcard of the Teopanzolco pyramid, he wrote his young friend Richard Ern:

I just spent a long time sitting on this pyramid and talking with an Indian shepherd boy who could neither read nor write but had a great deal to tell. It's beautiful here and not very hot at all, since the elevation is over two thousand meters. Everything is completely different from the States. There are apparently a great many poor people here. They often live in tiny huts, and the children often wear only shirts or nothing at all. The people look nice and are quite friendly. I'm looking

forward to getting back into your car and to seeing you again. Take
care, dear boy. Cordial greetings to you and your parents.

By June 17, Bonhoeffer and Lasserre were back in New York, which was
sweltering. And three days later, Bonhoeffer boarded a ship and headed back
home.

CHAPTER 8

BERLIN

1931–32

He told us of his colored friend with whom he had travelled through the States... he told of the piety of the negroes . . . At the end of the evening he said: "When I took leave of my black friend, he said to me: 'Make our sufferings known in Germany. Tell them what is happening to us, and show them what we are like.'"

—WOLF-DIETER ZIMMERMANN

Among the public there spread the expectation that the salvation of the German people would now come from Hitler. But in the lectures we were told that salvation comes only from Jesus Christ.

—INGE KARDING

Bonhoeffer returned to Berlin from America at the end of June. But he was home only a few days before he again left the country. His parents had hoped to lure him to Friedrichsbrunn, but even that couldn't compete with what awaited Bonhoeffer in Switzerland. Erwin Sutz had arranged to introduce him to Karl Barth.

Bonhoeffer left for Bonn on July 10. Not surprisingly his first impressions of the great theologian were favorable. He wrote his parents: "I have now met Barth and got to know him quite well at a discussion evening at his

119

house. I like him very much indeed, and am also very impressed by his lectures. . . . I think I shall gain a great deal from the time spent here."

In one of Barth's seminars—perhaps at that first discussion evening—a student had quoted Luther's famous maxim that "sometimes the curses of the godless sound better than the hallelujahs of the pious." Barth, pleased with what he heard, asked who had said it. It was Bonhoeffer. This was likely the first time they met. They soon became friends.

On July 23, the forty-five-year-old Barth invited the twenty-five-year-old Bonhoeffer to dinner. Bonhoeffer was alone with Dr. Barth, able to ask questions he had had for years. "I have been impressed even more by discussions with him than by his writings and his lectures," Bonhoeffer said. "For he is really all there. I have never seen anything like it before." He added, "There is with him an openness, a readiness for any objection which should hit the mark, and along with this such concentration and impetuous insistence on the point, whether it is made arrogantly or modestly, dogmatically or completely uncertainly, and not only when it serves his own theology."

In the next two years Bonhoeffer visited Barth often. In September 1932, just after Barth completed the first volume of his landmark *Church Dogmatics*, Bonhoeffer visited him on the Bergli in Switzerland. He also saw Sutz, who introduced him to the Swiss theologian Emil Brunner. In 1933, when a chair in theology opened at Berlin University, Bonhoeffer tried to leverage his family's connections in the Prussian Ministry of Culture on Barth's behalf. But Hitler had just taken power as Reichkanzler. Once that happened, everything was politicized, and no one who disdained Hitler's views would get an important position in academia or anywhere else. The chair went to Georg Wobbermin, who was cut of the same brown cloth as the new Reichkanzler. Barth wrote to Bonhoeffer afterward: "In the era of Reichkanzler Hitler, Wobbermin will certainly fill Schleiermacher's chair in a fashion more true to type than I should have done. I hear that you have come out strongly on my behalf. . . . I should undoubtedly have accepted. . . . [T]he world is in bad shape, but we don't want to let our pipe go out under any circumstances, do we?"

But at this point, Hitler's ascent to the chancellorship was still two years in the unimaginable future. Bonhoeffer had been in New York a mere nine months, but in some ways it seemed a lifetime. When he left, the Nazis were a tiny gray cloud on the horizon of an otherwise clear sky. Now, black and crackling with electricity, they loomed nearly overhead.

Bonhoeffer wrote Sutz that the "outlook is really exceptionally grim." He felt that they were "standing at a tremendous turning point in world history," that something was about to happen. But what? In his prescient way, Bonhoeffer sensed that whatever lay ahead, the church would be threatened. He wondered if it would survive at all. "Then what's the use of everyone's theology?" he asked. There were now an urgency and a seriousness to Bonhoeffer that had not been there before. Somehow he sensed he must warn people of what lay ahead. It was as if he could see that a mighty oak tree, in whose shade families were picnicking, and from whose branches children were swinging, was rotten inside, was about to fall down and kill them all. Others observed the change in him. For one thing, his sermons became more severe.

The Great Change

What's left of the Kaiser Wilhelm Memorial Church sits like Ozymandias in the midst of the bleak plastic-and-cement desert of Berlin's commercial district. Most of the area was turned to rubble during an RAF raid in 1943, and what remains of this once awe-inspiring cathedral—the pitted, busted hulk of the bell tower—now serves as a heavy-handed modernistic reminder of the destructiveness of war. But before the war, as they say, it was one of the glories of Berlin.

Bonhoeffer was asked to preach there on Reformation Sunday in 1932.* This was the day Germany celebrated Luther and the great cultural heritage of the Reformation. The people in the pews that day expected about what an American might expect from a July 4 service in a mainstream Protestant church: an uplifting, patriotic sermon. The Germans expected to be movingly inflated with pride at the miracle of their German Lutheran heritage and to have their egos sensitively stroked for the part they played in keeping this grand tradition alive by sitting in the hard pews when they might have been doing so many other things. Hindenburg, that stout, burly national icon, might well have been in the congregation that day, as this was the very church the great man attended. What a wonderful service it would be! And so, with the congregation having settled itself into this warm and pleasant

---

* He preached there a number of times during those years, filling in for his friend, the pastor Gerhard Jacobi, who became a close ally in the church struggles of the 1930s.

expectation, the sermon that Bonhoeffer delivered must have seemed like a nasty sucker punch followed by a wheeling roundhouse kick to the chops.

The Bible texts provided a clue of what lay ahead. The first was from Revelation 2:4–5: "Nevertheless I have somewhat against thee, because thou hast left thy first love. Remember therefore from whence thou art fallen, and repent, and do the first works; or else I will come unto thee quickly, and will remove thy candlestick out of his place, except thou repent." People familiar with Bonhoeffer's preaching, upon hearing these verses, might well have slipped out the side exit. On the other hand, if they had been in the mood to be blasted backward by a bracing philippic and had chosen to stay, they would not have been disappointed.

Bonhoeffer opened with the bad news: the Protestant church was in its eleventh hour, he said, and it's "high time we realized this." The German church, he said, is dying or is already dead. Then he directed his thunder at the people in the pews. He condemned the grotesque inappropriateness of having a celebration when they were all, in fact, attending a funeral: "A fanfare of trumpets is no comfort to a dying man." He then referred to the day's hero, Martin Luther, as a "dead man" whom they were propping up for their selfish purposes. It was as if he'd thrown a bucket of water on the congregation and had then thrown his shoes at them. "We do not see that this Church is no longer the Church of Luther," he said. He called it "unpardonable frivolity and arrogance" for them to blithely appropriate Luther's famous words, "Here I stand, I can do no other," for their own ends—as if these words applied to them and the Lutheran church of their day. So it went.

Nor was it the only sermon of its kind that he would preach that year. But what exactly did Bonhoeffer see, and whence this urgency to communicate what he saw? He seemed to want to warn everyone to wake up and stop playing church. They were all sleepwalking toward a terrible precipice! But few took him seriously. For many, Bonhoeffer was only one of those bespectacled and overserious academic types, with a good dose of religious fanaticism in the bargain. And he preached such depressing sermons!

One must wonder what Bonhoeffer meant to accomplish with these sermons. Did he really expect people in the pews to take what he was saying to heart? But what he said was indeed true, and he felt that God had chosen him to say what he was saying. He took the idea of preaching the Word of God extremely seriously and wouldn't have dared to speak his mere opinions from the pulpit. He also knew that a word might be delivered that had come straight from heaven and be rejected, just as the messages of the Old Testament prophets had been rejected and just as Jesus had been rejected. The prophet's role was simply and obediently to speak what God wished to say. Whether or not the message was received was between God and his people. And yet to preach such a burning message, and to know that it was God's Word for the faithful, who rejected it, was painful. But this was the pain of the prophetic office, and to be chosen by God as his prophet always meant, in part, that the prophet would share in God's sufferings.

Something had obviously happened to Bonhoeffer in the previous year and was happening still. Some have gone so far as to call it a conversion, which it can hardly have been. To Bonhoeffer and to others close to him, it was evident that his faith had somehow deepened in the previous year. And it was obvious that his sense of himself as called by God was becoming clearer.

A few years later, in January 1936, in the letter he wrote to Elizabeth Zinn, he described the change that had taken place in him during this time:

> I plunged into work in a very unchristian way. An . . . ambition that many noticed in me made my life difficult. . . . Then something happened, something that has changed and transformed my life to the present day. For the first time I discovered the Bible . . . I had often preached. I had seen a great deal of the Church, and talked and preached about it—but I had not yet become a Christian. . . . I know that at that time I turned the doctrine of Jesus Christ into something of personal advantage for myself . . . I pray to God that that will never happen again. Also I had never prayed, or prayed only very little. For all my loneliness, I was quite pleased with myself. Then the Bible, and in particular the Sermon on the Mount, freed me from that. Since then everything has changed. I have felt this plainly, and so have other people about me. It was a great liberation. It became clear to me that the life of a servant of Jesus Christ must belong to the Church, and step by step it became plainer to me how far that must go. Then came the crisis of 1933. This strengthened me in it. Also I now found others who shared that aim with me. The revival of the Church and of the ministry became my supreme concern. . . . My calling is quite clear to me. What God will make of it I do

not know . . . I must follow the path. Perhaps it will not be such a long one. (Phil 1:23). But it is a fine thing to have realized my calling . . . I believe its nobility will become plain to us only in coming times and events. If only we can hold out.

Somehow Bonhoeffer's time in New York, especially his worship at the "negro churches," played their part in all of this. He had heard the gospel preached there and had seen real piety among a suffering people. The fiery sermons and the joyous worship and singing had all opened his eyes to something and had changed him. Had he been "born again"?

What happened is unclear, but the results were obvious. For one thing, he now became a regular churchgoer for the first time in his life and took Communion as often as possible. When Paul and Marion Lehmann visited Berlin in 1933, they noticed a difference in their friend. Two years earlier, in New York, he hadn't been interested in going to church. He loved working with the children in Harlem, and he loved going to concerts and movies and museums, and he loved traveling, and he loved the philosophical and academic give-and-take of theological *ideas*—but here was something new. What had happened that Bonhoeffer should suddenly take attending church so seriously?

Bonhoeffer the Teacher

Just before leaving for Union, Bonhoeffer had qualified as a university lecturer in theology at Berlin University, so on his return he immediately took up his post there, giving seminars and lectures. But his way of teaching theology would not be what most people expected. The change that had been occurring in him would be visible behind the lectern and in the seminars too.

Wolf-Dieter Zimmermann was one of Bonhoeffer's students from those days and first encountered Bonhoeffer in the fall of 1932. There were only a handful of students in the lecture hall that first day, and Zimmermann was tempted to leave. But for some reason he was curious, and he stayed. He recalled the moment:

A young lecturer stepped to the rostrum with a light, quick step, a man with very fair, rather thin hair, a broad face, rimless glasses with a golden bridge. After a few words of welcome he explained the meaning and structure of the lecture, in a firm, slightly throaty way of speaking. Then he opened his manuscript and started on his lecture. He pointed out that nowadays we often ask ourselves whether we still need the Church, whether we still need God. But this question, he said, is wrong. We are the ones who are questioned. The Church exists and God exists, and we are asked whether we are willing to be of service, for God needs us.

Talk like this was rare from most German pulpits. From a university lectern it was simply unheard of. But Bonhoeffer had not suddenly become more emotional, or less rational. His style as a lecturer was "very concentrated, quite unsentimental, almost dispassionate, clear as a crystal, with a certain rational coldness, like a reporter." It was this combination of an adamantine faith with a logician's sparkling intellect that was so compelling. Ferenc Lehel, another student, said they "followed his words with such close attention that one could hear the flies humming. Sometimes, when we laid our pens down after a lecture, we were literally perspiring." Yet Bonhoeffer was not always serious and intense. There was a winking playfulness to him, too, that many friends remarked on over the years. When Lehel visited him at his home and was invited to stay for dinner, Lehel politely declined, but Bonhoeffer pushed him to stay: "It isn't just my bread, but our bread, and when we eat it together there will be twelve baskets left over."

Bonhoeffer often invited students home. He was involved in their lives, just as he had been involved in the lives of the little children in his Grunewald Sunday school class and with the young men in his Thursday Circle. Lehel remembered that Bonhoeffer had encouraged him in his faith:

> In my intellectual difficulties he stood by me, as a pastor, brotherly and friendly. When he recommended Karl Heim's *Glaube und Denken* to me he pointed out how Heim was able to feel at one with the doubter; how he did not indulge in cheap apologetics which from their lofty base fire upon the battlements of natural science. We must think with the doubter, he said, even doubt with him.

Another student, Otto Dudzus, recalled that Bonhoeffer invited students to the musical evenings at his parents' home:

Whatever he had and whatever he was, he made that accessible to others. The great treasure he possessed was the cultivated, elegant, educated, highly educated, open-minded home of his parents, which he introduced us to. The open evenings, which took place every week, or later every two weeks, had such an atmosphere that they became a piece of home for us, as well. Also, Bonhoeffer's mother entertained in the best possible way.

Even when Bonhoeffer went to London in 1934, his parents continued to treat these students like family, including them in the larger circle of their society and home. Bonhoeffer did not separate his Christian life from his family life. His parents were exposed to other bright students of theology, and his students were exposed to the extraordinary Bonhoeffer family.

Inge Karding, one of the few women students in Bonhoeffer's circle, remembered her first lecture with him:

My first impression of him was that he was so young! . . . He had a good face, and he had good posture. . . . He was very natural with us students . . . but there was, for such a young man, a certainty and dignity in him. . . . He always maintained a certain distance. . . . One wouldn't have trusted oneself to make a joke around him.

Albrecht Schönherr was another Bonhoeffer student:

He was not like he appears in many photographs. The pictures sometimes make him look plump and fleshy, but he had an athletic build, rather big, with a big forehead, a Kant-like forehead. But his voice did not go with his body. It was a little high, so that you could never be seduced by his voice. It would never sound demagogical. He actually was very glad about that, because he would never under any circumstances want to be a demagogue—to convey something to people through his voice, his appearance, or his "flair," rather than to speak to people through substance.

Bonhoeffer had always struggled with the "problem" of being charming. He mistrusted it and wanted the words and logic of what he said to be the only things to which others responded.

Nonetheless, a group of students formed around Bonhoeffer during this time. Their conversations overflowed the boundaries of the lecture halls and seminar rooms. They wanted to continue their conversations away from the strictures of the university. Some met once a week in Wolf-Dieter Zimmermann's attic room near the Alexanderplatz. It was very crowded, but they would stay for hours, smoking and talking. Bonhoeffer imposed a certain discipline even on these gatherings, as he had with his Thursday Circle. It was no aimless gabfest, but a controlled, serious exploration of questions. It consisted of "pure, abstract theorizing, in the attempt to grasp a problem in its fullness."

Bonhoeffer openly thought things through and taught his students to do the same. They followed lines of reasoning to their logical conclusions and considered every angle to have a sense of absolute thoroughness, so that nothing depended on mere emotion. He accorded theological ideas the same respect that his father or Karl-Friedrich accorded scientific ideas, or his brother Klaus accorded ideas of jurisprudence. Questions about the Bible and ethics and theology must be treated with the same rigorousness, and all cant and "phraseology" must be identified, exposed as such, and cut away and discarded. One wished to arrive at answers that could stand up to every scrutiny because one would have to live out those conclusions. They would have to become actions and would have to become the substance of one's life. Once one saw clearly what the Word of God said, one would have to act on it and its implications, such as they were. And actions in Germany at that time had serious consequences.

Students found Bonhoeffer extremely open-minded and patient. Hellmut Traub noted that Bonhoeffer was "extraordinarily reserved, ready to consider every fresh problem put to him, taking even the remotest ideas into account." The students learned how to take the time to think things through to the end. "His conservative nature, his scholarly education and his thoroughness prevented any quick result."

Around ten thirty they repaired to a nearby *Bierkeller* for more informal conversation. Bonhoeffer always picked up the tab.

One evening, Zimmermann said that Bonhoeffer brought the records of "negro spirituals" he had bought in New York:

He told us of his colored friend with whom he had travelled through the States . . . he told of the piety of the negroes. . . . At the end of the evening he said: "When I took leave of my black friend, he said to me: 'Make our sufferings known in Germany, tell them what is happening to us, and show them what we are like.' I wanted to fulfill this obligation tonight."

It is likely that he now began to think of the church as called by God to "stand with those who suffer."

Many of Bonhoeffer's students from this time became part of his life for years. Some would become involved in the ecumenical world with him, and many of them would later be part of the illegal seminaries at Zingst and Finkenwalde. Otto Dudzus, Albrecht Schönherr, Winfried Maechler, Joachim Kanitz, Jürgen Winterhager, Wolf-Dieter Zimmermann, Herbert Jehle, and Inge Karding were among them.

Bonhoeffer's interest was not only in teaching them as a university lecturer. He wished to "disciple" them in the true life of the Christian. This ran the gamut, from understanding current events through a biblical lens to reading the Bible not just as a theology student but as a disciple of Jesus Christ. This approach was unique among German university theologians of that era.

Bonhoeffer was able to get away with it because of his patrician cultural background and his intellectual brilliance. He spoke in a highly academic way, but in a way that also spelled out the implications of what he was saying to current events. In 1933, one student said, "Among the public, there spread the expectation that the salvation of the German people would now come from Hitler. But in the lectures we were told that salvation comes only from Jesus Christ."

Inge Karding said that Bonhoeffer once spoke to her about the seriousness of saying, "Heil!" (Hail!) to anyone but God. He didn't shrink from political commentary, and from the beginning he never felt what many others felt: that somehow politics was not related to Christian faith. She also recalled that Bonhoeffer unapologetically approached the Bible as the word of God. At a place like Berlin University, where the ghost of Schleiermacher still walked abroad in the night, and where Harnack's chair was still warm, this was positively scandalous:

[He said] when you read the Bible, you must think that here and now God is speaking with me. . . . He wasn't as abstract as the Greek teachers and all the others. Rather, from the very beginning, he taught us that we had to read the Bible as it was directed at us, as the word of God directly to us. Not something general, not something generally applicable, but rather with a personal relationship to us. He repeated this to us very early on, that the whole thing comes from that.

Bonhoeffer was not interested in intellectual abstraction. Theology must lead to the practical aspects of how to live as a Christian. Karding was surprised when Bonhoeffer asked his students whether they sang Christmas carols. Their answer was noncommittal, so he said, "If you want to be pastors, then you must sing Christmas carols!" For him, music was not an optional part of Christian ministry, but *de rigeur*. He decided to tackle this deficiency head-on. "On the first day of Advent," he said to her, "we will meet each other at noon . . . and we will sing Christmas carols." She remembered that he "played the flute wonderfully" and sang "magnificently."

Joachim Kanitz remembered that once Bonhoeffer told them that they should not forget that "every word of Holy Scripture was a quite personal message of God's love for us." Bonhoeffer then "asked us whether we loved Jesus."

Taking students on weekend trips into the country for retreats was another element of his practical instruction method. Sometimes they went to Prebelow, staying in the youth hostel there, and a number of times visited the cabin he bought in nearby Biesenthal. On one hiking trip, Bonhoeffer had them meditate on a Bible verse after breakfast. They had to find a place on the grass and sit quietly for an hour and meditate on that verse. Many of them found it difficult, as Bonhoeffer's Finkenwalde ordinands would find it difficult. Inge Karding was among them: "He taught us that the Bible goes directly into your life, [to] where your problems are."

Bonhoeffer was working out the ideas that would find their way into the illegal seminaries of the Confessing Church in a few years. For him, such things as meditating on Bible verses and the singing formed integral parts in a theological education. Bonhoeffer's recurring theme of incarnation—that God did not create us to be disembodied spirits, but flesh-and-blood human beings—led him to the idea that the Christian life must be modeled. Jesus did not only communicate ideas and concepts and rules and principles for living. He lived. And by living with his disciples, he showed them what life was supposed to look like, what God had intended it to look like. It was not merely intellectual or merely spiritual. It was all these things together; it was something more. Bonhoeffer aimed to model the Christian life for his students. This led him to the idea that, to be a Christian, one must live with Christians.

One student said she learned about the concepts of guilt and grace from the way Bonhoeffer treated them. On one retreat in 1933, Bonhoeffer and a group of students were hiking in some woods when they came upon a hungry family obviously looking for food. Bonhoeffer approached them warmly and asked whether the children were getting any hot food. When the man replied, "Not so much," Bonhoeffer asked if he could take two of them along. "We're going home now to eat," he said, "and they can get something to eat with us, and then we'll bring them right back."

A Confirmation Class in Wedding

Bonhoeffer's ability to connect with people in difficult circumstances was remarkable, but perhaps never quite so remarkable as when he taught a confirmation class at the Zionskirche in Wedding, a notoriously tough neighborhood in the Prenzlauer Berg district of North Berlin. He was given the assignment shortly after his ordination in November 1931.[*] Around the same time his superintendent, Otto Dibelius, also assigned him to a chaplaincy at the Charlottenburg Technical College. That was not very satisfying to him, but his colorful experiences with the rowdy confirmation class were quite the opposite.

The old minister at the Zionskirche, Superintendent Müller, desperately needed help with a class of fifty boys. Their behavior was almost beyond description. Bonhoeffer described this area as "wild" and as having "difficult social and political circumstances." Bonhoeffer had taught Sunday school to children in Harlem, but the difference was profound. The American separation of church and state made churchgoing private and voluntary, so if children were in church classes, it was likely because their parents wanted them there. If they misbehaved, they would answer to their parents. But in Germany most children went to confirmation classes as they went to school. It was effectively mandated by the state, and the parents of the children who

---

* Bonhoeffer was ordained on November 15, 1931, at St. Matthew's Church near Potsdam Palace.

would greet the young pastor likely thought about it as their children did. In any case, it kept their kids off the street for an hour or two. But if their children misbehaved, that was the teacher's affair. As far as many of them were concerned, the church was a corrupt institution, and if their kids could ladle out a bit of grief to this soft, golden-haired cleric, perhaps he had it coming.

Quite unlike the cherubs Bonhoeffer had taught in Harlem, he now faced a veritable gang of sawed-off hoodlums. He had been duly warned, but nothing could have prepared him for what lay ahead. The fourteen- and fifteen-year-old miscreants were so famously misbehaved—and had so expertly harassed the minister Bonhoeffer was replacing—that no sooner had Bonhoeffer taken over the class than the exasperated old fellow died— skipped off to that great confirmation class in the sky. Bonhoeffer was seriously convinced that the frail man's health failed chiefly as a result of this ungovernable class. Bethge described the initial meeting:

> The elderly minister and Bonhoeffer slowly walked up the stairs of the school building, which was several stories high. The children looked down on them from over the banisters, making an indescribable din and dropping refuse on the two men ascending the stairs. When they reached the top, the minister tried to force the throng back into the classroom by shouting and using physical force. He tried to announce that he had brought them a new minister who was going to teach them in the future and that his name was Bonhoeffer, and when they heard the name they started shouting "Bon! Bon! Bon!" louder and louder. The old man left the scene in despair, leaving Bonhoeffer standing silently against the wall with his hands in his pockets. Minutes passed. His failure to react made the noise gradually less enjoyable, and he began speaking quietly, so that only the boys in the front row could catch a few words of what he said. Suddenly all were silent. Bonhoeffer merely remarked that they had put up a remarkable initial performance, and went on to tell them a story about Harlem. If they listened, he told them, he would tell them more next time. Then he told them they could go. After that, he never had a reason to complain about their lack of attentiveness.

Bonhoeffer described the situation to Erwin Sutz: "At first the boys behaved as though they were crazy, so that for the first time I had real difficulties with discipline. . . . But what helped the most was that I simply told them stories from the Bible with great emphasis, particularly the eschatological passages."

His youth, athletic build, and aristocratic bearing helped Bonhoeffer earn their respect. But often he had a similarly extraordinary effect on people who were otherwise thought impossible. He would have such an effect on some of the prison guards near the end of his life too.

Years later, one of the boys recalled that, during class, a student pulled out a sandwich and began eating it: "This was nothing unusual in the north of Berlin. Pastor Bonhoeffer said nothing at first. Then he looked at him, calmly and kindly—but long and intensely, without saying a word. In embarrassment, the boy put his sandwich away. The attempt to annoy our pastor had come to nothing through his composure and kindness—and perhaps through his understanding for boyish tomfoolery."

It also fell to the patrician young pastor to visit the homes and parents of every one of the fifty students. Wedding was a squalid, poverty-stricken district, and many of the parents allowed him into their homes only because they felt they must. The halting conversations could be agonizing. Bonhoeffer thought it the worst aspect of his duties. In a letter to Sutz he wrote:

> I sometimes, indeed often, stand there and think that I would have been as well equipped to do such visits if I had studied chemistry. . . . To think of those excruciating hours or minutes when I or the other person try to begin a pastoral conversation, and how haltingly and lamely it goes on! And in the background there are always the ghastly home conditions, about which one really cannot say anything. Many people tell one about their most dubious way of life without any misgivings and in a free and easy way, and one feels that if one were to say something then they simply wouldn't understand.

Yet Bonhoeffer did not shrink from the task. Indeed, to be closer to all of these families and spend more time with the boys, he moved into a furnished room in the neighborhood at 61 Oderbergstrasse. Then he took a page from his dormitory experiences at Union and adopted an open-door policy, such that his new charges could visit him unannounced at any time. It was a bold and decisive about-face for the once solipsistic Bonhoeffer. His landlord was the baker whose shop occupied the street level below. Bonhoeffer instructed the baker's wife that the boys were to be allowed into his room in his absence. That Christmas he gave each boy a Christmas present.

Bonhoeffer told Sutz: "I'm looking forward to this time immensely. This is real work. Their home conditions are generally indescribable: poverty, disorder, immorality. And yet the children are still open; I am often amazed how a young person does not completely come to grief under such conditions; and of course one is always asking oneself how one would react to such surroundings."

Two months later, he wrote Sutz again:

> The second half of the term has been almost entirely given up to the candidates. Since New Year I have been living here in the north, so as to be able to have the boys here every evening, in turns of course. We have supper together and then we play something—I have taught them chess, which they now play with the greatest enthusiasm. . . . At the end of each evening I read something out of the Bible and after that a little catechizing, which often grows very serious. The experience of teaching them has been such that I can hardly tear myself away from it.

It was during this time that Bonhoeffer decided to rent a nine-acre parcel of land just north of Berlin and build a small cabin on it. The land was in Biesenthal, and the cabin was primitive, made of tar paper and wood. Inside were three bedsteads, a few stools, a table, and a paraffin stove. In a photo in front of this Thoreauvian hovel he strikes a heroic pose, wearing gaiters and smoking a pipe. He would retreat to this place often, sometimes with his students from the university, and sometimes with the boys from Wedding. As he had done with his flat in Berlin, he told them they were welcome anytime. As their confirmation approached, Bonhoeffer realized many of them didn't have a proper suit for the occasion or money to buy material for one, so he purchased a huge bolt of woolen cloth and cut enough material for each boy.

When one of the boys fell ill, Bonhoeffer visited him in the hospital two or three times a week, and before the operation, he prayed with him. The doctors were convinced his leg would have to be amputated, but quite miraculously it was saved. The boy made a complete recovery and was confirmed with the others.

The Sunday of their confirmation was March 13, 1932. That same day a national election was being held to determine who would be president. Nazi rowdies rode around in the backs of trucks with megaphones, stirring things up. A month earlier Hitler was found ineligible to run since he was born and reared in Austria. But this problem was strenuously shoved through a loophole, and he would run after all. So that Sunday was not a quiet one in Wedding. But even with this Nazi hubbub, the service went off without a hitch. Bonhoeffer's sermon to the boys was gentler than his other sermons of that time:

> Dear Confirmation Candidates!
> When in the last days before your confirmation I asked you many times what you hoped to hear in your confirmation address, I often received the answer: we want a serious warning which we shall remember all our lives. And I can assure you that whoever listens well today will receive a warning or two by the way; but look, life itself gives us enough and too many serious warnings today; and so today I must not make your prospect for the future seem harder and darker than it already is—and I know that many of you know a great many of the hard facts of life. Today you are not to be given fear of life but courage; and so today in the Church we shall speak more than ever of hope, the hope that we have and which no one can take from you.

He invited them to a service two days later so they could celebrate Communion together. That next weekend was Easter, and he took a large group of them to Friedrichsbrunn. His cousin Hans-Christoph came along to help manage them. Bonhoeffer wrote his parents:

> I am delighted to be able to be up here with the confirmation boys; even though they do not show any special appreciation of the woods and nature, they are enthusiastic about climbing in the Bode valley and playing *Fussball* on the field. It is often by no means easy to keep these predominantly antisocial boys under control. . . . I think that afterwards you will not notice any ill-effects on the house as a result of

these occupants. Apart from a broken windowpane, everything is as it was. . . . Only Frau S. [the housekeeper] is somewhat indignant at the proletarian invasion. . . . On Thursday it will all be over.

Five months later Bonhoeffer was at Friedrichsbrunn again, under different circumstances. Four generations of Bonhoeffers gathered to celebrate Julie Tafel Bonhoeffer's ninetieth birthday. Christel and Hans von Dohnanyi's son, Christoph, had not yet celebrated his second birthday. Nonetheless, in the well-worn family tradition, he memorized and recited a verse for his great-grandmother:

> When you were once as small as me
> One rode upon a steed;
> When I am someday old as you
> we'll travel to the moon.

Although many of them were not Christians, they embodied the values that made it possible for Bonhoeffer to become a Christian in a world that was quickly turning in every other direction, whether toward unbridled materialism or nationalistic emotionalism. They maintained decorum and civility amidst madness and barbarism. Bonhoeffer was therefore skeptical of the pietistic branches of the Christian faith that would have had him push away from his family and "the world."

Because he continued to remain in their midst as he did, the fullness of his life as a Christian pastor and theologian was not hidden from them. It was no small thing to become a theologian in a family whose father was one of the world's leading doctors and whose eldest son was splitting atoms with Planck and Einstein. But it was another thing entirely to move away from the theology of his distinguished and respected great-grandfather, Karl August Hase, or his esteemed Grunewald neighbor Adolf von Harnack, to the theology that had him talking to his students about loving Jesus or talking about God to the lower classes in their tenement flats in Wedding.

Bonhoeffer's family could not have helped noticing the change that had taken place in him between the time he had left for Manhattan and now, but the change was not an ungainly, embarrassing leap from which he would have to retreat slightly when he gained more maturity and perspective. It was by all accounts a deepening consistent with what had gone before. He never made any sharp turns that would give his family members cause for concern, nor did he attempt to "evangelize" them in any clumsy, desperate way. Rather, he continued to honor his mother and his father, was always respectful to his family members, and continued to uphold the values he had been raised with. His opposition to self-indulgent emotionalism and "phraseology" was the same as ever; his opposition to the National Socialists and all they represented was the same as ever. In light of all this, his faith, like the faith of his mother, Paula Bonhoeffer, was rather difficult to argue with, however one might have wished to do so.

A few years later, in 1936, Bonhoeffer wrote his brother-in-law Rüdiger Schleicher, who was as liberal theologically as Bonhoeffer was conservative. It says much about their relationship that he could write such things:

> First of all I will confess quite simply—I believe that the Bible alone is the answer to all our questions, and that we need only to ask repeatedly and a little humbly, in order to receive this answer. One cannot simply *read* the Bible, like other books. One must be prepared really to enquire of it. Only thus will it reveal itself. Only if we expect from it the ultimate answer, shall we receive it. That is because in the Bible God speaks to us. And one cannot simply think about God in one's own strength, one has to enquire of him. Only if we seek him, will he answer us. Of course it is also possible to read the Bible like any other book, that is to say from the point of view of textual criticism, etc.; there is nothing to be said against that. Only that that is not the method which will reveal to us the heart of the Bible, but only the surface, just as we do not grasp the words of someone we love by taking them to bits, but by simply receiving them, so that for days they go on lingering in our minds, simply because they are the words of a person we love; and just as these words reveal more and more of the person who said them as we go on, like Mary, "pondering them in our heart," so it will be with the words of the Bible. Only if we will venture to enter into the words of the Bible, as though in them this God were speaking to us who loves us and does not will to leave us along with our questions, only so shall we learn to rejoice in the Bible. . . .

If it is I who determine where God is to be found, then I shall always find a God who corresponds to me in some way, who is obliging, who is connected with my own nature. But if God determines where he is to be found, then it will be in a place which is not immediately pleasing to my nature and which is not at all congenial to me. This place is the Cross of Christ. And whoever would find him must go to the foot of the Cross, as the Sermon on the Mount commands. This is not according to our nature at all, it is entirely contrary to it. But this is the message of the Bible, not only in the New but also in the Old Testament. . . .

And I would like to tell you now quite personally: since I have learnt to read the Bible in this way—and this has not been for so very long—it becomes every day more wonderful to me. I read it in the morning and the evening, often during the day as well, and every day I consider a text which I have chosen for the whole week, and try to sink deeply into it, so as really to hear what it is saying. I know that without this I could not live properly any longer.

CHAPTER 9

THE FÜHRER PRINCIPLE

1933

The fearful danger of the present time is that above the cry for
authority . . . we forget that man stands alone before the ultimate
authority and that anyone who lays violent hands on man here is
infringing eternal laws and taking upon himself superhuman authority
which will eventually crush him.

The church has only one altar, the altar of the Almighty . . . before
which all creatures must kneel. Whoever seeks something other than
this must keep away; he cannot join us in the house of God . . . The
church has only one pulpit, and from that pulpit, faith in God will be
preached, and no other faith, and no other will than the will of God,
however well-intentioned.

—DIETRICH BONHOEFFER

On January 30, 1933, at noon, Adolf Hitler became the democratically elected chancellor of Germany. The land of Goethe,
Schiller, and Bach would now be led by someone who con-
sorted with crazies and criminals, who was often seen carrying
a dog whip in public. The Third Reich had begun.

Two days later, on Wednesday, February 1, a twenty-six-year-old theologian gave a radio address at the Potsdamerstrasse radio station. Bonhoeffer's speech was titled "The Younger Generation's Altered Concept of Leadership." It dealt with the fundamental problems of leadership by a *Führer*, explaining how such a leader inevitably becomes an idol and a "mis-leader." Before he could finish, the speech was cut off.

This story is usually told as though Bonhoeffer had bravely put himself forward to speak out against Hitler, whose henchmen ordered the microphones turned off and the broadcast ended. But the speech had been scheduled for some time and was not a response to Hitler's election. How Bonhoeffer came to give the speech is unclear. Wolf-Dieter Zimmermann may have recommended him; he worked at the radio division of the Evangelical Press Union. Karl Bonhoeffer had recently given two talks at the station as well. And Dietrich's speech was not specifically about Hitler, but about the popular concept of the so-called Führer Principle, which had been around for decades. (*Der Führer* literally means "the Leader.") It arose out of the popular German Youth Movement of the early twentieth century. The Führer and Adolf Hitler were not yet the same thing. Of course Hitler rode the concept of the Führer Principle right into the chancellorship and eventually came to embody it. He insisted on being called *der Führer* because he wished to fully exploit this principle for political gain. But in February 1933 the idea was not yet uniquely associated with him. Still, the timing of Bonhoeffer's speech, two days after Hitler's election, was uncanny.

The Nazis may have censored the broadcast, but it's also possible that Bonhoeffer and the station manager misunderstood each other, and he simply ran out of time. It's also unclear whether the Nazis could control the airwaves now as they certainly would in a few years. Still, the idea that such a speech should be cut off by the newly elected Nazis is tempting to believe and might indeed be what happened.

In any case, Bonhoeffer was upset that the speech ended prematurely, mainly because he didn't want his listeners to come away with the notion that he approved of Hitler. Anyone who heard the end of the speech would understand that the Führer Principle was disastrously misguided, but since no one heard the ending, many listening or half listening might have assumed Bonhoeffer's ruminations on this concept of the Leader were just part of the general acclamation. To redeem the situation, Bonhoeffer had the speech duplicated and sent it to many of his influential friends and relatives, along with a note explaining that the speech's conclusion had been cut off. The speech was also published in the *Kreuzzeitung*, a politically conservative newspaper, and Bonhoeffer was invited to give an extended version of the speech in early March at the College of Political Science in Berlin. Such things were still possible in early 1933.

But the circumstances of the broadcast mustn't obscure the uncanniness of the speech itself. Two days after Hitler's election, a young professor of theology delineated with incisiveness the most fundamental philosophical errors of a regime that hadn't existed when he wrote the speech, but that would from the week in which he was speaking and for the next twelve years lead a nation and half the world into a nightmare of violence and misery, which would in its last days include the murder of the man giving the speech. There was an oddly prophetic aspect to the whole thing. But the speech didn't mention politics or current events. Indeed, it was a philosophy lecture, but it spoke more clearly about the political situation than a thousand political speeches.

Apart even from its content, the speech itself, in its construction and its delivery, was everything a ranting Hitler speech was not. It was exceedingly measured and sedate and logical and precise. It was also intellectually complex. It was not entertaining, nor was it very much of a speech, but more like a scholarly lecture. It would have been difficult to follow for some. Even if the conclusion had been broadcast, many listeners might have thought it dull and shut it off before they heard the conclusion. But Bonhoeffer was not trying to win his audience over. In fact, he was interested in drawing attention away from himself and to the ideas he was presenting. That was at the heart of the difference between his idea of leadership and Hitler's. He was living out the principles of the speech in his very delivery of the speech. Bonhoeffer hated to draw attention to himself or to use his personality to influence or to win converts to his way of thinking. He felt this was deceptive, that it obscured the substance of one's ideas. He wanted to serve the ideas. Indeed, one of his most important ideas was that *ideas could stand on their own*.

To understand what went so wrong in Germany and to understand the genius of Bonhoeffer's speech, one must understand the history of the Führer Principle. Its profoundly misguided concept of leadership is dramatically different from more modern concepts of leadership. It enabled Hitler's rise to power and led to the horrors of the death camps. This Führer Principle was at the heart of Bonhoeffer's objection to Hitler. In his speech that day, Bonhoeffer laid out his thoughts on the subject.

He began by explaining why Germany was looking for a Führer. The First War and the subsequent depression and turmoil had brought about a crisis in which the younger generation, especially, had lost all confidence in the traditional authority of the kaiser and the church. The German notion of the Führer arose out of this generation and its search for meaning and guidance out of its troubles. The difference between real leadership and the false leadership of the Leader was this: real leadership derived its authority from God, the source of all goodness. Thus parents have legitimate authority because they are submitted to the legitimate authority of a good God. But the authority of the Führer was submitted to nothing. It was self-derived and autocratic, and therefore had a messianic aspect.

Bonhoeffer stated, "Whereas earlier leadership was expressed in the form of the teacher, the statesman, the father . . . now the Leader has become an independent figure. The Leader is completely divorced from any office; he is essentially and only 'the Leader.'" A true leader must know the limitations of his authority.

> If he understands his function in any other way than as it is rooted in fact, if he does not continually tell his followers quite clearly of the limited nature of his task and of their own responsibility, if he allows himself to surrender to the wishes of his followers, who would always make him their idol—then the image of the Leader will pass over into the image of the mis-leader, and he will be acting in a criminal way not only towards those he leads, but also towards himself. The true Leader must always be able to disillusion. It is just this that is his responsibility and his real object. He must lead his following away from the author-ity of his person to the recognition of the real authority of orders and offices. . . . He must radically refuse to become the appeal, the idol, i.e. the ultimate authority of those whom he leads. . . . He serves the order of the state, of the community, and his service can be of incomparable value. But only so long as he keeps strictly in his place. . . . [H]e has to lead the individual into his own maturity. . . . Now a feature of man's maturity is responsibility towards other people, towards existing orders. He must let himself be controlled, ordered, restricted.

The good leader serves others and leads others to maturity. He puts them above himself, as a good parent does a child, wishing to lead that child to someday be a good parent. Another word for this is *discipleship*. He continued:

> Only when a man sees that office is a penultimate authority in the face of an ultimate, indescribable authority, in the face of the authority of God, has the real situation been reached. And before this Authority the individual knows himself to be completely alone. The individual is responsible before God. And this solitude of man's position before God, this subjection to an ultimate authority, is destroyed when the authority of the Leader or of the office is seen as ultimate authority. . . . Alone before God, man becomes what he is, free and committed in responsibility at the same time.
>
> The fearful danger of the present time is that above the cry for authority, be it of a Leader or of an office, we forget that man stands alone before the ultimate authority and that anyone who lays violent hands on man here is infringing eternal laws and taking upon himself superhuman authority which will eventually crush him. The eternal law that the individual stands alone before God takes fearful vengeance where it is attacked and distorted. Thus the Leader points to the office, but Leader and office together point to the final authority itself, before which Reich or state are penultimate authorities. Leaders or offices which set themselves up as gods mock God and the individual who stands alone before him, and must perish.

Forty-eight hours had passed since Hitler's election, but with Bonhoeffer's speech the battle lines were drawn. According to Bonhoeffer, the God of the Bible stood behind true authority and benevolent leadership, but opposed the Führer Principle and its advocate Adolf Hitler. Of course Hitler never publicly denounced God. He knew well that there were many churchgoers in Germany who had some vague idea that real authority should come from their God, but unlike Bonhoeffer, they had no idea what this actually meant. To embody the kind of leadership that rejected this idea of submission to God's authority, one must at least give lip service to that God, else one would not last very long. Hitler was ultimately a practical man, and as all truly practical men, he was a cynical man.

So Hitler gave a speech that day too. He was just forty-three and had already toiled in the political wilderness half his life. Ten years had passed since the *Bierhall Putsch* that landed him in prison. Now he was the chancellor of Germany. The original come-back kid had triumphed over his enemies. But to convince his followers that his authority was legitimate, he must say the necessary things. Thus the opening words of his speech that day were: "We are determined, as leaders of the nation, to fulfill as a national government the task which has been given to us, swearing fidelity only to God, our conscience, and our *Volk*." If his conscience was not already a corpse, it might have felt a twinge as he spoke. Hitler then declared that his government would make Christianity "the basis of our collective morality." This statement, which was a lie, instantly annulled itself. He ended with another appeal to the God he did not believe in, but whose Jewish and Christian followers he would thenceforward persecute and kill: "May God Almighty take our work into his grace, give true form to our will, bless our insight, and endow us with the trust of our *Volk*!"

Years afterward, Bonhoeffer's father recorded his thoughts on Hitler's victory:

> From the start, we regarded the victory of National Socialism in 1933 and Hitler's appointment as Reichkanzler as a misfortune—the entire family agreed on this. In my own case, I disliked and mistrusted Hitler because of his demagogic propagandistic speeches . . . his habit of driving about the country carrying a riding crop, his choice of colleagues—with whose qualities, incidentally, we in Berlin were better acquainted than people elsewhere—and finally because of what I heard from professional colleagues about his psychopathic symptoms.

The Bonhoeffers saw through Hitler from the beginning, but no one believed his reign would last as long as it did. Surely the Nazis would have their moment, perhaps even a long moment, but then it would be gone. It was all a terrible nightmare that, come morning, would disappear. But morning never seemed to come.

What led Germany to this strange pass was itself strange. After the war, many were happy to wipe away the old order and rid themselves of the kaiser. But when the old monarch at last left the palace, the people who had clamored for his exit were suddenly lost. They found themselves in the absurd position of the dog who, having caught the car he was so frantically chasing, has no idea what to do with it—so he looks about guiltily and then slinks away. Germany had no history of democracy and no idea how it worked, so the country broke apart into a riot of factions, with each faction blaming the others for everything that went wrong. This much they knew: under the kaiser there had been law and order and structure; now there was chaos. The kaiser had been the symbol of the nation; now there were only petty politicians.

So the German people clamored for order and leadership. But it was as though in the babble of their clamoring, they had summoned the devil himself, for there now rose up from the deep wound in the national psyche something strange and terrible and compelling. The Führer was no mere man or mere politician. He was something terrifying and authoritarian, self-contained and self-justifying, his own father and his own god. He was a symbol who symbolized himself, who had traded his soul for the zeitgeist.

Germany wanted to restore its former glory, but the only means available was the debased language of democracy. So on January 30, 1933, the people democratically elected the man who had vowed to destroy the democratic government they hated. Hitler's election to office destroyed the office.

Four weeks later, Bonhoeffer preached at the Trinity Church in Berlin. It was the first time he had preached since Hitler had come to power. Bonhoeffer saw the new situation for what it was and was not afraid to preach what he saw:

> The church has only *one* altar, the altar of the Almighty . . . before which all creatures must kneel. . . . Whoever seeks something other than this must keep away; he cannot join us in the house of God. . . . The church has only one pulpit, and from that pulpit, faith in God will be preached, and no other faith, and no other will than the will of God, however well-intentioned.

The theme was the same as in his radio address, but now the altar before which idol worshipers would worship would not have said, "To an unknown false god." Now everyone knew who the false god was that would be worshiped. Now the Führer to whom the Führer Principle referred had a name. Hitler had stepped onto the altar. All that remained was to deal with those closed-minded troublemakers who still worshiped other gods.

When Hitler and the Nazis gained power on January 31, they held a fraction of the seats in the Reichstag. Their political opponents thought Hitler needed them and naively thought they could therefore control him. But this was like thinking one could open Pandora's box and let out two or three Furies. Hitler knew his opponents were divided and couldn't unite against him. He would play them off each other brilliantly and would consolidate his power with breathtaking speed and a calculating ruthlessness for which no one was prepared. On February 3, Goebbels wrote in his diary: "Now it will be easy to carry on the fight, for we can call on all the resources of the State. Radio and press are at our disposal. We shall stage a masterpiece of propaganda. And this time, naturally, there is no lack of money."

The Burning of the Reichstag

But how would the Nazis "carry on the fight"? First, they would burn down a building. Arson was the first part of their plan to consolidate their gains and, ultimately, to do away with the German constitution and give Hitler the rights of a dictator. It was a scheme at once foolproof and foolhardy: they would start a fire at the Reichstag, the seat of German democracy. Then they would blame it on the Communists! If the German people believed the Communists had tried to burn down the parliament building, they would see the need for extraordinary actions on behalf of the government. They would welcome giving up a few liberties to preserve the German nation against the Communist devils. So the fire was set and the Communists blamed and the Nazis triumphed. But just how it happened that night remains a mystery.

In his monumental chronicle of the period, *The Rise and Fall of the Third Reich*, historian and journalist William Shirer stated that the Nazi leaders were taken by surprise: "Out at Goebbels' home, Chancellor Hitler had arrived to dine *en famille*. According to Goebbels, they were relaxing, playing music on the gramophone and telling stories. 'Suddenly,' he recounted later in his diary, 'a telephone call from Dr. Hanfstaengl: "The Reichstag is on fire!"'"

But Goebbels had to consider the source of the information. Ernst "Putzi" Hanfstaengl* was a "strange but genial Harvard man" whose money and connections had greatly helped Hitler's rise to power over the last decade. In his undergraduate heyday he had composed numerous songs for the Harvard football games. One of them had been played just a month earlier when the SA Brownshirts** marched down Unter den Linden in Hitler's victory parade. Shirer described Hanfstaengl as an "eccentric, gangling man, whose sardonic wit somewhat compensated for his shallow mind," and whose raucous piano playing and "clowning soothed Hitler and even cheered him up after a tiring day." So when Goebbels took the call that night, he was convinced that Hanfstaengl was simply having a few laughs.

But the lanky goofball was deadly serious. First to the fire scene was the corpulent Hermann Göring, perspiring and puffing as he exclaimed, "This is the beginning of the Communist revolution! We must not wait a minute. We will show no mercy. Every Communist official must be shot where he is found. Every Communist deputy must this very night be strung up." The flabby fellow had been in on the plan to burn the building, but now was not the time for sincerity. A shirtless Dutchman of some mental deficiency was arrested on the spot and accused of the crime, but how he figured into things will probably never be clear. Marinus van der Lubbe was a twenty-four-year-old pyromaniac with Communist leanings, but it's highly doubtful that he was part of a larger Communist plot, as the Nazis claimed. But whether he was acting on his own unbalanced accord or was simply a Nazi dupe is hard to say. One thing was clear: he had used his shirt as tinder.

But suddenly the Bonhoeffer family found itself in the center of the national controversy. Karl Bonhoeffer, Berlin's top psychiatrist, was now called upon to examine Van der Lubbe. And Dietrich's brother-in-law Hans von Dohnanyi was named an official observer at the trial. Many people believed Göring's henchmen were behind the fire and hoped the incorruptible Karl Bonhoeffer would give evidence to support that belief and perhaps use his position and

---

* *Putzi*, which is a German word meaning "cute" or "little," was six feet six inches tall.

** SA refers to the *Sturm Abteilung* (Storm Section); the group became known as storm troopers or as Brownshirts, because of the color of their uniforms.

credibility to denounce the Nazis, whom he loathed. The major and vitally important trial was moved to Leipzig and then later, back to Berlin.

The affair weighed heavily on the family that year. Karl Bonhoeffer visited Van der Lubbe twice in March and six times that fall. His official report, later published in *Monatsschrift für Psychiatrie und Neurologie*, stated:

> [Van der Lubbe] was violently ambitious, at the same time modest and friendly; a scatterbrain, without any demand for intellectual clarity, but nevertheless capable of unwavering determination, incorrigibly closed to contradictory arguments. He was good-natured and not resentful, but he resisted all authority. This fundamentally rebellious tendency was probably his most questionable characteristic, and the one most likely to set him upon the disastrous road which he took. The early conversion to Communistic ideas certainly contributed to the same effect; but the undisciplined elements in his temperament made it unlikely in any case, that he would follow a quiet and orderly pattern through life. Something which was unusual in one way or another was to be expected from him. But he was not for that reason to be regarded as mentally ill.

This clinical and lucid report contained no mention of guilt or innocence, and for this reason Dr. Bonhoeffer received irate letters, presumably from both sides. Years later, he recalled his role:

> I had the opportunity of meeting some of the leading Party members. A large number of them had gathered to attend the proceedings in the Supreme Court at Leipzig. The faces I saw at this gathering were unpleasant. During the hearings, the impassiveness and painstaking objectivity of the President of the Court was a pleasant contrast to the undisciplined manner of the Party members in the witness box. The other defendant, [Communist Party leader] Dimitroff, gave an impression of intellectual superiority, which set Minister President Göring, who had been invited to attend, in an incomprehensible fury. As for Lubbe, he was, in human terms, a not unsympathetic young man, a psychopath and a muddleheaded adventurer who, during the proceedings, reacted with a kind of stupefied defiance that he lost only shortly before his execution.

In 1933, Germany effectively lost the rule of law when Hindenburg signed Hitler's emergency decree the day after the Reichstag fire, but in many ways it still remained a nation where, at least in the courtroom, the Reichstag president, Hermann Göring, and the working-class arsonist were essentially on equal footing. Acting as his own lawyer, the brilliant Dimitroff, who later became Bulgaria's prime minister, could openly taunt and ridicule the vain, red-faced Göring and get away with it. The whole world was watching, so the Nazis could not do as they liked. Not yet. For a time they still must suffer these grave indignities. The international press reported the trial and relished Göring's humiliation. *Time* magazine's accounts were fulsome in their mockery, saying that the "bull-throated" premier's voice had risen to a "jittery scream" when Dimitroff got the better of him. Their account of Göring's statements speaks for itself:

> Folding his great arms and brooding for a moment like a brown Jove, General Göring exclaimed, "I regret exceedingly that certain Communist leaders have been saved from the gallows. . . . So surprised was I when I heard the Reichstag was burning that I thought faulty electric wiring must have started some small fire. . . . As I rushed to the Reichstag in my car someone shouted 'Incendiarism!'" As though hypnotized by this word, Witness Göring paused for a long time, then rolled it out again, "Incendiarism!—when I heard that word the scales dropped from my eyes. All was perfectly clear. Nobody but the Communists could have done it!"

Van der Lubbe was found guilty and beheaded at the Leipzig prison, but there was not enough evidence to convict the leading Communists, who were exiled to the Soviet Union and welcomed there as heroes. The trial shone enough light on what had happened to lend evidence to the idea that the Nazis had unscrupulously been involved in the fire. But by the time the trial was over, it was all too late. The Reichstag fire had served Hitler's cynical purposes and provided the cover to ensure that his grip on the country was irreversible and total.

Indeed, it was on the very day after the fire, when the Reichstag was still smoldering, that he pressed the eighty-five-year-old Hindenburg to sign the Reichstag Fire Edict, a decree officially suspending those sections of the

German constitution that guaranteed individual liberties and civil rights. The senescent Hindenburg's signature in a stroke turned Germany from a democratic republic with a would-be dictator into a dictatorship with the hollow shell of a democratic government. The democracy itself had gone up in smoke, and the symbolism of the gutted parliament—now a charred, empty husk—was bitterly apt.

The words of the decree, produced and signed into effect before anyone had had time to think carefully about it, made possible most of the horrors ahead, including the concentration camps:

> Restrictions on personal liberty, on the right of free expression of opinion, including freedom of the press; on the rights of assembly and association; and violations of the privacy of postal, telegraphic and telephonic communications; and warrants for house searches, orders for confiscations as well as restrictions on property, are also permissible beyond the legal limits otherwise prescribed.

Within days the Nazi storm troopers were in the streets, arresting and beating their political opponents, many of whom were imprisoned, tortured, and killed. The ability to speak against them in the press was gagged; the ability to assemble publicly against them was illegal. But Hitler was not through. To formally and legally place the whole power of the government in his control required the Reichstag to pass the so-called Enabling Act. The Reichstag was functioning, albeit in a greatly restricted way. But this Enabling Act would formally take away its powers—for the good of the nation, of course—and for four years place them in the eager hands of the chancellor and his cabinet. And so, on March 23, like a snake swallowing its own tail, the Reichstag passed the law that abolished its existence.

With the tools of democracy, democracy was murdered and lawlessness made "legal." Raw power ruled, and its only real goal was to destroy all other powers besides itself.

 CHAPTER 10

THE CHURCH AND
THE JEWISH QUESTION

What is at stake is by no means whether our German members of congregations can still tolerate church fellowship with the Jews. It is rather the task of Christian preaching to say: here is the church, where Jew and German stand together under the Word of God; here is the proof whether a church is still the church or not.

—DIETRICH BONHOEFFER

Where books are burned, they will, in the end, burn people, too.

—HEINRICH HEINE

In the first months of Nazi rule, the speed and scope of what the Nazis intended and had begun executing throughout German society were staggering. Under what was called the *Gleichschaltung* (synchronization), the country would be thoroughly reordered along National Socialist lines. No one dreamed how quickly and dramatically things would change.

The Bonhoeffers always had access to privileged information, but as the shadow of the Third Reich fell across Germany, much of the information came from Christel's husband, lawyer Hans von Dohnanyi, at the German Supreme Court. The Bonhoeffers learned that something especially disturbing called the Aryan Paragraph would take effect April 7. It would result in a series of far-reaching laws that were cynically announced as the "Restoration of the Civil Service." Government employees must be of "Aryan" stock; anyone of Jewish descent would lose his job. If the German church, essentially a state church, went along, all pastors with Jewish blood would be excluded from ministry. That would apply to Bonhoeffer's friend, Franz Hildebrandt. Many were confused about how to respond. The pressure to get in line with the National Socialist wave sweeping the country was intense. Bonhoeffer knew someone must think it all through carefully, and in March 1933, he did so. The result was his essay, "The Church and the Jewish Question."

The Church and the Jewish Question

A group of pastors had been meeting in the home of Gerhard Jacobi, pastor of the Kaiser Wilhelm Memorial Church, to discuss developments in the country. Bonhoeffer planned to deliver his essay to them in early April.

The German church was in turmoil. Some church leaders felt the church should make peace with the Nazis, who were strongly opposed to communism and "godlessness." They believed the church should conform to the Nazi racial laws and the Führer Principle. They thought that by wedding the church to the state, they would restore the church and Germany to her former glory, before the Treaty of Versailles and the chaos and humiliation of the last twenty years. The moral degeneration of Weimar Germany was self-evident. Hadn't Hitler spoken of restoring moral order to the nation? They didn't agree with him on everything, but they believed that if the church's prestige were restored, they might be able to influence him in the right direction.

There was at this time a group that stood solidly behind Hitler's rise to power and blithely tossed two millennia of Christian orthodoxy overboard. They wanted a strong, unified Reichskirche and a "Christianity" that was strong and masculine, that would stand up to and defeat the godless and degenerate forces of Bolshevism. They boldly called themselves the *Deutsche Christen* (German Christians) and referred to their brand of Christianity as "positive Christianity." The German Christians became very aggressive in attacking those who didn't agree with them and generally caused much confusion and division in the church.*

---

* A more complete treatment of the German Christians follows on pages 171–175.

But perhaps the most grievous aspect of the church turmoil was the willingness of mainstream Protestant Christian leaders to consider adopting the Aryan Paragraph. They reasoned that Jews who were baptized Christians could form their own church and had no particular business expecting to be a part of a distinctly "German" church. In the 1930s, such racially ideological ideas were not nearly as foreign as they are today, nor can all who were open to them be dismissed as hate-filled anti-Semites.

The idea that the races should be "separate, but equal" was popular and widespread in the Jim Crow American South, and Bonhoeffer had seen it firsthand. He knew that such ideas were powerfully rooted in notions about human identity and community. Across Europe and the world, there had often been strong taboos against mixing races and ethnicities. So even though Bonhoeffer knew that what he was facing was inimical to Christian faith, he knew that such thinking was also widespread. It was indeed possible that a German theologian or pastor who genuinely bore no ill will toward Jews might be persuaded that the Aryan Paragraph was acceptable. Some believed that an ethnically Jewish person who was honestly converted to Christian faith should be part of a church composed of other converted Jews. Many sincere white American Christians felt that way about Christians of other races until just a few decades ago. Bonhoeffer knew that he couldn't simply attack such people as racists. He would have to argue logically against such ideas.

Unlike most Germans, Bonhoeffer had experienced the church far beyond the Lutheran churches of Germany. In Rome, he had seen Christians of many races and nationalities worshiping together; in the United States, he had worshiped with African American Christians in Harlem; and via the ecumenical movement, he had worshiped with other European Christians. The immediate question before him was, what is the church's response to the Jewish question? But the question that stood behind that question was still, *what is the church?*

"The fact, unique in history," he began, "that the Jew has been made subject to special laws by the state solely because of the race to which he belongs and quite apart from his religious beliefs, raises two new problems for the theologian, which must be examined separately."

He addressed the issue of the church's attitude toward the state and created common ground with his skeptical readers by paraphrasing Romans 13:

"There is no power, but of God; the powers that be are ordained of God."
In other words, governments are established by God for the preservation
of order. The church had no fundamental quarrel with the state being the
state, with its restraining evil, even by use of force. His dramatic opening
sentence seemed to overstate the case: "Without doubt, the Church of the
Reformation has no right to address the state directly in its specifically
political actions." But he was aware of his audience and wished to establish
that he shared their attitude here. He was also aware of speaking within
a tradition that took its cues from Luther, and Luther's attitude toward
the role of the state erred much on the side of the state, whom Luther
applauded in crushing the Peasants' Rebellion, for example. Bonhoeffer
must tread carefully.

Then he moved on to clarify that the church does, nonetheless, play a
vital role for the state. What is that role? The church must "continually ask
the state whether its action can be justified as legitimate action of the state,
i.e., as action which leads to law and order, and not to lawlessness and disorder." In other words, it is the church's role to *help the state be the state*. If the
state is not creating an atmosphere of law and order, as Scripture says it must,
then it is the job of the church to draw the state's attention to this failing.
And if on the other hand, the state is creating an atmosphere of "excessive
law and order," it is the church's job to draw the state's attention to that too.

If the state is creating "excessive law and order," then "the state develops its power to such an extent that it deprives Christian preaching and
Christian faith . . . of their rights." Bonhoeffer called this a "grotesque situation." "The church," he said, "must reject this encroachment of the order
of the state precisely because of its better knowledge of the state and of the
limitations of its action. The state which endangers the Christian proclamation negates itself."

Bonhoeffer then famously enumerated "three possible ways in which the
church can act towards the state." The first, already mentioned, was for the
church to question the state regarding its actions and their legitimacy—to
help the state be the state as God has ordained. The second way—and here
he took a bold leap—was "to aid the victims of state action." He said that
the church "has an unconditional obligation to the victims of any ordering
of society." And before that sentence was over, he took another leap, far
bolder than the first—in fact, some ministers walked out—by declaring that

the church "has an unconditional obligation to the victims of any ordering of society, *even if they do not belong to the Christian community*." Everyone
knew that Bonhoeffer was talking about the Jews, including Jews who were
not baptized Christians. Bonhoeffer then quoted Galatians: "Do good to
all men." To say that it is unequivocally the responsibility of the Christian
church to help all Jews was dramatic, even revolutionary. But Bonhoeffer
wasn't through yet.

The third way the church can act toward the state, he said, "is not just to
bandage the victims under the wheel, but to put a spoke in the wheel itself."
The translation is awkward, but he meant that a stick must be jammed into
the spokes of the wheel to stop the vehicle. It is sometimes not enough to
help those crushed by the evil actions of a state; at some point the church
must directly take action against the state to stop it from perpetrating evil.
This, he said, is permitted only when the church sees its very existence
threatened by the state, and when the state ceases to be the state as defined
by God. Bonhoeffer added that this condition exists if the state forces the
"exclusion of baptized Jews from our Christian congregations or in the prohibition of our mission to the Jews."

The church would be *"in statu confessionis* and here the state would be in
the act of negating itself." This Latin phrase, which means "in a state of confession," was originally used as a specifically Lutheran phrase in the sixteenth
century. By Bonhoeffer's time it had come to mean a state of crisis in which
the "confession" of the gospel was at stake. To "confess the gospel" simply
meant to speak forth the good news of Jesus Christ.* Bonhoeffer continued,
"A state which includes within itself a terrorized church has lost its most
faithful servant."

Bonhoeffer went on to say that to "confess Christ" meant to do so to
Jews as well as to Gentiles. He declared it vital for the church to attempt to
bring the Messiah of the Jews to the Jewish people who did not yet know
him. If Hitler's laws were adopted, this would be impossible. His dramatic
and somewhat shocking conclusion was that not only should the church

---

* The term *Confessing Church* in large part was coined in reference to the phrase *"in status
confessionis."* Those who believed that the German church had ceased to be the church of Jesus
Christ because of the adoption of the Aryan Paragraph decided that they must break away and
form the church anew. The new church was called the Confessing Church because it proclaimed
the gospel of Jesus Christ.

allow Jews to be a part of the church, but that this was precisely what the church was: it was the place where Jews and Germans stand together. "What is at stake," he said, "is by no means the question whether our German members of congregations can still tolerate church fellowship with the Jews. It is rather the task of Christian preaching to say: here is the church, where Jew and German stand together under the Word of God; here is the proof whether a church is still the church or not."

Many would have remembered Galatians 3:28, declaring that "there is neither Jew nor Greek, bond nor free, male nor female, for you are all one in Christ Jesus." To underscore his point, Bonhoeffer concluded with words from Luther's commentary on Psalm 110:3: "There is no other rule or test for who is a member of the people of God or the church of Christ than this: where there is a little band of those who accept this word of the Lord, teach it purely and confess against those who persecute it, and for that reason suffers what is their due."

In the spring of 1933, Bonhoeffer was declaring it the duty of the church to stand up for the Jews. This would have seemed radical to even staunch allies, especially since the Jews had not begun to suffer the horrors they would suffer in a few years. Bonhoeffer's three conclusions—that the church must question the state, help the state's victims, and work against the state, if necessary—were too much for almost everyone. But for him they were inescapable. In time, he would do all three.

The advent of the Nazi victory and the Nazis' attempt to co-opt the church resulted in chaos within the church itself, and in fighting and politicking among the many factions of the church. Bonhoeffer wanted to drown out the cacophony of voices and look at these things calmly and logically. He knew that if these questions were not addressed properly, one would be reduced to merely "political answers" or "pragmatic" answers. One could begin to veer away from the true gospel, toward worshiping a god made in one's own image, rather than God himself, the "eternally other" of whom Barth had spoken and written. And just as many well-meaning Christians at Union had unwittingly abandoned that God for many good reasons, so too many of the well-meaning Christians in Germany were now doing. They were convinced that if they bent their theology a bit, it wouldn't matter—the results would be all right in the end. Many of them honestly believed that under Hitler the opportunities for evangelism would increase. But Bonhoeffer knew that a church that did not stand with the Jews was not the church of Jesus Christ, and to evangelize people into a church that was not the church of Jesus Christ was foolishness and heresy. From the time Bonhoeffer finished writing "The Church and the Jewish Question," he saw this clearly and would stake everything on it. But it would be a long and lonely road.

The April 1 Boycott

One week after passage of the Enabling Act, Hitler declared a boycott of Jewish stores across Germany. The stated purpose was stopping the international press, which the Nazis maintained was controlled by the Jews, from printing lies about the Nazi regime. They always cast their aggressions as a defensive response to actions against them and the German people.

Goebbels spoke at a rally in Berlin that day, fulminating against the "Jewish atrocity propaganda," and everywhere across Germany SA men intimidated shoppers from entering Jewish-owned stores, whose windows had been daubed in black or yellow paint with stars of David and the word *Jude* (Jew). The SA also handed out pamphlets and held placards: "Deutsche Wehrt Euch! Kauft Nicht Bei Juden!" (Germans, protect yourselves! Don't buy from Jews!) Some signs were in English: "Germans, defend yourselves from Jewish Atrocity Propaganda—buy only at German shops!" Even the offices of Jewish doctors and lawyers were targeted.

Bonhoeffer's Jewish brother-in-law, Gerhard Leibholz, was a lawyer, and like many German Jews, he was a baptized Christian. Karl and Paula Bonhoeffer, fearing the situation, went to Göttingen to be with Sabine and Gerhard that weekend, while other family members checked in via telephone. That April, "the hope, so eagerly nourished, that Hitler would soon ruin himself by mismanagement was shattered," recalled Sabine. "National Socialism established itself with lightning swiftness."

On the day of the boycott in Berlin, Dietrich's grandmother was shopping. The patrician ninety-year-old was not about to be told where to shop. When SA men tried to restrain her from entering one store, she informed them that she would shop where she liked and did so. Later that day she did the same at the famous Kaufhaus des Westens, the world's largest department store, ignoring the silly kickline of SA men stationed in front. The story of Julie Bonhoeffer marching past Nazi gorillas was a favorite in the Bonhoeffer family, who saw in her an embodiment of the values they sought to live by.

The Lehmanns' Visit

In these first tumultuous days of April, two other events touched Bonhoeffer's life: the German Christians held a conference in Berlin, and the Lehmanns came to visit.

The German Christians' conference was a disturbing spectacle for anyone wary of Hitler's zeal to reorder German society. The lines between church and state were being blurred aggressively. It was one thing when the state was led by the Christian kaiser, but another when it was led by the anti-Christian Führer. Most Germans believed Hitler was basically "one of them," however, and they welcomed the Nazis' plans to reorder society, including the church.

Hermann Göring gave a speech to great acclaim, casting the reordering of society as mainly an "administrative" change. He refreshed the crowd on the basics of the Führer Principle and exhorted them to expect their Führer to *führer* (lead) in every aspect of German life, including the church. As part of the administrative overhaul, Göring explained that Hitler was proposing the office of a Reichsbischof, a man who could bring all of the disparate elements in the German church together. Hitler's choice for this position was one Ludwig Müller, a coarse former naval chaplain. The German Christians wanted a unified German church in accord with Nazi principles, and they fought toward that end. If England could have the Church of England, why shouldn't Germany have its own church, too—and on a firmly "German" foundation?

Paul and Marion Lehmann arrived in the last days of March. They had come to Bonn to hear Barth and then would spend a few days in Berlin to see their old friend. Ever the gracious host, Bonhoeffer took his Union friends everywhere, showing them the church in Wedding whose confirmation class he had taught, strolling with them along Unter den Linden, and taking them to the opera to see Richard Strauss's *Elektra*.*

---

* Strauss was caught in the cultural crossfire: the Nazis tried to co-opt him by giving him an official arts post. He accepted it, he later claimed, to protect his Jewish daughter-in-law. But Strauss was friends with the German Jewish writer Stefan Zweig and was later forced to resign for refusing to remove Zweig's name from an opera libretto he had written.

During their time in Berlin, the Lehmanns witnessed the April 1 boycott, as well as the disturbing spectacle of the German Christians' conference. Another person in Berlin that week would figure prominently in Bonhoeffer's life, though the two would not meet for six months. This was George Bell, the bishop of Chichester, visiting for an ecumenical meeting scheduled at the same time as the German Christians' conference. He got an unplanned but extremely valuable firsthand look at the ugly reality of the German Christian movement, one that would help him in his role as one of their principal adversaries in the years to come.

The Lehmanns spent time with the Bonhoeffer family at Wangenheimstrasse and marveled at their life there. To them, it was a world outside of time, a cultural bulwark against the gathering madness. The Lehmanns noticed that now and again Klaus Bonhoeffer rose and tiptoed to the door of the room where they were speaking to see that none of the servants was listening.

Even in early 1933 one couldn't know who could be trusted, and some of their conversations were vigorously anti-Nazi. Klaus and Dietrich agreed that Hitler and the Nazis couldn't last long, but the damage they were now doing to the nation was grave. The Bonhoeffers must do all they could to work against them, especially on their treatment of the Jews. These conversations can be seen as the first blushes of the resistance against Hitler already beginning to form.

And even at this early stage, it was not only talk. That April, Paul and Dietrich composed a letter to Rabbi Stephen Wise in New York. This was the rabbi whom Bonhoeffer heard preach in his synagogue on that Easter Sunday two years earlier. Wise was honorary president of the American Jewish Committee and an outspoken voice against the Nazis early on. He was connected to President Franklin Roosevelt, so Bonhoeffer and Lehmann thought through him they might alert Roosevelt to the brewing situation. Through the Reichstag Fire Edict, Hitler had made even writing such a letter a treasonable offense. Bonhoeffer knew he could end up in a concentration camp for his troubles, but he wrote the letter and sent it nonetheless.

Paul and Marion noticed that their friend Dietrich had changed in the two years since they had seen each other. In New York he exhibited a more playful and carefree attitude than they saw now. Under the circumstances, this was understandable. But there was something else: his attitude toward God was different. He seemed to take the whole thing more seriously.

Sabine and Gerhard

Ten days after the boycott of Jewish stores, Bonhoeffer was asked to preach another sermon, for a funeral. On April 11, Gerhard Leibholz's father died. For Dietrich, this was a difficult spot, one that he later admitted he had not negotiated well. Leibholz was ethnically Jewish, but unlike his son, he had not been baptized into the church. Bonhoeffer was forever considering all sides of a question, sometimes to a fault. Now he thought about how it might appear if someone who was speaking boldly against the Nazis on the Jewish issue preached at the funeral of a Jew who was not a member of the church. Would it seem merely incendiary? Would it destroy his chances for future action in the church? Would it destroy his credibility with those inside the church who already thought his ideas on this subject overly radical?

He wasn't sure what to do, but he was urged to consult with his district superintendent. Knowing the uproar it might cause, his superintendent strongly opposed the idea of Bonhoeffer's preaching, and so Dietrich declined. But he would soon deeply regret his action.

Sabine stayed in close contact with her family. Gerhard was a popular professor of law at Göttingen, so it wasn't long before they were directly affected by the mounting anti-Semitism. At one point, the National Socialist student leaders in Göttingen called for a boycott of his classes. Sabine recalled:

> I had often heard my husband's lectures and I went to the university on the actual day of the boycott in order to be there and to hear what the students would have to say. A few students were standing there in SA uniform, straddling the doorway in their jackboots as only these SA men could and not allowing anyone to enter. "Leibholz must not lecture, he is a Jew. The lectures are not taking place." Obediently the students went home. A corresponding notice had been posted on the blackboard.

After a while, Sabine and Gerhard needed only to walk down the street in Göttingen to breathe the poisonous atmosphere. People who recognized them crossed to the other side to avoid them. "In Göttingen," Sabine said, "many tried to collaborate. Lecturers who had not achieved further promotion now saw their opportunity." But a few were sickened at what was taking place and were not afraid to express their horror. The theologian Walter Bauer met them on the street and launched into a tirade against Hitler. When Gerhard lost his position, another professor approached him and, with tears in his eyes, said, "Sir, you are my colleague and I am ashamed to be a German." And a group of students from Gerhard's seminar went to the Ministry to ask that he be allowed to teach.

Many of Gert's relatives lost their jobs too. One Jewish school friend of Gerhard committed suicide. There was constant news of this sort. On Reformation Day, a few months after his decision not to preach at Gert's father's funeral, Bonhoeffer wrote Gert and Sabine in Göttingen:

> I am tormented even now by the thought that I didn't do as you asked me as a matter of course. To be frank, I can't think what made me behave as I did. How could I have been so horribly afraid at the time? It must have seemed equally incomprehensible to you both, and yet you said nothing. But it preys on my mind, because it's the kind of thing one can never make up for. So all I can do is ask you to forgive my weakness then. I know now for certain that I ought to have behaved differently.

Throughout 1933, the Nazis continued their campaign to legally bar Jews from state-affiliated institutions. More and more laws were enacted along the lines of the April 7 Reformation of the Civil Service. On April 22, Jews were prohibited from serving as patent lawyers, and Jewish doctors from working in institutions with state-run insurance. Jewish children were affected too. On April 25, strict limits were placed on how many of them could attend public schools. On May 6, the laws were expanded to include all honorary university professors, lecturers, and notaries. In June all Jewish dentists and dental technicians were prohibited from working with state-run insurance institutions. By the fall, the laws included the spouses of non-Aryans. On September 29, Jews were banned from all cultural and entertainment activities, including the worlds of film, theater, literature, and the arts. In October all newspapers were placed under Nazi control, expelling Jews from the world of journalism.

The aggressive attacks from the German Christians during April shocked a number of pastors and theologians into action. Their responses varied. George Schulz of the Sydow Brotherhood published a manifesto. Heinrich Vogel published his "Eight Articles of Evangelical Doctrine." Some Westphalian pastors published a declaration that, like Bonhoeffer's essay, roundly rejected as heresy the exclusion of baptized Jews from German churches. The Young Reformation movement came into being, representing a number of theological points of view—all opposed to the German Christians, but not agreed on much else. And Gerhard Jacobi, who would work arm in arm with Bonhoeffer in the church struggle, began meeting with other pastors at the Café am Knie in Charlottenburg. There were so many theological and political points of view in the opposition that they could never muster a single, focused plan of resistance. But they would try.

"Where Books Are Burned . . ."

In May 1933, the madness continued apace. *Gleichschaltung* was much discussed. This idea, which Göring referenced at the German Christians' conference in Berlin the previous month, meant that everything in German society must fall in line with the Nazi worldview. This included the world of books and ideas.

Karl Bonhoeffer had a front-row seat to see how the Nazis exerted pressure on the universities. When the Nazi minister for cultural affairs spoke at Berlin University, Bonhoeffer recalled with shame that even though he found the man's attitude insulting, neither he nor his colleagues felt sufficient courage to walk out in protest:

> Young and hitherto wholly unknown medical trainees came, as representatives of the Party, to suggest to the heads of hospitals that they immediately dismiss the Jewish doctors. Some allowed themselves to be persuaded. Any suggestions that such matters came under the jurisdiction of the Ministry and not of the Party were met with threats. The Dean tried to persuade faculty members to join the Party collectively. His attempt was foiled by individual refusals. Nor did the Ministry at first make any move to meet the demand for the dismissal of Jewish assistants. But doctors in individual hospitals were constantly spied upon to discover their attitude towards the Party.

He was at the University of Berlin another five years, and only with some effort did he manage to avoid displaying a portrait of Hitler.

Anti-Semitism had existed for decades among the students of German universities, but now they expressed it formally. That spring the German Students Association planned to celebrate an "Action against the un-German Spirit" on May 10.* At 11:00 p.m. thousands of students gathered in every university town across Germany. From Heidelberg to Tübingen to Freiburg to Göttingen, where the Leibholzes lived, they marched in torch-light parades and were then whipped into wild-eyed enthusiasm as Nazi officials raved about the glories of what the brave young men and women of Germany were about to do. At midnight the whole thing roared to grand effect in a great *Säuberung* (cleansing) where huge bonfires were lit and into which the students hurled thousands of books.

Thus Germany would be "purged" of the pernicious "un-German" thoughts of authors such as Helen Keller, Jack London, and H. G. Wells. Of course Erich Maria Remarque's books were included, as were those of many others, including Albert Einstein and Thomas Mann. In 1821, in his play *Almansor*, the German poet Heinrich Heine wrote the chilling words: "Dort, wo man Bücher verbrennt, verbrennt man am Ende auch Menschen." Heine was a German Jew who converted to Christianity, and his words were a grim prophecy, meaning, "Where books are burned, they will, in the end, burn people, too." That night across Germany his books were among those thrown into the crackling flames. Sigmund Freud, whose books were also burned that night, made a similar remark: "Only our books? In earlier times they would have burned us with them."

In Berlin the torchlight procession began at the Hegelplatz behind Berlin University, went through the university, and then eastward along Unter den Linden. The "anti-German" books followed in a truck, and at the Opernplatz stood the great pile of wood that would become the bon-fire. Then addressing the thirty thousand, the vampiric homunculus Joseph Goebbels ranted into the darkness: "German men and women! The age of arrogant Jewish intellectualism is now at an end! . . . You are doing the right thing at this midnight hour—to consign to the flames the unclean spirit

---

* It's unclear whether that date was chosen to mark the end of the Franco-Prussian War in 1871, but since that is the day Germany defeated France and marked the beginning of its emergence as a united Germany, it's likely.

of the past. This is a great, powerful, and symbolic act. . . . Out of these ashes the phoenix of a new age will arise. . . . O Century! O Science! It is a joy to be alive!"

As with so much else in the Third Reich, the scene had an undeniably macabre aspect to it: the midnight bonfire feeding like a succubus on the noble thoughts and words of great men and women. Goebbels, the propagandist, well knew that to stage a torchlight parade, followed by a bonfire at the stroke of midnight, evoked something ancient and tribal and pagan and invoked the gods of the German *Volk*, who represented strength and ruthlessness and blood and soil. The ritual was not meant to be Christian in any sense; indeed it was very much meant to be anti-Christian, though it wouldn't do to say so, since most of those present might have balked to hear such a thing, though they well felt it. The torches and the drums and the procession were meant to create an atmosphere of ominousness and foreboding and fear, and to summon forces who knew nothing of the weak virtues of the Christian faith, but stood in fundamental opposition to them and to the monotheistic religion of the despised Jews. It's no mistake that in the cities where the event was canceled by rain, it was rescheduled for June 21, the summer solstice.

Heinrich Heine's famous words about the book burnings are often quoted and today are inscribed at the Opernplatz as a memorial of the ghastly ritual. But another passage from Heine's works is perhaps more eerily prophetic of what would take place in Germany a century hence. They are the concluding words of his 1834 book, *Religion and Philosophy in Germany*:

Christianity—and that is its greatest merit—has somewhat mitigated that brutal German love of war, but it could not destroy it. Should that subduing talisman, the cross, be shattered, the frenzied madness of the ancient warriors, that insane Berserk rage of which Nordic bards have spoken and sung so often, will once more burst into flame. This talisman is fragile, and the day will come when it will collapse miserably. Then the ancient stony gods will rise from the forgotten debris and rub the dust of a thousand years from their eyes, and finally Thor with his giant hammer will jump up and smash the Gothic cathedrals. . . . Thought precedes action as lightning precedes thunder. . . . [W]hen you hear a crashing such as never before has been heard in the world's history, then you know that the German thunderbolt has fallen at last. At that uproar the eagles of the air will drop dead, and lions in the remotest deserts of Africa will hide in their royal dens. A play will be performed in Germany which will make the French Revolution look like an innocent idyll.

CHAPTER 11

NAZI THEOLOGY

*It's been our misfortune to have the wrong religion. Why didn't we have
the religion of the Japanese, who regard sacrifice for the Fatherland
as the highest good? The Mohammedan religion too would have been
much more compatible to us than Christianity. Why did it have to be
Christianity with its meekness and flabbiness?*

—ADOLF HITLER

*You'll see the day, ten years from now, when Adolf Hitler will occupy
precisely the same position in Germany that Jesus Christ has now.*

—REINHARD HEYDRICH

One sometimes hears that Hitler was a Christian. He was certainly not, but neither was he openly anti-Christian, as most of his top lieutenants were. What helped him aggrandize power, he approved of, and what prevented it, he did not. He was utterly pragmatic. In public he often made comments that made him sound pro-church or pro-Christian, but there can be no question that he said these things cynically, for political gain. In private, he possessed an unblemished record of statements against Christianity and Christians.

Especially early in his career, Hitler wished to appear as a typical German, so he praised the churches as bastions of morality and traditional values. But he also felt that, in time, the churches would adapt to the National Socialist way of thinking. They would eventually be made into vessels for Nazi

165

ideology, so it little served his purposes to destroy them. It would be easier to change what already existed and benefit from whatever cultural cachet they possessed.

In his famous diary, Joseph Goebbels, who was probably closer to Hitler than anyone, recorded some of the Führer's private thoughts about the clergy:

> The Fuehrer spoke very derogatorily about the arrogance of the higher and lower clergy. The insanity of the Christian doctrine of redemption really doesn't fit at all into our time. Nevertheless there are learned, educated men, occupying high positions in public life, who cling to it with the faith of a child. It is simply incomprehensible how anybody can consider the Christian doctrine of redemption as a guide for the difficult life of today. The Fuehrer cited a number of exceptionally drastic and in part even grotesque examples. . . . Whereas the most learned and wisest scientists struggle for a whole lifetime to study but one of the mysterious laws of nature, a little country priest from Bavaria is in a position to decide this matter on the basis for his religious knowledge. One can regard such a disgusting performance only with disdain. A church that does not keep step with modern scientific knowledge is doomed. It may take quite a while, but it is bound finally to happen. Anybody who is firmly rooted in daily life and who can only faintly imagine the mystic secrets of nature, will naturally be extremely modest about the universe. The clerics, however, who have not caught a breath of such modesty, evidence a sovereign opinionated attitude toward questions of the universe.

Hitler's attitude toward Christianity was that it was a great heap of mystical out-of-date nonsense. But what annoyed Hitler was not that it was nonsense, but that it was nonsense that did not help him get ahead. According to Hitler, Christianity preached "meekness and flabbiness," and this was simply not useful to the National Socialist ideology, which preached "ruthlessness and strength." In time, he felt that the churches would change their ideology. He would see to it.

Martin Bormann and Heinrich Himmler were the most passionately anti-Christian members of Hitler's inner circle, and they didn't believe the churches should adapt or could. They wanted the clergy crushed and the churches abolished, and they encouraged Hitler along these lines whenever possible. They hoped to accelerate the timetable for open warfare with the church, but Hitler was in no hurry. Whenever he attacked the churches, his popularity waned. Unlike his top men, Hitler had an instinctive political sense of timing, and now was not the time to take on the churches directly. Now was the time to pretend to be pro-Christian.

Hitler's architect, Albert Speer, was a firsthand witness to Hitler's cold-blooded approach: "Around 1937, when Hitler heard that at the instigation of the party and the SS vast numbers of his followers had left the church because it was obstinately opposing his plans, he nevertheless ordered his close associates, above all Göring and Goebbels, to remain members of the church. He too would remain a member of the Catholic Church, he said, although he had no real attachment to it."

Bormann despised Christians and Christianity, but couldn't yet say so publicly. In 1941, when the war was raging, he made his thoughts known, saying, "National Socialism and Christianity are irreconcilable." Speer commented:

> In Bormann's mind, the *Kirchenkampf*, the campaign against the churches, was useful for reactivating party ideology which had been lying dormant. He was the driving force behind this campaign. . . . Hitler was hesitant, but only because he would rather postpone this problem to a more favorable time. . . . "Once I have settled my other problems," he occasionally declared, "I'll have my reckoning with the church. I'll have it reeling on the ropes." But Bormann did not want this reckoning postponed. Brutally direct himself, he could ill tolerate Hitler's prudent pragmatism. . . . [So he] would draw one of the members of the entourage into telling him about seditious speeches a pastor or bishop had delivered, until Hitler finally became attentive and demanded details. . . . At some point [Bormann] would take a document from his pocket and begin reading passages from a defiant sermon or a pastoral letter. Frequently Hitler became so worked up that he began to snap his fingers—a sure sign of his anger—pushed away his food and vowed to punish the offending clergyman eventually.

But all of this was far in the future. In 1933, Hitler never hinted that he was capable of taking a stand against the churches. Most pastors were quite convinced that Hitler was on their side, partly because he had a record of pro-Christian statements that reached back to the first days of his political life. In a 1922 speech, he called Jesus "our greatest Aryan hero." Reconciling the idea of the Jewish Jesus as an Aryan hero is no less preposterous than trying to reconcile Hitler's ideal of the ruthless, immoral Nietzchean *Übermensch* with the humble, self-sacrificing Christ.

Hitler must be called a Nietzschean, although he likely would have bristled at the term since it implied that he believed in something beyond himself. This clashed with the idea of an invincible Führer figure, above whom none could stand. Still, Hitler visited the Nietzsche museum in Weimar many times, and there are photos of him posed, staring rapturously at a huge bust of the philosopher. He devoutly believed in what Nietzsche said about the "will to power." Hitler worshiped power, while truth was a phantasm to be ignored; and his sworn enemy was not falsehood but weakness. For Hitler, ruthlessness was a great virtue, and mercy, a great sin. This was Christianity's chief difficulty, that it advocated meekness.

Nietzsche called Christianity "the one great curse, the one enormous and innermost perversion . . . the one immortal blemish of mankind." He despised the Christian idea of virtue, considering it despicable and weak: "Society has never regarded virtue as anything else than as a means to strength, power and order." And of course, Nietzsche exalted the idea of strength personified in the Superman, or *Übermensch*, a cruel and ruthless champion of unbridled power—"the magnificent blond brute, avidly rampant for spoil and victory."

Hitler seems to have believed that Nietzsche had prophesied his coming and rise to power. In *The Will to Power*, Nietzsche prophesied the coming of a race of rulers, "a particularly strong kind of man, most highly gifted in intellect and will." Hitler believed the Aryan race was this "race of rulers." Nietzsche referred to these men as "lords of the earth." William Shirer said that Nietzsche's rantings along these lines met with Hitler's approval: "[They] must have struck a responsive chord in Hitler's littered mind. At any rate he appropriated them for his own—not only the thoughts but . . . often his very words. 'Lords of the Earth' is a familiar expression in *Mein Kampf*. That in the end Hitler considered himself the superman of Nietzsche's prophecy can not be doubted."

Hitler could hail Nietzsche as great as long as people understood that

Nietzsche existed principally to prepare the way for Hitler, to be his John the Baptist, as it were.

Among the first to portray Hitler in a messianic light was Houston Stewart Chamberlain, whom Shirer called "one of the strangest Englishmen who ever lived," and whom many considered to be one of the spiritual fathers of the Third Reich. Chamberlain believed Germany was meant to rule the world as a master race, and he prophesied that Hitler was the man to lead them:

> At the end of a fantastic life he could hail the Austrian corporal—and this long before Hitler came to power or had any prospect of it—as a being sent by God to lead the German people out of the wilderness. Hitler, not unnaturally, regarded Chamberlain as a prophet, as indeed he turned out to be. . . . He went to his grave . . . on January 11, 1927—with high hope that all he had preached and prophesied would yet come true under the divine guidance of this new German Messiah.

Before he died, Chamberlain met Hitler. He is another baffling character in a baffling story, a kind of satanic Simeon warbling an inverted *Nunc Dimittis*.

A New Nazi Religion

Since Hitler had no religion other than himself, his opposition to Christianity and the church was less ideological than practical. That was not the case for many leaders of the Third Reich. Alfred Rosenberg, Martin Bormann, Heinrich Himmler, Reinhard Heydrich, and others were bitterly anti-Christian and were ideologically opposed to Christianity, and wanted to replace it with a religion of their own devising. Under their leadership, said Shirer, "the Nazi regime intended eventually to destroy Christianity in Germany, if it could, and substitute the old paganism of the early tribal Germanic gods and the new paganism of the Nazi extremists."

Hitler wouldn't let them do this at first, hence his constant battle to rein them in. But he was not opposed to their doing it when the time was right. He couldn't take it very seriously, but he thought that the neopagan stew that Himmler was cooking up would probably be far more useful than Christianity because it would advocate such "virtues" as would be useful to the Third Reich.

Himmler was the head of the SS and was aggressively anti-Christian. Very early on, he barred clergy from serving in the SS. In 1935 he ordered every SS member to resign leadership in religious organizations. The next year he forbade SS musicians to participate in religious services, even out of uniform. Soon afterward he forbade SS members to attend church services. For Himmler, the SS was itself a religion, and its members, postulants in its priesthood. Many SS rituals were occultic in nature. Himmler was deeply involved in the occult and in astrology, and much of what the SS perpetrated in the death camps bore Himmler's saurian stamp.

Hans Gisevius, a member of the German military, would become one of the leaders in the conspiracy against Hitler. Like most in the conspiracy, Gisevius was a serious Christian. He was a friend of Niemöller and attended his church. One day around 1935 he was in a meeting with Himmler and Heydrich, who knew of his faith and argued with him about it. Gisevius wrote:

> Heydrich, who took a lively part in the discussion, paced energetically back and forth in the room. He never quite finished making his point, and as we were taking our leave he ran after me to get in a final word. Tapping me on the shoulder he said with a grin: "Just you wait. You'll see the day, ten years from now, when Adolf Hitler will occupy precisely the same position in Germany that Jesus Christ has now."

The SS was fiercely intent on this subject. Albert Speer recalled hearing Hitler privately mock Himmler's efforts: "What nonsense! [Hitler said.] Here we have at last reached an age that has left all mysticism behind it, and now he wants to start that all over again. We might just as well have stayed with the church. At least it had tradition. To think that I may some day be turned into an SS saint! Can you imagine it? I would turn over in my grave."

Rosenberg was one of the Nazi leaders most active in creating this "new religion." How they would get there was a point of some disagreement. Some, like Himmler, wanted to start fresh; while others thought it easier to turn the existing Christian churches into "Nazi" churches over time. Rosenberg was an "outspoken pagan" who, during the war, developed a thirty-point program for the "Nationale Reichskirche." That it was entrusted to an outspoken pagan shows how much respect Hitler had for the Christian church and its doctrines.

Rosenberg's plan is some of the clearest proof that exists of the Nazis' ultimate plans for the churches. A few points of his program illustrate what Hitler was open to approving and, under cover of war, would move toward:

13. The National Church demands immediate cessation of the publishing and dissemination of the Bible in Germany. . . .

14. The National Church declares that to it, and therefore to the German nation, it has been decided that the Fuehrer's *Mein Kampf* is the greatest of all documents. It . . . not only contains the greatest but it embodies the purest and truest ethics for the present and future life of our nation.

18. The National Church will clear away from its altars all crucifixes, Bibles and pictures of saints.

19. On the altars there must be nothing but *Mein Kampf* (to the German nation and therefore to God the most sacred book) and to the left of the altar a sword.

30. On the day of its foundation, the Christian Cross must be removed from all churches, cathedrals and chapels . . . and it must be superseded by the only unconquerable symbol, the swastika.

The German Christians

The most serious Christians in Germany recognized the incompatibility of Christianity and Nazi philosophy. Karl Barth said Christianity was separated "as by an abyss from the inherent godlessness of National Socialism."

But someplace in the deep and wide abyss betwixt these two existed a strange group who did not think there was an abyss, and who wished to create a seamless connection between National Socialism and Christianity. They saw no theological problem with this project, and during much of the 1930s, they constituted a powerful force in Germany. They formed the core of the opposition to Bonhoeffer, Niemöller, and other leaders in the Confessing Church side of the church struggle (*Kirchenkampf*) just beginning. To co-opt all who fancied themselves Germans and Christians, they called themselves the *Deutsche Christens*, "German Christians." The contortions required to pull together their idea of Germanness with their idea of Christianity can be painful to contemplate.

In her book, *Twisted Cross: The German Christian Movement in the Third Reich*, Doris Bergen wrote that "the 'German Christians' preached Christianity as the polar opposite of Judaism, Jesus as the arch anti-semite, and the cross as the symbol of war against Jews." Fusing the German *Volk* (people) with the German *Kirche* (church) meant stretching and twisting the definitions of both. Step one was to define *Germanness* as inherently in opposition to *Jewishness*. To make Christianity one with Germanness meant purging it of everything Jewish. It was an absurd project.

For starters, they decided the Old Testament must go. It was obviously too Jewish. At one German Christians' gathering in Bavaria, the speaker ridiculed the Old Testament as a saga of racial defilement. His remark that "Moses in his old age had married a Negro woman" drew boisterous laughter and enthusiastic applause. As late as 1939, they founded "the Institute for Research into and Elimination of Jewish Influence in German Church Life." Like the famous Jefferson Bible that omitted anything not to Jefferson's liking, this institute took a cut-and-paste attitude toward the Bible, excising anything that seemed Jewish or un-German. One of the leaders, Georg Schneider, called the whole Old Testament "a cunning Jewish conspiracy." He went on: "Into the oven, with the part of the Bible that glorifies the Jews, so eternal flames will consume that which threatens our people."

As for the New Testament, the German Christians quoted scriptures out of context and twisted the meaning to suit their anti-Semitic agenda. They used John 8:44 to great effect: "You are of your father the devil, and your will is to do your father's desires. He was a murderer from the beginning, and has nothing to do with the truth, because there is no truth in him. When he lies, he speaks out of his own character, for he is a liar and the father of lies" (ESV). Of course Jesus and all of his disciples were Jewish, and the Jews whom Jesus addresses here are religious leaders. It was only with them that he took such a harsh tone. The passage in which Jesus throws the money changers out of the temple was also popular with the German Christians. But to hone its barbed point, the phrase "den of thieves" was replaced with the German *Kaufhaus* (department store), most of which were then owned by Jews. The German Christians always painted Jesus as a non-Jew and often as a cruel anti-Semite. As Hitler had called him "our greatest Aryan hero," this was not much of a leap. Before the German Christians were through with him, the Nazarene rabbi would be a goose-stepping, strudel-loving son of the Reich.

The German Christians took the same line with church music. At their famous gathering in the Berlin *Sportpalast*, one of their leaders declared, "We want to sing songs that are free from all Israelite elements!" This would be difficult. Even the most German hymn of all, Luther's "Mighty Fortress Is Our God," contained a reference to Jesus as "Lord Sabaoth." But they were deadly earnest about purging their hymnbooks of such "Jewish" words as *Jehovah*, *Hallelujah*, and *Hosanna*. One author proposed changing *Jerusalem* to *heavenly abode*—and *cedars of Lebanon* to *firs of the German forest*.

As they bent themselves into pretzels, some German Christians realized it was a losing battle. So in 1937, a group of them stated that the written word of Scripture was the problem. "Whereas the Jews were the first to write out their faith," they said, "Jesus never did so." True "German" Christianity must therefore move beyond written words. "A demon always resides in the written word," they added.

Their efforts became more and more ridiculous. German Christians sometimes spoke of baptism as a baptism not into the body of Christ but into "the community of the *Volk*" and into the *Weltanschauung* of the Führer. Communion presented other difficulties. One pastor spoke of the bread symbolizing "the body of the earth that, firm and strong, remains true to the German soil," and the wine was "the blood of the earth." The paganism of it all escaped them.

But it wasn't merely the jots and tittles of their theology that were at issue. Their entire concept of Christianity was heretical. Ludwig Müller, the man whom Hitler would put forward as his choice to lead a "united German church"—in the new position of Reichsbischof—declared that the "love" of the German Christians had a "hard, warrior-like face. It hates everything soft and weak because it knows that all life can only then remain healthy and fit for life when everything antagonistic to life, the rotten and the indecent, is cleared out of the way and destroyed." This was not Christianity, but Nietzschean social Darwinism. Müller also publicly stated that the idea of grace was "un-German." A crew-cutted former naval chaplain and self-styled "lusty fellow" and "man's man" who sneered at theologians—Karl Barth was one of his favorite whipping boys—Müller was one of the staunchest advocates of the Nazification of the church in Germany. He would be the principal nemesis of the Confessing Church in the church struggle ahead.

But Müller was hardly alone in thinking that the love and grace of traditional Christianity had no place in the positive Christianity of the German Christians. Another German Christian declared that the teaching of "sin and grace . . . was a Jewish attitude inserted into the New Testament" and was simply too negative for Germans at that time:

> A people, who, like our own, has a war behind them that they did not want, that they lost, and for which they were declared guilty, cannot bear it, when their sinfulness is constantly pointed out to them in an exaggerated way. . . . Our people has suffered so much under the lie of war guilt that it is the task and duty of the church and of theology to use Christianity to give courage to our people, and not to pull them down into political humiliation.

How the German Christians justified twisting and bending the traditionally accepted meaning of the Scriptures and the doctrines of the church is complicated. One German Christian leader, Reinhold Krause, said that Martin Luther had left Germans with "a priceless legacy: the completion of the German Reformation in the Third Reich!" If Luther could break away from the Catholic church, it followed that nothing was written in stone. That was the weed in the garden of Protestantism. Even Luther had questioned the canonicity of some books of the Bible, especially the book of James, for what he took as its preaching of "salvation by works." And Bonhoeffer's professor, the liberal theologian Adolf von Harnack, had questioned the canonicity of much of the Old Testament. There's little question that the liberal theological school of Schleiermacher and Harnack helped push things along in this direction. But the other piece of this puzzle has to do with the confusion that inevitably arises when the Christian faith becomes too closely related to a cultural or national identity. For many Germans, their national identity had become so melted together with whatever Lutheran Christian faith they had that it was impossible to see either clearly. After four hundred years of taking for granted that all Germans were Lutheran Christians, no one really knew what Christianity was anymore.

In the end, the German Christians would realize that they were living in Barth's abyss after all. True Christians viewed them as confused, nationalistic heretics, and they could never satisfy the staunch anti-Semites on the Nazi side of the abyss. One Nazi leader sent the Gestapo a letter complaining that the *melody* to the hymn "Jerusalem, Thou City High and Fair" was played at memorial services for the German war dead. There were no offensive words, since only the melody was played, but even to evoke the memory of the words was unacceptable. That well-known hymn, which had been played at German memorial services for many years, was chosen by Paula Bonhoeffer for Walter's funeral in 1918.

CHAPTER 12

THE CHURCH STRUGGLE BEGINS

If you board the wrong train it is no use running along the corridor in the opposite direction.

—DIETRICH BONHOEFFER

A t first the German Christians were careful about hiding their most radical beliefs from the German people. To the casual observer, their conference in April 1933 was a model of theological soberness. But the German Christians were vocal that the German church must be united as a Reichskirche. Anything else smacked of the fractured Reichstag and the Weimar Republic. Everything must now be synchronized under the Führer's leadership and under the idea of *Gleichschaltung*—and the church must lead the way.

As a result of the April conference, many Germans were open to a single Reich church (*Reichskirche*). Few knew how this should happen or in what form, although Hitler had definite ideas. When the church leaders appointed a commission of three bishops to meet at Loccum that May to discuss the church's future, he saw an opportunity. In an effort to bring the wayward churches to heel, he shoehorned a fourth cleric into the trio. The skunk at the bishops' garden party was none other than Ludwig Müller, the aforementioned former naval chaplain whom Hitler had been proposing as his Reich bishop (*Reichsbischof*)—and who would head up the unified church being proposed.

But that May, Hitler's gambit to create a church in his own image did not succeed. The bishops agreed to put someone forward as Reich bishop. But it was not Müller; it was Friedrich von Bodelschwingh, a gentle, eminent, and deeply respected figure who ran a large community for people with epilepsy and other disabilities at Biesenthal in Westphalia.

Bodelschwingh was elected Reichsbischof on May 27, but no sooner had this kind soul been fitted for his mitre than the German Christians began to attack him, hoping to overturn the election by any means necessary. Müller led this charge, insisting that the "voice of the people" must be heeded. But many Germans found Müller's attacks shocking and distasteful. Bodelschwingh was patently a decent and apolitical man, who won the election fairly.

Despite the howlings against him, Bodelschwingh went to Berlin and set to work. On arriving, he asked Martin Niemöller for assistance. Pastor Niemöller had been a U-boat captain during the First War, who was awarded the Iron Cross for his bravery. He had initially welcomed the Nazis, hailing them as the heroes who would restore Germany's dignity, chase the Communists from the country, and restore moral order. Niemöller met with Hitler privately in 1932, and Hitler had given him his personal assurance that he would keep his hands off the churches and would never institute pogroms against the Jews. This was good enough for Niemöller, who was sure the Nazis' victory would bring about the national religious revival for which he had long prayed. But he soon saw that he had been taken in. When Niemöller finally turned against Hitler, he did so without any fear, and the sermons he gave at his overfilled church in Dahlem, a working-class section of Berlin, were listened to with the greatest interest, not least by members of the Gestapo. Niemöller knew this and mocked them openly from the pulpit. It was thought that if ever anyone outside the military could lead a movement against Hitler, Niemöller was the man. It was around the time of Bodelschwingh's election that Niemöller met Bonhoeffer and began to play a central role in the church struggle.

Bodelschwingh's short tenure as Reichsbischof was made increasingly miserable by the hue and cry of the German Christians. Amazingly, on June 18, in the midst of the turmoil, Franz Hildebrandt was ordained. Because he was a Jew, the question of his future in the church could not have been more pressing. What might the church look like if the theological roughnecks got their way? Bonhoeffer was there for the ceremony, which took place in the historic *Nikolaikirche* in Berlin. This was where Hildebrandt's spiritual hero, the famous seventeenth-century hymn writer Paul Gerhardt, had been ordained and later served as minister. Bonhoeffer knew many of Gerhardt's hymns by heart, and they would sustain him during his imprisonment.*

The German Christians' public attacks continued, and on June 19, they held a meeting at Berlin University. They had gained a foothold in the universities, and the students began agitating against Bodelschwingh. Bonhoeffer and many of his students attended the meeting, but Bonhoeffer didn't make any statements. He let his students argue with the German Christians. He and his students had planned to walk out en masse if the German Christians again proposed electing Ludwig Müller as Reichsbischof, which they must do, and eventually did. At that point Bonhoeffer and the pro-Bodelschwingh contingent stood and made for the exits. To Bonhoeffer's surprise, 90 percent of the people in the meeting walked out too. It was a bold slap in the face to the German Christians, and it showed how off-putting their behavior in the recent weeks had been.

Those who walked out gathered by a statue of Hegel and held an impromptu rally. But even among these young people, there was a gap between opposing the German Christians and opposing Hitler. They thought the German Christians too radical in wanting to bring Nazi doctrines into the church, but most of them still thought of themselves as patriotic Germans who were devoted to the country—and its Führer. So at the rally after walking out, they declared their submission to Hitler's leadership. Bonhoeffer said that "one student gave a *Heil* for the Reichskanzler, the rest following suit."

Three days later, there was another meeting. This time Bonhoeffer spoke. What he said is hard to fathom, but he was still hopeful, still thinking it must be possible for the church to resolve this issue amicably. First, he said that God was using this struggle in the German church to humble it, and no one had the right to be proud and self-justifying. Christians must humble themselves and repent. Perhaps something good would come of the struggle,

---

* Ironically, the minister of the *Nikolaikirche* before 1923 was Dr. Wilhelm Wessel, the father of Horst Wessel, whose composition "Raise High the Flag" became the infamously eponymous "Horst Wessel Song," the Nazis' official anthem.

but having humility and repentance was the only path forward. Bonhoeffer was speaking mostly to his own people, who understood that barring Jews from the church was wrong. They, who were on the right side of the issue, must guard against spiritual pride. Then he invoked Romans 14 and the idea of the "weaker brethren" in the church, who required extra grace and special accommodations. And he seemed to wonder whether those who were against the Aryan Paragraph should put up with it for the sake of the whole church and the "weaker brethren." His comments were quite radical and, in retrospect, overly generous.

Bonhoeffer even suggested convening a church council, as had been done in early church history at Nicea and Chalcedon. He believed the Holy Spirit could speak and solve the problem if they behaved like the church. But he was mostly speaking to liberal theologians for whom the notions of a council, heresy, or schism seemed archaic. He was calling the church to behave like the church, but his declarations fell on deaf ears.

Two days later it was all moot because the state intervened and all hell broke loose. In protest, Bodelschwingh resigned. Now the real church struggle would begin. On June 28, Müller ordered SA troops to occupy the church offices in Berlin. On July 2, an SA commando arrested a pastor. Those in the opposition held prayers of atonement and called for prayers of intercession. In the resultant chaos, Bodelschwingh met with Hindenburg to explain his side of the situation, and Hindenburg said he would convey Bodelschwingh's concerns to Hitler.

Bonhoeffer began to see that the opposition to Hitler and the German Christians was weak and divided, and he was gradually losing hope that anything positive could be done. It was all very depressing. Müller and the German Christians were not afraid to use the power of the state to force things to go their way and had been doing so rather effectively. But Bonhoeffer and Hildebrandt saw one possibility. They suggested that the churches effectively go on strike against the state to assert their independence. If the state did not pull back and let the church be the church, the church would cease behaving like the state church and would, among other things, stop performing funerals. It was a brilliant solution.

As would always be the case, their suggestion was too strong and too dramatic for most of the conciliatory Protestant leaders. Bonhoeffer's decisiveness was unsettling to them, since it forced them to see their own sins in what was happening. Just as the politically compromised military leaders would one day balk when they ought to have acted to assassinate Hitler, so the theologically compromised Protestant leaders now balked. They couldn't muster the will to do anything as stark and scandalous as staging a strike, and the opportunity was lost.

The Church Elections

Meanwhile, Hitler was moving ahead with his own plans for the church. He knew quite well how to deal with these Protestant pastors. "You can do anything you want with them," he once remarked. "They will submit . . . they are insignificant little people, submissive as dogs, and they sweat with embarrassment when you talk to them." With the cynicism he brought to every call for an "election," Hitler suddenly announced new church elections to be held July 23. This created an illusion of choice, but with the powers at the Nazis' disposal, there was little question who would win. Intimidation of every kind was brought to bear on the situation, with the serious threat that anyone opposing the German Christians could be accused of treason. And there was only one week between the announcement and the elections, making it virtually impossible to organize a viable opposition.

Despite the stacked odds, Bonhoeffer threw himself into the task. The Young Reformation movement chose candidates, and Bonhoeffer and his students wrote campaign leaflets and duplicated them. But on the night of July 17, before the leaflets could be distributed, the Gestapo broke into the Young Reformation offices and confiscated them. The German Christians had found a legal objection to the way the Young Reformation movement listed its candidates, and the Gestapo was dispatched to put a stop to it— "legally"—by confiscating the leaflets.

But Bonhoeffer was not intimidated, and borrowing his father's Mercedes, he and Gerhard Jacobi drove to Gestapo headquarters on Prinz-Albrecht-Strasse to redress the situation. Jacobi had been decorated with two Iron Crosses in the First War, and to bolster their credentials as patriotic Germans, he wore them into the lions' den of the Gestapo headquarters.

It was in the lightless basement of this notorious building that Bonhoeffer would be imprisoned, following the failure of the Stauffenberg assassination attempt in 1944. But now, in 1933, he still lived in a Germany that could be forced to behave with respect for the rule of law. So with the confidence of someone who knew his rights and was bold enough to claim them, Bonhoeffer stormed into the building and demanded to see the head of the Gestapo. Bonhoeffer convinced him that it was a case of electoral interference—which was forbidden, however cynically—and the leaflets were returned. He had to agree to change the title of the roster of candidates from "List of the Evangelical Church," to which the German Christians objected in that they wished to be thought of as the official "Evangelical Church," to the more neutral "Gospel and Church." The Gestapo threatened Bonhoeffer and Jacobi, making them personally responsible for seeing that the changes were made. They would be sent to concentration camps if leaflets without the changes were anywhere distributed.

In the meantime, as the German Christians and the Young Reformation movement campaigned for the election, Hitler showed that he knew how to deal with the Catholics too. Indeed, he had been dealing with them privately, and on July 20 he victoriously announced that a Concordat had been forged between the German Reich and the Vatican. It was a major public relations coup, since it gave the impression that he was reasonable on these matters and posed no threat to the churches. The text of the Concordat began:

> His Holiness Pope Pius XI and the President of the German Reich, moved by a common desire to consolidate and promote the friendly relations existing between the Holy See and the German Reich, wish to permanently regulate the relations between the Catholic Church and the state for the whole territory of the German Reich in a way acceptable to both parties. They have decided to conclude a solemn agreement.

The first article stated:

> The German Reich guarantees freedom of profession and public practice of the Catholic religion. It acknowledges the right of the Catholic Church, within the framework of the laws valid for all, to manage and regulate its own affairs independently, and, within the framework of its own competence, to issue binding laws and ordinances for its members.

These would be exposed as weasel words within a few years, but for now they did their job, holding off criticism and presenting a pacific face to the skeptical world.

Three days later the church elections were held. It was a predictable landslide, with the German Christians receiving about 70 percent of the votes. The biggest news was that Ludwig Müller was elected Reichsbischof. The bullheaded Müller was widely regarded as an uncouth hick; for many Germans, it was as if Gomer Pyle had become the archbishop of Canterbury. Müller was someone for whom "the ladies" and coarse language were not off-limits, especially as they burnished one's bona fides as a regular fellow of the Reich and not some fussy theologian. Behind his back, they mockingly referred to him as the *Reibi,* a foreshortening of *Reichsbischof* that also meant "Rabbi." For Bonhoeffer and those who would later become the Confessing Church, this was bad news. Bonhoeffer wrote Bishop Bell earlier in the week, saying that a "definite disqualification of Müller by the ecumenical movement would perhaps be the last hope—humanly spoken—for a recovery of the German church."

Müller and his German Christians had won the political battle, but Bonhoeffer and the others in the Young Reformation movement were not at all ready to concede the theological battle. In some ways the political loss freed them to fight on another plane. They now proposed to create a clear statement of faith—a "Confession of Faith"—to use against the German Christians. It would force a crisis and would force the German Christians to define themselves. Pastor Niemöller felt that this was the answer to the current situation, and he played a large part in persuading them to take this tack:

> Is there theologically a fundamental difference between the teachings
> of the Reformation and those proclaimed by the "German Christians"?
> We fear: Yes!—They say: No! This lack of clarity must be cleared up by
> a confession for our time. If this doesn't come from the other side—and
> there's no sign of it coming soon—then it must come from us; and it has
> to come in such a way that the others must say Yes or No to it.

A national synod was to be held in September; ideally this confession should be finished by then. Bonhoeffer and Hermann Sasse would go to Bodelschwingh's community at Bethel, to which he had returned after resigning as Reichsbischof, and in August 1933 they would write what came to be known as the Bethel Confession.

CHAPTER 13

THE BETHEL CONFESSION

The question is really: Christianity or Germanism? And the sooner the conflict is revealed in the clear light of day the better.

—DIETRICH BONHOEFFER

Early that summer of 1933, Bonhoeffer received an invitation from Theodor Heckel to become the pastor of a German-speaking congregation in London. Heckel, who knew Bonhoeffer through ecumenical contacts, was head of the church's Foreign Office, which oversaw all German-speaking parishes abroad—what they called "the diaspora." The idea of leaving Germany and the political troubles behind was appealing to Bonhoeffer, especially since Franz Hildebrandt was also thinking about going to London. So before going to Bethel, Bonhoeffer traveled to London.

He left after the July 23 election and on July 30 preached to the two congregations considering him. One, the church of St. Paul's, was in the East End. The other was in a southern suburb of London, called Sydenham, where the parsonage was located. Both congregations were impressed. Heckel glowingly recommended him to the departing pastor as someone "whom I personally feel to be quite outstanding." He also mentioned that Bonhoeffer spoke "a number of languages" and "has in addition a special Pauline advantage in that he is unmarried." But Heckel's warm feelings toward Bonhoeffer would change soon enough.

After the London sojourn, Bonhoeffer went to Bodelschwingh's Bethel

183

community in Biesenthal. As much as he had heard about this fabled place, he was quite unprepared for what he saw. Bethel (Hebrew for "house of God") was the fulfillment of a vision that Bodelschwingh's father had in the 1860s. It began in 1867 as a Christian community for people with epilepsy, but by 1900 included several facilities that cared for 1,600 disabled persons. The younger Bodelschwingh took it over at his father's death in 1910, and by the time of Bonhoeffer's visit, it was a whole town with schools, churches, farms, factories, shops, and housing for nurses. At the center were numerous hospital and care facilities, including orphanages. Bonhoeffer had never seen anything like it. It was the antithesis of the Nietzschean worldview that exalted power and strength. It was the gospel made visible, a fairy-tale landscape of grace, where the weak and helpless were cared for in a palpably Christian atmosphere.

Bonhoeffer attended services and wrote his grandmother about the people with epilepsy: their "condition of being actually defenseless may perhaps reveal to these people certain actualities of our human existence, in which we are in fact basically defenseless, more clearly than can ever be possible for us who are healthy." But even in 1933, the anti-gospel of Hitler was moving toward the legal murder of these people who, like the Jews, were categorized as unfit, as a drain on Germany. The terms increasingly used to describe these people with disabilities were *useless eaters* and *life unworthy of life*. When the war came in 1939, their extermination would begin in earnest. From Bethel, Bonhoeffer wrote his grandmother: "It is sheer madness, as some believe today, that the sick can or ought to be legally eliminated. It is virtually the same as building a tower of Babel, and is bound to avenge itself."

He often mentioned the Tower of Babel in his sermons as a picture of man's "religious" attempt to reach heaven on his own strength, and he had probably picked it up from Barth. But here he linked it with the Nazis' Nietzschean worldview in which strength was exalted and weakness was crushed and eliminated. One was about works, and the other was about grace.

Toward the end of the decade, the Nazis increased pressure on places like Bethel, and when the war began, they demanded that such places give up their patients for "mercy killings." Bodelschwingh was in the vanguard of this battle, valiantly fighting the Nazis over the issue, but by 1940 he had essentially lost. Karl Bonhoeffer and Dietrich, too, got involved in this battle, advising churches to pressure church-run hospitals and care facilities into refusing to turn over their patients to the Nazis. There was no room for the weak and the infirm in the National Socialist state, however. In August 1933, these horrors were all in the future, and Bethel was still an oasis of peace and a living testament to the best of true German Christian culture.

The Confession

From Bethel, Bonhoeffer wrote to his grandmother, telling her of his progress with the confession:

> Our work here gives us both trouble and pleasure. We want to attempt to extract from the "German Christians" some answer about their intentions. Whether we shall succeed is certainly very doubtful. For even if they nominally give some ground in their formulations, they are under such powerful pressure that sooner or later all promises must be overborne. It has become ever more evident to me that we are to be given a great popular national Church, whose nature cannot be reconciled with Christianity, and that we must prepare our minds for the entirely new paths which we shall then have to follow. The question is really: Christianity or Germanism? And the sooner the conflict is revealed in the clear light of day the better.

Their chief goal in writing the Bethel Confession was to spell out the basics of the true and historic Christian faith, which contrasted with Ludwig Müller's facile and inchoate "theology." Bonhoeffer and Sasse had the task of making the distinctions between the two sides crisp and clear.

After three weeks of work, Bonhoeffer was satisfied, but then the document was sent to twenty eminent theologians for their comments. By the time they were through, every bright line was blurred; every sharp edge of difference filed down; and every point blunted. Bonhoeffer was so horrified that he refused to work on the final draft. When it was completed, he refused to sign it. As would happen so often in the future, he was deeply disappointed in the inability of his fellow Christians to take a definite stand. They always erred on the side of conceding too much, of trying too hard to ingratiate themselves with their opponents. The Bethel Confession had become a magnificent waste of words. The final draft even contained a fawning line about "joyful collaboration" between church and state.

Bonhoeffer decided to accept the offer to pastor the German-speaking congregations in London. But first, licking his wounds, he retreated to Friedrichsbrunn and thought about what lay ahead. The failure of the Bethel Confession was a powerful shove in the direction of London, since he wasn't sure what else he could do in the church struggle. He decided that he would not officially begin until mid-October. The church's national synod would be held in September, and he wanted to be there. He would also attend two ecumenical conferences in Bulgaria, at Novi Sad and Sofia.

His main interest in attending the synod was to see whether they could fight off the part of the Aryan Paragraph or Aryan Clause that would prevent pastors of Jewish background *who had already been ordained* from serving as ministers. If the Aryan Paragraph were to take effect retroactively, Franz Hildebrandt's career as a minister would have ended before it began.

In the weeks approaching the synod, Bonhoeffer circulated a pamphlet he had written, "The Aryan Clause in the Church," laying out his position, especially in light of the developments since April, when he had written "The Church and the Jewish Question." In the pamphlet he rebutted the idea behind the "orders of creation" theology of the German Christians in which "ethnicity" was sacred and inviolable, and he rebutted the idea that the "opportunity for evangelism" that came of excluding Jews was worth anything. He also suggested that German clergy could no longer reasonably serve a church in which they were accorded special privileges over clergy of Jewish descent. In this pamphlet, Bonhoeffer was pointing toward schism. When the pamphlet was brought to the attention of Theodor Heckel in the Church Foreign Office, it was decided that unless he recanted his position, they would not send Bonhoeffer to London to represent the German church.

Even many of Bonhoeffer's allies in the theological battle thought that some of his statements in the pamphlet went too far. Martin Niemöller was still open to the possibility that the Aryan Paragraph might have to be allowed to apply to the churches. He felt that it was wrong, but he was not willing to break the church apart over it, not yet anyway. But Bonhoeffer had moved past this sort of pragmatic thinking. The "weaker brethren" argument that he had seemed willing to accept back in June no longer seemed relevant to him. He had become convinced that a church that was not willing to stand up for the Jews in its midst was not the real church of Jesus Christ. On that, he was quite decided.

He was far ahead of the curve, as usual. Some wondered whether he was just kicking against the goads, but when someone asked Bonhoeffer whether he shouldn't join the German Christians in order to work against them from within, he answered that he couldn't. "If you board the wrong train," he said, "it is no use running along the corridor in the opposite direction."

The Brown Synod

The national synod was held in Berlin on September 5. It was overwhelmingly dominated by the German Christians, and 80 percent of the delegates wore the brown shirts of the Nazi uniform, so it became known as the Brown Synod. It was less like a synod than a Nazi rally. Pastor Jacobi tried to make a motion, but was pointedly ignored. Opposition voices were shouted down. But the decision to remove *already ordained* non-Aryans was not passed, nor was the decision to remove spouses of non-Aryans from their posts. It was something positive, but under the circumstances, not much.

The next day a group of the opposition met at Jacobi's home. On September 7 they met at Niemöller's. For Bonhoeffer and Hildebrandt, the time for schism had arrived. A church synod had officially voted to exclude a group of persons from Christian ministry simply because of their ethnic background. The German Christians had clearly broken away from the true and historical faith. Bonhoeffer and Hildebrandt called for the pastors to stand up and be counted by resigning from office. But Bonhoeffer and Hildebrandt were voices crying in the wilderness. No one else was willing to go that far just yet.

Not even Karl Barth. On September 9, Bonhoeffer wrote the great theologian, asking whether this was the time for a *status confessionis*: "Several of us are now very drawn to the idea of the Free Church." He meant that they were willing to split from the German church. But Barth was convinced that they must not be the ones to leave; he said that they must wait until they were thrown out. They must continue to protest from within. "If there is schism," Barth wrote, "it must come from the other side." He even said that they must wait until there was a "clash over an even more central point."

Bonhoeffer and Hildebrandt wondered, *What could be more central than the Aryan Paragraph?* Bonhoeffer was so disturbed by Barth's response that he did not write Barth about his decision to go to London until well after he had left. Besides, he knew that Barth would have counseled him against it.

It was in reaction to the Brown Synod that the soon-to-be-famous *Pfarrernotbund* (Pastors' Emergency League) came into being. It grew out of the statement that Niemöller and Bonhoeffer drew up on September 7. Bonhoeffer and Hildebrandt could not persuade the others that now was the time for resignations and schism, but perhaps they could draw up a document summarizing their positions. The official protest to the Brown Synod was titled "To the National Synod," since a national synod was to be held later that month in Wittenberg.

Before they sent it to the church government, they sent it to Bodelschwingh, who sent a modified version of it to Reichsbischof Müller. Niemöller sent it to pastors across Germany. The statement contained four main points. First, it declared that its signers would rededicate themselves to the Scriptures and to the previous doctrinal confessions of the church. Second, they would work to protect the church's fidelity to Scripture and to the confessions. Third, they would lend financial aid to those being persecuted by the new laws or by any kind of violence. And fourth, they would firmly reject the Aryan Paragraph. Much to the surprise of Niemöller, Bonhoeffer, and all involved, the response to the statement was extremely positive. On October 20 the pastors across Germany who had signed this statement became an official organization, the Pastors' Emergency League, and by the end of the year, six thousand pastors had become members. This was a major first step toward what would soon come to be known as the Confessing Church.

In the last half of September, Bonhoeffer was in Sofia, Bulgaria, for an ecumenical conference of the World Alliance. The other ecumenical organization with which he had been affiliated, under the leadership of George Bell, the bishop of Chichester, was called Life and Work. Life and Work had a conference in Novi Sad during this time too. It was now that Theodor Heckel, who had recommended Bonhoeffer for his London pastorate, would reveal himself as someone all too willing to cooperate with the German Christians. As the official representative of the German church in the ecumenical setting, he presented an exceedingly rosy version of the grotesque events that had just transpired at the synod, in which Jews had officially been barred from having a life in the church. In Bonhoeffer's view, Heckel behaved despicably.

The only good news was that the others at the conference did not accept his version of the events. Under Bishop Bell's leadership, a resolution was passed declaring the "grave anxieties" of the "representatives of different churches in Europe and America in particular with regard to the severe action taken against persons of Jewish origin." Bell would soon become a close ally of Bonhoeffer in this struggle, and Bonhoeffer would be a pebble in Heckel's shoe for years to come, mostly because his would be the fearless and persistent voice telling Bell—and through Bell, the world—the truth about what was really happening in the church in Germany, despite the reports of "official representatives" like Heckel.

The ecumenical movement was an ally to Bonhoeffer in the years ahead, but as with his allies in the German church, the ecumenical movement was usually unwilling to follow his radical line. In the meantime he had some staunch allies. Danish Bishop Valdemar Ammundsen was one. He and a group of ecumenical leaders met privately with Bonhoeffer in Sofia, and Bonhoeffer gave them the full story on what was happening. After giving him a sympathetic hearing, they prayed for him, and he was deeply moved.

Bonhoeffer suggested that the ecumenical leaders delay officially recognizing the "new" German church led by Reichsbischof Müller. He suggested sending a delegation to investigate the situation for themselves. Bonhoeffer knew the Nazis had grave concerns about how they were being perceived in the world community, so the ecumenical movement had great leverage, which they must use.

At the conference in Novi Sad, a resolution on the Jewish question was passed, even more dramatic than the one in Sofia: "We especially deplore the fact that the State measures against the Jews in Germany have had such an effect on public opinion that in some circles the Jewish race is considered a race of inferior status."

They also protested the action of the German church against "ministers and church officers who by chance of birth are non-Aryan." They declared that this was a "denial of the explicit teaching and spirit of the Gospel of Jesus Christ." These were very strong words, and as a result of them, Heckel's position in the church was now jeopardized.

Bonhoeffer then returned to Germany for the national synod at Wittenberg, where Luther had famously inaugurated the Reformation. By now two thousand people had signed the manifesto of the Pastors' Emergency League. On the day of the synod, Bonhoeffer had the use of his father's Mercedes and chauffeur. He left 14 Wangenheimstrasse very early, with Franz Hildebrandt and their friend Gertrud Staewen. It was a gorgeous autumn morning. The back of the Mercedes was filled with boxes of the manifesto. That afternoon with friends they distributed them and nailed them to trees throughout Wittenberg.

An honor guard formed under the window of Ludwig Müller, causing the three to roll their eyes and cringe. While there, Bonhoeffer and Hildebrandt sent Müller a telegram demanding a response to the issue of the Aryan Paragraph, since he had not mentioned it in his morning speech. Unsurprisingly, he ignored it. That day Müller was unanimously elected Reichsbischof, and to make it all the more painful, the election took place in the church at Wittenberg Castle, over Luther's tomb. The always wisecracking Hildebrandt said that Luther must be turning over in his grave.

It was then decided that Müller was to be officially consecrated as Reich bishop on December 3 in the Cathedral at Magdeburg. The German Christians had won resoundingly. Once again, Bonhoeffer and Hildebrandt decided that the only solution was schism.

In October, Bonhoeffer turned his attention to London. His pastorate was to begin in two weeks, but Heckel made it clear that, given his recent activities, he might not be allowed to go. Heckel hoped to use this threat to get Bonhoeffer to change his positions, but Bonhoeffer was unrepentant, and boldly so. He told Heckel he would recant nothing he had said or written. Nor would he promise to refrain from "ecumenical" activities while he was in London, as Heckel tried to get him to do. In the meeting with Heckel he went so far as to demand a meeting with Reichsbischof Müller.

Bonhoeffer met with Müller on October 4. He explained that he would not represent the German Christian Reichskirche in England and reiterated what he had told Heckel, that he would continue speaking to the ecumenical movement. When the semi-educated Müller asked him to recant his signature on the Pastors' Emergency League statement, he answered that he would not, and quoted the Augsburg Confession in Latin at great length. Müller grew uncomfortable and cut him off. In the end, fearing Bonhoeffer would cause more trouble if prevented, Müller let him go to London.

Bonhoeffer had declared his loyalty to Germany, but he would not declare his loyalty to the "National Socialist state." That summed up Bonhoeffer's attitude going forward: he would be fiercely loyal to the church and to Germany, but would not pledge one atom of himself to Müller's pseudochurch or to the dictatorship that claimed to represent the great country and culture he cherished.

League of Nations

That October, to the delight of most Germans, Hitler declared that Germany was pulling out of the League of Nations. The announcement came just two days before Bonhoeffer was to leave for his London pastorate. As with so many of Hitler's most audacious moves, he presented it as something he had been forced to do by the actions of others. He had recently asked the League of Nations for "equality of status"—meaning he wanted them to grant Germany the right to build up its military to a level equal to those of the other major powers. When they predictably refused, he made the announcement. He calculated that the League of Nations did not have the will to stand up to him, and of course was quite correct. He also calculated that the German people would rejoice in his action, since it seemed like a further shaking off of the chains of humiliation that had come with Versailles. Here, too, he was quite right.

As ever, Hitler was uncannily in tune with the people's perception, which he had much to say about shaping. But it was a fact that at that time most Germans were wildly in favor of what he was doing. To be fair, they could have no idea of what was to come. And yet some did, Bonhoeffer and Hildebrandt chief among them.

Martin Niemöller did not. Like many on the right side of the church struggle at this time, he utterly separated the issues of church and state. To him, the German Christians' meddling in church affairs was one thing, but it was quite unconnected to what Hitler was undertaking elsewhere. So now—in the name of the Pastors' Emergency League, no less—Niemöller even sent a congratulatory telegram to the Führer, in which he swore their loyalty to him, and their gratitude.

Bonhoeffer and Hildebrandt were horrified. As a Jew, Hildebrandt was so disgusted by Niemöller's blindness to this issue that when Niemöller asked him to take a post in the Pastors' Emergency League, he declined. He wrote to Niemöller, expressing his feelings on the subject. He and Bonhoeffer often found themselves the lone voices, even among their allies in the Pastors' Emergency League. "I find it impossible," Hildebrandt wrote, "to understand how you can joyfully welcome the political move in Geneva when you yourselves refuse to adopt an unequivocal attitude toward a church which persistently denies us equality of status."

Many years later, after Niemöller had been imprisoned for eight years in concentration camps as the personal prisoner of Adolf Hitler, he penned these infamous words:

> First they came for the Socialists, and I did not speak out—
> because I was not a Socialist.
> Then they came for the Trade Unionists, and I did not speak out—
> because I was not a Trade Unionist.
> Then they came for the Jews, and I did not speak out—
> because I was not a Jew.
> And then they came for me—
> and there was no one left to speak for me.

When Hitler announced that Germany was leaving the League of Nations, he cannily announced that he would let the "German people" decide the issue in a November 12 plebiscite. He knew what the outcome would be, especially since the Nazis controlled all of the media and money in Germany.

Even the timing of the plebiscite was carefully chosen, and cynically. November 12 was one day after the fifteenth anniversary of Germany's humiliation at the hands of the Allies. In case anyone might have missed this, Hitler made it explicit in a speech. "See to it that this day shall later be recorded in the history of our people as a day of salvation!" he said. "That the record shall run: on an eleventh of November the German people formally lost its honor; fifteen years later came a twelfth of November and the German people restored its honor to itself!" And so that November 12 Germany once again ratified Hitler's leadership and "democratically" granted him overwhelming permission to thumb his nose at their enemies and all who had once brought them low. Now France, England, and the United States would see with whom they had been trifling!

The German Christians Overreach

It was a heady time for the Nazis. The day after the plebiscite, the German Christians decided to celebrate by staging a massive rally in their favorite arena, the Berlin *Sportpalast*. The great hall was festooned with Nazi flags and banners declaring "One Reich. One People. One Church." Twenty thousand gathered to hear the leader of the Berlin German Christians, an overwrought high-school teacher named Reinhold Krause. This was his moment in the sun, and he seized it. But he seems to have leaped to the national stage with such eagerness that he hurt himself—and the German Christians—very badly.

Unaware that his speech would be heard beyond the devoted audience in the *Sportpalast* that day, Krause let fly with what he and the more passionate figures in the German Christian movement had been saying among themselves all along, but had not yet said publicly. The moderate mask they had presented to most Germans would now be taken off.

In coarse, crude language, Krause demanded that the German church must once and for all divest itself of every hint of Jewishness. The Old Testament would be first, "with its Jewish money morality and its tales of cattle merchants and pimps!" The stenographical record notes that "sustained applause" ensued. The New Testament must be revised, too, and must present a Jesus "corresponding entirely with the demands of National Socialism." And it must no longer present an "*exaggerated* emphasis on the crucified Christ." This tenet was defeatist and depressing, which was to say Jewish. Germany needed hope and victory! Krause also mocked "the theology of the Rabbi Paul with its scapegoats and inferiority complex," and then he mocked the symbol of the cross, "a ridiculous, debilitating remnant of Judaism, unacceptable to National Socialists!" Furthermore, he demanded that every German pastor must take an oath of personal allegiance to Hitler! And the Aryan Paragraph that demanded the expulsion of every church member of Jewish descent must be heartily accepted by every German church!

Krause gave the performance of his life, but it was a fatal miscalculation for the German Christians. In the morning the press reported on the event, and most Germans beyond the packed *Sportpalast* were shocked and outraged. It was one thing to wish for a church that was relevant to the German people and that inspired Germans to rise from their defeat at the hands of the international community and the godless Communists. But to go as far as Krause had gone, mocking the Bible and St. Paul and so much else, was too much. From that moment, the German Christian movement was effectively doomed to Barth's abyss. Mainstream Protestants saw them as beyond the pale, as openly heretical and fanatically Nazi. And most of the Nazis, who were not Christians, simply thought of them as laughable.

The Nazis used the German Christians while it was convenient, giving them a chance to do what was likely impossible. It simply hadn't worked out. Müller hung in there for a time, but his star with Hitler was now on the wane. When the National Socialist project came to an end, Müller took his own life.

 CHAPTER 14

BONHOEFFER IN LONDON

1934–35

And I believe that the whole of Christendom should pray with us that it will be a "resistance unto death," and that the people will be found to suffer it.

—Dietrich Bonhoeffer

I n the late summer and fall of 1933, after Heckel invited him to pastor the two German congregations in London, Bonhoeffer thought about what to do. There were two main reasons to go. First, there was the grounding experience of honest "parish work" or "church work," as he sometimes called it. He had begun to see that the overemphasis on the cerebral and intellectual side of theological training had produced pastors who didn't know how to live as Christians, but knew only how to think theologically. Integrating the two was increasingly important to him. Second, he wished to push away from the church struggle in Germany, to gain perspective on the bigger picture, which, as far as he was concerned, went far beyond mere church politics. In a letter to Erwin Sutz, he wrote:

Although I am working with all my might for the church opposition, it is perfectly clear to me that this opposition is only a very temporary transition to an opposition of a very different kind, and that very few of those engaged in this preliminary skirmish will be part of the next struggle. And I believe that the whole of Christendom should pray with us that it will be a "resistance unto death," and that the people will be found to suffer it.

Even his closest allies, such as Franz Hildebrandt, could not see what he was seeing. He seemed to be operating on an impossibly high theological plane, seeing things in the distance that were invisible to those around him. It must have been frustrating for him and for them. Jean Lasserre's influence upon him had given Bonhoeffer a deep love for the Sermon on the Mount, and that opened the door to the perspective he now had on what was happening and what lay ahead.

There were other levels of meaning and depth to what he was facing. While Hildebrandt, Niemöller, and Jacobi were thinking about how to defeat Müller, Bonhoeffer was thinking about God's highest call, about the call of discipleship and its cost. He was thinking about Jeremiah and about God's call to partake in suffering, even unto death. Bonhoeffer was working it out in his head at the same time that he was thinking about what the next move should be with Heckel and the church struggle. He was thinking about the deep call of Christ, which was not about winning, but about submission to God, wherever that might lead. In the letter to Sutz, he said,

> Simply suffering—that is what will be needed then—not parries, blows or thrusts such as may still be possible or admissible in the preliminary fight; the real struggle that perhaps lies ahead must simply be to suffer faithfully. . . . [F]or sometime [the church struggle] hasn't even been about what it appears to be about; the lines have been drawn somewhere else entirely.

It's hard to escape the conclusion that Bonhoeffer was somehow thinking prophetically, that somehow he could see what was ahead of him, that at some point he would be able to do nothing more than "suffer faithfully" in his cell, praising God as he did so, thanking him for the high privilege of being counted worthy to do so.

On the other hand, on the much more mundane level of church politics—on the level of that "preliminary fight"—it seemed clear enough that he could be more effective from across the Channel. In London he would not be as directly under the authority of the Reichskirche, not as much under the watchful eye of the church or political authorities in Berlin. He would also be free to work with ecumenical contacts to tell the truth about what was happening inside Germany. This was important and would have been impossible while still in Germany.

It was during this period in London that he became close to the man who would become a dear friend as well as his most important ecumenical contact, George Bell, the bishop of Chichester.

There was one other man in the world whose influence and friendship meant as much as his relationship with Bishop Bell would mean to him. That man was Karl Barth. But Barth's apparent rebuff—on whether the approval of the Aryan Paragraph at the Brown Synod constituted a *status confessionis*—had been difficult to digest. So Bonhoeffer hadn't been inclined to tell Barth he was going to London. On October 24, a week or so after he arrived, he finally wrote Barth:

> If one were going to discover quite definite reasons for such decisions after the event, one of the strongest, I believe, was that I simply did not any longer feel up to the questions and demands that came to me. I feel that, in some way I don't understand, I find myself in radical opposition to all my friends; I became increasingly isolated with my views of things, even though I was and remain personally close to these people. All this has frightened me and shaken my confidence so that I began to fear that dogmatism might be leading me astray—since there seemed no particular reason why my own view in these matters should be any better, any more right, than the views of many really capable pastors whom I sincerely respect.

On November 20 came Barth's reply:

> Dear Colleague!
> You can deduce from the very way in which I address you that I do not regard your departure for England as anything but a necessary personal interlude. Once you had this thing on your mind, you were quite

right not to ask for my wise counsel first. I would have advised you against it absolutely, and probably by bringing up my heaviest artillery. And now, as you are mentioning the matter to me after the fact, I can honestly not tell you anything but "Hurry back to your post in Berlin!" . . . With your splendid theological armor and your upright German figure, should you not perhaps be almost a little ashamed at a man like Heinrich Vogel, who, wizened and worked up as he is, is just always there, waving his arms like a windmill and shouting "Confession! Confession!" in his own way—in power or in weakness, that doesn't matter so much—actually giving his testimony? . . . Be glad that I do not have you here in person, for I would let go at you urgently in quite a different way, with the demand that you must not let go of all these intellectual flourishes and special considerations, however interesting they may be, and think of only one thing—that you are a German, that the house of your church is on fire, that you know enough and can say what you know well enough to be able to help, and that you must return to your post by the next ship. Given the situation, shall we say the ship after next? . . . Please take it [this letter] in the friendly spirit in which it is intended. If I were not so attached to you, I would not let fly at you in this way.

With sincere greetings,
Karl Barth

Bishop George Bell

In London that fall, Bonhoeffer met Bishop George Bell, who would figure prominently in his life from that point forward. Bell was also the man to whom Bonhoeffer would direct his final words, just hours before he was executed. Bell and Bonhoeffer shared a February 4 birthday, although Bell was born in 1883. Bell and Karl Barth were two decades older than Bonhoeffer, and were the only men who ever functioned as anything like mentors. To his friends such as Franz Hildebrandt, Bonhoeffer would soon affectionately refer to Bell as Uncle George, though never to his face.

Bell was an impressive character. While a student at Christ Church, Oxford, he had won a major poetry award there, and after his appointment as chaplain to the famous Archbishop Randall Davidson, he went on to write

Davidson's biography, a monumental, definitive work of 1,400 pages. Bell got involved in the ecumenical movement after the First War and became one of its major figures. It was the ecumenical movement that brought him together with Bonhoeffer, who became his chief connection to the horrors unfolding in Germany. While dean of Canterbury, Bell had invited Dorothy Sayers and Christopher Fry as guest artists, but his most important invitation would be in 1935, when he commissioned T. S. Eliot to write the play *Murder in the Cathedral*, which dramatized the murder of Thomas à Becket that had taken place there in 1170. The play was an obvious criticism of the Nazi regime and premiered in the eponymous cathedral on June 15, 1935. Bell had also invited Gandhi to Canterbury and later provided the principal connection between him and Bonhoeffer.

Germany's relations with England at this time were complicated. Hitler desperately wanted to put forward an image of himself as someone the international community could trust, and throughout the thirties, he had many friends and allies in English aristocratic circles. Bishop Bell was not among them. In late 1933, the Nazis desperately hoped to curry favor with the Anglicans over the impending consecration of Ludwig Müller as Reichsbischof. Two leading German Christians, Joachim Hossenfelder and Professor Karl Fezer, were deputized to travel to England, there to spread the manure of Hitler's propaganda. Though not one of its witting consumers, Frank Buchman of the Oxford Movement had been the one to extend the invitation.

Buchman was an important evangelical Christian of the early twentieth century. He typified many well-meaning persons in being blind enough to Hitler's true nature to reach out to him when he might better have spoken out against him. But when Germany was reeling from the Weimar years, the man who unfailingly presented himself as an enemy of the godless Bolsheviks, and as a friend of the churches, was difficult to dismiss. In this, and in his desire to convert leaders to the Christian faith, Buchman seemed to have overlooked the biblical injunction to possess the wisdom of serpents. He naively hoped to convert Hitler and reached out to him and the German Christians.

But Hossenfelder and Fezer's fertilization campaign did not produce the growth they had hoped. The British papers were properly suspicious of Hitler's clerical envoys. Other than modest success with the pro-Hitler bishop of Gloucester, Arthur Cayley Headlam, they were generally rebuffed.

Bonhoeffer, however, had great success. His first meeting with George Bell was on November 21 in Chichester at the bishop's residence, and the two quickly became friends. Because Bell had been in Berlin the previous April, when the German Christians held their conference, he knew more of the situation in Germany than Bonhoeffer expected. In fact, on returning from his trip that April, Bell publicly alerted the international community about the anti-Semitism he had witnessed, and that September he had put forward a motion protesting the Aryan Paragraph and the German church's acceptance of it. In future years, Bonhoeffer would be Bell's principal source of information on what was happening in Germany, and Bell—who was a member of the House of Lords—would take this information to the British public, often through letters to the London *Times*. There can be little question that for the next decade, Bell and Bonhoeffer were vital to galvanizing British sentiment against Hitler and the Third Reich.

The London Pastorate

The London church where Bonhoeffer lived was in the southern suburb of Forest Hill. His flat consisted of two large rooms on the second floor of the parsonage, a rambling Victorian house on a hill surrounded by trees and gardens. Most of the other rooms were used by a private German school. The flat was drafty and always cold, and Bonhoeffer was perpetually getting, suffering, and recovering from the flu or some other ailment. The fireplaces were jerry-rigged with small coin-operated gas heaters that helped very little. There was also a problem with mice. Eventually Bonhoeffer and Hildebrandt gave up on keeping the mice out and simply stored their food in tins.

Paula Bonhoeffer tried to help her twenty-seven-year-old bachelor son set up housekeeping from a distance. She shipped several large pieces of furniture to him, including their Bechstein piano, which he played a great deal. She also hired a housekeeper for him.

Although he was physically removed from Berlin, Bonhoeffer managed to keep closely involved in the Sturm und Drang of the church struggle. For one thing, he traveled to Berlin every few weeks. And when he wasn't visiting Berlin, he was on the phone with someone there, whether Gerhard Jacobi, Martin Niemöller, or his mother, who was as immersed in the church struggle as anyone else. She fed her son every tidbit of information she gathered.

Bonhoeffer telephoned Germany so much that the local post office once actually lowered his monumental monthly phone bill, either out of disbelief that it could be accurate or out of pity.

Hildebrandt arrived in London on November 10. Bonhoeffer had said he would meet him at Victoria Station, but was nowhere to be seen. Hildebrandt thought he'd better call the parsonage, but didn't have the number and knew very little English. He was in the process of struggling to communicate his problem to the telephone operator when Bonhoeffer tapped on the kiosk window, having just arrived. Thereafter Bonhoeffer took it upon himself to teach Hildebrandt English and always sent him shopping, believing that "shopping will always teach the essentials."

That Christmas, Dietrich gave Hildebrandt an English Bible as a present; it was another way to speed up learning the language. But he also sent Hildebrandt out to buy the Christmas tree, having never changed his mind about shopping as the best method. Wolf-Dieter Zimmermann surprised them by arriving on Christmas Day, bearing a Strasbourg liver pâté. He stayed two weeks and would never forget how Bonhoeffer and Hildebrandt never stopped arguing, though he knew it was never personal:

> Usually we had a sumptuous breakfast about 11 a.m. One of us had to fetch *The Times* from which we learned, during breakfast, of the latest developments in the German Church struggle. Then each of us went about his own task. At 2 p.m. we met again for a light snack. Then there were conversations, interspersed with music, for both played the piano to perfection, solo or together. . . . Many evenings we spent together at home, only occasionally going to see a film or a play, or to other engagements. Such evenings at home were typical of our life in London: theological discussions, music, debates, story-telling, all following one another, passing into one another—till 2 or 3 a.m. Everything broke forth with an enormous vitality.

A friend from the church said there "was always an abundance of humour when Bonhoeffer was around." Bonhoeffer was constantly joking, whether verbally or in other ways. Sometimes he would start a piano duet in the wrong key until his partner figured out that he had done it on purpose.

Hildebrandt lived with Bonhoeffer in the parsonage for three months.

People were constantly visiting. While Zimmermann was there, another Berlin student arrived. Everyone marveled at how Bonhoeffer and Hildebrandt lived "in a state of permanent dispute" that was somehow never acrimonious. They obviously enjoyed the constant theological bickering. It constituted entertainment for them, allowing them to exercise their incredible wit, much of which went over the heads of anyone listening. Hildebrandt's biographers write that sometimes "when they were both involved in an argument Franz would produce his trump card, his clinching point. At this moment Dietrich would look up and say 'What was that? I'm sorry I didn't hear a word.'" Of course he had heard everything. And then the two of them would "dissolve into laughter."

There were plenty of other visitors. Bonhoeffer's sister Christel came to visit with her husband, Hans von Dohnanyi; and his sister Susanne came to visit with her husband, Walter Dress, who had been Bonhoeffer's friend for years and would be a member of the Confessing Church. According to Sabine, sometime during his stay in London, Bonhoeffer took in a St. Bernard dog. When the dog was killed by a car, Bonhoeffer was quite affected by it.

Bonhoeffer was responsible for two congregations, neither of which was large enough to support its own pastor. The Sydenham congregation numbered between thirty and forty, many of whom worked at the German embassy; and the St. Paul's congregation numbered about fifty, mostly tradesmen. Despite the small numbers, Bonhoeffer prepared his sermons as if he were preaching to thousands. Each sermon was written out by hand, and he mailed them to his friends in Germany, including Elizabeth Zinn.

These expatriate congregations in London were similar to the expatriate congregation he served in Barcelona. As with most ethnic churches abroad, they were the main cultural connection to the homeland. Consequently the theological side of things was less important. As in Barcelona, Bonhoeffer ambitiously introduced new activities to the congregation, including a Sunday school and youth group. He also supervised a nativity play at Christmas and a passion play at Easter.

Also as in Barcelona, his sermons were strong meat for parishioners used to much lighter fare. In fact, they were now more demanding and severe than those he had preached five years earlier. Bonhoeffer had changed much from the twenty-two-year-old in Barcelona; the circumstances of life had obviously grown darker. In some ways it was as if decades had passed. One sign of a deepening seriousness in him was his penchant for eschatological themes and a palpable longing for the "kingdom of heaven," which he communicated in his sermons. In a letter to Gerhard Leibholz, he wrote that "one feels such a tremendous longing for real peace, in which all the misery and injustice, the lying and cowardice will come to an end." He had believed these things five years earlier, but now he could feel them too.

CHAPTER 15

THE CHURCH BATTLE HEATS UP

He is a prisoner and he has to follow. His path is prescribed. It is the path of the man whom God will not let go, who will never be rid of God.

The question at stake in the German church is no longer an internal issue but is the question of the existence of Christianity in Europe.

—DIETRICH BONHOEFFER

I f Heckel and Müller thought letting Bonhoeffer go to London might mollify him somewhat or might keep him at arm's length from Berlin, they were mistaken. In London, Bonhoeffer was five times the trouble for them than he ever could have been back home. London gave Bonhoeffer a freedom he didn't have in Berlin, and he used it well. He deepened his relationships in the ecumenical world, and he made sure that whatever positive image Hitler's Germany might have in the English press was quickly corrected with facts.

And given his extraordinary gifts as a leader, he was soon shaping the opinions of other German pastors in London. At this crucial time, he would guide their individual and collective responses to the Reichskirche. Because of Bonhoeffer, the German churches in England even joined the Pastors'

Emergency League and, later, the Confessing Church. Of all the countries with German congregations, only one country—England—would take such a stand, all because of Bonhoeffer.

One German pastor in England to whom Bonhoeffer grew especially close was Julius Rieger, then in his early thirties. Pastor Rieger would work closely with Bonhoeffer and Bishop Bell in the years to come, and after Bonhoeffer's departure in 1935, he would become the principal German contact with Bell. Rieger was the pastor of St. George's Church in London's East End, which soon became the center for refugees from Germany. Bishop Bell became so involved in working with German refugees that he came to be thought of as the "bishop to refugees." When Sabine and Gerhard Leibholz were forced to leave Germany, Bell, Rieger, and St. George's Church were important connections for them. Rieger would also become close to Franz Hildebrandt, who became a pastor at St. George's when he was forced to leave Germany in 1937.

In mid-November 1933, following the German Christians' fiasco in the Berlin *Sportpalast*, the forces that had opposed the German Christians clamored for Müller's resignation. He was scheduled to be consecrated on December 3 all the same. What's more, the Reichskirche invited the German pastors in England to come home to attend the ceremony. The church government knew that a free trip home would be hard for the poorly paid pastors to resist, and their attendance would strengthen their ties to Müller and the Reichskirche, not to mention further legitimize the whole swastika-studded affair.

Bonhoeffer had other ideas. First he tried to convince all of the German pastors in England to stay away from the sham ceremony, and he succeeded with many of them. He persuaded those going to use the opportunity to deliver a document detailing their objections to Ludwig Müller. Titled "To the Reichskircharleitung," it catalogued the absurd statements and actions of Müller over the last few months. They would get their free trip home and could still register an official and detailed protest. Müller's consecration ceremony was eventually postponed, so the document was not delivered personally, but it was sent to the leaders of the Reichskirche nonetheless.

As a result of the outcry over the *Sportpalast* event, the German Christians were in an awful position, losing ground by the hour. The greatest proof of their rapid retreat was that Müller executed a shocking about-face and rescinded the Aryan Paragraph. Then the Janus-faced Heckel sent an epistolary olive branch to the German congregations in England, effectively saying there was nothing to fight about any longer, and mayn't we all get along?

Bonhoeffer was not tempted by this offer. Nor did he believe for a moment that any of the recent gains were permanent, which they weren't. In fact, they proved to be more temporary than he thought. In early January, Müller spun back around and bared his teeth again, rescinding his previous rescindment: the Aryan Paragraph was suddenly back on. Before he did this, though, he had given himself some cover. On January 4 of the new year, he enacted what came to be known as the "muzzling decree," although Müller originally had given it the more cheerful and Goebbelsesque title, "Decree for the Restoration of Orderly Conditions in the German Evangelical Church." This decree declared that discussions concerning the church struggle could not take place in church buildings or be conducted in church newspapers. Anyone who did so would be dismissed. And there was more to gasp at: he announced that all German church youth groups, called the Evangelical Youth, were to be merged with the Hitler Youth. Suddenly the battle was renewed.

Bonhoeffer knew that because they could threaten to leave the Reichskirche, the German congregations abroad had leverage that the churches inside Germany did not. The separation of the German churches in England from the official German church would be a serious blow to Germany's international reputation. The threat became explicit in a letter sent by Baron Schroeder, chairman of the Association of German Congregations abroad. "I fear fateful consequences," he wrote, "in the form of a secession of overseas German parishes from their home church which would deeply sadden me, on behalf of the past community of faith." This was no hollow threat. On Sunday, January 7, the German pastors sent a telegram to the Reichskirche: "For the sake of the Gospel and our conscience we associate ourselves with [the] Emergency League proclamation and withdraw our confidence from Reichsbischof Müller." This was tantamount to a declaration of war. In the original version that Bonhoeffer drafted, it went further, saying they "no longer recognize[d]" the Reichsbischof. That was too strong for some, so it was softened to the nonetheless electrically charged "withdraw our confidence." In either case, to declare such things to the Reichskirche was as close to the Rubicon of a *status confessionis* as the opposition churches had ever come. As events were unfolding, they would cross that river soon enough.

In fact, the very next day began a weeklong double-time march in that direction. On Monday the eighth, the Pastors' Emergency League planned to kick off its protest with a service at the magnificent and hugely important Berlin Cathedral, just across from the former kaiser's palace. This colossal cathedral, nearly four hundred feet tall and conceived as a Protestant answer to St. Peter's in Rome, was commissioned by Kaiser Wilhelm II in the 1890s on the site of the 1465 church that was the first Hohenzollern Court chapel. It was originally to be a visible and literal link between church and state, with a covered bridge connecting it with the palace, and was therefore a place of great symbolic significance for Germans. But the despotic Müller caught wind of their plans and decided to head them off at the pass by obtaining a police order to keep the massive doors shut. He had political power and was not afraid to use it.

But even Müller could not prevent the aggrieved faithful from gathering in the vast plaza outside the cathedral, which they did, and there they sang Luther's *Ein Feste Burg.** The gloves had come off. On Thursday the eleventh, in an effort to lend some civility to the escalating ugliness, the aged Hindenburg shuffled into the fray and summoned Reichsbischof Müller to a meeting. Now eighty-six and only months from death, the titular president of the Reich represented a living, wheezing link with Germany's glorious past under the kaiser. If anyone could influence Müller, surely he could. On the twelfth, Hindenburg met with Bodelschwingh and two other members of the Pastors' Emergency League. And on the thirteenth came the declaration of peace. The opposition pastors retracted their imminent threat to secede from the Reichskirche—but only for the time being. The only reason that Hindenburg was able to pull off this miracle was that a meeting with the Great Man of Peace was scheduled in just a few days.

On January 17, both sides were to meet with the Reichskanzler, Adolf Hitler. In early 1934, many in the Confessing Church, including Niemöller, still thought of Hitler as the reasonable one in all of this, as the man who would settle things in their favor. They were sure the smaller-minded men

---

*   The hymn "A Mighty Fortress Is Our God."

below him were to blame. It was Reichsbischof Müller who was Nazifying the church, not Hitler—and when they could finally meet with him, all would be clarified. So everyone had been willing to stand down and abate their breath until that meeting, since it meant waiting only four more days.

In the meantime they would count the seconds, and the tension would again ratchet upward. But Hitler postponed the meeting. And postponed it again, till the twenty-fifth. The eight days of additional waiting were an eternity of strained inaction.

Bonhoeffer followed every detail of these hemorrhoidal isometrics from England via his mother's almost daily updates. Because of the family's connections, he received extraordinary inside information, even while at his parsonage in Sydenham. And Paula Bonhoeffer was not only reporting on the mounting intrigue; she was a player in it. She wrote her son that it was strategically important to let Müller know that the truce was indeed only a truce, and said that she had been trying to get this message to him via her brother-in-law, General von der Goltz. She added that "we hope that our man in Dahlem," meaning Niemöller, "may get an audience" with Hindenburg.

Hindenburg seemed to be the key. He appeared to have a soft spot for the embattled Confessing Church and was thought to be of the opinion that Hitler should sack Müller. What they didn't know was that Göring wanted to prop Müller up, the better to stick it to the troublemaking theologians. So the London pastors sent a letter to Hindenburg, and Bonhoeffer persuaded Bishop Bell to send one too.

Hindenburg even forwarded the pastors' letter to Hitler. But with Göring and his other anticlerical henchmen whispering in his ear, Hitler was decidedly unreceptive. As far as he was concerned, the London pastors were merely spewing "internationalist Jewish atrocity propaganda." They had better watch themselves. The fawning Heckel passed along Hitler's gloomy impressions to them as a not-so-veiled threat, which they parried by calling it a threat. Meanwhile, everyone continued to wait for the meeting with Hitler.

God's Captive

During this tense time of waiting, Bonhoeffer preached his now rather famous sermon on the prophet Jeremiah. It was Sunday, January 21. Preaching on a Jewish Old Testament prophet was quite out of the ordinary and provocative, but that was the least of the sermon's difficulties. The opening words were typically intriguing: "Jeremiah was not eager to become a prophet of God. When the call came to him all of a sudden, he shrank back, he resisted, he tried to get away."

The sermon reflected Bonhoeffer's own difficult situation. It is extremely doubtful whether anyone in his congregations could understand what he was talking about, much less accept that it was God's word to them that Sunday. If they had ever been puzzled by their brilliant young preacher's homilies, they must have been puzzled now.

The picture that Bonhoeffer painted of Jeremiah was one of unrelieved gloom and drama. God was after him, and he could not escape. Bonhoeffer referred to the "arrow of the Almighty" striking down its "hunted game." But who was the "hunted game"? It was Jeremiah! But why was God shooting at the hero of the story? Before they found out, Bonhoeffer switched from arrow imagery to noose imagery. "The noose is drawn tighter and more painfully," he continued, "reminding Jeremiah that he is a prisoner. He is a prisoner and he has to follow. His path is prescribed. It is the path of the man whom God will not let go, who will never be rid of God." The sermon began to get seriously depressing. What was the young preacher getting at? Perhaps he was reading too many books. A little fresh air and fun now and again, that's what a man wants! As for Jeremiah, he could certainly use a little cheering up. But surely things would begin to look up for him soon! They continued listening, hoping for an upturn in Jeremiah's fortunes.

But alas, Pastor Bonhoeffer delivered an unrelenting homiletic bummer. He marched farther downhill:

> This path will lead right down into the deepest situation of human powerlessness. The follower becomes a laughingstock, scorned and taken for a fool, but a fool who is extremely dangerous to people's peace and comfort, so that he or she must be beaten, locked up, tortured, if not put to death right away. That is exactly what became of this man Jeremiah, because he could not get away from God.

If Bonhoeffer wanted to ensure that his congregation would never dream of following God too closely, this sermon was just the ticket. He then spoke of God driving Jeremiah "from agony to agony." Could it get worse?

> And Jeremiah was just as much flesh and blood as we are, a human
> being like ourselves. He felt the pain of being continually humiliated
> and mocked, of the violence and brutality others used against him.
> After one episode of agonizing torture that had lasted a whole night,
> he burst out in prayer: "O Lord, you have enticed me and I was enticed;
> you have overpowered me, and you have prevailed."

Bonhoeffer's congregation was lost. God maneuvered his beloved servant and prophet into imprisonment and agony? Somewhere along the line
they must have missed a crucial sentence! But they hadn't.

And what none of them could know was that Pastor Bonhoeffer was
talking, in some large part, about himself and about his future, the future
that God was showing him. He was beginning to understand that he was
God's prisoner, that like the prophets of old, he was called to suffer and to
be oppressed—and in that defeat and the acceptance of that defeat, there
was victory. It was a sermon that applied to anyone with ears to hear, but few
could actually hear it:

> [Jeremiah] was upbraided as a disturber of the peace, an enemy of
> the people, just like all those, throughout the ages until the present
> day, who have been possessed and seized by God, for whom God had
> become too strong . . . how gladly would he have shouted peace and
> *Heil* with the rest. . . .
>
> The triumphal procession of truth and justice, the triumphal pro-
> cession of God and his Scriptures through the world, drags in the wake
> of the chariot of victory a train of prisoners in chains. May he at the last
> bind us to his triumphal carriage so that, although in bonds oppressed,
> we may participate in his victory!

The Meeting with Hitler

Finally January 25 came, and both sides met with Adolf Hitler. It did not go
well for the opposition, who had come to the meeting hoping to be vindi-
cated and to see the rough-necked Müller get his comeuppance from the

Führer. But it was Niemöller, up to this point the most pro-Nazi figure in the Confessing Church, who got the worst of it.

Göring had had Niemöller's telephone tapped, and he opened the long-awaited meeting by producing the transcript of a call in which Niemöller had spoken ill of Hindenburg's influence on Hitler. Suddenly and un-forgettably—and for the first time for many in the room—the true colors of Hitler and his lieutenants shone vividly. In the transcript, Niemöller had cracked wise about Hindenburg's recent meeting with Hitler. Hitler was not amused. "This is completely unheard of!" he fumed. "I will attack this rebel-lion with every means at my disposal!"

"I was very frightened," Niemöller said later. "I thought, what do I answer to all his complaints and accusations? [Hitler] was still speaking, speaking, speaking. I thought, dear God, let him stop." In an attempt to put a better face on things, Niemöller declared truthfully, "But we are all enthusiastic about the Third Reich." Hitler exploded. "I'm the one who built the Third Reich!" he fumed. "You just worry about your sermons!" In that painful, sobering moment, Niemöller's fantasy that the Third Reich was a legitimate movement—something that existed in the world of real-ity, apart from Hitler's mind—was dashed. He now saw that the only prin-ciples of the Third Reich were the desires and will of the man ranting in front of him.

The rest of the meeting was no less dispiriting. Naturally, everyone pres-ent vowed fealty to Hitler and *his* Third Reich. Niemöller was able to speak with Göring afterward, but he was now banned from preaching nonethe-less. When the whole thing was over, there was no question who had won. Müller, the chuckle-headed chaplain, had again blundered upward.

Heckel's position was strengthened too. Two days after the meeting, he sent a letter to all the pastors abroad, effectively reiterating what had been agreed to at the meeting, and then saying, "Just as the front-line soldier is not in a position to assess the overall plan but must carry out the duties that immediately concern him, so I expect the clergy abroad to distinguish between their own particular task and the task of the church authorities in shaping the German Evangelical Church at home."

A major church figure was extending the Führer Principle to the ecclesi-astical and theological sphere, and using a martial simile to do so. It must have been depressing. Worse yet, Heckel decided it was time to visit London.

The principal reason for Heckel's visit was to stanch the bleeding of damaging information from Bonhoeffer and his ecumenical contacts. He knew that the disturbingly doughty Bonhoeffer would not get discouraged by a little bad news, such as what had happened at the meeting with Hitler. After all, when Niemöller was banned from preaching in his pulpit at Dahlem, Franz Hildebrandt—who was no less outspoken against the German Christians— would fill in.

On February 4, his twenty-eighth birthday, Bonhoeffer received letters from friends and family, but Hildebrandt's brilliantly funny letter outshone them all. It was a parody written in the archaic German of Luther—whose legacy was at the center of the *Kirchenkampf*—and with extraordinary wit and wordplay it combined teasing inside jokes with serious, but still funny cracks about the church struggle and their theological enemies. One inside joke was about a naked photo of Bonhoeffer as a two-year-old in the bathtub, which Paula Bonhoeffer had erred in showing to the incorrigible Hildebrandt; another concerned Bertha Schulze, a Berlin student of Bonhoeffer whom Paula Bonhoeffer had hired as her son's secretary and housekeeper in London, but who, because of what Hildebrandt referred to as "intentions" toward Bonhoeffer, had to find another job. She likely hadn't realized that Bonhoeffer had not yet resolved his relationship with Elizabeth Zinn, to whom he sent his sermons each week. Hildebrandt's high-spirited letter gives a real picture of the joy at the heart of their friendship and the hilarity of their constant teasing and bickering during the three months they were together in the London parsonage.

Bonhoeffer preached twice on his birthday, as he did every Sunday, but in the evening he gathered with a few friends and got a phone call from 14 Wangenheimstrasse, where the whole family had gathered, just to wish him a happy birthday. One of the letters he had received that day was from his father, who revealed something he had never said to his son before:

> Dear Dietrich,
> At the time when you decided to study theology, I sometimes thought to myself that a quiet, uneventful pastor's life, as I knew it from that of my Swabian uncle . . . would really almost be a pity for you. So far as uneventfulness is concerned, I was greatly mistaken. That such a crisis

should still be possible in the ecclesiastical field seemed to me, with my scientific background, to be out of the question. But in this as in many other things, it appears that we older folks have had quite wrong ideas about the solidity of so-called established concepts, views, and things. . . . In any case, you gain one thing from your calling—and in this it resembles mine—living relationships to human beings and the possibility of meaning something to them, in more important matters than medical ones. And of this nothing can be taken away from you, even when the external institutions in which you are placed are not always as you would wish.

Bishop Heckel Comes to London

The day after his birthday, Bonhoeffer gathered with the London pastors in anticipation of Heckel's visit. They wrote a memorandum, detailing their problems with the Reichskirche to use in the meeting. It took issue with the Reich church's use of force against its opponents and raised the general problem of Müller's leadership, since he obviously agreed with much of the most inane heresy of the German Christians. The memo also declared that the Aryan Paragraph "contradicts the clear meaning of the scriptures and is only one symptom of the danger to the pure gospel and the confession that is posed by the 'German Christians.'" It is significant that they put "German Christians" in quotation marks since the term must have especially nauseated them. It was offensive for its bold claim that those associated with it were Christians, which they could scarcely be from any theologically serious standpoint; and for the clear insinuation that those outside their fold were not true Germans. The memo ended by referring to Müller's crude disparagements of his opponents: "The Reichsbischof's language, as reported even in the daily press, which is otherwise allowed to say so little, includes such expressions as 'Pfaffen' and 'shriveled-up fellow citizens.' For pastors who are already subjected to enough hostility in their daily work, such insults out of the mouth of their highest minister really do not allow any confidence to grow."

Pfaffen was a combination of the German words *Pfarrer* (pastor) and *Affen* (apes). Hitler, too, was known to use the term *Pfaffen* to refer to the Protestant pastors. The other phrase was meant to malign his opponents as lacking in manly German vigor, which was the hallmark of true "positive Christianity" and one of whose chief manifestations was the use of crude, disparaging language.

When Heckel and his delegation arrived in London to meet the seven pastors, the lines between the two sides were drawn. Heckel thought he could achieve his aims nonetheless, which were not only to persuade them to fall in line, but to get them to sign an agreement he had drafted, in effect declaring their loyalty to the German Reichskirche. To obtain the signatures, he would use any means at his disposal, especially obfuscation and veiled threats. But he did not reveal the document until the end of the meeting. First Heckel presented the "General Plans" for the imminent "reorganization" of the Reichskirche.

When the meeting was opened for discussion, Bonhoeffer spoke first. He would not content himself with rebutting what Heckel said and implied, but characteristically leaped to the offensive, being aggressive, brilliant, and infuriatingly and yet earnestly polite as he did so. He described the Reichskirche's actions, repeating the issues in the memo, and then said that the question at hand was not how to unify with such a church, but how to secede from it. In Bonhoeffer's mind, the Reichskirche of Ludwig Müller was clearly and unrepentantly heretical. This was not something he was at liberty to overlook.

Heckel was not elected bishop that year for acceding to logic. He cleverly skated and pirouetted around every one of the memo's objections, as though each was simply a silly misunderstanding. He explained that Müller—who had instituted, rescinded, and then reinstituted the Aryan Paragraph—was actually *against* it after all! And had he mentioned that the Reichsbischof was particularly fond of the churches abroad? The Reichsbischof was a cheerful and conciliatory fellow if one gave him a chance. He had been presented with difficult choices. As for his public insults and foul language, that was merely the "soldier's slang" of the time! Müller was for many years a naval chaplain, and that sort of thing must be expected.

And what of the brazen attempt to combine all church youth groups with the Hitler Youth? Heckel said that no one else had difficulty with it, and as he now glided from obfuscation to veiled threats, he said that the beloved Führer gushingly described this conflation of church youth with the Hitler Youth "as the Christmas present that pleased him most." How Bonhoeffer must have cringed.

But Heckel was not through. Continuing in this threatening vein, he brought up the evidence they had against certain opposition clergy, and he spoke of the disciplinary actions taken against them. Niemöller was among this group, and Heckel said that if Niemöller did not shape up, the whole thing might come to a "terrible ending." Heckel did not neglect to mention the "treasonous" action of consorting with "foreign influences," referring specifically to an "English bishop" and a "Swedish bishop," but of course he did not say what he and everyone else in the room knew, that these were Bonhoeffer's allies, George Bell and Valdemar Ammundsen. He preferred to rely on everyone's powers of inference.

Bonhoeffer, however, seemed to have been strangely immune to intimidation. He continued to push back and do what he knew he must, but always in a respectful and measured way and at the appropriate times. This was not one of them, so he said little in response, and the meeting came to an end. But it was only the first of two that had been scheduled. They would meet again the next day.

Meanwhile, Heckel went to the Athenaeum Club, where he met with the "English bishop" to whom he had referred. Heckel was desperate to stop Bonhoeffer from working his ecumenical contacts, which was causing real trouble for the Reichskirche in the English press. But in case Heckel was not successful with the idealistic young pastor, he must try to get an agreement from the older and wiser Bishop Bell. Surely he would be more reasonable. At their meeting Heckel diplomatically suggested that Bell agree to stay out of the German church's business for at least the next six months. Bell was not so reasonable and refused.

For Heckel it was all quite infuriating. When he met with the London pastors the next day, the stakes were that much higher. He had struck out with Bell, so he desperately needed to succeed here and must not fail to get their signatures on the document he brought. But the seven pastors weren't signing anything. In fact, they had their own document, and they were brassy enough to push Heckel to sign it. If he wanted them to join the new Reichskirche, all he had to do was agree to their conditions. If the Reichskirche agreed that it was "founded on the Holy Scriptures of the Old and New Testaments," if it abolished the Aryan Paragraph once and for all, and if it agreed not to dismiss any pastors who agreed to these first points, and so on, they would all be only too happy to join the new Reichskirche. It was that simple.

Pushed into a corner, Heckel again resorted to veiled threats. He dared to suggest that if they were not "obedient" on these issues, they might come to be numbered with the "Prague emigrants." This was the pejorative term that the Nazis used to refer to their left-leaning political enemies, who had been forced to flee Germany when Hitler came to power, under threat of death. This went too far. Shortly after Heckel said that, Bonhoeffer and two others rose and left in protest.

Heckel returned to Berlin empty-handed and steaming. To say that he regretted having warmly promoted Bonhoeffer to his London pastorate was a great understatement. All it had done was give the high-handed hothead a protected and public platform from which to take potshots at the Reichskirche. A week later Heckel learned that Bonhoeffer had been invited to Lambeth Palace by the archbishop of Canterbury, Cosmo Lang. This must have been unbearably irksome, since just a few months earlier, the official Reichskirche delegation of Hossenfelder and Fezer had angled for such an invitation and were soundly rebuffed. Heckel had had enough. He now summoned Bonhoeffer to Berlin.

But before Bonhoeffer's visit, the stakes in this battle rose significantly for both men. Heckel had just been rewarded for his good behavior with the office of bishop. The Reichsbischof had also made him head of the church's Foreign Office. This meant that he now answered not just to the church, but to the state too. So his failure to improve Germany's image in the international press was more serious than ever. It was more serious for Bonhoeffer, too, since noncompliance with Heckel's edicts was now disobedience to the state and could be considered treasonous.

Bonhoeffer arrived in Berlin on March 5. When he met with Heckel, the newly minted bishop did not mince words. Bonhoeffer must henceforth refrain from all ecumenical activity. And in what was becoming a cliché, Heckel produced another document to sign; and again Bonhoeffer was too smart to sign it and smart enough not to say so defiantly, but to say that he would weigh the matter and respond in writing very soon. He flew back to London on March 10, and on March 18 he wrote his predictable response to Heckel: he would not sign.

On the Banks of the Rubicon

In Berlin, Bonhoeffer met with Martin Niemöller, Gerhard Jacobi, and other leaders in the Pastors' Emergency League. Their moment of truth had arrived. They saw that their efforts in the church struggle had largely been for naught, and as the leaders of the opposition, they planned to break ranks with the German Reichskirche. They agreed this was the *status confessionis* that Bonhoeffer had been saying it was all along, and they would hold the synod for a Free Church in Barmen at the end of May. It would be a watershed event and would officially and publicly separate them from the apostate Reich church. They had come to the banks of the Rubicon and were girding themselves for the crossing.

Now more than ever they would need the help and support of the churches outside Germany. Bonhoeffer felt the great urgency of the situation, and during the week in which he was formulating his response to Heckel, he contacted his friends in the ecumenical movement. On March 14 he wrote Henry Louis Henriod, the Swiss theologian who headed the ecumenical World Alliance. Bonhoeffer also wrote Bishop Bell. He wrote the letter in English:

> My dear Lord Bishop,
> . . . One of the most important things is that the Christian churches of the other countries do not lose their interest in the conflict due to the passage of time. I know that my friends are looking to you and your further actions with great hope. There is really a moment now as perhaps never before in Germany in which our faith in the ecumenical task of the churches can be shaken and destroyed completely or strengthened and renewed in a surprisingly new way. And it is you, my Lord Bishop, on whom it depends whether this moment shall be seized. The question at stake in the German church is no longer an internal issue but is the question of the existence of Christianity in Europe . . . even if the information of the newspaper is becoming of less interest, the real situation is as tense, as acute, as responsible as ever before. I shall only wish you would see one of the meetings of the Emergency League now—it is always in spite of all gravity of the present moments a real uplift to one's own faith and courage—Please do not be silent now! I beg to ask you once more to consider the possibility of an ecumenic delegation and ultimatum. It is not on behalf of any national or denominational interest that this ultimatum should be brought forward but it is in the name of Christianity in Europe. Time passes by very quickly and it might soon be too late.

On March 16, Henriod wrote Bell, underscoring the situation, and that same day Henriod replied to Bonhoeffer:

> My dear Bonhoeffer,
> Thank you for your letter of March 14th. As you say, the situation is becoming more critical and some action should be taken up without any delay by the Oecumenic movement. . . . I have written a few days ago already to the Bishop of Chichester, urging him to follow up his correspondence with Bishop Heckel by a strong letter. . . . Those who stand for the Gospel in Germany should not get desperate. There are declarations and messages which are coming out from various countries by pastors and others, which will indicate how much deep feeling there is outside Germany with regard to the situation of the government of the German Church. I can only repeat that stronger action might have been taken earlier if our best trusted friends in Germany had not urged us again and again even these last few days, not to break relationships with the German Church, as it is our only means of influencing the situation by getting at the present government again and again with strong criticisms.

On March 28, Bonhoeffer traveled to Lambeth and was received by Cosmo Lang, the archbishop of Canterbury. Bonhoeffer wrote Henriod again on April 7. His urgency and frustration are typical of his dealings with both the ecumenical movement and his allies in the Confessing Church:

> My dear Henriod!
> I would very much have liked to discuss the situation with you again, since the slowness of ecumenical procedure is beginning to look to me like irresponsibility. A decision must be made at some point, and it's no good waiting indefinitely for a sign from heaven that will solve the difficulty without further trouble. Even the ecumenical movement has to make up its mind and is therefore subject to error, like everything human. But to procrastinate and prevaricate simply because you're afraid of erring, when others—I mean our brethren in Germany—must make infinitely more difficult decisions every day, seems to me almost to run counter to love. To delay or fail to make decisions may be more

sinful than to make wrong decisions out of faith and love. . . . [I]n this particular case it really is now or never. "Too late" means "never." Should the ecumenical movement fail to realize this, and if there are none who are violent in order to take the kingdom of heaven by force (Matthew 11:12), then the ecumenical movement is no longer the church, but a useless association in which fine speeches are made. "If you do not believe, you will not be established"; to believe, however, means to decide. And can there be any doubt as to the nature of that decision? For Germany today it is the Confession, as it is the Confession for the ecumenical movement. We must shake off our fear of this world—the cause of Christ is at stake, and are we to be found sleeping? . . . Christ is looking down at us and asking whether there is anyone left who confesses faith in him.

In the midst of this whirlwind of ecumenical activity, Bonhoeffer served as the main pastor for two congregations, preaching twice each Sunday and carrying out his innumerable functions as a pastor. On April 11, he performed the funeral for a nineteen-year-old German girl in his parish.

On the twelfth he learned that Müller had nominated as *Rechtswalter* (legal administrator) over the German church a racist fanatic named Dr. August Jäger. In a speech the year before, Jäger had wackily declared, "The appearance of Jesus in world history ultimately represents a burst of Nordic light in the midst of a world tormented by symptoms of degeneracy." On April 15 Bonhoeffer wrote Bishop Bell:

The appointment of Dr. Jäger . . . is an ostentatious affront to the opposition and . . . means in fact that all power of the church government has been handed over to political and party authorities. It was much surprising to me that the *Times* gave a rather positive report to this appointment. Jäger is in fact the man with the famous statement about Jesus being only the exponent of Nordic race etc. He was the man who caused the retirement of Bodelschwingh and who was considered to be the most ruthless man in the whole church government. . . . So this appointment must be taken as a significant step towards the complete assimilation of the church to the state and party. Even if Jäger should try to make himself sympathetic to the churches abroad, by using mild words now, one must not be deceived by this tactic.

Bonhoeffer knew Jäger's appointment meant the Nazis were planning to be as brazen as possible; the ecumenical movement must act quickly and give them an ultimatum. The Reichskirche would do everything possible to curry favor with the churches abroad, so the ecumenical movement must remain strong and must refuse to recognize it as the true German church. It was also imperative that the ecumenical movement show solidarity with the pastors in the Emergency League.

In explaining the situation to his friend Erwin Sutz, Bonhoeffer showed a defiant side that we rarely see:

> The church regime ordered me to fly to Berlin and put before me some sort of declaration that I would refrain from all ecumenical activity from now on, which I didn't sign. This sort of thing is disgusting. They'd give anything to get me away from here, and for that reason alone I am digging in my heels. . . .
>
> Nat[ional] Socialism has brought about the end of the church in Germany and has pursued it single-mindedly. We can be grateful to them, in the way the Jews had to be grateful to Sennacherib. For me there can be no doubt that this is clearly the reality that we face. Naïve, starry-eyed idealists like Niemöller still think they are the real Nat[ional] Socialists—and perhaps it's a benevolent Providence that keeps them under the spell of this delusion.

The Barmen Declaration

All of Bonhoeffer's ecumenical efforts were beginning to pay off. Bishop Bell wrote his "Ascension Day Message" on the crisis in the German church, and on May 10 he sent it to the members of the ecumenical Life and Work organization around the world. It brought worldwide attention to the opposition pastors in Germany and put great pressure on the Reichskirche. Of course this made Heckel and Müller—and the Nazis in general—look bad. As with most of what Bell wrote about the German church struggle, Bonhoeffer worked closely with him in shaping the message. "The situation," it declared, is, beyond doubt, full of anxiety. . . . [A] revolution has taken place in the German State. . . . [T]he present position is being watched by members of the Christian Churches abroad not only with great interest, but with a deepening concern. The chief cause of anxiety is the assumption by the Reichsbischof in the name of the principle of leadership of autocratic powers unqualified by constitutional or traditional restraints which are without precedent in the history of the Church. . . . [T]he disciplinary measures which have been taken by the Church government against ministers of the Gospel on account of their loyalty to the fundamental principles of Christian truth have made a painful impression on Christian opinion abroad, already disturbed by the introduction of racial distinctions in the universal fellowship of the Christian Church. No wonder that voices should be raised in Germany itself making a solemn pronouncement before the whole Christian world on the dangers to which the spiritual life of the Evangelical Church is exposed.

On and on it went, spelling out the Nazi government's effect on the German churches. Two days after Bishop Bell mailed it to his ecumenical contacts, the full text appeared in the London *Times*.

It was obvious from this victory that Bonhoeffer's ecumenical activities alone were reason enough for him to be in London. He also continued his refugee work with Julius Rieger at St. George's. More Jewish refugees from Germany were arriving all the time. Life in Göttingen was getting so difficult for Sabine and her family that, in a year, they would arrive as refugees too. Two years later Hildebrandt would do the same. Bonhoeffer's work in London as a pastor and in the trenches of the church struggle held an appeal for him that was undeniable. On May 22, as he prepared for the Barmen synod, he wrote his grandmother:

Just now it is quite lovely here. We had a church excursion yesterday and were outdoors all day, in an area that is famous because at this time of year the whole forest floor is absolutely covered in blue, for hundreds of meters, by a kind of bellflower. Furthermore, I was greatly surprised to find wild rhododendrons in the woods, a whole lot of them, hundreds of bushes growing close together. . . . It's still very uncertain how much longer I shall be here. I recently had a letter . . . confirming my current leave of absence. . . . I assume that I shall then have to make a final decision whether to return to an academic career. I'm not so tremendously keen on it anymore.

The Birth of the Confessing Church

On the last three days of May 1934, the leaders of the Pastors' Emergency League held a synod in Barmen. It was there, on the Wupper River, that they wrote the famous Barmen Declaration, from which emerged what came to be known as the Confessing Church.*

The purpose of the Barmen Declaration was to state what the German church had always believed, to ground it in the Scriptures, and to differentiate it from the bastardized theology that had been coming from the German Christians. It made clear that the German church was not under the authority of the state; it repudiated the anti-Semitism and other heresies of the German Christians and their "official" church led by Müller. The principal author of the Barmen Confession was Karl Barth, who claimed to have produced the final version "fortified by strong coffee and one or two Brazilian cigars."

Since it was a watershed in the German church struggle of the Third Reich, and is a seminal document, we quote it at length here:

I. An Appeal to the Evangelical Congregations and Christians in
    Germany

8.01 The Confessional Synod of the German Evangelical Church met
    in Barmen, May 29–31, 1934. Here representatives from all the
    German Confessional Churches met with one accord in a confes-
    sion of the one Lord of the one, holy, apostolic Church. In fidelity
    to their Confession of Faith, members of Lutheran, Reformed, and
    United Churches sought a common message for the need and
    temptation of the Church in our day. . . . It was not their intention

---

* The term *confess* means "to give assent to" or "to acknowledge." It echoes Jesus' statement from the gospel of Matthew that "whoever confesses Me before men, him I will also confess before my Father who is in heaven" (10:32 NKJV). At first some called it the Confessional Movement. The German term for "Confessional Church" was *Bekennende kirche*, so it is sometimes abbreviated BK.

to found a new Church or to form a union. . . . Their intention was, rather, to withstand in faith and unanimity the destruction of the Confession of Faith, and thus of the Evangelical Church in Germany. In opposition to attempts to establish the unity of the German Evangelical Church by means of false doctrine, by the use of force and insincere practices, the Confessional Synod insists that the unity of the Evangelical Churches in Germany can come only from the Word of God in faith through the Holy Spirit. Thus alone is the Church renewed.

8.03 Be not deceived by loose talk, as if we meant to oppose the unity of the German nation! Do not listen to the seducers who pervert our intentions, as if we wanted to break up the unity of the German Evangelical Church or to forsake the Confessions of the Fathers!

8.04 Try the spirits whether they are of God! Prove also the words of the Confessional Synod of the German Evangelical Church to see whether they agree with Holy Scripture and with the Confessions of the Fathers. If you find that we are speaking contrary to Scripture, then do not listen to us! But if you find that we are taking our stand upon Scripture, then let no fear or temptation keep you from treading with us the path of faith and obedience to the Word of God, in order that God's people be of one mind upon earth and that we in faith experience what he himself has said: "I will never leave you, nor forsake you."

II. Theological Declaration Concerning the Present Situation of the German Evangelical Church

8.05 According to the opening words of its constitution of July 11, 1933, the German Evangelical Church is a federation of Confessional Churches that grew out of the Reformation and that enjoy equal rights. The theological basis for the unification of these Churches is laid down in Article 1 and Article 2(1) of the constitution of the German Evangelical Church that was recognized by the Reich Government on July 14, 1933:

Article 1. The inviolable foundation of the German Evangelical
Church is the gospel of Jesus Christ as it is attested for us in
Holy Scripture and brought to light again in the Confessions of
the Reformation. The full powers that the Church needs for its
mission are hereby determined and limited.

8.07 We publicly declare before all evangelical Churches in
Germany that what they hold in common in this Confession
is grievously imperiled, and with it the unity of the German
Evangelical Church. It is threatened by the teaching methods and actions of the ruling Church party of the "German
Christians" and of the Church administration carried on by
them. These have become more and more apparent during the
first year of the existence of the German Evangelical Church.
This threat consists in the fact that the theological basis, in
which the German Evangelical Church is united, has been continually and systematically thwarted and rendered ineffective
by alien principles, on the part of the leaders and spokesmen
of the "German Christians" as well as on the part of the Church
administration. When these principles are held to be valid,
then, according to all the Confessions in force among us, the
Church ceases to be the Church and the German Evangelical
Church, as a federation of Confessional Churches, becomes
intrinsically impossible.

8.09 In view of the errors of the "German Christians" of the pres-
ent Reich Church government which are devastating the
Church and also therefore breaking up the unity of the German
Evangelical Church, we confess the following evangelical truths:

8.10 1. "I am the way, and the truth, and the life; no one comes to
the Father, but by me." (John 14.6.) "Truly, truly, I say to you, he
who does not enter the sheepfold by the door, but climbs in by
another way, that man is a thief and a robber. . . . I am the door;
if anyone enters by me, he will be saved." (John 10:1, 9.)

8.11 Jesus Christ, as he is attested for us in Holy Scripture, is the one
Word of God which we have to hear and which we have to trust
and obey in life and in death.

8.12 We reject the false doctrine, as though the church could and would have to acknowledge as a source of its proclamation, apart from and besides this one Word of God, still other events and powers, figures and truths, as God's revelation.

8.15 We reject the false doctrine, as though there were areas of our life in which we would not belong to Jesus Christ, but to other lords—areas in which we would not need justification and sanctification through him.

8.17 The Christian Church is the congregation of the brethren in which Jesus Christ acts presently as the Lord in Word and sacrament through the Holy Spirit. As the Church of pardoned sinners, it has to testify in the midst of a sinful world, with its faith as with its obedience, with its message as with its order, that it is solely his property, and that it lives and wants to live solely from his comfort and from his direction in the expectation of his appearance.

8.18 We reject the false doctrine, as though the Church were permitted to abandon the form of its message and order to its own pleasure or to changes in prevailing ideological and political convictions.

8.19 "You know that the rulers of the Gentiles lord it over them, and their great men exercise authority over them. It shall not be so among you; but whoever would be great among you must be your servant." (Matt. 20:25, 26.)

8.20 The various offices in the Church do not establish a dominion of some over the others; on the contrary, they are for the exercise of the ministry entrusted to and enjoined upon the whole congregation

8.21 We reject the false doctrine, as though the Church, apart from this ministry, could and were permitted to give itself, or allow to be given to it, special leaders vested with ruling powers.

8.22-5. "Fear God. Honor the emperor." (1 Peter 2:17.) Scripture tells us that, in the as yet unredeemed world in which the Church also exists, the State has by divine appointment the task of providing for justice and peace. [It fulfills this task] by means of the threat and exercise of force, according to the measure of human judgment and human ability. The Church acknowledges

the benefit of this divine appointment in gratitude and reverence before him. It calls to mind the Kingdom of God, God's
commandment and righteousness, and thereby the responsibility
both of rulers and of the ruled. It trusts and obeys the power of
the Word by which God upholds all things.

8.23 We reject the false doctrine, as though the State, over and
beyond its special commission, should and could become the
single and totalitarian order of human life, thus fulfilling the
Church's vocation as well.

8.24 We reject the false doctrine, as though the Church, over and
beyond its special commission, should and could appropriate the
characteristics, the tasks, and the dignity of the State, thus itself
becoming an organ of the State.

8.26 The Church's commission, upon which its freedom is founded,
consists in delivering the message of the free grace of God to all
people in Christ's stead, and therefore in the ministry of his own
Word and work through sermon and sacrament.

8.27 We reject the false doctrine, as though the Church in human
arrogance could place the Word and work of the Lord in the
service of any arbitrarily chosen desires, purposes, and plans.

On June 4—again, thanks to Bishop Bell and Bonhoeffer—the full text of
the Barmen Declaration was published in the London *Times*. It was incendiary,
announcing to the world that a group of Christians in Germany had officially
and publicly declared their independence from the Nazified Reichskirche.
When one read it, it was easy to understand why they had done so.

As Bonhoeffer took great pains to make clear, the Barmen Declaration
did not constitute a secession from the "official" German church because
calling it a secession would give an appearance of legitimacy to that "official" German church. It was not the Confessing Church that had broken
away, but the Reichskirche. The Barmen Declaration signaled that a group
of pastors and churches acknowledged, repudiated, and officially distanced
themselves from that *de facto* secession. It reclarified what it—the legitimate
and actual German Church—actually believed and stood for.

To Bonhoeffer, because of the Barmen Declaration, the Confessing
Church had become *the* German church, and he believed that all true

Christians would recognize that the Reichskirche of the German Christians was officially excommunicated. But as it turned out, not everyone saw this as clearly as Bonhoeffer had expected.

Indeed, even some of his closest allies, such as George Bell and Bishop Ammundsen, did not see it that way. This would lead to some difficulties, especially since Bonhoeffer anticipated the ecumenical conference to be held in Fanø, Denmark, that August. Bonhoeffer had been asked to give a speech at Fanø and to organize the youth conference that was part of the larger conference, but he soon realized that he had bigger issues to worry about.

The troubles began when Bonhoeffer discovered that some German delegates invited to the Fanø conference were part of the Reichskirche led by Müller. First of all, Bonhoeffer was determined that the youth conference he was organizing would not recognize any delegates with ties to Müller's Reichskirche. Second, he was determined to prevent anyone from the Reichskirche from attending the larger Fanø conference. Either one was with those who had declared their separation from the Reichskirche, or one was with the Reichskirche. How had the ecumenical leaders failed to grasp that?

In June Bonhoeffer traveled to Berlin to meet with Niemöller and Karl Koch, president of the Confessing Synod. The three agreed that the powers that be in Geneva, where the ecumenical organization's offices were headquartered, would be expected to acknowledge the new situation and invite members of the Confessing Church to the conference and keep away all others.

Bonhoeffer immediately contacted the Fanø organizers, making his position clear:

> I have already written Herr Schönfeld that participation by our German delegation in Fanø will essentially depend on whether representatives of the present Reichskirchen leilung are to take part in the conference. In any case the members of our delegation are agreed that they will stay away from those Fanø meetings that are attended by representatives of the church government. It would be a good thing if this alternative is generally and clearly realized. And I hope that you, too, will help us to get the ecumenical movement to state openly, before it is too late, which of the two churches in Germany it is prepared to recognize.

So Bonhoeffer's participation was contingent on the understanding that the Confessing Church was now the true German church. If the leaders of the Confessing Church were not invited as such, no one from the Confessing Church would participate. If Heckel and the Reichskirche were there, they would be there alone. The silence of the Confessing Church would speak for itself.

But all of this would soon get awkward. Henriod wrote Bonhoeffer with bad news: an invitation had already been extended to Heckel and the Reichskirche's Foreign Office. Even though he was on Bonhoeffer's side, generally speaking, Henriod said that it was impossible to retract the invitation. It was also impossible for the ecumenical body to issue a second invitation to the Confessing Church, as such. The ecumenical leaders regarded the Confessing Church as a movement, not a church. But he added that if the Confessing Synod declared itself to be a second German church, that would be a different situation.

Bonhoeffer was exasperated. The Confessing Church had abundantly declared all that was necessary at Barmen. Furthermore, it was certainly *not* a second German church. It was the *only* German church. There could not be two. The Reichskirche had stepped away by being unrepentantly heretical, leaving the Confessing Church as the only remaining German church. Bonhoeffer's ecclesiology was quite crisp and clear, although those who didn't see things his way might have thought him fussy. But for him these things were bound by the doctrines of the Scriptures and the dogmas of the historical church. One must not sloppily blur such things. Either the Confessing Church was the one and only German Evangelical Church, adhering to the Scriptures and to the spirit of the Reformation and to the Constitution of the German Evangelical Church—or it was not. The Barmen Declaration had clearly and loudly declared to the world that they were theologically and legally that church.

On July 12 he wrote Henriod:

There is not the claim or even the wish to be a Free Church beside the *Reichskirche*, but there is the claim to be the only theologically and legally legitimate evangelical church in Germany, and accordingly you cannot expect this church to set up a new constitution, since it is based on the very constitution, which the *Reichskirche* has neglected. . . . [T]he

Confessional [*sic*] Church . . . [has] already once declared before the whole [of] Christianity, what their claim is. So, I feel strongly, that legally and theologically the responsibility for the future relationships between the German Church and the Ecumenic Movement rests with the Ecumenic Movement itself and its actions.

He asked Henriod to excuse his "lengthy explanation, but I should not like to be misunderstood by my friends."

But Henriod, who was the head of the Ecumenical Federation, simply did not see it this way. And he felt bound by the protocols and statutes of his organization. To Bonhoeffer, the idea that Geneva was unable to retract the invitation to Heckel, or to extend an invitation to the Confessing Church as things stood, seemed ridiculous. He now turned to Bell. And Bell turned to Ammundsen. Ammundsen wrote a kind letter, in which, by referring to the Confessing Church as a "Free Synod," he made it clear that he himself did not understand the situation as Bonhoeffer did. Even he still regarded the Confessing Church as some kind of alternative German "free" church. But he said that perhaps two members of the Confessing Church could be invited "in no official capacity," thereby doing an end run around the strange rules. Bonhoeffer, Bodelschwingh, and Koch were thus invited, and now had to think about whether to accept under these strange conditions. Meanwhile, Heckel caught wind of their invitation and tried to stop it.

During that summer of 1934, during all of this back-and-forth, dramatic changes were taking place in Germany. Taken together, they powerfully altered the political landscape, which would have a direct bearing on everyone's future for years to come and would immediately affect who would attend the ecumenical conference at Fanø.

The Night of the Long Knives

The terrible events that altered the political landscape of Germany that summer were Hitler's response to what looked like very bad news. There were rumors that things were at last unraveling for Hitler and his criminal administration. Bonhoeffer heard from his brother-in-law Dohnanyi that Hjalmar Schacht, the head of the German *Reichsbank*, was on the verge of resigning. President Hindenburg's doctors leaked the news that he was likely only months from death. Hitler feared that as soon as Hindenburg died, the conservatives and the army leaders would push hard for a return to the Hohenzollern monarchy. For them, the way forward to a greater and more unified Germany was away from the crass embarrassment that was Adolf Hitler and back to the golden days of the kaiser and aristocratic rule. But Hitler, having sniffed the political winds with typically canine sensitivity, would bound ahead of the situation. And with typical lupine ruthlessness, he would order a savage bloodbath that came to be known as the *Nacht der Langen Messer* (Night of the Long Knives).*

Hitler knew that he must keep the army generals from acting against him. And he knew that their greatest fear was losing their power to the SA. Ernst Röhm wanted his SA to become the new Nazi army, with him at its head, and since he had been at Hitler's side from the earliest days of the Nazi movement, how could Hitler deny him? But Hitler was for Hitler, so if his old comrade Ernst Röhm was giving the generals concern, and thereby threatening Hitler's own future, that was another bag of peanuts. To get the generals to cool their monarchist ardor, Hitler made a preemptive deal with them. He promised to keep Röhm at bay and prevent the SA from taking over. He had not built the Third Reich only to have that bull-necked pervert Röhm spoil everything!

Thus, on June 29, the extraordinary murder spree known as the Night of the Long Knives was unleashed, a ghastly tableau of blood-letting across Germany in which hundreds of people were slain in cold blood. Some were dragged out of bed and shot in their homes; some were killed by firing squads; others were sent to eternity sitting at their desks; wives were dispatched with their husbands; and ancient enemies from the failed putsch of 1923 were avenged, one with pickaxes. It was a foretaste of things to come. By far the most brazen act of all the carnage was the killing of two army generals, von Schleicher and von Bredow.

As for Ernst Röhm, he was awakened in his hotel room, dressed down personally by an irate Hitler, and then hauled off to a prison cell in Munich, where he was suggestively sequestered with a loaded revolver. But Röhm's taste for butchery did not extend to suicide, and it fell to two of his own SA men to end his sordid life.

---

* Absurdly, it was also referred to as Operation Hummingbird.

When it was all over, Hitler claimed that a Röhm putsch had been imminent, but with the help of Providence it had been avoided. He announced that 61 had been shot, although another 13 died while "resisting arrest." Dohnanyi told Bonhoeffer that the Ministry of Justice put the figure at 207 who were methodically hunted down and murdered; in later years the figure was put at 400 or even 1,000. In any event, it was a long list, and no previous enemy of Hitler, Göring, or Himmler was excluded. It was an opportunity to sweep every traitorous scoundrel from the ranks of the living! Many more were hauled off to concentration camps. As usual, Hitler raged that he had been provoked to his actions—that a coup was in the works, that indeed his own life had been threatened, and that these murders were in the best interests of the German *Volk*, for whom no sacrifice was too great!

On July 13, Hitler gave a speech to the Reichstag:

> If anyone reproaches me and asks why I did not resort to the regular courts of justice, then all I can say is this: In this hour I was responsible for the fate of the German people, and thereby I became the supreme judge of the German people. . . . Everyone must know for all future time that if he raises his hand to strike the State, then certain death is his lot.

It all had a chilling effect on most Germans. Bonhoeffer's student Inge Karding recalled the mood that followed this episode: "A crippling fear rose up like a bad odor within you."

As for the army generals, they had landed in a difficult spot, someplace in Hitler's pocket. To be fair, they had no idea that Hitler's promise to keep Röhm from taking over the armed forces would mean a limitless massacre. Nonetheless, the plans to restore the Hohenzollern dynasty were off. After all, Hitler had kept his part of the bargain, even if he had done so through mass murder and rampant lawlessness. And as far as Hitler was concerned, that waxworks annoyance Hindenburg was now free to depart this world when he wished, and the sooner the better, since Hitler had some particular ideas about who might replace him.

Austria was also experiencing violence and political turmoil, which culminated in the July 25 assassination of Chancellor Engelbert Dollfuss by Nazi agents. A staunch Catholic in a staunchly Catholic country, Dollfuss once said,

"For me the fight against National Socialism is essentially a fight in defense of the Christian conception of the world. Whereas Hitler wants to revive the old Germanic paganism, I want to revive the Christian Middle Ages." In the wake of his murder, further violence erupted in Austria, and many feared Hitler would send troops across the border. Mussolini sent Italian troops to prevent this, which they did. A week later, Hindenburg died.

When the war hero gave up the ghost on August 2 at the age of eighty-six, Hitler—lickety-split—announced his choice for Hindenburg's replacement. He would be Hindenburg's successor! As it turned out, he would remain chancellor too. The two offices of president and chancellor would be combined in one person (*c'est moi*), as this was the will of the German people. And if anyone doubted it, the object of their affection announced a plebiscite later that month when, as one might have foreseen, 90 percent of the German people voted *Ja*. How many did so with enthusiasm and how many out of fear cannot be known.

As for the army, they had been freed of the threat of Röhm and the SA, but the SS, under the superlatively despicable Heinrich Himmler, would give them far worse trouble. Hitler could have his cake and eat it too. Hitler was never content to contemplate gains when there was still more to be grabbed. Playing on the deeply patriotic mood that attended Hindenburg's death, Hitler summoned the officers and troops of the Berlin garrison to the Königsplatz where, by flickering torchlight, they renewed their oath of allegiance. But when their hands were raised, they found themselves swearing an oath that was not what they had expected. It was not an oath to the German constitution or to the German nation, but to the fellow with the mustache. According to what they were swearing, Hitler had become the living embodiment of the German will and law. The oath came quite to the point: "I swear by God this sacred oath, that I will render unconditional obedience to Adolf Hitler, the Führer of the German Reich and people, Supreme Commander of the Armed Forces, and will be ready as a brave soldier to risk my life at any time for this oath."

They pronounced these words en masse, frozen in their formations and unable to scratch their heads at what had just happened. But what had happened was that in their hour of grief and honor, they had been magnificently snookered. Germans in general, and military men in particular, took obedience and oaths extremely seriously, and these few words, assented to under some duress, would pay handsome dividends for the Führer in the years ahead. They would make executing any plans to remove him from office, whether via assassination or otherwise, very difficult indeed, as we shall see.

General Ludwig Beck was horrified. The noble tradition of the German army had been outwitted and defrauded, duped into dragging its colors through the mud. Beck called it "the blackest day of his life." He would resign in 1938 and become one of the leaders of the plots to assassinate Hitler, culminating in the final plot that would take place on July 20, 1944, the day before Beck took his own life.

With Hindenburg's death, the German people's connection to the comfort and stability of the old order under the kaiser was severed. Hindenburg had given many a sense of security. He was thought to be a stabilizing force and a check on the wildness of Hitler. Hitler knew this and had used Hindenburg to legitimize his leadership. But now Hindenburg was gone, and the German people found themselves far from shore, alone in a boat with a madman.

CHAPTER 16

THE CONFERENCE AT FANØ

*It must be made quite clear—terrifying though it is—that we are
immediately faced with the decision: National Socialist or Christian . . .*

✧

*My calling is quite clear to me. What God will make of it I do not know
. . . I must follow the path. Perhaps it will not be such a long one.
(Phil 1:23). But it is a fine thing to have realized my calling . . . I
believe its nobility will become plain to us only in coming times and
events. If only we can hold out.*

—DIETRICH BONHOEFFER

anø is a small island in the North Sea, a mile off the coast of Denmark.
On his way there, Bonhoeffer spent a few days in Copenhagen, visiting a childhood friend who was a lawyer in the German Embassy.
He then stopped at Esbjerg to see Franz Hildebrandt. Hildebrandt explained that because of the tense political situation in Germany following the Röhm putsch, the Dollfuss murder, and Hindenburg's death, Bodelschwingh and Confessing Synod President Koch would not attend the Fanø conference. Hildebrandt would accompany Bonhoeffer to the youth conference, but would leave before Heckel and his compatriots arrived. Since he was a non-Aryan and was not operating in the relative safety of a church outside Germany, Hildebrandt thought it wiser to avoid being seen by them. Hildebrandt would fill in for Bonhoeffer at Sydenham and

St. Paul's; and Jürgen Winterhager, Bonhoeffer's former student from Berlin who had been filling in for Bonhoeffer in London, would come to Fanø to assist Bonhoeffer.

Without Koch, Bodelschwingh, or Hildebrandt at Fanø, Bonhoeffer felt somewhat alone. Julius Rieger would be there, though, as would many of Bonhoeffer's Berlin students. But Müller and the German Christians had been emboldened by the recent events. In July, Interior Minister Wilhelm Frick decreed that discussion of the church disputes, both in public assemblies and in the press, was illegal. This decree was no different from Müller's previous "muzzling decree," except that now it was the state, not the church, that had issued it, so there was no chance to dispute it. It was the law of the land. State and church were being welded together at every point.

And after Hindenburg's death, the Reichskirche, drunk on the blood of the Röhm purge, held a synod where they ratified all of Müller's previous edicts. Perhaps most ominous of all, the synod declared that henceforth every new pastor was required upon his ordination to swear an oath "of service" to Adolf Hitler. Müller, the former navy chaplain, would not be outdone by the army, who had sworn their oath of personal fealty to the Führer. The oath that new pastors would take read: "I swear before God . . . that I . . . will be true and obedient to the *Führer* of the German people and state, Adolf Hitler."

Facing these circumstances, many in the Confessing Church literally feared for their lives, especially if they planned to say something impolitic on a world stage. They also knew that Bishop Bell's "Ascension Day Message" would be raised at Fanø, putting them in an awkward position. Many in the Confessing Church were not yet where Bonhoeffer was on these issues and felt uncomfortable taking part in anything that publicly condemned Germany. Even at that late date, they considered themselves patriotic Germans first, and were wary of anyone from the countries that had brought the shame of Versailles to Germany, with all the misery and suffering that had followed it.

Only four years earlier, when he arrived at Union, Bonhoeffer shared that position, but mainly as a result of his friendship with Jean Lasserre, he had begun to change his views. His subsequent experiences with Americans such as the Lehmanns and Frank Fisher, and with the Englishman George Bell and the Swede Valdemar Ammundsen, had expanded his view of the church in a way that precious few of his countrymen could have dreamed. There was no question that his brothers and sisters in Christ around the world were closer to him than the pseudo-Christian Nazis in the Reichskirche. But he knew that many in the Confessing Church were still liable to balk at taking decisive action at Fanø.

Weeks earlier, on August 8, Bonhoeffer had written Bishop Ammundsen:

Personally, to be quite frank, I am more afraid of many of our own supporters, when I think of Fanø, than of the German Christians. It's possible that many on our side may be terribly cautious for fear of seeming unpatriotic, not so much from anxiety as rather from a false sense of honor. Many people, even those who have been doing ecumenical work for quite some time, still seem incapable of realizing or believing that we are really here together purely as *Christians*. They are dreadfully suspicious, and it prevents them from being completely open. If only you, my dear Bishop, could manage to break the ice so that these people become more trusting and open. It is precisely here, in our attitude toward the state, that we must speak out with absolute sincerity for the sake of Jesus Christ and of the ecumenical cause. It must be made quite clear—terrifying though it is—that we are immediately faced with the decision: National Socialist *or* Christian. . . .

In my opinion, a resolution ought to be drawn up—no good can come of evading it. And if the World Alliance in Germany should then be dissolved—well, all right, then we have acknowledged that we were to blame, and that's better than vegetating along in a state of insincerity. Only the *complete truth* and *complete truthfulness* can help us now. I know that many of my German friends think otherwise. But I do beg you to try and understand this idea.

As far as he was concerned, the serious Christians in the ecumenical movement constituted the church, the true church beyond borders, and he was exhorting them to behave as such. At Fanø he would do so again.

The youth conference began on August 22, and Bonhoeffer led the devotions. One participant, Margarete Hoffer, recalled, "At our first devotions we were urgently told, as the watchword for our entire conference, that our work cannot and must not consist of anything but listening together to what the *Lord* says, and in praying together that we may hear aright. Listening in faith to the words of the Bible, hearing one another as listeners who obey; this is the core of all ecumenical work." Another participant, E. C. Blackman, said, "We started in the right atmosphere, for at our devotions on the first morning Bonhoeffer reminded us that our primary object was not to commend our own views, national or individual, but to hear what God would say to us."

The radical nature of what Bonhoeffer said and did at Fanø is difficult to overstate. One may draw a direct line from Fanø to Flossenbürg eleven years later. The prison doctor at Flossenbürg, having no idea whom he was watching, later recalled: "I saw Pastor Bonhoeffer kneeling on the floor, praying fervently to God . . . so certain that God heard his prayer. . . . I have hardly ever seen a man die so entirely submissive to the will of God." This was Bonhoeffer at Fanø. What made him stand out, to some as an inspiration, to others as an oddity, and to others as an offense, was that he did not hope that God heard his prayers, but knew it. When he said they needed to humble themselves and listen to God's commands and obey them, he was not posturing. He wanted to impart this vision of God and was saying that one must utterly trust God now and must know that hearing him is indeed all that matters. Many in the ecumenical movement and in the Confessing Church obviously didn't quite believe that. But Bonhoeffer knew that God could not help them unless they acted out of faith and obedience.

On Tuesday the twenty-eighth, Bonhoeffer preached at morning worship, taking as his text Psalm 85:8: "I will hear what God the LORD will speak: for he will speak peace unto his people, and to his saints: but let them not turn again to folly." Peace was an issue of ultimate concern to him, but that August it also had an immediate aspect that would have been obvious to everyone. The murder of Dollfuss had thrown Austria into turmoil, with Germany threatening to invade at any moment. At the same time Mussolini threatened to invade Ethiopia during the Abyssinian crisis.

Bonhoeffer's hope that the youth conference would result in some bold and substantive resolutions was not disappointed. The fifty delegates drew up two resolutions. The first said that God's commandments utterly trumped any claims of the state. It passed narrowly, with many of Bonhoeffer's Berlin students registering contrary votes. The second condemned Christian support for "any war whatsoever." A Polish delegate suggested emending it to a condemnation of "aggressive war" rather than "any war whatsoever," but that was not accepted by the others. There was a lively debate on conscientious objection, which spilled out, as all the larger scheduled discussions did, into smaller conversations among the participants. The German students were brave to discuss such things.

During the days, Bonhoeffer and the youth conference participants gathered on the Fanø beaches for informal discussions. Even in that relaxed setting, they remained dressed as they were during the official meetings: most men in their jackets, ties, shoes, and socks; the women in their starched dresses. During one seaside conversation, a Swede asked Bonhoeffer what he would do if war came. It was not an abstract consideration for anyone, least of all Bonhoeffer, whose three brothers had taken up arms and who himself had taken firm steps in that direction during his two-week stint as an Igel, with the Ulm Rifles. Just eighteen months earlier, on the very day that Hitler came to power, Bonhoeffer's brother Klaus declared, "This means war!" He saw quite presciently where Hitler intended to lead the country. According to those present, Bonhoeffer quietly scooped up a handful of sand and let it run out between his fingers as he pondered the question and his answer. Then looking calmly at the young man, he replied, "I pray that God will give me the strength then not to take up a weapon."

In the middle of it all, Bonhoeffer's sense of playful wit remained intact. Otto Dudzus, one of his students from Berlin, recalled being seated next to Bonhoeffer when a Russian priest of notable girth took the floor. Bonhoeffer scribbled a humorous couplet from the German nonsense-verse poet Christian Morgenstern and slipped it to him:

> Ein dickes Kreuz auf dickem Bauch,
> Wer spürte nicht der Gottheit Hauch?*

Dudzus said Bonhoeffer's contributions to the conference's theme and overall direction "can hardly be estimated highly enough. He effectively saw to it that it did not turn into an ineffectual academic discussion." His encouragement of Ammundsen and the others to take a stand behind a real resolution on the subject of Germany was heroic and visionary. He was a terrific

---

* With a big fat cross on a big fat gut, / Who'd fail to feel the breath of God?

exhorter, and many times in his life he would help others see clearly what he saw clearly, and make the logical connections and reach the logical conclusions that he knew one must.

In the end, Bonhoeffer did not participate in the official discussions about Bell's "Ascension Day Message," but he said all that was necessary to those who would discuss it. He felt that it was in good hands with the committee that had been chosen to draft the resolution, which consisted of Bishops Bell and Ammundsen, H. L. Henriod, and four others.

One was an American, Dr. Henry Smith Leiper, who would figure prominently in Bonhoeffer's fateful 1939 trip to the United States. Bonhoeffer had known Leiper at Union, but only in a casual way. Leiper was a special lecturer when Bonhoeffer was a Sloane Fellow. But in Fanø, Bonhoeffer went to Leiper's room to talk, telling him of the situation with Heckel, and how Heckel had informed him that he must leave London. Leiper recalled their conversation:

> When I asked what his reply had been to the Bishop's order, he said with a grim smile: "Negative." Amplifying that laconic remark he said: "I told him he would have to come to London to get me if he wanted me out of that church." With utter candor and fearless scorn he talked of what the followers of Christ must be prepared to do in resisting Nazi Caesarism and its penetration of spiritual domains. From that it was quite plain to me that he was prepared to fight the régime of Ludwig Müller. Yet at no point in our conversation did he show any concern for what might be the consequences of his decision to oppose openly the whole effort of Hitlerism to take over the control of the Church in Germany. Nor did he show the least doubt that the discerning Christians would have to deal realistically with the most dangerous and unscrupulous dictator who believed that he could achieve his plan for making what he called "practical Christianity" a source of power and influence for his political platform.
>
> It was very significant that Dietrich should have had such clear insights and could have reached such bold decisions so early in the official life of Hitler's thrust into the administrative life of the churches. From my own somewhat extensive experience in many earlier visits to Germany I knew that hardly any of his colleagues were as wise and fearless as he with respect to what was afoot. Nor were many of them as

defiant—at least openly—towards the tyranny which had loomed on the horizons of their country in the "miracle" of the Third Reich. . . . Dietrich was determined to approach the problems raised by the Nazi movement not merely from a theological or philosophical point of view but with directness of action.

This was likely Bonhoeffer's most important contribution at Fanø, and in many other circumstances, rousing others to action, away from mere theologizing. His thoughts on this would be expressed in his book *Discipleship*, in which anything short of obedience to God smacked of "cheap grace." Actions must follow what one believed, else one could not claim to believe it. Bonhoeffer was pushing the delegates at Fanø to see this, and he mainly succeeded.

He certainly succeeded in marshaling the leadership to respond to Bell's "Ascension Day Message" with a resolution. Leiper and the committee gave it a ringing endorsement. As much as Bell's original message had been an open-handed and public slap at Müller, so this resolution, ratifying Bell's message, was another. And while Bell's message was that of a single British clergyman, the resolution at Fanø was the united voice of a great multitude from around the world:

> The Council declares its conviction that autocratic Church rule, especially when imposed upon the conscience in solemn oath, the use of force, and the suppression of free discussion, are incompatible with the true nature of the Christian Church, and asks in the name of the Gospel for its fellow Christians in the German Church:
>
> "Freedom to preach the Gospel of our Lord Jesus Christ and to live according to His teaching;
>
> "Freedom of the printed word and of Assembly in the service of the Christian Community;
>
> "Freedom for the Church to instruct its youth in the principles of Christianity and immunity from the compulsory imposition of a philosophy of life antagonistic to the Christian religion."

On the morning of the twenty-eighth, Bonhoeffer gave his memorable "Peace Speech" to the assembly. "From the first moment," said Dudzus, "the assembly was breathless with tension. Many may have felt that they would never forget what they had just heard." Bonhoeffer said that first and foremost, the church must hear God's Word and must obey. Those from theologically liberal backgrounds were not used to the language or the tone he used. The idea that God was speaking, demanding anything, made some uncomfortable. Dudzus said that Bonhoeffer "charged so far ahead that the conference could not follow him." But it was hard to miss the power behind the words. The twenty-eight-year-old Bonhoeffer's words from that morning are still quoted:

> There is no way to peace along the way of safety. For peace must be dared, it is itself the great venture and can never be safe. Peace is the opposite of security. To demand guarantees is to want to protect oneself. Peace means giving oneself completely to God's commandment, wanting no security, but in faith and obedience laying the destiny of the nations in the hand of Almighty God, not trying to direct it for selfish purposes. Battles are won, not with weapons, but with God. They are won when the way leads to the cross.

"He was not concerned here with the helpless exchange of open-ended questions," said Bethge, "but with the direct demand that certain decisions be risked." He was demanding—no, it was not he, but God who was demanding—that those listening obey. He "passionately exhorted this carefully convened assembly to justify its right to exist by imposing the Gospel of peace in its fullest extent." He was telling them that God had given them the power as his church to be a prophetic voice in the midst of the world, and they must take up their God-given authority and behave like the church that, by the power of the Holy Spirit, was God's answer to the problems of the world.

But who among his hearers knew what to make of it all? Bethge recalled that Bonhoeffer "used the word 'council' which must have shocked some of his listeners. But he wanted to lead them beyond the idea that they were merely an advisory or opinion-forming body. A council proclaims, commits, and resolves, and in the process commits and resolves itself." If ever Bonhoeffer was a Jeremiah or a Jonah, it was there on the island off the coast of Denmark at the end of August 1934.

His Berlin students who had been at the youth conference were not allowed to watch from the main assembly hall, where the dignitaries were gathered, but a friend of Bonhoeffer wheedled someone into letting them listen from an upstairs gallery. As soon as it was over, they were hustled out. One student recalled that Bonhoeffer's last sentences were unforgettable: "What are we waiting for? The time is late." After Bonhoeffer finished, the leader of the conference came to the podium and stated that it wasn't necessary to comment on the speech; its meaning had been clear to everyone.

In the evenings and often late into the night the Berlin students gathered to continue discussing the issues. Bonhoeffer warned them to be careful, to know who was around when they spoke. Then one day they saw a Danish newspaper with the headline: "German Youth Speak Freely: 'Hitler Wants to Be Pope.'" Someone had wormed his way into their discussions and heard them speaking about Hitler's takeover of the church. It was disastrous. Bonhoeffer was sure when they tried to reenter Germany, they would encounter difficulties. He did all he could to defuse the situation, playing it down in conversations on the phone and with others at the conference. In the end nothing happened. Germany was not yet a police state.

Heckel and other members of the Reichskirche delegation were at the Fanø conference, but they were about their master's business, which consisted of saying as little of substance as possible. Heckel evaded speaking on the Jewish question by pursuing a strategy of double-barreled flatulence: on the twenty-fifth he delivered a paper on ecumenical issues that lasted an hour and a half; two days later he delivered a paper on church and state. The London *Times* called the first speech "a brilliant ascent into the stratosphere of pure ecclesiastical dogma." Somehow word reached Müller that Heckel was not making the crackerjack impression one had hoped. Leaving nothing to chance, he immediately dispatched a special envoy, Walter Birnbaum, along with Dr. August Jäger, the ruthless crank who had called the incarnation a "burst of Nordic light into world history." The two men hustled to Copenhagen, only to discover that the ecumenical conference was being held at Fanø on the other side of Denmark. With the Reichskirche's image at stake, they resourcefully chartered a sea plane and zoomed two hundred miles west before making their doubly splashy entrance, to the great consternation of Heckel.

Jäger did not speak, but his colleague's theology was no less buggy. Birnbaum requested permission to address the assembly and coughed up a flowery garland of anecdotes about some Germans who had become Christians as a result of National Socialism. Julius Rieger deemed it "absurd rigmarole." Heckel was nettled that the Reichsbischof had felt the need to send these two; their presence and comments made his position even more difficult. But Heckel knew how to game the system at these conferences as well as anyone. Once again he laced on his skates and zipped about confusingly to the best of his abilities: he denied certain things outright, lodged protests, inserted boilerplate baloney into the official minutes, and deadpanned that the situation in Germany was better than ever for "proclaiming the Gospel."

Nonetheless, to Bonhoeffer's delight, the conference voted through a resolution that declared "grave anxiety" at the situation in Germany. It said that "vital principles of Christian liberty" had been threatened and declared that the use of force, "an autocratic church rule," and "the suppression of free discussion" were "incompatible with the true nature of the Christian Church." It went on: "The Council desires to assure its brethren in the Confessional Synod of the German Evangelical Church of its prayers and heartfelt sympathy in their witness to the principles of the Gospel and of its resolve to maintain close fellowship with them."

What especially stung was that Koch, the president of the Confessing Synod, was openly and pointedly elected to the Universal Council of the World Alliance. Heckel protested bitterly, but in vain. There was one action, however, that justified the Nazis' expense in sending him there. He lobbied for a small, seemingly benign insertion to the resolution, saying that the council wanted to stay in "friendly contact with all of the groups in the German Evangelical Church." Doing that effectively put the Reichskirche *and the Confessing Church* in the category of "groups," which was devastating for the future. Bonhoeffer's claim that the Confessing Church was in fact *the* German church, and that the German Christians and their Reichskirche were heretical and could not be recognized as the German church, had been defused by Bishop Heckel's deft parliamentary procedure.

At the time, however, that was not evident. Bonhoeffer thought they had achieved a bold leap forward, and future ecumenical conferences would build on their progress. Everyone was buoyant. But according to Bethge, the ecumenical movement would never go any further in its commitment to the Confessing Church. "Fanø," he wrote, "did not represent a first step, but a short-lived climax."

Göttingen

Before returning to London, Bonhoeffer would do some more traveling. His first trip was to Göttingen to see Sabine and her family. Things might get markedly worse at any time, so that year they bought a car in case they needed to get away for any reason. They would, and soon enough. They already left Göttingen frequently and stayed with her parents in Berlin, where the situation was less volatile for Jews. At school their daughters, Marianne and Christiane, were sometimes subjected to ridicule. Sabine remembered:

> One little friend actually called out to [Christiane] over the fence, "Your father is a Jew." One day a notice-board was fixed to one of the trees in front of the school on which was written "The Father of the Jew is the Devil." Every day our two children passed under this piece of rabble-rousing on their way to school. Then a box with the Nazi newspaper *Der Stürmer* with its abominations was set up opposite the school. It contained anti-Semitic matter, fantastic accounts of sexual crimes and sadistic ritual acts allegedly practised by the Jews and fabricated stories of the most obscene kind. The elder school children thronged in front of this.

The Leibholzes' house was on the Herzberger Landstrasse, where many Göttingen professors had homes. The SA often marched down the street on Sunday mornings. Many years later, Sabine said, "It still makes me shudder to remember their marching songs, 'Soldiers, comrades, hang the Jews, shoot the Jews.'" Dietrich's love for his twin sister was no small part of the courage that he sometimes showed in his dealings with the Nazis.

After Göttingen, Bonhoeffer went to Würzburg and met with some Confessing Church leaders. In his standard role of leader and exhorter, he helped them acknowledge that they were indeed a church and not just a movement, and he persuaded them to declare so emphatically and promptly. They finally did so at Dahlem that October. Their failure to be clear about this earlier had cost them dearly at Fanø, and they mustn't let it happen again. They also discussed Müller's upcoming consecration and the importance of keeping ecumenical figures away.

Next, Bonhoeffer visited Jean Lasserre in his working-class parish in France's Artois region. A number of the ecumenical delegates met there after Fanø. Some of them went out and did street preaching. Lasserre marveled at Bonhoeffer's ease in communicating with people so different from him and his circumstances: "He really spoke the Gospel to the people in the street."

CHAPTER 17

THE ROAD TO ZINGST AND FINKENWALDE

It is high time we broke with our theologically based restraint towards the state's actions—which, after all, is only fear. "Speak out for those who cannot speak." Who in the church today realizes that this is the very least that the Bible requires of us?

The restoration of the church must surely depend on a new kind of monasticism, which has nothing in common with the old but a life of uncompromising discipleship, following Christ according to the Sermon on the Mount. I believe the time has come to gather people together to do this.

—Dietrich Bonhoeffer

Back in London, Bonhoeffer wondered what he would do next. Because of his talents and family connections, there were always many possibilities, and he seemed to like keeping his options open.

Earlier that year, the leaders of the Confessing Church realized they must think about opening their own seminaries. The Reichskirche required that all university theological students prove their Aryan racial purity. The previous June, Jacobi and Hildebrandt suggested that Bonhoeffer run a Confessing

Church seminary. A month later, Niemöller assigned Bonhoeffer to take over the Berlin-Brandenburg district seminary, effective the following January, but Bonhoeffer was hardly settled on it. Synod President Koch preferred that Bonhoeffer remain in London, but if he wanted to continue his studies at the University of Berlin, he needed to decide soon; his leave of absence could not last forever. Although academia had lost its charms for him, Bonhoeffer hated to have the possibility of it taken away.

On September 11 he wrote Erwin Sutz:

> I am hopelessly torn between staying here, going to India and return-ing to Germany to take charge of a preachers' seminary shortly to be opened there. I no longer believe in the university, and never really have believed in it—to your irritation. The entire education of the younger generation of theologians belongs today in church cloister-like schools, in which pure doctrine, the Sermon on the Mount and worship are taken seriously—as they never are (and in present circum-stances couldn't be) at the university. It is also high time we broke with our theologically based restraint towards the state's actions—which, after all, is only fear. "Speak out for those who cannot speak"—who in the church today realizes that this is the very least that the Bible requires of us?

One week later he made his decision. He would accept the director-ship of the new Confessing Church seminary. But he said he could not start till spring. He planned to prepare for the experience by using the remain-ing months of 1934 traveling across England, making a study of a number of Christian communities. After that he would finally go to India and visit Gandhi, as he had long planned to do. But it was now part of his larger thinking on how God meant for Christians to live. As the church battle and the political situation grew difficult, he wondered if Gandhi's methods of Christian social resistance were something God was calling the church toward. Was that how he and other Christians were supposed to fight? Was the idea of winning the current church struggle, as they were now fighting it, a red herring?

He knew something was deeply wrong with the church as it then existed, and not just with the Reichskirche and the German Christians, but with the best of the church, with the Confessing Church, and with the current form of Christianity in Germany in general. He felt that what was especially missing from the life of Christians in Germany was the day-to-day reality of dying to self, of following Christ with every ounce of one's being in every moment, in every part of one's life. This dedication and fire existed among pietist groups like the Herrnhüter, but he thought that they bordered on being "works" oriented and overly "religious" in the Barthian sense. They had pushed away from the "world" too much, had pushed away the very best of culture and education in a way that he didn't feel was right. Christ must be brought into every square inch of the world and the culture, but one's faith must be shining and bright and pure and robust. It must be free of cant and "phraseology" and mere religiosity, or the Christ whom one was bringing into the world and the culture was not Christ at all, but a tawdry man-made counterfeit. Bonhoeffer advocated a Christianity that seemed too worldly for traditional Lutheran conservatives and too pietistic for theological liberals. He was too much something for everyone, so both sides misunderstood and criticized him.

In any case, he had long felt that Gandhi could provide some clues for him. Gandhi was not a Christian, but he lived in a community that endeavored to live by the teachings set forth in the Sermon on the Mount. Bonhoeffer wanted Christians to live that way. So he would travel to India to see it practiced by non-Christians. At Fanø he asked the assembled Christians: "Must we be put to shame by the non-Christian people in the East? Shall we desert the individuals who are risking their lives for this message?" Was it possible that, just as Christ had been sent to the Gentiles "to provoke his own people (the Jews) to jealousy," Christ was operating among non-Christians in a way that could force the church to action? That May, he had written his grandmother:

> Before I tie myself down anywhere for good, I'm thinking again of going to India. I've given a good deal of thought lately to the issues there and believe that there could be important things to be learned. In any case it sometimes seems to me that there's more Christianity in their "heathenism" than in the whole of our Reichskirche. Christianity did in fact come from the East originally, but it has become so westernized and so permeated by civilized thought that, as we can now see, it is almost lost to us. Unfortunately I have little confidence left in

the church opposition. I don't at all like the way they're going about things and really dread the time when they assume responsibility and we may be compelled yet again to witness a terrible compromising of Christianity.

Bonhoeffer was already looking beyond the Confessing Church, whose birth he had only just midwifed. He saw too much compromise already. One thing was certain: the evil of Hitler could not be defeated with mere religion. He longed to see a church that had an intimate connection with Christ and was dedicated to hearing God's voice and obeying God's commands, come what may, including the shedding of blood. But how could one hear the voice of God, much less obey God, when prayer and meditating on the Scriptures were not even being taught in German seminaries? Neither were worship and singing taught. He would teach all of that in the seminary he was going to run, come spring.

Meanwhile, Barth was attempting to meet with Hitler. Many in the Confessing Church still thought Hitler might be reasoned with. The war and the death camps and the Final Solution were years in the future. There was still hope that this madman might not be so mad after all or that his wildness might yet be domesticated. Bonhoeffer had already seen through this, which was why he was already looking far past it for something else, something more pure and true. He had long moved past thinking that anything currently being discussed might be the solution. In his letter to Sutz, he referred to Barth's idea:

From now on, I believe, any discussion between Hitler and Barth would be quite pointless—indeed, no longer to be sanctioned. Hitler has shown himself quite plainly for what he is, and the church ought to know with whom it has to reckon. Isaiah didn't go to Sennacherib either. We have tried often enough—too often—to make Hitler aware of what is going on. Maybe we've not yet gone about it in the right way, but then Barth won't go about it the right way either. Hitler is not in a position to listen to us; he is *obdurate*, and as such he must compel *us* to listen—it's that way round. The Oxford movement was naïve enough to try and convert Hitler—a ridiculous failure to recognize what is going on. *We* are the ones to be converted, not Hitler.

In an earlier letter to Sutz he had referred to Hitler as a Sennacherib figure. He seemed to believe that the utter wickedness of Hitler, like that of Sennacherib, would cleanse the church, would blow away the chaff. But why hadn't others yet seen this? Why had people like the evangelist Frank Buchman been taken in by Hitler, thinking they might be able to convert him? Why didn't others see that unless they first recognized evil, it would continue to have power and cause destruction? In this letter, Bonhoeffer referred to Karl Brandt, who was Hitler's personal physician, and whom Sutz met on an Alpine tour.

> What sort of man is Brandt? I don't understand how any man can stay on in Hitler's entourage, unless he is either a Nathan or else shares the guilt for what happened on June 30 and July 25, and for the lie served up on August 19—and shares the guilt for the next war! Please forgive me, but for me these things are really so serious, I don't feel like being witty about them anymore.

Bonhoeffer's asking about Brandt helps us understand what life must have been like for Germans in the Third Reich, especially in the early days when most people were still completely in the dark about what lay ahead, and about what Hannah Arendt so famously called the "banality of evil." Bonhoeffer wondered how someone could keep company with Adolf Hitler, whom he knew had given himself over to evil, and he wondered about what kind of man Brandt was.

Sutz didn't know, but history tells us that Brandt was the principal architect and codirector of the T-4 euthanasia program in which scores of thousands of persons with mental and physical disabilities were removed from hospitals and places like Bodelschwingh's Bethel community and murdered. Brandt also performed innumerable forced abortions on women deemed "genetically inferior," "racially deficient" (Jewish), or mentally or physically disabled. Abortions were legal except in the cases of "healthy Aryan" fetuses. Brandt also oversaw and participated in many of the unspeakably sadistic "medical experiments" carried out on concentration camp inmates. In fact, he was the lead medical defendant at the Nuremberg trials, where he was convicted and sentenced to death. Vocally unrepentant to the bitter end, he was hanged in 1948.

The Church Struggle Continues

On September 23, a tacky riot of swastikas and a brown-shirted honor guard sullied the hallowed Lutheran ground of the Berlin Cathedral. It was the "consecration" of Reichsbischof Johann Heinrich Ludwig Müller. But ecumenical leaders from around the civilized world skipped the gaudy spectacle, turning the beef-witted Müller's moment of triumph into a lonely Nazi farce. Still, Müller felt that at long last he had received his due, and he would honor his beloved Führer by bringing unity to the German Evangelical Church, even if he must do it with an ax.

A few days later, Bonhoeffer received a mysterious postcard from Franz Hildebrandt. It said only "Luke 14:11." It was the verse for the day of Müller's ceremony, and Bonhoeffer would have instantly gotten the joke. It was Jesus' words for the Pharisees—and Hildebrandt's words for Müller: "For every one who exalts himself will be humbled, and he who humbles himself will be exalted" (NIV). As it turned out, the words were not merely appropriate, but prophetic. No sooner had the ceremony ended than all hell broke loose. The church struggle burst into flame again, and within no time the Reichsbischof was in Dutch with the displeased Führer.

The trouble began when the saber-scarred Dr. August Jäger had within a single week placed the bishops of Württemberg and Bavaria under house arrest. Jäger did most of Müller's dirtiest work, but this time, it backfired badly. Supporters of both bishops took to the streets, and suddenly the world press was again focused on the German church's troubles. *Time*'s coverage was particularly embarrassing:

> A wildly enthusiastic crowd hustled the brave Bishop into his automobile, swept the police and S.S. troops aside, trotted beside the car all the way to his house shouting *"Heil* Meisser! *Pfui* Müller!" Another crowd stayed by the church, solemnly chanting Martin Luther's great "Ein feste Burg ist unser Gott!" . . . [The following day the] angry crowd tramped off to assemble in front of Nazidom's holiest shrine, Adolf Hitler's original Brown House. While S.S. Troops stood undecidedly on guard, the Protestants spat at the bronze swastikas on either side of the door, yelled defiance at Bishop Müller and Adolf Hitler himself. . . . [T]he Meisserites published a bitter manifesto:

"In a Church which calls itself a church of the gospel, the gospel is cast out and despotism and lying have gained control. . . . Realm Bishop Ludwig Müller and August Jaeger are responsible for this ravagement. Satan does his work through them. Therefore we cry to God to make us free."

In the meantime, the members of the Confessing Church thought it time for another synod. They needed to officially establish themselves as a church by creating an administrative organization, and on October 19 they convened in Dahlem, issuing the famous Dahlem Resolution: "We call upon the Christian congregations, their pastors and elders, to ignore any instructions received from the former Reichskirche government and its authorities and to refrain from cooperating with those who wish to continue to obey that same church government. We call upon them to adhere to the directions of the Confessional synod of the German Evangelical Church and its recognized bodies."

No one could say they weren't an official church anymore. Bonhoeffer was quite pleased. The synod also enacted a resolution accusing Müller of violating the constitution of the German Evangelical Church.

Bonhoeffer heard from his brother-in-law Dohnanyi that as a result of these very public troubles, Hitler had begun to turn his attention to the church struggle. He couldn't trust Müller to keep the lid on the situation, so he took matters into his own hands. He revoked the high-handed legislation that the Reichskirche had enacted that summer and publicly distanced himself from the Reich church. Then in a burst of Nordic light, August Jäger resigned. Things were looking up for the Confessing Church.

Bonhoeffer knew they must act on what they had resolved at Dahlem, and quickly, because Müller was neither down nor out, but had only been a little bloodied and would soon be counterpunching. Bonhoeffer made plans to attend a meeting of all German pastors in England, on November 5, at Christ Church in London. Forty-four vestry members and clergy representing nine congregations attended. Bonhoeffer and Julius Rieger spoke. Out of the meeting came a resolution that thrilled Bonhoeffer: "The elders assembled here in Christ Church declare that they intrinsically hold the same position as the Confessing Church, and that they will immediately initiate the necessary negotiations with the church authorities arising from this." Bonhoeffer wrote Bell with the news: "I am very happy about it."

Things had to be formalized, so copies of the resolution were sent to Heckel in the Foreign Office and to Karl Koch at the Confessing Synod, and a letter was enclosed:

> The German Evangelical congregations in Great Britain have heard with great pleasure that, as a result of the Führer's declarations, the conscious profession of loyalty to the Third Reich and its Führer is not identical with membership in any one church group. These congregations have been based, some of them for centuries, upon the Bible and the Confession, and therefore consider the Confessional church to be the rightful successor of the German Evangelical Church Federation.

One may imagine Heckel's gorge rising. Worse yet, the rebellion was in danger of spreading around the world: the proactive London pastors had sent a copy of the resolution with a separate letter to other German congregations overseas, urging them to take a stand on the resolution. For Heckel, this was grievous news. On November 13 Heckel telephoned the German Embassy in London and spoke with First Secretary Prince Bismarck, saying that the pastors' action might result in "unfavorable international repercussions." Bismarck was unmoved and replied that it wasn't in his jurisdiction to do anything about it. Looking for a point of leverage, Heckel then telephoned one of the pastors, Pastor Shreiner at the German Church in Liverpool. He learned enough to understand that the pastors were not united with Bonhoeffer on every issue. He would try to exploit their differences. He also discovered procedural irregularities he could make use of. To secede, each church was to submit a written notice from its own church council. This had not been done, and Heckel surmised that if he dealt with each church individually, he would find less resolve and more points of difference. But there was something else he might do. Although Müller's star had begun to wane, he was still despised enough by the Confessing Church opposition that his dismissal would cheer them greatly. Perhaps Heckel could bump Müller out of the sled to slow the Confessing wolves.

Helmut Rössler

Finally Heckel contacted the young pastor of a German congregation in Heerlen, Holland, and persuaded him to side against the London pastors.

Perhaps he would help persuade the others in the "diaspora," too, by sending a "circular letter" to them in which he explained the dangers of jumping ship to the Confessing Church? The young pastor had just begun his pastorate and was willing to be of service. He sent an eloquently persuasive letter to the twenty overseas pastors in France, Luxembourg, Belgium, and Holland. It's unclear how or why Bonhoeffer received the letter, or whether the pastor sent it to him out of courtesy, but when Bonhoeffer did receive it, he was knocked backward. Its author was his old friend Helmut Rössler. Rössler had been one of the fellow students in Berlin chosen to oppose Bonhoeffer's doctoral thesis, along with Bonhoeffer's brother-in-law Walter Dress. In the spring of 1927 he and Walter had even come to Friedrichsbrunn. They had lost touch with each other, and now Rössler had surfaced on the side of the enemy. It was a grievous development.

In his letter, Rössler argued that the German Evangelical Churches abroad must not join the Confessing Church. If the Confessing Church won, he said, "the Church Struggle might well end in a drift toward the establishment of free churches, as in America, in which event the tie that has existed since Luther's day between the Evangelical Church and the German state would cease to be." Of course, Bonhoeffer had seen the American system and thought it a fine idea. It was certainly far better than remaining in a church that was patently no longer the church. Rössler also pointed out that joining the Confessing Church would jeopardize one's funding:

> I can well understand that many colleagues in the ministry might have a sense of belonging inwardly to the Confessing Church and would not understand why they shouldn't simply give way to it. But as things are now, to do so would be to stab the Church Foreign Office in the back, just when, aware of its ultimate responsibility for German Protestantism worldwide, it is struggling to find a real solution for the *whole* church that does not necessitate the complete disintegration of what now exists. . . . [I]ndividual demonstrative acts by congregations abroad could do more harm than good, quite aside from the fact that congregations abroad that intervene in internal German church disputes may at any time easily incur accusations of treason and have a hard time refuting them.

Rössler's cynical mention of *Dolchstoss* (stab-in-the-back) and treason must have set Bonhoeffer off. For someone so famously controlled, he
responded with an obviously emotional letter on November 20:

My dear Rössler,
And so the two of us meet again! in such an official way and once again,
on opposite sides of an issue. . . . I really and truly hadn't expected
this—that you had listened to Heckel's siren song. . . . And there is
even everyone's favorite cheap shot, "treason against our fatherland."
That you fell under the spell of these siren songs, like an innocent
youngster—I'm amazed and wish I could still be that innocent. I was,
for a long time, especially with regard to the Foreign Office, until I got
to know it better. . . . Heckel's path . . . is the path of good tactics but
not the path of faith. . . . I know the arguments in favor of Heckel's line
by heart. But the line is false. It is not we who would "stab the Church
Foreign Office in the back" but rather the Foreign Office itself that is
betraying our congregations abroad to a pseudo-church for the con-
temptible purpose of getting the pastors paid.

Bonhoeffer was especially disgusted to know that Heckel, who had
always pretended to be above the fray and not in the German Christian
camp, had been at the Berlin Cathedral to give his blessing at Müller's instal-
lation as Reichsbischof:

This, instead of refusing to associate himself with the powers of darkness—what does Christ have to do with Belial? . . . What is called
for here is an immediate, uncompromising No. There *is* no more communion between us and this kind of a church, and since that is so, we
should say so. We have waited long enough. . . . I know, and can document it with the definitive testimony of a colleague, that Heckel told a
colleague . . . that he had to become a German Christian! Furthermore
he has defended that church regime when he was here and to ecumenical partners as well. . . . He demanded a written declaration from me
that I would withdraw from all ecumenical activities. He ordered me to
fly to Berlin for this purpose, but of course he didn't get my signature!
Finally, if one really looks at this "situation of the whole church," one

should draw the right conclusions and realize that the supposed integrity of the Church Foreign Office cannot allow it to preserve its tie with a church regime that is so unchristian. . . . [T]here is no credible excuse for the use of tactics when it comes to a central decision in and of faith. That is what this is all about. Here in London we hope that we have made such a decision; since then we feel confident, whatever may happen. It was no longer possible to act otherwise.

Finally it grew rancorous:

Now to a personal question. Did Heckel ask you to write this letter or did he know you were writing it? Its scope is too precisely directed toward us here in London for us not to suspect this. Furthermore, we thought we detected that the envelopes had been addressed on the Foreign Office typewriter! I would regret this alliance very deeply. . . . I used to have quite good relations with Heckel—almost a friendship, so this whole business is doubly painful for me. On a human basis I sometimes feel terribly sorry for him. But there's nothing for it; we have chosen separate ways. And now I am honestly afraid that our friendship too, yours and mine, is threatened by such a parting of the ways. So I am asking you, could we not get together some time? We could clear up so many things! I look forward to your reply soon. Best regards to your wife.

As ever,
Dietrich Bonhoeffer

Rössler wrote his response to Bonhoeffer on December 6. Their exchange affords a rare and poignant window into how complicated and painful this church struggle must have been. Rössler was obviously no unthinking party hack.

My dear Bonhoeffer,
I'll begin my answer at the end: would you be able to be, and remain, friends with a Communist? Yes! With a Frenchman? Yes! With a Mohammedan, a Hindu, or a heathen of the Batak faith? I would think so. With a Christian, a German, who "betrays the gospel"??—well, I don't think that's what I am. But I protest with all my might against

seeing the relation between the opposing sides in the church today as the fulfillment of Matt. 10:35.* The differences may lie deep as an abyss, but they have absolutely no effect on blood relationships and bonds of friendship; they are poles apart in matters of the mind, but not of faith! So even if you were a fanatic of the Confessing Church . . . I would not take this to mean any destruction of our relationship with each other. I could not make any sense of that at all. My opinion of intellectual differences and battles is much too low, compared with my high estimation of the true mystery of our calling and mission in history, to allow me to think otherwise.

2. Of course I wrote my circular letter by agreement with Heckel, to give my brothers in the ministry abroad some insight into the struggles and the position of our church authorities. I am in no way ashamed of this "alliance," not even if it leaves me open to the charge of being too ambitious. . . .

3. If you are going to call me an innocent youngster, then I will have to call you a naïve child, if you equate the Confessing Church with Christ and Müller's government with Belial. Only once in your letter did you mention any foreboding that the Confessing Church could also be a tactical path that attracts all sorts of people. How can it escape our notice that this is already the case, that it is already a collection of the most disparate minds, from [theologically liberal] neo-Protestantism to the [conservative fundamentalist] sanctification sects and fanatics of the confessions, all working together? The Confessing Church isn't any more the true church than the German Christian Church. The true church lies hidden within each of them.

Some of this must have struck a chord, especially Rössler's points concerning the Confessing Church. We have no record of a response from Bonhoeffer, but he may have partly responded to it by leaving the church struggle and training young Confessing Church ordinands how to become disciples of Jesus Christ so that they might go out and do the same. In any case, that's what he would soon do.

---

* "For I am come to set a man . . . against his father, and the daughter against her mother."

During the fall of 1934, as he was still in the middle of the church struggle, Bonhoeffer's pastoral life in London continued. At his St. Paul's church, he sang in a choir performance of Brahms's *Requiem*. And he worked with refugees at St. George's.

Hitler's endless campaign to undo the Versailles Treaty now reached westward, toward the Saar region. He announced there would be a plebiscite in January to determine whether the inhabitants of the Saar wanted to become a part of Germany. When Hitler came to power in 1933, many Communists and other enemies of his found asylum in the Saar region. Bonhoeffer and Julius Rieger knew that if the German-speaking inhabitants voted to join the Third Reich, that asylum would end and thousands of German refugees would head toward London. Bishop Bell also worked with refugees, so much so that at one point he considered leaving his diocese to devote himself exclusively to this work.

Hitler was also continuing his efforts to establish warmer relations with England. As part of this initiative, the Nazi Foreign Minister Joachim von Ribbentrop paid a visit to Bishop Bell on November 6. Bell used the meeting to forthrightly detail the serious abuses to which Confessing Church pastors had been subjected in the Third Reich. Ribbentrop and his family lived in Dahlem, and in preparation for his role as an ambassador to Great Britain he had approached Martin Niemöller about joining the church, saying, "The English will expect it of me." Predictably, Niemöller judged this reason "utterly insufficient" and did not comply. Ribbentrop returned to visit Bell again in 1935. Later that year Bell had the dubious honor of meeting with Hitler's beetle-browed deputy, Rudolf Hess.

Bishop Bell's prominence made him tremendously helpful to Bonhoeffer, who needed introductions to the heads of Christian colleges around England as he prepared for his tour of them. Bell also wrote to Gandhi in India, trying to help Bonhoeffer finalize the plans for his long-delayed trip there:

> A friend of mine, a young man, at present German Pastor in London . . . is most anxious that I should give him an introduction to you. I can most heartily commend him. He expects to be in India for the first two or three months of 1935. . . . He is a very good theologian, a most earnest man, and is probably to have charge of the training of Ordination candidates for the Ministry in the future Confessional Church of Germany.

He wants to study community life as well as methods of training. It would be a very great kindness if you could let him come to you.

In early November, Bonhoeffer's mail included a letter from India:

Dear friend,
I have your letter. If you . . . have enough money for return passage and can pay your expenses here . . . you can come whenever you like. The sooner the better so as to get the benefit of such cold weather as we get here. . . . With reference to your desire to share my daily life, I may say that you will be staying with me if I am out of prison and settled in one place when you come. But otherwise . . . you will have to be satisfied with remaining in or near one of the institutions that are being conducted under my supervision. If . . . you can live on the simple vegetarian food that these institutions can supply you, you will have nothing to pay for your boarding and lodging. Yours sincerely, [Gandhi]

In mid-January, Dietrich wrote his eldest brother to tell him about choosing to lead an illegal seminary. Karl-Friedrich was not a Christian and had for some time been a socialist in his thinking and politics, but Bonhoeffer always felt the freedom to speak to him honestly:

Perhaps I seem to you rather fanatical and mad about a number of things. I myself am sometimes afraid of that. But I know that the day I became more "reasonable," to be honest, I should have to chuck my entire theology. When I first started in theology, my idea of it was quite different—rather more academic, probably. Now it has turned into something else altogether. But I do believe that at last I am on the right track, for the first time in my life. I often feel quite happy about it. I only worry about being so afraid of what other people will think as to get bogged down instead of going forward. I think I am right in saying that I would only achieve true inner clarity and honesty by really starting to take the Sermon on the Mount seriously. Here alone lies the force that can blow all of this idiocy sky-high—like fireworks, leaving only a few burnt-out shells behind.

The restoration of the church must surely depend on a new kind of monasticism, which has nothing in common with the old but a life of uncompromising discipleship, following Christ according to the Sermon on the Mount. I believe the time has come to gather people together and do this.

Forgive me for these rather personal ramblings, but they just came to me as I thought about our time together recently. And after all, we do have an interest in each other. I still have a hard time thinking that you really find all these ideas of mine completely mad. Things do exist that are worth standing up for without compromise. To me it seems that peace and social justice are such things, as is Christ himself.

I recently came across the fairy tale of "The Emperor's New Clothes," which really is relevant for our time. All we are lacking today is the child who speaks up at the end. We ought to put it on as a play.

I hope to hear from you soon—in any case, my birthday is coming soon.

Warm greetings to you all,
Dietrich

 CHAPTER 18

ZINGST AND FINKENWALDE

Theological work and real pastoral fellowship can only grow in a life which is governed by gathering round the Word morning and evening and by fixed times of prayer.

Do not try to make the Bible relevant. Its relevance is axiomatic . . . Do not defend God's Word, but testify to it . . . Trust to the Word.

—DIETRICH BONHOEFFER

onhoeffer preached his last sermons in London on March 10, and shortly afterward he left for his tour of Christian communities. As for the trip to Gandhi, it was postponed yet again. Bonhoeffer visited Low Church Anglican communities, such as Wycliffe Hall, Oxford, and High Church Anglican communities too. He visited a Quaker community near Birmingham and a Methodist college in Richmond. He visited Presbyterian, Congregationalist, and Baptist communities, ending up on March 30 in Edinburgh, where he visited his Union teacher, John Baillie.

On April 15 he left London for Berlin, to report for duty as the imminent head of the first seminary in the Confessing Church. Twenty-three ordinands were ready, but there was still no place to house them, although many of them had already arrived in Berlin. Two days later, Bonhoeffer and Franz Hildebrandt drove around Berlin's Brandenburg district, looking at possible

properties. Nothing was found. They were offered the use of a church building called Burkhardt House in Berlin, until then the home of educational and
social service offices. It was a decidedly pedestrian alternative to the idyllic
locations that Bonhoeffer had been visiting—there were no greenswards or
sheep-proof ha-has—but he was grateful for anything. Still, his dream of
creating something along the lines of the monastic communities he had seen
in those greener settings would be difficult to realize here.

Then on April 25, he received word that the Rhineland Bible School on
the Baltic coast was available until June 14. The ramshackle retreat center,
intended for summer use, lay just behind the dunes and beach, which at that
time of the year could be brutally cold and windy. But there were a half-
timbered farmhouse and a number of unheated thatched cottages where the
ordinands could live. Everyone was young and up for an adventure, including Bonhoeffer. The next day Bonhoeffer led his flock of ordinands two hundred miles north to the sea, there to inaugurate the experiment in Christian
living he had been dreaming about.

Zingst

Until one day in 1874, Zingst was an island in the Baltic Sea. Then a storm
created a hundred-yard-wide land bridge to the Pomeranian coast, overnight transforming the island into a peninsula, which it has remained. It was
to that young peninsula that Bonhoeffer and his ordinands traveled, at the
end of April 1935, with the plan of opening a seminary in the brand-new
Confessing Church.

In this resort village, Bonhoeffer would bring into being what had been
forming in his mind for years. When Martin Niemöller asked Bonhoeffer to
run a seminary on behalf of the Confessing Church, he had no idea what
they had set in motion. Bonhoeffer could be theologically unpredictable, so
as a gentle bulwark against this, they sent along Wilhelm Rott as his assistant.
Rott was known to be of sound, solid theology. But Rott never had cause to
question Bonhoeffer's theology or methods, nor was he aware that he had
been sent there for this reason. It all seemed perfectly natural as it unfolded,
perhaps because a good number of the ordinands had been Bonhoeffer's students in Berlin, and were used to his methods.

Bonhoeffer had in mind a kind of monastic community, where one aimed to live in the way Jesus commanded his followers to live in his Sermon on the Mount, where one lived not merely as a theological student, but as a disciple of Christ. It would be an unorthodox experiment in communal Christian living, in the "life together" as Bonhoeffer would so famously put it. No one in the Lutheran tradition had ever tried such a thing. The knee-jerk reaction away from anything that smacked of Roman Catholicism was strong, but Bonhoeffer had long before moved past such parochialism and was willing to bear criticisms. He felt that Lutheran Christianity had slid away from Luther's intentions, just as Luther felt that the Roman Catholic Church had moved away from St. Peter's and, more important, from Christ's. Bonhoeffer was interested in a Holy Spirit–led course adjustment that hardly signaled something new.

In his book *Discipleship*, Bonhoeffer would deal with the theological aspect of this Lutheran drift away from Luther's initial understanding of gratitude for God's grace and toward the ingratitude of what he called cheap grace. Bonhoeffer saw that a large part of the problem was Lutheran theological education, which produced not disciples of Christ, but out-of-touch theologians and clerics whose ability to live the Christian life—and to help others live that life—was not much in evidence. The rubber and the road were strangers, and the church was out of touch with the people to whom it was supposed to minister. As far as that went, Ludwig Müller and the German Christians were dead on in some of their criticisms, but their soapy solution was simply to be a dedicated National Socialist. To them, all that business about doctrine was folderol that didn't matter to the man in the street. Bonhoeffer's attitude was that it must be made real to the man in the street, and that was where the church was failing. That's what this experiment on the Baltic seashore was all about.

The actual location was remote, about a hundred yards from the dunes, with a main building and some outbuildings. They couldn't see any other farmhouses, and they were a mile from the small town of Zingst itself. Bonhoeffer must have smiled to learn that, just a few miles south, lay the small town of Barth.

Four of the twenty-three ordinands came from Saxony, Eberhard Bethge among them. They were at the official preachers' seminary in Wittenberg, but had chosen to side with the Dahlemites of the Confessing Church, so Müller had them expelled. Bethge arrived a day or two later, on one of the last days of April, just after the evening meal. He immediately ran out to the beach, where everyone was playing soccer, as they often did at that part of the day. He greeted his three friends from his hometown of Magdeburg and asked where *Herr Direktor* was. They pointed out Bonhoeffer. Bethge had never heard of him before and knew nothing of his leadership in the church struggle. Bethge was surprised at how young and athletic Bonhoeffer looked, and at first he found it impossible to differentiate him from the students. When Bonhoeffer finally realized that another ordinand had arrived, he left what he was doing, greeted Bethge, and invited him to take a walk along the beach.

Bonhoeffer asked Bethge about his family and upbringing, the expulsion by Müller, and his experiences in the church struggle. Bethge was taken aback that the head of this new seminary would ask such personal questions and take such a sincere interest in him. The ordinands were used to a great gap between them and their teachers, and when Bonhoeffer, a few days later, asked them not to call him *Herr Direktor*, but *Bruder* (Brother) Bonhoeffer, they were amazed.

As they walked and talked on the beach that evening, neither young man could imagine how important their meeting would seem later. They had quite different upbringings. One was a sophisticate from the exclusive Grunewald circle of Berlin, whose father was a famous doctor, skeptical of his son's choice of profession; the other was a simple country boy from the small village of Zitz, in Saxony, where his father was a village pastor who had inspired his son to follow in his footsteps. Bethge's father had died twelve years earlier.

The two men soon saw that they were more in tune with each other than anyone else in their lives. Each had extraordinary intellectual and aesthetic sensibilities in literature, art, and music. They didn't know they would soon become such close friends that many of the other ordinands would grow jealous of their relationship. They had no inkling that their friendship, not yet begun, would become the means by which Bonhoeffer's writings were preserved and disseminated throughout the world for generations; or that sixty-five years in the future, when Bethge died, their names would be inextricably intertwined. They were still strangers now, as they made their U-turn and headed back to the Zingst farmhouse.

Everyone had only been there for a few days when, on May 1, an important event took place between Bonhoeffer and his ordinands. Across Germany, the day was celebrated not just as May Day, but as an official day to recognize Germany's workers. On that particular May Day a new law regarding military conscription went into effect, and that evening, Hitler gave a speech. The ordinands and Bonhoeffer were gathered around the radio to listen.

At that time even these ordinands in the Confessing Church had few qualms about Hitler; certainly none of them felt toward him the way Bonhoeffer did. They still thought the church struggle separate from politics and had few qualms about the idea of military conscription. Undoing Versailles and doing one's duty for Germany went hand in hand with doing one's duty to God. In people's minds, the church and the state were still linked as they had been under the kaiser, and to the extent that the Weimar Republic had undermined this connection, any move back in that direction was welcomed. And because members of the Confessing Church had been attacked by the German Christians as being less than patriotic, they were perhaps keener than most to want to prove otherwise if the opportunity presented itself.

At some point in the speech, Bonhoeffer asked a question that made it clear he was not of the same mind as everyone else. Most of the students were taken aback. Someone asked him to clarify his thinking, and he said they should discuss it when the speech was over. For most of these ordinands, it was the very first time they had heard anyone in authority deviate from the standard Lutheran line, which was that serving one's country could be only a good thing. In that gathering, Bonhoeffer was alone in having strong misgivings about Hitler and the war that he knew Hitler was maneuvering the country toward.

Most of the ordinands in that course and the subsequent four courses would end up serving in the military, and Bonhoeffer never tried to argue them out of it or make an issue of it. He was not a committed pacifist in that sense and was certainly not convinced that Christians must be conscientious objectors. Bonhoeffer was respectful of the students' points of view. He never wanted his classes or the seminary to become a cult of personality, centered on him. He was interested only in persuading via reason. Forcing his thoughts on others was something he thought of as fundamentally wrong, as worthy of a "mis-leader."

Finkenwalde

The humble accommodations at Zingst had to be vacated by June 14, and a more permanent home found as soon as possible. They considered a number of properties, including Ziethen Castle in Kremmen. They finally settled on the former von Katte estate in Finkenwalde, a small town not far from Stettin in Pomerania. The estate had been the home of a private school, but the Nazis frowned on such places. Along with many others like it, it soon became vacant. The estate was looking for a new tenant when the Confessing Church came across it. It possessed a number of outbuildings and a manor house to which a "poorly constructed" school building had been added, spoiling its beauty. A commercial enterprise had also done its part to mar the surroundings: a rear portion of the property was now a gravel pit, a vulgar gash on the otherwise pristine grounds of the once magnificent Pomeranian estate.

The manor house was in a state of terrible disrepair. One of those who procured it called it "a veritable pigsty." Before they could move into their new home, much work had to be done. Many of the ordinands were without a home for twelve days and had to stay in youth hostels in Griefswald. Another group went ahead to paint and clean up the battered property.

Bonhoeffer inaugurated Finkenwalde with his first lecture there on June 26. At that point the manor house was still empty. Funds had to be raised for furnishings and much else, but everything seemed to have been done with good cheer, including fund-raising. One of the ordinands, Winfried Maechler, wrote a poem, "Ordinands' Humble Request," that in clever verse asked for assistance. It was sent to Confessing Church congregations and to individuals, many of whom were thrilled to help. Maechler's thank-you letters were in verse too.

The landed gentry of Pomerania were strongly against Hitler and the Nazis, and they were generally devout Christians too. Many of these families practically adopted the Finkenwaldians as their personal project, wanting to help the brave, fledgling enterprise however they could. The mother of Ewald von Kleist-Schmenzin made all of the covers for their chairs. Wilhelm Gross, a sculptor, lent his talents to the transformation of the gym into a chapel. And very often food was delivered from one of the farm estates. One day the phone rang and the ordinands learned that someone had sent Pastor Bonhoeffer a live pig. It was at the local freight yard, waiting to be picked up.

Bonhoeffer and the ordinands themselves donated to the fledgling enterprise. Bonhoeffer donated his entire theological library, including his great-grandfather von Hase's invaluable Erlangen edition of Martin Luther's works. He brought his gramophone, too, and his many recordings, the most prized and exotic of which were the Negro spirituals he had bought in Manhattan.

Music formed a huge part of the communal life at Zingst and Finkenwalde. Each day around noon everyone gathered to sing hymns or other sacred music. Joachim Kamnitz, one of Bonhoeffer's Berlin students, usually led the singing. One day Bethge said he'd like to teach them Adam Gumpelzhaimer's "Agnus Dei." He told them about Gumpelzhaimer, who lived in the sixteenth century and wrote sacred music and hymns, especially polychoral motets. Bonhoeffer was intrigued. His musical knowledge went back to Bach, but Bethge was familiar with the music that preceded him. He widened Bonhoeffer's horizons to that earlier sacred music and to composers such as Heinrich Schutz, Johann Schein, Samuel Scheidt, Josquin des Prez, and others, and that music was incorporated into the repertoire of Finkenwalde.

There were two pianos in the manor house. Bethge said that Bonhoeffer "never turned down a request to join in playing one of Bach's concertos for two pianos." He also said that Bonhoeffer particularly loved singing a part in Schutz's vocal duets, "Eins bitte ich vom Herren" and "Meister, wir haben die ganze Nacht gearbeitet." Bonhoeffer had always been an extraordinary sight reader, and he amazed his students with his musical talents and passions. He loved Beethoven, and Bethge said "he could sit down at the piano and simply improvise the *Rosenkavalier*. That impressed us greatly." There weren't many seminaries in Germany where music was such an integral part of things. In their first month at Zingst, the sun sometimes warmed things up enough that Bonhoeffer took the classes outdoors, usually to a windless spot in the dunes, and a few times they sang there too.

The Daily Routine

At Zingst and Finkenwalde, Bonhoeffer emphasized a strict daily routine and the spiritual disciplines. That aspect of the seminary existence most resembled what Bonhoeffer found at the communities he visited. But the specifics of what filled the daily routine were of his own devising and borrowed from many traditions.

Each day began with a forty-five-minute service before breakfast, and ended with a service just before bed. One student from Finkenwalde, Albrecht Schönherr, recalled that the morning service began within minutes of waking:

> Bonhoeffer requested us not to say a single word to each other before the service. The first word to come was supposed to be God's word. But this was not so simple, because we spent all the time in a room in which we slept six or eight at a time, and we slept on old featherbeds, [on top of] hay mattresses. These mattresses had been used for generations. When you lay down on them, there was a huge dust explosion.

The services took place not in the chapel, but around the large dinner table. They began by singing a choral psalm and a hymn chosen for that day. Then there was a reading from the Old Testament. Next they sang "a set verse from a hymn," using the same verse for several weeks, followed by a New Testament reading. Schönherr described the order of the service:

> We sang a great deal, prayed the Psalms, usually several psalms, so that we went through the whole Psalter in a single week. Then there was a whole chapter of the Old Testament, a piece from the New Testament, and a prayer which Bonhoeffer offered himself. . . . This prayer, however, was very important, because it treated whatever we were dealing with, whatever we truly needed to ask of God. Then came breakfast, which was very modest. Then came half an hour of meditation. Then everybody went to his room and thought about the Scripture until he knew what it meant for him today, on that day. During this time there had to be absolute quiet; the telephone couldn't ring, nobody could walk around. We were supposed to concentrate completely on whatever it was that God had to say to us.

One meditated on the same verse for an entire week, a half hour each day. Wolf-Dieter Zimmermann recalled that they were not allowed to look

at the text in the original language or to consult reference books or commen-
taries. They must deal with the verse as though it was God's word to them
personally. Many seminarians chafed at the practice, but Bonhoeffer's former
Berlin students were used to his ways. They had been with him on retreats
at his cabin in Biesenthal and at the youth hostel in Prebelow, and they had
been his guinea pigs. Their easy acceptance of these practices made it easier
for the other ordinands to accept them, but at times it was difficult. Once,
when Bonhoeffer was away for a few days, he returned to find that the daily
Scripture meditations had not been continued. He made it clear that he was
not pleased.

It wasn't only ordinands who were bothered by the practice of meditation on Scripture verses. In a letter in October 1936, Karl Barth wrote that
he was disturbed by what he described as

> an almost indefinable odor of a monastic eros and pathos. I can hardly
> say that I am very happy about it . . . I cannot go with the distinction
> in principle between theological work and devotional edification. . . .
> Do not regard this as a criticism of your efforts simply because the basis
> of my knowledge and my understanding is still far too scanty. But you
> will at least understand from this the questions that I would put to you
> despite all my sympathies.

Bonhoeffer was no authoritarian, but he had a traditional respect for order
and would not allow his ordinands to get the impression that they were his
equals. The authority of a servant leader, as opposed to the authoritarian-
ism of the mis-leader, came from God and was a leadership of serving those
below oneself. That was Christ's example to the disciples, and Bonhoeffer
strove to lead that way too.

Bethge remembered that early on—they had been at Zingst a few
days—Bonhoeffer asked for help in the kitchen. There were no immediate
volunteers, so Bonhoeffer locked the door and began to wash the dishes.
When others tried to come in to help, he wouldn't unlock the door. He never
mentioned a word about it, but the point was made. He wanted to transmit
the same culture of selflessness here that had been practiced in his home
as a child. Selfishness, laziness, self-pity, poor sportsmanship, and the like

were not tolerated. He made that legacy of his upbringing a part of these seminaries.

Another aspect of this "life together" that proved quite difficult was Bonhoeffer's rule never to speak about a brother in his absence. Bonhoeffer knew that living according to what Jesus taught in the Sermon on the Mount was not "natural" for anyone.

Whatever they thought of the disciplines and the daily devotions, no one at Finkenwalde could complain that there was no fun. Most afternoons and evenings a time was set aside for hiking or sports. Bonhoeffer was forever organizing games, just as his mother had done in their family. There was a lot of table tennis, and anyone looking for Bonhoeffer would try the table tennis room first. They also played soccer. Schönherr recalled that "Bonhoeffer was always at the head of the pack because he was such a fantastic runner." He had always been competitive, and Bethge remembered that "he hated to lose when we tried shot-putting—or stone-putting—down the beach."

Albrecht Schönherr remembered that after dinner and recreation, around ten o'clock, there was another service of about three-quarters of an hour, "as the last note of a day with God. After that, silence and sleep. That was the way the day went."

Bonhoeffer wrote Barth, partially in response to his concern about Finkenwalde's "monastic" atmosphere. Bonhoeffer himself was critical of "pietistic" communities, but he knew that regarding all emphasis on prayer and spiritual disciplines as "legalism" was equally erroneous. He had seen that at Union, too, where students prided themselves on avoiding the legalism of the so-called fundamentalists without expressing any real theology. To Barth, he wrote:

> Work at the seminary gives me great joy. Academic and practical work are combined splendidly. I find that all along the line the young theologians coming into the seminary raise the very questions that have been troubling me recently, and of course our life together is strongly influenced by this. I am firmly convinced that in view of what the young theologians bring with them from the university and in view of the

independent work which will be demanded of them in the parishes . . . they need a completely different kind of training which life together in a seminary like this unquestionably gives. You can hardly imagine how empty, how completely burnt out most of the brothers are when they come to the seminary. Empty not only as regards theological insights and still more as regards knowledge of the Bible, but also as regards their personal life.

On an open evening—the only one in which I shared—you once said very seriously to the students that you sometimes felt as though you would rather give up all lectures and instead pay a surprise visit on someone and ask him, like old Tholuck, "How goes it with your soul?" The need has not been met since then, not even by the Confessing Church. But there are very few who recognize this sort of work with young theologians as a task of the church and do something about it. And it is really what everyone is waiting for. Unfortunately I am not up to it, but I remind the brothers of each other, and that seems to me to be the most important thing. It is, though, certain that both theological work and real pastoral fellowship can only grow in a life which is governed by gathering round the Word morning and evening and by fixed times of prayer. . . . The charge of legalism does not seem to me to fit at all. What is there legalistic in a Christian setting to work to learn what prayer is and in his spending a good deal of his time in this learning? A leading man in the Confessing Church recently said to me: "We have no time for meditation now, the ordinands should learn how to preach and to catechize." That seems to me either a complete mis-understanding of what young theologians are like today or a culpable ignorance of how preaching and catechism come to life. The questions that are seriously put to us today by young theologians are: How do I learn to pray? How do I learn to read the Bible? If we cannot help them there we cannot help them at all. And there is really nothing obvious about it. To say, "If someone does not know that, then he should not be a minister" would be to exclude most of us from our profession. It is quite clear to me that all these things are only justified when alongside them and with them—at just the same time!—there is really serious and sober theological, exegetical and dogmatic work going on. Otherwise all these questions are given the wrong emphasis.

Preaching the Word

Bonhoeffer took preaching seriously. For him a sermon was nothing less than the very word of God, a place where God would speak to his people. Bonhoeffer wanted to impress this idea on his ordinands, to help them see that preaching was not merely an intellectual exercise. Like prayer or meditation on a scriptural text, it was an opportunity to hear from heaven, and for the preacher, it was a holy privilege to be the vessel through whom God would speak. Like the incarnation, it was a place of revelation, where Christ came into this world from outside it.

But as with so much else, Bonhoeffer knew that the best way to communicate what he thought and felt about homiletics was by doing it. Delivering a real sermon during an actual service was infinitely better than giving a lecture on homiletics. The ordinands must see in him someone who lived what he meant to teach them, just as Jesus did. The teaching and the living must be two parts of the same thing.

Yet even when he was not preaching, but merely talking about sermons, he wanted to communicate practical things to his ordinands. Bethge remembered some of Bonhoeffer's advice: "Write your sermon in daylight; do not write it all at once; 'in Christ' there is no room for conditional clauses; the first minutes on the pulpit are the most favorable, so do not waste them with generalities but confront the congregation straight off with the core of the matter; extemporaneous preaching can be done by anyone who really knows the Bible."

In 1932 Bonhoeffer told Hildebrandt: "A truly evangelical sermon must be like offering a child a fine red apple or offering a thirsty man a cool glass of water and then saying: Do you want it?" At Finkenwalde he effectively said the same thing: "We must be able to speak about our faith so that hands will be stretched out toward us faster than we can fill them. . . . Do not try to make the Bible relevant. Its relevance is axiomatic. . . . Do not defend God's Word, but testify to it. . . . Trust to the Word. It is a ship loaded to the very limits of its capacity!"

He wished to impress upon his ordinands that when one truly presented the Word of God, it would undo people because it had the innate power to help them see their own need and would give the answer to that need in a way that was not larded over with "religion" or false piety. The grace of God, without filters or explanation, would touch people.

Bonhoeffer's teaching on prayer was similar. Every morning at the devotions, he offered a longish extemporaneous prayer. Most seminarians in the Lutheran tradition would have first thought this overly pietistic. But Bonhoeffer was unapologetic about such things. The life of prayer and communion with Jesus must be at the center. One's whole ministry arose from it. Wilhelm Rott remembered that Bonhoeffer often talked about these things while sitting on the large staircase in the main manor house at Finkenwalde, holding a cigarette and a cup of coffee: "Another lasting impression made upon me was Bonhoeffer's complaint how much we lacked the 'love of Jesus.' . . . Real faith and love were identical for him. Here was the very heart and core of the existence of this highly intellectual Christian. We felt it in the improvised prayers of the morning and evening devotions; they sprang from the love of the Lord and of his brethren."

Acedia and Tristizia

Once a month, on a Saturday evening, all of the ordinands took part in a Communion service. One such Saturday before this service, Bonhoeffer broached the subject of personal confession between them. It had been Luther's idea that Christians should confess to one another instead of to a priest. Most Lutherans had thrown that baby out with the bathwater and didn't confess to anyone. Confession of any kind was considered overly Catholic, just as extemporaneous prayer was criticized as too pietistic. But Bonhoeffer successfully instituted the practice of confessing one to another. Perhaps not surprisingly, Bonhoeffer chose Eberhard Bethge as his confessor.

Bonhoeffer felt comfortable sharing with Bethge what he called *acedia* or *tristitia*—a "sadness of the heart" that we might typically call depression. He suffered from it but rarely showed it, except among close friends. Gerhard Jacobi said, "In private conversation he made a less calm and harmonious impression. One noticed at once what a sensitive person he was, what a turmoil he was in, and how troubled." And it's doubtful that Bonhoeffer discussed it with anyone but Bethge. He knew that Bethge's towering intellect and his mature and well-established faith were up to the task of dealing with him in his complexities, even in his doubts, such as they were. He knew that Bethge could function in the role of pastor to him, which he did, and not just at Finkenwalde, but thenceforth. He touched on his depression years later, in a letter to Bethge from Tegel prison: "I wonder why it is that we find some days so much more oppressive than others, for no apparent reason. Is it growing pains—or spiritual trial? Once they're over, the world looks quite a different place again."

There was little question that Bonhoeffer was sometimes extremely intense, that his brilliant and overactive mind could lead him into temporary cul-de-sacs of agitation. But in Bethge, he had a friend to whom he could show this worst side. Bethge was as naturally sunny as Bonhoeffer could be intense. Bonhoeffer mentioned it in another letter from Tegel: "I don't know anyone who does not like you, whereas I know a great many people who do not like me. I don't take this at all hardly for myself; wherever I find enemies I also find friends, and that satisfies me. But the reason is probably that you are by nature open and modest, whereas I am reticent and rather demanding."

The Junkers of Pomerania

In the charming rural atmosphere of Pomerania, Bonhoeffer first became acquainted with the landed gentry of the region, the Junkers (pronounced YUN-kers), who were untitled aristocratic families.* Pomerania was a world apart from Berlin and Grunewald. The metropolitan climate of liberal intellectualism was replaced by the conservative and almost feudal world of landed estates. But the traditional values and fealty to high standards of culture were strikingly similar. Most of the families were members of the Prussian military officers' class, from whom virtually all the conspirators against Hitler would come. Bonhoeffer quickly felt at home with them, and the wealthy estate owners would be his most loyal supporters. And from their daughters he would choose the woman he wanted to marry.

Bonhoeffer's first contacts with these families occurred when Finkenwalde sent out fund-raising letters. They included the Bismarcks of Lasbeck and the Wedemeyer family from Pätzig. He also met the von Schlabrendorff family and their son, Fabian von Schlabrendorff.**

---

* Bonhoeffer became friendly with a number of these families and got to know many of the men who would in a few years be involved in the conspiracy against Hitler.

** Fabian would become vitally involved in the Resistance against Hitler and would end up in a cell close to Bonhoeffer in the Gestapo prison. Ewald von Kleist-Schmenzin, a conservative Christian with a large estate in the region, was also part of the conspiracy. In 1933 Kleist-

Ruth von Kleist-Retzow

By far the most significant friendship that Bonhoeffer would enjoy among these noble families was the one with Ruth von Kleist-Retzow, a vital woman of sixty-eight when they met. Like Bishop George Bell, she shared Bonhoeffer's February 4 birthday, and they became so close over the next decade that he often called her Grandmother, mainly because he spent much time with her grandchildren, several of whose confirmations he personally oversaw, at her insistence. With Eberhard Bethge he sometimes playfully referred to her as Tante Ruth, just as with Franz Hildebrandt he had sometimes called Bishop Bell "Uncle George."

Bonhoeffer and Tante Ruth shared impressive aristocratic backgrounds. She was the daughter of the Count and Countess von Zedlitz-Trützschler. Her father was the governor of Silesia, and she had grown up in the palace at Oppern, cutting her capers among the social circles of her class until, at age fifteen, she fell madly in love with her future husband, Jürgen von Kleist. Three years later they married, and he whisked her from her palace home to the starkly rural world of his large agricultural estate in Kieckow. Their marriage was very happy, and they were devotedly Christian in the pietistic mold that flourished in Pomerania for generations.

But soon after she bore him a fifth child, Ruth's husband died, leaving her a widow at age twenty-nine. She moved with her children to a large townhouse in Stettin, leaving Kieckow to the capable care of the estate manager. After the First War, her son Hans-Jürgen fixed up the house at Klein-Krössin so that she could live there—it was one of Kieckow's properties—while he and his family moved into the manor house at Kieckow. Over the next years, Bonhoeffer spent many weeks at Kieckow and Klein-Krössin; in the thirties he retreated there to work on his *Nachfolge* (*Discipleship*), and in the forties he worked on his *Ethics* there.

Ruth von Kleist-Retzow was a strong-willed and accomplished woman who had no patience for wishy-washy clerics. The brilliant, cultured, and heroically combative Pastor Bonhoeffer seemed an answer to her prayers. She helped him and Finkenwalde in any way she could and advocated for the

---

Schmenzin sought an interview with Hindenburg to prevent Hitler from becoming chancellor, and in 1938 General Beck would send him to London to seek British assurances that they would not allow Hitler to get away with marching into Czechoslovakia.

Finkenwalde cause among the region's other families. The Finkenwaldians received much of their food from the farms of these families, and thanks to their advocacy, some ordinands would find posts as pastors in the churches of the region. The old system of patronage, whereby the families were able to appoint the pastors of local churches, still held firm.

Frau von Kleist-Retzow was overseeing the education of several of her grandchildren at that time: sixteen-year-old Hans-Otto von Bismarck and his thirteen-year-old sister, Spes; twelve-year-old Hans-Friedrich Kleist of Kieckow; and two Wedemeyer children from Pätzig: thirteen-year-old Max and his fifteen-year-old sister, Ruth-Alice. Maria von Wedemeyer came to Stettin the following year, when she was twelve. They lived with their grandmother in her Stettin townhouse, and on Sundays she shepherded them out to Finkenwalde to hear the fascinating young pastor. Beginning in the autumn of 1935, Bonhoeffer instituted the practice of regular Sunday services at the Finkenwalde chapel, which outsiders could attend. Frau von Kleist-Retzow was thrilled to come and hear Bonhoeffer preach, and she was even more thrilled to bring her grandchildren to hear him. Ruth-Alice remembered:

> One day we found ourselves sitting . . . beneath the pulpit occupied by Dietrich Bonhoeffer. . . . Grandmother had apparently read some of his writings before that date. . . . So there Grandmother sat, a handsome, dignified figure surrounded by her youthful grandchildren—an unwonted apparition in the former school gymnasium that had been converted into a makeshift place of worship. We all got carried away by the lusty singing of the twenty ordinands. The subject of Bonhoeffer's sermon—one I have never forgotten—was Aaron's blessing.
>
> What followed—[table] tennis in the garden, a discussion between Grandmother and Pastor Bonhoeffer, a modest but cheerful meal at the seminary's big horseshoe table, a Shakespeare reading with everyone taking part—was the prelude to much to-ing and fro-ing between Finkenwalde and Grandmother's. . . . The ordinands dropped in whenever they visited the office of the Pomeranian Council of Brethren, which was on the same street. The latest developments in ecclesiastical policy, a continual spur to decision-making, were enthusiastically discussed. Being a woman versed in theology and rich in human experience, but above all a fighter, Grandmother was completely in her

element. Before long she was meditating each morning, under Dietrich's instruction, on the same biblical texts as his ordinands.

Ruth von Kleist-Retzow not only adopted Bonhoeffer's spiritual disciplines; she decided at age seventy to learn New Testament Greek. She was not about to waste the opportunities available to her with Dietrich Bonhoeffer nearby. She even cajoled him into considering overseeing the confirmation of four of her grandchildren: Spes von Bismarck, Hans-Friedrich von Kleist-Retzow, and Max von Wedemeyer and his sister, Maria. Bonhoeffer took the responsibility extremely seriously, meeting and speaking with each of them and their parents. In the end he took on only three. Maria, who was twelve, didn't seem mature enough for such a serious undertaking.

Bonhoeffer "always had some distance around him, some reserve," said Ruth-Alice. But there was something compelling about him when he was preaching. "When you saw him preaching," she said, "you saw a young man who was entirely in God's grasp." In some ways it was particularly difficult for the younger generations whose parents and grandparents were so adamantly opposed to the Nazis. Bonhoeffer and Finkenwalde made it easier for them. He was an encouragement. "In those days," Ruth-Alice recalled, "the Nazis were always marching and saying, 'The future belongs to us! We are the future!' And we young ones who were against Hitler and the Nazis would hear this and we wondered, 'Where is our future?' But there in Finkenwalde, when I heard this man preaching, who had been captured by God, I thought: 'Here. Here is our future.'"

CHAPTER 19

SCYLLA AND CHARYBDIS

1935–36

The proclamation of grace has its limits. Grace may not be proclaimed to anyone who does not recognize or distinguish or desire it . . . The world upon whom grace is thrust as a bargain will grow tired of it, and it will not only trample upon the Holy, but also will tear apart those who force it on them.

Only he who cries out for the Jews may sing Gregorian chants.

—DIETRICH BONHOEFFER

I n 1935, as he embraced his call to be the director of the Confessing Church's seminary at Finkenwalde, Bonhoeffer's relationship with the Confessing Church grew more awkward. He became a lightning rod for controversy, both inside and outside the Confessing Church. And in 1936, the Nazis themselves would take notice of him.

The Scriptures said that faith without works is dead, that faith "is the evidence of things not seen." Bonhoeffer knew that one could see some things only with the eyes of faith, but they were no less real and true than the things one saw with one's physical eyes. But the eyes of faith had a moral component. To see that it was against God's will to persecute the Jews, one must choose to open one's eyes. And then one would face another uncomfortable choice: whether to act as God required.

Bonhoeffer strove to see what God wanted to show and then to do what God asked in response. That was the obedient Christian life, the call of the disciple. And it came with a cost, which explained why so many were afraid to open their eyes in the first place. It was the antithesis of the "cheap grace" that required nothing more than an easy mental assent, which he wrote about in *Discipleship*. Bonhoeffer "was a person about whom one had the feeling that he was completely whole," said one Finkenwalde ordinand, "a man who believes in what he thinks and does what he believes in."

That summer Bonhoeffer wrote the essay "The Confessing Church and the Ecumenical Movement" in which he took both sides to task. He was the principal point of connection between them, seeing the best and the worst in both. But each saw the best in itself and the worst in the other. Because of the still unhealed wounds from the First World War, many in the Confessing Church were suspicious of anyone, even Christians, from other countries; and they felt that many in the ecumenical movement were theologically sloppy. On the other side, many in the ecumenical movement thought the Confessing Church was overly concerned with theology and overly nationalistic. Both sides had good points.

But Bonhoeffer wanted them to fight their common enemy, National Socialism, and he tried to get them to do so, despite many roadblocks. He was horrified that the ecumenical movement was still willing to talk to the Reichskirche of Müller, Jäger, and Heckel. And he was horrified that the Confessing Church was still willing to talk to Hitler and was unwilling to confront him. Action was the only thing these bullies feared, but neither the ecumenical movement nor the Confessing Church seemed prepared to act. They preferred to keep up a meaningless and endless dialogue and played into their enemies' hands. The announcement of the Nuremberg Laws against the Jews was a case in point.

The Nuremberg Laws and the Steglitz Synod

On September 15, 1935, the Nuremberg Laws were announced. These Laws for the Protection of German Blood and German Honor stated:

Entirely convinced that the purity of German blood is essential to the further existence of the German people, and inspired by the uncompromising determination to safeguard the future of the German nation, the Reichstag has unanimously resolved upon the following law, which is promulgated herewith:

Section 1 1. Marriages between Jews and citizens of German or kindred blood are forbidden. Marriages concluded in defiance of this law are void, even if, for the purpose of evading this law, they were concluded abroad. 2. Proceedings for annulment may be initiated only by the Public Prosecutor.

Section 2 1. Extramarital intercourse between Jews and subjects of the state of Germany or related blood is forbidden.

Section 3 Jews will not be permitted to employ female citizens of German or kindred blood as domestic workers under the age of 45.

Section 4 1. Jews are forbidden to display the Reichsflagge or the national colors. 2. On the other hand they are permitted to display the Jewish colors. The exercise of this right is protected by the State.

The Nuremberg Laws represented what has been called a second, "more ordered" phase of Jewish persecution. Jews, who were once legal citizens of Germany, were becoming subjects of the Third Reich. Their citizenship was vanishing, legally, in the center of Europe, in the twentieth century. Bonhoeffer had known of this pending legislation through Dohnanyi, who tried to thwart it, or blunt it, in vain.

Bonhoeffer saw the enactment of these laws as an opportunity for the Confessing Church to speak out clearly, in a way they had not yet been able to do. The Nazis had drawn a line in the sand and everyone could see it.

But the Confessing Church was again slow to act. It was guilty of the typically Lutheran error of confining itself to the narrow sphere of how church and state were related. When the state is trying to encroach upon the church, this is a proper sphere of concern. But for Bonhoeffer, the idea of limiting the church's actions to this sphere alone was absurd. The church had been instituted by God to exist for the whole world. It was to speak into the world and to be a voice in the world, so it had an obligation to speak out against things that did not affect it directly.

Bonhoeffer believed it was the role of the church to *speak for those who could not speak.* To outlaw slavery inside the church was right, but to allow it to exist outside the church would be evil. So it was with this persecution of the Jews by the Nazi state. Boldly speaking out for those who were being persecuted would show the Confessing Church to be the church, because just as Bonhoeffer had written that Jesus Christ was the "man for others," so the church was his body on this earth, a community in which Christ was present—a community that existed "for others." To serve others outside the church, to love them as one loved oneself, and to do unto them as one would have others do unto oneself, these were the clear commands of Christ.

Around that time, Bonhoeffer made his famous declaration: "Only he who cries out for the Jews may sing Gregorian chants." As far as he was concerned, to dare to sing to God when his chosen people were being beaten and murdered meant that one must also speak out against their suffering. If one was unwilling to do this, God was not interested in one's worship.

The willingness of Lutherans to keep the church out of the world reflected an unbiblical overemphasis on Romans 13:1–5,* which they had inherited from Luther. They had never been forced to deal with the boundary of this scriptural idea of obedience to worldly authorities. The early Christians stood up against Caesar and the Romans. Surely the Nuremberg Laws would force the Confessing Church to take a stand against the Nazis.

One day, from his home church in Dahlem, Franz Hildebrandt called Finkenwalde with alarming news. The Confessing Synod was proposing a resolution conceding the state's right to enact the Nuremberg legislation. It was the last straw for him. Hildebrandt was ready to resign from the Pastors' Emergency League and to leave the Confessing Church. Bonhoeffer decided he must do something, so he and a group of ordinands would go to Berlin, to see whether they might influence things at the synod, which would be held

---

* "Everyone must submit himself to the governing authorities, for there is no authority except that which God has established. The authorities that exist have been established by God. Consequently, he who rebels against the authority is rebelling against what God has instituted, and those who do so will bring judgment on themselves. For rulers hold no terror for those who do right, but for those who do wrong. Do you want to be free from fear of the one in authority? Then do what is right and he will commend you. For he is God's servant to do you good. But if you do wrong, be afraid, for he does not bear the sword for nothing. He is God's servant, an agent of wrath to bring punishment on the wrongdoer. Therefore, it is necessary to submit to the authorities, not only because of possible punishment but also because of conscience" (NIV).

in Steglitz. Bonhoeffer was not a delegate and couldn't speak at the synod, but he could be an encouragement to those who saw things as he did. He wanted them to see that the Nuremberg Laws gave them an extraordinary opportunity to take a stand.

The trip was an anticlimax. The synod did not approve the resolution, and it also failed to take a stand. The National Socialists' strategy of dividing and conquering its opponents, of confusing and delaying, was working with the Confessing Church. Bonhoeffer knew that something of this unwillingness to speak out with boldness had to do with money. The state provided financial security for the pastors of Germany, and even pastors in the Confessing Church would jeopardize their incomes only to a certain point.

Family

During this period, Bonhoeffer's struggles with depression continued. There was much to be discouraged about, not least his church's unwillingness to speak out against the monstrous Nuremberg Laws. These laws would affect his own family. As a non-Aryan family, Sabine and Gert had suffered, but now the Nuremberg Laws would make things worse. They were forced to dismiss many women who worked for them. "There were tears," Sabine wrote. The women had been increasingly harried for working in a Jewish household. SA men making deliveries to the home would say things like, "What, are you still working with Jews?" Some professors who had been their friends distanced themselves, fearing for their jobs. The more Sabine heard through her sister Christel von Dohnanyi, the more she knew that she, Gert, and the girls would have to leave Germany, hard as that was to fathom. When Christel told Sabine of what was happening in the concentration camps, long before others knew, she couldn't hear any more and asked her to stop.

Bonhoeffer's grandmother, then ninety-three, had a friend whose Jewish family member was forced to give up a legal practice as a result of the new laws. In what would end up being her last letter to Dietrich, she asked his help: "This fifty-four-year-old man is traveling around the world looking for work so that he can finish raising his children. . . . A family's life destroyed! . . . Everything is affected, down to the smallest details. Can you actively advise or help us here? . . . I hope you can give some energetic thought to this and perhaps know some way out."

That October of 1935, Bonhoeffer's parents moved from their vast home on Wangenheimstrasse in Grunewald to a new house that they had built in Charlottenburg. It was smaller, but still large enough for guests. Dietrich would always have a room on the top floor. Grandmother Julie Tafel Bonhoeffer moved with them into this new home, but after Christmas, she contracted pneumonia and died in January. Her influence on Karl Bonhoeffer and his children was incalculable. On January 15, taking as his text Psalm 90, which the family read every year on New Year's Eve, Bonhoeffer preached at her funeral:

> A refusal to compromise over the right principle, free speech for the free individual, that fact that one's word once given is binding, clarity and common sense in one's opinions, candor and simplicity of life in private and in public—these were factors that went to her very heart. . . . She could not bear to see these values despised or to see the rights of an individual violated. For this reason her last years were clouded with the great sorrow that she bore for the fate of the Jews among our people, a burden which she shared with them and a suffering which she, too, felt. She stemmed from another age, from another spiritual world, and this world does not descend with her into the grave. . . . This heritage for which we thank her lays duties upon us.

The Trip to Sweden

On February 4, 1936, Bonhoeffer celebrated his thirtieth birthday. He had always felt overly conscious of his age and thought thirty impossibly old. It was the last such milestone he would see. And it was the celebration of this birthday that would for the first time bring him into the sights of the Nazis.

It began innocently enough in one of the many postprandial conversations with his ordinands in the main hall at Finkenwalde. A fire blazed in the huge eighteenth-century copper brazier that he had bought in Spain. They had been celebrating Bonhoeffer's birthday in the usual manner, with singing and other tributes to the honoree, and when the evening was winding down, they got into a rather free-wheeling conversation about gift giving. Someone brightly suggested that perhaps the person celebrating a birthday should not be the one to receive the gifts, but to give them—and his friends should be the recipients. When Bonhoeffer took the bait and inquired what everyone might want, they settled on the idea of a trip to Sweden. Would he organize one for them? As it turned out, he would.

The trip to Sweden was one of many examples of Bonhoeffer's generosity. One ordinand at Gross-Schlönwitz, Hans-Werner Jensen, said that "serving his brothers became the center of Bonhoeffer's life. He avoided keeping them in tutelage; he only wanted to help them." Jensen recalled other incidents of Bonhoeffer's generosity. When Jensen was at Stolp hospital with appendicitis, he was transferred from the third-class ward to a private room. "The orderly told me that a good-looking gentleman with glasses had been in that morning declaring he would bear the cost. . . . Another time we were making our way home after an open evening in Berlin. Bonhoeffer bought the tickets for all of us at the station. When I wanted to repay him, he just answered: 'Money is dirt.'"

This was a grand opportunity to show his ordinands the church beyond Germany. He had captivated them many times with tales of his trips abroad. And he had explained that the church was something that transcended national boundaries, that it extended throughout time and space. There were many good reasons for such a trip, not least to afford his ordinands some measure of the culturally broadening experiences he'd had in spades. Bonhoeffer also knew strengthening Finkenwalde's ties to the ecumenical church abroad would be helpful in safeguarding it from Nazi interference.

He immediately contacted his ecumenical friends in Sweden and Denmark. Plans for the trip had to be made as quickly and quietly as possible, because once Bishop Heckel caught wind of it, there would surely be trouble. He would do all he could to stop it, and he could do much. But not if they left before he heard about it. Nils Karlström, who was the secretary of the Ecumenical Committee in Uppsala, understood Bonhoeffer's situation and went to great pains to help. His official invitation, which was a crucial matter, since Heckel would look into the propriety of every detail of the trip, came on February 22. Three days later Bonhoeffer sent official notice of the trip to his superiors, as well as to the Foreign Ministry, where a Bonhoeffer family friend was the head of the Justice Department. He thought this would give him some cover, but it backfired. Someone else saw it and contacted Heckel, who in turn gave them a bad report on Bonhoeffer. As a result, the Foreign Ministry wrote to the German Embassy in Stockholm: "The Reich and Prussian Ministries for Church Affairs, and the Church Foreign Office, warn against Pastor Bonhoeffer because his influence is not conducive to German interests. Government and church departments have the strongest objections to his visit which has just now become known."

On March 1, the twenty-four ordinands, with Bonhoeffer and Rott, boarded a ship in the port of Stettin and sailed northward to Sweden, unaware that the Foreign Ministry had taken an interest in their trip. Bonhoeffer knew of the dangers of such a trip and had warned his ordinands to be very careful about what they said, especially to newspaper reporters. Whatever they said would be blown up into the cartoon proportions of typical newspaper headlines. Bonhoeffer didn't want a repeat of the "Hitler Wants to Be Pope" fiasco.

News of the trip made Heckel look bad with the Reich government. On March 3, the Swedish press put the seminarians' visit on their front pages, and the next day, their visit to Archbishop Eidem in Uppsala made the papers too. On the sixth, in Stockholm, they called on the German ambassador, Prince Victor zu Wied. The prince, having just read the warning letter about this troublemaker, received Bonhoeffer and his associates with obvious coolness. Bonhoeffer didn't know why, but later recalled that a life-sized portrait of Hitler in the room glowered at them.

With their arrival in Stockholm came many more articles and photographs. Each column inch of international coverage made Heckel look worse. He must do something immediately, and as usual, the resourceful cleric would do everything possible. First, he fired off a letter to the Swedish church. Next, he wrote a letter to the Prussian church committee, taking them to task. But this time, he would bring out the big artillery and blast Bonhoeffer officially and in writing, in terms that moved the whole dispute to another level:

> I feel impelled . . . to draw the attention of the provincial church committee to the fact that the incident has brought Bonhoeffer very much into the public eye. Since he can be accused of being a pacifist and an enemy of the state it might well be advisable for the provincial church committee to disassociate itself from him and to take steps to ensure that he will no longer train German theologians.

A corner had been turned. Heckel placed Bonhoeffer at the mercy of the Nazi state. Bethge wrote that "no form of denunciation was more fatal than the description 'a pacifist and an enemy of the state,' especially when this was used officially and in writing."

The immediate upshot was that Bonhoeffer's right to teach at Berlin University was officially revoked. He had given a lecture there on February 14, which turned out to be his last. His long relationship with the world of academia ended forever. He would protest and appeal, but there was no way to rescind the judgment. And yet, in the topsy-turvydom of Hitler's Germany in which academia was closed to Jews, it can hardly have been entirely disheartening. His brother-in-law Gerhard Leibholz was forced to "retire" that April. In some ways the judgment was a badge of honor.

"An Atrocious Piece of False Doctrine"

On April 22, Bonhoeffer delivered a lecture titled "The Question of the Boundaries of the Church and Church Union." It was typically measured, thorough, and definitive, to the point of being elegant and beautiful, like a winning equation. In it, he explained how the Confessing Church was not solely concerned with dogma, but neither was it unconcerned with dogma. In a memorable and hideous turn of phrase, he said that the Confessing Church "takes its confident way between the Scylla of orthodoxy and the Charybdis of confessionlessness." He talked about the boundaries of engagement, explaining the vital difference between engaging "another church"— such as the Greek Orthodox Church or the Roman Catholic Church—and an institution that was "anti-church," such as the German Christians. One could have differences with another church, but engage in a dialogue to further mutual understanding. One could *not* have a dialogue with an institution that was "anti-church." This lecture on the eternal question, *What is the church?* helped his students make clear, biblical sense of a confusing issue at a confusing time in German church history.

But someplace in this beautiful landscape, planted like a time bomb, was a single sentence. It would soon explode and effectively obliterate every sentence around it and cause a firestorm of controversy. Bonhoeffer did not think of it that way when he wrote it, and he had never imagined that it would become a focal point of the lecture. The controversial sentence was this: "Whoever knowingly separates himself from the Confessing Church in Germany separates himself from salvation."

The condemnations were thundering. When the lecture was published in the June issue of *Evangelische Theologie*, the paper quickly sold out. Bonhoeffer's essay led Hermann Sasse, who had cowritten the Bethel Confession with him, to declare that the Confessing Church as "distinct from the confessional movement upheld by the Lutheran churches, is a sect, the worst sect in fact ever to have set foot on the soil of German Protestantism. " Merz said that Bonhoeffer's declaration was "the ecstatic effusion of a hitherto level-headed man, contradicting everything that was essential to Luther." General Superintendent Ernst Stoltenhoff called it "nothing more than an atrocious piece of false doctrine."

Bonhoeffer wrote to Erwin Sutz:

My paper has made me the most reviled man of our persuasion. . . . Things are approaching the stage when the beast before which the idol worshippers bow down will bear the caricature of Luther's features. . . . Either the Barmen Declaration is a true confession of the Lord Jesus Christ which has been brought about through the Holy Spirit, in which case it can make or divide a church—or it is an unofficial expression of the opinion of a number of theologians, in which case the Confessing Church has been on the wrong track for a long time.

Memo to Hitler

Bonhoeffer's hopes for the Confessing Church were raised again in the spring of 1936 when he learned that the church administration was preparing a document that forthrightly criticized the Nazis' policies against the Jews, among other things. It was a brave but measured document, and it was being written for the eyes of one man. It was a memorandum from the Confessing Church to Adolf Hitler.

The memo was written in such a way as to invite its maniacal reader into a conversation. It was neither demanding nor accusatory, but asked questions, and as such was calling Hitler's bluff, asking him to clarify things, giving him the benefit of the doubt. Was the "de-Christianization" of the German people official government policy? What did the Nazi Party mean by the term *positive Christianity*? It also noted that party ideology was forcing German citizens to hate Jews, and as a result, Christian parents faced difficulties with their children since Christians were not supposed to hate anyone. Hildebrandt was involved in drafting it, and Niemöller was among the signers.

The document was hand delivered to the Reich chancellery on June 4. Besides the copy for Hitler, only two other copies existed, both closely guarded. It was all a calculated gamble, since Hitler could respond negatively. As it turned out, Hitler did not respond at all. Days passed, then weeks. Had he ever received it?

After six weeks, disastrous news: they heard news of the memo from a London newspaper. On July 17, the *Morning Post* published an article about it. How could the British press have known about it since it had not been made public? Now Hitler would look bad in the eyes of the world at the very moment the Confessing Church had hoped to give him an opportunity to react privately, to save face. And it got worse: a week later a Swiss newspaper published the memo in its entirety. It appeared that the Confessing Church had leaked the memo to the international press with the intention of making Hitler look bad. But no one who had written the memo had a copy of it. Some suspected that Hitler himself had leaked the memo to make the Confessing Church look bad. Indeed, the church now appeared traitorous, having used the international press against the German government. As a result, many mainline Lutherans distanced themselves even further from the Confessing Church.

So what happened? It turned out that two of Bonhoeffer's former students, Werner Koch and Ernst Tillich, and Dr. Friedrich Weissler, a lawyer for the Confessing Church, were behind the leak. They had been frustrated with Hitler's lack of response, and they thought they could force his hand. All three were arrested and sent to Gestapo headquarters and interrogated. In the fall they were sent to the concentration camp at Sachsenhausen. Weissler, for the crime of being Jewish, was separated from his brethren and died within the week.

The Olympics were to begin in two weeks, so Hitler delayed taking immediate action against the trio. After all, international visitors and media were on hand, and more than four million tickets were sold. For now, he wished to appear magnanimous and tolerant.

The Confessing Church now made a bold move. Since the horse was out of the barn, the memo would be read from pulpits across Germany "to provide unmistakable evidence that the church had not completely lost its voice about the flagrant injustice." Furthermore, the text of the memo would be printed onto a million pamphlets and distributed. By criticizing Hitler publicly, the Confessing Church was swimming against a surging tide of popular opinion for Hitler. He was in high regard among even those who had been his detractors a year or two earlier, and the Olympics would be a crowning achievement. Anyone criticizing the buoyant Hitler at that high-water mark in Germany's resurrection from the Versailles grave was likely to be thought a griping fussbudget. Or an enemy of the state.

Olympiad

That summer the Olympic Games afforded Hitler a singular opportunity to show the cheerful, reasonable face of the "new Germany." Goebbels, who spared no expense in building his cathedrals of deceit, erected a veritable Chartres of trickery and fraud. The propagandist Leni Riefenstahl was even making a film of the spectacle.

The Nazis did their best to portray Germany as a Christian nation. The Reichskirche erected a huge tent near the Olympic stadium. Foreigners would have no idea of the internecine battle between the German Christians and the Confessing Church; it simply looked like there was an abundance of Christianity in the midst of Hitler's Germany. At St. Paul's Church, the Confessing Church sponsored a series of lectures: Jacobi, Niemöller, and Bonhoeffer spoke. "Not a bad evening yesterday," Bonhoeffer wrote. "The church packed; people were sitting on the altar steps and standing everywhere. I wish I could have preached instead of giving a lecture." Most of the Confessing Church lectures were packed. The Reichskirche sponsored lectures by "approved" university theologians, all thinly attended.

Bonhoeffer had mixed feelings about whether the Confessing Church should participate. Serious Christians in Germany were at war with something that was unrepentantly evil, that would not listen to reason and would not compromise. One must act and be prepared to face the consequences. As ever, he seemed alone in seeing this. The ecumenical movement continued its interminable dialogue, and the leaders of the Confessing Church did much the same, straining at gnats and swallowing camels.

The evangelical American leader Frank Buchman, who was the head of the Oxford Movement, was in Berlin now, hoping to bring the gospel of Christ to Hitler and the other Nazi leaders. His colleague Moni von Cramon had made the acquaintance of Himmler, with whom Buchman lunched during this time. The year before, Himmler told Cramon: "As an Aryan I must have the courage to take the responsibility for my sins alone." He rejected as "Jewish" the idea of putting one's sins on someone else's shoulders. He was even less interested in what Buchman had to say. Later in August Buchman made his tragic remark: "I thank heaven for a man like Adolf Hitler, who built a front line of defense against the anti-Christ of Communism." It was a throwaway comment made in an interview with the *New York World-Telegram* from his office at Calvary Church on Park Avenue and Twenty-first Street, and it did not reflect his wider thinking on the subject. Still, it illustrates how easily even the most serious Christians were initially taken in by Hitler's conservative pseudo-Christian propaganda.

After the Olympics, Bonhoeffer went to Chamby, Switzerland, for the Life and Work conference. The memo to Hitler would be read by Confessing Church pastors across Germany on August 23. Bonhoeffer asked his superiors whether he might stay in Switzerland, since it would be valuable to have someone outside Germany who was familiar with the memo, who could get word to the international press about it and about how Hitler was dealing with those who proclaimed it.

A number of brave pastors read the proclamation from their pulpits on the appointed day. One was Gerhard Vibrans, a close friend of Bonhoeffer and Bethge. At the end of the service the village schoolmaster spied the village policeman. "Arrest this traitor!" he cried. The policeman shrugged that he had no orders to do so. The Gestapo nonetheless had taken the names of those who read the proclamation.

Cast Ye Not Your Pearls Before Swine

In the fall of 1936, Ludwig Müller surfaced again, causing ripples with a pamphlet titled "Deutsche Gottesworte" ("German Words of God"). In the avuncular tone of an iconic chain-restaurant pitchman, the Reibi addressed his constituency in the foreword: "For you, my comrades in the Third Reich, I have not translated the Sermon on the Mount but Germanicized it. . . . Your *Reichsbischof*." Müller was only too happy to help his Aryan friend Jesus communicate more effectively with the people of the Third Reich. And since meekness was not an acceptable "German" attitude, Müller had given his comrades something more in keeping with the hearty Germanic image he wished to promote: "Happy is he who always observes good comradeship. He will get on well in the world." Müller obviously meant this self-lampooning hokum as evangelistic. But to what did he wish to convert his ignorant readership?

The German Christians had convinced themselves that "evangelizing" Germany was worth any price, including eviscerating the gospel by preaching hatred against the Jews. But Bonhoeffer knew that twisting the truth to sell it more effectively was not confined to the German Christians. Members of the Confessing Church had also shaved the truth betimes.

For Bonhoeffer, the challenge was to deliver the Word of God as purely as possible, without feeling the need to help it along or to dress it up. It alone had the power to touch the human heart. Any frippery would only dilute the power of the thing itself. He had told his ordinands of this time and again. Let this power speak for itself, unhindered.

But practically speaking, it was difficult to know where to draw the line in proclaiming the gospel. Was it so easy to say that Frank Buchman was casting pearls before swine in trying to reach Himmler? This question would come up in a very practical way for some of the ordinands who were dispatched to parishes not terribly interested in what they had to offer. It could be discouraging. Gerhard Vibrans was sent to a tiny village east of Magdeburg that seemed populated almost exclusively by dullards:

> My parish of six hundred souls at Schweinitz is a very poor one; on average only one or two people go to church there every Sunday. . . . [E]very Sunday, wearing my vestments, I make a pilgrimage through the whole village primarily to bring home to the people that it is Sunday. . . . The people try to comfort me by saying that I will get my salary even though no one goes to church.

He said that on Trinity Sunday no one at all showed up, "apart from the woman sexton." Bonhoeffer's response to Vibrans was simple, practical, and biblical: "If one village will not listen we go to another. There are limits." He was echoing Jesus' injunction to the disciples that they shake the dust from their sandals and leave a village where they were not welcomed (Matt. 10:14). But Bonhoeffer was not cavalier about it, and his heart went out to Vibrans, who had been about as faithful a servant as anyone could have imagined: "Your loyal observance of our advice almost puts me to shame. Don't take it too literally or one day you might get fed up with it."

Bonhoeffer visited the village and preached there. He later wrote Vibrans and said that he should write his congregation "telling them that this is possibly the last offer of the Gospel to them, and that there are other communities whose hunger for the Word cannot be satisfied because there are too few workers."

In the spring of 1937, Bonhoeffer wrote a dramatic paper titled "Statements about the Power of the Keys and Church Discipline in the New Testament." He was trying to get the church to take itself seriously, to grasp what power God had given it, an awesome and frightening power that needed to be understood and used as God intended. Just as he spoke to his ordinands about preaching the Word, he now spoke to the whole Confessing Church. The paper begins:

> 1. Christ has given his church power to forgive and to retain sins on earth with divine authority (Matt. 16:19; 18:18; John 20:23). Eternal salvation and eternal damnation are decided by its word. Anyone who turns from his sinful way at the word of proclamation and repents, receives forgiveness. Anyone who perseveres in his sin receives judgement. The church cannot loose the penitent from sin without arresting and binding the impenitent in sin.

There was nothing wishy-washy about it. Later he touched on the concept of cheap grace—without using the term—and he commented on how the ecumenical movement and the Confessing Church had sometimes engaged in well-intentioned dialogue with Hitler and the Reichskirche:

> 3. "Do not give dogs what is holy; and do not throw your pearls before swine, lest they trample them underfoot and turn to attack you" (Matt. 7:6). The promise of grace is not to be squandered; it needs to be

protected from the godless. There are those who are not worthy of the sanctuary. The proclamation of grace has its limits. Grace may not be proclaimed to anyone who does not recognize or distinguish or desire it. Not only does that pollute the sanctuary itself, not only must those who sin still be guilty against the Most Holy, but in addition, the misuse of the Holy must turn against the community itself. The world upon whom grace is thrust as a bargain will grow tired of it, and it will not only trample upon the Holy, but also will tear apart those who force it on them. For its own sake, for the sake of the sinner, and for the sake of the community, the Holy is to be protected from cheap surrender. The Gospel is protected by the preaching of repentance which calls sin sin and declares the sinner guilty. The key to loose is protected by the key to bind. The preaching of grace can only be protected by the preaching of repentance.

He had made similar comments before, in many contexts. He had warned the Confessing Church leaders much as the prophets of the Old Testament had done. And like the prophets, he had warned in vain.

But in 1937, the true nature of the beast with whom they had been dealing would suddenly reveal itself. The wolves, no longer needing to creep along under their sheepskins, would toss them away and come running.

The Nazis Crack Down

In 1937, the Nazis abandoned all pretense of being even-handed and came down hard on the Confessing Church. That year more than eight hundred Confessing Church pastors and lay leaders were imprisoned or arrested. Their leader, the outspoken Martin Niemöller of Dahlem, was among them. On June 27, he preached what would be his last sermon for many years. Crowds had overflowed his church week after week. That final Sunday, Niemöller was no less outspoken than he had always been. From the pulpit he declared, "We have no more thought of using our own powers to escape the arm of the authorities, than had the Apostles of old. No more are we ready to keep silent at man's behest when God commands us to speak. For it is, and must remain, the case that we must obey God rather than man." That Thursday he was arrested.

Even when being brutal, the Nazis were canny and careful. They were exceedingly sensitive to public opinion, and their approach to the Confessing Church was mostly one of ever-increasing and ever-tightening regulations. Their methods were "not so much aimed at banning the Confessing Church directly," Bethge said, "but gradually liquidating it through intimidation and the suppression of individual activities."

They forbade the reading of intercessory prayer lists from the pulpit and revoked passports; Niemöller's passport had been revoked earlier in the year. In June the Nazis declared that all collections taken during services of the Confessing Church were illegal. In July all "duplicate communication" would be subject to the Nazis' Editorial Law and would receive the same treatment as newspapers. For example, the Finkenwalde circular letters that Bonhoeffer wrote to his former pupils must now be signed personally by him. He put the words *Personal Letter* at the top of each copy. The welter of inane regulations and unjust laws overwhelmed the Confessing pastors, who were constantly running afoul of one of them and being arrested.

Over the next few years, Bonhoeffer felt a keen responsibility toward any Finkenwaldians taken to prison. He visited many of them and stayed in touch with their wives and parents. To the parent of one, he wrote:

> It is often difficult for us to grasp God's way with his church. But we may attain peace in the certainty that your son is suffering for the sake of the Lord and that the church of Jesus intercedes for him in prayer. The Lord confers great honor on his servants when he brings them suffering. . . . [Your son], however, will pray that you place everything in God's hands and that you will give thanks for everything that God may visit on you and on his church.

He wanted them to know that they were part of a larger community of resistance. To this end, and as a way to generally bring some relief to the harried young wives of imprisoned pastors, Bonhoeffer arranged for them to stay at the country home of Ruth von Kleist-Retzow at Klein-Krössin. She, too, became a supporter and encourager of many of the brethren and their families. When Werner Koch was imprisoned in a concentration camp, she wrote him: "We live in strange times, but we should be eternally thankful that poor, oppressed Christianity is acquiring greater vitality than I have ever known in the course of my seventy years. What testimony to its real existence!" Bonhoeffer sent Koch's wife to Frau von Kleist-Retzow to enjoy her peerless Christian hospitality. The rambling house, built in the old half-timbered German style, was surrounded by gardens and tall chestnut trees. She even raised young geese in her large country kitchen and had three guest rooms, named Hope, Contentment, and Joy.

Niemöller Arrested; Hildebrandt Departs

On the morning of July 1, Bonhoeffer and Bethge were in Berlin. The arrests of the Confessing Church pastors had been increasing, so they went to Niemöller's house in Dahlem to strategize with him and Hildebrandt. But they found only Hildebrandt and Niemöller's wife. The Gestapo had arrested Niemöller just moments earlier.

The four of them were talking about what to do next when several black Mercedes pulled up to the house. Knowing these to be Gestapo, Bonhoeffer, Bethge, and Hildebrandt made for the back door and were there stopped by Herr Höhle, a Gestapo official already familiar to them and most of the Confessing Church. The three men were escorted back into the house, searched by another officer, and then placed under house arrest, where they remained for seven hours, during which time they sat and watched as the Niemöllers' house was searched. The Gestapo's meticulous perseverance was eventually rewarded with the discovery of a safe behind a picture, and the thousand marks within, belonging to the Pastors' Emergency League.

Niemöller's ten-year-old son, Jan, remembered that anyone who showed up at the house that day was detained and fell under suspicion. "The house became full," he said. Somehow the inimitable Paula Bonhoeffer got wind of the situation. Bonhoeffer saw his parents' car pass several times, his mother peeking out. Everyone but Niemöller was released that afternoon. Things had entered a new phase.

Niemöller was in jail for eight months, but on the day of his release the Gestapo promptly rearrested him. They were known for this unpleasant tactic. Hitler could not abide the freedom of someone so outspokenly against him, so he honored Pastor Niemöller with the distinction of being a "personal prisoner" of the Führer for the next seven years, which Niemöller spent in Dachau. He was freed by the Allies in 1945.

Meanwhile, Hildebrandt would preach at Dahlem, his sermons no less fiery than Niemöller's. Still, he began to see that, as a Jew, it might be time for him to make an exit. Passports were being revoked, and he might not be able to leave when it was more convenient. His last sermon was July 18.

There were always Gestapo officers in the congregation. They meant to intimidate the parishioners and pastors, but at Dahlem they failed consistently. Niemöller teased them from the pulpit, sometimes asking a congregant to "pass a Bible to our policeman friend." This Sunday, in direct contravention of the new laws, Hildebrandt read aloud the list of those for whom intercessory prayers were being asked. He then took up an extra collection explicitly for the work of the Confessing Church. He instructed that the money be placed on the Lord's Table at the altar, where it was dedicated to God and God's work with a prayer. The Gestapo usually turned a blind eye to such breaches of the laws, but that day the officer did not. At the end of the service he brazenly went forward and took the money.

After this, Hildebrandt was arrested. A scene ensued in which Hildebrandt protested his arrest. Then the congregation joined in, growing louder and louder. The noisy crowd followed as the Gestapo officers escorted Hildebrandt outside to their car. The congregation crowded around the car, continuing their protest, and watched as the Gestapo officers tried to start the car and failed. After several embarrassing minutes, the humiliated Gestapo officers conceded defeat, got out of the car, and began walking with their prisoner toward headquarters. They preferred to do their work quietly, under cover of night when possible, but now as they walked down the street, they were the objects of a jeering congregation, outraged that their pastor was being taken from them, and letting everyone within earshot know about it. What's more, the Gestapo were unwittingly marching their prisoner in the wrong direction. Hildebrandt and his parishioners knew it, but they were not in a mood to help the Gestapo, who appeared more and more foolish with each step. In the end Hildebrandt was taken to the Gestapo headquarters on the Alexanderplatz.

The following day, the Gestapo took him back to his apartment, where another stash of money belonging to the Confessing Church was discovered and confiscated. But one of the officers was stricken with a bad toothache during the search, forcing him to end things prematurely, and leaving untouched a second Confessing Church fund.

Hildebrandt was then taken to the Plötzensee prison. Bonhoeffer and his other friends feared for his life there. As a Jew, he was much more likely to be mistreated. The Bonhoeffer family made an all-out effort to secure his release. Hans von Dohnanyi stepped into the fray and was able to get him out two days earlier than the prescribed twenty-eight. The early release enabled him to leave for Switzerland undetected by the authorities. Without this extraordinary intervention, he would have had to remain in the country and likely would have been rearrested as Niemöller had. As a non-Aryan, he probably would not have survived. From Switzerland, Hildebrandt went to London where he immediately became assistant pastor with his old friend Julius Rieger at St. George's. There he continued to work with refugees, and with Bishop Bell and his other ecumenical contacts. But Bonhoeffer would miss his friend.

The End of Finkenwalde

In Berlin, the Confessing Church planned a service of intercession to be held at Niemöller's church in Dahlem on August 8. The church was cordoned off, but Niemöller's congregation, like its pastor, was made of sterner stuff than most, and things erupted into another demonstration against the Nazis. The crowds refused to disperse for hours. Two hundred and fifty of the faithful were arrested and taken to the Alexanderplatz.

Throughout the summer of 1937, Bonhoeffer oversaw the fifth six-month course at Finkenwalde. He was also completing work on his manuscript for a book on the Sermon on the Mount that had been taking form in his thoughts since about 1932. The book, to be called *Nachfolge* (*Discipleship*), appeared in November 1937. It would become one of the most influential Christian books of the twentieth century.

When the summer term was over, Bonhoeffer and Bethge took a holiday trip to the Königsee and to Grainau, near Ettal, in the Bavarian Alps. After this they went up to Göttingen to visit Sabine and Gerhard and their girls. It was in Göttingen that he received a surprise telephone call from Stettin, informing him that the Gestapo had closed down Finkenwalde. The doors had been sealed. An era had ended.

For the next six weeks, Bonhoeffer and Bethge stayed in Berlin at his parents' home on Marienburgerallee. They stayed in Bonhoeffer's attic room, where there were two beds and many bookshelves.* From the window one looked down at the house and backyard next door, where Bonhoeffer's sister Ursula and her husband, Rüdiger Schleicher, lived. Bethge became a member of the Bonhoeffer family, eating every meal with them and enjoying these intelligent and cultured people, all of whom were passionately opposed to the Nazis. At night Bethge and Bonhoeffer discussed the latest news from Dohnanyi. It was getting more and more grim, especially with regard to the Jews.

They spent many evenings at the Schleichers' home, where the grand piano was. Bethge and Dietrich and the others would sing, with Dietrich usually playing accompaniment. Dietrich's eleven-year-old niece, Renate, was the designated page turner. Like her uncle, she had inherited the von Hase coloring—the flaxen hair and piercing blue eyes—of her grandmother, Paula Bonhoeffer. Neither she nor the twenty-eight-year-old Bethge had the slightest inkling that in six years they would be married.

The Collective Pastorates

During these six weeks, Bonhoeffer tried everything to appeal the closing of Finkenwalde. But it was clear by the end of 1937 that Finkenwalde would not reopen. Still, Bonhoeffer knew this didn't have to mean the end of the illegal seminaries. They would continue in the form of a *Sammelvikariat* (collective pastorates).

The process began by finding a church whose senior pastor was sympathetic to the Confessing Church and placing a number of "apprentice vicars" with him. Theoretically, they would be assisting him, but would actually receive education in the Finkenwalde mode. Each ordinand would be registered by the local police as an assistant to the local pastor, but would live with other ordinands in groups of seven to ten. In 1938 there were two such collective pastorates, both in the eastern wilds of Pomerania. The first, at Köslin, was about a hundred miles northeast of Stettin. The second was even more remote, about thirty miles farther east.

The superintendent of the Köslin district was the father of Fritz Onnasch, a Finkenwalde graduate. He placed ten ordinands with five Confessing

---

* One may visit this room today. Bonhoeffer's bookshelves, desk, and piano are still there.

Church pastors in his area. All of them lived in his vicarage. Bonhoeffer also lived there when necessary. Onnasch was the director of studies. The superintendent in Schlawe was Eduard Block, who employed Bethge and Bonhoeffer as assistant ministers under him. In Schlawe, Bethge would be the director of studies. This group of ordinands lived east of Schlawe in what Bethge described as "the rambling, wind-battered parsonage in Gross-Schlönwitz, at the boundary of the church district."

Bonhoeffer split his time between these idylls, traveling between Köslin and Schlawe on his motorcycle, weather permitting. He taught at Schlawe during the latter half of the week and remained through the weekend. Bonhoeffer often traveled the two hundred miles to Berlin and phoned almost every day, usually speaking with his mother, who continued to be his principal conduit of information about the church and political struggles.

Bonhoeffer was an eternal optimist because he believed what God said through the Scriptures. He knew that whatever befell him or the faithful brethren would open new opportunities in which God would operate, in which his provision would become clear. In his 1937 end-of-the year summation to the Finkenwalde graduates, he wrote, "We can already tell you today that the new ways by which we are being led give us great cause for thankfulness." A letter from one of the ordinands during this time gives a picture of what life at Schlönwitz was like:

> I did not come to Schlönwitz in a glad or hopeful frame of mind. . . .
> I shuddered at the prospect of this period of mental and physical
> straitening. It was to my mind a necessary evil . . . which one must
> endure gracefully and get through as well as possible on grounds of
> self-discipline . . . but then everything turned out quite different from
> what I had feared. Instead of entering the stuffy world of theological
> bigotry, I found myself in one which combined much of what I loved
> and needed; clear theological work in companionship with others,
> who never let one be wounded by feeling one's own incompetence,
> but who made the work a joy; brotherhood under the Word which
> united us all without respect of person; and at the same time an appre-
> ciation of all that gives charm to the fallen creation; music, literature,
> sport and the beauty of the earth; a magnanimous way of living . . .
> when I look back I can see a clear picture. . . . The brothers sitting in

the afternoon over coffee and bread and jam. The chief returns after a long absence . . . now we get the latest news, and the world breaks into the quiet and simplicity of our country life in Pomerania. . . . [D]oes it dull the exactness of your theological vision, if I tell you that it was the peripheral things which [were] enhanced by appreciation of the central one?

In 1939 the vicarage in Schlawe was no longer available, but even this was no hardship. The ordinands relocated to Sigurdshof, an even more remote location than Gross-Schlönwitz. It was as if a bird were leading them farther and farther away from the cares of the present and into a realm deep in the heart of a German fairy tale. Bethge wrote:

> The small house was two miles south of the village on the estate, and it was more secluded than anywhere they had lived up to that point. Four tiny windows looked out the front onto a little-used courtyard, under an overhanging roof and through luxurious climbing plants. In the back the idyllic Wipper River flowed by. There was a water pump beneath the nearest trees, where a vast forest began that merged with the Varzin woods of the Bismarck estate to the south. There was no electricity. . . . Anyone who did not find even this situation quiet enough could withdraw to a hunting lodge farther away in the forest. In the summer they could use the count's fishing skiff on the pond and the tennis court at the Tychow manor house.
>
> We are anxious about our coal; and besides that, we have no paraffin, so we have to use candles. We all stay in one room, and someone plays [an instrument] or reads aloud.

In letters to his parents describing the situation, Bonhoeffer wrote:

> I arrived here yesterday. . . . Yesterday afternoon I could not stop myself from joining the skiers in the snow-covered wood. It was really lovely, and so peaceful that everything else seemed like an apparition. Generally speaking, I really feel more and more that life in the country, especially in times like these, has much more human dignity than in towns. All the manifestations of the masses simply fall away. I think

the contrast between Berlin and this secluded farmstead is particularly striking now.

We are now fairly snowed in and cut off. The postal van can't get through, and we can get nothing except now and then by sled. . . . Minus 28 degrees. . . . Under the circumstances the work goes well. The forester has let us have two loads of wood and two hundred kilograms of coal, and that will do for a few weeks. Of course, the food supply is rather difficult too, but we still have enough. If I had my way, I think I should like to leave town for good.

The black ice here is indescribable after a good deal of flooding. Up to within ten yards of the house the meadows have turned into a magnificent skating rink. . . . We have enough fuel for a week.

For two days we have been deep in snow with almost uninterrupted snowstorms.

CHAPTER 20

MARS ASCENDING

1938

Confirmands today are like young soldiers marching to war, the war of Jesus Christ against the gods of this world. It is a war that demands the commitment of one's whole life. Is not God, our Lord, worthy of this struggle?

—DIETRICH BONHOEFFER

My dear lady, we have fallen into the hands of criminals. How could I ever have imagined it!

—HJALMAR SCHACHT, FORMER HEAD OF THE GERMAN REICHSBANK

The year 1938 was hugely tumultuous for Germany and for Europe. It was certainly so for the Bonhoeffers, and for Dietrich it did not begin well at all. On January 11 he was arrested at a Confessing Church meeting in Dahlem. Gestapo officers appeared, arrested all thirty people, and interrogated them at the Alexanderplatz headquarters for seven hours before releasing them. But the biggest news of the day was that Bonhoeffer learned he was henceforth banned from Berlin. The Gestapo put him and Fritz Onnasch aboard a train bound for Stettin that evening.

The first term of the collective pastorates had begun, and Bonhoeffer was grateful he had not been banned from continuing that work. But to be

302

cut off from Berlin now, when political developments were beginning to look encouraging, was devastating. He expected to commute between Berlin and Pomerania, much as he had been doing since 1935. His parents' home was the center of his universe, and at this moment, with the Nazi government beginning to wobble and raise everyone's hopes that Hitler might be on his way out, it was a terrible time to be kept away.

But knowing many people in high places, Bonhoeffer was almost never without recourse. He made a plan to meet his parents to discuss what might be done. He obviously couldn't travel to them, so in early February they came to Stettin and met him at the home of Ruth von Kleist-Retzow. Karl Bonhoeffer's eminence was somehow brought to bear on the situation, and he persuaded the Gestapo to make the ban exclusively related to work. So Dietrich could still travel to Berlin for personal and family matters.

Bonhoeffer had many reasons to hope that Hitler's luck would suddenly run out. From his position in the Ministry of Justice, Hans von Dohnanyi saw and heard things before they were filtered by the Nazi propaganda machine, and he conveyed what he learned to his extended family. The previous fall, Hitler's government was put in a difficult spot when Hjalmar Schacht, the architect of Germany's booming economy, resigned in a public protest. In January 1938, events began to unfold that would lead to another major crisis. Perhaps they were all on the threshold of the departure of the irascible vegetarian who had been destroying their country for the previous five years.

Hitler's troubles began on November 5, 1937. He summoned his generals to a meeting in which he spelled out his plans for war. As anyone paying attention had known, Hitler had been intent on war from the beginning. Now it was at hand. He told the stunned generals that he would first attack Austria and Czechoslovakia to eliminate the possibility of trouble on Germany's eastern flank, and it was imperative that England be mollified for the moment since the English were a serious military threat. War with England and France was probably in the offing soon enough. For four hours the megalomaniac scrawled a recipe of how he would soon have the world agog at his military genius: "I'll cook them a stew that they'll choke on!"

The generals left this meeting in various states of shock and fury. What they had just heard was distilled madness. The foreign minister, Baron von Neurath, literally had several heart attacks. General Beck found it all "shattering." Beck would lead the conspiracy to assassinate Hitler in which Dohnanyi and Bonhoeffer would soon become involved, and it was what Beck heard from Hitler that day that set him on his mutinous course. But all the generals were nonplussed by Hitler's naked and blind aggression. They had begun to describe him as "mentally ill" and "blood thirsty." What he was planning was nothing short of national suicide.

But these gentlemen from the Prussian officer tradition were all too well-bred to know how to deal with someone as vulgar as Hitler. On the one hand, he was an uncouth embarrassment, a feral clod hardly to be taken seriously. On the other hand, he was the legal head of their beloved Germany, to whom they had sworn oaths. For most of these men, he presented some kind of obscene Chinese puzzle. Most of them loved their country and hated Hitler, and they rightly saw his war plans as breathtaking in their foolhardiness and immorality. They were convinced that he would smash their great nation on the rocks, and they were quite right. From that meeting forward, they were intent on removing him.

Beck did all he could to influence the generals to stage a coup d'etat. Finally, to make as bold a public statement as possible, he resigned. This ought to have shaken the nation to its roots—and to have defenestrated the Nazis en masse. But by maintaining his dignified aristocratic bearing, Beck fluffed the full effect of his exit. He didn't want to draw too much attention to himself, for that would have been unseemly, so he departed with such nobility that hardly anyone heard him go. His parting shot had just enough English on it that he quite missed the pocket.

Hans Gisevius said that Beck "was still so deeply immersed in the traditions of the Prussian officers' corps that he wished to avoid even the faintest semblance of an attack upon the authority of the state." In time Beck would begin to see that he was in a new world, where the state as he knew it had been dismantled and dumped in a swamp. But Beck hadn't seen this quite yet. His successor, Franz Halder, was not nearly as passive, and he described Hitler as "the very incarnation of evil."

The Fritsch Affair

One of these dignified men was at the center of the crisis that threatened to topple Hitler, and that had Dohnanyi and Bonhoeffer wide-eyed with interest. That man was the commander in chief of the army, General Wilhelm von Fritsch.

The troubles began when Fritsch made the mistake of trying to talk Hitler out of his war plans. Hitler had no patience for these upper-class cowards. For him the question was not whether Fritsch might have a point, but how to silence such troublemakers. The puffy and pomaded Luftwaffe chief Hermann Göring had an idea. Göring had been ogling the top spot in the German military for some time, and he had recently been successful in getting rid of the previous head of the army in an underhanded fashion. That man, Field Marshal Blomberg, was drummed out in a scandal involving his new wife, whom Göring accused of having been a prostitute, which she had been. The dapper older gent hadn't any idea that his secretary's past might splash to the surface, but when it did, he bowed and took his exit.

Göring had known he would; with these men of honor, it didn't take much to embarrass them and send them packing. Could it work again? But this time Göring had no facts to work with. Still, he would come up with something. What he came up with was despicable. Himmler would provide the damning information. It involved a shifty eyewitness who would say that Fritsch had a homosexual liaison in a "dark alley near the Potsdam railroad station in Berlin with an underworld character by the name of 'Bavarian Joe.'" Confronted with this startlingly seamy accusation, Fritsch was understandably speechless.

It must be said that the Nazi leaders, including Hitler, had no moral difficulties with homosexuality. Many of the early figures in the Nazi movement were homosexuals, Ernst Röhm and his strutting cronies chief among them. Hitler has plausibly been connected to such activity. But in the Third Reich an accusation of homosexuality was without peer in smearing someone's reputation. So with the breathtaking cynicism that was their trademark, Hitler and the Nazis employed this tactic innumerable times against their political enemies; and the concentration camps were full of sad cases whose real reasons for being there need never be disclosed, as long as they bore the stigma of a pink triangle.

But General Fritsch was indeed innocent of the stipulated act and vowed to defend his honor. Dohnanyi was in the midst of trying to shed light on what happened. It was soon discovered that Fritsch had been deliberately confused with a "bedridden retired cavalry officer" named Frisch. Frisch had indeed cavorted in the dark alley; Fritsch had not. Himmler and the Gestapo knew everything, but their desire to be rid of Fritsch was paramount, so they tried to frame him with a deliberate typographical error. Who would bother about one little *t* in the inky ocean of the Third Reich? They almost succeeded. But not quite.

When the foul stunt became known to Fritsch, he vowed that justice would be done. The military court of honor would exonerate him, and the evidence of Himmler's machinations would publicly expose him and his SS for what they were. Heydrich, too, would also be implicated, flushed out, and chased back to his submarine cavern. The guilt of the Gestapo and the SS was such that it seemed the whole thing might drive Hitler from office. And if Hitler tried to suppress the evidence, the army was ready to act. Plans for a coup were being made, and Dohnanyi and Bonhoeffer watched with bated breath.

But as we know, none of this happened. Like some Houdini from hell, Hitler again wriggled free. But how? As usual, it was the fumfering inaction of the German army officer corps, bound and gagged by their misplaced scruples. In time the bloodthirsty devils with whom they were playing patty-cake would strangle them with the guts of their quaint scruples. Though it can scarcely be believed, Fritsch was convinced it would be unseemly for a man of his social standing to publicly protest the accusations. Joachim Fest wrote that Fritsch's "inability to come to terms with the coarse new world in which he suddenly found himself is evidenced in his almost comic yet poignant plan, devised with Beck's approval, to challenge Himmler . . . to a duel." He might as well have suggested playing chess with a shark. Another German conservative had once said that Hitler "had something alien about him, as if he sprang from an otherwise extinct primeval tribe." He was a damned conundrum! By the time any of these fine fellows had drawn a bead on him, it was too late. That year, former *Reichsbank* head Hjalmar Schacht exclaimed to a dinner companion: "My dear lady, we have fallen into the hands of criminals. How could I ever have imagined it!"

Hitler further wiped the slate clean by announcing on the morning of February 4—Bonhoeffer's thirty-second birthday—a drastic reordering of the whole German military. It was a bold, sweeping decree: "From now on I take over personally the command of the whole armed forces." In a single stroke he erased the whole problem of Fritsch and much else by abolishing the War Ministry and creating in its place the *Oberkommando der Wehrmacht*

(OKW), making himself its head. The top spot that Göring had coveted no longer existed, but Hitler happily kicked his bejeweled *Arsch* upstairs by granting him the head-swelling title of field marshal. Wilhelm Keitel was named chief of the OKW precisely because he lacked leadership qualities and wouldn't interfere with Hitler's wishes. Hitler had once told Goebbels that Keitel "possessed the brains of a movie usher." Thus the trouble that might have ended Nazi rule evaporated.

If ever a golden opportunity was lost to put Hitler and the Nazis on an early train and deliver Germany from the unthinkable fate that awaited her, the flubbed Fritsch Affair was it. But it was from this lowest of low points that much of the resistance to Hitler would emerge. The main figure of the various opposition groups that sprang up now was Hans Oster, who became the head of the Central Division of the Abwehr (German Military Intelligence). On the civilian side, Carl Goerdeler would be the principal leader. Goerdeler was the mayor of Leipzig who, in 1933, boldly refused to raise the swastika at Leipzig city hall, and in 1937 he refused to remove a public statue of the Jewish composer Felix Mendelssohn. In his absence the Nazis removed it anyway, and Goerdeler resigned, but he thenceforward worked tirelessly against Hitler and the Nazis.

The Austrian *Anschluss*

Having successfully dealt with the Fritsch Affair, Hitler could once again settle down and peacefully focus on how to take over Europe. Appropriately enough, his first toddling steps toward war and conquest were in the direction of his birthplace, Austria. In March 1938, he brought an entire nation into the Nazi fold with the annexation (*Anschluss*) of Austria. For many Germans, the *Anschluss* was a giddy moment. What had been taken from them through Versailles would now be returned to them—with interest—by their benevolent Führer. Public figures eager to curry favor with the increasingly popular dictator would outdo each other in contorted calisthenics of sycophancy. In ecclesiastical circles, Bishop Sasse of Thuringia was first in line, aching to say 'thank you' to his Führer, and doing so by demanding that all of the pastors under him take a personal "oath of loyalty" to Hitler. His telegram to Hitler has been preserved: "My *Führer*, I report: in a great historic hour all the pastors of the Thuringian Evangelical Church, obeying an inner command, have with joyful hearts taken an oath of loyalty to *Führer* and Reich. . . . One God—one obedience in the faith. Hail, my *Führer!*" In short order other bishops, afraid to be left out of the riot of gratitude, vigorously supplied "inner commands" to their flocks too.

The new head of the Reichskirche was Dr. Friedrich Werner, and as a triple-jointed sycophant, he wouldn't be outdone. His grand sense of occasion alone would catapult him into the lead because, for his obsequious gesture, he chose the Führer's birthday. On April 20 he published in the *Legal Gazette* a sweeping ordinance demanding that every single pastor in Germany take an oath of obedience to Adolf Hitler. There was nothing "inner" about it.

> In the recognition that only those may hold office in the church who are unswervingly loyal to the Führer, the people and the Reich, it is hereby decreed: Anyone who is called to a spiritual office is to affirm his loyal duty with the following oath: "I swear that I will be faithful and obedient to Adolf Hitler, the Führer of the German Reich and people, that I will conscientiously observe the laws and carry out the duties of my office, so help me God." . . . Anyone who refuses to take the oath of allegiance is to be dismissed.

Many Confessing Church pastors felt that taking this oath would be like bowing down to a false god. Just as early Christians had refused to worship images of Caesar, and Jews had refused to worship the statue of Nebuchadnezzar, so they refused to take this oath to Adolf Hitler. But the messianic attitude toward Hitler was widespread, and few dared to stand against it. With each of his triumphs, the pressure to join the adulation increased. That April, Bonhoeffer had been in Thuringia when he passed the famous Wartburg castle in Eisenach. It was here that Luther, freshly excommunicated by Pope Leo X, had translated the New Testament into German in 1521. After the *Anschluss*, Bonhoeffer saw that the great cross atop the castle had been eclipsed by a monstrous flood-lit swastika.

Werner's decree that all German pastors must take this "oath of allegiance" to Hitler brought bitter division to the Confessing Church at a time when things were already fragile. Many Confessing pastors were tired of fighting, and they thought that taking the oath was a mere formality, hardly worth losing one's career. Others took the oath, but with torn consciences, heartsick over what they were doing. But Bonhoeffer and others saw it as a cynical calculation on Werner's part, and pushed the Confessing Church to stand against it. But the church did not. Karl Barth wrote from Switzerland:

> I am most deeply shocked by that decision and the arguments used to support it, after I have read and reread them. . . . Was this defeat possible, permissible or necessary? Was there and is there really no one among you at all who can lead you back to the simplicity of the straight and narrow way? . . . No one who beseeches you not to jeopardize the future credibility of the Confessing Church in this dreadful way?

On the bright side, that April Bonhoeffer presided over the confirmation of three of Ruth von Kleist-Retzow's grandchildren, Spes von Bismarck, Hans-Friedrich von Kleist-Retzow, and Max von Wedemeyer. The service was held at the church in Kieckow, and in keeping with the environment of the Prussian military class, Bonhoeffer employed a martial simile in his sermon: "Confirmands today are like young soldiers marching to war, the war of Jesus Christ against the gods of this world. It is a war that demands the commitment of one's whole life. Is not God, our Lord, worthy of this struggle? Idolatry and cowardice confront us on all sides, but the direst foe does not confront us, he is within us. 'Lord, I believe; help thou mine unbelief.'"

Ruth von Kleist-Retzow was there, beaming with pride over her grandchildren and over Dietrich. Her children and their spouses, and her other grandchildren were there, too, including Maria von Wedemeyer, to whom Bonhoeffer would propose marriage four years hence. Both young men confirmed that day would be killed in the war not yet begun: Friedrich in 1941, and Max in 1942. Max's father, also in attendance, would be killed too. But Bonhoeffer's relationships with these genuinely noble families were a brilliant bright spot during otherwise dark times.

Escape from Germany

On May 28, Hitler informed his military commanders of his plans to march into Czechoslovakia and end its cartographical existence. Compulsory civilian service was enacted in June, and throughout the summer, Germany leaned toward war. The time for the generals to stage their coup had come. In August, Ewald von Kleist-Schmenzin met with Winston Churchill, then a member of Parliament, to discuss whether England would help the Germans trying to bring about a new government. "We will give you everything," Churchill said, "but first bring us Hitler's head!" The generals were working on it.

The sense of imminent war caused the Leibholzes to wonder whether their days in Germany would soon be over. A law was about to take effect requiring every Jewish person's passport to be emended if the person's given name was not obviously Jewish: Israel had to be added as a middle name for men, and Sarah, for women. Hans von Dohnanyi urged the Leibholzes to leave while they could. If war broke out, Germany's borders would be sealed. Sabine and Gert heard stories of Jews being abducted at night and humiliated. Every time the doorbell rang they were frightened, not knowing what trouble lay behind it. They had traveled to Switzerland or Italy on vacations and felt the freedom of being outside Germany. "Each time that we journeyed back to Göttingen," Sabine recalled, "something like an iron band seemed to tighten round my heart with every kilometre that brought us nearer to the town."

Finally they made preparations to leave. It was a monumental and heart-wrenching decision. Sabine and Gert first went to Berlin where they discussed all the final details with the family, who already had begun to use code words in phone and written communications. They still hoped that with the imminent coup of which Dohnanyi was informing them, they would be able to return before very long. Perhaps they would be away only a few weeks. But they could not take chances; they must go.

When they returned to Göttingen on September 8, Bethge and Bonhoeffer followed from Berlin in Bonhoeffer's car. The plan was to accompany them for part of the journey to the Swiss border the following day. Everything must be done with utter secrecy. Even the girls' nanny must not know.

The next day was a Friday. The nanny woke the girls at six thirty and began to get them ready for school. Suddenly their mother came into the room and announced that they were not going to school. They would be going on a trip to Wiesbaden! Eleven-year-old Marianne suspected something was afoot. They never went to Wiesbaden. But she was wise enough to know that if they were about to leave their home, she mustn't let on. Sabine told the girls' nanny they would be back on Monday.

Normally, Marianne walked to school with her best friend, Sybille, but this morning Marianne told her they were going to Wiesbaden for the weekend. When Sybille said good-bye, Sabine realized she might never see her again. "I must try to remember what she looks like," she thought.

The Leibholzes' car was packed full, but not too full. It must appear as though they were only going away for a weekend. Anything else might arouse suspicions when they got to the border, near Basel. They drove away in the two cars.

When they felt it was safe, Sabine told the girls that they weren't going to Wiesbaden after all. They were going to cross the Swiss border. "They may close the frontier because of the crisis," she said.

Many years later Marianne recalled that day:

The roof of our car was open, the sky was deep blue, the countryside looked marvelous in the hot sunshine. I felt there was complete solidarity between the four grown-ups. I knew that unaccustomed things would be asked of us children from now on but felt proud of now being allowed to share the real troubles of the adults. I thought if I could do nothing against the Nazis myself I must at the very least co-operate with the grown-ups who could. Christiane and I spent most the time singing in the car, folk songs and rather militant songs about freedom, my mother, Uncle Dietrich and "Uncle" Bethge singing with us. I enjoyed the various descants. Uncle Dietrich taught me a new round, *Über die Wellen gleitet der Kahn.*

During the drive, my uncle seemed to me just as I always remember him: very strong and confident, immensely kind, cheerful and firm.

We stopped at Giessen and pick-nicked by the wayside. The grown-ups' mood did not strike me as depressing. Then all of a sudden they said it was getting late and that we must hurry. "We have to get across the frontier tonight, they may close it at any moment." We children settled in our car, our parents got in, and I remember Uncle Dietrich and "Uncle" Bethge waving farewell to us until they became tiny and were cut off by a hill. The rest of the drive was no longer cheerful. My parents drove as fast as they could, we stopped talking so that they could concentrate. The atmosphere was tense.

We crossed the Swiss border late at night. Christiane and I

pretended to be asleep and very angry at being wakened, to discourage the German frontier guards from doing too much searching of the car. My mother had put on a long, very brown suede jacket, whose brownness was meant to pacify the German officials. They let our car through and the Swiss let us in. My parents were not to cross the German border again till after the war.

After seeing Sabine, Gert, and the girls off, Bonhoeffer and Bethge returned to Göttingen, where they stayed in the Leibholzes' house for several weeks. There Bonhoeffer wrote his small devotional classic, *Life Together.* Bethge recalled Bonhoeffer working on the manuscript at Gerhard's desk almost constantly, while Bethge studied Barth's *Church Dogmatics*. During breaks, they played tennis. Bonhoeffer had begun the short book with the intention of writing something for the ordinands while the experience and his thoughts were fresh. But eventually he realized his thinking on Christian community might have a wider audience. The book has become a classic of devotional literature.

While Bonhoeffer wrote, the Czechoslovakian crisis was front and center. Hitler publicly maintained that the German-speaking populations of Europe belonged to Germany. The Austrian *Anschluss* had been portrayed not as an act of aggression, but as a benevolent father welcoming his children home. The Sudetenland situation was portrayed in the same way. But larger issues were at stake. France and England would not stand for it. Italy, at that time led by Mussolini, was inclined to side with Hitler. The generals knew Hitler's plans were naked aggression and would lead Germany into a world war she would lose. Bonhoeffer knew a coup was imminent. He and Bethge stayed in close contact with the family at Marienburgerallee.

During this time, Karl Barth wrote a letter to a friend that included the following sentence: "Every Czech soldier who fights and suffers will be doing so for us too, and I say this without reservation—he will also be doing it for the church of Jesus, which in the atmosphere of Hitler and Mussolini must become the victim of either ridicule or extermination." Somehow the letter was made public and caused a terrific uproar. For many in the Confessing Church, he had gone too far, and they would distance themselves from him.

---

* He had already dictated parts of it at Gross-Schlönwitz. Hans-Werner Jensen, an ordinand, recalled typing it to Bonhoeffer's dictation.

Peace in Our Time: Munich, 1938

The army generals were aching for Hitler to march on Czechoslovakia, not because they thought it wise, but because they thought it so patently foolish that it would give them the opportunity they had been waiting for. They would seize Hitler and take over the government. A number of possibilities were open to them. One was to declare him insane and unfit for leadership, and the first piece of evidence would be his insistence on invading Czechoslovakia when it would bring certain disaster and ruin to Germany. But they also had connections to a highly esteemed German psychiatrist who shared their diagnosis of the nation's leader, and their political views. Karl Bonhoeffer was waiting in the wings. His expert testimony would come in handy, and he was indeed convinced from a clinical perspective that Hitler was a pathological madman. They had thought that going about everything through legal means would expose Hitler's crimes, would avoid the grim possibility of sparking a civil war, and would avoid turning him into a martyr, since his popularity was soaring. But Hitler must make the first move. When he did, the army would stage its coup, and everything would be different.

The most immediate benefit for the Bonhoeffer family would be that the Leibholzes could return to Germany. They did not anticipate leaving forever, which was likely why Bonhoeffer and Bethge remained at their home in Göttingen after their departure. They all knew from Dohnanyi that the generals were preparing a putsch. One way or another, the former Viennese vagrant might be given the bum's rush at any moment. But what played out on the world stage in the weeks ahead was stranger than fiction.

As things stood that September, Hitler was on the verge of marching into Czechoslovakia, and all of the European leaders were expecting him to do so. It seemed inevitable. And they were preparing to stop him by military means, and would have succeeded, as Germany was simply not ready to wage war on the scale that would have been necessary. So the scene was set. It was as if Hitler had crept out onto a ledge, made his outrageous demands, and would not come back inside. He certainly wasn't about to embarrass himself before the crowds by crawling back in the window. The whole world watched him from below, and the generals watched him from inside, looking out the window at him on the ledge. They knew his position was impossible and were expecting him to fall, and if necessary, they were prepared to give him a little "Putsch." The whole world would cheer. The breathtaking climax of this magnificent drama was destroyed by Britain's prime minister, Neville Chamberlain, who suddenly appeared in the unprecedented role of appeaser *ex machina*. It was as though he had commandeered a hot air balloon, floated by, and offered Herr Hitler a nice, civilized ride to the ground.

Hitler accepted, although he was thunderstruck by Chamberlain's unsolicited and unnecessary offer. He was not one-tenth as thunderstruck as the generals, who had been a hair's breadth from action and couldn't fathom why Chamberlain would have done such a thing! And Chamberlain was willing to meet with Hitler personally, wherever Hitler wished, with no concern for protocol. The sixty-nine-year-old prime minister had never been in an airplane before, but he would now fly seven hours from London to Berchtesgaden on the far side of Germany to meet with the ill-mannered tyrant.

His badly timed efforts would serve for generations as the textbook example of cheap grace in geopolitical terms: it was "peace" on the house, with a side order of Czechoslovakia. The accord was immediately denounced by Goerdeler, who called it "outright capitulation." Far away in London, Winston Churchill called it the "first foretaste of a bitter cup." Even worse than saving Hitler from his own destruction, it bought Hitler time to build up Germany's armed forces. In a year, when he surged across Poland on all cylinders, Hitler would laugh at Chamberlain.

That October, when the rebounding Nazis demanded that every Jew in Germany have a *J* stamped on his passport, it was clear the Leibholzes could not return. They would leave Switzerland for London. There Bonhoeffer connected them with Bishop Bell and Julius Rieger, who welcomed them as they had welcomed so many Jewish refugees from the Third Reich. Franz Hildebrandt, whom they knew very well, was also on hand to help them get established. Gerhard eventually was able to get a lectureship at Magdalen College, Oxford, where C. S. Lewis was then.

Kristallnacht, "9.11.38"

Bonhoeffer often spoke of Jesus Christ as the "man for others," as selflessness incarnate, loving and serving others to the absolute exclusion of his needs and desires. Similarly, the church of Jesus Christ existed for "others." And since Christ was Lord over the whole world, not just the church, the church existed to reach out beyond itself, to speak out for the voiceless, to defend the weak and fatherless. In 1938, Bonhoeffer's views on this subject were particularly sharpened as a result of the disturbing events of November 9. It was now, for the first time, that his gaze was in a new way directed away from his own trials and toward the trials of God's people, the Jews.

The infamous events of that week began November 7, when a seventeen-year-old German Jew shot and killed an official in the German Embassy in Paris. The young man's father had recently been put in a crowded boxcar and deported to Poland. For that and for the Nazis' other abuses against the Jews he had his revenge. But the man he killed was not the German ambassador, Count Johannes von Welczeck, as he had intended. It was the third secretary of the embassy, Ernst vom Rath, who happened to cross the angry young man's path at the wrong time. Ironically, vom Rath was opposed to the Nazis, in part because of their vicious anti-Semitism. As with the burning of the Reichstag, the shooting was just the pretext that Hitler and the Nazi leaders needed. In a "spontaneous" series of demonstrations, evils would be unleashed against the Jews of Germany on a terrible scale.

Hitler gave the command to take action against the Jews, but to execute this action, he looked to the services of Reinhard Heydrich, Himmler's second in command at the SS. One of the most sinister figures in the evil pantheon of the Third Reich, Heydrich had an icy mien that suggested something one might encounter in the lightless world of the Marianas Trench. At 1:20 a.m., following the vom Rath assassination, he sent an urgent Teletype message to every Gestapo station across Germany. The orders gave explicit directions on how to perpetrate the events of what has come to be known as the *Kristallnacht* (Night of Broken Glass). Homes and businesses were destroyed and looted, synagogues were set aflame, and Jews were beaten and killed.

Bonhoeffer was in the far eastern wilds of Pomerania when these events began. The Gestapo in Köslin had gotten the Teletype message, too, and the synagogue there was burned. But Bonhoeffer did not know of it, having already set off for Gross-Schlönwitz to begin his second half of the week of teaching. It was only later the next day that he heard what had happened across Germany. In a conversation about it with his ordinands the next day, someone put forth the accepted theory about the "curse" upon the Jews. The young ordinands did not condone what had happened and were genuinely upset about it, but they quite seriously suggested that the reason for the evils must be the "curse" that the Jews bore for rejecting Christ. Bonhoeffer knew the young men were neither hateful nor anti-Semitic, but he firmly refuted their interpretation. They were in error.

In his Bible that day or the next, Bonhoeffer was reading Psalm 74. This was the text he happened to be meditating upon. What he read startled him, and with his pencil he put a vertical line in the margin to mark it, with an exclamation point next to the line. He also underlined the second half of verse 8: "Sie verbrennen alle Häuser Gottes im Lande." ("They burn all of God's houses in the land.") Next to the verse he wrote: "9.11.38." Bonhoeffer saw this as an example of God speaking to him, and to the Christians in Germany. God was telling him something through his Word that day, and as he meditated and prayed, Bonhoeffer realized that the synagogues that had been burned in Germany were God's own. This was when Bonhoeffer most clearly saw the connection: to lift one's hand against the Jews was to lift one's hand against God himself. The Nazis were attacking God by attacking his people. The Jews in Germany were not only not God's enemies; they were his beloved children. Quite literally, this was a revelation.

In the circular letter to the Finkenwalde community a few days afterward, Bonhoeffer reflected on this, and to make his bold point, he added other verses into the mix: "I have lately been thinking a great deal about Psalm 74, Zech. 2:8 and Rom. 9:4f. and 11:11–15. That leads us to very earnest prayer." Taken all together, he was preaching a provocative sermon. The verse in Zechariah is: "For thus said the LORD of hosts, after his glory sent me to the nations who plundered you, for he who touches you touches the apple of his eye" (ESV). The verses in Romans 9 are: "They are Israelites, and to them belong the adoption, the glory, the covenants, the giving of the law, the worship, and the promises. To them belong the patriarchs, and from their race, according to the flesh, is the Christ who is God over all, blessed forever. Amen" (ESV). And in Romans 11: "So I ask, did they stumble in order that they might fall? By no means! Rather through their trespass salvation has come to the Gentiles, so as to make Israel jealous. Now if their trespass means riches for the world, and if their failure means riches for the Gentiles, how much more will their full inclusion mean! Now I am speaking to you Gentiles. Inasmuch then as I am an apostle to the Gentiles, I magnify my ministry in order somehow to make my fellow Jews jealous, and thus save some of them" (ESV).

Bonhoeffer was using the words of Jews—David, Zechariah, and Paul—to make the point that the Jews are God's people, that the Messiah came from them and came for them first. He had never abandoned them, but longed to reach those who were the "apple of His eye." If Christianity has come to the Gentiles, it came in some large part so that the Jews could receive their Messiah. Bonhoeffer was identifying the evil done to the Jews as an evil done to God and God's people, but he was not taking that next theological leap to suggest that Christians were not meant to take the gospel of Christ to the Jews. On the contrary, he stood against this idea by quoting these verses, and he stood against the Nazis who had forbidden Jews from being a part of the German church.

For Bonhoeffer to take such a theological stand on the subject of the Jews was exceedingly rare. But he knew that God had spoken to him that morning. Bethge said that Bonhoeffer never wrote anything about contemporary events in his Bible. This was the only time he had done so.

Hans-Werner Jensen recalled that Bonhoeffer's awareness of what the Jews were going through immediately following *Kristallnacht* caused him to be "driven by a great inner restlessness, a holy anger. . . . During those ugly days we learned to understand—not just human revenge, but the prayer of the so-called psalms of vengeance which give over to God alone the case of the innocent, 'for his name's sake.' It was not apathy and passiveness which Dietrich Bonhoefer derived from them, but for him prayer was the display of the strongest possible activity."

Throughout 1938, the inability of the Confessing Church's leaders to be bold and stand firm disheartened Bonhoeffer, not least because the pastors were not receiving the encouragement and support they desperately needed. He wrote in his Advent letter that year:

I'm not quite sure how we have largely got into a way of thinking which is positively dangerous. We think that we are acting particularly responsibly if every other week we take another look at the question whether the way on which we have set out is the right one. It is particularly noticeable that such a "responsible reappraisal" always begins the moment serious difficulties appear. We then speak as though we no longer had "a proper joy and certainty" about this way, or, still worse, as though God and his Word were no longer as clearly present with us as they used to be. In all this we are ultimately trying to get round what the New Testament calls "patience" and "testing." Paul, at any rate, did not begin to reflect whether his way was the right one when opposition and suffering threatened, nor did Luther. They were both quite certain and glad that they should remain disciples and followers of their Lord. Dear brethren, our real trouble is not doubt about the way upon which we have set out, but our failure to be patient, to keep quiet. We still cannot imagine that today God really doesn't want anything new for us, but simply to prove us in the old way. That is too petty, too monotonous, too undemanding for us. And we simply cannot be constant with the fact that God's cause is not always the successful one, that we really could be "unsuccessful": and yet be on the right road. But this is where we find out whether we have begun in faith or in a burst of enthusiasm.

Bonhoeffer himself encouraged and supported his persecuted brothers in Christ however he could. Many pastors had been arrested that year, and that Christmas Fritz Onnasch was arrested. Bonhoeffer wrote the Finkenwalde brothers in December: "This time the annual balance sheet pretty well speaks for itself. Twenty-seven of your circle have been in prison, in many cases for several months. Some are there still and have spent the entire Advent in prison. Of others, there cannot be anyone who has not had some sort of experience either in his work or in his private life of the increasingly impatient attacks by the anti-Christian forces."

Bonhoeffer began to wonder whether the Confessing Church's fight was over. He had always felt that there was another battle to which God was calling him. One thing he knew: he would not fight with a gun on any front. He was not a pacifist, as some have said, but he saw that the war into which Hitler was plunging Germany was an unjust war. But it was coming soon enough, and he knew that he would be called up to serve. Then what?

Entering the Conspiracy

It's impossible to say when Bonhoeffer joined the conspiracy, mainly because he was always in the midst of it, even before it could have been called a conspiracy. The Bonhoeffer family had relationships with many powerful people in the government, most of whom shared their anti-Hitler views. Karl Bonhoeffer was close to Ferdinand Sauerbruch, a famous Berlin surgeon who was anti-Nazi and who influenced Fritz Kolbe, a German diplomat, to join the Resistance. Kolbe became America's most important spy against Hitler. Paula Bonhoeffer was close to her cousin, Paul von Hase, the military commander in Berlin. He was fiercely against Hitler and would play a central role in the July 20, 1944, Valkyrie plot. When Dietrich was arrested and imprisoned at Tegel, von Hase's stature made a significant difference in how he was treated. Bonhoeffer's brother Klaus, who was the top lawyer for Lufthansa, was well connected to business and other leaders, and their brother-in-law Rüdiger Schleicher, also a lawyer, was close to the head of the army's legal department, Dr. Karl Sack.

Then there was Hans von Dohnanyi, who was one of the conspiracy's leaders. In 1933 he was assigned to the Reichsjustizminister, Franz Gürtner, and for the first time he had a blood-spattered front-row seat at the inner workings of the Nazi leadership. But he deftly avoided any connection to the party, which caused him serious trouble now and again. In 1938 his troubles mounted, but he escaped the pressures of Berlin by becoming a justice of the Supreme Court at Leipzig. He still returned to Berlin each week to give a lecture and thus stayed in close touch with the Resistance, especially General Hans Oster and Carl Goerdeler. He stayed at his in-laws' house on Marienburgerallee, where he saw much of his young brother-in-law, Dietrich.

During 1938, Dohnanyi helped Ewald von Kleist-Schmenzin provide British intelligence with information about Hitler and the Nazis, trying to influence them into taking a tough stand against Hitler before he marched into Austria and the Sudetenland. Their principal contact was Churchill, not yet in power as prime minister. But in October 1938, Dohnanyi's involvement in the conspiracy grew dramatically.

At that point, Hitler was preparing to take by force the part of Czechoslovakia that Chamberlain had neglected to hand him on a silver charger. The head of the Abwehr was Wilhelm Canaris. Knowing Dohnanyi's position on Hitler, Canaris appointed Dohnanyi to his staff and asked him to compile a file of the Nazis' atrocities. A year later, when the war against Poland was launched, Dohnanyi documented the barbarity of the SS

Einsatzgruppen, even though many of the top generals themselves knew nothing about it. Canaris knew that the evidence of these atrocities would be crucial in convincing those generals and others to join the coup when the time came. That information would also help to convince the German people of the criminality of Hitler and thereby destroy his sway over them. And it would give the new government the necessary authority.

Much of this information collected by Dohnanyi found its way to his brothers-in-law and their families. Before others in Germany knew of them, the Bonhoeffers heard of the mass murders in Poland, the systematic burning of synagogues there, and much else. Things that no one would know about for years were known in the Bonhoeffer household almost as quickly as they happened. Dohnanyi kept a file of these things. It was labeled the Chronicle of Shame, although later it became known as the Zossen File because it was eventually hidden in Zossen. Its discovery there by the Nazis would lead to Dohnanyi's execution and to the execution of many others, including his three brothers-in-law, Rüdiger Schleicher and Klaus and Dietrich Bonhoeffer.

Even before Bonhoeffer chose to join the conspiracy, he provided counsel to Dohnanyi and a number of its leaders. He was not quite ready to move beyond that. To know where he stood in all of this, and to hear from God, he would first have to travel back to the United States.

CHAPTER 21

THE GREAT DECISION

1939

I have had the time to think and to pray about my situation and that of my nation and to have God's will for me clarified. I have come to the conclusion that I have made a mistake in coming to America. I must live through this difficult period of our national history with the Christian people of Germany. I shall have no right to participate in the reconstruction of Christian life in Germany after the war if I do not share the trials of this time with my people. My brothers in the Confessing Synod wanted me to go. They may have been right in urging me to do so; but I was wrong in going. Such a decision each man must make for himself. Christians in Germany will face the terrible alternative of either willing the defeat of their nation in order that Christian civilization may survive, or willing the victory of their nation and thereby destroying our civilization. I know which of these alternatives I must choose; but I cannot make that choice in security.

—DIETRICH BONHOEFFER TO REINHOLD NIEBUHR, JULY 1939

O n January 23, Bonhoeffer's mother informed him that she had seen a notice ordering all men born in 1906 and 1907 to register with the military. Bonhoeffer's hand would now be forced. He couldn't declare himself a conscientious objector.

That could bring about his arrest and execution. And it would have wide ramifications: if a Confessing Church leader was unwilling to take up arms for Germany, the whole Confessing Church would be put in a bad light. It would give the other Confessing Church pastors the idea that Bonhoeffer believed they must do the same, which he did not. It was all terribly problematic.

There was one possible solution. Bonhoeffer might be able to have his military call-up deferred for a year. Perhaps in the meantime he might return to America and work in the ecumenical movement. As he thought about the possibilities, he decided he must speak with Reinhold Niebuhr, who had been his professor at Union. Niebuhr was giving the prestigious Gifford Lectures in Edinburgh that year and would soon be in Sussex, England. Bonhoeffer wanted to visit Sabine and Gert, for whom living abroad had not been easy. And he wanted very much to see Bishop Bell. It was decided: he would go to England.

But Hitler was again threatening to march on Prague. If he did, any hope of a deferment would vanish, since there were no deferments during wartime. On March 10, Bonhoeffer and Bethge took a night train to Ostend on the Belgium coast. Because of the tense political situation, Bonhoeffer did not sleep until they crossed the border. If Hitler decided to march, their train could have been halted inside Germany, and no one could leave. The next day they made the Channel crossing. On March 15, Hitler breached Chamberlain's Munich agreement by devouring more of Czechoslovakia. To save face, the British prime minister vowed to declare war if Hitler marched on Poland.

War was coming. That much was obvious. Bonhoeffer was quite unclear about what to do, and on March 25, he wrote Bishop Bell:

> I am thinking of leaving Germany sometime. The main reason is the compulsory military service to which the men of my age (1906) will be called up this year. It seems to me conscientiously impossible to join in a war under the present circumstances. On the other hand, the Confessing Church as such has not taken any definite attitude in this respect and probably cannot take it as things are. So I should cause a tremendous damage to my brethren if I would make a stand on this point which would be regarded by the regime as typical of the hostility of our

church toward the state. Perhaps the worst thing of all is the military oath which I should have to swear. So I am rather puzzled in this situation, and perhaps even more because I feel it is really only on Christian grounds that I find it difficult to do military service under the present conditions, and yet there are only few friends who would approve of my attitude. In spite of much reading and thinking concerning this matter I have not yet made up my mind what I would do under different circumstances. But actually as things are I should have to do violence to my Christian conviction, if I would take up arms "here and now." I have been thinking of going to the Mission Field, not as an escape out of the situation, but because I wish to serve somewhere where service is really wanted. But here also the German foreign exchange situation makes it impossible to send workers abroad. With respect to British Missionary Societies I have no idea of the possibilities there. On the other hand, I still have the great desire to serve the Confessing Church as long as I possibly could.

That, in a nutshell, was Bonhoeffer's difficulty, and it illustrated his thinking that Christians cannot be governed by mere principles. Principles could carry one only so far. At some point every person must hear from God, must know what God was calling him to do, apart from others. Bonhoeffer did not believe it was permissible for him to take up arms in this war of aggression, but he also did not feel that he could make an absolute rule out of this, or declare it and put the Confessing Church in a difficult spot. He was looking for a way out that would allow him to obey his conscience, but that would not force *others* to obey his conscience.

On other issues he was all too willing to take a stand and push others to do the same. The Aryan Paragraph was one example. But taking up arms for Germany was more complicated. He couldn't make an issue of it, even though it would be nearly impossible to avoid. Still, there had to be a way. He would pray toward that end and seek counsel from those he knew and trusted, like Bishop Bell.

In England he was thrilled to see Franz Hildebrandt again and Julius Rieger. He had meetings with colleagues in the ecumenical movement, most of them discouraging. On March 29 he traveled with the Leibholzes to Oxford, and on April 3, with Julius Rieger and Gerhard Leibholz, he went to

Sussex to see Niebuhr, hoping for assistance. Bonhoeffer explained that getting a solid and official invitation to teach at Union for a year would solve his dilemma, and it would be needed quickly. Niebuhr realized the urgency of the situation and leaped into action. He would pull what strings he could.

The next day, the Reichskirche published the Godesberg Declaration, signed by Dr. Werner. It declared that National Socialism was a natural continuation of "the work of Martin Luther" and stated that the "Christian faith is the unbridgeable religious opposite to Judaism." It also said: "Supra-national and international church structure of a Roman Catholic or world-Protestant character is a political degeneration of Christianity."

The Provisional Committee of the World Council of Churches wrote a manifesto in response, drafted by Karl Barth. It repudiated the idea that race, national identity, or ethnic background had anything to do with actual Christian faith and declared, "The Gospel of Jesus Christ is the fulfillment of the Jewish hope. . . . The Christian church . . . rejoices in the maintenance of community with those of the Jewish race who have accepted the Gospel." The man who had pushed for the manifesto was Willem A. Visser 't Hooft, a Dutchman whom Bonhoeffer had known in ecumenical circles and who now had a key position in the ecumenical movement. When Bonhoeffer learned he would be in London, he asked Bell to arrange a meeting. They met at Paddington Station. Years later, Visser 't Hooft recalled their time together:

> We had heard a great deal about each other, but it was surprising how quickly we were able to get beyond the first stage of merely feeling our way into the deeper realm of real conversation—that, in fact, he was soon treating me as an old friend. . . . We walked up and down the platform for a long time. He described the situation of his church and country. He spoke in a way that was remarkably free from illusions, and sometimes almost clairvoyantly, about the coming war. . . . Had not the time now come to refuse to serve a government that was heading straight for war and breaking all the commandments? But what consequences would this position have for the Confessing Church?

Bonhoeffer also traveled to Chichester to meet with Bell. Before he left England, he wrote Bell to thank him for his counsel and understanding: "I do not know what will be the outcome of it all, but it meant much to me to realise that you see the great conscientious difficulties with which we are faced." Bonhoeffer returned to Berlin on April 18, hopeful that something would come of his meeting with Niebuhr. He had been in England five weeks, during which the chance of war considerably increased.

Two days later, Germany celebrated Hitler's fiftieth birthday, and once again the sinuous Dr. Werner tied himself into a ribbon for the epochal occasion: he published another glowing tribute to Hitler in the official journal of the German Reichskirche: "[We celebrate] with jubilation our Führer's fiftieth birthday. In him God has given the German people a real miracle worker. . . . Let our thanks be the resolute and inflexible will not to disappoint . . . our Führer and the great historic hour."

Even worse, another church publication, *Junge Kirche*, once an organ of truth and theological orthodoxy, had gone over to the dark side, painting Hitler in brightly messianic colors: "It has today become evident to everyone without exception that the figure of the Führer, powerfully fighting his way through old worlds, seeing with his mind's eye what is new and compelling its realization, is named on those few pages of world history that are reserved for the initiators of a new epoch. . . . The figure of the Führer has brought a new obligation for the church too."

Bonhoeffer knew that he might be called up any day, but all he could do was wait and pray. Niebuhr set a number of things in motion. On May 1 he wrote to Henry Leiper in New York, singing Bonhoeffer's praises and urging Leiper to act quickly, saying "time is short." Leiper knew Bonhoeffer from ecumenical circles, and they had spent time at Fanø in 1934. Niebuhr also wrote Henry Sloane Coffin, the president of Union, asking his help. And Niebuhr wrote Bonhoeffer's friend Paul Lehmann, then teaching at Elmhurst College outside Chicago. Within days, Niebuhr's letters generated a hive of activity across the Atlantic: phone calls were made, meetings were called, plans were changed, and more letters were written, all in the frantic but excited hopes of rescuing Bonhoeffer from imminent danger, not to mention bringing the brilliant young theologian into their spheres of orbit. There was a giddy tone to the whole affair, and Bonhoeffer had no idea of the extraordinary efforts being made on his behalf.

On May 11, Leiper sent Bonhoeffer a formal letter offering a joint position with Union and with Leiper's organization, the Central Bureau of Interchurch Aid. For Leiper, Bonhoeffer would serve as pastor to German refugees in New York. He would also lecture in the theological summer school of Union and Columbia, and in the fall he would lecture during Union's regular term. The grand position that Leiper had created just for him should occupy Bonhoeffer for "at least the next two or three years." Meanwhile, Paul Lehmann, thrilled at the prospect of having his old friend back, fired off urgent letters to more than thirty colleges—no mean feat in the days before computers—asking whether they would be interested in Bonhoeffer lecturing. In the first line of each letter he dropped Niebuhr's weighty name, saying that Niebuhr was the chairman of the committee "venturing to bring Bonhoeffer to your attention." He described Bonhoeffer as "one of the ablest of the younger theologians and one of the most courageous of the younger pastors who have undertaken the task of the faithful exposition and perpetuation of the Christian faith in the present critical time in Germany."

But even as these efforts were being made, Bonhoeffer was far from settled on his course of action. Complicating things was a letter from his friend Adolf Freudenberg, who said that if Bonhoeffer were to accept the post of a pastor for refugees, it would be impossible for him to return to Germany while it was still under National Socialist rule. Bonhoeffer never liked to be without options.

The situation in the Confessing Church seemed increasingly hopeless too. Its revulsion toward Karl Barth over his letter calling every Czech soldier who died fighting Hitler a martyr disturbed Bonhoeffer. That the Confessing Church could distance itself from the author of the Barmen Confession grieved him. This and many other things made him feel that there was little left for him to do in Germany. America seemed to be the direction that God had for him. Still, he wasn't sure.

Before he left for America, he met with about ten students and friends in Dudzus's apartment. Albrecht Schönherr, Winfried Maechler, Gerhard Ebeling, and Bethge were among them. "Bonhoeffer explained to us why he was leaving for America," Dudzus recalled, "and we talked about how to continue his work, the work of Finkenwalde. The seminary was outlawed, but it existed illegally in the forms of underground meetings. We spoke about how that should be pursued and discussed many necessary things with each other. And at some point during the discussion he asked us, quite unexpectedly if we would grant absolution to the murderer of a tyrant."

At that time, no one but Bethge knew that Bonhoeffer was involved in the Resistance. Later on in conversations he used an example of a drunken driver killing pedestrians on a main street like the Kurfürstendamm in Berlin. He said it would be the responsibility of everyone to do all they could to stop that driver from killing more people. A year or two later, Bonhoeffer knew what few others knew, that the killing of the Jews was beyond anything they had conceived. He felt a responsibility to stop it, to do anything he could. But now, before he left for America, he was still working these things out.

On May 22, Bonhoeffer received a notice to report for military duty, and he realized he must act quickly. He contacted the necessary authorities, informing them of the official invitations from Union and Leiper. On June 4 he was on his way to America.

Back to America

Bonhoeffer kept a journal during his trip to America and wrote numerous postcards and letters, mostly to Bethge, who passed the information to everyone else. Bonhoeffer took an evening flight from Berlin to London: "We are now flying over the channel in a wonderful sunset. It is ten o'clock and still very bright. All is well with me." On the seventh he boarded a ship at Southampton: "This card is to send you all my last best wishes before we get on the Atlantic and there is no more post. We have just left Southampton and will be docking at Cherbourg in a couple of hours. My cabin is very roomy, and everywhere else there is a remarkable amount of space on the ship. The weather is glorious and the sea quite calm." On the eighth he bumped into a young man who had studied at Union. "It was like an answer to a prayer," he wrote. "We spoke of Christ in Germany and America and Sweden, from where he had just come. The task in America!" He was still thinking forward, about his time in America, but in his letter to Bethge on the ninth, he already felt a sense of separation from Germany and the "brethren" that is striking: "You may be working over there and I may be working in America, but we are both only where he is. He brings us together. Or have I missed the place where he is? Where he is for me? No, God says, 'You are my servant.'" June 11 was a Sunday, but there were no church services. Bonhoeffer had agreed to have private devotions each day at the same time as Bethge. This was one of the things about Finkenwalde that had captivated him: the daily meditation on the Scriptures and the sense of union with those doing the same thing at the same hour. But the ship was nearing New York, and the time change made that confusing: "But I am altogether with you, today more than ever," he wrote. Then he seemed to soar away, being ruthlessly honest about discerning his motives and God's will:

> If only the doubts about my own course had been overcome. One's own searching into the depths of one's heart which is nevertheless unfathomable—"He knows the secrets of the heart." When the confusion of accusations and excuses, of desires and fears, makes everything with us so obscure, he sees quite clearly into all our secrets. And at the heart of them all he finds a name which he himself has inscribed: Jesus Christ. So too one day we shall see quite clearly into the depths of the divine heart and there we shall then be able to read, no, to see, a name: Jesus Christ. So we would celebrate Sunday. One day we shall know and see what today we believe; one day we shall hold a service together in eternity.

> The beginning and the end, O Lord, are thine;
> The span between, life, was mine.
> I wandered in the darkness and did not discover myself;
> With thee, O Lord, is clarity, and light is thy house.
> A short time only, and all is done;
> Then the whole struggle dies away to nothing.
> Then I will refresh myself by the waters of life,
> And will talk with Jesus for ever and ever.

Twenty-six Days

On June 12, 1939, a week shy of eight years since leaving New York, Bonhoeffer entered the great harbor of America for the second time. But things were quite different now, for him and for the city. The Manhattan skyline did not seem to grin at him as it did the last time, nor had it sprouted a single new tooth since his departure. The building frenzy and the vibrancy and the ferment of the Jazz Age were gone. The Great Depression that had then taken its first steps was now ten years old.

At the dock, Bonhoeffer was met by the Reverend Macy, from the Federal Council of Churches, who took him to the Parkside Hotel. The next morning, a Tuesday, he met Henry Leiper for breakfast: "[He] greeted me most kindly and fetched me. First discussion of the future. I am taking as the firm starting point for everything that I want to go back in a year at the latest. Astonishment. But I am quite clear that I must go back."

He had not been in New York for twenty-four hours, but Bonhoeffer was already deeply out of sorts. He was sure that he must go back. Leiper was sure that Bonhoeffer would be there for longer and was taken aback. What happened? Later in the day after making phone calls, Bonhoeffer went up to Union and settled in the so-called Prophet's Chamber, a well-appointed guest suite directly over the seminary's main entrance. A vast room with high ceilings and wood paneling, it has a set of east windows that look out on Broadway and 121st Street, and a set of west windows that have "a fine view overlooking the quadrangle." He was being given the star treatment. But a higher honor yet awaited him: at four o'clock he was to meet Dr. Coffin at Grand Central. Coffin invited Bonhoeffer to his country estate in the Berkshires, near the Massachusetts border.

Henry Sloane Coffin epitomized the East Coast liberal establishment. Elected to Skull and Bones at Yale, he became pastor of Manhattan's prestigious Madison Avenue Church in 1910. When he became president of Union in 1926, *Time* put him on its cover. Coffin had known the twenty-four-year-old Bonhoeffer of 1930, the brilliant Sloane Fellow with a doctorate from Berlin University who took the Bible and himself so seriously, who championed Barth and Luther; but the Bonhoeffer he would meet today was something else. He came with the greatest recommendations from Niebuhr, who rather alarmingly—but also rather accurately—said that if Union didn't make room for him, he would likely end up in a concentration camp. Although Coffin was a staunch theological liberal, he respected Bonhoeffer and his Barthian views.

On the two-and-a-half-hour train ride north, the patrician fifty-nine-year-old American and the patrician thirty-three-year-old German discussed the church situation in America. But as they spoke, Bonhoeffer's mind continued to churn about the situation back home, wondering how long he should stay in America, whether he ought to have come at all. But ever the master of his emotions, he didn't betray any of this inner turmoil to his host, neither on the train nor in the three days he was with him and his family in their country home. His diary gives us his thoughts:

13th June, 1939—The country house in Lakeville, Connecticut, is in the hills, fresh and luxuriant vegetation. In the evening thousands of fire-flies in the garden, like flying fire. I had never seen them before. Quite a fantastic sight. Very friendly and "informal" reception. All that's missing is Germany, the brethren. The first lonely hours are hard. I do not understand why I am here, whether it was a sensible thing to do, whether the results will be worthwhile. In the evening, last of all, the readings and thoughts about work at home. I have now been almost two weeks without knowing what is going on there. It is hard to bear.

14th June, 1939—Breakfast on the verandah at eight. It poured during the night. Everything is fresh and clean. Then prayers. I was almost overcome by the short prayer—the whole family knelt down—in which we thought of the German brethren. Then reading, writing, going out to issue invitations for the evening. In the evening about twenty-five people, pastors, teachers, with wives and friends. Very friendly conversations without getting anywhere.

15th June, 1939—Since yesterday evening I haven't been able to stop thinking of Germany. I would not have thought it possible that at my age, after so many years abroad, one could get so dreadfully homesick. What was in itself a wonderful motor expedition this morning to a female acquaintance in the country, i.e., in the hills, became almost unbearable. We sat for an hour and chattered, not in a silly way, true, but about things which left me completely cold—whether it is possible to get a good musical education in New York, about the education of children, etc., etc., and I thought how usefully I could be spending these hours in Germany. I would gladly have taken the next ship home. This inactivity, or rather activity in unimportant things, is quite intolerable when one thinks of the brethren and of how precious time is. The whole burden of self-reproach because of a wrong decision comes back again and almost overwhelms one. I was in utter despair.

Torn between his hatred of wasted words and his deep respect for mannerly behavior, he was the very definition of unsettled. When he returned from his jaunt and his polite conversation with the well-meaning female acquaintance he tried to lose himself in his work. But he was interrupted by another invitation to take a ride into the Massachusetts hills. He accepted and went, but reproved himself for going: "I still hadn't found peace for Bible reading and prayer." Nonetheless it was a glorious ride. They drove through a long stretch of laurel trees and came upon a view that reminded him of Friedrichsbrunn. But during the whole time, the burden of Germany and whether he should return remained.

That evening they drove to a local movie theater. The offering was *Juarez*, a historical drama starring Bette Davis and Paul Muni. If Bonhoeffer hoped to lose himself in another world, he was disappointed. Muni played Benito Juarez, the noble, democratically elected president of Mexico who locked horns with Claude Rains as Napoleon III, a cynical European dictator bent on creating an empire. Caught between them was the idealistic and young Hapsburg emperor Maximilian I, who was duped by France into assuming the leadership of Mexico, but whose devotion to the Mexican people was a moving picture of a truly noble monarch. The movie's rather pedantic theme of what constitutes legitimate leadership and its several parallels to what was swimming through Bonhoeffer's mind are startling. In his diary, Bonhoeffer simply deemed it a "good film."

Alone in his room that evening, he wrote Leiper, reiterating that he must go back "within a year at the latest" and explaining himself more fully, obviously feeling guilty for having led anyone astray in expectations. But then at long last he found peace in the Scriptures, into which he had longed to wade all day and in which he now settled himself: "How glad I was to begin the readings again in the evening and find 'My heart shall rejoice in thy salvation' (Ps. 13.5)."

The next morning he returned to New York and visited the World's Fair in Queens. He spent the afternoon there, amidst the crowds. When he returned to his room that evening, he was delighted to have solitude again, to think and pray. In his diary he wrote, "One is less lonely when one is alone." He jotted down his fresh impressions of New York: "How much cleaner New York is than London! No smoking in the subway or on the street. Technically more advanced, too, or more up to date (ventilation in every subway). And how much more international New York is than London. Of the people to whom I talked today at least half spoke a dreadfully broken English."

The next day, Saturday, he was alone again. He spent most of it in the Union library, working. He studied issues of the *Christian Century* for an essay he was writing. But all the while he was pining for a letter from Germany, telling him of the situation there. Nothing in his life could quite compare with what he felt. He was more unsettled, more profoundly out of sorts, than ever. He seemed cut off from a part of himself, divided from himself by an ocean, wandering the streets of New York like a ghost:

> It is almost unbearable. . . . Today God's Word says, "I am coming soon" (Rev. 3.11). There is no time to lose, and here I am wasting days, perhaps weeks. In any case, it seems like that at the moment. Then I say to myself again, "It is cowardice and weakness to run away here now." Will I ever be able to do any really significant work here? Disquieting political news from Japan. If it becomes unsettled now I am definitely going back to Germany. I cannot stay outside [Germany] by myself. That is quite clear. My whole life is still over there.

The next day was Sunday. His restlessness, his search for peace and an answer, continued; and from the west windows of his room, he could see high up, just beyond the roof of Union, a sculpture of the angel Gabriel holding his trumpet. Gabriel faced north and crowned the spire over the altar at Riverside Church. Bonhoeffer knew that the tepid liberal preaching at Riverside was extremely unlikely to meet with his approval, much less be a conduit by which God would speak to him about his situation. But he could not live a hundred yards away and not visit. Sooner or later, he must at least taste the lukewarm waters there. But this morning Bonhoeffer burned to hear something from God.

Riverside was the church Rockefeller had built for Harry Emerson Fosdick, which had opened to such fanfare in 1930. In 1939, Fosdick was still the most famous liberal preacher in America, and Riverside was America's premier pulpit of theological liberalism.* Bonhoeffer was in a mood to hear

---

* Bonhoeffer probably didn't know that Fosdick was one of the most vocal proponents of appeasing Hitler. He championed moral equivalency, which argued that the phenomenon of Hitler and fascism came into being because of the faults of America and its policies.

God in the preaching of his Word, even if it was not in the precise form he liked. But he was in no mood for what he heard that morning at Riverside. The text for the sermon was from James, but not from the James of the New Testament. It was from the American philosopher William James, whose works Bonhoeffer had studied nine years earlier. The usually exceedingly gracious and tolerant Bonhoeffer had been aching for something of God, but he had come to the wrong place. In his diary he wrote, "Quite unbearable." The empty preaching set him off, and he poured out his disgust to his diary:

> The whole thing was a respectable, self-indulgent, self-satisfied religious celebration. This sort of idolatrous religion stirs up the flesh which is accustomed to being kept in check by the Word of God. Such sermons make for libertinism, egotism, indifference. Do people not know that one can get on as well, even better, without "religion"? . . . Perhaps the Anglo-Saxons are really more religious than we are, but they are certainly not more Christian, at least, if they still have sermons like that. I have no doubt at all that one day the storm will blow with full force on this religious hand-out, if God himself is still anywhere on the scene. . . . The tasks for a real theologian over here are immeasurable. But only an American himself can shift all this rubbish, and up till now there do not seem to be any about.

To find the word of God, he returned to his room and the daily texts, the Moravian *Losungen*. "How good the readings are today!" he wrote, "Ps. 119:115; Matt.13:8." He was elated by the verses. The first was, "Depart from me, you evil ones, so that I may obey my God's commands." The second: "Still others fell on good ground, and produced a crop; some 100, some 60, and some 30 times what was sown."

He was again alone all day and missed his brothers in Christ: "Now I must begin to learn again how fortunate I have been hitherto always to have been in the company of the brethren. And Niemöller has been alone for two years. To imagine it! What a faith, what a discipline, and what a clear act of God!" Bonhoeffer would be alone in prison for two years, and by the time the war was over, Niemöller would have been imprisoned for eight. But that was in the future. Right now he longed for peace and for the Word. So again he left Union and walked south on Broadway, seven blocks, to another church.

The preacher at this church, Dr. McComb, was reviled as a fundamentalist by Fosdick and the others up the street. But what Bonhoeffer found there thrilled him:

> Now the day has had a good ending. I went to church again. As long as there are lonely Christians there will always be [church] services. It is a great help after a couple of quite lonely days to go into church and there pray together, sing together, listen together. The sermon was astonishing (Broadway Presbyterian Church, Dr. McComb) on "our likeness with Christ." A completely biblical sermon—the sections on "we are blameless like Christ," "we are tempted like Christ" were particularly good.

To have found biblical preaching in New York City, and on this day of all days, when he was desperately trying to hear God's voice, was an answer to his prayers. Here, in this "fundamentalist" Presbyterian Church on Broadway, he heard God's Word preached. At this critical juncture he did something he had never done before: he took a stand with the so-called fundamentalists against their adversaries at Riverside and Union. Referring to McComb's church, he declared, "This will one day be a center of resistance when Riverside Church has long since become a temple of Baal. I was very glad about this sermon."

He repented of the anti-Americanism stirring in him over the last days and boldly equated the fundamentalists with the Confessing Church. Here they were fighting the corrupting influences of the theologians at Union and Riverside, and at home the fight was against the Reichskirche. It was a staggering equation. Here is the church, he seemed to say, marginalized here as we are marginalized there.

> This sermon opened up to me an America of which I was quite ignorant before. Otherwise I would have become quite ungrateful in these days for all the protection which God has given me. With my intention and inner need to think incessantly of the brethren over there and their work I would almost have avoided the task here. It began to seem treacherous not to have all my thoughts over there. I still have to find the right balance. Paul writes that he thinks of his congregation

"without ceasing" in his prayers and yet at the same time he devoted himself completely to the task in hand. I must learn to do that. It will probably only come with prayer. God, grant me in the next few weeks clarity about my future and keep me in the communion of prayer with the brethren.

On Monday there was still no news from Germany. The next day was the important meeting with Leiper. But he was aching for news from the brethren: "I want to know how work is going over there, whether all is well or whether they need me. I want to have some sign from over there before the decisive meeting tomorrow. Perhaps it is a good thing that it has not come."

His thoughts were also on the international situation:

The news about China is disquieting. Will one be able to get home in time if it gets serious? Spent the whole day in the library. Wrote English lectures. I have great difficulty with the language. They say that I speak English well, and yet I find it so utterly inadequate. How many years, how many decades has it taken to learn German, and even now one does not know it! I will never learn English. That is already one reason for going back home soon. Without language one is lost, hopelessly lonely.

He had never felt more alone, and he had never felt more German. He was all alone in New York City in the warm month of June. Paul Lehmann was in Chicago. That evening, after working all day struggling to write in English, he took the subway to Times Square. He watched the newsreel for an hour and then took the subway back uptown, walked up Broadway to Union, made a left through the great entrance, then upstairs to his huge room. He wrote in his diary, read the Scriptures, and prayed. But his sense of being out of sync with himself and with the brothers in Germany was inescapable. Before he went to sleep, he even complained about the time difference: "It disturbs me that we do not keep the same time as Germany. It hinders and prevents prayer together. It is the same every evening. But: 'We thank thee, O God, . . . that thy name is so near' (Ps. 75:1)."

On the morning of June 20, he finally got a letter from his parents. But still nothing from the brethren. That day he would have his important lunch meeting with Henry Leiper. They met at the National Arts Club on Gramercy Park. Afterward he wrote in his diary: "The decision has been made. I have refused. They were clearly disappointed, and rather upset. It probably means more for me than I can see at the moment. God alone knows what."

Years later, Leiper recalled their lunch meeting there, under the famous tiled ceiling of the exclusive club. He had obviously looked forward to the lunch as much as Bonhoeffer had dreaded it; he expected to discuss the nature of the work they would do together. "What was my surprise and dismay," Leiper said, "to learn from my guest that he had just received an urgent appeal from his colleagues in Germany to return at once for important tasks which they felt he alone could perform." We do not know to what Bonhoeffer was referring. It's possible his parents' letter included a coded reference to the conspiracy, something that seemed urgent to him and that had decided his course. In any case, he was determined to obey God and was sure he was doing so in deciding to return to Germany. He knew that the consequences of his obedience were God's business. "I did not press him for details of what that work might be," Leiper recalled. "It was abundantly clear from his manner and his tenseness that he felt it something he could not refuse to undertake."

That evening in his diary Bonhoeffer ruminated about the decision, puzzled by the strange mystery of it all:

> It is remarkable how I am never quite clear about the motives for any of my decisions. Is that a sign of confusion, of inner dishonesty, or is it a sign that we are guided without our knowing, or is it both? . . . Today the reading speaks dreadfully harshly of God's incorruptible judgement. He certainly sees how much personal feeling, how much anxiety there is in today's decision, however brave it may seem. The reasons one gives for an action to others and to one's self are certainly inadequate. One can give a reason for everything. In the last resort one acts from a level which remains hidden from us. So one can only ask God to judge us and to forgive us. . . . At the end of the day I can only ask God to give a merciful judgement on today and all its decisions. It is now in his hand.

Somehow he was again at peace. The next day was a scorcher. He worked through the morning and in the afternoon went across Central Park to the cool marble shelter of the vast Metropolitan Museum of Art. He revived himself by drinking a cool draught of European culture. He was particularly taken with El Greco's *View of Toledo* and Hans Memling's *Head of Christ*.

He spent the evening with German friends, the Bewers, where his sense of alienation and his homesickness were further relieved. J. W. Bewer was an Old Testament scholar, whom Bonhoeffer had known from his year at Union and who had just published a book on Micah. "It was so good to think and speak again in German," he wrote. "I have never felt the resistance which the English language offers to my thoughts so strongly as here in New York. In this language I always feel dissatisfied with myself."

But this evening his thoughts turned to his future:

> Of course I still keep having second thoughts about my decision. One could have also given quite different reasons: first, I am here (and perhaps the very misunderstanding was a guidance); they say that it was like the answer to a prayer when my coming was announced; they would like to have *me*; they cannot understand why I refuse; it upsets all their plans for the future; I have no news from home and perhaps everything is going well without me, etc. Or one could ask: have I simply acted out of a longing for Germany and the work there? And is this almost incomprehensible and hitherto almost completely unknown homesickness an accompanying sign from above to make refusal easier for me? Or, is it not irresponsible towards so many other men simply to say no to one's own future and that of many others? Will I regret it? I may not. . . . The reading is again so harsh: "He will sit as a refiner of gold and silver" (Mal. 3:3). And it is necessary. I don't know where I am. But he knows; and in the end all doings and actions will be pure and clear.

The next day, the twenty-second, he received an invitation from his relatives the Boerickes to visit in Philadelphia the next week. But still no other mail from the brethren at Sigurdshof. Unbeknownst to him, they were doing fine and had chosen Hellmut Traub as their new director. Bonhoeffer was reading Niebuhr, but found the book disappointing. That evening he wandered to a newsreel theater: "nothing special." Then he read the newspapers:

> Bewer calms me down. It is unbearable over here for a German; one is

simply torn in two. . . . [E]ven to be responsible, to have to reproach oneself, for having come out unnecessarily, is certainly crushing. But we cannot part ourselves from our destiny, much less here, outside; here everything lies solely on one's own shoulders, and one has no voice and no rights in a foreign land. . . . It is strange how strongly I have been moved by these particular thoughts in the last few days and how all thoughts about the *Una Sancta* make slow progress. . . . I have been writing in bed since yesterday evening. . . . All that remains now is the readings and intercessions. In the morning a discussion with Bewer and Van Dusen about the future. I want to go back in August. They urge me to stay longer. But if nothing happens in the meantime I shall stick by 12th August. I shall then stay with Sabine.

At lunch with David Roberts and his wife, he discussed the racial situation in America, as well as what Roberts described to him as a marked increase in American anti-Semitism. He told of having seen a sign posted on the road leading to a mountain resort: "1000 feet—too high for Jews." Another one read: "Gentiles preferred."

On the twenty-third, he read in his room and then took a walk to the Hudson. Sitting on the bank, he thought of Sigurdshof, so far away: "Why don't I hear anything?" He finished the Niebuhr book with mixed feelings and remained disappointed at what continued to pass for theology at Union: "No thinking in the light of the Bible here." He closed the day's diary entry with a judgment on the quality of music he heard from his room: "They have just finished a conference on hymn-book revision below. They drag the chorales dreadfully, and use too much pedal. The clavichord is better. Readings and intercessions."

Finally on Saturday, the twenty-fourth, he received a letter: "That is a great relief." Reflecting on the American church scene, he was fascinated that tolerance trumped truth. His analysis was remarkably similar to the report he wrote in the summer of 1931, trying to make sense of his year at Union:

I now often wonder whether it is true that America is the country without a reformation. If reformation means the God-given knowledge of the failure of all ways of building up a kingdom of God on earth, then it is probably true. But is it not also true of England? The voice of

Lutheranism is there in America, but it is one among others: it has never been able to confront the other denominations. There hardly ever seem to be "encounters" in this great country, in which the one can always avoid the other. But where there is no encounter, where liberty is the only unifying factor, one naturally knows nothing of the community which is created through encounter. The whole life together is completely different as a result. Community in our sense, whether cultural or ecclesiastical, cannot develop there. Is that true?

That evening he wrote postcards and noted in his diary: "The newspaper grim again today. Readings: 'The one who believes does not flee' (Isa. 28.16). I'm thinking of work at home." Later, this *Losung* text was said to have been the key to his decision, the one that spoke the most loudly of them all: "The one who believes does not flee." To stay now was to flee. And to flee from America was to believe, to trust in the Lord.

He jotted a tittle of sarcasm under the last word of the day: "Tomorrow is Sunday. I wonder if I shall hear a *sermon?*"

In the morning, hoping to do so, he visited a Lutheran Church on Central Park:

Sunday, 25th June 1939—Sermon on Luke 15, on the overcoming of fear. Very forced application of the text. Otherwise lively and original, but too much analysis and too little Gospel. It came home when he said of the life of the Christian that it is like the daily joy of the person who is on the way home. Again no real exposition of the text. It is very poor.

After the service, he lunched with the Bewers and spent the afternoon and evening with Felix Gilbert, a historian about his age whom he knew from Berlin. His last words in the diary that evening are: "Today is the anniversary of the Augsburg Confession. It makes me think of the brethren at home. Rom. 1.16. ['For I am not ashamed of the gospel of Christ, for it is the power of God to salvation, for everyone who believes, for the Jew first and also for the Greek' (NKJV).]"

26th June 1939— . . . Today I read by chance in II Timothy 4, "Do thy diligence to come before winter," Paul's petition to Timothy. Timothy is to share the suffering of the apostle and not to be ashamed. "Come before winter"—otherwise it might be too late. That has been in my mind all day. It is for us as it is for soldiers, who come home on leave from the front but who, in spite of all their expectations, long to be back at the front again. We cannot get away from it any more. Not because we are necessary, or because we are useful (to God?), but simply because that is where our life is, and because we leave our life behind, destroy it, if we cannot be in the midst of it again. It is nothing pious, more like some vital urge. But God acts not only by means of pious emotions, but also through vital ones. "Come before winter"—it is not a misuse of Scripture if I take that to be said to *me*. If God gives me grace to do it.

27th June 1939—Letter from my parents. Great joy, quite surprising. Work lunchtime and afternoon in the library. . . . In the evening a visit from Professor Richardson, long conversation. He is an Englishman. One seems to stand nearer to him than to the Americans. I wonder if the Americans do not understand us at all because they are people who left Europe so as to be able to live out their faith for themselves in freedom? i.e. because they did not stand fast by the last decision in the question of belief? I feel that they would understand the fugitive better than the one who stays. Hence the American tolerance, or rather, indifference in dogmatic questions. A warlike encounter is excluded, but so too is the true passionate longing for unity in faith.

28th June 1939— . . . The newspaper reports get more and more disturbing. They distract one's thoughts. I cannot imagine that it is God's will for me to remain here without anything particular to do in case of war. I must travel at the first possible opportunity.

That same day he got a letter from Paul Lehmann, still under the impression that all systems were go. Lehmann had gone to considerable trouble to arrange invitations for Bonhoeffer:

You cannot know with what joy and relief your letter was received. . . . Marion and I have been eagerly awaiting word of your arrival in

Union. Now that you are there we can scarcely wait until you are here with us. . . . I do know that it is unthinkable that you should return until America has had the fullest opportunity to be enriched by your contribution to its theological hour of destiny. At least, I like to think of it in this way. . . . So that you must see this also as a responsibility.

Bonhoeffer realized he needed to tell Lehmann about his recent decision and sent a postcard immediately: "Things have changed for me entirely. I am going back to Germany on August 2nd or even July 25th. The political situation is so terrible. But, of course, I should like to have a word from you before I leave. I am enjoying a few weeks in freedom, but on the other hand, I feel, I must go back to the 'trenches' (I mean of the church struggle.)"

The next day he continued to ponder the state of the American church:

29th June 1939—The separation of church and state does not result in the church continuing to apply itself to its own task; it is no guarantee against secularization. Nowhere is the church more secularized than where it is separated in principle as it is here. This very separation can create an opposition, so that the church engages much more strongly in political and secular things. That is probably important for our decisions over there.

On the thirtieth, Bonhoeffer wrote Lehmann with a fuller explanation:

30th June 1939—Thank you so much for your good letter, which is so full of friendship and hope for the future. I can hardly find it in my heart to tell you that in the meantime I have had to decide to return to Germany with the next weeks. My invitation to come over here was based on a misunderstanding to the effect that I intended to remain in America indefinitely. Therefore it was proposed to make me responsible for the care of Christian refugees here, a work which, necessary as it is, would have prevented any possibility of my returning to Germany. It must be done by a refugee. In the meantime everything has been decided and set in order with the Confessing Church; I return in July or August. I certainly regret it in some ways, but on the other hand I am glad that I shall very soon be able to help again over there. I am drawn back into the struggles of the brothers.

But that very day Bonhoeffer received a telegram from Karl-Friedrich in Chicago, and he decided to move his departure date up yet again. He would leave in one week:

30th June 1939—Telegram from Karl-Friedrich, who is coming from Chicago. There is much to discuss. He has been offered an excellent professorship there; it means a decision once for all. Then my questions. As in the present situation I would in any case have gone in four weeks at the latest, with things as they are I have decided to go on the eighth with Karl-Friedrich. If war breaks out I do not want to be here, and it is impossible to get any objective news about the situation. That was a [big] decision.

The next day Karl-Friedrich arrived. Bonhoeffer put on his tourist hat, and the two brothers spent the day in Midtown Manhattan:

1st July 1939— . . . with K. F. into town, bought presents, [Radio City] Music Hall, cinema, the largest. Dreadful. Gaudy, ostentatious, vulgar colors, music and flesh. One can only find this sort of fantasy in a big city. K. F. disagrees. . . . I could not get away all day from thinking about the situation in Germany and in the church. . . . The readings are again very good. Job 41.11, "God says, Who has given to me, that I should repay him? Whatever is under the whole heaven is mine." Rom. 11.36: "By him and through him and to him are all things. To him be glory for ever. Amen." The earth, nations, Germany, and above all, the church, cannot fall from his hand. It was dreadfully hard for me to think and to pray "Thy will be done" in view of the present situation. But it must be. Tomorrow is Sunday. May God make his Word find a hearing in all the world.

Sunday, 2nd July, 1939—Church, Park Avenue. Rev. Gorkmann (Radio preacher) on "Today is ours," no text, no echo of the Christian proclamation. Rather a disappointment. . . . The Americans speak so much

about freedom in their sermons. Freedom as a possession is a doubtful thing for a church; freedom must be won under the compulsion
of a necessity. Freedom for the church comes from the necessity of
the Word of God. Otherwise it becomes arbitrariness and ends in a
great many new ties. Whether the church in America is really "free,"
I doubt. They are lonely Sundays over here. Only the Word makes
a true community. I need some good communal prayers in my own
language. The news is not good. Will we arrive in time? Reading: Isa.
35.10! ["And the ransomed of the LORD shall return, and come to Zion
with singing, with everlasting joy on their heads. They shall obtain
joy and gladness, and sorrow and sighing shall flee away" (NKJV).]
Intercessions.

On Monday Bonhoeffer attended lectures by Coffin and Niebuhr,
then spent the rest of the day writing an article and talking with a student.
He noted in his diary: "Morning prayers by Coffin were very poor. I must
take care not to be remiss with Bible reading and prayer. Letter from Paul
Lehmann." Lehmann had received Bonhoeffer's letter with the disappointing
news: "I cannot tell you how deeply it troubles both Marion and me. I write
now, believe me, with great heaviness of spirit."

The next morning Bonhoeffer met with Coffin and then with Niebuhr,
who invited him for dinner. But that day, the only Fourth of July he spent in
the United States, Bonhoeffer had lunch in the Empire State Building with
Karl-Friedrich.

5th July, 1939—The nearer my departure comes the fuller the days
become. . . . Conversation at lunch with two students from the
Southern States on the Negro problem. . . . It would be good to stay
another four weeks. But the price is too high. Letter from Eberhard,
great joy.

The next two days were so full he didn't have time for his diary. On the
sixth he went downtown to book his ticket on the ship. On the way uptown
he visited the Stock Exchange. At two thirty he met Paul Lehmann back at
the Prophet's Chamber. They had not seen each other since 1933, so it was
a delightful reunion.

The next morning, Bonhoeffer's last in America, Paul Lehmann tried to talk Bonhoeffer out of leaving. He knew what his friend was returning to. But the decision was made: Bonhoeffer had set his face toward Berlin. He had been in New York twenty-six days.

That evening Paul took him down to the ship and said good-bye.

7th July, 1939—Farewell half past eleven, sail at half past twelve. Manhattan by night; the moon over the skyscrapers. It is very hot. The visit is at an end. I am glad to have been over and glad that I am on the way home. Perhaps I have learnt more in this month than in a whole year nine years ago; at least I have acquired some important insight for all future decisions. Probably this visit will have a great effect on me. *In the middle of the Atlantic Ocean* . . .

9th July, 1939—Conversation with Karl-Friedrich about theological matters. Read a great deal. The days are noticeably shorter by the loss of an hour. Since I have been on the ship my inner uncertainty about the future has ceased. I can think of my shortened time in America without reproaches. Reading: "It is good for me that I was afflicted, that I might learn thy statutes" (Psa. 119.71). One of my favorite verses from my favorite psalm.

Bonhoeffer was in England ten days. He did not visit Bishop Bell, but he saw Franz Hildebrandt and Julius Rieger, and he spent time with his beloved Sabine, Gerhard, and the girls. They knew that war was imminent, that any day the world would change.

Some sense of what was ahead touched Bonhoeffer while he was staying with the Leibholzes. He was teaching Marianne and Christiane English nursery rhymes when he was interrupted with the grim news that Paul Schneider, among the bravest of the Confessing Church pastors, had been beaten to death at Buchenwald. Bonhoeffer knew that it was right he was going back. Now he would say good-bye to Sabine and her family and return to Germany.

He arrived in Berlin on July 27 and immediately traveled to Sigurdshof to continue his work. But unbeknownst to him, Hellmut Traub had ably

taken over where Bonhoeffer had left off. Traub recalled his surprise at seeing Bonhoeffer suddenly returned to them:

> I was happy to know that Bonhoeffer was not in Germany, but safe from
> the coming reign of terror, and the catastrophe which I was convinced
> would follow. He must not perish in it. He knew about the resurgence of
> the Church, about the inner necessity (and not just the external neces-
> sity conditioned by the German Christians) of the Confessing Church
> whose destiny he had helped to shape; the best of liberal theology from
> Harnack's time, as well as the most recent movement of dialectical the-
> ology, were alive in him, and equally so an amazingly extensive general,
> philosophical, literary and artistic education. His openness and his free
> and unprejudiced conviction that the Church must undergo a change,
> renew itself, justified the confidence he enjoyed in foreign churches. . . .
> He was practically predestined to rebuild the Protestant church after
> the débâcle which most certainly was in store for us. . . . Over and
> above this, and apart from the great danger of his situation, Bonhoeffer
> was sure to find no mercy, as he was bound to be a conscientious objec-
> tor. There was no room for him in this present-day Germany, because
> we believed that *then*, later, we would be in real, deepest need of him;
> *then* his time would come.
>
> And then one day, after a short message that he was returning,
> Bonhoeffer stood before us. This was quite unexpected—indeed, there
> was always something extraordinary about him, even when the cir-
> cumstances were quite ordinary. I was immediately up in arms, blurting
> out how could he come back after it had cost so much trouble to get
> him into safety—safety for us, for our cause; here everything was lost
> anyway. He very calmly lit a cigarette. Then he said that he had made
> a mistake in going to America. He did not himself understand now
> why he had done it. . . . It is this fact—that he abandoned in all clarity
> many great possibilities for his own development in the free countries,
> that he returned to dismal slavery and a dark future, but also to his
> own reality—which gave to everything he told us then a strong and
> joyful firmness, such as only arises out of realized freedom. He knew
> he had taken a clear step, though the actualities before him were still
> quite unclear.

Life at the two collective pastorates in eastern Pomerania continued that August. But the sense of war was imminent, and they were so close to Poland, where it would surely begin, that Bonhoeffer thought it too dangerous to remain there. He decided they must leave. So the Köslin and Sigurdshof terms were prematurely ended, and on August 26, Bonhoeffer was back in Berlin.

CHAPTER 22

THE END OF GERMANY

You can't wage war with Salvation Army methods.

—ADOLF HITLER

Back in March, when Hitler had marched on Prague, Neville Chamberlain set down his teacup and took notice. It was then, exchanging one of his carrots for a stick, he vowed that Britain would defend Poland if Hitler attacked it. That time had come. But Hitler couldn't simply attack. He must first make it look like self-defense. So on August 22, he told his generals, "I shall give a propagandist reason for starting the war; never mind whether it is plausible or not. The victor will not be asked afterward whether he told the truth."

The plan was for the SS, dressed in Polish uniforms, to attack a German radio station on the Polish border. To make the whole thing authentic, they would need German "casualties." They decided to use concentration camp inmates, whom they vilely referred to as *Konserven* (canned goods). These victims of Germany would be dressed as German soldiers. In the end only one man was murdered for this purpose, via lethal injection, and afterward shot several times to give the appearance that he had been killed by Polish soldiers. The deliberate murder of a human being for the purposes of deceiving the world seems a perfectly fitting inaugural act for what was to follow. This took place on schedule, August 31.

In "retaliation," German troops marched into Poland at dawn on September 1. Göring's Luftwaffe rained hell from the skies, deliberately killing civilians. Civilians were murdered more carefully on the ground. It was a coldly deliberate act of terror by intentional mass murder, never before seen in modern times, and it was the Poles' first bitter taste of the Nazi ruthlessness they would come to know so well. The outside world would not hear details for some time. It knew only that German forces were cutting through Poland like the proverbial hot knife through butter as Panzer divisions neatly erased thirty and forty miles of Poland per day.

But Hitler gave a speech to the Reichstag, casting himself in the role of aggrieved victim. "You know the endless attempts I made for a peaceful clarification and understanding of the problem of Austria," he said, "and later of the problem of the Sudetenland, Bohemia and Moravia. It was all in vain." Poland had refused his gracious offers of peace and with a callousness not to be borne. The Poles rewarded his good faith with violence! "I am wrongly judged if my love of peace and patience are mistaken for weakness or even cowardice. . . . I have therefore resolved to speak to Poland in the same language that Poland for months past has used toward us." The long-suffering and peace-loving Führer could take it no more: "This night for the first time Polish regular soldiers fired on our own territory. Since 5:45 A.M. we have been returning the fire, and from now on bombs will be met with bombs." Admiral Canaris, the head of the Abwehr, had long dreaded this hour. He was overcome with emotion at the implications of it all. Hans Bernd Gisevius, a diplomat whom Canaris had recruited to work with him in the Resistance, was at OKW headquarters that day. They ran into each other in a back stairway, and Canaris drew Gisevius aside. "This means the end of Germany," he said.

It now only remained for Britain to declare war. But Hitler and von Ribbentrop doubted the British would do so. As with Austria and Czechoslovakia, they would probably prefer a "diplomatic" solution. Indeed, for two days the British engaged in diplomatic back and forth, but at some point someone lent Chamberlain a vertebra, for against Hitler's calculations, on Sunday, Great Britain declared war.

That morning Dietrich and Karl-Friedrich were a few minutes from home, discussing the events of the last days. It was a warm, humid morning, with low-hanging cloud cover over the city. Suddenly there were sirens. It was noon. Dietrich quickly pedaled his bicycle back to the house on Marienburgerallee and waited for something to happen. But no planes flew over Berlin. There would be no immediate air retaliation. It was all a bit strange and anticlimactic. But World War II had begun.

September 1939

During the first weeks of the war, Bonhoeffer considered his situation. He had gotten a yearlong deferral from military service, and he was on friendly terms with the powers that be in Schlawe. But what would happen after his year was up? He considered a job as a military chaplain; he might even be assigned to a hospital. His mother met with her cousin Paul von Hase, the Berlin commandant, to discuss this possibility, and an application was filed. Bonhoeffer didn't hear back until February: the response was negative. Only those already on active duty were eligible for chaplaincy posts.

Meanwhile, many men who had been part of Finkenwalde, Köslin, Schlawe, and Sigurdshof had already been called up. On the third day of fighting, one was killed. By war's end more than 80 of the 150 young men from Finkenwalde and the collective pastorates had been killed. Bonhoeffer wrote a circular letter to the brethren on September 20:

> I have received the news, which I pass on to you today, that our dear brother Theodor Maass was killed in Poland on 3rd September. You will be as stunned by this news as I was. But I beg you, let us thank God in remembrance of him. He was a good brother, a quiet, faithful pastor of the Confessing Church, a man who lived from word and sacrament, whom God has also thought worthy to suffer for the Gospel. I am sure that he was prepared to go. Where God tears great gaps we should not try to fill them with human words. They should remain open. Our only comfort is the God of the resurrection, the Father of our Lord Jesus Christ, who also was and is his God. In him we know our brothers and in him is the biding fellowship of those who have overcome and those who still await their hour. God be praised for our dead brother and be merciful to us all at our end.

The war put Bonhoeffer in a strange position. He had always been a man of seeming contradictions, and the war would magnify them. He knew he could not fight for Hitler's Germany, but he was extraordinarily supportive when it came to the young men who did not see things his way. He also knew he had options they did not. Albrecht Schönherr remembered the climate:

Through the Nazi propaganda and this whole blurring of the situation, we had the feeling, well, in the end we really must step in; the Fatherland must be defended. Not with a very good conscience, of course not. Above all not with enthusiasm. . . . After all, it was very clearly the case that whoever refused the draft in the case of war would be beheaded, would be executed. Was this the point at which we should give up our lives, and thereby also our care for our family, and everything which was important to us? Or was it not yet the point? Bonhoeffer did not say, you may not go. . . . If you see it from today's perspective you see it much more critically. Above all, because we now know everything which happened. But at that time we didn't perceive things with complete clarity. I know that Bonhoeffer himself was sad that he had supported a man who completely refused the draft and then was executed. It was a very strange situation in which we all stood.

Through the Looking Glass

In the middle of October, when the fighting in Poland ended, it seemed safe to resume the collective pastorates, at least the one in Sigurdshof. Eight ordinands arrived there, and Bonhoeffer picked up where he had left off. He alternated between the otherworldly fairyland idyll of the Pomeranian woods and the churning intrigue of *über*-present Berlin. That winter was one of the most severe on record, but it was a joy to escape to that primitive snowbound world, so far from the gritty concerns of the war.

And yet he could never escape it much. In Berlin he met with Dohnanyi, who told him everything, as he always had. But Bonhoeffer now heard things he had not heard before, things that would fundamentally alter his thinking. It was worse than anything he had dreamed. And what Bonhoeffer now knew would make him feel more alone than ever because many in the church and ecumenical world were expending great energies toward ending the war. But Bonhoeffer was not. He now believed that the principal goal was to remove Hitler from power. Only afterward could Germany negotiate for peace. Knowing what he knew, any peace with Hitler was no better than war. But he couldn't say such things, even in ecumenical circles. This was when he began to realize that he was already part of the conspiracy to remove Hitler. He couldn't even share what he knew with his best friends. It had become too dangerous. More than ever now, he was alone with God, and he looked to God's judgment upon his actions.

What *did* Bonhoeffer know?

Dohnanyi told him that now, under the dark cover of war, Hitler had unleashed horrors that beggared description, that made the usual horrors of war quaint things of the past. Reports from Poland indicated that the SS were committing unspeakable atrocities, things unheard of in civilized times. On September 10, a group of SS men had brutally overseen the forced labor of fifty Polish Jews, who spent the day repairing a bridge. When the work was completed, the SS herded the workers into a synagogue and murdered them. That was only one example. On a widespread systematic level, the Wehrmacht's advances in Poland were accompanied by the intentional mass murder of civilians.

Dohnanyi's primary source was his boss, Admiral Canaris. It was so disturbing that Canaris insisted on a meeting with Wilhelm Keitel, the head of the German military. They met in Hitler's private railroad train on September 12, and Canaris questioned the OKW chief about the heinous evils, which would destroy Germany. What Canaris could not have known at that civilized meeting was that it would continue and would get much worse. It would not only destroy Germany, but would do so more completely than he had ever dared to fear. The German culture and civilization that he, Dohnanyi, and Bonhoeffer knew and loved would be obliterated from history. Future generations would be convinced that nothing good could ever have existed in a country that produced such evil. They would think only of these evils. It would be as if these unleashed dark forces had grotesquely marched like devils on dead horses, backward through the gash in the present, and had destroyed the German past too.

Canaris and the others in the German military leadership thought that Hitler's bestial nature was unfortunate, but they had no idea it was something that he cultivated and celebrated, that it was part of an ideology that had been waiting for this opportunity to leap at the throats of every Jew and Pole, priest and aristocrat, and tear them to pieces. The German generals had not seen the dark river of blood bubbling beneath the surface of the new Germany, but suddenly here it was, gushing like a geyser. Despite all the hints and warnings, it was too gruesome to be believed.

Hitler's hour had arrived, and on the first of September, a brutal new

Darwinism broke over Europe: the Nietzschean triumph of the strong over the weak could at last begin. The weak who could be useful would be brutally enslaved; all others would be murdered. What seemed so offensive to the international community—that Hitler would take the territory of the Polish people by force—was nothing compared to what the Nazis were doing. Their racial ideologies demanded more than territory; Poland must become a giant slave labor camp. The Poles were to be treated as *Untermenschen* (sub-humans). Their lands would not merely be occupied; they themselves would be terrorized and broken into utter docility, would be dealt with as beasts. The Germans would not tolerate the possibility of failure or the slightest manifestation of mercy. Brutality and mercilessness would be aggressively cultivated as virtues.

In his diary Canaris wrote, "I pointed out to General Keitel that I knew that extensive executions were planned in Poland and that particularly the nobility and the clergy were to be exterminated." Canaris was referring to the plan that the SS called the "housecleaning of Jews, intelligentsia, clergy and the nobility." All Poles with leadership abilities were to be killed. Soon after his appointment as governor general of Poland, Hans Frank declared, "The Poles shall be the slaves of the German Reich."

There had been warnings all along, the loudest being Hitler's book, *Mein Kampf*. The entire Western world might have saved itself wondering what lay ahead. But who could believe it? On August 22, Hitler boldly told his generals that in the prosecution of the coming war, things would take place that were not to their liking. At other times he referred to the brutality ahead as "devil's work." He once declared, "You can't wage war with Salvation Army methods." He planned these things all along, and in that August 22 meeting, he warned the generals that they "should not interfere in such matters, but restrict themselves to their military duties."

There was something in the German psyche that responded to this sort of suggestion too well. But there were some brave souls who did consider the larger picture. Niemöller was certainly one. Now Canaris was another. So he protested to Keitel. But in vain. Canaris didn't understand that these brutalities were at the very core of the dark vision Hitler was now, at last, bringing into reality. Keitel did not concern himself with such things above his pay grade. He told Canaris: "The Führer has already decided on this matter."

Since the SS perpetrated the most wicked acts, Hitler could keep the worst of it from his military leaders. But reports leaked out. Many generals were beside themselves. General Blaskowitz sent Hitler a memo describing the horrors he had seen. He was profoundly concerned about the effect on the German soldiers. If hardened military leaders were disturbed, one can imagine the effect these things would have on the young men who had never seen a battlefield. General Bock read Blaskowitz's memo and found its descriptions "hair-raising." General Petzel and General Georg von Küchler opposed what they were seeing in the strongest terms possible. They demanded an end to the murder of civilians. General Ulex called the "ethnic policy" a "blot on the honor of the entire German people." General Lemelsen had one SS leader arrested for ordering the shooting death of fifty Jews.

But no one would get in any trouble. Hitler saw to it that a blanket amnesty was declared on all such men arrested. But because reports of these monstrous acts began to circulate and be verified, many in the military leadership were finally willing to take a stand and join a coup against Hitler.

Some generals, however—Brauchitsch was one—were less bothered. In January 1940, Blaskowitz wrote another memo and sent it to Brauchitsch; he described the attitude in the army toward the SS as alternating "between abhorrence and hatred," and said "every soldier feels sickened and repelled by the crimes committed in Poland by agents of the Reich and government representatives." Brauchitsch only shrugged. He didn't want the army sullied with these evildoings, but if the SS was doing most of the dirty work, he wouldn't make a fuss.

The nobler-minded generals would, and did, but they came to realize that making a fuss was not succeeding. More Jews and Poles were being butchered every day. They must plan another coup. Many of them were Christians and had no qualms about calling what they saw evil, and felt a duty to stop it at all costs. Many felt that to be good Germans and faithful Christians at that time meant turning against the man leading their country.

They knew that if they weren't careful to plan other details of the coup, the death of Adolf Hitler might bring worse things. Two things were vital. First, they must communicate with British officials to guarantee that they, the conspirators, would be recognized as separate from Hitler and the Nazis. If the death of Hitler only emboldened the British to destroy Germany, little would be gained. Second, they must get enough of the army leaders on their side to pull it off *in toto*. If they succeeded only in killing Adolf Hitler, other Nazis would likely seize control and continue his work.

The Nazi Worldview at Home

Just as Hitler had been planning for years to enslave the Poles and kill the Jews, he had been planning to murder every German with a disability. Now he could do just that. As early as 1929 he had publicly proposed that 700,000 of the "weakest" Germans be "removed" per year. Before the war, the out-cry over such actions would have been deafening. But now, with everyone's attention on the war, this domestic nightmare could begin; the fog of war would cover a multitude of sins at home too.

Preparations for the T-4 euthanasia program had been under way for years. Now they hit the ground running. In August 1939 every doctor and midwife in the country was notified that they must register all children born with genetic defects—retroactive to 1936. In September, when the war began, the killing of these "defectives" began. In the next few years five thousand small children were killed. It wasn't until later that fall that attention was formally focused on the other "incurables." In her excellent book, *For the Soul of the People*, Victoria Barnett tells the story:

> It is unlikely that the first institutions to receive the forms were aware of their purpose. For each patient, a form was to be filled out giving in detail the nature of the patient's illness, the length of time already spent in institutions, and the patient's racial status. The cover letter told institutions' directors that filling out the forms was a necessary statistical measure and that a mass transfer of certain patients to other institutions might be necessary because of wartime demand for medical facilities. Three state-appointed experts would review the completed forms, select those patients to be "transferred," and provide for their removal from the home institution.

As soon as the Polish campaign was under way, a number of adult patients deemed the least "fit" were put on buses for these "transfers." The places to which these poor souls were transferred would murder them. At first the method was via injection, and later on via carbon monoxide gas. The parents or relatives of these patients had no idea of these goings-on until they received a letter in the mail, informing them of the death of their loved one, who had already been cremated. The cause of death was usually given as pneumonia or a similarly common ailment, and the ashes of their loved one's remains arrived shortly thereafter.

Hitler's memo on this subject was postdated September 1, to coincide with the beginning of the war. The rationale given for the killings was that the patients were taking up medical facilities and beds that should be used by soldiers wounded while fighting for the fatherland. When the Third Reich was straining to battle its enemies, the cost of caring for the "incurables" was prohibitive. They must "give their lives" for the greater cause just as everyone else, and just as the parents of soldiers must "make the ultimate sacrifice" of their sons for the war effort, so too must the parents of these patients. The T-4 program was run by Hitler's personal physician, Karl Brandt, the man Erwin Sutz had met while hiking in the Alps.

The methods of killing used at these euthanasia centers and the methods of cremation were the first attempts by the Nazis to undertake mass killings. The lessons learned in murdering these helpless patients helped the Nazis streamline their killing and cremation methods, which would culminate in the death camps, where hundreds of thousands and then millions of innocents were killed.

Putsch Plans Renewed

Toward the end of September, everyone in Germany was sure that peace was at hand. Hitler had gotten what he wanted—Poland—and that would be that. But on September 27, the day of Warsaw's surrender, Hitler convened his generals and announced plans to make war on the western frontier too. He would attack Belgium and Holland. And then France and England. And Denmark and Norway. Again, the generals were thunderstruck by what they heard, and plans to do away with this madman were now dusted off and updated.

Beck also told Dohnanyi to update his Chronicle of Shame, for which they would one day hang. To that end, Dohnanyi obtained actual film footage of many SS atrocities in Poland. To avoid another *Dolchstoss* (stab-in-the-back) legend from arising when Hitler was killed and Germany "defeated" by the Allies, it was vital to have proof of the Nazi atrocities. There were more conversations and meetings, and Bonhoeffer was at the center of many of them.

But as the military geared up for more war—and as the conspirators geared up for a new coup attempt—a fresh surprise stopped everyone in his tracks. Behold, that unpredictable magus, Adolf Hitler, would now with a flourish produce from his hindquarters a withered olive branch and wave it before the goggling world. In a speech to the Reichstag on October 6, he again struck a pose of profound magnanimity, and with a face so straight that the rest of the world seemed askew, Hitler proposed peace: "My chief endeavor has been to rid our relations with France of all trace of ill will and render them tolerable for both nations. . . . Germany has no further claims against France. . . . I have devoted no less effort to the achievement of Anglo-German understanding, nay, more than that, of an Anglo-German friendship."

It was a performance. Of course the unspoken terms of his absurd *Diktat* were that no one mention the blood-soaked piece of German-occupied territory formerly known as Poland. Nor the place once upon a time known as Czechoslovakia. If no one was foolish enough to bring them up, peace was in the offing. But Chamberlain, like a woman scorned, would hear no more sweet talk. If Hitler wished to be believed, he said, "acts—not words alone—must be forthcoming." Chamberlain rejected Hitler's proposal on October 13.

Meanwhile the generals realized they must act quickly. The putsch must happen *before Hitler attacked the West.* Once German armies marched on Belgium and Holland, it would be harder than ever to get Britain to take the conspirators seriously, especially since many of them had been in charge of the bloody juggernaut across Poland. And Hitler was not about to sit on his heels. If he couldn't convince Britain to give him the peace terms he liked, he would take them by force. In his typically gentlemanly way, he said to General Halder: "[The] British will be ready to talk only after a beating." Military plans were being made to march westward as soon as possible. And the conspirators rushed to pull together their own plans.

But these plans consisted of far more than figuring out how to squeeze off a clean shot at Herr Hitler. First, the conspirators must make sure that Britain and other powers knew of their existence and were willing to support them when they made their fateful move. They didn't want Britain and

France to simply take advantage of Hitler's sudden demise to mete out their own harsh justice on Germany. They needed peace assurances from these countries. And they couldn't take their eyes off Russia in the east. Stalin was always waiting for any moment of weakness when he might pounce and tear away another piece of Europe at bargain basement prices. For the conspirators, cultivating friendly foreign contacts, and convincing them that the conspiracy was credible, was a vital part of the whole.

This was where Dietrich Bonhoeffer would come in. His role in reaching out to the British would be a crucial one over the next few years. His connections with Bishop Bell and others—and Bell's connections with top men in the British government—were significant. Bonhoeffer also had connections in Norway and America. But would this pastor really take that last step beyond providing emotional and intellectual support for others and actively participate along with them? That remained to be seen.

CHAPTER 23

FROM CONFESSION TO CONSPIRACY

Bonhoeffer introduced us in 1935 to the problem of what we today call
political resistance . . . The escalating persecution of the Jews generated
an increasingly hostile situation, especially for Bonhoeffer himself.
We now realized that mere confession, no matter how courageous,
inescapably meant complicity with the murderers.

—EBERHARD BETHGE

We will have to move through a very deep valley, I believe much
deeper than we can sense now, before we will be able to ascend the
other side again.

—DIETRICH BONHOEFFER

Bonhoeffer was in the heart of the conspiracy, lending emotional support and encouragement to those more directly involved, such as his brother Klaus and his brother-in-law Dohnanyi. He didn't have qualms about it. But for him to become more officially involved was something else entirely.

Bonhoeffer's situation was a complicated one. As a leader in the Confessing Church, he had more difficult choices than if he had been acting alone. Whatever he chose to do, he must consider others, just as he had done when he rejected becoming a conscientious objector. He wasn't free to do as he pleased. Bonhoeffer never arrived at decisions easily, but once he saw things clearly, he moved forward. After his return from New York, he was not yet clear about what God was leading him to do.

It must have been sometime during this period that his sister-in-law Emmi Bonhoeffer provocatively tried to prod him toward more serious involvement. Neither Emmi nor Klaus was a Christian, so it was inevitable that when her husband was risking his life, she might think of her pastor brother-in-law as being too comfortably above the fray. Perhaps he had the tendency toward being so "spiritually minded" that he was "no earthly good." Emmi thought enough of Dietrich to share her thoughts directly. "You Christians are glad when someone else does what you know must be done," she said, "but it seems that somehow you are unwilling to get your own hands dirty and do it." She wasn't suggesting that Bonhoeffer become an assassin, but his involvement was not what her husband's or Dohnanyi's was. Bonhoeffer carefully considered what she said. He said that no one should be glad that anyone was killing anyone else, and yet he knew what she was getting at; she had a point. Still, he wasn't decided on what to do.

Meanwhile, with or without Bonhoeffer, the conspiracy moved ahead with renewed vigor. Dohnanyi got in touch with Dr. Joseph Müller, a Munich lawyer with strong ties to the Vatican. Sometimes referred to by those in the conspiracy as "Herr X," Müller was a man of great physical strength. Since childhood, friends had called him *Ochsensepp* (Joe Ox). Müller's assignment in October 1939 was to travel to Rome, seemingly on official Abwehr business. But in reality he was to make contact with the British ambassador to the Holy See and gain some assurance of peace from the British if those in the conspiracy could oust Hitler. Müller succeeded; the British terms required Germany to shed the lands added during Hitler's binge of the previous two years. But Müller went further. He convinced the pope to agree to act as an intermediary between Britain and the fledgling German government that formed following Hitler's demise. It was all very promising. Bonhoeffer and Müller immediately hit it off, and a year later, Müller provided Bonhoeffer's entree to the Alpine monastery at Ettal. But for now, Bonhoeffer continued traveling between Sigurdshof and Berlin.

The conspirators planned to launch the coup when Hitler gave the green light to attack the West. But he would set a date, everyone would gear up, and at the last minute, Hitler would call it off. He did this twenty-nine times over several months, driving everyone half mad. The chain of command in pulling off a full-blown military coup was terribly complicated, and unfortunately it was General Brauchitsch who must give the final go-ahead. It had been very difficult to convince him to be involved, and the whip-sawing of emotions from the constant postponements sapped what little courage he had. Numerous opportunities were lost. When Hitler finally issued the order to go in May 1940, the unwieldy coup tripped over itself and nothing happened. They had failed.

From Confession to Resistance

On March 15 the last group of ordinands finished their term, and two days later the Gestapo closed Sigurdshof. They had discovered it at last, and the golden era that began at Zingst in early 1935 had ended. Bonhoeffer could no longer teach ordinands. He would have to think about what was next, and his options were being winnowed down. He was moving ineluctably toward deeper involvement in the conspiracy, but exactly what this would mean was still unclear.

No one has better attempted to explain the seeming paradox of a Christian involved in a plot to assassinate a head of state than Eberhard Bethge. He helps show that Bonhoeffer's steps toward political resistance were not some unwarranted detour from his previous thinking, but were a natural and inevitable outworking of that thinking. Bonhoeffer always sought to be brave and to speak the truth—to "confess"—come what may; but at some point merely speaking the truth smacked of cheap grace. Bethge explained:

> Bonhoeffer introduced us in 1935 to the problem of what we today call political resistance. The levels of confession and of resistance could no longer be kept neatly apart. The escalating persecution of the Jews generated an increasingly intolerable situation, especially for Bonhoeffer himself. We now realized that mere confession, no matter how courageous, inescapably meant complicity with the murderers, even though there would always be new acts of refusing to be co-opted and even though we would preach "Christ alone" Sunday after Sunday. During

the whole time the Nazi state never considered it necessary to prohibit such preaching. Why should it?

Thus we were approaching the borderline between confession and resistance; and if we did not cross this border, our confession was going to be no better than cooperation with the criminals. And so it became clear where the problem lay for the Confessing Church: we were resisting by way of confession, but we were not confessing by way of resistance.

All his life, Bonhoeffer had applied the same logic to theological issues that his father applied to scientific issues. There was only one reality, and Christ was Lord over all of it or none. A major theme for Bonhoeffer was that every Christian must be "fully human" by bringing God into his whole life, not merely into some "spiritual" realm. To be an ethereal figure who merely talked about God, but somehow refused to get his hands dirty in the real world in which God had placed him, was bad theology. Through Christ, God had shown that he meant us to be in this world and to obey him with our actions in this world. So Bonhoeffer would get his hands dirty, not because he had grown impatient, but because God was speaking to him about further steps of obedience.

Crossing the Line

After months of postponement, Hitler ordered his armies to march west in May. On the tenth, German units attacked Holland. The Dutch succumbed in five days. Belgium was next, and soon German tanks roared across France. On June 14, German troops marched into Paris, and three days later *le mot oncle* was heard round the world. It was a stunning collapse.

Meanwhile, on the far side of the continent, Bonhoeffer and Bethge were visiting the pastorate of one of the Finkenwalde brothers in eastern Prussia. After a pastors' meeting that morning, they took a ferry across to the peninsula and found an outdoor café in the sun. It was in Memel, which is today in Lithuania. Suddenly a trumpet fanfare on the radio loudspeakers announced a special news flash: *France had surrendered!* Twenty-two years after Germany's humiliation, Hitler had turned the tables.

People went wild. Some of them leaped up and stood on chairs; others stood on tables. Everyone threw out his arm in the Nazi salute and burst into "Deutschland über Alles" and then the "Horst Wessel Song." It was a pandemonium of patriotism, and Bonhoeffer and Bethge were pinned like beetles. At least Bethge was. Bonhoeffer, on the other hand, seemed to be a part of it. Bethge was flabbergasted: along with everyone else, his friend stood up and threw out his arm in the "Heil, Hitler!" salute. As Bethge stood there gawking, Bonhoeffer whispered to him: "Are you crazy? Raise your arm! We'll have to run risks for many different things, but this silly salute is not one of them!" Bethge's extraordinary friend and mentor had schooled him in many things over the previous five years, but this was something new.

It was then, Bethge realized, that Bonhoeffer crossed a line. He was behaving conspiratorially. He didn't want to be thought of as an objector. He wanted to blend in. He didn't want to make an anti-Hitler statement; he had bigger fish to fry. He wanted to be left alone to do the things he knew God was calling him to do, and these things required him to remain unnoticed. Bethge said that one cannot fix a date when Bonhoeffer passed into being a part of the conspiracy in any official way. But he knew at that café in Memel, when Bonhoeffer was saluting Hitler, that his friend was already on the other side of the border. He had crossed from "confession" to "resistance."

Hitler's Greatest Triumph

Three days later in some woods north of Paris, a curious scene was unfolding. Hitler, to whom mercy was a sign of subhuman weakness, arranged for the French to sign the terms of their surrender in the forest of Compiegne on the very spot where they had the Germans sign the armistice in 1918. That black day of humiliation was fresh in Hitler's mind, and he would now make the most of the opportunity to reverse it. Forcing his vanquished foes to return to the site of Germany's humiliation was only the beginning. Hitler would clamber to oxygen-free heights of pettiness by having the very railroad car in which that armistice had been signed removed from the museum in which it was kept and hauled all the way back into this forest glade. Pneumatic drills were employed to remove the museum wall, and the railroad car was taken out and back again into the past where the fateful wound had been inflicted on the German nation. If this gesture wasn't enough, Hitler had the very chair in which Foch had sat delivered to him, so that he could sit in it, inside the railroad car, there in the forest of Compiegne. With such a penchant for symbolism, it's a wonder he resisted putting the Treaty of Versailles into a safe and casting it into the middle of the Atlantic Ocean.

Hitler and Germany had waited twenty-three years for this triumphant moment, and if ever Adolf Hitler became the Savior of the German nation, this was it. Many Germans who had reservations and misgivings about Hitler now changed their opinions. He had healed the unhealable wound of the First War and Versailles. He had restored a broken Germany to her former greatness. The old had passed way, and behold, he had made all things new. In many people's eyes he was suddenly something like a god, the messiah for whom they had waited and prayed, and whose reign would last a thousand years.

In his book *Ethics*, which he worked on during this time, Bonhoeffer wrote about the way people worship success. The topic fascinated him. He referred to it in his letter from Barcelona many years earlier, in which he observed the fickleness of the crowds at bullfights, how they roared for the toreador one moment and for the bull the next. It was success they wanted, success more than anything. In *Ethics*, he wrote:

> In a world where success is the measure and justification of all things the figure of Him who was sentenced and crucified remains a stranger and is at best the object of pity. The world will allow itself to be subdued only by success. It is not ideas or opinions which decide, but deeds. Success alone justifies wrongs done. . . . With a frankness and off-handedness which no other earthly power could permit itself, history appeals in its own cause to the dictum that the end justifies the means. . . . The figure of the Crucified invalidates all thought which takes success for its standard.

God was interested not in success, but in obedience. If one obeyed God and was willing to suffer defeat and whatever else came one's way, God would show a kind of success that the world couldn't imagine. But this was the narrow path, and few would take it.

For the German Resistance, it was a depressing time. Nonetheless, their efforts continued on several fronts. There were always a number of groups and plans moving forward simultaneously. Around this time, Fritz-Dietlof von der Schulenburg joined forces with a member of the Kreisau Circle. Others planned to have the great conqueror picked off by snipers as he swanned down the Champs-Elysées in the inevitable victory parade. But the parade never materialized.

For the Nazis, the sense of victory was so great that in Poland, Hans Frank took the opportunity to order cold-blooded mass executions on a vast scale. He would make hay while the sun shone.

Bonhoeffer Misunderstood

After Hitler's success in France, a new day had dawned. Bonhoeffer and so many in the Resistance had been convinced that Hitler would ruin Germany by dragging it into a miserable military defeat. But who could have dreamed he would destroy Germany through success, through an ever-escalating orgy of self-love and self-worship? Actually Bonhoeffer considered it in the truncated speech given two days after Hitler came to power. He knew that if Germany worshiped any idol, it would incinerate its own future, as those who worshiped Moloch did by burning their children.

After the fall of France, many understood that Hitler was destroying Germany through success. That July, Bonhoeffer was thinking about the implications of this when he spoke at a Potsdam meeting of the Old Prussian Council of Brethren. But what he said was widely misinterpreted and added to his growing sense of alienation from the Confessing Church.

Bonhoeffer said that Germany had given its full assent to National Socialism and to Hitler. He called it a "historic yes." Before the French victory, there had been great possibilities for Hitler's quick defeat and the end of National Socialism, but these had vanished. They who stood against Hitler must get used to it, must try to understand the new situation and act accordingly. It would be a long haul, not a short one, and different tactics were in order. Bonhoeffer often spoke hyperbolically, for effect, and sometimes it backfired, as it did now.

He had once told a student that every sermon must contain "a shot of heresy," meaning that to express the truth, we must sometimes overstate something or say something in a way that will sound heretical—though it must certainly not be heretical. But even in using this phrase, "a shot of heresy," Bonhoeffer betrayed his habit of saying things for effect that could easily be misinterpreted. Many seized on that phrase to claim that Bonhoeffer was unconcerned with orthodox theology. Bonhoeffer often fell into such traps, and for this reason he might be the most misunderstood theologian who ever lived.

That day in Potsdam he was trying to shake the cobwebs from everyone's understanding, and it happened again. By saying that Hitler had won, he was trying hard—in retrospect, too hard—to get his listeners to wake up and change course. So now, when he spoke of how National Socialism had won, some in his audience thought he was giving his assent to this victory. They seriously thought he had said, in effect, "If you can't beat 'em, join 'em." In the next few years, after he began work for the Abwehr—ostensibly as an agent of the German government, but of course as a member of the Resistance—many remembered what he said that day and thought he actually had gone over to the "other" side and was working for Hitler and the Nazis.

What Is Truth?

Bonhoeffer obviously meant that those opposed to Hitler must rethink their approach to the new situation in Germany. Bonhoeffer was quite willing to do this, to forgo his previous position of outward opposition to the regime and suddenly pretend to be in step with it. But of course it was only so that he could be in opposition to it on another, more fundamental level.

This involved deception. Many of the serious Christians of Bonhoeffer's day were theologically unable to follow him to this point, nor did he ask them to. For many of them, such deception as Bonhoeffer would soon be involved in was no different from lying. Bonhoeffer's willingness to engage in deception stemmed not from a cavalier attitude toward the truth, but from a respect for the truth that was so deep, it forced him beyond the easy legalism of truth telling.

In Tegel prison several years later, Bonhoeffer wrote the essay "What Does It Mean to Tell the Truth?" in which he explored the subject. "From the moment of our lives in which we become capable of speech," it begins, "we are taught that our words must be true. What does this mean? What does 'telling the truth' mean? Who requires this of us?"

God's standard of truth entailed more than merely "not lying." In the

Sermon on the Mount, Jesus said, "You have heard it said . . . but I say unto you." Jesus took the Old Testament laws to a deeper level of meaning and obedience, from the "letter of the Law" to the "Spirit of the Law." Following the letter of the law was the dead "religion" of which Barth, among others, had written. It was man's attempt to deceive God into thinking one was being obedient, which was a far greater deception. God always required something deeper than religious legalism.

In the essay Bonhoeffer gave the example of a girl whose teacher asks in front of the class whether her father is a drunkard. She says no. "Of course," Bonhoeffer said, "one could call the child's answer a lie; all the same, this lie contains more truth—i.e., it corresponds more closely to the truth—than if the child had revealed the father's weakness before the class." One cannot demand "the truth" at any cost, and for this girl to admit in front of the class that her father is a drunkard is to dishonor him. How one tells the truth depends on circumstances. Bonhoeffer was aware that what he called the "living truth" was dangerous and "arouses the suspicion that the truth can and may be adapted to the given situation, so that the concept of truth utterly dissolves, and falsehood and truth draw indistinguishably close to each other."

Bonhoeffer knew that the flip side of the easy religious legalism of "never telling a lie" was the cynical notion that there is no such thing as truth, only "facts." This led to the cynical idea that one must say everything with no sense of propriety or discernment, that decorum or reserve was "hypocrisy" and a kind of lie. He wrote of that in his *Ethics* too:

> It is only the cynic who claims "to speak the truth" at all times and in all places to all men in the same way, but who, in fact, displays nothing but a lifeless image of the truth. . . . He dons the halo of the fanatical devotee of truth who can make no allowance for human weaknesses; but, in fact, he is destroying the living truth between men. He wounds shame, desecrates mystery, breaks confidence, betrays the community in which he lives, and laughs arrogantly at the devastation he has wrought and at the human weakness which "cannot bear the truth."

For Bonhoeffer, the relationship with God ordered everything else around it. A number of times he referred to the relationship with Jesus Christ as being like the *cantus firmus** of a piece of music. All the other parts of the music referred to it, and it held them together. To be true to God in the deepest way meant having such a relationship with him that one did not live legalistically by "rules" or "principles." One could never separate one's actions from one's relationship to God. It was a more demanding and more mature level of obedience, and Bonhoeffer had come to see that the evil of Hitler was forcing Christians to go deeper in their obedience, to think harder about what God was asking. Legalistic religion was being shown to be utterly inadequate.

Dohnanyi's boss, General Oster, had said that National Socialism was "an ideology of such sinister immorality that traditional values and loyalties no longer applied." Bonhoeffer knew that God had the answer to every difficulty, and he was trying to understand what God was saying to him about his situation. He had moved past mere "confession" and into conspiracy, which involved a measure of deception that many of his colleagues in the Confessing Church would not have understood. Soon, when he became a double agent for Military Intelligence under the command of Admiral Canaris, he had moved into a very lonely place indeed.

The Prayerbook of the Bible

As his role in the conspiracy developed, Bonhoeffer continued his pastoral work and his writings. He would write until the last months of his life, but the last book he published in his lifetime was *Das Gebetbook der Bibel* (*The Prayerbook of the Bible*), which appeared in 1940. That a book on the Old Testament Psalms was published then is a testimony to Bonhoeffer's devotion to scholarly truth and to his willingness to deceive the leaders of the Third Reich.

Bonhoeffer scholar Geffrey Kelly wrote, "One should make no mistake about it; in the context of Nazi Germany's bitter opposition to any manner of honoring of the Old Testament, this book, at the time of its publication, constituted an explosive declaration both politically and theologically." The book was a passionate declaration of the importance of the Old Testament to Christianity and to the church, and it was a bold and scholarly rebuke to Nazi efforts to undermine anything of Jewish origin.

---

* A pre-existing melody forming the basis of a polyphonic composition.

Because of this, Bonhoeffer got into a battle with the Board for the Regulation of Literature. As he would do in many interrogations in prison later on, he played dumb, claiming the book was merely scholarly literary exegesis. He well knew that all true exegeses and scholarship pointed to the truth, which, for the Nazis, was far worse than a hail of bullets. Bonhoeffer also said that the board's prohibitions against his "religious writings" were unclear, and he hadn't understood that he ought to have submitted this manuscript to them.

The incident illustrates Bonhoeffer's sense of what it meant to "tell the truth." Obeying God by publishing this pro-Jewish book—and cannily pretending that he had no inkling the National Socialists would object to its contents—was being true. He knew that if he had sent the manuscript to them beforehand, it would never have seen the light of day. Bonhoeffer had little doubt that God wished him to publish the truth in the book. He did not owe the Nazis the truth about the manuscript any more than the hypothetical little girl in his essay owed her class the truth about her father's vices.

In the book, Bonhoeffer linked the idea of Barthian grace with prayer by saying that we cannot reach God with our own prayers, but by praying "his" prayers—the Psalms of the Old Testament, which Jesus prayed—we effectively piggyback on them all the way to heaven. We must not confuse what we do naturally, such as "wishing, hoping, sighing, lamenting, rejoicing," with prayer, which is *unnatural* to us and which must be initiated from outside us, by God. If we confuse these two things, "we confuse earth and heaven, human beings and God." Prayer cannot come from us. "For that," he wrote, "one needs Jesus Christ!" By praying the Psalms, we "pray along with Christ's prayer and therefore may be certain and glad that God hears us. When our will, our whole heart, enters into the prayer of Christ, then we are truly praying. We can pray only in Jesus Christ, with whom we shall also be heard."

The idea would have seemed impossibly "Jewish" for the Nazis, and it was too "Catholic" for many Protestants, who saw in recited prayers the "vain repetition" of the heathen. But Bonhoeffer only wanted to be biblical. The ordinands at Finkenwalde and afterward prayed the Psalms every day. Bonhoeffer was firm: "The Psalter filled the life of early Christianity. But more important than all of this is that Jesus died on the cross with words from the Psalms on his lips. Whenever the Psalter is abandoned, an incomparable treasure is lost to the Christian church. With its recovery will come unexpected power."

In one slim book, Bonhoeffer was claiming that Jesus had given his imprimatur to the Psalms and to the Old Testament; that Christianity was unavoidably Jewish; that the Old Testament is not superseded by the New Testament, but is inextricably linked with it; and that Jesus was unavoidably Jewish. Bonhoeffer also made clear that the Psalms spoke of Jesus and prophesied his coming. The following March he would find that publishing this small exegetical tract resulted in his being forbidden to publish anything again.

Bonhoeffer Joins the Abwehr

On July 14, 1940, Bonhoeffer was preaching at a church conference in Königsberg when the Gestapo arrived and broke up the meeting. They cited a new order forbidding such meetings, and the conference ended. No one was arrested, but Bonhoeffer saw that his ability to continue such pastoral work was coming to an end. He and Bethge forged ahead, visiting parishes in East Prussia, including what were then the German towns of Stallupönen, Trakehnen, and Eydtkuhnen.* Stalin's troops were very near, and the general mood was anxious. So after his tour of these villages, Bonhoeffer returned to Berlin and spoke with Dohnanyi about his plans going forward.

There was great rivalry between the Abwehr and the Gestapo, since they occupied separate spheres, just as the CIA and the FBI do in the United States. Dohnanyi reasoned that if the Abwehr officially employed Bonhoeffer, the Gestapo would be forced to leave him alone. It made sense for many reasons. Bonhoeffer would have great freedom of movement to continue his work as a pastor, and he would have the cover needed to expand his activities for the conspiracy. Another benefit was that as an invaluable member of Germany's Military Intelligence, Bonhoeffer was unlikely to be called into military service. He would ostensibly be performing an important duty for the fatherland. That was a huge boon since he had never resolved what he would do if he was drafted.

---

* After the war these towns became part of the Soviet Union, and after the breakup of the Soviet Union, they became part of Kaliningrad Oblast, an exclave of Russia.

Dohnanyi, Bethge, Bonhoeffer, Gisevius, and Oster discussed this arrangement in a meeting at the Bonhoeffer home that August. They decided to move forward. For starters they would send Bonhoeffer on assignment to East Prussia, especially since war with Russia seemed imminent, and it would be a natural place for him to go since he had plenty of pastoral business there. If the Gestapo thought it odd that a Confessing Church pastor should be used on Abwehr business, they could say that the Abwehr used Communists and Jews, too, which they did. The "front" of a pastorate in the Confessing Church was ideal camouflage for the Abwehr's activities. Besides, they were Military Intelligence, engaged in complex and mysterious missions. Who was the Gestapo to question them?

So the day had come. Bonhoeffer had officially joined the conspiracy. He would be enfolded into the Abwehr's protection and, in the guise of a member of Military Intelligence, would be protected by Oster and Canaris. The levels of deception were several. On the one hand, Bonhoeffer would be actually performing pastoral work and continuing his theological writing, as he wished to do. Officially this work was a front for his work as a Nazi agent in Military Intelligence. But unofficially his work in Military Intelligence was a front for his real work as a conspirator against the Nazi regime.

Bonhoeffer was pretending to be a pastor—but was only pretending to be pretending, since he really *was* being a pastor. And he was pretending to be a member of Military Intelligence working for Hitler, but—like Dohnanyi, Oster, Canaris, and Gisevius—he was in reality working *against* Hitler. Bonhoeffer was not telling little white lies. In Luther's famous phrase, he was "sinning boldly." He was involved in a high-stakes game of deception upon deception, and yet Bonhoeffer himself knew that in all of it, he was being utterly obedient to God. For him, that was the *cantus firmus* that made the dizzying complexities of it all perfectly coherent.

That September, however, the RSHA (*Reichssicherheitshauptamt*), which had a bitter rivalry with the Abwehr, caused Bonhoeffer further trouble. The RSHA was led by the waxy lamprey Reinhard Heydrich, who worked directly under Himmler. The RSHA now informed Bonhoeffer that because of what they termed "subversive activities," he was no longer allowed to speak in public. Even worse, he must report regularly to the Gestapo at Schlawe, in faraway eastern Pomerania, where he was still officially in residence. His possibilities for working with the Confessing Church were shrinking to nothing. They could still legally use him as a teacher, but after this restriction, the Confessing Church decided to give him a leave of absence for "theological study."

Bonhoeffer did not take these accusations lying down. It was important to counterpunch and to preserve the illusion that he was devoted to the Third Reich. Once again playing dumb, he wrote an indignant letter to the RSHA, protesting the characterization of him as anything less than patriotic. He also cited his distinguished ancestors and relatives, something he would never have done under normal circumstances, since it would have struck him as prideful and ridiculous. But he did it all with a perfectly straight face, even ending the letter with a harrumphing "Heil Hitler!" for good measure. But the letter did not solve his problem, so again he turned to Dohnanyi.

As a result of the conversation with Dohnanyi, his role with the Abwehr would get more serious, and the cat-and-mouse game with Hitler's henchmen would begin in earnest. First of all, Dohnanyi wanted to get him away from the RSHA's interference. It wouldn't do to have him in Pomerania any longer. But Berlin would be worse yet. So it was contrived to assign him Abwehr duties that took him to Munich.

Dohnanyi went to Munich in October and discussed the situation with his colleagues. Meanwhile, Bonhoeffer laid low in Klein-Krössin, working on his *Ethics* and waiting for the high sign. At the end of October he got the go-ahead and went to Munich, officially registering at the town hall as a Munich resident. His aunt, Countess Kalckreuth, would provide accommodations in her home. Her address was his "official" residence, just as Superintendent Eduard Block's address was his "official" residence in Schlawe. How many nights he actually spent in either place was another story.

Once he registered as a Munich resident, the local Abwehr could request his services, which they did. Bonhoeffer became a so-called *V-Mann*, or *Vertrauensmann* (the literal translation means "confidence man") and was working undercover. He was still "officially" a civilian and could continue to do what he liked, to work on his *Ethics*, minister as a pastor, and work for the Confessing Church.

Ettal Monastery in the Alps

In Munich, Bonhoeffer reconnected with Joseph Müller, who was attached to the Abwehr office there and was an active leader of the conspiracy.

Bonhoeffer's work with the Resistance in Munich was now through Müller. It was Müller who wangled an invitation for Bonhoeffer to live at Ettal, a picturesque Benedictine monastery nestled in the Garmisch-Partenkirchen region of the Bavarian Alps. For Bonhoeffer, it was a small dream come true. Here, in this Catholic bastion of resistance against the Nazis, he found profound peace and quiet, far from the mental noise of Berlin. The abbey dated to 1330, but most of the buildings were built in the eighteenth century in the baroque style. Bonhoeffer became friendly with the prior and abbot, who invited him to stay as their guests as long as he liked, and beginning in November, he lived there through the winter.

On November 18 he wrote Bethge: "Received most warmly; I eat in the refectory, sleep in the hotel, can use the library, have my own key to the cloister, and yesterday had a long and good conversation with the abbot." It was all quite an honor, but especially so for a non-Catholic. The Ettal *Kloster* (cloister) was a two-and-a-half-mile walk from Oberammergau, where every ten years since 1634 the residents put on their famous passion play.

Bonhoeffer enjoyed the routine of the monastic existence and made progress with his writing. At Finkenwalde he instituted the monastic habit of having someone reading aloud during mealtimes. The ordinands were not fond of the practice, and after a while, he discontinued it. But at Ettal it was the custom, as it had been for many centuries. Bonhoeffer enjoyed it, but found it curious that nondevotional books, such as historical works, were read in the same chanting tone used in the church liturgy. "Sometimes, when the subject matter is humorous," he said to his parents, "it is impossible to suppress a smile." While he was there, the abbot, Father Angelus Kupfer, and some of the priests were reading Bonhoeffer's book *Life Together* and planned to discuss it with the author afterward.

His long conversations with the abbot and other priests gave him a renewed appreciation for Catholicism and informed his writing of *Ethics*, especially the parts dealing with natural law, which was absent from Protestant theology and which absence he meant to correct.

Munich was about ninety minutes away by train, and Bonhoeffer made many trips there. He sometimes stayed with his aunt, but more often than not he stayed at a Catholic hostel, the Hotel Europäischer Hof.

That year Bonhoeffer did his Christmas shopping in Munich. He was extremely thoughtful and generous about gift giving. He gave a number of friends and relatives framed prints of the *Birth of Christ* by Stephan Lochner. Each Christmas now he had the additional task—self-imposed—of putting together packages for each of the Finkenwalde brethren, who were scattered throughout Germany, and many of whom were soldiers. He mailed numerous books, and in a Munich shop purchased one hundred postcards of Albrecht Altendorfer's *Holy Night* to include in these Christmas parcels. He wrote to Bethge: "The picture seems quite timely to me: Christmas amid the rubble."

Bonhoeffer's ministry to the brethren of Finkenwalde continued in these packages and in frequent letters. That Christmas he sent out ninety such packages and letters; it seems that he had to type the letter over many times, using carbon copies to make it a bit less draining. That year's Christmas letter was another beautiful "sermon meditation," this time on Isaiah 9:6–7 ("For unto us a child is born . . ."). He ruminated on the idea that things had changed forever, that they could never go back to the way things were before the war. But he explained that the idea one could ever go back to a time before troubles and death was false to begin with. The war was only showing them a deeper reality that always existed:

> Just as time-lapse photography makes visible, in an ever more com-pressed and penetrating form, movements that would otherwise not be thus grasped by our vision, so the war makes manifest in particularly drastic and unshrouded form that which for years has become ever more dreadfully clear to us as the essence of the "world." It is not war that first brings death, not war that first invents the pains and torments of human bodies and souls, not war that first unleashes lies, injustice, and violence. It is not war that first makes our existence so utterly precarious and ren-ders human beings powerless, forcing them to watch their desires and plans being thwarted and destroyed by more "exalted powers." But war makes all of this, which existed already apart from it and before it, vast and unavoidable to us who would gladly prefer to overlook it all.

Because of the war, he explained, they could see things as they truly are. The promise of Christ is therefore all the more real and desired.

On December 13 he wrote to Bethge: "It has been snowing here for forty-eight hours without a break, and snow banks are piling up even higher than those we saw last year—out of the ordinary even here." Because of the constant air raids over Berlin, Dohnanyi and Bonhoeffer's sister Christine decided to enroll their children, Barbara, Klaus, and Christoph, at the school in Ettal. Christine often visited. That Christmas they were all together, amidst the Alpine snow and ice. The beauty of the surroundings was not lost on Bonhoeffer. He wrote Bethge that the "insurmountable quality [of the mountains] sometimes lies like a burden on my work."

That Christmas Bethge visited too. Bonhoeffer tried out his snowshoes, and everyone skied. As is traditional in Germany, everyone opened presents on Christmas Eve. One present came all the way from Bonhoeffer's pastor friend Erwin Schutz in the wilds of Gross-Schlönwitz. "Dear Brother Schutz," Bonhoeffer wrote later, "it was truly a great surprise, an excitement without equal, when under the noses of several of my nephews and nieces your package was opened and a real live rabbit emerged." After opening the presents, everyone went to High Mass in the resplendent church of the abbey.

Bonhoeffer's parents sent him a French dictionary. He knew he would soon be spending some time in Geneva and had asked for one. They also sent him a magnifying glass that had belonged to his brother Walter, now dead more than twenty-two years. Walter had been the naturalist of the family. On the twenty-eighth he wrote his parents, thanking them for their gifts and reflecting on the "new reality" that, for a while, things weren't going to change. But he was determined to look for the deeper truth hidden in the midst of an otherwise bleak situation: "Last year when . . . we came to the end of the year, we probably all thought that this year we would be decisively further along and would see more clearly. Now it is questionable at the very least whether this hope has come true. . . . It almost seems to me as if we must come to terms with it over the long haul, to live more deeply out of the past and the present—and that means out of gratitude—than from any vision of the future."

He wrote something similar to Schutz: "We will have to move through a very deep valley, I believe much deeper than we can sense now, before we will be able to ascend the other side again. The main thing is that we let ourselves be led entirely and not resist and become impatient. Then it will all go right." He had settled in for the long haul, come what may.

At Ettal, Bonhoeffer often met with members of the conspiracy, such as Justice Minister Gürtner and Carl Goerdeler, the former mayor of Leipzig. Müller sometimes stopped by daily. During that Christmas, Bonhoeffer and Bethge met with Dohnanyi and Vatican representatives, including Pope Pius XII's personal secretary, Robert Leiber. Bethge and Bonhoeffer took a long walk in the Alpine cold with Gürtner during his visit, and they discussed the difficulty the Confessing Church was having in its dealings with the Reichskirche.*

In January 1941 Bonhoeffer traveled to Munich to see Justus Perels, the head lawyer for the Confessing Church. Perels was working hard to lobby the Reich government on its treatment of Confessing Church pastors; so many of them were being drafted and sent into battle that the Confessing Church was being decimated. This was intentional on the part of the Nazis. Perels hoped to persuade them to use the same policy for the Confessing Church as for the Reichskirche.

While in Munich, Bonhoeffer accompanied Perels to see a Beethoven opera, *Creatures of Prometheus*, performed as a pantomime. Bonhoeffer was "not too excited about it." They also took in a film on the life of Schiller, which Bonhoeffer described to Bethge as "terrible: pathetic, clichéd, phony, unreal, unhistorical, badly acted, kitsch! Go see it yourself. This is the way I imagined Schiller as a junior in high school."

For the first time in five years, Bonhoeffer and Bethge were apart for a significant length of time. Bonhoeffer had grown deeply dependent on him. He trusted Bethge to criticize and help shape his theological ideas, and while he was working on his *Ethics*, he missed being able to try out and explore his ideas with his dear friend. They prayed together almost daily for years; they worshiped together daily; and most intimate of all, each was the other's confessor. Each knew the other's private struggles and would intercede for him. On February 1, Bonhoeffer celebrated his own birthday by sending Bethge a birthday letter and reflecting on their friendship:

> That the two of us could be connected for five years by work and friendship is, I believe, a rather extraordinary joy for a human life. To have a person who understands one both objectively and personally, and whom one experiences in both respects as a faithful helper and adviser—that is truly a great deal. And you have always been both

---

* Gürtner had a touch of the flu at that time, and perhaps as a result of this walk, he died one month later.

things for me. You have also patiently withstood the severe tests of such a friendship, particularly with regard to my violent temper (which I too abhor in myself and of which you have fortunately repeatedly and openly reminded me), and have not allowed yourself to be made bitter by it. For this I must be particularly grateful to you. In countless questions you have decisively helped me by your greater clarity and simplicity of thought and judgment, and I know from experience that your prayer for me is a real power.

Trip to Geneva

On February 24, the Abwehr sent Bonhoeffer to Geneva. His main purpose was to make contact with Protestant leaders outside Germany, let them know about the conspiracy, and put out feelers about peace terms with the government that would take over. Müller was having similar conversations at the Vatican with Catholic leaders. But at first, Bonhoeffer couldn't even get into Switzerland. The Swiss border police insisted that someone inside Switzerland vouch for him as his guarantor. Bonhoeffer named Karl Barth, who was called, and assented, but not without some misgivings.

Like others at the time, Barth was perplexed about Bonhoeffer's mission. How could a Confessing Church pastor come to Switzerland in the midst of war? It seemed to him that Bonhoeffer must have somehow made peace with the Nazis. This was one of the casualties of the war, that trust itself seemed to die a thousand deaths.

Such doubts and questions from others would plague Bonhoeffer, but he certainly wasn't free to explain what he was doing to those outside his inner circle. This represented another "death" to self for him because he had to surrender his reputation in the church. People wondered how he escaped the fate of the rest of his generation. He was writing and traveling, meeting with this one and that one, going to movies and restaurants, and living a life of relative privilege and freedom while others were suffering and dying and being put in excruciating positions of moral compromise.

For those who knew that Bonhoeffer was working for the Abwehr, it was all the worse. Had he finally capitulated, this high-minded patrician moralist, who always was so unyielding and who demanded that others must be similarly unyielding? Was he the one who had said that "only those who cry out for the Jews may sing Gregorian chants" and who had put himself in the place of God by outrageously declaring that there was no salvation outside the Confessing Church?

Even if Bonhoeffer could have explained that he was in fact working against Hitler, many in the Confessing Church would still have been confused, and others would have been outraged. For a pastor to be involved in a plot whose linchpin was the assassination of the head of state during a time of war, when brothers and sons and fathers were giving their lives for their country, was unthinkable. Bonhoeffer had come to a place where he was in many ways very much alone. God had driven him to this place, though, and he was not about to look for a way out any more than Jeremiah had done. It was the fate he had embraced, and it was obedience to God, and he could rejoice in it, and did.

While in Switzerland, Bonhoeffer wrote Sabine and Gert in Oxford, something he couldn't do from Germany. How he missed them! He also wrote Bishop Bell. In Geneva he visited with Erwin Sutz, to whom he reportedly remarked, "You can rely on it, we shall overthrow Hitler!" Bonhoeffer met with Karl Barth, too, but even after a long conversation, Barth was not fully at ease with Bonhoeffer's connection to the Abwehr.

Bonhoeffer also met with two contacts from the ecumenical world, Adolf Freudenberg and Jacques Courvoisier. But his principal meeting in Geneva was with Willem Visser 't Hooft, whom he had last seen at Paddington Station in London. Bonhoeffer told him everything about the situation in Germany and Visser 't Hooft would pass along the information to Bishop Bell—who would pass it along to the Churchill government. Bonhoeffer spoke about the Confessing Church's continuing struggle with the Nazis, and told about the pastors being arrested and persecuted in other ways, and of the euthanasia measures. Very little information of this kind had escaped Germany since the war had begun. If only Bell could succeed in bringing this information to someone like British Foreign Minister Anthony Eden, Bonhoeffer's trip would have been a success.

Bonhoeffer was in Switzerland a month. When he returned to Munich at the end of March, he discovered a letter from the Reich Writers' Guild informing him that he was henceforth prohibited from writing. He had gamely tried to avoid this and had even registered with them—something he obviously thought loathsome and did to preserve the appearance of being a "good German" in their eyes. He had even gone so far as to submit the required "proof" of his "Aryan ancestry." But even this unpleasant ruse had been insufficient to offset the offensively pro-Jewish content of his book on the Psalms.

As he had done when prohibited from speaking publicly, Bonhoeffer again protested vigorously, maintaining that his writing was scholarly and did not fall into the categories they suggested. They actually rescinded the initial fine against him—a small miracle—but did not agree that his work was exempt on scholarly grounds. Expressing the Third Reich's strong bias against Christianity, they wrote, "Only those theologians who occupy chairs at state colleges are exempted. Moreover, because of their overwhelming dogmatic allegiance, I cannot readily recognize clergymen as specialists in this sense." In the end, the prohibition against writing did not affect him overmuch. He would not publish again during his lifetime, but he would write much. He continued work on his magnum opus *Ethics* and would do so for some time to come.

Bonhoeffer spent the Easter holiday with his family at Friedrichsbrunn. The Bonhoeffers had been coming to the untouched beauty of the Harz Mountains since before the First War. For all of them, and especially for Bonhoeffer, who was seven when they bought the forester's lodge, it was a link to the timeless world beyond their present difficulties. In the magical woods that brought to mind the world of the tales of Jacob and Wilhelm Grimm, nothing had changed from the golden days when they were children, when Walter was alive and walked with his little brother, Dietrich, to look for strawberries or mushrooms. Three years later, after a year of imprisonment at Tegel, he would write about Friedrichsbrunn and how its memory touched him:

> In my imagination I live a good deal in nature, in the glades near Friedrichsbrunn. . . . I lie on my back in the grass, watch the clouds sailing in the breeze across the blue sky, and listen to the rustling of the woods. It's remarkable how greatly these memories of childhood affect

one's whole outlook: it would seem to me impossible and unnatural
for us to have lived either up in the mountains or by the sea. It is the
hills of central Germany, the Harz, the Thuringian forest, the Weser
mountains, that to me represent nature, that belong to me and have
fashioned me.

But it was not yet merely a memory. Now he was still here, free to roam
the woods and lie in the meadows and enjoy his family. Easter was April 13,
and the whole family had come here to celebrate. But after everyone left,
Bonhoeffer stayed behind to work on his *Ethics* in the peace and quiet; he had
written a great deal here over the years. There was still no electricity—they
would not install it for another two years—but there was a coal stove, which
was necessary at this time of year. But there was no coal. For some reason it
hadn't been delivered. Bonhoeffer kept warm by burning wood, and whenever he needed a break from his writing, he stepped outside and chopped
some. When the family first arrived, they noticed that some of the wood that
had been stacked there was gone. They never knew who had taken it, but
when Bonhoeffer finally left, he made a small mark on the wall to show how
high the stack was, and told his parents about it. This way they would know
if any of it went missing after he had gone.

 CHAPTER 24

PLOTTING AGAINST HITLER

The German people will be burdened with a guilt the world will not forget in a hundred years.

—HENNING VON TRESCKOW

Death reveals that the world is not as it should be but that it stands in need of redemption. Christ alone is the conquering of death.

—DIETRICH BONHOEFFER

I am sure that there are very many in Germany, silenced now by the Gestapo and the machine-gun, who long for deliverance from a godless Nazi rule, and for the coming of a Christian order in which they and we can take our part.

—BISHOP GEORGE BELL

Since the fall of France a year earlier, the coup had stalled. Hitler's victories had been so stunning and rapid that most generals had lost all confidence in their ability to oppose him. His popularity soared. In recent months Yugoslavia, Greece, and Albania were conquered, and General Rommel had triumphed in North Africa. Hitler seemed unstoppable, so most generals floated along with the rising German tide and could not be persuaded to lift a finger against him.

Dohnanyi and Oster knew that persuading the top generals was the only hope of toppling Hitler. It had been earlier hoped that a grassroots movement could have brought the Nazis down from below. But once Martin Niemöller was imprisoned, this possibility evaporated. His bold defiance of the Nazis and his leadership qualities made him the perfect candidate. This was doubtless why Hitler sent the fiery Christian to a concentration camp. Now it had to come from above, and that meant the generals.

Some generals were the noble leaders of the conspiracy, ready to act at any time. But many others were less noble and wise, and their desire to be unmired from the swamp and ignominy of Versailles was so strong that it overrode their extreme revulsion toward Hitler. Many reasoned that once he had served his purposes, he would falter and be replaced by someone less brutal; if necessary, they would see to that. But not while they were winning so spectacularly, not while they were rolling back Versailles. Many also felt that killing Hitler would make a martyr of him. Another stab-in-the-back legend would arise, and they would be cast forever in the roles of Brutus and Cassius to Hitler's Caesar. Why risk anything? The gelatinous Brauchitsch epitomized those who had firmly resolved to blow with the wind. "I myself won't do anything," he said, "but I won't stop anyone else from acting."

Beck, Dohnanyi, Oster, Canaris, Goerdeler, and the other conspirators did what they could during this year of Hitler's successes, but essentially they were stuck.

The Commissar Order

Then came June 6, 1941, and the notorious Commissar Order. Hitler was about to launch his campaign against Russia, code named Operation Barbarossa, and his bitter contempt for the "eastern races" such as the Poles and the Slavs would again be on full display. The Commissar Order instructed the army to shoot and kill all captured Soviet military leaders. Hitler had allowed the army to avoid the most gruesome horrors in Poland. He knew they didn't have the stomach for it, and the soulless SS *Einsatzgruppen* had done the foulest and most inhuman deeds. But now he ordered the army itself to carry out the butchery and sadism in contravention of all military codes going back for centuries. The generals took notice. Even the weakest-willed among them saw that they had been gaily riding along on the back of a tiger.

Murdering all captured Red Army leaders was unthinkable, but Hitler was not interested in old-fashioned ideas about morality and honor. He would show them the brutal road to victory and now belched diabolical aphorisms of perfectly circular logic. "In the East," he said, "harshness is kindness toward the future." The leaders of the German military "must demand of themselves the sacrifice of overcoming their scruples." In explaining the need for the Commissar Order, he absurdly stated that the Red Army leaders must, "as a rule, immediately be shot for instituting barbaric Asian methods of warfare."

Henning von Tresckow was a typical Prussian with a strong sense of honor and tradition who had come to despise Hitler early on. He was the first officer at the front to contact the conspirators. When he heard about the Commissar Order, he told General Gersdorf that if they weren't able to convince Bock to have it canceled, "the German people will be burdened with a guilt the world will not forget in a hundred years." He said the guilt would fall not only on Hitler and his inner circle, "but on you and me, your wife and mine, your children and mine." For many generals this was the turning point. The indefatigably weak-willed Brauchitsch was so shocked by the Commissar Order that he brought it up with Hitler, who promptly hurled an inkwell at the venerable general's head.

Hitler launched Operation Barbarossa on June 22, 1941. Germany was at war with the Soviet Union. The sense of invincibility around Hitler was still strong, but now there arose for the first time the question of whether Hitler ought to quit while he was ahead. Wouldn't his winning streak sometime come to an end? There was something that gave sane men pause, something about the endless white terrain of Russia. Hitler, however, was unburdened by such sanity, and despite the long odds of success, the march of the German armies toward Moscow now began.

The conspiracy leaders bided their time. Hitler's Commissar Order helped them recruit many generals, and as its brutal implications were witnessed firsthand, their ability to win converts would increase. Meanwhile, Oster and Dohnanyi continued their work under the protection of Admiral Canaris. If ever anyone led a double life, Canaris did. He took morning horseback rides in Berlin's Tiergarten with Heydrich, the piscine ghoul, and yet was at this very time using his power to undermine Heydrich and the

Nazis at every turn. The gangsterism of Hitler sickened him. On a trip to Spain, while riding through the countryside in his open car, he stood and gave the Hitler salute to every herd of sheep he passed. "You never know," he said, "whether one of the party bigwigs might be in the crowd."

Bonhoeffer's next trip for the Abwehr would not be until September, when he would again travel to Switzerland. In the meantime he continued writing *Ethics* and doing pastoral work. With the help of Oster and Dohnanyi, Bonhoeffer got exemptions and deferments for a number of pastors in the Confessing Church. He hoped to keep them from danger, but also to keep them functioning as pastors since the needs of their flocks were greater than ever. It was mostly a losing battle, as were so many, but Bonhoeffer nonetheless waged it with vigor and was grateful for small successes.

Much of Bonhoeffer's pastoral work was now via correspondence. In August he wrote another circular letter to the hundred or so former ordinands. In it one finds words that shed light on his own death:

> Today I must inform you that our brothers Konrad Bojack, F. A. Preuß, Ulrich Nithack, and Gerhard Schulze have been killed on the eastern front. . . . They have gone before us on the path that we shall all have to take at some point. In a particularly gracious way, God reminds those of you who are out on the front to remain prepared. . . . To be sure, God shall call you, and us, only at the hour that God has chosen. Until that hour, which lies in God's hand alone, we shall all be protected even in greatest danger; and from our gratitude for such protection ever new readiness surely arises for the final call.
>
> Who can comprehend how those whom God takes so early are chosen? Does not the early death of young Christians always appear to us as if God were plundering his own best instruments in a time in which they are most needed? Yet the Lord makes no mistakes. Might God need our brothers for some hidden service on our behalf in the heavenly world? We should put an end to our human thoughts, which always wish to know more than they can, and cling to that which is certain. Whomever God calls home is someone God has loved. "For their souls were pleasing to the Lord, therefore he took them quickly from the midst of wickedness" (Wisdom of Solomon 4).
>
> We know, of course, that God and the devil are engaged in battle

in the world and that the devil also has a say in death. In the face of death we cannot simply speak in some fatalistic way, "God wills it"; but we must juxtapose it with the other reality, "God does not will it." Death reveals that the world is not as it should be but that it stands in need of redemption. Christ alone is the conquering of death. Here the sharp antithesis between "God wills it" and "God does not will it" comes to a head and also finds its resolution. God accedes to that which God does not will, and from now on death itself must therefore serve God. From now on, the "God wills it" encompasses even the "God does not will it." God wills the conquering of death through the death of Jesus Christ. Only in the cross and resurrection of Jesus Christ has death been drawn into God's power, and it must now serve God's own aims. It is not some fatalistic surrender but rather a living faith in Jesus Christ, who died and rose for us, that is able to cope profoundly with death.

In life with Jesus Christ, death as a general fate approaching us from without is confronted by death from within, one's own death, the free death of daily dying with Jesus Christ. Those who live with Christ die daily to their own will. Christ in us gives us over to death so that he can live within us. Thus our inner dying grows to meet that death from without. Christians receive their own death in this way, and in this way our physical death very truly becomes not the end but rather the fulfillment of our life with Jesus Christ. Here we enter into community with the One who at his own death was able to say, "It is finished."

Bonhoeffer corresponded with the brethren individually too. He received a letter from one Finkenwaldian who had resisted meditating on the biblical texts. But in the midst of war, he told Bonhoeffer that he kept up the practice on his own. When it was too difficult to meditate on the verses, he had simply memorized them, which had a similar effect. He said that just as Bonhoeffer had always told them, the verses "opened out at an unexpected depth. One has to live with the texts, and then they unfold. I am very grateful now for your having kept us to it."

His correspondence with so many is a testament to his faithfulness as a pastor. Although not himself on the front lines, he heard from many of the brethren who were, encouraging them by return mail and praying for them.

One of them, Erich Klapproth, wrote that the temperature was forty below zero: "For days at a stretch we cannot even wash our hands, but go from the dead bodies to a meal and from there back to the rifle. All one's energy has to be summoned up to fight against the danger of freezing, to be on the move even when one is dead tired." Klapproth wondered whether they would ever be allowed to return home again, to resume their calm and quiet lives. Shortly thereafter, Bonhoeffer learned that he had been killed.

Hearing that his dear friend Gerhard Vibrans had been killed hit him particularly hard: "I think the pain and feeling of emptiness that his death leaves in me could scarcely be different if he had been my own brother."

Bonhoeffer's larger efforts for the Confessing Church did not stop. The war gave the Nazis ample opportunities to harm the churches. Toward the end of 1941, Bonhoeffer helped Perels draft a Petition to the Armed Forces:

> The hope of Protestant Christians that the antichurch measures would cease, at least for the length of the war, has been bitterly disappointed. . . . [A]t the same time, antichurch measures at home are taking on ever harsher forms. In congregations the impression is gradually emerging that the calamity of the war and the absence of the clergy are here being intentionally exploited by the party and the Gestapo to destroy the Protestant church even during the war itself.

The document cited many forms of abuse. Himmler was trying to destroy the Confessing Church most vigorously, and all Confessing Church pastors who had not been drafted were forced to abandon their pastorates and given jobs of "some useful activity." The Gestapo's treatment of pastors at interrogations was "now in general the same as that of criminals." Another example showed the Nazi leadership's bitter hatred of Christians and Christianity:

> A prominent layman of the Protestant church, whose son had been killed in the East, was forced to endure great abuse through an anonymous communication. He had announced the death of his son with the following words: "Fallen in faith in his Lord and Savior. . . ." The communication speaks of "shame on the sanctimonious clan and their degenerate blood" that has denounced the son as a believer in an "obscure itinerant preacher."

Finally Christians across Germany were battling against the euthanasia measures:

> The killing of so-called unworthy lives, which has now become better known in the congregations and has claimed its victims from them, is viewed by Christians of all confessions with the deepest alarm and with revulsion, especially in connection with the general abrogation of the Ten Commandments and any security of law and thus as a sign of the anti-Christian stance of leading authorities in the Reich.

Second Trip to Switzerland

In September Bonhoeffer was back in Switzerland for the Abwehr. Again he met with Visser 't Hooft. Things were looking bad for the Resistance since Hitler's armies had been thus far successful in the Russian campaign. But Bonhoeffer had a different impression. "So this is the beginning of the end," he said when they greeted each other. Visser 't Hooft was puzzled. Did Bonhoeffer mean it was the beginning of the end for Stalin and the Soviets? "No, no," Bonhoeffer replied, "Hitler is nearing an end, through a surfeit of victories." Bonhoeffer was convinced that Hitler was nearing the end of his charmed run. "The old man will never get out of this," he said.

By the fall of 1941, however, all hopes that the conspiracy could get Britain's assurances of a negotiated peace were gone. The war had dragged on too long. With Germany fighting Russia, Churchill saw it as all or nothing. He was not interested in the conspiracy—if one even existed. He took a defiant stance that branded every German a Nazi and turned a deaf ear to the voices of the conspirators. Bishop Bell spoke on their behalf nonetheless. He tried to raise British awareness that there were men and women in Germany eager for Hitler's demise. Earlier that year he had given a speech at a large demonstration criticizing the British government for talking of victory, but not of any mercy toward those suffering outside Britain. In no small part from conversations with Bonhoeffer and the Leibholzes, Bell knew whereof he spoke: "I am sure that there are very many in Germany, silenced now by the Gestapo and the machine-gun, who long for deliverance from a godless Nazi rule, and for the coming of Christian order in which they and we can take our part. Is no trumpet call to come from England, to awaken them from despair?"

Churchill and his Foreign Secretary Eden were unmoved. Still, Bonhoeffer would persevere. He wrote a long memorandum in which he explained, among other things, that the Allied indifference to those who might stage a coup against Hitler was discouraging them from staging it. If the good Germans in the conspiracy thought that after risking their lives they would be treated by the British and their allies as indistinguishable from the Nazis, there was precious little incentive to do so: "The question must be faced whether a German government which makes a complete break with Hitler and all he stands for, can hope to get such terms of peace that it has some chance to survive. . . . It is clear that the answering of this question is a matter of urgency, since the attitude of opposition groups in Germany depends upon the answer given."

Bonhoeffer naively thought he might receive some word from the British government after this memorandum was circulated in the proper circles. None came. In one conversation that September in Geneva, Visser 't Hooft asked Bonhoeffer what he prayed for. "If you want to know the truth," Bonhoeffer replied, "I pray for the defeat of my nation. For I believe that is the only way to pay for all the suffering which my country has caused in the world." Fresh reports were coming back from the front lines, and what Bonhoeffer heard through Dohnanyi was monstrous. Hitler must be stopped at any price.

As Germany's armies moved toward Moscow, the barbarism of the SS had again been given the freedom to express itself. It was as if the devil and his hordes had crawled out of hell and walked the earth. In Lithuania, SS squads gathered defenseless Jews together and beat them to death with truncheons, afterward dancing to music on the dead bodies. The victims were cleared away, a second group was brought in, and the macabre exercise was repeated.

As a result of such things, many more in the army leadership were driven to the conspiracy. At one point officers came to Field Marshal Bock and begged him with tears in their eyes to stop "the orgy of executions" in Borisov. But even Bock was powerless. When he demanded that the SS commander in charge of the massacres be brought to him, the civilian commissioner, Wilhelm Kube, laughed defiantly. Hitler had given the SS free rein, and even a field marshal could do nothing about it.

It was during this time that Count Peter Yorck von Wartenburg and his cousin von Stauffenberg overcame their fundamental feelings against conspiracy. Both were devoutly Christian and had been raised in the caste of German military aristocracy. What they witnessed was a reversal and mockery of every value they held dear. Stauffenberg would take the lead in the famous July 20, 1944, attempt to kill Hitler, as we shall soon see.

Operation 7

When Bonhoeffer returned from Switzerland in late September, he learned of more horrors. But these were being perpetrated *inside* Germany. A new decree required all Jews in Germany to wear a yellow star in public. Things had now moved into a new realm, and Bonhoeffer knew it was but a foretaste of things to come. At the Dohnanyis' house that September, Bonhoeffer famously said that, if necessary, he would be willing to kill Hitler. It would not come to that, but Bonhoeffer had to be clear that he was not assisting in the fulfillment of a deed he was unwilling to do. He stipulated, however, that he would first have to resign from the Confessing Church. Bonhoeffer knew that most of its members would not share his position on this matter, but more important, he did not want to implicate them in something that he was undertaking alone. His role in the conspiracy was between him and God alone; that much he knew. And he knew that being chosen by God, as the Jews were chosen, and as the prophets were chosen, was something unfathomable. It was the highest honor, but a terrible one, one that none would ever seek.

It was around this time that Bonhoeffer became involved in a complex plan to save seven Jews from death. It would be his first serious assignment for the Abwehr. It was code named U7 for *Unternehmen 7* (Operation 7) for the number of Jews first involved; the number eventually doubled. Admiral Canaris wanted to help two Jewish friends and their dependents, and Dohnanyi, two of his lawyer friends. They would smuggle the seven Jews into Switzerland for the ostensible purpose of having them tell the Swiss how well the Germans were treating Jews.

As far as those in Himmler's circles were concerned, the Jews were expected to lie on behalf of the Nazis, and by speaking well of the Nazis to the Swiss authorities, they would be granted their freedom. At first, some of the Jews believed this was actually expected of them and refused to participate. Dohnanyi had to convince them, at great risk to himself, that it was a counteroperation, and that he wanted them to tell the truth to the Swiss authorities, and to go free. He made it clear that he, Colonel Oster, Admiral Canaris, Count Moltke, and others were involved in a conspiracy against Hitler.

But the operation proved complex and time-consuming. First Dohnanyi had to get the Jews off the deportation lists, and then he had to officially make them Abwehr agents, as he had done for Bonhoeffer. Then he had to convince Switzerland to take them in, which was the greatest difficulty. The Swiss were officially neutral in the war, so they refused to help German Jews. At this impasse, Bonhoeffer, Justus Perels, and Wilhelm Rott (Bonhoeffer's assistant at Zingst) used their ecumenical contacts. They appealed to Swiss churchmen in what was clearly a life-and-death situation. If these Jews did not escape Germany soon, they would be transported to a terrible fate. Rott pleaded with the president of the Federation of Swiss Churches, knowing what they were asking was officially impossible: "What we now ask you is whether, by urgent representations and official action by the Swiss churches, the door might possibly be opened for just a few, or at least for one solitary case for which we specially plead." Despite Rott's begging, the Swiss were unmoved. Bonhoeffer then wrote Barth, asking for help.

The Swiss had their price. Dohnanyi had to secure a large amount of foreign currency to be sent to Switzerland, since these men and women wouldn't be able to work in the country. This last detail of foreign currency, like a hanging thread, was eventually noticed and then pulled by the Abwehr's archnemeses Himmler and Heydrich* until things began to unravel, eventually leading to Bonhoeffer's arrest. But it was what the Nazis were doing to the Jews that pushed Bonhoeffer and many in the conspiracy to action in the first place. When their death sentences were finally handed down in 1945, and they could speak without endangering others, both Bonhoeffer's brother Klaus and his brother-in-law Rüdiger Schleicher shocked their captors by telling them boldly that they had entered the conspiracy primarily for the sake of the Jews.

Hitler Stumbles

In October, Dohnanyi and Oster met with Fabian von Schlabrendorff and Major General Henning von Tresckow, who believed that things were again ripe for toppling Hitler. The generals on the Russian front were becoming increasingly

---

* Gisevius tells us that these two miscreants were often called the Black Twins.

annoyed with Hitler's interference. Between this and the continuing sadism of the SS, many were finally ready to turn against him. And as Bonhoeffer prophesied, Hitler had come to the end of his unbroken string of successes.

In November 1941 German troops under the command of Field Marshal von Rundstedt were roaring toward Stalingrad when on November 26 in Rostov, they suffered a serious defeat and began to retreat. That was the first time any of Hitler's forces were decisively routed. It was not something the Führer's hubris could accommodate. He was personally affronted and now, from a thousand miles away at Wolfsschanze, his bunker in the woods of East Prussia, Hitler demanded that Rundstedt hold the line at all costs. His troops must pay any price and bear any burden. Rundstedt wired back that it was "madness" to attempt to do so. "I repeat," Rundstedt continued, "that this order be rescinded or that you find someone else." Hitler relieved Rundstedt of his command and did so.

The tide was turning for Adolf Hitler. The rest of his eastern armies were now charging into the white jaws of the notorious Russian winter, whose fury increased with each day. Thousands of soldiers were dying from severe frostbite. Fuel was freezing. Fires had to be started under tanks in order to start them. Because of the cold, machine guns ceased firing. Telescopic sights were useless.

Still, despite the entreaties of other generals, Hitler mercilessly drove his armies forward, and on December 2, a single German battalion pushed close enough to glimpse the fabled golden spires of the Kremlin, fourteen miles away. That was as close as the Germans would get. On December 4 the temperature fell to thirty-one below zero. On the fifth it fell to thirty-six below zero. Generals Bock and Guderian knew they had come to the end of their abilities and resources. They must retreat. Brauchitsch, the commander in chief of the army, determined to resign his post. On the sixth the Russians attacked the German lines with such shattering force that the once invincible armies of Adolf Hitler turned tail and went into full retreat. They were chased back across the endlessly bleak landscape, and it was to their great credit that they survived the retreat at all. Napoleon's armies had not fared as well.

The reversal pierced Hitler like a dagger, but the news on December 7 of the sneaky Japanese attack on Pearl Harbor revived his spirits. He especially rejoiced at the underhandedness of the attack, saying that it corresponded to his "own system," and in that eternally sunny way of his he interpreted the mass murder of Americans as an encouraging sign from Providence, just when he needed one. The U.S. declaration of war against Japan and Germany spelled the beginning of the end for Hitler, who would be fighting a war on two fronts until the day of his suicide. But Hitler could not see the grim future. At the moment, he still had his mind on Russia where he was busily snow-shoveling a fresh path to world domination.

First, he would cashier the generals whom he blamed for the shameful disaster. He should have done so long ago. Bock was replaced. Guderian was dismissed. Hoepner was stripped of his rank and forbidden to wear his uniform. Sponeck was imprisoned and sentenced to death. General Keitel, as a reward for years of faithful fawning, got away with a blistering dressing-down, during which the Führer denounced the highly decorated inverte-brate as a *dummkopf*. Brauchitsch responded to the fiasco with coronary failure and turned in his resignation.

This was catastrophic for the conspirators, who had been courting Brauchitsch for some time and had lately gotten his assent to their plans. Now their wobbly linchpin pulled himself out. The conspiracy leaders must turn their attention to his replacement. But Brauchitsch's replacement would be disinclined to participate. This was because Hitler, always inclined to cut out the middleman, appointed himself as Brauchitsch's replacement. As commander in chief of the army, he would oversee all military operations going forward. Before it was all over, Hitler would be doing everything himself. If there had been tennis courts at Wolfsschanze, surely the Führer would have overseen the schedule for those using them too.

The Conspirators Regroup

With Brauchitsch gone, the conspiracy had to find another way forward. There were other reasons to be disheartened, not least the dashed chances for a negotiated peace with Britain and her allies. But there was no time to be lost in hand-wringing. The escalating deportations of Jews to the east saw to that. But for their escape four years earlier, Bonhoeffer's beloved Sabine and her husband and girls might well be in a boxcar on their way to certain death. Bonhoeffer thought of Franz Hildebrandt. He thought of Jewish friends at the University of Berlin and of childhood friends from Grunewald. The extermination of "world Jewry" under the Orwellian aegis of the Final Solution had begun. At a conference at Wannsee early in 1942, the fate of all Jews within reach of the Third Reich had been sealed. The importance of killing Hitler and derailing the progress of his hellish vision for the world was more urgent than ever. But how?

The conspirators' plans were roughly the same as before: Hitler would be assassinated; General Beck, who had resigned in protest four years earlier, would lead the coup and likely become the head of a new government. According to Gisevius, Beck "stood above all parties . . . [as] the only general with an unimpaired reputation, the only general who had voluntarily resigned." Having Beck as the leader of a new German government gave many generals the courage to move forward.

Meanwhile the larger conspiracy went ahead on several fronts, with the Abwehr planning to send Bonhoeffer on a mission to Norway in early April. For the first time, though, in February 1942, Dohnanyi learned that the Gestapo was watching him and Bonhoeffer. Dohnanyi's telephone had been tapped, and his correspondence was being intercepted. Martin Bormann and the cadaverous Heydrich were likely behind it. Aware of the increasing danger, Bonhoeffer drew up a will, which he gave to Bethge; he did not want to alarm his family.

Bonhoeffer was meeting regularly with his brother Klaus, who as the top lawyer for Lufthansa had many high-level business contacts. Klaus was able to bring his colleague Otto John into the conspiracy, and John drew in the Prussian Prince Louis Ferdinand. The number of people involved became quite large. There were roughly two main groups conspiring against Hitler. The first was centered on Canaris and Oster and the Abwehr. But another group, led by Count Helmuth von Moltke, was now beginning to form. It was called the Kreisau Circle.

The Kreisau Circle

The Kreisau Circle took its name from the place of its first meeting, the Kreisau estate of Moltke.* Von Moltke was a member of the Prussian House of Lords and a scion of an illustrious military family. His father commanded Germany's forces at the outset of the First World War and served as aide-de-camp to Kaiser Wilhelm II. His great-uncle, Field Marshal Helmuth Graf

---

* *Kreis* means "circle"; the repetition of *Kreisauer Kreis* is lost in translation.

von Moltke, was the legendary military genius whose celebrated victories in the Austro-Prussian and Franco-Prussian wars prepared the way for the creation of the German Empire in 1870.*

Like many in the Kreisau Circle, Moltke was a committed Christian. Canaris drafted him into the conspiracy at the outset of the Polish campaign when he documented many human rights abuses. In October 1941 he wrote, "Certainly more than a thousand people are murdered in this way every day, and another thousand German men are habituated to murder. . . . What shall I say when I am asked: And what did you do during that time?" In another letter he wrote, "Since Saturday the Berlin Jews are being rounded up. Then they are sent off with what they can carry. . . . How can anyone know these things and walk around free?"

Before his execution in 1945, Moltke wrote his wife that he stood before the court "as a Christian and nothing else" and said that "what the Third Reich is so terrified of" was that he had discussed with Protestant and Catholic clergymen "questions of the practical, ethical demands of Christianity. Nothing else: for that alone are we condemned . . . I just wept a little, not because I was sad or melancholy . . . but because I am thankful and moved by this proof of God's presence." To his sons, he wrote that he had tried to help the victims of the Nazis and to try to prepare the way for a change to new leadership: "In that my conscience drove me . . . and in the end that is a man's duty." He believed that only by believing in God could one be a total opponent to the Nazis. Early on he tried to convince the Nazis to abide by the Geneva Convention, but Keitel dismissed it as a "notion of chivalry of a bygone era." Moltke later helped deport Jews from Germany.

The other main figure of the Kreisau Circle was Count Peter Graf Yorck von Wartenburg, whose cousin Count Claus Schenk von Stauffenberg would lead the failed Valkyrie plot on July 20, 1944. But the Kreisau Circle was staunchly opposed to assassination. Its conspiracy was mostly limited to discussing how Germany should be run after Hitler's removal, so there was not extensive contact with the Abwehr conspirators. After the first meeting at Moltke's estate, they gathered at Yorck's villa in Berlin's Lichterfelde neighborhood. Yorck eventually changed his mind about the assassination and became a principal figure in the Stauffenberg plot.

---

* He was also a celebrated linguist, but famously taciturn, and therefore said "to be silent in seven languages."

✦✦ CHAPTER 25

BONHOEFFER SCORES
A VICTORY

*If there are men in Germany also ready to wage war against the
monstrous tyranny of the Nazis from within, is it right to discourage
or ignore them? Can we afford to reject their aid in achieving our end?*
— BISHOP GEORGE BELL TO BRITISH FOREIGN MINISTER ANTHONY EDEN

Von Moltke and Bonhoeffer met for the first time during their trip
to Norway, which had recently been handed over to Hitler by
the Nazi collaborator Vidkun Quisling, whose surname became an
improper noun, meaning "traitor." For his treachery, Quisling was
made prime minister of the new puppet government on February 1, 1942.
But on the day he took office, Quisling struck a belligerent pose with the
Norwegian church, forbidding one of its leaders, Provost Fjellbu, to hold
a service at the nationally symbolic Nidaros Cathedral in Trondheim. This
caused a firestorm of resistance and linked the Norwegian church to the
wider Norwegian resistance in a way that was publicly disastrous for the new
puppet government and the Nazis in general. In April, the Abwehr decided
to send Bonhoeffer to Norway to help the situation, although of course he
was going there to do precisely the opposite.

Quisling removed Fjellbu from office on February 20. But unlike what had
happened in Germany, the Norwegian church leaders were both united and
firm: every Norwegian bishop immediately severed his connections to the gov-

ernment. In March Quisling overreached again, establishing a Norwegian version of the Hitler Youth. A thousand teachers immediately struck in protest.

In April it was again the church's turn to oppose Quisling. On Maundy Thursday, Bishop Berggrav, the heroic leader of the pastors' resistance, was put under house arrest. So on Easter, April 5, every pastor in Norway did what their bishops did six weeks earlier and what Bonhoeffer had begged the German pastors to do in July 1933: they went on strike. Bonhoeffer had been in Kieckow and Klein-Krössin during March, working on his *Ethics*. But when Berggrav was imprisoned, Dohnanyi summoned him to Berlin and briefed him on his new assignment.

The bravery of the Norwegian church during this episode cheered Bonhoeffer. He was eager to travel there and encourage them, offering the benefit of his experience. On April 10, he took the train from Stettin to Sassnitz on the northern coast. He and Dohnanyi were to meet von Moltke there and then take the ferry to Trelleborg in Sweden.

Von Moltke was among those who did not believe assassinating Hitler was permissible morally and who thought it would make a martyr of him and lead to a worse government under his vile lieutenants. His principal interest was in having plans ready for a socialistic, democratic government when the Nazi regime collapsed. Four weeks hence, a group would begin discussions about this at Moltke's estate in Kreisau; it would be the first of the Kreisau Circle. Bonhoeffer couldn't attend because he would be going to Switzerland then, but he and Moltke would have plenty of time to discuss their views since the ferry they missed was the last one that day. So they dined together and saw a movie.

The next morning, with no word on the ferry, they took a long walk to clarify their game plan for Norway. Von Moltke and Bonhoeffer walked four miles north along the coast to the chalk cliffs of Stubbenkammer and four miles back, not seeing a soul the entire time, save one solitary woodsman. After the three-and-a-half hour walk, they returned to the hotel to learn that there was still no news of the ferry. They decided to have lunch. Von Moltke was a year younger than Bonhoeffer, but had been married ten years. In a letter to his wife, Freya, he wrote, "As we were sitting at table (!), the ferry appeared suddenly in the window, coming out of the fog. It was truly marvelous. So we rushed to the harbor, where we were told that the ship would depart two hours later, so we should hurry."

They caught this ferry, but it got stuck in the ice for two hours, causing them to miss the last train from Malmö to Oslo. They stayed overnight in Malmö and in the morning continued to Oslo. Bonhoeffer's experience in the German church struggle gave him special authority with the Norwegian church leaders. He took the same stand that he had taken years earlier in Germany, but this time his advice was heeded. He told them that this was an opportunity to show the world—and everyone in Norway—just how brutal the Nazis were. They mustn't back down. According to Berggrav's account years later, Bonhoeffer "insisted on bitter resistance—even as far as martyrdom." Neither Bonhoeffer nor Moltke was able to meet with him in his prison cell, but they got a message to him, and their mission to persuade the Norwegian government to free him was successful. The day they left Stockholm, Berggrav was released.

Bonhoeffer and Moltke returned to Berlin and reported to Dohnanyi. They had enjoyed each other's company, but a few weeks later, when the Kreisau Circle met for the first time, Bonhoeffer was on his third journey to Switzerland for the Abwehr.

The Third Trip to Geneva

When he arrived in Geneva, Bonhoeffer was disappointed that Visser 't Hooft was not there, not least because he wished to talk to him about his recent trip to Norway. He learned that Visser 't Hooft was traveling in Spain and England, and in England he presented to a gathering called the Peace Aims Group the memorandum that Bonhoeffer had drawn up the previous September, although by this time it had become somewhat dated due to changed circumstances. The main reason for being in England was to meet with Sir Stafford Cripps, who had a prominent position in Churchill's War Cabinet. He gave Cripps a memorandum written by Adam von Trott zu Solz, who worked at the Foreign Office and would become a vital figure in the Kreisau Circle.* His memorandum was meant to make its way through Cripps to Churchill. Bonhoeffer knew little about the Trott memorandum or about Visser 't Hooft's intended contact with Cripps since all of that had come out of the world of the Kreisau Circle rather than from the world of

---

* Trott was a descendant of John Jay, the first chief justice of the U.S. Supreme Court.

the Abwehr conspiracy. The lack of communication between the two groups was unintentional; it was typical in the secret world of military intelligence and wartime conspiracies.

In Geneva, Bonhoeffer again visited with Erwin Sutz. He also spent time with Adolf Freudenberg, who had been the second pastor at St. George's in London, where he helped Rieger and Hildebrandt with German refugees. One evening at the Freudenbergs', Bonhoeffer saw Frau Visser 't Hooft and others in the ecumenical movement. But he did less important things too. He spent one delightful afternoon shopping with Frau Freudenberg. Adolf Freudenberg remembered that his decision to go slumming at a certain eatery did not meet with Bonhoeffer's approval:

> We knew a romantic but rather dingy beer garden situated above the murmuring waters of the Arve, which had been a great success with all our guests. But not with Dietrich: the waitress, the way she served the meal, the importunate animals, like a cat, a dog, an old duck, a half-naked turkey, begging for food and pestering the customers—all this offended his sense of beauty and dignity, and we soon left.

The Trip to Sweden

During this rather aimless visit to Geneva, Bonhoeffer learned something on May 23 that would lead to his greatest success in the new field of foreign policy: Bishop Bell would be in Sweden for three weeks. Such information was hard to come by during the war, especially for Germans, so to coordinate plans with someone like Bell was impossible. That Bell would be in neutral Sweden where Bonhoeffer might see him was too good to pass up since it presented the possibility of getting word of the conspiracy to the British government. Since Bell had direct connections to the Churchill government, Bonhoeffer must do everything possible to catch him before he left Sweden.

Bonhoeffer must leave Geneva immediately. Arrangements would have to be made through the Abwehr, which could always be complicated, not to say dangerous. Bonhoeffer hustled back to Berlin to speak with Dohnanyi and Oster. Canaris got Bonhoeffer a special courier pass through the Foreign Ministry, and on May 30 he boarded a plane for Stockholm.

In the tangled huggermuggery of secret intelligence missions, one hand often didn't know what the other was doing. And no one was sure whom to trust. A sometime opponent of Bonhoeffer named Hans Schönfeld was at that moment in Sweden and had met with Bishop Bell on the twenty-fourth. Schönfeld and Bonhoeffer had a number of conflicts over the years. Schönfeld was not connected to the Confessing Church, and in the ecumenical sphere he had been in league with the perfidious Bishop Heckel. He was at Fanø when Bonhoeffer gave his peace speech and was quite upset, hoping to hear something more pro-German. He even thought Bonhoeffer should have used the opportunity to defend the racist *Volk* theology that many Germans adopted. Of course Bonhoeffer did nothing of the kind, knowing it was anti-Semitism in clerical robes. But suddenly Bonhoeffer and Schönfeld found themselves on the same side of the conspiracy against Hitler.

When Bell and Schönfeld met, Bell was wary since he knew of Schönfeld's connection to the Reichskirchenleitung. Schönfeld's general attitude was a bit like the attitude that Churchill cynically associated with German "peace feelers." They wanted Britain to go easy on Germany when the war was over, and they didn't want to concede the territories that they had conquered using their barbaric methods. There was little humility or shame for what their government had been doing. That was why Churchill wouldn't give Germans the time of day, even those claiming to represent a conspiracy against Hitler. Schönfeld was not quite like that, but since Bell didn't know him, Bell was cordial, though ultimately cool and noncommittal.

But now Bonhoeffer was on his way. On Whitsunday, May 31, he arrived in Stockholm, where he learned that Bell was in Sigtuna at the Nordic Ecumenical Institute. Bonhoeffer hurried there, surprising his old friend. They hadn't seen each other since the spring of 1939, just before Bonhoeffer left for New York. It seemed that several lifetimes had passed for both men, and yet here they were, as if they had only seen each other yesterday.

Bell brought Bonhoeffer welcome news of Sabine and Gert. The Bonhoeffer family had been anxious about the Leibholzes and vice versa; there had been no communication in three years. Bell told Bonhoeffer that the last he heard, Bonhoeffer was a soldier on his way to fight in Norway! A mutual friend knew that Bonhoeffer had been in Sweden and assumed that he must have been on his way to fighting in Norway. After all, what else would a German be doing in Sweden? After the two old friends caught up on personal news, they moved to the subject of the conspiracy.

Bonhoeffer now learned that Schönfeld was in Sigtuna too. It was initially confusing, but in the end it proved fortuitous because, from a slightly different point of view, Bonhoeffer could corroborate most of what Schönfeld had said. And he could add to it, giving Bell names of those in the conspiracy whom Schönfeld hadn't known. Bonhoeffer knew through Oster and Schlabrendorff that the two generals who would initiate the coup were Field Marshals von Boch and von Kluge. Such details made it clear to Bell—and would make it clear to his contacts in London—that there were reality and depth to the conspiracy. But how Schönfeld and Bonhoeffer should both come to meet with Bell on behalf of the conspiracy is unknown.

Bonhoeffer observed that despite their differences, Schönfeld had changed in some ways and was fundamentally trustworthy. Indeed he was risking his life to be here, speaking covertly to the representative of an enemy nation about a plot to assassinate Hitler. His connection to the conspiracy seems to have been with the Kreisau Circle, since he spoke of a future post-Nazi government along socialistic lines. Bonhoeffer spoke of more conservative possibilities, including a return to a Hohenzollern monarchy with the Prussian prince, Louis Ferdinand, to whom he was connected via his brother Klaus.*

Bonhoeffer and Schönfeld diverged in their general attitude. Schönfeld presented an attitude of German strength and sought favorable peace terms. He suggested, for example, that the British could not win the war, so it was in the best interests to cut a deal with the conspirators. Bonhoeffer came from a position of deliberate weakness, one that hoped to appeal to a sense of Britain's justice and mercy. He expressed deep humility and shame over Germany's sins, and he felt that he and every German must be willing to suffer for those sins. They must show the world that they were seriously repentant. He wanted to demonstrate to the world the sincerity of their grief and their solidarity with those who had suffered and were suffering. He had no desire to minimize the evils committed in the name of Germany: "Christians do not wish to escape repentance, or chaos, if it is God's will to bring it upon us. We must take this judgement as Christians." Christians must be like Jesus in their willingness to suffer for others, and Germany must now do this before the world. God could be trusted to sort out the details. Christians were obligated, like Christ, to pay the price for the sins of others, to lead the way in that. He

---

* Ferdinand had befriended Henry Ford and for a time worked in a Ford factory in Detroit. He was also friendly with President Franklin Delano Roosevelt.

knew Germany would never recover unless the Germans adopted an attitude of repentance. It was his, and the wider church's, role to exhort them in that.

Bell minced no words in letting both men know that they should not get their hopes up regarding Churchill's response to their overtures. The odds had become increasingly long. Nonetheless, they discussed such specifics as how they would communicate with Britain if she wished to communicate, including codes and locations. At first Sweden was to be the place, but Bishop Björquist, who was the head of the Nordic Ecumenical Institute, didn't think that was possible because of Sweden's neutrality. Switzerland would have to be the meeting place for representatives of Britain and the German conspiracy. Bethge stated that Björquist's attitude may have stemmed from a fundamental uneasiness with Bonhoeffer as a result of the ten-day trip to Sweden in 1936 with his Finkenwalde ordinands. Björquist was close to the Reichskirche and to Bishop Heckel, and was himself an advocate of *Volkskirche* theology. Like many mainstream Lutherans then, Björquist regarded Bonhoeffer as an Episcopal bishop might today regard an evangelical, and going out on a limb with him seemed a bit frightening.

While in neutral territory, Bonhoeffer wrote Sabine and Gert. He wrote in English, possibly to avoid raising suspicions if the letter fell into the wrong hands:

> June 1, 1942
> My dears,
> What an indescribable joy to have heard from you through George! It still seems to me like a miracle. . . . You will have heard, of course, as we have here in Sweden, that all persons of non-aryan descent who are outside of Germany have been in general expatriated. As far as I can tell the future of your fatherland that is a good thing for you and will make your return only easier on that day for which we are all longing. So I hope, you do not worry about it.
> My heart is full of thanks for these last days. George is one of the very great personalities I have met in my life. Please, give my love to the girls. . . . Charles and his wife will go to the countryside in the north to friends of mine for several weeks. That will do them good.
> > Much love from
> > Dietrich

"Charles and his wife" was one of the code names the family used during the war. It referred to his parents, Charles being the English cognate for
Karl. They were going to Pomerania as guests of Ruth von Kleist-Restow at
her estate in Klein-Krössin. Bonhoeffer couldn't have dreamed that in one
week he would be there, and that as a result, his life would change forever.

That same day he wrote Bishop Bell, also in English:

June 1, 1942
My Lord Bishop,
Let me express my deep and sincere gratitude for the hours you have
spent with me. It still seems to me like a dream to have seen you, to have
spoken to you, to have heard your voice. I think these days will remain
in my memory as some of the greatest of my life. This spirit of fellowship and of Christian brotherliness will carry me through the darkest
hours, and even if things go worse than we hope and expect, the light
of these few days will never extinguish in my heart. The impressions of
these days were so overwhelming that I cannot express them in words.
I feel ashamed when I think of all your goodness and at the time I feel
full of hope for the future.

God be with you on your way home, in your work and always. I
shall think of you on Wednesday. Please pray for us. We need it.
Yours most gratefully, Dietrich

Bishop Bell well knew the level of Churchill's cynicism to German overtures, but his meeting with Bonhoeffer had strengthened his resolve to do
what he could. That Visser 't Hooft had been in London to present Trott's
memorandum also encouraged him. On June 18, Bell sent a letter concerning the Sigtuna meetings to Foreign Minister Anthony Eden and requested
a meeting:

Dear Mr. Eden,
I have just got back from Sweden with what seems to me very important confidential information about proposals from a big opposition
movement in Germany. Two German Pastors, both of them well known
to me for 12 years or more (one of them an intimate friend), came

expressly from Berlin to see me at Stockholm. The movement is backed
by leaders of both the Protestant and Catholic Churches. They gave me
pretty full particulars, and names of leading persons in the civil administration, in the labour movement and in the Army, who are involved.
The credentials of these pastors are such that I am convinced of their
integrity and the risks they have run.

Bell met with Eden on June 30 and presented a long memorandum with
the details of his discussions with Schönfeld and Bonhoeffer. Two weeks
later, having heard nothing, he bumped into Sir Stafford Cripps. Cripps gave
him encouraging news about his own meeting in May with Visser 't Hooft
and about the general reception of Adam von Trott's memorandum. Cripps
said he would put in a good word with Eden. But when it came, four days
later, the news was very bad: "Without casting any reflection on the bona
fides of your informants, I am satisfied that it would not be in the national
interest for any reply whatever to be sent to them. I realize that this decision
may cause you some disappointment, but in view of the delicacy of the issues
involved I feel that I must ask you to accept it."

There is no doubt that the bitter British refusal to help these Germans
in fighting Hitler had much to do with Churchill's desire to mollify Stalin,
with whom Churchill's government had that May signed a treaty of alliance.
Bethge said that "London carefully avoided anything that might resemble a
lack of loyalty to the alliance." Ironically, the future coiner of the term *Iron
Curtain* was being sensitive to its future architect.

But Bell did not give up. He wrote Eden on July 25, still pressing his suit:

I found much evidence on many sides in Sweden, in addition to my
information from the two Pastors, of the existence of a sharp distinction between the Nazis as such and a very large body of other Germans.
It is the drawing of this distinction (with its consequences) by the
Government in the most emphatic way which is so anxiously awaited
by the opposition. . . .

Mr. Churchill said in his first speech as Prime Minister in the
House of Commons on May 13th, 1940 that our policy was "to wage
war against a monstrous tyranny never surpassed in the dark and lam-
entable catalogue of human crimes," and that our aim was "victory at all

costs." If there are men in Germany also ready to wage war against the monstrous tyranny of the Nazis from within, is it right to discourage or ignore them? Can we afford to reject their aid in achieving our end? If we by our silence allow them to believe that there is no hope for any Germany, whether Hitlerite or anti-Hitlerite, that is what in effect we are doing.

Gerhard Leibholz had been in close touch with Bell and knew what they were up against. In a letter to Sutz about Bell's efforts, he wrote that "unfortunately, many of his friends and ours do not possess his breadth of judgment, and will have difficulty freeing themselves from erroneous prejudices." As a Jew, Leibholz was keenly aware of the anti-Semitism in Britain, which accounted for some indifference to the plight of European Jewry; as a German, he was keenly aware of anti-German attitudes that were no less racially motivated. According to journalist Joachim Fest, "there was the conviction in Britain, by no means confined to readers of the gutter press, that Germans were innately evil, or at any rate inclined to be so, as result of their historical and cultural heritage."

Leibholz urged Bell to take the memorandum to the American ambassador in Britain, John Gilbert Winant. Bell did so on July 30, and Winant was more encouraging. He promised to pass the information to Roosevelt, but Bell never heard from him again. Roosevelt had bluntly rebuffed other overtures from those connected to the German conspiracy.

On August 4, Eden posted his obtuse reply:

My dear Lord Bishop,
Thank you very much for your letter of July 25th about the German problem.

I am very conscious of the importance of what you say about not discouraging any elements of opposition in Germany to the Nazi regime. You will remember that in my speech at Edinburgh on May 8th I devoted quite a long passage to Germany and concluded by saying that if any section of the German people really wished to see a return to a German state based on respect for law and the rights of the individual, they must understand that no one would believe them until they had taken active steps to rid themselves of their present regime.

For the present I do not think that it would be advisable for me to go any further in a public statement. I realize the dangers and difficulties to which the opposition in Germany is exposed, but they have so far given little evidence of their existence and until they show they are willing to follow the example of the oppressed peoples of Europe in running risks and taking active steps to oppose and overthrow the Nazi rule of terror I do not see how we can usefully expand the statements which have already been made by members of the Government about Germany. I think these statements have made it quite clear that we do not intend to deny to Germany a place in the future Europe, but that the longer the German people tolerate the Nazi regime the greater becomes their responsibility for the crimes which that regime is committing in their name.

> Yours sincerely,
> Anthony Eden

Diplomatic decorum prevented Eden from expressing his true sentiments, but he jotted them in the margin of Bell's letter for posterity: "I see no reason whatsoever to encourage this pestilent priest!"

On the positive side of things, Heydrich was dead. At the end of May, the albino stoat had been ambushed by Czech Resistance fighters while he was riding in his open-topped Mercedes. Eight days later, the architect of the Final Solution fell into the hands of the God of Abraham, Isaac, and Jacob.

CHAPTER 26

BONHOEFFER IN LOVE

*Why am I suddenly so cheerful these days? . . . The incredible fact
remains, he actually wants to marry me. I still fail to grasp how
that can be.*

—MARIA VON WEDEMEYER

J ust after his trip to Sweden, Bonhoeffer went to Klein-Krössin to visit
his dear friend Ruth von Kleist-Retzow on June 8, 1942. Her granddaughter Maria happened to be there. She had just graduated from
high school, and before embarking on a year of national service, she
decided to spend some time visiting family. "Foremost among these visits,"
she recalled,

> was one to my grandmother, to whom I had always been close. The
> feeling was mutual, because she thought I resembled her as a young
> girl. I had been there a week when the celebrated Pastor Bonhoeffer
> came to stay. I was a bit put out at first, to be honest, but it very
> soon emerged that the three of us got on extremely well together. The
> other two conversed in such a way that I not only felt I understood
> what they were talking about but was cordially encouraged to join in.
> Which I did.
>
> I'm afraid I used to take a cocky tone with my grandmother, which
> amused her, and which I maintained even when Dietrich turned up. We
> talked about future plans. Grandmother pronounced my plan to study

mathematics a silly whim, but Dietrich, perhaps for that very reason, took it seriously.

We went for a stroll in the garden. He said he'd been to America, and we noted with surprise that I'd never before met anyone who had been there.

Maria left the next morning, so they didn't have much time together, but Bonhoeffer was smitten. As ever, he needed time to process what he was feeling and thinking. But he was taken aback at how affected he had been by the short time spent with this beautiful, intelligent, and confident young woman. She was eighteen.

Until that June, Bonhoeffer thought of her as the twelve-year-old girl too young to take on as a confirmand in 1936 when he agreed to teach her elder brother and two cousins. He had seen her a few times since then in Klein-Krössin and in Kieckow, but perhaps he had not really seen her at all. She was a beautiful and vivacious young woman, and she hoped to study mathematics. Bonhoeffer deeply admired the Pomeranian aristocratic class, but he was surprised to find such an ambition among its women. It would have been typical among the Grunewald set, but here it was a revelation.

Bonhoeffer knew Maria's family well. Besides his abiding friendship with her grandmother, he had spent much time with her brother Max, who was two years her senior and whom she adored. Max was then a lieutenant serving on the eastern front. Bonhoeffer knew her parents, too, Hans and Ruth von Wedemeyer; a couple more devoutly Christian—and anti-Hitler—did not exist.

Hans von Wedemeyer had been close to Franz von Papen, the Reich chancellor before Hitler. Von Papen was one of the principal figures deluded into thinking he might somehow control Hitler. Hans von Wedemeyer was under no such illusions. His wife recalled his reaction the night Hitler became chancellor: "I had never seen him in a mood of such utter despair, nor did I ever do so again." Von Papen became Hitler's vice chancellor, and von Wedemeyer stayed on his staff, but after three months, he could no longer be party to any of it, and quit. It was well he did. One year later, during the Night of the Long Knives, his successor was murdered at his desk.

In 1936 the Nazis came after Wedemeyer for his staunchly anti-Nazi political stance. They launched a press campaign against him and tried to legally bar him from managing his Pätzig estate. In the denouement to the kangaroo court procedures, the Nazi judge forced him to stand for forty-five minutes as he ranted against him, citing his "reprehensible attitude and debased character." Most of his friends strongly counseled him not to appeal the verdict, but he appealed nonetheless. He prepared his case for a year with help from his cousin Fabian von Schlabrendorff, who became a central figure in the plot against Hitler. Wedemeyer was ultimately cleared of all charges.

Wedemeyer and his wife were also the leaders of the Berneuchen movement, an evangelical movement that aimed to breathe life into the staid Lutheran churches. They hosted a gathering at Pätzig each year.

Hans was now the leader of an infantry battalion near Stalingrad. Like so many of his era, he was caught between his hatred of Hitler and his love of country. The Prussian military class did not shrink from duty, but as with so many others, it disturbed Hans that the man commanding Germany's armies was so fundamentally unworthy of his position and so intrinsically opposed to all that Hans knew to be right and true.

That week, in the charmed surroundings of Klein-Krössin, Bonhoeffer worked on his book. Whether he and Ruth spoke about Maria as a potential wife is unknown. It's likely the thought crossed her mind, since she was the most ardent supporter of the union once the couple publicly discussed its possibility. She was also outspoken and strong-willed, and that she suggested the idea to Bonhoeffer cannot be ruled out.

The thirty-six-year-old Bonhoeffer knew that Maria was probably too young or that he was probably too old. He had long ago decided against marriage. When his relationship with Elizabeth Zinn ended six years earlier, he ruled out marriage as incompatible with the life to which he felt called.

Two weeks after leaving Klein-Krössin, Bonhoeffer wrote one of the Finkenwalde ordinands, Gustav Seydel, who had announced his own engagement. Bonhoeffer's response gives us a glimpse into his thoughts on this issue:

> I would like to tell you how greatly I rejoice with you. What always delights me in news like this is the self-assured glimpse into the future and the confidence that there is a reason to look forward to the next day or the next year, the joyful grasping hold of happiness where God

still gives it to us. This is—don't misunderstand me—a protest against all false, inauthentic apocalypticism that is becoming so widespread today, and I hail it as a sign of authentic and healthy faith. As earthly human beings we have to take account of an earthly future. For the sake of this future we must accept tasks, responsibilities, and joys and sorrows. We need not despise happiness simply because there is so much unhappiness. We should not arrogantly push away the kind hand of God because God's hand is otherwise so hard. I think it is more important to remind one another of this in these days than of many other things, and I received your wedding announcement gratefully as a fine testimony to this very thing. . . . May God also prepare you through this divine kindness to bear again the divine hardship if necessary.*

We know these thoughts did not arise simply because of meeting Maria since Bonhoeffer wrote something similar to Erwin Sutz the previous September:

Over the years I have written many a letter for the wedding of one of the brothers and preached many a wedding sermon. The chief characteristic of such occasions essentially rested in the fact that, in the face of the "last" times (I do not mean this to sound quite so apocalyptic), someone dares to take a step of such affirmation of the earth and its future. It was then always very clear to me that a person could take this step as a Christian truly only from within a very strong faith and on the basis of grace. For here in the midst of the final destruction of all things, one desires to build; in the midst of a life lived from hour to hour and from day to day, one desires a future; in the midst of being driven out from the earth, one desires a bit of space; in the midst of widespread misery, one desires some happiness. And the overwhelming thing is that God says yes to this strange longing, that here God consents to our will, whereas it is usually meant to be just the opposite.

Weeks later, Bonhoeffer spoke to Eberhard Bethge about Maria. As with any-

---

* Seydel was killed in action in the Ukraine in October 1943.

thing, he was trying to work out what he thought God was saying to him. On June 25, he wrote Bethge:

> I have not written to Maria. It is truly not time for that yet. If no further meetings are possible, the pleasant thought of a few highly charged minutes will surely eventually dissolve into the realm of unfulfilled fantasies, a realm that in any case is already well populated. On the other side, I do not see how a meeting could be brought off that would be inconspicuous and not painful for her. Even Mrs. von Kleist cannot be expected to arrange this, at least not at my initiation; for I am in fact still not at all clear and decided about this.

On the twenty-seventh, Bonhoeffer flew to Venice with Dohnanyi on Abwehr business. A week later he was in Rome, and on July 10 he was back in Berlin. He planned to be back at Klein-Krössin ten days later, but could not return until August 18. He had no contact with Maria since their meeting. But now, while he was again in Klein-Krössin, tragedy struck. Maria's father was killed at Stalingrad. He was fifty-four.

Hans von Wedemeyer had been commanding a regiment that, like most at that time, was fatigued and depleted. On the night of August 21, the Russians launched a shell attack, and he was hit. In Hanover, Maria heard of her father's death and immediately traveled home to Pätzig. On hearing the news her brother Max wrote his mother: "When my thoughts turn to you, Mother, I'm not worried about you. It's only when I think of dear Maria, with her passionate temperament and extreme sensitivity, that I wonder how she'll fare."

Bonhoeffer stayed with Ruth von Kleist-Retzow until the twenty-sixth. On August 21, he wrote Max:

> Dear Max,
> You have lost your father. I believe I can sense what that means for you and am thinking of you very much. You are still very young to be without a father. But you have learned from him to honor the will of God in everything God gives and in everything God takes away. You have learned from him that a person's strength comes solely from being united with the will of God. You know that God loved your

father and that God loves you and that it was your father's wish and prayer that you continue to love God, no matter what God sends you and requires of you. Dear Max, as heavy as your heart must be now, let that which your father by God's goodness planted in you now grow strong. Pray to God with your whole heart to help you preserve and prove what has been given you. You have your mother, your grandmother, your siblings, who will help you; but help them as well. How greatly they will need it. In such times one must struggle through a great deal for oneself alone. You will have to learn out there how one sometimes must come to terms with something alone before God. It is often very difficult, but these are the most important hours of life.

The following day he wrote Frau von Wedemeyer:

My dear lady,
It was around seven years ago that your spouse sat in my Finkenwalde room to speak about the confirmation instruction that Max was to receive at that time. I have never forgotten that meeting. It accompanied me throughout the period of instruction. I knew that Max had already received and would continue to receive what was decisive from his parents' home. It was also clear to me what it means for a boy today to have a godly father who at the same time stands in the thick of life. When in the course of those years I then came to know almost all your children, I was often extremely impressed by the power of the blessing that emanates from a father who believes in Christ. This is essentially one and the same impression that has become so important to me in my encounters with your entire extended family. . . . This blessing is, of course, not something purely spiritual, but something that works its way deep into earthly life. Under the right blessing, life becomes healthy, secure, expectant, active, precisely because it is lived out of the source of life, strength, joy, activity. . . . If human beings have passed on to loved ones and to many the blessing they have themselves received, then they have surely fulfilled the most important thing in life; then they have surely themselves become persons happy in God and have made others happy in God.

Bonhoeffer returned to Klein-Krössin on September 1 for two days, and again for two days on September 22. Neither time did he see Maria. But he saw her on October 2 in Berlin. It was their first meeting since early June.

Ruth von Kleist-Retzow was in Berlin for an eye operation at the Franciscan hospital, and she had asked Maria to nurse her there. At the sickbed of Maria's grandmother, the two bumped into each other again. Her thoughts toward him had not been along the lines of his toward her, nor had Bonhoeffer allowed his thoughts to get very far anyway. In any case, he was at the hospital in the role of pastor, and Maria had just lost her father.

Years later, Maria recalled, "Dietrich's frequent visits [at the hospital] surprised me, and I was impressed by his devotion. We often had long talks together at this time. It was a reunion under different circumstances than in June. Being still deeply affected by my father's death, I needed Dietrich's help." They spent more time together than would have been possible under other circumstances. As a native Berliner, Bonhoeffer played the role of host. One day he invited Maria to lunch, suggesting they go to a small restaurant near the hospital. He said because of the ownership, it was actually the safest place for them to talk freely. It was owned by Hitler's brother.

On October 15 Bonhoeffer invited Maria to a Bonhoeffer family gathering at his sister Ursula's home. It was a farewell celebration for his nephew Hans-Walter Schleicher, who was headed off to war the next day. Bonhoeffer thought he would be traveling then and had written Hans-Walter a few days earlier. Given what he knew was happening in Hitler's war, it is natural that he would feel protective toward his nephew. The letter offers a glimpse of his attitude toward those with whom he would soon be mixing in prison:

> Hans-Walter,
> You are, of course, entering into your life as a soldier differently from most of your contemporaries. You have a foundation of values. You have received certain fundamental concepts of life. You know—perhaps partly still unconsciously, but that doesn't matter here—what treasures a good family life, good parents, right and truth, humanity and education, and tradition are. You yourself have been making music for years

and in recent years have read many books, all of which has not simply washed over you without any effect. And finally, you also somehow know what the Bible, the Lord's Prayer, and church music are. Out of this, however, you have received an image of Germany that can never be entirely lost to you, that will accompany you into the war, and for which you will stand up wherever you are and no matter who might confront you. Perhaps as a soldier you are freer for this than we others. But it is clear, and you yourself know it as well, that because of this you will face conflicts, not only with those who are coarse by nature, whose power will shock you in the next few weeks, but simply because you, precisely because you come from a family of this kind, are different from most other people, different even into the smallest externals. The important thing is thus only that one conceive the ways one has an edge on others (and you definitely do!) not as your due but as a gift, and that you place yourself entirely at others' disposal and truly like them, despite their different way of being.

That evening Maria met Bonhoeffer's parents and siblings. Bethge was likely there too. That evening, after returning to her aunt's home, where she was staying, Maria wrote in her diary:

> I had a very interesting talk with Pastor Bonhoeffer. He said it was a tradition with us that young men should volunteer for military service and lay down their lives for a cause of which they mightn't approve at all. But there must also be people able to fight from conviction alone. If they approved of the grounds for war, well and good. If not, they could best serve the Fatherland by operating on the internal front, perhaps even by working against the regime. It would thus be their task to avoid serving in the armed forces for as long as possible—and even, under certain circumstances, if they wouldn't reconcile it with their conscience, to be conscientious objectors.
>
> Oh, it's all so logically clear and obvious. But isn't it terrible, when I think of my father?

Her diary from the next day showed Bonhoeffer was not shy in sharing something of his role in the conspiracy. Of course Maria's uncle Henning von Tresckow was a major figure in the conspiracy, and she was related to many of the others, including von Schlabrendorff.

> Oct. 16. I now know that a man like Dietrich, who truly feels he has an inner mission to help his country and is a personality capable of form-ing an objective opinion, is right to be useful to Germany in another way and avoiding military service for as long as possible. And it's very responsible of him to seek out the genuinely right course of action. It's so easy to become a grumbler, a person who condemns and carps at everything on principle and sees an ulterior motive behind it.

Two days later, a Sunday, Bonhoeffer was at the hospital to visit Ruth von Kleist-Retzow. He performed morning devotions there, taking as his text Ephesians 5:15–21. Maria recalled:

> Oct. 18th. "Make the most of your time!" Pastor Bonhoeffer took morn-ing service today. "Time belongs to death, or, still more so, to the devil. We must buy it from him and return it to God, to whom it must really belong."—"If we inquire the will of God, free from all doubt and all mistrust, we shall discover it."—"Always give thanks for all things."—"Everything we cannot thank God for, we reproach him for."

Bonhoeffer's sense of propriety and his desire to be a pastoral comfort to Maria must have made it easier to avoid thinking too much about a future with her. Neither seemed to have breathed a word indicating this was more than a family pastor ministering to an older woman and her granddaughter who had just lost her father. And yet they enjoyed each other's company; per-haps the constraints of the situation made it easier to relax with each other.

Then on October 26, fresh tragedy struck. Maria's brother Max was killed. On the thirty-first, Bonhoeffer wrote her:

> Dear Miss von Wedemeyer,
> If I might be allowed to say only this to you, I believe I have an inkling of what Max's death means for you.
> It can scarcely help to tell you I too share in this pain.
> At such times it can only help us to cast ourselves upon the heart of

God, not with words but truly and entirely. This requires many difficult hours, day and night, but when we have let go entirely into God—or better, when God has received us—then we are helped. "Weeping may endure for the night, but joy comes in the morning" (Psalm 30:5). There really is joy with God, with Christ! Do believe it.

But each person must walk this way alone—or rather, God draws each person onto it individually. Only prayers and the encouragement of others can accompany us along this way.

If ever there was a time to put aside thoughts of a romantic relationship, this was it. Other than his conversations with Bethge, it's doubtful Bonhoeffer mentioned his feelings to anyone. Maria had no such feelings to speak of, and therefore cannot have seen him as more than a friendly and devout pastor friend. It was in that context that Bonhoeffer expected to travel to Pomerania to be at Max's memorial service.

But somehow, Maria's grandmother, who had been watching them from her hospital bed for weeks—and had doubtless noticed their chemistry in June—had other ideas. She foolishly mentioned them to her daughter. Maria's mother now sent Bonhoeffer a letter asking him not to come to the funeral. He was stunned. Frau von Wedemeyer felt her daughter was too young to be engaged to Pastor Bonhoeffer and thought any discussion of it inappropriate at such a time. Bonhoeffer was shocked to think any of this could be in the open. That anyone was discussing these things when he himself had not discussed them was a horror. On the eleventh, after getting the letter from Maria's mother, Bonhoeffer called Ruth von Kleist-Retzow immediately, knowing she had started the trouble.

Maria was blindsided by the whole thing. She wrote Bonhoeffer a letter saying that she had learned that her mother "had asked you not to come for the memorial service, just because of some stupid family gossip which Grandmother has rather encouraged." As far as Maria was concerned, there was nothing to it, except that she was embarrassed.

Bonhoeffer responded:

November 13, 1942
Dear Miss von Wedemeyer,
Your letter has brought a salutary clarity into an unnecessarily confused

situation. With my whole heart I thank you for this, as well as for the courage with which you have taken the bull by the horns. You will surely understand that I was unable to find your mother's request entirely comprehensible; what I did understand readily—because it corresponds to my own feelings—was simply the wish not to be worried and burdened by something else altogether in these difficult days and weeks. Whatever else may have spurred her request was not spelled out in the letter, and I had no right to inquire about it. . . .

You, as much as or perhaps even more than I, will perceive as a painful inner burden that things not suitable for discussion were brought out into the open. Let me say openly that I cannot easily quite come to terms with your grandmother's behavior; I told her countless times that I did not wish to discuss such things, in fact that this would do violence to all parties. I believed that it was because of her illness and age that she could not cherish silently in her heart what she believed she was witnessing. My conversations with her were often difficult to endure; she did not heed my request. I then interpreted your premature departure from Berlin within that context and was grieved by it. . . . We must make great effort to bear no hard feelings toward her.

But in this letter, in a sidewise, ever-so-gentle way, Bonhoeffer took the opportunity of this opening up of things, however unintended, to hint his way forward:

. . . only from a peaceful, free, healed heart can anything good and right take place; I have experienced that repeatedly in life, and I pray (forgive me for speaking thus) that God may grant us this, soon and very soon.

Can you understand all this? Might you experience it just as I do? I hope so, in fact, I cannot conceive of anything else. But how difficult this is for you too!

. . . Please forgive me this letter, which says so clumsily what I am feeling. I realize that words intended to say personal things come only with tremendous difficulty to me; this is a great burden for those around me. Your grandmother has often enough reproached me severely for my aloofness; she herself is so completely different, but people must of course accept and bear one another as they are. . . . I am writing your grandmother very briefly, urging her to silence and patience. I will write to your mother tomorrow, that she not get upset at whatever your grandmother may be writing; the thought of it horrifies me.

What Maria really thought after reading his letter is unknown, but this might have been her first inkling that he had feelings for her. He wrote her again two days later, on November 15. Between what was happening in the Wedemeyer family and all else in the world around them, it was a tumultuous and confusing time. Bonhoeffer mentioned the suicide of a prominent composer of church music, Hugo Distler, in despair at the deportation of Jewish friends: "Now I hear that he took his own life in his office at the cathedral, Bible and cross in hand. . . . He was thirty years old. I am quite shaken by this. Why was no one able to help him?"

Frau von Wedemeyer was displeased about the spate of letters and must have had unpleasant conversations with her mother and daughter. On the nineteenth she called Bonhoeffer at his parents' home. She said Maria did not wish to receive any more letters, although it's as likely that Frau von Wedemeyer herself made this decision on her daughter's behalf. Bonhoeffer wrote Maria later that day:

Dear Miss von Wedemeyer,
Your mother called me this morning and told me of your wish. The telephone is a very inadequate means of communication, not least because I was unable to be alone during the conversation. Please forgive me if I have burdened you too greatly with my letters. I had not wished this but desired your peace of mind. It appears—this was how I was obliged to understand your mother—that at the moment we are unable to give this to each other. So I ask it of God for you and for us and will wait until God shows us our way. Only in peace with God, with others, and with ourselves will we hear and do God's will. In this we may have great confidence and need not become impatient or act rashly.

Do not think I failed to understand that you do not want to respond and cannot and most likely also did not wish to receive this letter. But if the timing proves feasible for me to come again to Klein-Krössin at some point in the not too distant future, your wishes would not forbid this? This is what I understand, in any case.

Please forget every word that hurt you and burdened you further beyond what has already been laid on you by God.

I have written to your mother that I needed to write you briefly once more.—

God protect you and us all.

Sincerely yours,
Dietrich Bonhoeffer

Bonhoeffer Proposes

What happened next is anyone's guess, but the well-meaning grandmother's big mouth had flushed the bird from its hiding place. It wasn't supposed to happen this way; suddenly everything was out in the open. On November 24, Bonhoeffer traveled to Pätzig to visit with Frau von Wedemeyer. Somehow, in a thunderclap of time, Bonhoeffer had decided he wanted to marry Maria von Wedemeyer. He was going to ask her mother's permission to propose.

Bonhoeffer respected Frau von Wedemeyer, but feared she might be overly pious. He wrote Bethge three days later: "Contrary to my fears that the house would have an excessive spiritual tone, its style made a very pleasant impression." Frau von Wedemeyer was "calm, friendly, and not overwrought, as I had feared." She was not unalterably opposed to the match, but "given the enormity of the decision," she proposed a yearlong separation. Bonhoeffer responded that "these days a year could just as well become five or ten and thus represented a postponement into the incalculable." Nonetheless he told Frau von Wedemeyer that he "understood and recognized her maternal authority over her daughter." Bonhoeffer didn't expect it would really be a year, but didn't want to force the issue, especially since Frau von Wedemeyer had been recently widowed.

When they finished their conversation, Frau von Wedemeyer asked Bonhoeffer to talk to her mother, to let her know where things stood. Maria's grandmother promptly blew up on hearing that her daughter would take such a severe stand, and Bonhoeffer realized the feisty Ruth would probably cause more trouble. Bonhoeffer didn't see Maria during his visit, but gathered from her mother that she was generally amenable to the separation, although she obviously had little say in the matter.

During this very same time, Eberhard Bethge proposed marriage to Bonhoeffer's sixteen-year-old niece, Renate Schleicher. Her parents, Ursula and Rüdiger, were concerned about the match for similar reasons, Bethge then being thirty-three. Bonhoeffer wrote Bethge with the details of his visit to Klein-Krössin and then turned to Bethge's situation. The Schleichers had also suggested a lengthy separation. "If it begins to look ominous for you," Bonhoeffer said, ". . . I shall in that case say something about my own situation; then for once they will consider your situation not only from Renate's perspective but also from your own. But for now I shall hold my peace."

Maria's diary three days, a month, and six weeks later show us the progress of her feelings:

Nov. 27th. Why am I suddenly so cheerful these days? I feel safe, for one thing, because I can now postpone all my musings, deliberations and worries till later. But shelving them surely can't be responsible for this sense of relief. Ever since Mother told me on the phone about her meeting with Dietrich, I feel I can breathe freely again. He made a considerable impression on Mother, that's obvious—he couldn't fail to.

The incredible fact remains, he actually wants to marry me. I still fail to grasp how that can be.

19 December 1942. Pätzig.

I thought coming home might be the one thing that could shake my resolve. I still believed I was under the influence of Grandmother, or rather, of her own exaggerated and unrealistic idea, but it isn't true. The innermost reality still stands, even though I don't love him. But I know that I will love him.

Oh, there are so many superficial arguments against it. He's old and wise for his age—a thoroughgoing academic, I suppose. How will I, with my love of dancing, riding, sport, pleasure, be able to forgo all those things? . . . Mother says he's an idealist and hasn't given it careful thought. I don't believe that.

10 Jan 1943. On the way here I had the talk with Mother, the one I had longed for so eagerly but feared so greatly. It caused tears—hot, heavy tears—"and yet, what happiness to be loved. . . ." Was it good and productive? I pray so, because I feel that it was, and is, crucial to my life. I pray, too, that I didn't just talk Mother round but convinced her—that she isn't just giving in to me but can look upon it as the proper course.

"Today I Can Say Yes to You"

Bonhoeffer had no communication with Maria since November, but on January 10 Maria spoke with her mother and uncle Hans Jürgen von Kleist-Retzow, who was her guardian, and persuaded them to allow her to write Bonhoeffer. She wrote on the thirteenth:

Dear Pastor Bonhoeffer,

I've known, ever since arriving home, that I must write to you, and I've looked forward to doing so.

I recently spoke with my mother and my uncle from Kieckow. I'm now able to write to you, and to ask you to answer this letter.

It is so difficult for me to have to put in writing what even in person can scarcely be spoken. I wish to rebut every word that wants to be spoken here, because words are so clumsy and forceful with things that want to be said gently. But because I have experienced that you understand me so well, I now have the courage to write you, although I actually have no right at all to reply to a question you have not even asked me. Today I can say Yes to you from my entire, joyful heart.

Please understand my mother's reluctance to waive the delay she imposed on us. She still can't believe, from past experience, that our decision will hold good. And I myself am always saddened to think that Grandmother has told you only nice things about me, so you form a false picture of me. Perhaps I should tell you a lot of bad things about myself, because it makes me unhappy to think that you could love me for what I'm not.

But I can't believe that anyone can like me so much for what I really am. I certainly have no wish to hurt you, but I must say this anyway:

If you've realized that I'm not good enough, or that you no longer want to come to me, I beg you to say so. I can still ask you that now, and how infinitely harder it will be if I'm forced to recognize it later on. I myself am quite convinced that I need some more time in which to put my decision to the test, and because I know my time in the Red Cross will be hard, it's essential to me.

This is our business alone, isn't it, not anyone else's. I'm so scared of what other people say, even Grandmother. Can you grant this request?

Thank you from the bottom of my heart for all you've done for me recently. I can only guess how difficult it must have been, because I myself have often found it hard to endure.

Yours, Maria

Bonhoeffer wrote back immediately. For the first time he addressed her by her Christian name, and early in the second paragraph, in the phrase "dear Maria, I thank you for your word," switched to the informal *du*:

Dear Maria,
The letter was under way for four days before just now—an hour ago— arriving here! In an hour the mail is being picked up again, so at least an initial greeting and thanks must go with it—even if the words I wish to say now have not yet emerged. May I simply say what is in my heart? I sense and am overwhelmed by the awareness that a gift without equal has been given me—after all the confusion of the past weeks I had no longer dared to hope—and now the unimaginably great and blissful thing is simply here, and my heart opens up and becomes quite wide and overflowing with thankfulness and shame and still cannot grasp it at all—this "Yes" that is to be decisive for our entire life. If we were now able to talk in person with each other, there would be so infinitely much—yet fundamentally only always one and the same thing—to say! Is it possible that we will see each other soon? And where? Without having to be afraid of others' words again? Or for one reason or another shall this still not happen? I think now it must happen.

And now I cannot speak any differently than I have often done in my own heart—I want to speak to you as a man speaks to the girl with whom he wants to go through life and who has given him her Yes—dear Maria, I thank you for your word, for all that you have endured for me and for what you are and will be for me. Let us now be and become happy in each other. Whatever time and calm you need to compose yourself, as you write, you must have, in whatever form is good for you. You alone can know that. With your "Yes" I can now also wait peacefully; without the Yes it was difficult and would have become increasingly difficult; now it is easy since I know that you want this and need it. I wish in no way to push or frighten you. I want to care for you and allow the dawning joy of our life to make you light and happy. I understand well that you wish to be entirely alone for a time yet—I have been alone long enough in my life to know the blessing (though, to be sure, also the dangers) of solitude. I understand and understood also throughout these past weeks—if not entirely without pain—that for you it cannot be easy to say Yes to me, and I will never forget that. And it is this, your Yes, which alone can give me the courage as well no longer to say only No to myself. Say no more about the "false image" I could have of you. I want no "image," I want you, just as I beg you with my whole heart to want not an image of me but me myself; and you must know those are two different things. But let us not dwell now on the bad that lurks and has power in every person, but let us encounter each other in great, free forgiveness and love, let us take each other as we are—with thanks and boundless trust in God, who has led us to this point and now loves us.

This letter must be off immediately so that you will receive it tomorrow. God protect you and us both.

Your faithful Dietrich

With that, Dietrich Bonhoeffer was engaged. They would look back on January 17 as the official date. It would be an engagement like few in the world. Of course, had either known what was ahead, they would have arranged things quite differently. But no one knew what was ahead, nor could know. But Bonhoeffer had cast his cares and expectations upon God. He knew that he and his engagement to Maria were in God's hands.

They were still obliged to wait. But now it was a different kind of waiting. In a sense they already belonged to each other and could enjoy belonging to each other, even as they were apart. Bonhoeffer had much to occupy him. Though he wasn't quite sure of it yet, the Gestapo was on his tail, and the conspiracy was racing forward with yet another plan to kill Hitler.

When six days passed and Bonhoeffer had not heard from her, he wrote again, even if it was only to tell Maria that all was well and that she should not feel rushed. "At the moment," he said, "it seems to me as if it were in fact God commanding us to wait until we are shown the way."

The next day, Sunday the twenty-fourth, he received her letter. She asked him whether they might wait six months before they corresponded. Whether her mother had persuaded her to ask this is not known, and it seemed to surprise Bonhoeffer, but he was too happy to be bothered by much. He was in love.

My dear Maria,
Now the letter is here, your kind letter—I thank you for it and thank you anew each new time I read it, indeed to me it is almost as if I were experiencing now for the first time in my life what it means to be thankful to another person, what a profoundly transforming power gratitude can be—it is the Yes—this word so difficult and so marvelous, appearing so seldom among mortals—from which all this springs—may God from whom every Yes comes grant that we may speak this Yes always thus and always more and more to one another throughout our entire life.

From every word of your letter I have sensed with joyful certainty that it will be good between us. The life together, toward which through God's goodness we hope to move, is like a tree that must grow from deep roots silent and hidden, strong and free.

He also asked Maria to inform her grandmother of their new situation and to keep from having any further misunderstandings with the strong-willed woman.

The day after Bonhoeffer's thirty-seventh birthday, he heard from Ruth von Kleist-Restow. Maria had told her the news.

You know utterly without saying how I desire to receive you fully as a son, when the time comes. That it should still take so long is probably the decision of [her] mother and Hans-Jürgen, I am *presuming*. Perhaps this is the right thing for M., so that she remains quite clear. And if it appears too long for her and you, then there will be means and ways to shorten it. What does time mean today anyway? . . . Oh, I am happy.
Grandmother

CHAPTER 27

KILLING ADOLF HITLER

Shall I shoot? I can get inside the Führer's headquarters with my revolver. I know where and when the conferences take place. I can get access.

—WERNER VON HAEFTEN TO DIETRICH BONHOEFFER

F rau von Wedemeyer's concern about Bonhoeffer was not merely his age; it was also his work for the Abwehr. She might even have known of his involvement in the conspiracy. Whatever he was doing was uncertain and dangerous. Drawing an eighteen-year-old girl into a relationship with someone whose future was so uncertain seemed selfish. At any moment he could be arrested or worse. That Frau von Wedemeyer had just lost her husband and son underscored the uncertainty of things. So she agreed to the engagement but stipulated that it not be made public for a period. Bonhoeffer told his parents in February, but besides them and Bethge, it remained a secret.

Maria's sister, Ruth-Alice von Bismarck, was four years older. She and her husband had similar concerns about the danger of Bonhoeffer's work and about what seemed like his selfishness in proposing. Didn't he realize how she might be hurt if he were arrested, imprisoned, or killed? Wasn't the decent thing to wait, as so many others were doing during these tumultuous times? Indeed, as a result of his part in Operation 7, the Gestapo had already stumbled onto Bonhoeffer's trail the previous October.

Operation 7 was ultimately successful, but one of its many details caught the Gestapo's attention when a customs search officer in Prague discovered a currency irregularity leading to Wilhelm Schmidhuber. Schmidhuber was a member of the Abwehr who visited Bonhoeffer at Ettal in December 1940. The Gestapo wasted no time in finding him. He was interrogated about the smuggling of foreign currency abroad, a grave crime during wartime, even if done under the aegis of the Abwehr. Schmidhuber led them to Bonhoeffer's Catholic friend, Joseph Müller. It was all greatly troubling, especially when Schmidhuber was transferred to the infamous Gestapo prison on Prinz-Albrecht-Strasse in Berlin. He surrendered information implicating Dohnanyi, Oster, and Bonhoeffer. Now it was entirely a race against time. The coup against Hitler and his regime must be launched before the Gestapo made their move and arrested their hated Abwehr rivals.

"Guilt and Freedom"

Bonhoeffer knew he might be arrested and even killed, but he had come to terms with that reality. He had also come to terms with moving forward with marriage under such circumstances, as his letters to Seydel and Sutz show. He saw it as an act of faith in God to step out in freedom and not to cringe from future possibilities.

This thinking also affected his involvement in the conspiracy. In December 1942, he spoke with a church colleague Oskar Hammelsbeck:

> Bonhoeffer confided to me that he was actively and responsibly involved in the German resistance against Hitler, following his moral conviction that "the structure of responsible action includes both readiness to accept guilt and freedom" (*Ethics*, p. 209). "If any man tries to escape guilt in responsibility he detaches himself from the ultimate reality of human existence, and what is more he cuts himself off from the redeeming mystery of Christ's bearing guilt without sin, and he has no share in the divine justification which lies upon this event" (*Ethics*, p. 210).

Bonhoeffer knew that to live in fear of incurring "guilt" was itself sinful. God wanted his beloved children to operate out of freedom and joy to do what was right and good, not out of fear of making a mistake. To live in fear and guilt was to be "religious" in the pejorative sense that Bonhoeffer so often talked and preached about. He knew that to act freely could mean inadvertently doing wrong and incurring guilt. In fact, he felt that living this way meant that it was impossible to avoid incurring guilt, but if one wished to live responsibly and fully, one would be willing to do so.

Bonhoeffer's student Wolf-Dieter Zimmermann remembered an extraordinary evening in November 1942. Bonhoeffer was visiting him and his wife at their small house near Berlin. Also there was Werner von Haeften, the younger brother of Hans-Bernd von Haeften, who had been in Bonhoeffer's confirmation class in Grunewald two decades earlier. Bonhoeffer visited Hans-Bernd in Copenhagen on his way to Fanø, and Hans-Bernd became part of the conspiracy through the Kreisau Circle. But Werner was more deeply involved: he was adjutant for Stauffenberg, who would lead the July 20, 1944, plot. At Zimmermann's house, he prodded Bonhoeffer about whether it was permissible to kill Hitler. Zimmermann recalled the conversation:

> Werner von Haeften, an old friend of my family, was now a staff lieutenant of the Army High Command. At the beginning he was rather silent, and we did not ask him about his duties in detail. Suddenly he turned to Bonhoeffer and said: "Shall I shoot? I can get inside the Führer's headquarters with my revolver. I know where and when the conferences take place. I can get access." These words frightened us all. They had such an explosive effect that at first each of us endeavored to calm the others down. The discussion lasted for many hours. Bonhoeffer explained that the shooting by itself meant nothing: something had to be gained by it, a change of circumstances, of the government. The liquidation of Hitler would in itself be no use; things might even become worse. That, he said, made the work of the resistance so difficult, that the "thereafter" had to be so carefully prepared. Von Haeften, who came from an old officers' family, was a gentle type, enthusiastic, idealistic, but also a man of Christian convictions who believed in inherited traditions. He was one of Niemöller's confirmands. Now he suddenly developed enormous energy and was not content with "theoretical" reflections. He kept asking questions, digging more deeply, he saw his chance and wondered whether he should take it. He reiterated that he might be one of the very few who were able to act, to intervene. He did not consider his life of great importance. Bonhoeffer, on the other hand, exhorted him over and over

again to be discreet, to plan clearly and then to see all unforeseen compli-
cations through. Nothing should be left to chance. At last von Haeften's
questions became direct: "Shall I . . . ? May I . . . ?" Bonhoeffer answered
that he could not decide this for him. The risk had to be taken by him,
him alone. If he even spoke of guilt in not making use of a chance, there
was certainly as much guilt in light-hearted treatment of the situation.
No one could ever emerge without guilt from the situation he was in. But
then that guilt was always a guilt borne in suffering.

The two men talked for hours. We others only made some marginal
comments. No decision was taken. Werner von Haeften returned to his
duties without being given any direction. He had to decide for himself.
And later, he did decide. As aide-de-camp to Stauffenberg he was one
of those who were involved in the abortive attempt on Hitler's life. He
was also one of those who, in the evening of 20th July 1944, were shot
in the courtyard of the Army High Command in the Bendlerstrasse.
Eye-witnesses tell us that he faced death calmly and bravely.

Operation Flash

In January and February 1943, as the Gestapo gathered information on
Bonhoeffer and Dohnanyi, preparations were under way for a coup attempt in
March. The Gestapo's noose was tightening, but if the coup succeeded, every-
one's problems would be over. The code name for this effort was Operation
Flash, doubtless because its literally brilliant climax involved the detonation of
an explosion aboard Hitler's plane as it squired its passenger over Minsk.

The principal players were General Friedrich Olbricht, General Henning
von Tresckow, and von Tresckow's aide-de-camp and cousin Fabian von
Schlabrendorff, who was married to Maria von Wedemeyer's cousin Luitgard
von Bismarck. Schlabrendorff also figured prominently in the July 20 plot as
Stauffenberg's aide-de-camp. Von Tresckow was Maria's uncle, and Olbricht
had been helpful in getting military exemptions for many Confessing
Church pastors.

The plan was for Schlabrendorff to plant a bomb on Hitler's plane in
Smolensk, where he would be on March 13 for a brief visit to the troops on
the eastern front. Years later, Schlabrendorff explained that "the semblance of
an accident would avoid the political disadvantages of a murder. For in those

days Hitler still had many followers who, after such an event, would have put up a strong resistance to our revolt." As soon as it was confirmed that the Führer's remains had been properly scattered across Minsk, the generals would launch their coup. Schlabrendorff and Tresckow had experimented with numerous bombs, but in the end the honor of exploding the myth and the man Adolf Hitler fell to an English bomb. The mechanisms and fuses of German bombs made enough noise that they might be discovered. But Schlabrendorff and Tresckow found an English bomb; it was a book-sized plastic explosive with no clockwork and no fuse, hence no ticking or hissing. When Schlabrendorff pressed a certain button, a vial holding a corrosive chemical would be broken. The released chemical would eat away the wire holding back the spring that, once sprung, would strike the detonator cap, which would explode the bomb and then: *curtains*.

The special explosive was available only to the Abwehr, so Dohnanyi would have to take it via train from Berlin to Smolensk on the Russian front. By then Dohnanyi had recruited Bethge to work for the Abwehr so that he, too, might avoid military service, especially since he was about to marry Dohnanyi's niece Renate Schleicher. As it happened, Bethge was obliged to borrow Karl Bonhoeffer's Mercedes to drive Dohnanyi to the night train that would carry him to Russia. Dr. Bonhoeffer had no idea his official physician's car was being used to transport explosives meant to kill Hitler, nor did Bethge have any idea he was chauffeuring such a thing. He delivered Dohnanyi and the bomb to the station, and Dohnanyi and the bomb made their way to Smolensk.

On the thirteenth Tresckow and Schlabrendorff, in the possession of the bomb, were twice so close to Hitler that they were tempted to explode the bomb prematurely. But in both cases the generals meant to lead the coup were also present, so they adhered to the original plan of getting the bomb onto Hitler's plane. But how? Meanwhile, they lunched with the Führer. Years later, the well-bred Schlabrendorff recalled the grim spectacle of Hitler at table: "To see Hitler eat was a most disgusting sight. His left hand he placed upon his thigh, while with his right hand he stuffed his food, consisting of all sorts of vegetables, into his mouth. As he did so he did not lift his hand to his mouth, but kept his right arm flat on the table and brought his mouth down to his food."

As the famously vegetarian Reichsführer indecorously bolted his meat-less mush, the horrified aristocratic generals around him indulged in polite conversation. During what certainly must have been an exceedingly tense meal, not least because some knew it was the final meal for all those boarding the Führer's plane, General Tresckow casually asked a favor of his table mate, Lieutenant Colonel Heinz Brandt. Brandt was in Hitler's entourage, and Tresckow asked whether he would mind taking a gift of brandy to Rastenberg to give to his old friend, General Stieff. Tresckow implied the brandy was payment for a gentlemanly wager. Brandt agreed, and a little while later, just as they headed to the airfield, Schlabrendorff handed Colonel Brandt the package. Just before, he pressed the magic button, *presto*, setting things in motion, and knowing that approximately one half hour later, somewhere far above the earth, the final buzzer would sound over the Third Reich.

If Hitler did not board the plane soon, it could be embarrassing. But he did board the plane, along with his entourage and Brandt. The counterfeit brandy was placed safely beneath them all, in the cargo hold, and at last the plane took off, accompanied by its detail of fighter planes. They would be the ones to radio the first news of the Führer's startling demise. All that remained was the agony of waiting.

The extent to which Hitler planned his movements and activities to avoid assassination was impressive. All his meals were prepared by a chef he brought with him wherever he went, and like some ancient despot, he made sure that each dish set before him was first tasted by his personal quack physician, Dr. Theodor Morrell, while Hitler watched. He also wore a fantastically heavy hat. On the sly, Schlabrendorff hefted this fabled chapeau when the generals were meeting at Kluge's quarters. It was "heavy as a cannon ball," lined with three and a half pounds of steel. As for Hitler's plane, it was divided into several compartments. His personal cabin, Schlabrendorff explained, "was armor-plated and had a contrivance for descent by parachute. According to our computation, however, the explosive charge in the bombs was sufficient to blow up the whole plane, including the armored cabin. Even if that should not happen, such essential parts of the plane would be torn off that it was bound to crash."

For two hours they heard nothing. Then came the impossible news: Hitler landed safely in East Prussia. The attempt had failed. Everyone was too filled with fear to be depressed about the outcome. They knew that the bomb had likely been discovered. But General Tresckow remained calm and coolly telephoned Hitler's headquarters, asking to speak with Brandt. When Brandt came on the line, Tresckow asked whether the brandy had been delivered to Stieff. It had not. Tresckow explained that he'd given Brandt the wrong package. Would he mind terribly if the next day Schlabrendorff stopped by to exchange it for the right one? As it turned out, he was headed that way on official business.

With great courage, since he had no idea what would greet him when he arrived, Schlabrendorff took a train thither and paid the dreaded visit. No one seemed to know he was there to retrieve an unexploded bomb. All was quite well until Brandt handed him the bomb. Brandt gave the package an inadvertent jerk, nearly causing Schlabrendorff to have a heart attack and to expect a belated and unwelcome *ka-boom*. But of such there was none. They amiably exchanged packages: Schlabrendorff gave Brandt a package containing actual brandy, and Brandt handed Schlabrendorff the ersatz version.

On the train to Berlin, Schlabrendorff locked the door of his sleeper car and opened the package to see what had gone wrong. Everything had worked perfectly: the vial had been broken; the corrosive liquid had dissolved the wire; the wire had released the spring; the spring had sprung; and the detonator cap had been struck. But the detonator cap had not ignited the explosive. Either it was an extremely rare dud, or the cold in the luggage compartment was to blame. In either case, the mysteriously durable Führer had again escaped death.

Everyone was shattered at the failure, but this feeling was offset by relief that the bomb had not been discovered. It all might have ended far worse. On the morning of March 15, Schlabrendorff showed Dohnanyi and Oster the undetonated bomb. But why cry over spilled milk? They would simply have to try again. Hitler would be in Berlin on the twenty-first, accompanied by Himmler and Göring. The opportunity to send this unholy trio into the next world together was too good to be true. They were rarely together in public, but they were scheduled to attend ceremonies for *Heldengedenktag* (Heroes' Memorial Day) at the Zeughaus on Unter den Linden. Then they were to examine captured Soviet weaponry. The conspirators again went to work.

The Overcoat Bombs

But there were difficulties. To begin with, it would have to be a suicide mission. Nonetheless, Major Rudolf-Christoph von Gersdorff on Kluge's staff bravely volunteered for the honor. He would meet Hitler and his entourage after the ceremony and lead them through the exhibit of captured weaponry.

He would carry two bombs in his overcoat, of the same type that had failed to detonate in Hitler's plane, but the fuses would be shorter. They wanted to rig them with much quicker fuses, but settled for fuses that should take ten minutes. Hitler was supposed to be there for half an hour. Once the fuses were triggered and the vials broken, it would take ten interminable minutes for the wire to be dissolved, releasing the spring. While Gersdorff was telling the Führer about the weaponry, he would know that, minute by minute, he was approaching his own death. The night before, Gersdorff met Schlabrendorff in his room in the Eden Hotel, and Schlabrendorff gave him the bombs. Everything was prepared.

The next day, a Sunday, most of the Bonhoeffer clan was assembled at the Schleicher home at 41 Marienburgerallee. They were rehearsing for their musical performance at the seventy-fifth birthday of Karl Bonhoeffer, ten days hence. They had chosen Walcha's cantata "Lobe den Herrn" ("Praise the Lord"). Bonhoeffer played piano, Rüdiger Schleicher played violin, and Hans von Dohnanyi was in the choir. It was a terrific act of self-discipline to keep their minds on the music since these three and Christine were aware of what was unfolding six miles away in the Zeughaus. Any moment it would happen or had already happened.

They kept their eyes glued to the clocks; their ears cocked for the ringing of the phone with the call that would change everything and that they would celebrate for the rest of their lives. Dohnanyi's car was parked at the front door, ready to carry him to where he was needed as soon as he himself knew. The end of the nightmare called the Third Reich was imminent. The tapped phone calls and the shadowing by the Gestapo that had been increasing these past months would end, and they would all turn their great talents and energies to the long and hard but welcome work of restoring their beloved Germany to something of which they might once more be proud.

The large group continued to rehearse, not knowing that the Zeughaus ceremony had been delayed an hour, wondering why the phone did not ring. Gersdorff waited as planned, the bombs in his military overcoat. At last Hitler arrived, gave a short speech, and proceeded to the exhibition with his remoras, Göring, Himmler, General Keitel, and the head of the navy, Admiral Karl Dönitz.

When Hitler approached him, Gersdorff reached inside his coat and pressed the buttons. Now it would happen. The vials were broken, and the acid began to eat away slowly at the wires. Gersdorff greeted the Führer and with extraordinary bravery and discipline began the acting job of a thousand lifetimes, pretending to be concerned with the Russian weaponry and giving the Führer details as they proceeded. But Hitler suddenly decided to end his visit. In a moment he walked out a side door onto Unter den Linden and was gone. What was to have taken half an hour had taken a few minutes. Gersdorff was still wearing an overcoat laden with explosives about to go off. There was no "shut off" switch. The acid was doing its corrosive work, dissolving the metal wire further with every second. As soon as Hitler was gone, Gersdorff rushed into a restroom and ripped the fuses from the two bombs. Instead of dying that afternoon as planned, this brave man lived to 1980. But Hitler had escaped again.

The Bonhoeffer family received no happy phone call that day. And the Gestapo was closing in.

Ten days later, the occasion of Karl Bonhoeffer's seventy-fifth birthday was grandly celebrated. Though none of them knew it that day, this was the last, magnificent performance the Bonhoeffer family would give. In some ways it was a fitting and crowning moment for the extraordinary family, for whom such performances had been a tradition over the years. In five days their lives would change dramatically. They would never gather like this again.

But here they were now, singing "Praise the Lord." Everyone was there that day, including their former governess Maria Czeppan and Bethge, who would officially become a member of the family in a month. The only ones missing were the Leibholzes, still in England. But even they managed to make an appearance of sorts, sending a congratulatory telegram through Erwin Sutz.

With exquisite irony, Hitler was represented too. For Karl Bonhoeffer's lifetime of service to Germany, an official from the Reich's Ministry of Culture showed up to award him the nation's coveted Goethe medal. It was presented to him in front of the assemblage, along with a special certificate: "In the name of the German people I bestow on Professor Emeritus Bonhoeffer the Goethe medal for art and science, instituted by the late Reichspräsident Hindenburg. The *Führer*, Adolf Hitler."

In five days other representatives of Hitler's government would come to the house at 43 Marienburgerallee. They would come not to praise anyone, and their arrival would not be expected.

 CHAPTER 28

CELL 92 AT TEGEL PRISON

I can't go on like this. I have to know—are you really in danger?
—MARIA VON WEDEMEYER

Who stands fast? Only the man whose final standard is not his reason, his principles, his conscience, his freedom, or his virtue, but who is ready to sacrifice all this when he is called to obedient and responsible action in faith and in exclusive allegiance to God—the responsible man, who tries to make his whole life an answer to the question and call of God.
—DIETRICH BONHOEFFER

The isolated use and handing down of the famous term 'religionless Christianity' has made Bonhoeffer the champion of an undialectical shallow modernism which obscures all that he wanted to tell us about the living God.
—EBERHARD BETHGE

On April 5, Bonhoeffer was at home. Around noon, he called the Dohnanyis. Their phone was answered by an unfamiliar man's voice. Bonhoeffer hung up. He knew what was happening: the Gestapo had finally made their move. They were at the Dohnanyis, searching the house. Bonhoeffer calmly went next door to see Ursula and told her what had happened and what would likely happen next: the Gestapo would arrive and arrest him too. She prepared a large meal for him, and then Bonhoeffer went back home to put his papers in order, since the Gestapo would be having a good look around, as was their habit. He had prepared for this moment for a long time and even left a few notes specifically for their benefit.

Then he returned to the Schleichers and waited. At four o'clock Bonhoeffer's father came over and told him that two men wished to speak with him. They were upstairs in his room. It was Judge Advocate Manfred Roeder and a Gestapo official named Sonderegger. Bonhoeffer met them, and taking his Bible with him, he was escorted to their black Mercedes and taken away. He would never return.

The Engagement to Maria

In the three months between his engagement and his arrest, Bonhoeffer had been in the midst of a moratorium on communication with Maria. The agreement was that they would wait a year before marrying. Maria had asked that they not write each other for six months, presumably beginning in late January, after their engagement. It was a long time to wait, but Bonhoeffer was willing to do so with joy, as he said in his letter. Maria had another way of dealing with it. She would write Dietrich, but would not mail the letters. She wrote her letters in her diary. Perhaps the idea was that Dietrich could read them once the separation was over.

And so in February and March, while the Gestapo was closing in on Bonhoeffer and Dohnanyi, Maria wrote to him in her diary a few times. She often expressed concern that he hardly knew what he was getting in her, that her youth and free-spirited personality made her somehow unworthy of him. He went to great pains to assure her she was mistaken. Nonetheless, in her "letter" to him on February 3, she wrote him from Pätzig:

> If you could see me here like this, I think there are times when you wouldn't care for me at all. For instance when I ride like a maniac and talk dialect to the farmhands. I sometimes give a start and think you'd be sorry to see me that way. When I play the gramophone and hop across the room on one foot, pulling on a stocking with a huge great hole in it, I flop down on the bed in horror at the thought that you might see me

like that. I also do far worse things. I smoke a cigar because I've never smoked one but simply have to know what it's like, and then I feel so ghastly that I can't eat any lunch or supper. Or I get up in the night, put on a long dress, and dance wildly around the drawing-room, or go for a walk with Harro [the dog] and sleep all next morning.

I can understand you'd find that awful, and I'll certainly try not to do it when you're here, but it happens of its own accord sometimes, and I have to let off steam somehow. Still, I'm sure the Red Cross will improve my behavior a bit and save you the job.*

Maria didn't seem to know of the danger facing her fiancé in the months before his arrest—until her overly talkative grandmother gave her reason to worry in a letter on February 16. The letter hinted at Bonhoeffer's danger enough to upset Maria significantly. She "wrote" him again in her diary:

I can't go on like this. I have to know—are you really in danger? What am I doing, Dietrich? Forgive my weakness. I must call you. I must hear from your own lips what is going on. Why don't you keep me posted? I don't understand you. Perhaps you don't realize what you're doing to me. I find the thought that something might happen to you unbearable, don't you realize that? Don't you sense that, ever since I've known, I haven't been able to shake off my fears for your safety?

I did say you could call me or write to me! Tell me you're all right, Dietrich, and that you aren't getting impatient, because all I've heard comes from Grandmother, not from you. Oh, Dietrich, just tell me that, I beg you.

For three weeks she kept her worries between herself and her diary, but on March 9, she broke the rules of engagement and telephoned him in Berlin. Whether her mother knew of the phone call is unclear. The next day, Maria even wrote an actual letter and mailed it:

I've spoken to you and heard your voice. Dietrich, dearest, can you still remember every word we exchanged? "Hey," you said, "what's the

---

* She expected to begin a nursing job in Hanover soon.

matter?" And oh, how the tears rolled down my cheeks although I'd tried so hard not to cry and certainly hadn't done so since the lunch break. And at first you didn't understand what I was driving at. I put it so stupidly, didn't I? But then you laughed. It was so lovely, that laugh. To think you could laugh like that! I'm grateful to you for that most of all. When you laughed and told me not to worry, I knew all at once that it wasn't true, what Grandmother had said, and that all my worrying and weeping had been quite unnecessary and that you were all right and glad that I'd called you. That was why you laughed, wasn't it, because you were glad. Afterwards, I laughed too.

That same day, Bonhoeffer wrote Maria. What they had decided about communicating going forward is unknown, but it appears both had had enough of the noncommunication. They were madly in love and wanted to be together, and if they could not be together, they must at least write each other.

Dear Maria,
My heart is still pounding audibly, and everything inside me has undergone a kind of transformation—from joy and surprise, but also from dismay that you were worried. I'm always doing silly things like this. If you were here and we could talk to each other I'd have told you what I stupidly told your grandmother. No, you needn't have a moment's worry—I'm not worried either. You do, of course, know from the little we've said to each other that danger exists not only out there [on the battlefronts] but here at home as well, sometimes rather less so, sometimes rather more. What man of today has the right to shun it and shrink from it? And what woman of today should not share it, however gladly the man would relieve her of that burden? And how indescribably happy it makes the man if the woman he loves stands by him with courage, patience, and above all—prayer. Dear, good Maria, I'm not being fanciful—something to which I'm far from prone—when I tell you that your presence-in-spirit has been a manifest help to me in recent weeks. That I should have caused you distress, however, genuinely saddens me a great deal. So now please be calm and confident and happy again, and think of me as you have hitherto and as I so constantly think of you.

Two weeks later Bonhoeffer wrote again, telling her about his hospital visit with her grandmother. She didn't seem to be doing well, and Bonhoeffer knew she continued to be troubled over the "memories of last winter's difficulties—which we, of course, have put far behind us." He thought a letter from Maria would put her at ease. In fact, she had been planning to visit her grandmother, and wrote Bonhoeffer on March 26, telling him so. She also had good news. She had been "temporarily exempted" from the *Reichsarbeitsdienst*, a national program that put unmarried young women into a kind of military service. Maria had dreaded this and was happy to work as a nurse instead. When a year later the threat again reared its head, Bonhoeffer's father hired Maria to work for him as his secretary at the Bonhoeffer home. Renate's marriage to Bethge was also sped up so she could avoid the odious military service.

Just ten days after this letter, Maria sensed something was wrong. In her diary on April 5, she wrote Dietrich again. "Has something bad happened?" she asked. "I'm afraid it's something very bad." She had no idea that he had been arrested that day, but she felt a deep foreboding and recorded it in her diary. She had no communication with Bonhoeffer or his family during this time.

On April 18 she was in Pätzig for the confirmation of her younger brother Hans-Werner. By then her feelings about her situation had boiled over, and she had resolved to defy her mother's insistence that she and Bonhoeffer not see each other. She said as much to her brother-in-law Klaus von Bismarck that day. But a short time after she had done so, she and the Bismarcks returned to the manor house where they spoke with her uncle Hans-Jürgen von Kleist. He knew about Bonhoeffer's arrest and told them of it. It was the first Maria had heard.

Now it was too late to see Bonhoeffer. For the rest of her life, Maria regretted not having defied her mother's wishes earlier. Her mother came to regret her actions on this score and reproached herself, and Maria took pains to forgive her.

First Days at Tegel

The Gestapo had been gathering information on their rivals in the Abwehr for a long time. They had wanted nothing more than to bring this rogue organization to heel. But Canaris was so canny, and Oster and Dohnanyi had been so careful, that it was nearly impossible to get to the bottom of what they were up to. Still, the Gestapo had a feeling the Abwehr was a bastion of intrigues and perhaps even conspiracy against the Reich, and in their thorough way, the Gestapo uncovered what they could until they had enough information to make their arrests. Then they would strike.

On the day Bonhoeffer was arrested, they also arrested Dohnanyi and Joseph Müller, who were taken to the Wehrmacht prison on the Lehrter Strasse for ranking officers. Bonhoeffer's sister Christine was arrested, too, as was Müller's wife. Both were taken to the women's prison in Charlottenburg. Bonhoeffer alone had been taken to Tegel military prison.

Months later, Bonhoeffer wrote an account of his first days there:

> The formalities of admission were correctly completed. For the first night I was locked up in an admission cell. The blankets on the camp bed had such a foul smell that in spite of the cold it was impossible to use them. Next morning a piece of bread was thrown into my cell; I had to pick it up from the floor. A quarter of the coffee consisted of grounds. The sound of the prison staff's vile abuse of the prisoners who were held for investigation penetrated into my cell for the first time; since then I have heard it every day from morning till night. When I had to parade with the other new arrivals, we were addressed by one of the jailers as "scoundrels," etc. etc. We were all asked why we had been arrested, and when I said I did not know the jailer answered with a scornful laugh, "You'll find that out soon enough." It was six months before I got a warrant for my arrest. As we went through the various offices, some NCOs, who had heard what my profession was, wanted now and then to have a few words with me. . . . I was taken to the most isolated cell on the top floor; a notice, prohibiting all access without special permission, was put outside it. I was told that all my correspondence would be stopped until further notice and that, unlike all the other prisoners, I should not be allowed half an hour a day in the open air, although, according to the prison rules, I was entitled to it. I received neither newspapers nor anything to smoke. After forty-eight hours my Bible was returned to me; it had been searched to see whether I had smuggled inside it a saw, razor blades, or the like. For the next twelve days the cell door was

opened only for bringing food in and putting the bucket out. No one said a word to me. I was told nothing about the reason for my detention, or how long it would last. I gathered from various remarks—and it was confirmed later—that I was lodged in the section for the most serious cases, where the condemned prisoners lay shackled.

For the first twelve days Bonhoeffer was treated as a felon. The cells around him held men condemned to death, one of whom wept through Bonhoeffer's first night, making sleep impossible. On the cell wall Bonhoeffer read the wry graffito of a previous occupant: "In a hundred years it'll all be over." But from this bleakest nadir things would improve over the weeks and months. The bulk of the eighteen months that Bonhoeffer would spend at Tegel were nothing like these first days.

But there was one way in which they were identical. From the beginning of his time until the end, Bonhoeffer maintained the daily discipline of scriptural meditation and prayer he had been practicing for more than a decade. Each morning he meditated for at least half an hour on a verse of Scripture. And he interceded for his friends and relatives, and for his brothers in the Confessing Church who were on the front lines or in concentration camps. Once he got his Bible back he read it for hours each day. By November he had read through the Old Testament two and a half times. He also drew strength from praying the Psalms, just as they had done at Zingst, Finkenwalde, Schlawe, Sigurdshof, and elsewhere. Bonhoeffer once told Bethge, who was about to embark on a trip, that it was all the more important to practice the daily disciplines when away, to give oneself a sense of grounding and continuity and clarity. And now, rudely thrust into an atmosphere intensely different from his parents' home, he practiced these same disciplines.

He was at first on the prison's uppermost floor, the fourth, but was soon transferred to the third, to "a cell looking south with a sweeping view across the prison yard to the pine forest." This seven-by-ten cell, number ninety-two, was immortalized in the book *Love Letters from Cell 92.** It featured a plank bed, a bench along one wall, a stool, a necessary bucket, a wooden door with

---

* The editor of these extraordinary letters is Maria's sister, Ruth-Alice von Bismarck. Before her premature death from cancer in 1977, Maria gave her sister permission to publish the letters, which tell the story of her relationship with Dietrich Bonhoeffer and give context and background not found elsewhere.

a tiny circular window through which the guards might observe him, and a not-so-small window above his head providing daylight and fresh air. It might have been worse. Bonhoeffer's family lived seven miles south and visited often, providing him with food, clothing, books, and other things. In the postscript to his first letter home, nine days after arriving, Bonhoeffer asked for "slippers, bootlaces (black, long), shoe polish, writing paper and envelopes, ink, smoker's card, shaving cream, sewing things and a suit I can change into."

Bonhoeffer had lived simply before. For three months at Ettal he had lived in a monk's cell, and he had been on the move over the last years. Even his room at 43 Marienburgerallee was furnished in a spartan way.

And his situation would improve on all counts. At first he had to adhere to the strict one-letter-every-ten-days rule, and these letters could be only one page. This chafed at him terribly. But Bonhoeffer quickly ingratiated himself with a number of the guards, who were able to sneak other letters out for him. The happy result was a gushing torrent of epistolary activity far beyond the few "official" letters he wrote on the ten-day cycle. Between November 1943 and August 1944, Bonhoeffer wrote two hundred very crowded pages to his friend Eberhard Bethge alone. He didn't have his piano, but in time he would have many books and papers. His parents would send small gifts of all kinds, including flowers for his birthday, as would Maria. She even brought him a huge Christmas tree in December, though it was too large to put in his cell and remained in the guards' room. She brought him an Advent wreath instead. He would post favorite works of art around, and would have his tobacco.

But Bonhoeffer's outlook did not depend on these amenities. His first letter home painted a picture of his attitude:

> Dear Parents! I do want you to be quite sure that I'm all right.* I'm sorry
> that I was not allowed to write to you sooner, but I was all right during
> the first ten days too. Strangely enough, the discomforts that one gener-
> ally associates with prison life, the physical hardships, hardly bother me
> at all. One can even have enough to eat in the mornings with dry bread
> (I get a variety of extras too). The hard prison bed does not worry me

---

* The English translation in *Letters & Papers from Prison* is much less emphatic than what the German sentence indicates. The German "Vor allem . . . dir wissen und auch wirklich glauben, das es mir gut geht" is better translated, "Above all, I want you to know and also to really believe that I am doing well."

a bit, and one can get plenty of sleep between 8 p.m. and 6 a.m. I have been particularly surprised that I have hardly felt any need at all for cigarettes since I came here; but I think that in all this the psychic factor has played the larger part. A violent mental upheaval such as is produced by a sudden arrest brings with it the need to take one's mental bearings and come to terms with an entirely new situation—all this means that physical things take a back seat and lose their importance, and it is something that I find to be a real enrichment of my experience. I am not so unused to being alone as other people are, and it is certainly a good spiritual Turkish bath. The only thing that bothers me or would bother me is the thought that you are being tormented by anxiety about me, and are not sleeping or eating properly. Forgive me for causing you so much worry, but I think a hostile fate is more to blame than I am. To set off against that, it is good to read Paul Gerhardt's hymns and learn them by heart, as I am doing now. Besides that, I have my Bible and some reading matter from the library here, and enough writing paper now.

You can imagine that I'm most particularly anxious about my fiancée at the moment. It's a great deal for her to bear, especially when she has only recently lost her father and brother in the East. As the daughter of an officer, she will perhaps find my imprisonment especially hard to take. If only I could have a few words with her! Now you will have to do it. Perhaps she will come to you in Berlin. That would be fine.

The seventy-fifth birthday celebrations were a fortnight ago today. It was a splendid day. I can still hear the chorale that we sang in the morning and evening, with all the voices and instruments: "Praise to the Lord, the Almighty, the King of Creation. . . . Shelters thee under his wings, yea, and gently sustaineth." That is true, and it is what we must always rely on.

Spring is really coming now. You will have plenty to do in the garden; I hope that Renate's wedding preparations are going well. Here in the prison yard there is a thrush which sings beautifully in the morning, and now in the evening too. One is grateful for little things, and that is surely a gain. Good-bye for now.

I'm thinking of you and the rest of the family and my friends with gratitude and love,

your Dietrich.

Bonhoeffer's upbringing made it certain that he would not allow himself self-pity; he was repulsed by it in others and would not tolerate it in himself. His parents knew that he would be brave and strong, which gave them great comfort. All their children were like that and would be so to the very end. This was on display in Walter's final letter in 1918, downplaying his suffering and expressing concern for his fellow soldiers.* So what Bonhoeffer wrote now was written to put them at ease. But this letter and many of the letters he wrote were read by Manfred Roeder, the man prosecuting him. Bonhoeffer was writing on two levels: on one level to his parents, but on another to the hostile set of eyes trolling for incriminating evidence. But he was not merely trying to avoid saying anything incriminating: he was also using this and other letters to paint a particular picture for Roeder. He wanted to give Roeder a general framework in which to interpret things Bonhoeffer said during his interrogations. Even in an innocuous and truthful letter such as this first one, Bonhoeffer simultaneously engaged in a larger deception.

Why exactly had he been arrested in the first place? Bonhoeffer would be executed for his involvement in the plot to kill Hitler, but he was not arrested for that reason. In April 1943 the Nazis didn't have any inkling of Bonhoeffer's involvement in the conspiracy, or that there was a conspiracy at all. The conspiracy would remain hidden until the failed Stauffenberg bomb plot more than a year later. For the next fifteen months, his imprisonment, and Dohnanyi's, was for more innocuous reasons. One centered on Operation 7, which the Gestapo took for a money-laundering scheme. They couldn't fathom that Bonhoeffer and the others were mostly concerned with the fate of the Jews. Another reason had to do with the Abwehr's attempts to obtain military exceptions for the pastors of the Confessing Church. So Bonhoeffer was arrested for relatively minor reasons. In a way, he was arrested for his relationship with Dohnanyi more than anything else.

Because Bonhoeffer and the others knew the Nazis were ignorant of the conspiracy, they continued their multilevel game of deception. The conspiracy was ongoing while they were behind bars, and they knew that any moment Hitler would probably be assassinated and they would be set free. So they must do all they could to keep the conspiracy from being discovered. They must say nothing to tip off the Gestapo to anything besides

---

* See page 27.

what the Gestapo already knew, which was not much. They would pretend to be innocent of the charges leveled against them, and would pretend that there was nothing else worth looking into beyond those charges. And they would succeed.

Strategy

As part of their larger ruse, Dohnanyi and Bonhoeffer wanted to preserve the fiction that Bonhoeffer was an innocent pastor who knew little or nothing of the larger issues. This way, all of the focus would be on Dohnanyi, whose brilliant legal mind and greater knowledge of intricate details could better parry Roeder's attacks. To that end, Dohnanyi wrote a letter to Bonhoeffer at Easter, instead of to his parents, because he knew the letter would be read by Roeder, and he wished to shape things in Roeder's eyes. That letter, written on Good Friday, April 23, reads:

> My dear Dietrich, I don't know if I'll be allowed to send you this greeting, but I'll try. The bells are ringing outside for the service. . . . You can't imagine how unhappy I am to be the reason why you, Christel, the children, and my parents should have to suffer like this, and that my dear wife and you should have your freedom taken away. *Socios babuisse malorum** may be a comfort, but the *babere*** is a terribly heavy burden. . . . If I knew that you all—and you personally—did not think hardly of me, I'd feel so relieved. What wouldn't I give to know that you were all free again; what wouldn't I take on myself if you could be spared this affliction.

One reason the Bonhoeffer family could function as such a hotbed of sedition was their formidable intelligence, and their ability to comfortably communicate on several levels at once, with the confidence of being understood as they did so. Now, Bonhoeffer could write letters home and Dohnanyi could write the above letter to Bonhoeffer knowing that what they wrote would be read and understood on two levels. Bonhoeffer knew

---

* "To have company in distress," from the aphorism "Misery loves company."
** "Having (company)."

his parents would know what he wrote to them was written, in part, to fool Roeder—and he trusted them to be able to tease out what was meant for them and what was meant for Roeder. To some extent they had been functioning like this for years, since anything one said in the Third Reich might be overheard by the wrong party, but now they would hone it to a sharpness that allowed them to run circles around those who opposed them.

They had also worked out ahead of time how to communicate if any of them was imprisoned, and they now used these methods. One involved putting coded messages in the books they were allowed to receive. Bonhoeffer got many books from his parents and would send them back when he was finished with them. To indicate there was a coded message in the book, they underlined the name of the book's owner on the flyleaf or inside cover. If *D. Bonhoeffer* was underlined, the receiver knew there was a message. The message itself was communicated through a series of the tiniest pencil marks under letters on pages in the book. Every three or every ten pages—the number seemed to vary—a barely visible pencil dot would be put under a letter on that page. Ten pages later another letter would be marked with a dot. These marks would begin at the back of the book and proceed toward the front, so in the course of a three-hundred-page book one might have room for a thirty-letter communication. These were usually extremely important and dangerous messages, such as what Dohnanyi had communicated to his interrogator, so that Bonhoeffer could corroborate that information and not get tripped up or caught contradicting something Dohnanyi said. One message was "O. now officially acknowledges the Rome coding card." In this case, "O" referred to Oster. The prosecutor, Roeder, thought that the coding card indicated a greater crime, but eventually it was shown to be part of the standard Abwehr secrecy for official purposes. Another one of the coded book messages was: "I'm not certain that the letter with Hans's corrections has been found, but think so." It could all get a bit baroque, but the Bonhoeffers were up to it.

Renate Bethge recalled that she and the other younger ones often had the task of looking for the barely visible pencil markings since younger eyes were much better at seeing them. They would even use a pencil eraser to see whether the marks had been made with a pencil or were merely tiny irregularities in the actual printing of the book. Christopher von Dohnanyi recalled another way they were able to slip messages past the Nazis: "You could take a glass for jam or marmalade . . . there was a double lid. The lid had a double cardboard. Between this cardboard and the metal, my mother and we would cut little rounds, and there we would write the most dangerous things!" Hans von Dohnanyi wrote entire letters in miniature script on this secret circular stationery.

Throughout his eighteen months at Tegel, Bonhoeffer's basic pose of the simple and idealistic pastor unconcerned with political issues worked well. He played dumb brilliantly, both in the interrogations and in the often long letters that he wrote to Roeder: "I am the last person to deny that I might have made mistakes in work so strange, so new and so complicated as that of the *Abwehr*. I often find it hard to follow the speed of your questions, probably because I am not used to them." He acted the archetypical Lutheran pastor of that time, an unworldly ecclesiastical naïf who knew little of high-level intrigue; the sophisticated jurisprudential supergenius Dohnanyi knew everything important: "It was my brother-in-law who suggested to me that with my church connections, I should enter the service of the *Abwehr*. Despite considerable inner scruples, I took advantage of his offer because it provided me with the war work that I had wanted ever since the beginning of hostilities, even making use of my ability as a theologian."

He danced out on a limb, pretending that working for the Abwehr assuaged his hurt over the Gestapo's accusations, which had led to his being banned from preaching and writing:

> This had meant a great inner release, since I saw it as a welcome opportunity of rehabilitating myself in the eyes of the state authorities, which I was anxious to do in view of the offensive and, to me, completely unjustified charge against me. The knowledge that I was being used by a military department was, therefore, to me personally of great importance. I made a great sacrifice for this chance of rehabilitation and for my work in the service of the Reich, namely the offering of all my ecumenical connections for military use.

Bonhoeffer always pretended to have the typical Lutheran attitude toward state authorities, which came from a simplistic understanding of Romans 13. He feigned disbelief and umbrage at the very insinuation that he would question the state:

I cannot believe that this is the charge that is really leveled against me. Would I, in that case, have turned to an old officers' family, all of whose fathers and sons have been in the field since the beginning of the war, many of them winning the highest decorations and making the greatest sacrifice of life and limb, to find my future wife, who has herself lost both her father and her brother at the front? Would I, in that case, have abandoned all the commitments that I had undertaken in America and returned to Germany before the outbreak of war, where I naturally would expect to be called up at once? Would I, in that case, have volunteered as an army chaplain immediately after the war broke out?

Little did these theologically ignorant Nazis know that the man with whom they were dealing had worked out a theological defense of deception against the likes of them. In some ways he was their worst nightmare. He was not a "worldly" or "compromised" pastor, but a pastor whose very devotion to God depended on his deceiving the evil powers ranged against him. He was serving God by taking them all for a long ride.

"After Ten Years"

Bonhoeffer had written an essay a few months before his arrest, titled "After Ten Years: A Reckoning Made at New Year 1943." At Christmas 1942, he gave copies to Bethge, Dohnanyi, and Hans Oster, and he hid a fourth copy in the ceiling of his attic room. The essay is an assessment of what they had been through and learned in the extraordinary experiences of the ten years since Hitler's ascension, and it helps us see more of the thinking that led him and all of them to the extraordinary measures they had been taking and would continue to take against the Nazi regime. And it confirms Bonhoeffer's crucial role in the conspiracy, that of its theologian and moral compass. He helped them see precisely why they had to do what they were doing; why it was not expedient, but right; why it was God's will.

He opened by framing things:

One may ask whether there have ever before in human history been people with so little ground under their feet—people to whom every available alternative seemed equally intolerable, repugnant, and futile, who looked beyond all these existing alternatives for the source of their strength so entirely in the past or in the future, and who yet, without being dreamers, were able to await the success of their cause so quietly and confidently. . . .

The great masquerade of evil has played havoc with all our ethical concepts. For evil to appear disguised as light, charity, historical neces- sity, or social justice is quite bewildering to anyone brought up on our traditional ethical concepts, while for the Christian who bases his life on the Bible it merely confirms the fundamental wickedness of evil.

Then he dismissed the standard responses to what they were up against and showed why each would fail. "Who stands fast?" he asked. "Only the man whose final standard is not his reason, his principles, his conscience, his freedom, or his virtue, but who is ready to sacrifice all this when he is called to obedient and responsible action in faith and in exclusive allegiance to God—the responsible man, who tries to make his whole life an answer to the question and call of God."

This was how Bonhoeffer saw what he was doing. He had theologically redefined the Christian life as something active, not reactive. It had nothing to do with avoiding sin or with merely talking or teaching or believing theologi- cal notions or principles or rules or tenets. It had everything to do with living one's whole life in obedience to God's call through action. It did not merely require a mind, but a body too. It was God's call to be fully human, to live as human beings obedient to the one who had made us, which was the fulfillment of our destiny. It was not a cramped, compromised, circumspect life, but a life lived in a kind of wild, joyful, full-throated freedom—that was what it was to obey God. Whether Dohnanyi or Oster understood all of this as Bethge would have is doubtful, but they were brilliant men who surely understood enough of it to seek Bonhoeffer's counsel and participation in what they were doing.

Bonhoeffer talked about how the German penchant for self-sacrifice and submission to authority had been used for evil ends by the Nazis; only a deep understanding of and commitment to the God of the Bible could stand up to such wickedness. "It depends on a God who demands responsible action in a bold venture of faith," he wrote, "and who promises forgiveness and consola- tion to the man who becomes a sinner in that venture." Here was the rub: one must be more zealous to please God than to avoid sin. One must sacrifice oneself utterly to God's purposes, even to the point of possibly making moral mistakes. One's obedience to God must be forward-oriented and zealous and free, and to be a mere moralist or pietist would make such a life impossible:

> If we want to be Christians, we must have some share in Christ's large-heartedness by acting with responsibility and in freedom when the hour of danger comes, and by showing a real sympathy that springs, not from fear, but from the liberating and redeeming love of Christ for all who suffer. Mere waiting and looking on is not Christian behaviour. The Christian is called to sympathy and action, not in the first place by his own sufferings, but by the sufferings of his brethren, for whose sake Christ suffered.

Bonhoeffer spoke of death too:

> In recent years we have become increasingly familiar with the thought of death. We surprise ourselves by the calmness with which we hear of the death of one of our contemporaries. We cannot hate it as we used to for we have discovered some good in it, and have almost come to terms with it. Fundamentally we feel that we really belong to death already, and that every new day is a miracle. It would probably not be true to say that we welcome death (although we all know that weariness which we ought to avoid like the plague); we are too inquisitive for that—or, to put it more seriously, we should like to see something more of the meaning of our life's broken fragments. . . . We still love life, but I do not think that death can take us by surprise now. After what we have been through during the war, we hardly dare admit that we should like death to come to us, not accidentally and suddenly through some trivial cause, but in the fullness of life and with everything at stake. It is we ourselves, and not outward circumstances, who make death what it can be, a death freely and voluntarily accepted.

Life at Tegel

As the head of the Abwehr, Admiral Canaris did all he could to provide cover for Dohnanyi and Bonhoeffer. This would change in February 1944 when he was finally bested by the Gestapo and Himmler and ousted. But during the first ten months at Tegel, Bonhoeffer and Donhanyi were confident of Canaris's protection.

Bonhoeffer had a further advantage at Tegel, and a very significant one. His uncle Paul von Hase was the military commandant of Berlin and therefore was the big boss, high above the top warden at Tegel prison. When the guards at Tegel learned of this, everything changed. It can hardly have been imagined. Von Hase's nephew was a prisoner! It was as if they had a celebrity in their midst. And not only because of his uncle, but because of the great mystery that attended Bonhoeffer's imprisonment. He was a pastor and quite clearly an enemy of the Nazi state. Many of them were quietly against the Nazis, too, so there grew an undeniable fascination with Bonhoeffer. And as they got to know him, they found him genuinely kind and generous— quite shockingly so, for many of them—even to those guards whom others despised. He was a genuinely good man, a living rebuke to the forces that oppressed them and over which they had little power.

Bonhoeffer was soon given privileges in the prison, sometimes because of who his uncle was, but more often because others in the unpleasant environment found him to be a source of comfort to them and wanted him around. They wished to speak with him, to tell him their problems, to confess things to him, and simply to be near him. He counseled some condemned prisoners and some guards too. One of them, Knoblauch, became so enamored of Bonhoeffer that he eventually went to great lengths to help him escape, as we shall see. Bonhoeffer was also allowed time alone in his cell with others, contrary to explicit orders. And he was allowed to spend a time in the sick bay where he functioned much like a prison pastor instead of a prisoner. In general, Bonhoeffer spent quite a bit of time working pastorally at Tegel, so much so that he sometimes even felt he was taking too much time away from his own writing and reading.

The only Christmas that Bonhoeffer spent at Tegel was in 1943. Harald Poelchau, one of the official prison pastors, asked him to help write a sheet that would be distributed to the prisoners. On it Bonhoeffer wrote a number of prayers, including the following:

> O God,
> Early in the morning do I cry unto thee.

Help me to pray,
And to think only of thee.
I cannot pray alone.
In me there is darkness,
But with thee there is light.
I am lonely, but thou leavest me not.
I am feeble in heart, but thou leavest me not.
I am restless, but with thee there is peace.
In me there is bitterness, but with thee there is patience;
Thy ways are past understanding, but
Thou knowest the way for me.

Poelchau remembered Bonhoeffer's courtliness, even in prison:

One day he asked me to have a cup of coffee with him. . . . [H]e told me of his neighbour in the next door cell, an English officer, who had invited both of us if I could risk locking him in the other cell. We slipped across at a propitious moment, and had a little party, with a primus stove propped up in the heap of sand which was in a corner of each cell for use during air raids. We had coffee, white bread which had been saved for the occasion, and we had talk, both serious and gay, which helped us to forget the war.

Bonhoeffer's noble bearing and generosity were noted by many, even up until his last day. At Tegel he used his own money to pay for legal help for a young prisoner who couldn't afford it; another time he imposed upon his own defense lawyer by asking him to take the case of a fellow prisoner.

When in the summer of 1943 he was offered a cooler cell on the second floor of the prison, he refused it, knowing that his own cell would only be given to someone else. And he knew that much of his better treatment was because of who his uncle was. He wrote that when the prison authorities found out who his uncle was, "it was most embarrassing to see how everything changed from that moment." He was immediately offered larger food portions, but refused them, knowing it would have been at the expense of other prisoners. Bonhoeffer was sometimes grateful for the small mercies of the preferential treatment and sometimes disgusted by it. Some of the prison staff actually apologized to him after they found out who his uncle was. "It was painful," he wrote.

Bonhoeffer was outraged by injustice, and the way many of the senior guards abused prisoners infuriated him, but he used his position to speak out for those who had no power. At one point he even wrote a report on prison life, intending to draw the authorities' attention to those things that needed improving. He knew his position as von Hase's nephew would bring some attention to these problems, so he gave chapter and verse of the injustices he observed, being the voice for the voiceless just as he had always preached those in the church must do.

Maria von Wedemeyer

Bonhoeffer's relationship with Maria was a source of strength and hope for him now. When she learned of his arrest, Bonhoeffer's future mother-in-law was moved to allow the engagement to be made public. He was very grateful for this kindness. It gave him and Maria more hope that their future together was a reality, soon to come. They had been expecting to have to keep mum about it, even to the family, until the official "year" was up, which meant November. Everyone was convinced Bonhoeffer would be released quite soon, once Roeder got his questions answered and things generally cleared up, and so the marriage would take place soon too. Bonhoeffer could not write Maria during his first two months at Tegel, so he wrote her through his parents, who passed along the salient parts of his letters.

In the meantime, on May 23, she visited his parents in Berlin, where she was received as Dietrich's fiancée. Maria even spent a long time alone in Bonhoeffer's room. She wrote him the next day from Hanover:

> My dear, dear Dietrich,
> You thought of me yesterday, didn't you? I sense how constantly you were at my side, how you went with me through all those unfamiliar rooms to meet all those people, and how everything suddenly seemed familiar, homely, and very dear. I'm so happy about that day in Berlin, Dietrich—so inexpressibly happy and grateful to you and your parents. I think my happiness is so deeply, firmly rooted that sorrow simply can't reach that far, however immense it may sometimes seem.

I like your parents. The moment your mother greeted me I knew I couldn't fail to, and that you're giving me infinitely more than I ever dreamed. Oh, I fell in love with everything. Your house, the garden, and—most of all—your room. I don't know what I wouldn't give to be able to sit there again, if only to look at the ink-blots on your desk pad. Everything has become so real and clear to me since I met you at your parents' home yesterday. The desk where you wrote your books and your letters to me, your armchair and the ashtray, your shoes on the shelf and your favorite pictures. . . . I never thought I could miss you and long for you more than I do, but I've done so twice as much since yesterday.

. . . My dearest Dietrich, every morning at six, when we both fold our hands in prayer, we know that we can have great faith, not only in each other but far, far above and beyond that. And then you can't be sad any more either, can you? I'll write again soon.

Whatever I think or do, I'm always
Your Maria

In her next letter, on May 30, she marveled that it was a year since their fateful meeting at Klein-Krössin: "So it's really a year ago already. Just imagine, I find it almost incomprehensible that you should be the gentleman who I met at that time, and with who I discussed first names, *Lili-Marlen*,* daisies, and other matters. Grandmother told me what you remembered about it, and I blushed with retrospective horror at all the silly things I said."

At the beginning of June, Roeder granted Bonhoeffer permission to write Maria. After his first letter, she wrote the following:

June 9, 1943
Dearest Dietrich,
You wrote such a lovely letter . . . the very fact that I can expect another one like it in ten days' time puts me in an incredibly good mood. But when I read it I become almost too happy, and I suddenly think I'll have to awaken from this dream and realize that none of it is true, and laugh at myself for ever having dared to presume such

---

* A popular song of the era, especially among the troops. The German military broadcasting station ended with it each night.

happiness. So you see, my happiness is still so much greater than my sadness—you really must believe that. It won't be long before we see each other again, I'm quite certain, and I say that to you and myself night and morning. . . .

You say you want to hear some wedding plans? I've got more than enough. We must become officially engaged as soon as we're together again. Very few of my family are in the know yet. . . . You won't get away without an engagement party, but we'll marry soon after that. I'd like it to be in summer, when Pätzig looks its best. I've always looked forward so much to showing you Pätzig in August especially. What you've seen of it up to now doesn't count. I'd pictured that August in every detail. How I would meet your train, how I would go for walks with you and show you all my favorite places, views, trees and animals, and how much you would like them too, and then we would have a common home there. Don't be depressed and miserable. Think how happy we'll be later on, and tell yourself that perhaps all this had to happen for us to realize how lovely our life will be and how grateful for it we must be. . . . You must start choosing the hymns and texts right away. I'd like "Sollt ich meinem Gott nicht singen"* and the 103rd Psalm. . . . Please fit them in. As for the rest I'm open to persuasion and suggestion. You know Pätzig church, of course. . . .

We'll have a honeymoon, too! Where? And what then? Then, what matters most is that we're happy, the two of us. Nothing else will count for much, will it?

I've requested a transfer to the Augusta Hospital in Berlin, and am now waiting to be posted there. It could happen with the next few days. Being near you would be so much nicer, and I look forward to being able to visit your parents more often. Think how wonderful it will be when you're free again.

My dear Dietrich, if only I could relieve you of even a little of your burden. There's nothing I wouldn't give for a chance to do so. I'm with you every moment, yet so terribly far away, and I long so inexpressibly much to be with you in reality. You know, don't you, that I'm always

Your Maria

---

* "Shall I not praise my God?"

Maria obtained a visitor's permit for June 24, although Bonhoeffer did not know she would be coming. It would be the first of seventeen visits. Sixteen of them were between that date and June 27 of the following year, 1944.* The last visit was on August 23, 1944, one month after the July 20 assassination attempt. But on that June day in 1943, when Maria first came to see Dietrich, their hopes for an early trial and release were very much alive, and they were constantly thinking about their upcoming marriage.

The visits were always somewhat awkward since they were never alone but were chaperoned, as it were, by Roeder. In fact, in their first meeting on June 24, Roeder surprised Bonhoeffer by bringing Maria into the room. Bonhoeffer was quite nonplussed. What did it mean that she was there? It was a despicable tactic. "I found myself being used as a tool by the prosecutor, Roeder," Maria wrote years later. "I was brought into the room with practically no forewarning, and Dietrich was visibly shaken. He first reacted with silence, but then carried on a normal conversation; his emotions showed only in the pressure with which he held my hand."

When their time together was over, Roeder took Maria in one direction, while Bonhoeffer had to leave by another door. They hadn't seen each other since November. Now they'd been given these precious moments, and suddenly the visit was over. But just as Maria was about to leave the room, she manifested the independent spirit and strong will for which she was famous: when she looked back and saw her beloved Dietrich leaving through the door across the room, she impetuously, and obviously against the wishes of Roeder, ran back across the room and hugged her fiancée one last time.

When Bonhoeffer returned to his cell, he continued the letter he had been writing to his parents:

> I have just come back from seeing Maria—an indescribable surprise and joy! I had learned of it only a minute before. It's still like a dream— really an almost unimaginable situation—what will we think of it one day? What one can say at such a time is so trivial, but that's not the main thing. It was so brave of her to come; I wouldn't have dared to suggest it to her. It's so much more difficult for her than for me. I know where I

---

* In 1943, Maria visited Bonhoeffer on June 24, July 30, August 26, October 7, November 10 and 26, and December 10 and 22. In 1944, she visited him on January 1 and 24, February 4 (his birthday), March 30, April 18 and 25, May 22, June 27, and August 23.

am, but for her it is all unimaginable, mysterious, terrifying. Think how things will be when this nightmare is over!

Maria's early letters were full of ideas and plans for their wedding. She wrote that she'd started work on her trousseau, and with one letter she included a picture she had drawn of all the furniture in her room so that they could figure out how to furnish their new home together. She also told him that her grandmother had decided to give them her "blue sofa from Stettin, plus armchairs and table." She wondered which pastor should perform their wedding and confessed to Bonhoeffer that the previous September, before either of them knew what the next months would bring and she thought of him principally as a pastor, she had written in her diary that she'd like *him* to perform her wedding. "What a shame that's impossible!!!" she said.

Maria continued the conceit of writing to Bonhoeffer in her diary. After their second meeting, on July 30, she wrote:

I was sitting on the red plush sofa when you came in. Seeing you like that, I very nearly called you *"Sie."** A well-fitting dark suit, a formal bow to the *Oberst Gerichtsrat*** . . . strangely unfamiliar.

But when I looked into your eyes I saw that dear, dark light in them, and when you kissed me, I knew I'd found you again—found you more completely than I'd ever possessed you before.

It was all so different from the first time. You were calmer and more relaxed. But more confident, too. I sensed that most of all, and it was that which descended on my sad, dispirited heart and made me cheerful and happy. The things one talks about at such times! . . . car-driving, the weather, the family.*** And yet it meant so much and outweighed the intervening month of loneliness. You caught hold of me at one point. Although I was inwardly so calm, I was shivering. It felt so good, your warm hand, that I wished you would leave it there, although it transmitted a current that filled me up and left no room for thoughts.

---

* In German, *Sie* is the formal and polite mode of address, and *du* is the informal mode, saved for close friends and family members.

** Judge Advocate of colonel's rank; in this case, Roeder.

*** Most of their discussions were overheard by Roeder, who sat nearby.

About this time Bonhoeffer's writing privileges were extended to a letter every four days instead of every ten. He decided he would alternate letters between his parents and Maria. Because all letters were censored, they sometimes took ten days to reach the recipient, even though, in the case of his parents, the letter had less than seven miles to travel from his cell to their home. Bonhoeffer and Maria often wrote to each other immediately after a visit. They didn't want to write too close to an upcoming visit, since they then risked seeing each other before the letter arrived.

After this second visit, on July 30, Maria wrote Bonhoeffer that on the train back to Pätzig, she had run into her uncle Gerhard Tresckow. He was the brother of Henning von Tresckow, who was central to the two major assassination attempts on Hitler. Maria told Bonhoeffer that even though her uncle was "not in the know" about her engagement, he reminded her that when she was twelve, she had invited him to her wedding, and he said he was "determined not to miss it."

She also continued planning their future together, saying that the blue sofa from her grandmother "will go better in your room," since it would fit right in with theological discussions, bookshelves, and cigarette smoke. And the grand piano "will go in the living room." Their letters to each other were playful and filled with declarations of love. That August, Bonhoeffer wrote, "You can't possibly imagine what it means to me, in my present predicament, to have you. I'm under God's special guidance here. I feel sure. To me, the way in which we found each other such a short time before my arrest seems a definite indication of that. Once again, things went 'hominum confusione et dei providentia.'"*

In this letter Bonhoeffer wrote his famous line about their marriage being a "'yes' to God's earth." His very engagement was his way of living out what he believed. He did everything, including become engaged to Maria, "unto God." It was not a calculation, but an act of faith:

> When I consider the state of the world, the total obscurity enshrouding our personal destiny, and my present imprisonment, our union—if it wasn't frivolity, which it certainly wasn't—can only be a token of God's grace and goodness, which summon us to believe in him. We would have

---

* According to man's confusion and God's providence.

to be blind not to see that. When Jeremiah said, in his people's hour of direst need, that "houses and fields [and vineyards] shall again be bought in this land,"* it was a token of confidence in the future. That requires faith, and may God grant it to us daily. I don't mean the faith that flees the world, but the faith that endures *in* the world and loves and remains true to that world in spite of all the hardships it brings us. Our marriage must be a "yes" to God's earth. It must strengthen our resolve to do and accomplish something on earth. I fear that Christians who venture to stand on earth on only one leg will stand in heaven on only one leg too.

A Wedding Sermon from a Prison Cell

Bonhoeffer was not the only member of the family engaged to be married. His sixteen-year-old niece, Renate, was on the verge of marrying his best friend, Eberhard. If they didn't marry soon, she would be called up to serve in the *Reichsarbeitsdienst*. The thought of military conscription under the Hitler regime was far more odious to the Schleichers than that their daughter should marry her beloved Eberhard a year or two too soon. The date was set for May 15. Bonhoeffer had hoped to preach at this wedding, but even the earliest hopes of release would not be soon enough. He wrote a sermon nonetheless. It did not get to them in time to be read at the wedding, but like so much else that he wrote, this sermon found an audience far greater than he could have hoped. It has become a small classic, read by many on their anniversaries.

As in his letter to Maria, in which he described their marriage as a "'yes' to God's earth," he affirmed God's role in Bethge's upcoming wedding by affirming the couple's own role in it. He knew that to celebrate God aright, one must fully understand and celebrate humanity itself. Bonhoeffer was constantly trying to correct the idea of a false choice between God and humanity, or heaven and earth. God wanted to redeem humanity and to redeem this earth, not to abolish them. As he often did to be as clear as possible, he almost overstated his point:

We ought not to be in too much of a hurry here to speak piously of God's will and guidance. It is obvious, and it should not be ignored, that

---

* Jeremiah 32:15.

it is your own very human wills that are at work here, celebrating their triumph; the course that you are taking at the outset is one that you have chosen for yourselves; what you have done and are doing is not, in the first place, something religious, but something quite secular. . . . Unless you can boldly say today: "This is *our* resolve, *our* love, *our* way," you are taking refuge in a false piety. "Iron and steel may pass away, but our love shall abide for ever." That desire for earthly bliss which you want to find in one another, and in which, to quote the medieval song, one is the comfort of the other both in today and in soul—that desire is justified before God and man.

Bonhoeffer was trying to reclaim everything for God, just as he had been doing for twenty years. He was saying that it's not just some "religious" part of this marriage that is important, but the whole thing. The freedom to choose a mate is a gift from God, who created us in his image. And the "desire for earthly bliss" is not something we steal from behind God's back, but is something he has desired that we should desire. We mustn't separate that part of life and marriage from God, either by trying to hide it from him as belonging to us alone or by trying to destroy it altogether through a false piety that denies its existence.

Earthly bliss and humanity belong to God, not in any cramped "religious" sense, but in the fully human sense. Bonhoeffer was a champion of God's idea of humanity, a humanity that he invented and, by participating in it through the incarnation, that he redeemed. But just as soon as Bonhoeffer tacked far enough in one direction and made his "fully human" point, he tacked back the other way, making the "fully God" point too:

You yourselves know that no one can create and assume such a life from his own strength, but that what is given to one is withheld from another; and that is what we call God's guidance. So today, however much you rejoice that you have reached your goal, you will be just as thankful that God's will and God's way have brought you here; and however confidently you accept responsibility for your action today, you may and will put it today with equal confidence into God's hands.

So it's both, but to see each clearly is necessary before one puts them together. And then he brought the two things together:

> As God today adds his "Yes" to your "Yes," as he confirms your will with his will, and as he allows you, and approves of, your triumph and rejoicing and pride, he makes you at the same time instruments of his will and purpose both for yourselves and for others. In his unfathomable condescension God does add his "Yes" to yours; but by doing so, he creates out of your love something quite new—the holy estate of matrimony.

Bonhoeffer was trying with all his might to express the almost inexpressible paradox of a proper relation to God. He had a very high view of marriage: it is "more than your love for each other," and it "has a higher dignity and power, for it is God's holy ordinance, through which he wills to perpetuate the human race till the end of time." Perhaps the sermon's most memorable sentence is this: "It is not your love that sustains the marriage, but from now on, the marriage that sustains your love."

Reading

Bonhoeffer never expected to be imprisoned long. At first he simply wished to get as much information to the prosecutor as possible, with the hopes of getting a trial date. The charges were relatively minor, and he and Dohnanyi could put up a good defense and hoped to win. But Canaris and Sack, working behind the scenes on Dohnanyi's and Bonhoeffer's behalf, thought it better to drag things out. They wished to avoid the confrontation of a trial, especially since the plans to assassinate Hitler were going forward. When that happened, the trial would be moot. So the months passed and the legal battle raged. By October, Bonhoeffer marked six months at Tegel. It had all gone on far longer than he'd ever thought.

Between visits from his family and Maria, and the reading and writing and other things, he made the best of it. Karl and Paula Bonhoeffer visited on October 12, bringing dahlias from their garden. The next day he wrote

them, saying that a verse from the poet Theodor Storm's* "October Lied"
kept running through his head:

> Und geht es draussen noch so toll,
> unchristlich oder christlich,
> ist doch die Welt, die schöne Welt
> so gänzlich unverwüstlich.**

All that is needed to bring that home to one is a few gay autumn flowers, the view from the cell window, and half an hour's "exercise" in the
prison yard, where there are, in fact, a few beautiful chestnut and lime
trees. But in the last resort, for me at any rate, the "world" consists
of a few people whom I should like to see and to be with. The occa-
sional appearances of you and Maria, for a brief hour as though from
a great distance, are really the thing for which and from which I principally live. If, besides that, I could sometimes hear a good sermon on
Sundays—I sometimes hear fragments of the chorales that are carried
along the breeze—it would be still better. . . .

I've again been doing a good deal of writing lately, and for the
work that I have set myself to do, the day is often too short, so that
sometimes, comically enough, I even feel that I have "no time" here for
this or that less important matter! After breakfast in the morning (about
7 o'clock) I read some theology, and then I write till midday; in the
afternoon I read, then comes a chapter from Delbrück's *World History*,
some English grammar, about which I can still learn all kinds of things,
and finally, as the mood takes me, I write or read again. Then in the
evening I am tired enough to be glad to lie down, though that does not
mean going to sleep at once.

The amount of reading and writing that Bonhoeffer did in his eighteen
months at Tegel is decidedly impressive. In a letter to Eberhard Bethge in
December, he wrote:

---

* Danish-German poet, 1817–88.

** Although the storm is raging yet; / beneath each spire or minaret, / behold the world, the
glorious world / has not been destroyed.

In a rather haphazard way I've recently been reading a history of Scotland Yard, a history of prostitution, finished the Delbrück—I find him really rather uninteresting in his problems—, Reinhold Schneider's sonnets—very variable in quality, some very good; on the whole all the newest productions seem to me to be lacking the *hilaritas*—"cheerfulness"—which is to be found in any really great and free intellectual achievement. One has always the impression of a somewhat tortured and strained manufacture instead of creativity in the open air. . . . At the moment I'm reading a gigantic English novel which goes from 1500 to today, by Hugh Walpole, written in 1909. Dilthey is also interesting me very much and for an hour each day I'm studying the manual for medical staff, for any eventuality.

That was just the tip of the iceberg. Months before, he wanted to read Adalbert Stifter's medieval epic *Witiko* and had been pestering his parents about finding a copy, but they could not. To his amazement, he found one in the prison library. He was thrilled. Goebbels's purges of all "un-German" literature from every library had not touched the nineteenth century much. In a series of letters to his parents, Bonhoeffer spoke of his reading:

I read some Stifter almost every day. In this atmosphere, there's something very comforting about the sheltered and sequestered world of his characters—he's old-fashioned enough only to portray likeable people—and it focuses one's thoughts on the things that really matter in life. Here in a prison cell I outwardly and inwardly revert to the simplest aspects of existence; Rilke, for instance, leaves me cold.

Most people would find its thousand pages, which can't be skipped but have to be taken steadily, too much for them, so I'm not sure whether to recommend it to you. For me it's one of the finest books I know. The purity of its style and character-drawing gives one a quite rare and peculiar feeling of happiness . . . its *sui generis*. . . . So far, the only historical novels that have made a comparable impression on me are *Don Quixote* and Gotthelf's *Berner Geist*.

In my reading I'm now living entirely in the nineteenth century. During these months I've read Gotthelf, Stifter, Immermann, Fontane, and Keller with new admiration. A period in which people would write such clear and simple German must have had quite a healthy core. They treat the most delicate matters without sentimentality, the most serious without flippancy, and they express their convictions without pathos; there is no exaggerated simplifying or complicating of a language or subject matter; in short, it's all very much to my liking, and seems to me very sound. But it must have meant plenty of hard work at expressing themselves in good German, and therefore plenty of opportunity for quiet.

Bonhoeffer's cultural standards were obviously high. In a letter to Bethge, he said that his fiancée's generation had

grown up with very bad contemporary literature, and they find it much more difficult to approach earlier writing than we do. The more we have known of the really good things, the more insipid the thin lemonade of later literature becomes, sometimes almost to the point of making us sick. Do you know a work of literature written in the last, say, fifteen years that you think has any lasting quality? I don't. It is partly idle chatter, partly propaganda, partly self-pitying sentimentality, but there is no insight, no ideas, no clarity, no substance and almost always the language is bad and constrained. On this subject I am quite consciously a *laudator temporis acti.*[*]

Bonhoeffer was able to smuggle letters to Bethge starting in November 1943. Once this avenue was open to him, he poured out a torrent of writing to the one friend who had the theological, musical, and literary chops to keep up with him. "I can't read a book or write a paragraph," he said to Bethge, "without talking to you about it or at least asking myself what you would say about it."

Bonhoeffer's Innermost Thoughts

The letters to Bethge opened up far more than opportunities to discuss culture. That he could do with his parents and did. But with Bethge he

---

[*] "Praiser of times past," taken from Horace's *Ars Poetica*.

could discuss things he couldn't discuss with anyone else. Bethge was the one soul on earth to whom Bonhoeffer could show his weaknesses, with whom he could explore his innermost thoughts, whom he could trust not to misunderstand him. With everyone else, Bonhoeffer seemed to feel an obligation to play the role of pastor, to be strong. But Bethge was the one person from whom Bonhoeffer could receive ministry. He had functioned as Bonhoeffer's confessor and pastor since Finkenwalde and was no stranger to the darker side of his friend.

In his first letter to Bethge, Bonhoeffer let him know that the depression that sometimes plagued him was not an issue. He feared that Bethge must have been concerned about him on this score:

> 18 November 1943
>
> . . . after these long months without worship, penitence and eucharist and without the *consolatio fratrum*—once again be my pastor as you have so often been in the past, and listen to me. There is so infinitely much to report, that I would like to tell both of you, but today it can only be the essentials, so this letter is for you alone. . . . During this time I have been preserved from any serious spiritual trial. You are the only person who knows how often *accidie, tristitia*, with all its menacing consequences, has lain in wait for me; and I feared at the time that you must be worrying about me on that account. But I told myself from the beginning that I was not going to oblige either man or devil in any such way—they can do what they like about it for themselves; and I hope I shall always be able to stand firm on this.
>
> At first I wondered a good deal whether it was really for the cause of Christ that I was causing you all such grief; but I soon put that out of my head as a temptation, as I became certain that the duty had been laid on me to hold out in this boundary situation with all its problems; I became quite content to do this, and have remained so ever since (1 Peter 2.20; 3:14).*

---

* "For what credit is it if, when you are beaten for your faults, you take it patiently? But when you do good and suffer, if you take it patiently, this is commendable before God . . . But even if you should suffer for righteousness' sake, you are blessed. 'And do not be afraid of their threats, nor be troubled'" (NKJV).

Bonhoeffer said the Psalms and Revelation were a great comfort to him during those days, as were the hymns of Paul Gerhardt, many of which he knew by heart. So Bonhoeffer was not "naturally" strong and courageous. His equanimity was the result of self-discipline, of deliberately turning to God. Two weeks later he told Bethge about the air raids: "Now there's something I must tell you personally: the heavy air raids, especially the last one, when the windows of the sick-bay were blown out by the land mine, and bottles and medical supplies fell down from the cupboards and shelves, and I lay on the floor in the darkness with little hope of coming through the attack safely, led me back quite simply to prayer and the Bible."

Again and again in various accounts, people write about how strong Bonhoeffer was during the air raids, how he was a comfort and bulwark to those around him when everyone believed death was at hand. But his strength was borrowed from God and lent to others. Because Bonhoeffer was not afraid to share his weaknesses and fears with Bethge, the courage he expressed can be seen as real. He seems genuinely to have entrusted himself to God and therefore had no regrets or real fears:

23 January 1944

. . . when all possibility of co-operating in anything is suddenly cut off, then behind any anxiety about him there is the consciousness that his life has now been placed wholly in better and stronger hands. For you, and for us, the greatest task during the coming weeks and perhaps months, may be to entrust each other to those hands. . . . Whatever weaknesses, miscalculations, and guilt there is in what precedes the facts, God is in the facts themselves. If we survive during these coming weeks or months, we shall be able to see quite clearly that all has turned out for the best. The idea that we could have avoided many of life's difficulties if we had taken things more cautiously is too foolish to be entertained for a moment. As I look back on your past I am so convinced that what has happened hitherto has been right, that I feel that what is happening now is right too. To renounce a full life and its real joys in order to avoid pain is neither Christian nor human.

9 March 1944

When people suggest in their letters . . . that I'm suffering here, I reject the thought. It seems to me a profanation. These things must not be dramatized. I doubt very much whether I am "suffering" any more than you or most people are suffering today. Of course, a great deal here is horrible, but where isn't it? Perhaps we've made too much of this question of suffering, and been too solemn about it. . . . No, suffering must be something quite different, and have a quite different dimension, from what I have so far experienced.

11 April 1944

I heard someone say yesterday that the last years had been completely wasted as far as he was concerned. I'm very glad that I have never yet had that feeling, even for a moment. Nor have I ever regretted my decision in the summer of 1939, for I'm firmly convinced—however strange it may seem—that my life has followed a straight and unbroken course, at any rate in its outward conduct. It has been an uninterrupted enrichment of experience, for which I can only be thankful. If I were to end my life here in these conditions, that would have a meaning that I think I could understand; on the other hand, everything might be a thorough preparation for a new start and a new task when peace comes.

Bonhoeffer had been resigned to missing Eberhard and Renate's wedding the previous May. But when he learned they were expecting a child, Bonhoeffer was sure he would be out in time to preach at the baptism. The child was even named after him, and he was the godfather. As the date drew near, however, he realized that he would not be out in time for this, either:

9 May 1944—It's painful to me, to be sure, that the improbable has happened, and that I shall not be able to celebrate the day with you; but I've quite reconciled myself to it. I believe that nothing that happens to me is meaningless, and that it is good for us all that it should be so, even if it runs counter to our own wishes. As I see it, I'm here for some purpose, and I only hope I may fulfil it. In the light of the great purpose all our privations and disappointments are trivial. Nothing would be more unworthy and wrongheaded than to turn one of those rare occasions of joy, such as you're now experiencing, into a calamity because of my present situation. That would go entirely against the grain, and would

Bonhoeffer and Eberhard Bethge during the summer of 1938, in the parish house at Gross-Schlönwitz. *(Art Resource, NY)*

Dr. Karl Barth (left) *(Getty Images)*

Martin Niemoller (left) and Rev. Otto Dibelius (right) flank the Bishop of Chichester, George Bell before a German-English service at the Marienkirche in Berlin, October 27, 1946. *(AP Images)*

September 1, 1939. Hours after the Nazis' unprovoked attack on Poland *Der Führer* addresses the Reichstag: "You know the endless attempts I made for a peaceful clarification and understanding of the problem of Austria, and later of the problem of the Sudentenland, Bohemia, and Moravia. It was all in vain. I am wrongly judged if my love of peace and patience are mistaken for weakness or even cowardice . . . from now on bombs will be met with bombs!" Later that day Hans Bernd Gisevius ran into Admiral Canaris at OKW headquarters. "This means the end of Germany," he said. *(Art Resource, NY)*

A plaque at the Berlin Opernplatz on the site where 30,000 students gathered at midnight to burn the books of "un-German" authors and to hear Joseph Goebbels declare: "The age of arrogant Jewish intellectualism is now at an end!" On the left is a quote from the German poet Heinrich Heine: "Where books are burned, they will, in the end, burn people, too." On the right: "In the middle of this plaza on May 10, 1933 Nazi students burned the works of hundreds of authors, publishers, philosophers, and scientists." *(Eric Metaxas photo)*

Heinrich Himmler (1900-1945), the chicken farmer who became head of the Nazi SS and Gestapo. *(Getty Images)*

Reinhard Heydrich (1904-1942). He and Himmler were known as "the Black Twins." *(Getty Images)*

2009 rear view of the Wannsee Estate. Here Heydrich in January 1942 presented his plans for the "Final Solution to the Jewish question," to exterminate the Jews of Europe. Today the building is a Holocaust museum. *(Eric Metaxas photo)*

July 20, 1944. Wolfsschanze, East Prussia. Hours after Stauffenberg's bomb fails to kill him, the mysteriously durable Führer poses with Martin Borman (left), Alfred Jodl, and others.
(Getty Images)

Later that day, Hitler greets Goebbels. "It was Providence that spared me," he later declared. "This proves that I'm on the right track. I feel that this is the confirmation of all my work."
(Getty Images)

Dr. Carl Goerdeler, the Mayor of Leipzig, faces the "People's Court" of the notorious Ronald Freisler, who sentenced him to death for his role in the July 20th assassination plot. Freisler also sentenced Dietrich's brother Klaus and his brother-in-law Rüdiger Schleicher to death. *(Getty Images)*

Tegel military prison in Berlin, where Bonhoeffer was held for eighteen months before his transfer to the underground Gestapo prison on Prinz-Albrecht-Strasse. The "x" marks the cell where he first stayed. He was later transferred to Cell 92 on the 3rd floor. *(Getty Images)*

The manuscript for Bonhoeffer's poem "Wer Bin Ich?" ("Who Am I?"), written during his time at Tegel prison. (Art Resource, NY)

WHO AM I?

Who am I? They often tell me
I stepped from my cell's confinement
Calmly, cheerfully, firmly,
Like a squire from his country-house.
Who am I? They often tell me
I used to speak to my warders
Freely and friendly and clearly,
As though it were mine to command.
Who am I? They also tell me
I bore the days of misfortune
Equally, smilingly, proudly,
Like one accustomed to win.

Am I then really all that which other men tell of?
Or am I only what I myself know of myself?
Restless and longing and sick, like a bird in a cage,
Struggling for breath, as though hands were
compressing my throat,
Yearning for colors, for flowers, for the voices of birds,
Thirsting for words of kindness, for neighborliness,
Tossing in expectation of great events,
Powerlessly trembling for friends at an infinite distance,
Weary and empty at praying, at thinking, at making,
Faint, and ready to say farewell to it all?

Who am I? This or the other?
Am I one person today and tomorrow another?
Am I both at once? A hypocrite before others,
And before myself a contemptibly woebegone weakling?
Or is something within me still like a beaten army,
Fleeing in disorder from victory already achieved?
Who am I? They mock me, these lonely questions of mine.
Whoever I am, Thou knowest, O God, I am Thine!

The site at Flossenburg Concentration Camp where Bonhoeffer was executed at dawn on April 9, 1945, along with Admiral William Canaris, Colonel Ludwig Gehre, General Major Hans Oster, and others. The plaque reads: "In resistance against dictatorship and terror, they gave their lives for freedom, justice, and humanity." After witnessing Bonhoeffer's death, the Flossenburg doctor reported: "In the almost fifty years that I worked as a doctor, I have hardly ever seen a man die so entirely submissive to the will of God."

Bonhoeffer once had preached: "No one has yet believed in God and the kingdom of God. No one has yet heard about the realm of the resurrected, and not been homesick from that hour, waiting and looking forward joyfully to being released from bodily existence. . . . Death is hell and night and cold, if it is not transformed by our faith. But that is just what is so marvelous, that we can transform death."

(Eric Metaxas photos)

undermine my optimism with regard to my case. However thankful we may be for all our personal pleasures, we mustn't for a moment lose sight of the great things that we're living for, and they must shed light rather than gloom on your joy.

A week later he sent them "Thoughts on the Day of the Baptism of Dietrich Wilhelm Rüdiger Bethge." Like his sermon for their wedding, it is a small masterpiece. In the letter with this essay he wrote, "Please harbor no regrets about me. Martin [Niemöller] has had nearly seven years of it, and that is a very different matter."

"Religionless Christianity"

Sometime in April 1944, Bonhoeffer experienced a renewed surge in theological thinking, but because of his circumstances, he was able to communicate his ruminations only in the letters smuggled to Bethge. There would be no time to write another book, though he would try. He seemed to have been working on a book until the time that he was taken to the Gestapo prison that October, but the manuscript was never found. The sometimes inchoate thoughts in the letters to Bethge are all we have, and they have tangled his legacy. Many know Bonhoeffer only as the one who coined the dubious concept of *religionless Christianity*. And ironically many in the "God is dead" movement have regarded him as a kind of prophet.

Bonhoeffer felt free to share his deepest thoughts with his friend Eberhard Bethge, but he was an extremely guarded person otherwise, and it's almost certain that if he had known that his private and ill-expressed theological thoughts would have found their way into seminary discussions of the future, he would have been not only embarrassed but deeply disturbed. When Bethge asked whether he could share the letters with some of the brethren from Finkenwalde—"Would you, I wonder, allow these sections to be given to people like Albrecht Schönherr, Winfried Maechler and Dieter Zimmermann?"—Bonhoeffer demurred. "I would not do it myself as yet," he wrote, "because you are the only person with whom I venture to think aloud, as it were, in the hope of clarifying my thoughts." Later, in the same letter, he wrote, "Incidentally, it would be very nice if you didn't throw away my theological letters, but sent them from time to time to Renate, as they must surely be a burden for you there. I might like to read them again later for my work, perhaps. One can write some things in a more natural and lively way in a letter than in a book, and in letters I often have better ideas than when I'm writing for myself."

It was on this basis that Bethge felt free after Bonhoeffer's death to share some of these letters with other theologians. The strange theological climate after World War II and the interest in the martyred Bonhoeffer were such that the few bone fragments in these private letters were set upon as by famished kites and less noble birds, many of whose descendants gnaw them still. All of which has led to a terrific misunderstanding of Bonhoeffer's theology and which lamentably washed backward over his earlier thinking and writing. Many *outre* theological fashions have subsequently tried to claim Bonhoeffer as their own* and have ignored much of his ouevre to do so. Generally speaking, some theologians have made of these few skeletal fragments something like a theological Piltdown man, a jerry-built but sincerely believed hoax.

The most tortured interpretations have fixed on his reference to "religionless Christianity." In a 1967 lecture at Coventry Cathedral in England, Eberhard Bethge said that the "isolated use and handing down of the famous term 'religionless Christianity' has made Bonhoeffer the champion of an undialectical shallow modernism which obscures all that he wanted to tell us about the living God." A principal passage is this one from Bonhoeffer's letter to Bethge on April 30, 1944:

> What is bothering me incessantly is the question what Christianity really is, or indeed who Christ really is, for us today. The time when people could be told everything by means of words, whether theological or pious, is over, and so is the time of inwardness and conscience—and that means the time of religion in general. We are moving towards a completely religionless time; people as they are now simply cannot be religious any more. Even those who honestly describe themselves as "religious" do not in the least act up to it, and so they presumably mean something quite different by "religious."

---

* It seems likely someone will eventually claim that Bonhoeffer's relationship with Bethge partook of more than *philos* and *storge*.

In a nutshell, he saw a situation so bleak, by any historical measures, that he was rethinking some basic things and wondered whether modern man had moved beyond religion. What Bonhoeffer meant by "religion" was not true Christianity, but the ersatz and abbreviated Christianity that he spent his life working against. This "religious" Christianity had failed Germany and the West during this great time of crisis, for one thing, and he wondered whether it wasn't finally time for the lordship of Jesus Christ to move past Sunday mornings and churches and into the whole world. But this was simply an extension of his previous theology, which was dedicatedly Bible centered and Christ centered.

Bonhoeffer never had time to work out much of his new thinking. But overeager theologians have built diminutive Ziggurats from these few scattered bricks. Bonhoeffer also wrote, "In what way are we [the church] . . . those who are called forth, not regarding ourselves from a religious point of view as specially favoured, but rather as belonging wholly to the world? In that case Christ is no longer an object of religion, but something quite different, really the Lord of the world. But what does that mean?"

Bonhoeffer was thinking in a new way about what he had been thinking and saying for two decades: God was bigger than everyone imagined, and he wanted more of his followers and more of the world than was given him. Bonhoeffer recognized that standard-issue "religion" had made God small, having dominion only over those things we could not explain. That "religious" God was merely the "God of the gaps," the God who concerned himself with our "secret sins" and hidden thoughts. But Bonhoeffer rejected this abbreviated God. The God of the Bible was Lord over everything, over every scientific discovery. He was Lord over not just what we did not know, but over what we knew and were discovering through science. Bonhoeffer was wondering if it wasn't time to bring God into the whole world and stop pretending he wanted only to live in those religious corners that we reserved for him:

> It always seems to me that we are trying anxiously in this way to reserve some space for God; I should like to speak of God not on the boundaries but at the centre, not in weaknesses but in strength; and therefore not in death and guilt but in man's life and goodness. . . . The church stands not at the boundaries where human powers give out, but in the

middle of the village. That is how it is in the Old Testament, and in this sense we still read the New Testament far too little in the light of the Old. How this religionless Christianity looks, what form it takes is something that I'm thinking about a great deal and I shall be writing to you again about it soon.

Bonhoeffer's theology had always leaned toward the incarnational view that did not eschew "the world," but that saw it as God's good creation to be enjoyed and celebrated, not merely transcended. According to this view, God had redeemed mankind through Jesus Christ, had re-created us as "good." So we weren't to dismiss our humanity as something "un-spiritual." As Bonhoeffer had said before, God wanted our "yes" to him to be a "yes" to the world he had created. This was not the thin pseudohumanism of the liberal "God is dead" theologians who would claim Bonhoeffer's mantle as their own in the decades to come, nor was it the antihumanism of the pious and "religious" theologians who would abdicate Bonhoeffer's theology to the liberals. It was something else entirely: it was God's humanism, redeemed in Jesus Christ.

Bonhoeffer's Magnum Opus

Bonhoeffer thought of *Ethics* as his magnum opus. It is the book that he never quite finished. He had worked on it for years, at Ettal and at Klein-Krössin and at Friedrichsbrunn and in his attic bedroom in Berlin. And now he worked on it in his cell at Tegel. In 1943, to Bethge, he said, "I sometimes feel as if my life were more or less over, and as if all I had to do now were to finish my *Ethics*." Although Bonhoeffer never finished it to his satisfaction, it can be seen, along with his *Discipleship* and *Life Together*, as essentially complete,* and as indisputably important in forming a full understanding of Dietrich Bonhoeffer.

The book opens with these lines: "Those who wish even to focus on the problem of a Christian ethic are faced with an outrageous demand—from the outset they must give up, as inappropriate to this topic, the very two questions that led them to deal with the ethical problem: 'How can I be good?' and 'How can I do something good?' Instead they must ask the wholly other, completely different question: 'What is the will of God?'"

---

* Eberhard Bethge edited the surviving manuscript.

For Bonhoeffer, there is no reality apart from God and no goodness apart from him. All pretense to that effect is Barth's pejorative notion of religion, a scheme to subvert God altogether and make a fallen humanistic path to heaven alone. It is Barth's Tower of Babel, and it is the fig leaf that tries to fool God, but fails.

"All things appear as in a distorted mirror," Bonhoeffer wrote, "if they are not seen and recognized in God." So God is not merely a religious concept or religious reality. God is the one who invented reality, and reality can only be seen truly as it exists in God. Nothing that exists is outside his realm. So there are no ethics apart from doing God's will, and God—indeed, Jesus Christ—is the nonnegotiable given in the equation of human ethics:

> In Jesus Christ the reality of God has entered into the reality of this world. The place where the questions about the reality of God and about the reality of the world are answered at the same time is characterized solely by the name: Jesus Christ. God and the world are enclosed in this name . . . we cannot speak rightly of either God or the world without speaking of Jesus Christ. All concepts of reality that ignore Jesus Christ are abstractions.
>
> As long as Christ and the world are conceived as two realms bumping against and repelling each other, we are left with only the following options. Giving up on reality as a whole, either we place ourselves in one of the two realms, wanting Christ without the world or the world without Christ—and in both cases we deceive ourselves. . . . There are not two realities, but only one reality, and that is God's reality revealed in Christ in the reality of the world. Partaking in Christ, we stand at the same time in the reality of God and in the reality of the world. The reality of Christ embraces the reality of the world in itself. The world has no reality of its own independent of God's revelation in Christ. . . . [T]he theme of two realms, which has dominated the history of the church again and again, is foreign to the New Testament.

Bonhoeffer believed that, historically speaking, it was time for everyone to see these things. The evilness of the Nazis could not be defeated via old-fashioned "ethics," "rules," and "principles." God alone could combat it.

Under "normal" circumstances, he said, people are concerned with ideas of right and wrong. They try to do right, as they see it, and try to avoid doing what is wrong. This would never suffice, but at the time of the Nazis, the failure of such a "religious" approach had become more obvious. "Shakespeare's characters are among us," he wrote. "The villain and the saint have little or nothing to do with ethical programs." Hitler had made the true reality of the human condition less avoidable; evil had stepped to the center of the world stage and removed its mask.

In the book, Bonhoeffer examined and dismissed a number of approaches to dealing with evil. "Reasonable people," he said, think that "with a little reason, they can pull back together a structure that has come apart at the joints." Then there are the ethical "fanatics" who "believe that they can face the power of evil with the purity of their will and their principles." Men of "conscience" become overwhelmed because the "countless respectable and seductive disguises and masks in which evil approaches them make their conscience anxious and unsure until they finally content themselves with an assuaged conscience instead of a good conscience." They must "deceive their own conscience in order not to despair." Finally there are some who retreat to a "private virtuousness." He added,

> Such people neither steal, nor murder, nor commit adultery, but do good according to their abilities. But . . . they must close their eyes and ears to the injustice around them. Only at the cost of self-deception can they keep their private blamelessness clean from the stains of responsible action in the world. In all that they do, what they fail to do will not let them rest. They will either be destroyed by this unrest, or they will become the most hypocritical of all Pharisees.

Bonhoeffer was speaking about himself as much as about anyone. In light of the events in Germany at that time, everyone was trapped in a situation of ethical impossibilities. In light of the monstrous evils being committed all around, what could one do and what should one do? In letters from his ordinands, we read of how tortured they were in knowing when to protest and when to accede, when to go to war, even if they knew it was unjust, and when to take a stand. One of them wrote to Bonhoeffer about having to kill prisoners and was obviously torn up about it, knowing that if he didn't comply, he would himself be killed. This sort of thing had become commonplace. Who could fathom the horrors of the concentration camps where Jews, hoping to preserve their own lives, were forced to do unspeakable things to other Jews? The utter evilness of evil now showed itself clearly, and it showed up the bankruptcy of man's so-called ethical attempts to deal with it. The problem of evil is too much for us. We are all tainted by it and cannot escape being tainted by it.

But Bonhoeffer did not take a moralistic tone. He put himself in the mix of those perplexed by the problem of evil and likened all of us to the figure of Don Quixote. Don Quixote was for Bonhoeffer an important picture of the human condition. In his *Ethics*, he wrote that in our efforts to do good we, like that "knight of the doleful countenance," are tilting at windmills. We think we are doing good and fighting evil, but in fact, we are living in an illusion. There was no moral condemnation in what Bonhoeffer said, however. "Only the mean-spirited can read the fate of Don Quixote," he wrote, "without sharing in and being moved by it." This is our universal predicament as human beings.

The solution is to do the will of God, to do it radically and courageously and joyfully. To try to explain "right" and "wrong"—to talk about ethics— outside of God and obedience to his will is impossible: "Principles are only tools in the hands of God; they will soon be thrown away when they are no longer useful." We must look only at God, and in him we are reconciled to our situation in the world. If we look only to principles and rules, we are in a fallen realm where our reality is divided from God:

> "Be wise as serpents and innocent as doves" is a saying of Jesus (Matt.
> 10:16). As with all of his sayings, it is he himself who interprets it. No
> one can look at God and at the reality of the world with undivided gaze
> as long as God and the world are torn apart. Despite all efforts to pre-
> vent it the eyes still wander from one to the other. Only because there
> is one place where God and the reality of the world are reconciled with
> each other, at which God and humanity have become one, is it possible
> there and there alone to fix one's eyes on God and the world together
> at the same time. This place does not lie somewhere beyond reality in
> the realm of ideas. It lies in the midst of history as a divine miracle. It
> lies in Jesus Christ the reconciler of the world.

Bonhoeffer was saying that apart from Jesus Christ, we cannot know what is right or do right. We must look to him in every situation. Only in him can the fathomless evil of the world be dealt a death blow. To those for whom Bonhoeffer's few words on religionless Christianity were the sine qua non of all he ever said, this uncompromising Christocentrism would be strong meat, as are his pronouncements in *Ethics* on a number of other issues, such as abortion:

> Destruction of the embryo in the mother's womb is a violation of the right to live which God has bestowed upon this nascent life. To raise the question whether we are here concerned already with a human being or not is merely to confuse the issue. The simple fact is that God certainly intended to create a human being and that this nascent human being has been deliberately deprived of his life. And that is nothing but murder.

But Bonhoeffer saw both sides of such issues. God's grace must not be removed from the picture:

> A great many different motives may lead to an action of this kind; indeed in cases where it is an act of despair, performed in circumstances of extreme human or economic destitution and misery, the guilt may often lie rather with the community than with the individual. Precisely in this connexion money may conceal many a wanton deed, while the poor man's more reluctant lapse may far more easily be disclosed. All these considerations must no doubt have a quite decisive influence on our personal and pastoral attitude towards the person concerned, but they cannot in any way alter the fact of murder.

Visitors at Tegel

At the heart of Bonhoeffer's theology was the mystery of the incarnation. In a circular letter he wrote, "No priest, no theologian stood at the cradle in Bethlehem. And yet, all Christian theology has its origin in the wonder of all wonders that God became man. Alongside the brilliance of holy night there burns the fire of the unfathomable mystery of Christian theology." It was because of this that he embraced the humanity of Jesus Christ in a way that religious pietists could not, and it was because of this that he felt justified in embracing the good things of this world as gifts from the hand of God, rather than as temptations to be avoided. So even in prison, Bonhoeffer's enjoyment of people and life was very much alive.

His favorite times during these eighteen months at Tegel were when he could entertain visitors, even under Roeder's watchful eye, although as the months passed, guards sometimes allowed him time alone with visitors.

On November 26, 1943, Bonhoeffer was afforded the unique treat of a visit from the four people in the world he loved most: Maria, his parents, and Eberhard Bethge. They came together, and when Bonhoeffer returned to his cell, he was beside himself:

> It will be with me for a long time now—the memory of having the four people who are nearest and dearest to me with me for a brief moment. When I got back to my cell afterwards, I paced up and down for a whole hour, while my dinner stood there and got cold, so that at last I couldn't help laughing at myself when I found myself repeating over and over again, "That was really great!" I always hesitate to use the word "indescribable" about anything, because if you take enough trouble to make a thing clear, I think there is very little that is really "indescribable"— but at the moment that is just what this morning seems to be.

The good cheer of Bonhoeffer's family under all circumstances can be seen in the way they turned even the prison visits into small celebrations. This time they brought a number of presents with them, including a cigar from Karl Barth. Maria had made an Advent garland for him, and Bethge gave him several remarkably large hard-boiled eggs.* That Christmas, Maria gave him the wristwatch her father was wearing when he was killed. Bonhoeffer's parents also gave him an heirloom: "great-grandfather's goblet from 1845, which is now standing on my table with evergreen in it." Just over a month later, on his birthday, Bonhoeffer's mother gave him another heirloom, the Herzliebschränkchen, an exquisite little cupboard of carved rosewood that once belonged to Goethe, who had given it to his friend Minna Herzlieb.

---

* Some sources have mistaken them for actual ostrich eggs because Bonhoeffer jokingly referred to them that way in a letter to Bethge.

Like the goblet, it had come into the family through his great-grandfather, Karl August von Hase.

On his thirty-eighth birthday, Bonhoeffer received a visit from Maria, who unwittingly bore some hard news. One of the books she passed along to him that day contained a coded message from his parents: Admiral Canaris had been dismissed from office. The Gestapo and RSHA had achieved what they had always longed for. They had brought the renegade Abwehr under their jurisdiction. Canaris functioned effectively for a short time longer, but the most important development that came from this hard turn of events was a positive one. The leadership of the conspiracy to assassinate Hitler did not die but was placed in fresh hands. A new group of conspirators would emerge, headed by Colonel Claus von Stauffenberg. And this group would succeed where the others had failed time and again.

CHAPTER 29

VALKYRIE AND THE STAUFFENBERG PLOT

It's time now for something to be done. He who has the courage to act must know that he will probably go down in German history as a traitor. But if he fails to act, he will be a traitor before his own conscience.

—CLAUS SCHENK VON STAUFFENBERG

I want you to wait with me and be patient, and the more patient the longer this goes on. And now, don't be sad. Tell me what you think and act as you must. But always rest assured that I love you very much and hold you very dear.

—DIETRICH BONHOEFFER TO MARIA VON WEDEMEYER

On June 30, 1944, Paul von Hase, the military commandant of Berlin, entered the gates of Tegel prison. His purpose? The prisoner in cell 92, Dietrich Bonhoeffer. It was almost as if Hitler had suddenly showed up for lunch. Bonhoeffer wrote Bethge that it was "most comical how everyone goes about flapping his wings and—with a few notable exceptions—tries to outdo everyone else in undignified ways. It's painful, but some of them are in such a state now that they can't help it." The appearance must have been somewhat frightening, not least to the head of Tegel, Maetz, who already treated Bonhoeffer with sycophantic deference. And now the reason Bonhoeffer was treated this way had arrived. Incredibly, von Hase stayed for more than five hours. Bonhoeffer said his uncle "had four bottles of *Sekt* [German champagne] brought—a unique event in the annals of this place." Bonhoeffer thought that his uncle likely paid the visit to show everyone that he stood with his nephew and also to make it clear "what he expects from the jittery and pedantic M[aetz]." It was "most remarkable," Bonhoeffer thought, that his uncle would dare to take sides, as it were, against the Nazi prosecution and with his prosecuted nephew.

His uncle's bold appearance suggested that the coup was imminent, that Hitler would soon be dead and they could all begin life again. Bonhoeffer already knew things were in motion, but his uncle's visit strongly confirmed it. Von Hase was not only aware of the coup; he was an integral part of it. The plans for this plot, code named Valkyrie, had been in existence for a year, but events had never been favorable for their execution. Until now.

Preparations for the Coup

In truth, the situation was still far from ideal. But the level of desperation had increased. The conspirators moved from thinking prudently to simply wanting to act. For the longest time they wanted to kill Hitler so that they could get better peace terms from the Allies, but as Churchill's cold shoulder flirted with absolute zero, they realized that every passing day took them further from their goal. The war raged, and fresh Allied casualties were added to the toll, as were the innocent deaths of Jews and others. It was hopeless to look for anything from the Allies, but they came to the conclusion that this no longer mattered. Now it was simply about doing the right thing, come what may. Stauffenberg said, "It's time now for something to be done. He who has the courage to act must know that he will probably go down in German history as a traitor. But if he fails to act, he will be a traitor before his own conscience."

Maria's uncle Henning von Tresckow said something similar: "The assassination must be attempted, *coute que coute* [whatever the cost]. Even if it fails, we must take action in Berlin. For the practical purpose no longer matters; what matters now is that the German resistance movement must take the plunge before the eyes of the world and of history. Compared to that, nothing else matters."

The final and famous July 20 plot would be led by Stauffenberg, a devout Catholic from an aristocratic family. His disgust for Hitler skyrocketed when he saw the way the SS treated Polish prisoners of war in 1939. This, coupled with the murder of the Jews, helped him decide to do all possible to end Hitler's reign. In late 1943 he told his fellow conspirator Axel von dem Bussche: "Let's get to the heart of the matter: I am committing high treason with all my might and main."

Stauffenberg brought much-needed energy and focus to the task; he was also the one chosen to do the deed itself. Von Hase's visit made it clear to Bonhoeffer that action was imminent. Blowing up Hitler—along with any two or three of his scaly paladins—was still the ideal.

And so a date was set. On July 11, Stauffenberg visited Hitler at the Obersalzberg. He carried the bomb in his briefcase. But when Stauffenberg arrived, he realized that Himmler was absent. General Stieff strongly opposed going forward with the plan. "My God," said Stauffenberg to Stieff, "shouldn't we do it?" Back in Berlin, everyone was waiting, hoping. But Stieff prevailed. When Goerdeler heard that they hadn't gone ahead, he was furious. "They'll never do it!" he said.

But Stieff and Fellgiebel knew there would be plenty of opportunities. Sure enough, Stauffenberg was summoned to Hitler's East Prussian headquarters four days later. Once again, he arrived with the bomb in his briefcase and once again, Himmler was not there and once again, Stieff insisted they wait. This time Stieff was joined by Fellgiebel. Stauffenberg was upset, but unless Fellgiebel and Stieff were with him, his hands were tied. It had taken great effort to win over Fellgiebel, and his role in the larger plot was crucial. Once again, Stauffenberg returned to Berlin.

Still, everyone knew an attempt was imminent. On the sixteenth, Bonhoeffer wrote to Bethge: "Who knows—it may be that it will not have to be too often now, and that we shall see each other sooner than we expect. . . . We shall very soon now have to be thinking a great deal about our journey together in the summer of 1940, and my last sermons." Bonhoeffer was speaking in coded language. His last sermons were the ones he preached at the collective pastorates in East Prussia, which was his oblique way of referring to Hitler's Wolfsschanze headquarters. And that was precisely where the bomb went off.

July 20, 1944

The name Adolf is a contraction of the Old German *Adelwolf*, meaning "noble wolf." Hitler was aware of this etymology, and in his mystical and eerie way, he adopted the Teutonic and totemic symbol of the wolf as his own. The wild carnivorous and Darwinian ruthlessness of the beast appealed to him, and he had identified with it early on. In the 1920s he sometimes registered at hotels as Herr Wolf; the Obersalzberg house was bought under that name; and the Wagner children called him "Onkel Wolf."* He named his military headquarters during the Battle of France *Wolfsschlucht* (Wolf's Gorge), and the command post on the eastern front, *Werwolf* (Werewolf). But the most famous of his lupine haunts was his military headquarters in East Prussia, *Wolfsschanze* (Wolf's Lair).

On July 19, Stauffenberg was ordered to be at Wolfsschanze the next day for a one o'clock meeting. He knew this was the chance for which he had been patiently waiting. The next morning, July 20, he arose at five, and before he left, he told his brother Berthold, "We have crossed the Rubicon." He drove to the airport with his adjutant, Werner von Haeften, who had spoken for hours to Bonhoeffer about killing the Führer. Now he was on his way to do it. With them was Stauffenberg's briefcase, containing important papers and, swaddled in a shirt, another one of those cunning plastic bombs that had bedeviled the conspirators time and again. But this time, as history tells us, it did not fail to explode. In the end, its explosion would kill thousands, but not as intended.

They stopped at a Catholic chapel where Stauffenberg went to pray. Father Wehrle let him in, since the chapel was locked at that hour. Ten days earlier, Stauffenberg had asked him the question that had been on his mind: "Can the Church grant absolution to a murderer who has taken the life of a tyrant?" Father Wehrle said that only the pope could grant absolution in such a case, but he would look into it further. Haeften had broached this question with Bonhoeffer eighteen months before.**

At the airport Stauffenberg said, "This is more than we dared hope

---

* Hitler adored the composer Richard Wagner (1813–83). He met his widow, Cosima, in 1923 and in subsequent years spent much time with Wagner's children and grandchildren at their home in Bayreuth.

** See pages 425–26.

for. . . . Fate has offered us this opportunity, and I would not refuse it for anything in the world. I have searched my conscience, before God and before
myself. This man is evil incarnate."

Their three-hour plane ride got them to Rastenberg around ten. They
were picked up by a staff car and driven into the gloomy East Prussian woods
surrounding Hitler's headquarters. They rode past the pillbox fortifications,
past the mine fields, past the electrified barbed wire fence—and then past
the slavishly devoted SS guards who patrolled the area. Stauffenberg was
now in the "safe" zone, where the Führer was otherwise unprotected. All that
remained was to trigger the bomb, put the bomb near the Führer, slip out of
the room before it blew up, slip past the SS guards, who by then would be
in a frenzy of alertness, past the electrified fence and the mine fields and the
pillbox fortifications. And he would do all these things.

But there were still three hours before the meeting. First they would have
breakfast. Afterward Stauffenberg rendezvoused with Fellgiebel, who was to
inform the conspirators in Berlin when the bomb went off. Also, as the chief
of signals at OKW, he was able to effectively seal off Wolfsschanze from the
world by cutting all communications—phone, radio, and telegraph—just
long enough for the Valkyrie plans to get under way. After squaring things
with Fellgiebel, Stauffenberg made his way to the office of General Keitel,
the chief of OKW. But the unpleasant Keitel sprang some grievous news:
Mussolini was on his way! *Il Duce* was due at two thirty. Stauffenberg's presentation to Hitler must be moved up to twelve thirty. What's more, Keitel
said that Hitler would be in a hurry, so Stauffenberg must hustle things along
during his presentation. Stauffenberg wondered if the meeting would be too
brief for the fuse. But he had an idea: he would trigger the fuse *before* he
arrived at the meeting. Then Keitel delivered another surprise: because of
the heat, the meeting would not be in the underground bunker, but in the
conference barracks, above ground. Since the walls of the subterranean bunker would have confined the blast, multiplying its effect, this was bad news.
Still, the bomb was powerful enough.

Just before twelve thirty, Keitel said it was time. They must leave immediately. But before they left Keitel's office, Stauffenberg asked if he could
wash up; he was hoping to arm the bomb in the lavatory. When he saw the
lavatory wasn't the ideal place, he asked Keitel's aide where he could change
his shirt. Keitel's aide took Stauffenberg to another room where Stauffenberg

closed the door, quickly opened his briefcase, unwrapped the bomb, put on the shirt in which it was wrapped, and crushed the vial. The bomb would explode in ten minutes. Stauffenberg hurried to Keitel's car and in a moment they arrived at the conference barracks.

By the time Keitel and Stauffenberg entered the room where Hitler was meeting, four of the ten minutes had vanished. Hitler cursorily acknowledged Stauffenberg and continued listening to the presentation by General Heusinger. Stauffenberg glanced around the room and saw more trouble: Himmler and Goebbels were not there. Nonetheless, he took his place near Hitler, placing the briefcase under the table. It was just six feet from the Führer's legs, which—unless he moved—should be separated from their ill-tempered master in five minutes.

But something called a socle would literally get in the way, would divide the vector of the historic blast away from the intended target. A socle is a massive plinth used as a support. In the case of the huge oaken table in this map room, there were two of them, one at either end. The table itself was approximately eighteen feet by five feet, and each of the two monstrous socles was nearly as wide as the table. This freakish, legless table would play a part in the murders of Dietrich Bonhoeffer, his brother Klaus, and his two brothers-in-law; Stauffenberg and Haeften; and hundreds of other conspirators, not to mention the millions of innocents at that moment suffering in miserable desperation in death camps. It is a fact and a mystery that the course of history hinged on a quirk of furniture design.

Stauffenberg knew there were three minutes before the bomb detonated. It was time to go. Stauffenberg suddenly excused himself, mumbling something about needing to get a final set of figures over the phone for his presentation. For someone to leave the presence of Adolf Hitler was quite unprecedented, but Stauffenberg had pressing reasons. He walked out of the building, fighting the powerful temptation to break into a sprint. Behind him in the room, Heusinger continued to drone on until one of his sentences was prematurely punctuated by an explosion so powerful that Stauffenberg, now about two hundred yards away, saw bluish-yellow flames shoot out the windows, accompanied by some of the high-ranking men who had milliseconds earlier been dully gazing at maps.

The oaken table was in smithereens. Hair was on fire. The ceiling had descended to the floor. Several men lay dead. But contrary to what

Stauffenberg believed as he rushed toward the airfield, none of these dead men was "evil incarnate." Hitler was fine and dandy, albeit cartoonishly mussed. His secretary, Gertraud Junge, recalled, "The Führer looked very strange. His hair was standing on end, like quills on a hedgehog, and his clothes were in tatters. But in spite of all that he was ecstatic—after all, hadn't he survived?"

"It was Providence that spared me," Hitler declared. "This proves that I'm on the right track. I feel that this is the confirmation of all my work." His extraordinary survival amidst this smoke and death was proof positive that he was straddling the very zeitgeist. Still, his buttocks were badly bruised, and the explosion had blasted his pants into a hula skirt of tatters. Ever the romantic, he had them shipped to Eva Braun at Berchtesgaden as a memento of her beloved Führer's uncanny durability, with a note: "I have sent you the uniform of that wretched day. Proof that Providence protects me and that we no longer have to fear our enemies."

But after shipping his pants to Eva, Hitler turned to the German *Volk*, to whom Eva must ever play second fiddle. He must assure them that he was all right. A radio microphone was rigged up around midnight, and all Germany heard the voice of the Führer:

> If I speak to you today, I do so for two special reasons. In the first place, so that you may hear my voice and know that I myself am sound and uninjured; and in the second place, so that you may also hear the particulars about a crime that is without peer in German history. An extremely small clique of ambitious, conscienceless, and criminal and stupid officers forged a plot to eliminate me and, along with me, to exterminate the staff of officers in actual command of the German *Wehrmacht*. The bomb, which was planted by Colonel Count von Stauffenberg, burst two yards from my right side. It injured several of my colleagues; one of them has died. I myself am wholly unhurt. . . . The clique of usurpers is . . . an extremely small band of criminal elements who are now being mercilessly exterminated. . . . This time an accounting will be given such as we National Socialists are wont to give. . . . I wish especially to greet you, my old comrades in the struggle, for it has once more been granted me to escape a fate which holds no terrors for me personally, but which would have brought terror down upon the heads of the

German people. I see in this another sign from Providence that I must and therefore shall continue my work.

After that, there was martial music and Göring came on to speak:

Comrades of the *Luftwaffe*! An inconceivably base attempt at the murder of our Führer was committed today by Colonel Count von Stauffenberg on the orders of a miserable clique of one-time generals who, because of their wretched and cowardly conduct of the war, were driven from their posts. The Führer was saved as by a miracle. . . . Long live our Führer, whom Almighty God so visibly blessed on this day!

Then another military march, followed by the head of the navy, Dönitz:

Men of the Navy! Holy wrath and immeasurable rage fill our hearts at the criminal assault which was intended to take the life of our beloved Führer. Providence wished to have it otherwise; Providence guarded and protected the Führer; thus Providence did not desert our German Fatherland in its fated hour. An insanely small clique of generals. . . .

The truth was too hard to bear: it was a vast conspiracy of Germany's elites, and it had existed longer and was far wider than they had ever dreamed. The blow of such news to Hitler's ego must have been shattering, and like all such, he wouldn't stand for it. He would wipe out every trace of opposition and torture information from any conceivable source. The wives and children and other family members and friends of anyone connected to this conspiracy would be hunted down, arrested, and sent to concentration camps. The end of the conspiracy had begun.

There was but one "church" newspaper still operating in the Third Reich. A few days after the coup, it offered up another bouquet of propaganda:

The frightful day. While our brave armies, courageous unto death, are struggling manfully to protect their country and to achieve final victory, a handful of infamous officers, driven by their own ambition, ventured on a frightful crime and made an attempt to murder the Führer. The Führer was saved and thus unspeakable disaster averted from our people. For this we give thanks to God with all our hearts and pray, with all our church, congregations, for God's assistance and help in the grave tasks that the Führer has to perform in the most difficult times.

But another newspaper took a similarly reproachful tone toward the conspirators. The *New York Times* declared that those who had attempted "to kidnap or kill the head of the German state and commander in chief of the Army" had done something one would not "normally expect within an offi-cers' corps and a civilized government." And Winston Churchill, who had done his best to starve the conspiracy to death, now kicked its corpse, calling the attempt a case of "the highest personalities in the German Reich murder-ing one another."

Bonhoeffer Hears of the Plot's Failure

Listening to the radio in the sick bay on July 21, Bonhoeffer heard the news of the failed assassination attempt. He knew the ramifications. But he would not take his emotional cues from circumstances. His equanimity amidst this fiasco is evidenced in his letter to Bethge, written that day:

> All I want to do today is to send you a short greeting. I expect you are often with us here in your thoughts and are always glad of any sign of life, even if the theological discussion stops for a moment. These theo-logical thoughts are, in fact, always occupying my mind; but there are times when I am just content to live the life of faith without worrying about its problems. At those times I simply take pleasure in the days' readings—in particular those of yesterday and today; and I'm always glad to go back to Paul Gerhardt's beautiful hymns.

The readings, or *Losungen*, for July 20 were: "Some boast of chariots and some of horses; but we boast of the name of the Lord our God" (Ps. 20:7) and "If God is for us, who can be against us?" (Rom. 8:31). The readings for the next day were: "The LORD is my shepherd. I shall not want" (Ps. 23:1) and "I am the good shepherd; I know my own and my own know me" (John 10:14).

That he would have taken real comfort in these cannot be doubted, nor that he would have taken them as God's particular words to him in that blackest of hours. He also expressed more theological thoughts:

During the last year or so I've come to know and understand more and more the profound this-worldliness of Christianity. The Christian is not a *homo religiosus*, but simply a man, as Jesus was a man. . . . I don't mean the shallow and banal this-worldliness of the enlightened, the busy, the comfortable, or the lascivious, but the profound this-worldliness, characterized by discipline and the constant knowledge of death and resurrection.

Bonhoeffer famously said that he could "see the dangers" of his own book *Discipleship*, "though I still stand by what I wrote." What he meant was that with the Christian life that he advocated in that book, there is always the temptation to become religious in the pejorative, Barthian sense, to use the Christian faith as a means to escape life rather than as a means to live life more fully. He continued,

I discovered later, and I'm still discovering right up to this moment, that it is only by living completely in this world that one learns to have faith. . . . One must completely abandon any attempt to make something of oneself, whether it be a saint, or a converted sinner, or a churchman (a so-called priestly type!), a righteous man or an unrighteous one, a sick man or a healthy one. By this-worldliness I mean living unreservedly in life's duties, problems, successes and failures, experiences and perplexities. In so doing we throw ourselves completely into the arms of God, taking seriously not our own sufferings, but those of God in the world—watching with Christ in Gethsemane. That, I think, is faith; that is *metanoia*;* and that is how one becomes a man and a Christian (cf. Jer. 45!). How can success make us arrogant, or failure lead us astray, when we share in God's sufferings through a life of this kind?

I think you see what I mean, even though I put it so briefly, I'm glad to have been able to learn this, and I know I've been able to do so

---

* The New Testament Greek word for "repentance."

only along the road that I've travelled. So I'm grateful for the past and present, and content with them. . . .

May God in his mercy lead us through these times; but above all, may he lead us to himself. . . .

Good-bye. Keep well, and don't lose hope that we shall all meet again soon. I always think of you in faithfulness and gratitude.

Your Dietrich

With the letter Bonhoeffer included a poem. He said that he "wrote these lines in a few hours this evening. They are quite unpolished. . . . I can see this morning that I shall again have to revise them completely. Still, I'm sending them to you as they are, in the rough. I'm certainly no poet!" But he was, and the poem is a distillation of his theology at that time:

Stations on the Road to Freedom

Discipline
If you set out to seek freedom, then learn above all things
to govern your soul and your senses, for fear that your passions
and longing may lead you away from the path you should follow.
Chaste be your mind and your body, and both in subjection,
obediently steadfastly seeking the aim set before them;
only through discipline may a man learn to be free.

Action
Daring to do what is right, not what fancy may tell you,
valiantly grasping occasions, not cravenly doubting—
freedom comes only through deeds, not through thoughts taking wing.
Faint not nor fear, but go out to the storm and the action,
trusting in God whose commandment you faithfully follow;
freedom, exultant, will welcome your spirit with joy.

Suffering
A change has come indeed. Your hands, so strong and active,
are bound; in helplessness now you see your action
is ended; you sigh in relief, your cause committing

to stronger hands; so now you may rest contented.
Only for one blissful moment could you draw near to touch freedom;
then, that it might be perfected in glory, you gave it to God.

Death
Come now, thou greatest of feasts on the journey to freedom eternal;
death, cast aside all the burdensome chains, and demolish
the walls of our temporal body, the walls of our souls that are blinded,
so that at last we may see that which here remains hidden.
Freedom, how long we have sought thee in discipline, action, and suffering;
dying, we now may behold thee revealed in the Lord.

At the end of July, he sent Bethge some "Miscellaneous Thoughts": "Please excuse these rather pretentious 'pensées.' They are fragments of conversations that have never taken place, and to that extent they belong to you. One who is forced, as I am, to live entirely in his thoughts, has the silliest things come into his mind—writing down his odd thoughts!"

Appropriately enough, one of them reads, "Absolute seriousness is never without a dash of humor." Another one reiterates his theme that being a Christian is less about cautiously avoiding sin than about courageously and actively doing God's will: "The essence of chastity is not the suppression of lust, but the total orientation of one's life towards a goal. Without such a goal, chastity is bound to become ridiculous. Chastity is the *sine qua non* of lucidity and concentration." And the final one seems to reprise his poem: "Death is the supreme festival on the road to freedom."

Aftermath

Two days later Bonhoeffer heard that Canaris had been arrested. He would soon hear more about the failed plot. Werner von Haeften had died bravely, leaping into a hail of bullets intended for Stauffenberg. Stauffenberg died bravely, too, moments later. Just before being executed, he shouted: "Long live sacred Germany!"

Henning von Tresckow and others took their own lives, most of them for fear of revealing the names of others under torture. Before he did so, Tresckow spoke to Schlabrendorff, who recalled his words:

The whole world will vilify us now, but I am still totally convinced that we did the right thing. Hitler is the archenemy not only of Germany but of the world. When, in a few hours' time, I go before God to account for what I have done and left undone, I know I will be able to justify in good conscience what I did in the struggle against Hitler. God promised Abraham that He would not destroy Sodom if just ten righteous men could be found in the city, and so I hope that for our sake God will not destroy Germany. None of us can bewail his own death; those who consented to join our circle put on the robe of Nessus. A human being's moral integrity begins when he is prepared to sacrifice his life for his convictions.

Everyone remotely involved in the conspiracy was now arrested and interrogated. Most were tortured. On August 7 and 8 the first of the conspirators were subjected to the *Volksgerichtshof* (People's Court), presided over by Roland Freisler, whom William Shirer has called a "vile and vituperative maniac" and "perhaps the most sinister and bloodthirsty Nazi in the Third Reich after Heydrich." Freisler greatly admired the Moscow show trials of the 1930s and wished to emulate them; he was a man after Hitler's own heart. As for the People's Court, it was created by Hitler to try "cases of treason" in 1934 when the outcome of the Reichstag fire trial before the German Supreme Court did not produce the desired outcome.

On August 8, Bonhoeffer's uncle General Paul von Hase was sentenced to death by Freisler and hanged that day at Plötzensee prison. He was fifty-nine years old. His wife was arrested, as were the spouses and relatives of many in the conspiracy. On August 22, Hans von Dohnanyi was taken to Sachsenhausen concentration camp. On September 20, the Chronicle of Shame files (henceforth known as the Zossen files) were discovered at Zossen. For Bonhoeffer and Dohnanyi, this was the disaster of disasters. Dohnanyi had been keeping them since 1938, documenting the criminal horrors of the Nazis. The discovery brought everything into the light, and they knew it. The pretense was over.

But the bravery of the men who had stood against the evil regime came to light now too. Many of these beaten and broken men managed to make statements for posterity during their trials, things that must have knocked Freisler and the other devoted Nazis back on their heels. Ewald von Kleist-

Schmenzin said that committing treason against Hitler's regime was "a command from God." Hans-Bernd von Haeften said Hitler would go down in the annals of world history as a "great perpetrator of evil." Von der Schulenberg said to the court: "We resolved to take this deed upon ourselves in order to save Germany from indescribable misery. I realize that I shall be hanged for my part in it, but I do not regret what I did and only hope that someone else will succeed in luckier circumstances." And many others made similar statements. Hitler soon forbade further reportage of the trials.

Maria Loses Hope

Even in the months before the failed July 20 assassination attempt, there were signs from Maria that all of the waiting and stress was taking a toll. Her letters to Bonhoeffer came further and further apart, and she began suffering from headaches, insomnia, and even fainting fits. According to her sister, Ruth-Alice, there were "many indications that she was going through an emotional crisis." Her relatives noticed that each time she returned from Tegel, she seemed "desperate," as though it was dawning on her that the situation with Dietrich was not getting any better. In June she wrote him a letter about their situation. It has not survived, but Bonhoeffer's reply to it on June 27 gives us an idea of what she was feeling:

> My dearest, most beloved Maria,
> Many thanks for your letter. It didn't depress me at all; it made me happy, boundlessly happy, because I know that we couldn't speak to each other in such a way unless we loved each other very much—far more so than either of us realizes today. . . . None of what you wrote surprised or dismayed me. It was all more or less as I thought. What entitled me to believe, when we've seen so little of each other, that you could love me at all, and how could I have failed to rejoice in the smallest token of your love? . . .
> So it sometimes torments you to think of me? My dearest, dearest Maria, isn't it enough for you to know that you've made me glad and happy—more so than I ever hoped to be in all my days? Isn't it enough for you, if you're beginning to doubt your love for me, that I love you as you are, and that I want nothing from you—no

sacrifice, nothing; just you yourself? The one thing I do *not* want is that you should be or become unhappy because you feel the lack of something—because I'm failing to provide you with what you seek in me. On White Monday* you felt you "couldn't go on." So tell me, *can* you go on without me? And, if you feel you can, can you still do so if you know that *I* can't go on without *you*? No, it's all quite impossible. Don't torment yourself, dearest Maria. I know how you feel, and it's absolutely inevitable. To pretend otherwise would be untrue and insincere. But, being the way we are, we nonetheless belong together and will remain together, and I won't let you go; I shall hold you tight, so that you know we belong together and must stay together. . . .

I'm especially grateful for what you wrote about the years I told you of.** When I didn't hear for so long, I was afraid you might have been dismayed, though I didn't really believe so. And I detect in what you say a repetition of the "yes" you wrote me on 13 January 1943, and it's that "yes" to which I cling whenever I have to wait for a letter for any length of time. That's when I hear it again and again, that "Yes, yes, yes!," and become overwhelmed and happy at the sound of it.

So now you won't be coming again for a while. Dearest Maria, if you find it too tiring, it goes without saying that you're right not to do so. On the other hand, can there be anything in our lives more important at this stage than to see each other again and again? May we not be forcibly erecting a barrier between us if we deliberately forgo that? . . .

Let me be quite frank. We don't know how often we shall see each other again in this life, the times being what they are, and it depresses me a great deal to think that we may later reproach ourselves for something irremediable. Of course there are extraneous obstacles, like illness or bans on travel, which are unavoidable, but inward obstacles, no matter how insuperable they may seem at the time, can never absolve us of subsequent self-reproach. . . .

Betrothed couples belong together, and never more so than when one of them is in my present predicament. No one knows better than I,

---

* A holiday celebrated after Pentecost Sunday.
** See page 66, letter about his relationship with Elizabeth Zinn.

dearest Maria, that I'm subjecting you to unparalleled sacrifices, privations and exertions, and no one would more readily spare you them. How gladly I would forgo the pleasure a visit from you brings me in my solitude, but I strongly feel that I mustn't do so for our own sake and that of our future marriage. I have to exact this sacrifice from you— without being able to recompense you for it in any way—for the sake of our love. It goes without saying that you can't come if you're ill, or if it overtaxes you physically, but we must overcome the spiritual difficulties together! . . .

I've told you quite frankly how I feel. I'm untroubled by all that has gone before, but we alone are responsible for the future, and in that respect everything must be clear, straight-forward and unconstrained, mustn't it? Above all, we must submit our lives to a single consideration—that we belong together—and act accordingly.

It isn't easy to have to discuss these things by letter, but God has willed it so. We simply mustn't lose patience. God's will and our subjection to it are quite beyond dispute. I'm as averse to being pitied as you are, but I want you to wait with me and be patient, and the more patient the longer this goes on. And now, don't be sad. Tell me what you think and act as you must. But always rest assured that I love you very much and hold you very dear.

> Yours,
> Dietrich

Maria visited on June 27, so it's unclear whether she received his letter before or after her visit. Bonhoeffer wrote again on August 13:

My dearest Maria,

It always takes so long these days for our letters to reach their destination. It's probably the fault of the air raids. . . . I've received only one letter from you in almost six weeks, and I'm afraid my parents' news of you was similar the last time they visited me. But you know, letters are such a feeble token of our belonging to each other that our thoughts and prayers are bound to express it best of all. And that they do whether or not letters arrive, don't they? So now you've started work in Berlin.* Hard work has for centuries been extolled as the finest remedy for troubles and cares. Many people consider the most beneficial aspect of work to be its tendency to numb the psyche. Personally, I think what really matters is that the right kind of work renders one unselfish, and that a person whose heart is filled with personal interests and concerns develops a desire for such unselfishness in the service of others. So I hope from the bottom of my heart, dearest Maria, that your new job grants you that boon, and that the greater its difficulties, the greater will be your sense of spiritual liberation. I certainly believe that, given your natural and inherited vitality, not to say craze for hard work, you won't find a job like that too much for you. You've no idea how liberated I myself would feel if I were once more able to work for others instead of solely for myself. However, I'm thankful anew every day to be able to immerse myself in my books and learn so much that is new to me, and to jot down one or two of the ideas and references I need for my work. I've recently, and with great enjoyment, reread the memoirs of Gabriele von Bülow von Humboldt.** She was separated from her fiancé for three whole years, shortly after her engagement! What immense patience and forbearance people had in those days, and what great "tensile strength"! Every letter was over six weeks in transit. They learned to do what technology has deprived us of, namely, to commend each other daily to God and put their trust in him. We are now relearning that, and we should be thankful, however hard it is.

My beloved Maria, let us never lose faith in what befalls us; all of it is bestowed on us by good, kindly hands. I shall be thinking of you a great deal on the 22nd.*** Father is with God. He is only a step or two ahead of us. Let us think of him and Max with joy in our hearts and pray that Mother continues to find the consolation that has been hers throughout the past two years. Good-bye for now, beloved Maria, and may God preserve us all.

With all my faithful heart,
Dietrich

---

* It seemed that Maria was to begin a job with the Red Cross.

** She was a German noblewoman of the nineteenth century.

*** It was the anniversary of her father's death.

After this letter, Dietrich's parents informed him that Maria had decided to move in with them and help them at their home in Berlin. Ostensibly she was to perform secretarial duties for Dr. Bonhoeffer, whose office was on the first floor of their home. Dietrich wrote her,

My dearly beloved Maria,

So now, entirely of your own volition and without my having repeated my request, you've made the big decision to come here and help my parents. I just can't tell you how happy I am. I couldn't believe it at first, when my parents told me, and I still can't quite grasp how it happened or what made it possible. . . . I had just begun to reconcile myself to the idea that you would be recalled to the Red Cross, and that we wouldn't see each other again for ages. Now all that has changed completely, and it's a godsend from my point of view. I'm bound to worry about you during air raids, it's true, but I shall know that you're near me every hour of every day. How wonderful! What a wonderful decision of yours! I'm so grateful to you!

. . . May I beg a very great favor? Help Mama to cope with all her recurrent worries, dearest Maria, and please be very patient with her. That's the best turn you could do me. It may be that the good Lord has sent you to her precisely because she needs an outstanding daughter-in-law at this time, and the better you get to know Mama the more you'll sense that she really wants nothing for herself (*too* little, perhaps!), and that all her wishes, actions and thoughts are centered on others. Let us pray to God you succeed. And then—I shall see you again soon!! Dearest Maria, we must summon up all our strength again and be patient. Let us not lose heart. God has seen to it that the human heart is stronger than any power on earth. Good-bye for now, dearest Maria, and thank you for everything, everything!

I embrace and kiss you tenderly.

Yours, Dietrich

Maria visited Bonhoeffer again on August 23. As things turned out, it was the last time they saw each other. Bonhoeffer wrote to Bethge that day: "Maria was here today, so fresh and at the same time steadfast and tranquil in a way I've rarely seen."

Bonhoeffer Plans His Escape

In September, Bonhoeffer determined that he would escape from Tegel. His freedom to walk around had been extraordinary, and escape was always a very real option. But for various reasons, he had not done so. Now the avenues of hope that made staying there worthwhile were closed. Nearly everyone working for the conspiracy had been arrested. It was all over. The Nazis had solid evidence of what they had been doing, and in brutal interrogations, they would get more information. The only reason Hitler didn't have everyone executed was that he wanted to get as much information as possible. He wanted every name and every detail of the monstrous evil that had been done behind his back all those years. If ever there was a time to escape, this was it. There was no question the war would be over soon. Even if the Germans hadn't succeeded in killing Hitler, the Allies would do the job soon enough.

Bonhoeffer's closest friend among the guards, Corporal Knoblauch, volunteered to help. Word was passed to the family that they must procure a mechanic's uniform in Dietrich's size and deliver it to Knoblauch's home, four miles east of Tegel. They must also get food coupons and money. Knoblauch would hide everything in one of the small garden houses that Germans kept (and still keep) on the outskirts of the city. He and Bonhoeffer would go there after the escape. As for the escape itself, Bonhoeffer would put on the mechanic's uniform and simply walk out of the prison with Knoblauch at the end of his day's guard duties. The biggest hurdle was whether Bonhoeffer could remain hidden and leave the country before he was caught.

On September 24, a Sunday, Bonhoeffer's sister Ursula, her husband, Rüdiger, and their daughter Renate drove to Knoblauch's home and delivered a package containing the mechanic's uniform, the coupons, and the money. Everything was ready for an escape, except for the details regarding how Bonhoeffer would get out of the country. It's unclear why Bonhoeffer didn't proceed with the escape that week, but the lack of definite plans on how to escape Germany probably stopped him.

The following weekend another event caused him to forget about escaping altogether. On Saturday, the thirtieth, Klaus Bonhoeffer saw a car parked near his house. It caused him to turn around immediately and drive away. Klaus's wife, Emmi, was away at Schleswig-Holstein visiting their children, who had been sent there because of the Allied bombing. Klaus was sure the car was a Gestapo car, and if he had gone home, he would have been arrested and taken away, so he drove to Ursula's house on Marienburgerallee, where he stayed overnight. During this painful episode, Ursula succeeded in talking her brother out of suicide, something that, after Klaus had been arrested, tortured, and sentenced to death, she came to regret.

The noose was getting tighter by the day. The same Saturday in which Klaus showed up looking for refuge, their cousin, the wife of General Paul von Hase, was released from prison and showed up at their door. Von Hase had been executed by the People's Court, and she had nowhere to go. Because of her husband's role in the conspiracy, none of her relatives would take her in, save Ursula and Rüdiger Schleicher.

Around the same time that day Corporal Knoblauch arrived to discuss the details of Dietrich's flight from Germany; the Schleichers were to get a false passport and arrange a flight to Sweden. But Ursula and Rüdiger explained that the plan had been thrown off course. Klaus was about to be arrested. Dietrich's escape would only make everyone related to him look more guilty.

The next morning, Sunday, the Gestapo arrived and took Klaus away. On Monday Knoblauch returned to the Schleichers and informed them that Dietrich had decided against escape. It could only make things worse for everyone, especially for Klaus, and the Gestapo would have no compunction about going after his parents or Maria. It never came to that, but that Wednesday, the Gestapo came again to Marienburgerallee and arrested Rüdiger. Now two Bonhoeffer brothers and two Bonhoeffer brothers-in-law were imprisoned.

And that Sunday, October 8, 1944, Bonhoeffer's eighteen months at Tegel came to an end. He was secretly moved to the Gestapo prison on Prinz-Albrecht-Strasse. Dietrich Bonhoeffer was now in the custody of the state.

The Gestapo Prison

Bonhoeffer's four months in the Gestapo prison were markedly different from his time at Tegel. The cells were underground. Bonhoeffer's was eight by five feet, and he had no opportunity to see the light of day. There was no prison yard in which to walk, no thrushes to hear sing, and no friendly guards. Admiral Canaris said to him, "It's hell in here." Also there were Carl Goerdeler, Joseph Müller, General Oster, and Judge Sack. Maria's cousin, Fabian von Schlabrendorff, was there too. It seemed that everyone who had been working for the conspiracy was behind bars. Even Eberhard Bethge had been arrested, although he was not being held in this terrible place.

When Bonhoeffer was first interrogated, he was threatened with torture. He was told that the fate of his parents, his other family members, and his fiancée hung on his confession. He was able to speak with von Schlabrendorff and characterized his interrogations as "frankly repulsive." Nothing leads us to believe he was ever tortured, but his brother Klaus and most of the others were. In his book *They Almost Killed Hitler*, Schlabrendorff wrote of what he himself suffered. When Schlabrendorff thought he would be released, Bonhoeffer asked him to visit his father and suggest that he try to get a personal meeting with Himmler. But Schlabrendorff was not released during that time.

What Dohnanyi endured is another story. His health suffered greatly. During one Allied bombing, he suffered a stroke that caused him to become partially paralyzed and blind. Still, he was accorded no mercy by the Nazis, who knew that he was one of the conspiracy leaders, and would do anything to get information from him. His sufferings were such that he persuaded his wife, Christine, to smuggle a diphtheria baccillus into the prison. If he could infect himself with it, he would not be able to be interrogated.

In a letter to Maria, Bonhoeffer had once written:

> Stifter once said, "Pain is a holy angel, who shows treasures to men which otherwise remain forever hidden; through him men have become greater than through all joys of the world." It must be so and I tell this to myself in my present position over and over again—the pain of longing which often can be felt even physically, must be there, and we shall not and need not talk it away. But it needs to be overcome every time and thus there is an even holier angel than the one of pain, that is the one of joy in God.

But Bonhoeffer could not write to Maria anymore. She made the trek to the prison a number of times, hoping for permission to visit. Each time she was denied. As harsh as the conditions were, they were not as bad as they might have been. Himmler and the SS knew the war was winding down, and not in Germany's favor, so they were putting out "peace feelers" and knew they could use these prisoners as bargaining chips. Thus they allowed Bonhoeffer to write Maria at Christmas.

19 December 1944
My dearest Maria,
I'm so glad to be able to write you a Christmas letter, and to be able, through you, to convey my love to my parents and my brothers and sisters, to thank you all. Our homes will be very quiet at this time. But I have often found that the quieter my surroundings, the more vividly I sense my connection with you all. It's as if, in solitude, the soul develops organs of which we're hardly aware in everyday life. So I haven't for an instant felt lonely and forlorn. You yourself, my parents—all of you including my friends and students on active service—are my constant companions. Your prayers and kind thoughts, passages from the Bible, long-forgotten conversations, pieces of music, books—all are invested with life and reality as never before. I live in a great, unseen realm of whose real existence I'm in no doubt. The old children's song about the angels says "two to cover me, two to wake me," and today we grownups are no less in need than children of preservation, night and morning, by kindly, unseen powers. So you mustn't think I'm unhappy. Anyway, what do happiness and unhappiness mean? They depend so little on circumstances and so much more on what goes on inside us. I'm thankful every day to have you—you and all of you—and that makes me happy and cheerful.

Superficially, there's little difference between here and Tegel. The daily routine is the same, the midday meal is considerably better, breakfast and supper are somewhat more meager. Thank you for all the things you've brought me. I'm being treated well and by the book. The place is well heated. Mobility is all I lack, so I do exercises and pace up and down my cell with the window open. . . . I'm glad I'm allowed to smoke! Thank you for thinking of me and doing all you can for me. From my point of view, knowing that is the most important thing of all.

We've now been waiting for each other for almost two years, dearest Maria. Don't lose heart! I'm glad you're with my parents. Give my fondest love to our mother and the whole family. Here are another few verses that have occurred to me in recent nights. They're my Christmas greeting to you, my parents, and my brothers and sisters. . . . In great love and gratitude to you, my parents, and my brothers and sisters.

I embrace you.

Yours, Dietrich

The following poem—which Bonhoeffer enclosed with his letter—has become famous throughout Germany and is included in many school textbooks. It is also sung in churches as a hymn.

POWERS OF GOOD

With every power for good to stay and guide me,
comforted and inspired beyond all fear,
I'll live these days with you in thought beside me,
and pass, with you, into the coming year.
The old year still torments our hearts, unhastening;
the long days of our sorrow still endure;
Father, grant to the souls thou hast been chastening
that thou hast promised, the healing and the cure.
Should it be ours to drain the cup of grieving
even to the dregs of pain, at thy command,
we will not falter, thankfully receiving
all that is given by thy loving hand.
But should it be thy will once more to release us
to life's enjoyment and its good sunshine,
that which we've learned from sorrow shall increase us,
and all our life be dedicate as thine.
Today, let candles shed their radiant greeting;
lo, on our darkness are they not thy light
leading us, haply, to our longed-for meeting?
Thou canst illumine even our darkest night.
When now the silence deepens for our hearkening,
grant we may hear the children's voices raise
from all the unseen world around us darkening
their universal paean, in thy praise.

While all the powers of good aid and attend us,
boldly we'll face the future, come what may.
At even and at morn God will befriend us,
and oh, most surely on each newborn day!

Henceforward, the information on Bonhoeffer becomes scarce. Most of what we know about him during this four-month period comes from Schlabrendorff. His account, from the book *I Knew Dietrich Bonhoeffer*, is as follows:

I must admit that I was filled with alarm when I caught sight of Dietrich Bonhoeffer. But when I saw his upright figure and his imperturbable glance, I took comfort, and I knew that he had recognized me without losing his composure. . . . The very next morning I was able to have a word with him in the washroom which had facilities for several people, though the rule was that the prisoners were not allowed to speak to one another, and this was normally strictly watched. We had known each other for some time before the war began, and our relationship had become even closer through Dietrich Bonhoeffer's engagement to my cousin Maria von Wedemeyer. Dietrich let me know immediately that he was determined to resist all the efforts of the Gestapo, and to reveal nothing of what our friends' fates made it our duty to keep dark. A few days later he was transferred from cell 19 to cell 24. This made him my neighbour, and gave us the chance to communicate with one another and have short conversations every day. In the morning we hurried together into a niche of the washroom where we could have a shower, and we eagerly indulged in this opportunity, though the water was cold, for in this way we could escape the supervision of our warders and have a brief exchange of thoughts. In the evenings this was repeated and the doors of our cells remained open until all the prisoners of our corridor had returned. During that time we were eagerly talking to one another through the slits in the hinges of the door separating us. Finally, we saw one another during the air-raid warnings which happened every day and night, and where we seized every opportunity to inform each other of our thoughts and experiences. Only someone who has been in strict solitary confinement for a long period of time is able to understand what this chance of talking to somebody meant for us during those long months. Dietrich Bonhoeffer told me of his interrogations. . . . His noble and pure soul must have suffered deeply. But he betrayed no sign of it. He was always good-tempered, always of the same kindliness and politeness towards everybody, so that to my surprise, within a short time, he had won over his warders, who were not always kindly disposed. It was significant for our relationship that he was rather the hopeful one while I now and then suffered from depressions. He always cheered me up and comforted me, he never tired of repeating that the only fight which is lost is that which we give up. Many little notes he slipped into my hands on which he had written biblical words of comfort and hope. He looked with optimism at his own situation too. He repeatedly told me the Gestapo had no clue to his real activities. He had been able to trivialize his acquaintance with Goerdeler. His connection with Perels, the justiciary of the Confessing Church, was not of sufficient importance to serve as an indictment. And as for his foreign travels and meetings with English Church dignitaries, the Gestapo did not grasp their purpose and point. If the investigations were to carry on at the present pace, years might pass till they reached their conclusions. He was full of hope, he even conjectured that he might be set free without a trial, if some influential person had the courage to intercede on his behalf with the Gestapo. He also thought he had represented his relation to his brother-in-law, *Reichsgerichtsrat* von Dohnanyi, in a plausible way to his interlocutors, so that this was not a heavy charge against him. When Dohnanyi was also delivered to the Prinz-Albrecht-Strasse prison, Dietrich even managed to get in touch with him. When we returned after an air-raid warning from our cement shelter, his brother-in-law lay on a stretcher in his cell, paralyzed in both legs. With an alacrity that nobody would have believed him capable of, Dietrich Bonhoeffer suddenly dived into the open cell of his brother-in-law. It seemed a miracle that none of the warders saw it. But Dietrich also succeeded in the more difficult part of his venture, in emerging from Dohnanyi's cell unnoticed and getting into line with the column of prisoners who were filing along the corridor. That same evening he told me that he had agreed with Dohnanyi upon all essential points of their further testimony. Only once he thought things had taken a turn for the worse, for he had been threatened with the arrest of his fiancee, his aged parents and his sisters unless his statements were more comprehensive. Then he judged the time had come frankly to declare that he was an enemy of National Socialism. His attitude, so he had stated, was rooted in his Christian convictions. In his talks with me he stuck to his opinion that no evidence could be produced which justified a prosecution for high treason.

As neighbours in our prison cells we also shared joy and sorrow in our personal and human life. The few things which we possessed and which we were allowed to accept from our relations and friends we exchanged according to our needs. With shining eyes he told me of the letters from his fiancee and his parents whose love he felt near him even in the Gestapo prison. Each Wednesday he received his laundry parcel which also contained cigars, apples or bread, and he never omitted to share them with me the same evening when we were not watched; it delighted him that even in prison you were able to help your neighbour, and let him share in what you had.

On the morning of 3rd February 1945 an air raid turned the city of Berlin into a heap of rubble; the buildings of the Gestapo Headquarters were also burnt out. Tightly squeezed together we were standing in our air-raid shelter when a bomb hit it with an enormous explosion. For a second it seemed as if the shelter were bursting and the ceiling crashing down on top of us. It rocked like a ship tossing in the storm, but it held. At that moment Dietrich Bonhoeffer showed his mettle. He remained quite calm, he did not move a muscle, but stood motionless and relaxed as if nothing had happened.

On 7th February 1945 in the morning I spoke to him for the last time. On the same day around noon the number of his cell was called up amongst others. The prisoners were divided into two groups. Bonhoeffer was transported to Buchenwald, the concentration camp near Weimar.

"The Scoundrel Is Dead!"

The first days of February 1945 were eventful, to say the least. The war was winding down, but the cruel injustice of Hitler's regime continued nonetheless. On February 2, the notorious Roland Freisler of the People's Court sentenced Klaus Bonhoeffer and Rüdiger Schleicher to death. On February 3, Schlabrendorff was about to be sentenced to death by Freisler too. But on that day, the American Eighth Air Force unleashed nearly one thousand B-17 Flying Fortress bombers on Berlin. Within a short period they dropped three thousand *tons* of bombs. "For two hours," Bethge wrote, "squadron after squadron flew over Berlin in the bright blue winter sky, transforming the area east of the zoo into a wilderness of smoke and ash." The American bombs hit the Gestapo prison where Bonhoeffer was being held. The damage was so severe that he and most other prisoners would have to be transferred.

The People's Court was hit badly. Freisler was preparing to sentence Schlabrendorff when the American bombs struck. In one of those moments for which the word *Schadenfreude* seems to have been invented, the supremely wicked Freisler was brained by a ceiling beam and dispatched to another bar of justice altogether, one with which he seemed to have been less well acquainted. As a result of Freisler's unscheduled appearance in that other court, Schlabrendorff's exit from this world was delayed by decades.* But things that day would get stranger still.

As the American bombs rained upon the People's Court, the brother of Rüdiger Schleicher, Dr. Rolf Schleicher, was in the Berlin subway station. He was a senior staff doctor in Stuttgart and had come to Berlin to appeal the death sentence handed down by Freisler on his brother. But no one was allowed to leave the safety of the station until the bombing ceased. When he was allowed above ground, Dr. Schleicher passed the People's Court in which Freisler had sentenced his brother the day before. He saw that it had been bombed heavily and was burning. Someone noticed his doctor's uniform and haled him into the courtyard to help with one of the wounded. It was some important person who needed attention. Dr. Schleicher went over to the man and saw that there was nothing he could do, since the man was already dead. Dr. Schleicher also saw to his amazement that the dead man was Roland Freisler, whose keening voice had mocked his brother Rüdiger one day earlier, before gloatingly pronouncing the death sentence upon him.

Dr. Schleicher was pressed to write a death certificate, but refused to do so until he could see the minister of justice, Otto Thierack. Thierack was

---

* Schlabrendorff lived until 1980.

"quite shocked" by the eerily apt "coincidence" and told Schleicher that the execution of his brother Rüdiger would be delayed until an official "plea for mercy" had been submitted. When Dr. Schleicher arrived at his brother's house at Marienburgerallee later that day, he was able to utter the triumphant words: "The scoundrel is dead!"

Bonhoeffer Leaves Berlin

In the early afternoon of February 7, Bonhoeffer and a number of other prominent prisoners were taken from their cells and made to wait near two vans that would take them to the concentration camps at Buchenwald and Flossenbürg. There were twenty men, all principal figures in the conspiracy. A more stunning array of personages can hardly be imagined.

Among them was the former chancellor of Austria, Dr. Kurt von Schuschnigg, whose treatment by the Gestapo was one of the blackest marks in the pages of the Third Reich. Here, too, was Dr. Hjalmar Schacht, former head of the *Reichsbank*, who had enabled Hitler's rise to power and later fought in vain against the monster he'd helped create. Schacht had spoken against the treatment of the Jews early on and was part of the 1938 plot. Like so many others, he was arrested after the failed Stauffenberg plot. And here stood Admiral Canaris, General Oster, and Judge Sack. Bonhoeffer would join these three at Flossenbürg in two months. Also here were General Halder, General Thomas, and Oster's colleague, Theodor Strünck. All of these would get on the van for Flossenbürg.

Standing in front of the other van was a second group. It included General von Falkenhausen, who had been the governor of Belgium during Germany's occupation in the First War; Commander Franz Liedig, the navy corvette captain who had worked under Canaris; Ludwig Gehre, who had also been an Abwehr officer under Canaris; Gottfried Count Bismarck, a grandson of Otto von Bismarck; and the nearly seventy-year-old Count Werner von Alvensleben, who in 1934 had refused to take the infamous oath of allegiance to Hitler, and who had been persona non grata with the Nazis ever since. Dr. Hermann Pünder was here, too; he was a Catholic politician who had been the secretary of state just before Hitler. And Dr. Joseph Müller was here. Müller had been viciously mistreated by the Gestapo for years, but he gave them none of the information they so violently sought.

Payne Best described Müller as "one of the bravest and most determined men imaginable."

And here, too, was Dietrich Bonhoeffer, who had just celebrated his thirty-ninth birthday in a Gestapo cell and now saw the first daylight in four months. For most here it had been far longer. Wherever they were headed, to be outdoors in this extraordinary company lifted everyone's spirits. It was clear the war was ending and Hitler was finished. Whether any here lived to see it was another story.

When it was time to board the van, Bonhoeffer and Müller were hand-cuffed. Bonhoeffer protested in vain. Müller, who had suffered a thousand times worse, offered a word of encouragement to his friend and fellow believer. "Let us go calmly to the gallows as Christians," he said. Bonhoeffer was an ambassador in chains. Now he would take a long journey, two hundred miles south to Buchenwald.

CHAPTER 30

BUCHENWALD

His soul really shone in the dark desperation of our prison . . .
[Bonhoeffer] had always been afraid that he would not be strong
enough to stand such a test but now he knew there was nothing in life
of which one need ever be afraid.

—Payne Best, in a letter to Sabine

B
uchenwald was one of the Nazi centers of death.* But it was not
merely a place where people died; it was a place where death was
celebrated and worshiped. As much as Bodelschwingh's community
at Bethel had been a living embodiment of the gospel of life, where
the weak were cared for and loved, Buchenwald and its equivalents throughout the Third Reich were living embodiments of the satanic worldview of
the SS, where weakness was preyed upon and crushed. Human beings were
sometimes murdered for their skin, which was used to make souvenir items
such as wallets and knife cases for members of the SS. The heads of some
prisoners were shrunken and given as gifts. Bonhoeffer had heard of these
abominable practices through Dohnanyi, but few other Germans knew of
them at this time. When Emmi Bonhoeffer boldly told neighbors that in
some camps the fat of human beings was used to make soap, they refused to
believe her, convinced such tales were anti-German propaganda.

---

* The name Buchenwald means "Beech Forest." Though it was not an extermination camp per se,
56,545 people were killed there, through forced labor, shooting, hanging, or medical experiments
before the Allies liberated it in April 1945.

Bonhoeffer spent seven weeks at Buchenwald. He was not in the main compound, but just outside it in the cold makeshift prison cellar of a yellow tenement-style building constructed to house Buchenwald staff. It was five or six stories high, and its dank cellar had previously been used as a military jail for the SS. Now it would hold more illustrious prisoners, seventeen of them, in twelve cells.*

The Cast of Characters at Buchenwald

We have no letters from Bonhoeffer during this period, but one of the men he met at Buchenwald, the British intelligence officer Captain S. Payne Best, wrote an account of his years in German captivity titled *The Venlo Incident*. From this book we get most of the information about Bonhoeffer's last two months. Best arrived at Buchenwald on February 24, with three other prisoners. One was another British officer, Hugh Falconer; the second was Vassily Kokorin, a Soviet air force officer and nephew of Stalin's protegé Molotov; the third was General Friedrich von Rabenau, who joined Bonhoeffer in his small cell.

The sixty-year-old Rabenau was a Christian whose faith led him to oppose Hitler early on. In 1937 he was among the signers of the Declaration of Ninety-Six Evangelical Church Leaders Against the Theology of Alfred Rosenberg, which denounced and rebutted Rosenberg's anti-Christian, pro-Nazi philosophy. In 1942 he was sent into early retirement and spent the next two years getting his doctorate in theology from Berlin University, just as Bonhoeffer had done. He was also active in the Resistance, serving as a liaison between Beck and Goerdeler. Rabenau was also the author of a lengthy and highly regarded biography of the German military leader Hans von Seeckt, which Bonhoeffer had read. We know from Pünder, who shared the small cell next to theirs, that Rabenau continued to work on his auto-biography at Buchenwald, and it seems likely that Bonhoeffer was writing, too, though nothing survived. We also know from Pünder that Rabenau and Bonhoeffer spent hours discussing theology, and that Pünder enjoyed listening

---

* Cells 1, 2, 3, 4, 6, 7, and 8—all on one side of the cellar—were very small. Cell 5, also on that side, was about twice as large as the others. On the opposite side were cells 9, 10, 11, and 12, also twice as large as the smaller cells. Between the two rows of cells were two brick walls with one opening between them, so that each of the two rows of cells opened onto a corridor, and there was a central corridor between them, leading to the cellar entrance.

to their discussions. Rabenau and Bonhoeffer also played chess on a set given to Rabenau by Payne Best.

Best was one of the principal figures in the 1940 debacle that came to be known as the Venlo Incident, from which he took the title for his book. Though his book is a work of nonfiction, Best portrays himself as part Colonel Nicholson from *Bridge on the River Kwai*, part Terry Thomas, and part Baron von Munchausen. That Best was larger-than-life was not lost on him, but he could poke fun at himself too. In his book, he quoted a description of himself from someone else's memoir:

> As particularly noticeable Mr. Best must be mentioned, the Secret Service man who was "stolen" from Holland in 1940; really, a model for the figure of the well-known international caricature of the Englishman. Very tall, very gaunt, and even stooping a little through emaciation, with hollow leathery cheeks, prominent teeth, a monocle, flannel trousers, a check jacket, and—a cigarette. Always showing his big false horse's teeth in an obliging smile and displaying that trustworthy discretion which engenders deepest confidence.

Best then commented on her description: "Including her comments on my teeth, I accept, and indeed am flattered by her word picture, especially since the teeth were not my own but a construction of the Sachsenhausen dentist, who possibly had used his art to make my appearance better conform to his idea of an Englishman."

Seeing Bonhoeffer's last days through the funhouse monocle of Captain Best's personality can be strange, but his indefatigable good humor sometimes lightens the grim spectacle. In his defense, Best's six years at the Sachsenhausen concentration camp can only have sharpened his penchant for dark humor.

Also in this cellar were the former German ambassador to Spain, Dr. Erich Heberlein, and his wife, Margot. Best described them: "Of the Heberleins, the grey mare was undoubtedly the better horse. A mixture of Irish and Spanish blood cannot fail to produce something vivid and out of the ordinary. . . . she was as big a trial to her captors as two British prisoners, which is saying a lot. Her husband? A charming man, a diplomat of the old school, with impeccable manners and the impaired digestion of his class."

According to Best, Müller's cell mate, Captain Gehre, was a "spare, dark, good-looking man of about thirty." In fact, Gehre was fifty. After the Stauffenberg debacle, the Gestapo hunted him. He and his wife decided to escape via suicide. He shot her dead, then turned the gun on himself, but succeeded only in shooting out an eye. The Gestapo caught, tortured, and interrogated him. He would die with Bonhoeffer, Canaris, Oster, and Sack on April 9 at Flossenbürg.

Count von Alvensleben was in cell number four, with Colonel von Petersdorff. Petersdorff had been wounded six times in the First War and is described by Best as "a wild, adventurous fellow" who had opposed Hitler from the beginning. He was at the Lehrterstrasse prison on February 3 when American bombs buried him in his cell. His lungs and kidneys were injured, but he had not received any treatment and was now quite sick. His cell mate Alvensleben was typical of many arrested after the July 20 plot in that he had done nothing more than be on friendly terms with some of the plotters. Thousands had been arrested for this crime. Anyone related by blood was guilty of *Sippenhaft* (liability of kin), whereby relatives of the accused were arrested and punished: wives, parents, and children too. Some small children were taken away from parents, never to be seen again.

Another of the seventeen prisoners was Dr. Hoepner, brother of General Erich Hoepner, a central figure in the July 20 plot. He was among the first hanged at Plötzensee in a ghastly spectacle Hitler had filmed for his sadistic enjoyment. Best described this brother as "the only man whom I met during my imprisonment who was an abject coward." Best's cell was next to Hoepner's, and Best got into terrific arguments with the warders. He had become something of an expert at dealing with concentration camp guards, having been in their company for six years by then, and seemed to take great pride in refusing to give them an inch. But hearing these arguments, Hoepner got "into such a state of nerves that he collapsed on to the floor of the cell." Twice doctors had to attend to him because of these nervous spells.

In fairness to Hoepner, it was a brutal situation. Even the supremely doughty Best thought so: "This has been a hell of a month and has taken more out of me than the whole of my previous imprisonment. Doubt much whether shall ever get home. Probably shall be liquidated by a pistol bullet if our troops get too near. Only real hope is to destroy them and see no reason to spare those of us who are in their power—thorough!"

In cell five, one of the larger cells, was General von Falkenhausen. Best thought him "one of the finest men I have ever met." In the First War he was awarded the *Pour le Mérite.*˙ According to Schuschnigg, Falkenhausen now wore his full uniform "with bright red lining," the *Pour le Mérite* hung around his neck. In the next cell was the British squadron leader Hugh Falconer, and next to him, Kokorin. Müller and Gehre shared cell number eight. The last two inmates in this small prison with Bonhoeffer were quite unlike the others. The first we know only as "Heidl." Isa Vermehren described her: "An indefinable and most unpleasant young lady of whom no one could discover what was her real name, nationality, or language—she was put down as a spy and the only doubt was whether she had only spied for the Gestapo or whether she had been clever enough to ply her noble profession in the interests of two sides at the same time."

Best described her as "a short, fair, thickset girl in her early twenties who, but for her stature, might have posed as a model for a youthful Germania," but who was "always one of our problems." She had boarded at the brothel at Sachsenhausen and had "picked up much of the language and manners of her hostesses." Kokorin was taken with her, but was alone in this regard.

By many light-years the strangest of all who shared the last two months of Bonhoeffer's life were Dr. Waldemar Hoven and Dr. Sigmund Rascher, two of the most evil characters in the Third Reich. When Bonhoeffer arrived, Hoven was a prisoner, but in three weeks, because of a shortage of doctors, he was set free. As the chief doctor at Buchenwald, Hoven had overseen the killings of many inmates, some sick and some healthy. He also had the distinction to be a paramour of the infamously cruel Ilse Koch, wife of the camp commandant. A witness at the Nuremberg trials, a man who was an inmate at Buchenwald and had worked with Hoven, testified,

> Dr. Hoven stood once together with me at the window of the pathological section and pointed to a prisoner not known to me who crossed the place where the roll calls were held. Dr. Hoven told me: "I want to see the skull of this prisoner on my writing desk by tomorrow evening." The prisoner was ordered to report to the medical section, after the physician had noted down the number of the prisoner. The corpse was delivered on the same day to the dissection room. The post-mortem

---

˙ The highest German decoration for bravery.

examination showed that the prisoner had been killed by injections. The skull was prepared as ordered and delivered to Dr. Hoven.

The thirty-six-year-old Rascher took Hoven's place around February 28. Best met him in the lavatory one morning, "a little man with a ginger moustache" who was "a queer fellow; possibly the queerest character which has ever come my way." Rascher told Best that he had "planned and supervised the construction of the gas chambers and was responsible for the use of prisoners as guinea pigs in medical research." Best said,

> Obviously, he saw nothing wrong in this and considered it a matter of expediency. As regards the gas chambers he said that Himmler, a very kind-hearted man, was most anxious that prisoners should be exterminated in a manner which caused them least anxiety and suffering, and the greatest trouble had been taken to design a death chamber so camouflaged that its purpose would not be apparent, and to regulate the flow of the lethal gas so that the patients might fall asleep without recognizing that they would never wake. Unfortunately, Rascher said, they had never quite succeeded in solving the problem caused by the varying resistance of different people to the effects of poison gases, and always there had been a few who lived longer than others and recognized where they were and what was happening. Rascher said that the main difficulty was that the numbers to be killed were so great that it was impossible to prevent the gas chambers being overfilled, which greatly impeded any attempts to ensure a regular and simultaneous death-rate.

Why Rascher was there is unclear. He had been on Himmler's personal staff and was chief "medical officer" at Dachau. Rascher's principal claims to infamy are his "experiments" on human subjects. They began when he realized no one knew what occurred when aviators were subjected to high altitudes. He wrote Himmler with a proposal:

> Esteemed *Reichsführer!*
> My sincere thanks for your cordial wishes and flowers on the birth of my second son. This time, too, it is a strong boy, though he has come three weeks too early. I will permit myself to send you a picture of both children at an opportune moment.

For the time being I have been assigned to the *Luftgaukommando VII,* Munich, for a medical course. During this course, where researches on high-altitude flights play a prominent part (determined by the some-what higher ceiling of the English fighter plans), considerable regret was expressed at the fact that no tests with human material had yet been possible for us, as such experiments are very dangerous and nobody volunteers for them. I put, therefore, the *serious* question: can you make available two or three professional criminals for these experiments? . . . The experiments, from which the subjects can, of course, die, would take place with my cooperation. They are essential for researches on high-altitude flight and cannot be carried out, as has been tried, with monkeys, who offer entirely different test-conditions. I have had a very confidential talk with a representative of the Air Forces Surgeon who makes these experiments. He is also of the opinion that the question could only be solved by experiments on human persons (feeble-minded could also be used as test material).

I hope sincerely, highly esteemed *Reichsführer* that, in spite of the immense burden of work you carry, you are in the best of health.

With my heartiest wishes, I am with *Heil Hitler* your gratefully devoted

Sigmund Rascher

Permission was "gladly" granted. One Austrian inmate described one experiment:

I have personally seen through the observation window of the decom-pression chamber when a prisoner inside would stand a vacuum until his lungs ruptured. . . . They would go mad and pull out their hair in an effort to relieve the pressure. They would tear their heads and face with their fingers and nails in an attempt to maim themselves in their mad-ness. They would beat the walls with their hands and head and scream in an effort to relieve pressure on their eardrums. These cases usually ended in the death of the subject.

About two hundred inmates were subjected to these horrors before the "experiments" were concluded. About half died; those who survived were soon murdered, ostensibly to prevent their testifying about what they experienced. Rascher was highly praised for the information he ferreted out, and he soon had another idea. What of the extremely low temperatures to which aviators were subjected? An account from the Nuremberg trials tells the story:

> A prisoner was placed naked on a stretcher outside the barracks in the evening. He was covered with a sheet and every hour a bucket of cold water was poured over him. The test person lay out in the open like this into the morning. Their temperatures were taken. Later Dr. Rascher said it was a mistake to cover the subject with a sheet and to drench him with water. . . . In the future the test person must not be covered.

Rascher hoped to use Auschwitz instead of Dachau for these experiments because it was colder there, and the larger "size of the grounds causes less of a stir in the camp. (The test persons yell when they freeze.)" Rascher was forced to make do at Dachau. He wrote Himmler: "Thank God, we have had another intense cold snap at Dachau. Some people remained out in the open for 14 hours at 21 [F] degrees, attaining an interior temperature of 77 degrees, with peripheral frostbite."

Another method was putting the "test persons" into tanks of icy water. At the Nuremberg trials, a Dachau prisoner who had the misfortune to serve as an "orderly" for Rascher said that as these victims froze to death, their temperature, heartbeats, and respiration were regularly recorded. In the beginning Rascher did not permit anesthesia; but "the test persons made such a racket that it was impossible" to continue without it.

When some Luftwaffe medics learned of these experiments, they objected on religious grounds. Himmler was outraged at their objections. He decided to circumvent their objections by transferring Rascher to the SS, where Christian qualms were not a problem. This is his letter to the Luftwaffe's Field Marshall Erhard Milch:[*]

---

[*] Milch's father was Jewish. When rumors of this arose in 1935, the Gestapo launched an investigation, prompting Göring to step in and see to it that Milch was given a proper alibi (his mother was falsely made to testify that Milch's Jewish father was not actually his father, but that his Aryan uncle was his father). He was also given an official *Deutschblütigkeitserklärung* (German Blood Certificate). Göring was affronted by the Gestapo's actions and during this time made his famous statement: "Wer Jude ist, bestimme ich!" ("I decide who is a Jew!").

Dear Comrade Milch:

You will recall that through General Wolff I particularly recommended to you for your consideration the work of a certain SS Führer, Dr. Rascher, who is a physician of the *Luftwaffe* on leave. These researches which deal with the behavior of the human organism at great heights, as well as with manifestations caused by prolonged cooling of the human body in cold water, and similar problems which are of vital importance to the air force in particular, can be performed by us with particular efficiency because I personally assumed the responsibility for supplying asocial individuals and criminals who deserve only to die from concentration camps for these experiments.*

Unfortunately you had no time recently when Dr. Rascher wanted to report on the experiments at the Ministry for Aviation. I had put great hopes in that report, because I believed that in this way the difficulties based mainly on religious objections, which oppose Dr. Rascher's experiments—for which I assumed responsibility—could be eliminated.

The difficulties are still the same as before. In these "Christian medical circles" the standpoint is being taken that it goes without saying that a young German aviator should be allowed to risk his life but that the life of a criminal—who is not drafted into military service—is too sacred for this purpose and one should not stain oneself with this guilt. . . .

We two should not get angry about these difficulties. It will take at least another ten years until we can get such narrow-mindedness out of our people. But this should not affect the research work which is necessary for our young and splendid soldiers and aviators.

I beg you to release Dr. Rascher, medical officer in reserve, from the *Luftwaffe* and to transfer him to me to the *Waffen-SS*. I would then assume the sole responsibility for having these experiments made in this field, and would put the results, of which we in the SS need only a part for the frost injuries in the East, entirely at the disposal of the air force. However, in this connection I suggest that with liaison between you and Wolff a *"non-Christian" physician should be charged.* . . .

---

* Many of these "professional criminals" were so labeled for the "crime" of *Rassenschande*, which meant "race pollution," and which specifically meant that they had had consenting sexual relations with a German woman.

I would be grateful to you if you will give the order to put the low pressure chamber at our disposal again, together with step-up pumps, because the experiments should be extended to include even greater altitudes.

Cordial greetings and *Heil Hitler*
SS *Reichsführer* Himmler

Rascher conducted four hundred such "freezing" experiments on three hundred persons. A third froze to death. The others were gassed or shot afterward.

At Buchenwald, the warders were supposed to keep the prisoners well enough to be interrogated. At midday they received soup, and in the evenings they were given "bread, fat, and marmalade." They had gotten permission to take daily exercise by walking up and down the central corridor for a half hour. The seventeen prisoners were not supposed to have contact with anyone, and the exercise was to be taken alone or with one's cell mate. But the logistics of locking and unlocking cells and keeping the time of each prisoner's exercise proved tiring for the guards, who preferred staying in their heated guard room with few responsibilities. Eventually they let the prisoners out in groups of six or more, giving them quite a bit of contact.

At first each single person or each couple, in cases where cells were occupied by two people, were supposed to confine their promenade to separate passages, but very soon [said Best] we all got together and talked with each other freely. By shifting the hour when I went out from day to day, I was gradually able to meet and talk to all my fellow prisoners. In the morning, too, all cell doors were unlocked at the same time, generally between 6 and 8 a.m., and we men forgathered in the lavatory while the trusties cleaned out the cells and made our beds.

We may assume that over the course of his two months, Bonhoeffer had contact with most of the prisoners.

Best explained that Rascher had very seriously thought that the experiments he had conducted were "fully justified by the great value of the scientific results obtained." He added,

> He quite obviously saw nothing wrong in exposing a couple of dozen people to intense cold, in water or air, and then attempting their resuscitation. He was in fact very proud of having discovered a technique which he said would save the lives of thousands who would otherwise have died from exposure, and said that his imprisonment was due to the fact that he had attempted to publish the results of his research into this question in a Swiss medical journal so that it might benefit British seamen who, after rescue from the sea when their ships were torpedoed, frequently died without recovering consciousness.

Best's take on Rascher is a puzzle:

> I was not at the time greatly shocked by his stories, nor, when they got to know him, were any of our fellow prisoners. We were all far too hardened to surroundings where sudden death was the order of the day. At any moment an order might come for some or all of us to be gassed, shot, or hung [sic], and subconsciously we were all so much engaged in the struggle for survival that no one had the energy to expend in sympathy for the sufferings of unknown and anonymous people who, after all, were already dead; besides, Rascher was such a good comrade to us all. This is where the queer contradiction in his character comes in, for throughout our association with him he was distinguished by his bravery, unselfishness, and loyalty. In the difficult days that were to come he was the life and soul of our party, and although he well knew the risk, never hesitated to stand up to the brutal set of guards who had us in their power.

It's impossible to think Bonhoeffer shared this perspective. And the contrast between Rascher and Bonhoeffer could not be starker. Best described Bonhoeffer as "all humility and sweetness; he always seemed to me to diffuse an atmosphere of happiness, of joy in every smallest event in life, and of deep gratitude for the mere fact that he was alive. . . . He was one of the very few men that I have ever met to whom his God was real and ever close to him."
Best wrote to Sabine in 1951, describing her brother as "different; just

quite calm and normal, seemingly perfectly at his ease . . . his soul really shone in the dark desperation of our prison." Best said Bonhoeffer "had always been afraid that he would not be strong enough to stand such a test but now he knew there was nothing in life of which one need ever be afraid." He was also "cheerful, ready to respond to a joke."

Falconer said of Bonhoeffer and Rabenau: "I think they were the only pair of prisoners sharing a cell who got on really well together and enjoyed each other's company." Both Falconer and Best remarked on the bickering and mistrust that went on among the other Germans. Best wrote:

> When I first made contact with the other prisoners what struck me most forcedly was the intense distrust of most of the Germans of each other; almost every one of them warned me to be careful of some other as he was a Gestapo spy. . . . This atmosphere of suspicion was typical of Nazi Germany, though it seemed to me strange that these people imprisoned by the Gestapo, had so little inclination to form a common front and pull together.

Best was sure that if they banded together, they could easily escape. The warders were terrified about what would happen to them once the Allies reached them, and Best was sure they could be persuaded to escape with their own prisoners. It began to seem obvious that the Americans were making great advances from the west, while the Russians were pushing in from the east. Germany had grown thinner and thinner. It couldn't be long before they were liberated. One of the guards, Sippach, said he would flee the camp before the Americans could get to him. But another, Dittman, said he would fight till the last moment and would save two bullets: one for Best, whom he despised, and one for himself. "You will never leave this place alive!" he told Best, who spent a good deal of time proving his mettle with the warders, so much so that Rascher once advised him "to be more careful[,] as Buchenwald was very different to [sic] Sachsenhausen."

Bonhoeffer and everyone else hung on in the cold and hunger, knowing that any moment they might be liberated or killed. At one point they got news about the war's progress that made them realize the Americans were indeed close. The guards were so nervous that they let General von Falkenhausen listen to the daily war bulletins on the guard room radio, so he could explain to them, with his extraordinary military mind, just how close Germany was to defeat.

March 30 was Good Friday. We may assume that Bonhoeffer continued his daily meditations, prayers, and hymn singing, even if only quietly or in his head. On April 1, Easter, the thunder of the American guns could be heard in the distance. They were someplace across the Werra River. It would all be over soon. It must have seemed fitting that now, on the day that Bonhoeffer and all of Western Christendom celebrated the resurrection of the risen Christ, hope arrived.

Sometime that day the chief guard, Sippach, told the prisoners to get ready to leave. Where were they going? No one knew. Few had many belongings to transport. Best, however, had a typewriter, a suitcase, and three large boxes. They heard nothing more that day, but the next day Dittman, the other guard, told everyone they should be ready to leave on foot. Best was irate at having to jettison some of his belongings. But the situation was dire. Food was scarce and vehicles were scarce, and even if they could get a vehicle, getting fuel was impossible. It surprised no one that they would have to walk, even with some of them in ill health.* Gehre and Müller and von Petersdorff were in the worst shape of all, but everyone was weak from lack of food and constant cold. But all day they heard nothing further.

On the afternoon of Tuesday, April 3, Sippach announced they would leave within the hour. But hours passed. At ten that evening, word came. They would not have to travel on foot after all, but the van that would carry them was designed to accommodate eight people without luggage. They were sixteen and had luggage. It was fueled by wood, fed into a generator, so that much of the front section of the van was filled with wood. Once under way, the passenger area would become filled with choking wood smoke. Nonetheless, they were leaving Buchenwald.

---

*	As the Allies approached, the Nazis were desperately evacuating concentration camps throughout Germany, forcing their weak prisoners on marches and shooting many of them along the way.

 CHAPTER 31

ON THE ROAD TO FREEDOM

[Bonhoeffer] was very happy during the whole time I knew him, and did a great deal to keep some of the weaker brethren from depression and anxiety.

—HUGH FALCONER IN A LETTER TO GERHARD LEIBHOLZ, OCTOBER 1945

This is the end . . . For me the beginning of life.

—DIETRICH BONHOEFFER

No one has yet believed in God and the kingdom of God, no one has yet heard about the realm of the resurrected, and not been homesick from that hour, waiting and looking forward joyfully to being released from bodily existence . . . Death is hell and night and cold, if it is not transformed by our faith. But that is just what is so marvelous, that we can transform death.

—DIETRICH BONHOEFFER, FROM A SERMON DELIVERED
IN LONDON, NOVEMBER 1933

The sixteen prisoners—an oddball crew by any standards—crammed themselves into the van along with their luggage.* Many of them were literally unable to move an inch. It was quite an assemblage: bemedaled and aristocratic army generals, a naval commander, a diplomat

---

* Payne Best's account says sixteen, although it's unclear who was missing from the original seventeen prisoners.

and his wife, a depressed Russian air force officer, a Catholic lawyer, a theologian, a woman of questionable morals, and a concentration camp "doctor." But as soon as they all got into this space and the back door was locked, the air raid alert sounded. The guards abandoned them in the locked van and high-tailed it to a safer place, as far from the cellar and its stores of munitions as their legs could carry them. The prisoners waited in the back of the van in the blackness, not knowing whether they would be hit by a bomb. Finally the all clear was sounded, and the military personnel returned and started the engine. The van moved a hundred yards and halted. The wood-fueled engine continued to idle, and within moments the van was filled with fumes, which they inhaled, prompting the man who had helped design the gas chambers to cry out: "My God, this is a death van; we are being gassed!"

Rascher knew whereof he spoke. The Germans had used gas vans to kill people with mental disabilities and others in the euthanasia programs since 1940. Afterward they had used them to kill Jews. These vans were so filled with people that those inside could barely breathe to begin with. When the engine was started, the exhaust was pumped directly into the interior of the van, so that by the time the van arrived at its destination, the passengers had become corpses and were unloaded straight into the crematorium ovens.

Payne Best noticed some light coming through what seemed to be a vent and asked their resident expert whether such things were to be found in gas vans. Rascher said they were not, so if they died this way, it would likely be unintentional. Eventually the van began moving again and the fumes abated enough to make breathing possible, but Rabenau and both women, Margot Heberlein and Heidl, fainted.

They had left sometime after ten and traveled through the night, joggling along at fifteen miles per hour, covering eight or nine miles every hour because every hour they stopped to clean the flues and restock the generator with wood. Each time this procedure took place the passengers had to wait in the darkness in discomfort, and each time the engine was difficult to restart. It had to run for fifteen minutes before it had enough power to move the vehicle forward again. And when it idled, the van's interior was refilled with exhaust gases. Best summed it up: "It was a hell of a journey." He recalled the details:

There was no light, we had nothing to eat or drink nor, but for the generosity of Bonnhöfer [sic], who, although a smoker, had saved up his scanty ration of tobacco and now insisted in contributing it to the common good, anything to smoke. He was a good and saintly man. Literally, we could none of us move an inch for our legs were embedded in luggage and our arms pinned to our sides; we had even small articles of baggage wedged behind us on the seats so that our sterns rested on the sharp edges of the wooden bench and soon became the seat of neuralgic pains. We jogged and joggled along through the night, running an hour and stopping an hour, stiff, tired, hungry, thirsty, until a faint suspicion of light appeared at the ventilator. There came a time when nature, even after a sleepless night, makes certain demands, and soon there were cries from all sides, "I can't wait any longer, they must stop so that I can get out," and we started hammering against the sides of the van until it came to a sudden stop, the door was opened and a voice called: "What's all this?" Our needs were explained with the delicacy required by the presence of two ladies which the inquirer then crudely and loudly detailed to his mates outside.

The three guards argued over the request. Eventually the van doors were opened, and all got out. It was not the best place to have stopped, being devoid of such flora or undulations in the terrain as the ticklish situation required. In the distance there was a copse of trees to which the two women repaired with all alacrity, accompanied by one of the guards. The other two guards trained their machine guns on the fifteen men who were free to let nature take its course. "The ladies were prompter than we," wrote Best, "and although our backs were turned to their approach we were all of us conscious of over-exposure."

It was now daylight. They had been on the road for some seven or eight hours, and had in their fits and starts traveled about a hundred miles. The prisoners still had no idea where they were headed. Much of the wood had been consumed, and "by the exercise of great ingenuity," Hugh Falconer managed to repack things so that they had much more room than before. Two people could stand by the window of the van door, and all took their turns. The guards also gave them two loaves of bread and a large wurst, which they divided. There was even something to drink.

At one point someone at the window recognized a village, and they reasoned that they must have been traveling south and were therefore likely on

their way to Flossenbürg. But since Flossenbürg was known to be an extermination camp, this conclusion was not a happy one. After thirteen hours of
this travel, it was noon and they had reached Weiden, a small town of about
thirty thousand in northern Bavaria. Flossenbürg lay ten miles east.

In Weiden they stopped at the police station, and the guards went in.
Upon returning, the friendlier of the three told his captives: "You will have
to go farther. They can't take you here. Too full." But what did that mean?
A concentration camp sage was there in the van to make sense of it all. Dr.
Rascher pronounced them all unlikely to be marked for death. Flossenbürg,
he said, was never so full that it wouldn't bend the rules to welcome another
load of corpses. Or soon-to-be corpses. It was only for living, breathing prisoners that it could be "too full." If they had been marked for death, they
would have been happily accommodated. So this was good news. It seemed
they wouldn't be killed that day.

They had been headed for Flossenbürg all along, but not as people
intended to be killed and cremated; and Flossenbürg had turned them away.
Where would they go now? The guards got back in and continued southward. Just as they reached the edge of town a car passed them and motioned
for them to pull over. Two policemen stepped out, and one opened the
door of the van. What happened next is unclear, but it seems that perhaps Flossenbürg had room for three prisoners after all. Liedig's and Müller's
names were barked, so they gathered their things and got out. Bonhoeffer's
name might have been called, too, but he was in the back of the van. For
some reason Gehre got out instead. Bethge said that Bonhoeffer deliberately leaned back in the van to avoid being seen, implying that he had been
called to step out too. Payne Best's account said that Gehre was called along
with Liedig and Müller. Perhaps Gehre wished to stick close to Müller, with
whom he'd shared a cell and to whom he'd grown close, and there was
enough ambiguity for him to do so. Perhaps the policemen assumed he was
Bonhoeffer. In any event, Gehre, Liedig, and Müller bade good-bye to their
companions and went with the policemen. It was now Wednesday afternoon, April 4. Best wrote:

> After leaving Weiden there was a marked change in the attitude of the
> three SS guards. They had obviously left Buchenwald with orders to take
> us to Flossenbürg, and for so long they had felt themselves constricted

by the sense of an authority guiding them. When Flossenbürg refused to receive us they were apparently sent off on vague instructions to continue a southward course until they found some place where they could deposit us, and so, in a measure, they felt that they shared our lot and like us were just sailing along into the blue with no certain destination.

The van, with Bonhoeffer and thirteen companions, continued its wheezing, clanking journey southward toward no place in particular. They were like the troupe of actors from Bergman's *Seventh Seal*, cheerful and peripatetic, but shadowed as they went by the hooded, dark figure of Death. Even Heidl was somehow transformed from a cut-rate Mata Hari into a fresh-faced *Mädl*. What a difference from the horror of their long night in the cramped, befumed blackness. Now when the van stopped so the guards could restoke the generator and clean the flues, the guards opened the van doors and asked their prisoners if they'd like to step out and have a stretch. And they did this every hour. Someone semi-affectionately dubbed their van *Grüne Minna* (Green Minnie).

Sometime that afternoon they stopped in front of a farmhouse. Heidl and Mrs. Heberlein were allowed inside to wash up, and the men took turns outside at the pump. What a strangely jolly scene it must have been, these august figures weary from hunger and lack of sleep standing outside in the sunshine around the pump: Best, Pünder, von Alvensleben, von Petersdorff, Falconer, Kokorin, Hoepner, and von Rabenau. And here were Sigmund Rascher and Dietrich Bonhoeffer. These last two alone of all the company still together shared a fate in the weeks ahead. But no one knew of it. For now all was brightness and freedom and fresh air. To stand outside in the afternoon sun in front of a Bavarian farmhouse after two months at Buchenwald was something.

The farmer's wife emerged carrying several loaves of rye bread and a jug of milk. Best said that it was "real good rye bread such as none of us had tasted for years." And then back into the van, which was much roomier now. Several of them could take a nap. "The window over the door was left open," Best told us, "and as it was a lovely day everything looked bright in our cage." They rambled like this through town after town, southward through the Naab Valley. Many of them had almost forgotten that Germany, with its natural beauty and farm villages, was a real place in the present and not just a memory.

After about six hours, they had gone fifty miles, and as the daylight began to wane, they found themselves approaching the town of Regensburg. Regensburg is a medieval city where the Danube and Regen rivers meet. The van wandered around in the city, stopping again and again as the guards tried to find a place for their passengers to spend the night. Time and again they failed, got back in the van, and drove on.

After dark they ended up at the main entrance to the state prison. This time the guards opened the van doors and told everyone to get out. When they climbed the stairs into the building, one of the prison guards began ordering them uncivilly, prompting one of their own guards to interrupt him, explaining that they were not ordinary prisoners, but special prisoners who must be treated with courtesy. "Oh!" said a Regensburg guard. "More aristocrats! Well, put them with the other lot on the second floor."

They dragged their luggage up steep iron stairs to the second floor and were greeted by "a very decent elderly warder" who let them choose their own cell mates. As seemed to be the case everywhere, things were very tight. The men had to sleep five to a cell, with three straw mattresses covering the cell floor. Bonhoeffer shared his cell with Pünder, von Rabenau, von Falkenhausen, and Hoepner.

But everyone was famished. The guards said that getting any kind of food at that point was impossible because the kitchens were closed, but the hue and cry was so great that the guards realized they must think of something. Even the other "aristocrats" in the other cells on the floor loudly added their requests to the din. The guards eventually returned with "a large bowl of quite passable vegetable soup, a hunk of bread, and a cup of 'coffee.'"

In the morning the cell doors were opened and the men allowed down the corridor to the lavatory. But what a sight they saw: crowding the entire corridor were men, women, and children, all family members of the men who were executed and arrested in the Stauffenberg plot. In fact, a number of Stauffenberg's family were here.* Here, too, were the seventy-three-year-old industrialist Fritz Thyssen and his wife. Thyssen had been one of those who had supported Hitler and helped his rise to power, only to be later horrified at what he had done. The events of *Kristallnacht* in 1938

---

* The Countess Nina von Stauffenberg, pregnant with their fifth child, had been arrested immediately after her husband's death on July 20. Their four children had been taken to an orphanage and given different names. Their mother gave birth to her fifth child while imprisoned.

caused him to resign his government post. When the war broke out, he sent a telegram to Göring, telling of his opposition to it, and he and his wife immigrated to Switzerland. But they were arrested by the Nazis and spent most of the war in Sachsenhausen and Dachau. General Fritz Halder's wife was here, as was the daughter of General Ulrich von Hassell, who had been executed. Her sons, ages two and four, had been taken away from her, and Best wrote that she was "distracted with the fear that she might never find them again." The cabaret singer and film actress Isa Vermehren was here too. She was the sister of Erich Vermehren, another Resistance figure. Falkenhausen and Petersdorff seemed to know many of those here gathered, as did Bonhoeffer.

Best found himself being introduced to this one and that one so that it seemed more like a festive reception than a line to use the bathroom in a prison. The German aristocrats seemed to know one or another or to be related. The Vermehrens were related to Franz von Papen, who had been planning to attend Dietrich and Maria's wedding.

It seemed that the inmates had taken control of the prison. They wanted to continue talking with each other and would not return to their cells. Eventually the guards only managed to lure them back by putting their breakfast inside the cells. But even now, Bonhoeffer spent most of the time talking through the small door opening to the widow of Carl Goerdeler and telling her all he could about her husband's last days at the Gestapo prison. Goerdeler had been executed on February 2.

In a short time, the air raid siren sounded, and everyone had to be let out again and taken into the prison basement. Best said that "the fun started again" with everyone talking and catching up, putting together pieces of their individual puzzles. There was a railroad switching yard next to the prison that had already been bombed into oblivion, so there didn't seem to be much left to destroy. After the all clear, the crowd ascended to the second-floor corridor and again resisted the guards' efforts to put them in their cells. This time they succeeded completely.

Around five that afternoon, one of the guards who had driven the van from Buchenwald showed up and declared it was time to leave. The fourteen Buchenwald prisoners gathered their things, said their good-byes, and went down to their van again. Everyone's spirits were considerably improved as they again headed southeast out of Regensburg, along the Danube.

But no sooner were they a few miles outside of town than the van violently lurched—and stopped dead. Hugh Falconer was an engineer, and the guards prevailed upon him for his opinion. The steering was broken. Falconer pronounced it irreparable. Regensburg was several miles back, but there was nothing between them and it or anything ahead of them. They were on a lonely and deeply dispiriting bare stretch of road, literally blasted with shell craters on the side where the railroad tracks ran. Here and there lay the burnt skeletons of cars that had been caught in the Allied fire. When a lonely bicycle approached them from the opposite direction, the guards stopped the rider and asked that he inform the police in Regensburg, so they could send another van. The bicyclist said he would and pedaled off into the distance. Meanwhile they sat, waiting. They had no food or drink. Darkness descended and it got cold. No one came. Then it started to rain. Hours passed. Best said that the guards were quite miserable and seemed frightened, now behaving more like "comrades in distress." The rains increased and the night wore on. No one ever came.

Finally dawn came. The guards opened the doors of the van so everyone could get out. But now, even as the morning wore on, not a single car was seen. At last a motorcycle appeared. The guards wouldn't take any chances, so after they had stopped it, one of them rode on the back of it into Regensburg. It was the morning of April 6, the Friday after Easter.

Midmorning the guard returned with the news that the cyclist had indeed done as promised and had informed the police of their situation. The police had sent a driver out to them. But for reasons unknown, the driver stopped two hundred yards short of where they were, turned back, and said he never found them.

It was eleven o'clock before help arrived. What rolled to a stop in front of them was a huge bus with large plate-glass windows and comfortable upholstered seats. The ragtag band gathered their luggage and got on board. But they bade adieu to their three Buchenwald guards, who remained with the expired green heap. The bus had arrived with its own detail of about ten machine-gun-toting SD men.*

The bus took them along the southern side of the Danube at twice the speed of their previous vehicle, without having to stop. In about an hour

---

* The SD was a separate arm of the SS.

they were in Straubing. None of the prisoners knew where they were going, but the SD contingent obviously intended to cross the river. But the Allies had bombed the bridge. They continued along to the next bridge, which had also been bombed; and then to the next and the next. Eventually they came to a pontoon bridge and crossed, now heading northeast into the Bavarian countryside.

The landscape grew hillier and more wooded, and the roads winding and narrow. They were heading toward Schönberg, though Bonhoeffer and his companions did not know it. They knew nothing, except that they were exhausted and hungry, but more comfortable than they had been in ages. They did not know whether they were all riding to their deaths or to freedom. It was like a strange dream, this bus ride through the Bavarian forest on an afternoon in early April.

Then some village girls flagged them down and asked for a lift. They got on and wondered who these people were. Here were ten young SD men with tommy guns and a band of disheveled aristocrats. But when they asked the guards who they were, they told the girls that they were a film company, on their way to shoot a propaganda film. What was true and what was not true at this point was difficult to say. No one knew where they would sleep or whether they would ride all night. They were heading east, past the Mettin monastery. They hadn't eaten in more than twenty-four hours. Best spied a possibility:

> The country seemed to be strong on poultry, and so many hens wanted to cross the road that our driver had quite a job dodging them, though we rather hoped that one might meet with an accident—we would all have enjoyed some nice roast fowl. I suggested to one of our guards that perhaps we might stop and see if we could beg some eggs at one of the farms, and the idea received immediate approval, but when the guard returned with a capful of eggs we got none and were left to tighten our belts and hope that we were approaching our next meal.

In the early afternoon they came to the small Bavarian village of Schönberg and stopped in front of the village school, a squarish white building of four stories. They had reached their destination. The population of Schönberg had been 700, but in recent months, as the Red Army pushed farther west, more refugees fled ahead of the advance. Many had come to Schönberg and stayed. By now there were 1,300 of them, so food was exceedingly scarce—and now more political prisoners had arrived. As it happened, the large group of aristocrats that they had left behind in Regensburg had already arrived here. So the number of political prisoners was 150.

Bonhoeffer and his fellow prisoners were taken into the school and shown into a large room on the first floor. This was to be their common cell. The room had been a girls' infirmary and was set up with rows of beds. It was all very cheering. The blankets were in bright colors, and there were inviting white featherbeds too. Best said that despite the "fatigue and hunger we were all in the highest spirits, nervous, excited, and almost hysterical in our laughter." There were large windows on three sides of the room, so that everyone could look out and drink in the green scenery of the valley.

Each person chose his bed, and the Heberleins took Heidl out of harm's way down one end of the room, positioned between them. Bonhoeffer took a bed next to Kokorin. In the giddy spirit of the moment everyone wrote his name above his bed, "with humorous comments devised by Rascher."

Bonhoeffer sunned himself at one of the windows, praying and thinking. He spent time talking with Pünder and spent time with Kokorin. They even exchanged addresses. Bonhoeffer still had a few books with him: a volume of Goethe, a Bible, and *Plutarch's Lives*.

After their initial settling in, they became aware of their hunger and banged on the door of their room till a guard arrived. At their request for food he scratched his head and went away to fetch Lieutenant Bader. Best called Bader a "hard-bitten thug" who was "a member of the chief Gestapo execution gang and passed his life in traveling from one concentration camp to another, like a pest officer engaged in the extermination of rats." His presence was not encouraging, but he treated them cordially enough. Still, there was no food to be had in the town. The 1,300 refugees had descended like locusts and there wasn't a blade of grass left. There was food in Passau, but Passau was twenty-five miles away, and for such a trip they would need petrol, of which they had none. Nor were there telephones. There was simply nothing to be done.

But the resourceful Margot Heberlein had done something with nothing before. She asked a guard if she might use the W. C. and on her way fell upon the housekeeper, a kindly older woman. Thirty minutes later this woman reappeared with potatoes and some jugs of hot coffee. Everyone was grateful and devoured every crumb, but even so, they remained hungry. But there really was nothing to do but go to sleep. After months on the plank beds of Buchenwald, the promise of a night in these beds may have been better than food. The madcap highlight of the evening was when the screen placed between the men and the two women fell down. Best wrote:

> Of course "Heidl" very clumsily knocked over the screen just as Mrs. Heberlein's clothing had reached an abbreviated stage and her own had practically ceased. . . . In the end though we all got to bed, the light was turned out, and there were sincerely meant cries of good night all round. My bed was so soft that I seemed to float on air and very soon I was fast asleep; really, the first sound sleep for almost a week.

When they awoke the following day, there was no breakfast. But Best had an electric razor among his possessions, and since there was a working outlet, each man took a turn using it. At some point some kind soul from the village who had heard of the "special prisoners" and their predicament sent over potato salad and two large loaves of bread. Again, they were grateful, but this was all the food they would have that day, and it was likely the last food Bonhoeffer ever ate. It was Saturday, April 7.

Hugh Falconer wrote to Gerhard Leibholz in Oxford that fall:

> [Bonhoeffer] was very happy during the whole the time I knew him, and did a great deal to keep some of the weaker brethren from depression and anxiety. He spent a good deal of time with Wasily Wasiliew Kokorin, Molotov's nephew, who was a delightful young man although an atheist. I think your brother-in-law divided his time with him between instilling the foundations of Christianity and learning Russian.

Bonhoeffer's Last Day

The next day, April 8, was the first Sunday after Easter. In Germany it is called Quasimodo Sunday.* Dr. Pünder asked Bonhoeffer to hold a service

---

* The term *Quasimodo Sunday* comes from the two Latin words (*quasi* meaning "as if" and *modo* meaning "in the manner of") that begin the *introit* of the Roman Catholic Mass for that day. They are taken from 1 Peter (2:2: "as newborn babes . . .") and literally mean "as in the style of" or "as in the manner of." Victor Hugo's eponymous hunchback of Notre Dame was named Quasimodo because he was supposedly born on that Sunday in the church calendar.

for them. Pünder was Catholic, as were a number of others. This, and the fact that Kokorin was an atheist, caused Bonhoeffer to demur. He didn't wish to impose. But Kokorin himself insisted.

So less than twenty-four hours before he left this world, Bonhoeffer performed the offices of a pastor. In the bright Schönberg schoolroom that was their cell, he held a small service. He prayed and read the verses for that day: Isaiah 53:5 ("With his stripes we are healed") and 1 Peter 1:3 ("Blessed be the God and Father of our Lord Jesus Christ! By his great mercy we have been born anew to a living hope through the resurrection of Jesus Christ from the dead" RSV). He then explained these verses to everyone. Best recalled that Bonhoeffer "spoke to us in a manner which reached the hearts of all, finding just the right words to express the spirit of our imprisonment and the thoughts and resolutions which it had brought."

The other prisoners in the schoolhouse hoped that they might be able to get Bonhoeffer to hold a service for them as well. But there would not be any time for this. Best described what happened:

> He had hardly finished his last prayer when the door opened and two evil-looking men in civilian clothes came in and said:
>
> "Prisoner Bonhoeffer. Get ready to come with us." Those words "Come with us"—for all prisoners they had come to mean one thing only—the scaffold.
>
> We bade him good-bye—he drew me aside—"This is the end," he said. "For me the beginning of life."

Bonhoeffer also asked Best to remember him to Bishop Bell. Six years later, in a letter to the Bonhoeffer family, Best recalled what he had written about Bonhoeffer in his book, where he had said that he "was a good and saintly man." But in the letter he went further: "In fact my feeling was far stronger than these words imply. He was, without exception, the finest and most lovable man I have ever met."

Bonhoeffer's family had not heard of him since he had left the Gestapo prison two months earlier, so to leave some clue of his whereabouts, he took a blunt pencil and wrote his name and address in the front, middle, and back of the volume of Plutarch—the one his family had given him for his birthday two months earlier—and left it behind. One of Carl

Goerdeler's sons who was at the schoolhouse took the book and gave it to the Bonhoeffers years later. Bonhoeffer had been with Goerdeler in the last days before his execution in Berlin, and now, when he ran down the stairs of the schoolhouse to enter the van that would take him to his own execution, he bumped into Goerdeler's widow, who bade him his final friendly good-bye.

Bonhoeffer was on his way to Flossenbürg at last. The journey that Sunday afternoon was about a hundred miles in a north-northwesterly direction. He had his volume of Goethe with him. And he seemed to know where he was headed on that Sunday afternoon.

Bonhoeffer's sentence of death was almost certainly by decree of Hitler himself, as were the death sentences of Oster and Dohnanyi. Even Hitler must have known that all was lost for him and for Germany, and that killing others made no particular sense, but as he was every atom a petty man, he was accustomed to diverting exceedingly precious resources of time, personnel, and gasoline for the purposes of his own revenge.

The wheels for Bonhoeffer's execution were set in motion on April 4 when a significant chunk of Canaris's diary turned up by happenstance at Zossen, where Dohnanyi's files had been hidden. The next day this incriminating material was in Hitler's hands in Berlin, and what the madman read in its pages catapulted him far beyond the borders of reason. Here, as far as he was concerned, was the thing itself—the blood-stained poniard that had been plunged into the back of the Third Reich, that had sabotaged it from the beginning. Here was the reason for the failure of his otherwise predestined and prophesied triumph. If not for such evil traitors, of whom Canaris was chief, he might that moment be striding like a god across one of the great boulevards he was to build, instead of down here in the gray bunker where he scuttled like a rat beneath the rubble of the city that was to have been the crown of his kingdom of a thousand years. So three weeks before taking his own life, in what was one of his final eruptions, Hitler railed against the men who had done this to him and gave instructions to Rattenhuber, the SS commander assigned to him: "Destroy the conspirators!" Thus were the fates of Canaris, Oster, Sack, and Bonhoeffer sealed.

But to the last Hitler would preserve the fiction of legality in the German state. The corpse of German jurisprudence must be exhumed to create the image of lawfulness. So the SS prosecutor Huppenkothen must go through his paces, must travel with his documents—including Canaris's incriminating diary—all the way to Flossenbürg to set up a "summary court-martial." He traveled there on April 7. Also there for the charade was Dr. Otto Thorbeck, an SS judge. So that Saturday night, Canaris, Oster, Dr. Sack, Strünck, Gehre, and Bonhoeffer would be tried and executed in the morning.

But Bonhoeffer was not in Flossenbürg on Saturday the seventh. Hadn't he been sent there from Buchenwald? Fabian Schlabrendorff was at Flossenbürg, and twice he was screamed at by an official insisting that he must be Bonhoeffer. But Schlabrendorff was not Bonhoeffer. Bonhoeffer's old friend Joseph Müller was also at Flossenbürg and he, too, was screamed at by someone insisting that he was Bonhoeffer. Liedig, too, was accused of being Bonhoeffer, but was not. Where was Bonhoeffer?

Finally someone realized what had happened: a mistake had been made back in Weiden, four days earlier, when Liedig, Müller, and Gehre hopped out of the green van and Bonhoeffer remained inside. Bonhoeffer must be with that group at the schoolhouse in Schönberg. Two men were dispatched to travel the hundred miles to fetch him and bring him back to Flossenbürg. They arrived just after he had finished conducting the Sunday service.

The Beginning of Life

Bonhoeffer arrived at Flossenbürg sometime late on Sunday. Bethge wrote:

> The summary court, with Thorbeck as chairman, Huppenkothen as prosecutor, and the camp commandant Kögl as assistant, declared that it sat for a long time. It examined—its officers claimed later—each prisoner individually and confronted them with each other: Canaris and Oster, Sack, Strünck and Gehre, and finally Dietrich Bonhoeffer as well. After midnight Canaris returned to his cell after an absence of some time and signaled by knocking signs to the man in the next cell, the Danish colonel Lunding, that it was all up with him.

Whether Bonhoeffer slept, we cannot know. There were only a few hours between the end of the "summary court" trial and the dawn that brought his execution. It is worth noting that Flossenbürg, a place so closely associated with Bonhoeffer, is a place where he spent perhaps twelve hours.

We know that Bonhoeffer thought of death as the last station on the road to freedom, as he put it in his poem, "Stations on the Road to Freedom."* Even if millions have seen Bonhoeffer's death as tragic and as a prematurely ended life, we can be certain that he did not see it that way at all. In a sermon he preached while a pastor in London, he said:

No one has yet believed in God and the kingdom of God, no one has yet heard about the realm of the resurrected, and not been homesick from that hour, waiting and looking forward joyfully to being released from bodily existence.

Whether we are young or old makes no difference. What are twenty or thirty or fifty years in the sight of God? And which of us knows how near he or she may already be to the goal? That life only really begins when it ends here on earth, that all that is here is only the prologue before the curtain goes up—that is for young and old alike to think about. Why are we so afraid when we think about death? . . . Death is only dreadful for those who live in dread and fear of it. Death is not wild and terrible, if only we can be still and hold fast to God's Word. Death is not bitter, if we have not become bitter ourselves. Death is grace, the greatest gift of grace that God gives to people who believe in him. Death is mild, death is sweet and gentle; it beckons to us with heavenly power, if only we realize that it is the gateway to our homeland, the tabernacle of joy, the everlasting kingdom of peace.

How do we know that dying is so dreadful? Who knows whether, in our human fear and anguish we are only shivering and shuddering at the most glorious, heavenly, blessed event in the world?

Death is hell and night and cold, if it is not transformed by our faith. But that is just what is so marvelous, that we can transform death.

The camp doctor at Flossenbürg was H. Fischer-Hüllstrung. He had no idea whom he was watching at the time, but years later, he gave the following account of Bonhoeffer's last minutes alive:

---

*   See pages 485–86.

On the morning of that day between five and six o'clock the prisoners, among them Admiral Canaris, General Oster, General Thomas and
Reichgerichtsrat Sack were taken from their cells, and the verdicts of the
court martial read out to them. Through the half-open door in one
room of the huts I saw Pastor Bonhoeffer, before taking off his prison
garb, kneeling on the floor praying fervently to his God. I was most
deeply moved by the way this lovable man prayed, so devout and so
certain that God heard his prayer. At the place of execution, he again
said a short prayer and then climbed the steps to the gallows, brave and
composed. His death ensued after a few seconds. In the almost fifty
years that I worked as a doctor, I have hardly ever seen a man die so
entirely submissive to the will of God.

Bonhoeffer thought it the plain duty of the Christian—and the privilege
and honor—to suffer with those who suffered. He knew that it was a privilege to be allowed by God to partake of the sufferings of the Jews who had
died in this place before him. According to Schlabrendorff, the crematorium
at Flossenbürg was not working, so the bodies of the men hanged that morning were burned in piles, and in this, too, he had the honor to be joined to
the millions of other victims of the Third Reich.

Prince Philip of Hesse had been a prisoner at Flossenbürg for years and was
there that April. In the guard room that Monday morning, he found some
books, including Bonhoeffer's volume of Goethe. The books were later taken
from him and burned too.

Two weeks later, on April 23, the Allies marched into Flossenbürg. In
another week Hitler committed suicide, and the war was over. At that point
neither Maria nor anyone in Bonhoeffer's family knew what had become of
him. His sister Sabine did not hear about her brother's death until May 31:

Pastor [Julius] Rieger telephoned to us from London and asked whether
we were home because he had something to say to us. Gert's reply on
the telephone was "We would be very glad to see you."

Soon from the window I saw our friend arriving at the house. The
moment I opened the door to him I felt fear. The expression of his face

was so pale and drawn that I knew that something serious had happened. We quickly entered the room where Gert was, and then Pastor Rieger said with deep sadness, "It's Dietrich. He is no more—and Klaus too. . . ."

"Oh no, no!" groaned Gert from the very depths of his spirit.

Rieger laid the telegram before us on the table. Then he pulled his New Testament out of his coat pocket and began to read from Mt. 10. To this day I still do not know how I lived through those moments except by clinging to every word: ". . . Behold I send you forth as sheep in the midst of wolves. . . . But beware of men: for they will deliver you up to the councils and will scourge you. . . . But when they deliver you up, take no thought how or what ye shall speak, for it shall be given you in that same hour what ye shall speak. For it is not ye that speak, but the Spirit of your Father which speaketh in you. . . . There is nothing covered that shall not be revealed; and hid that shall not be known. . . .

"Whosoever, therefore, shall confess me before men, him will I confess also before my Father which is in heaven. But whosoever shall deny me before men, him will I also deny before my Father which is in heaven. . . . And he that taketh not his cross and followeth after me is not worthy of me. He that findeth his life shall lose it: and he that loseth his life for my sake shall find it."

Pastor Rieger also read us all the other verses of the tenth chapter, and reminded us of the fact that Dietrich had given so particularly beautiful an exposition of them in *The Cost of Discipleship*.

Apart from this, I no longer know what happened during the rest of this day, but I have not forgotten Gert's face streaming with tears or the sobbing of the children.

. . . Somehow I had been living wholly for the moment when I could be re-united with Dietrich in a new and better Germany; the moment when we would tell each other our adventures and exchange our news about all that had taken place in these difficult years.

. . . I had always hoped that the Allied troops had firm plans of their own for sending in paratroops to take possession of the concentration camps before the ground troops came too near to them, and for liberating their inmates. Many of the English had joined with us in believing that this would be the case—though perhaps in telling us this they were only trying to allay our anxieties. In any case it remained nothing more than a dream. Whether it really did belong to the realm of the impossible I am, it is true, unable to judge. But I could not rid myself of the suspicion that it was not done because the conduct of the war had become so embittered, a fact which is also illustrated by the disastrous policy towards the German opposition. The Bishop of Chichester had written to us that at the time Churchill was dedicated "to fighting, to the exclusion of all else."

That July, after they had learned of the deaths of their son Klaus and their son-in-law Rüdiger Schleicher, Karl and Paula Bonhoeffer wrote to Sabine and Gert. Communication between Berlin and the outside world had been nearly impossible. They had heard Dietrich had been killed, but had not had any confirmation of it yet.

23rd July 1945

My dearest children,

We have just been told that an opportunity has arisen for us to send you our greetings and news. It is now three years, I believe, since we received the last letters from you. Now we have just heard that Gert sent a telegram to Switzerland in order to obtain news of the fate of our dear Dietrich. From this we conclude that you are all still alive, and that is a great consolation for us in our deep sorrow over the fate of our dear Klaus, Dietrich and Rüdiger.

Dietrich spent eighteen months in the military prison at Tegel. Last October he was handed over to the Gestapo and transferred to the SS prison in Prinz-Albrechtstrasse. During the early days of February he was taken from there to various concentration camps such as Buchenwald and Flossenbürg near Weiden. We did not know where he was.

His fiancée, Maria von Wedemeyer, who was living with us at this time, attempted to find out for herself where he was. But in this she was unsuccessful. After the victory of the Allies we heard that Dietrich was still alive. But later we received news that he had been murdered by the Gestapo a little before the Americans arrived.

Meanwhile, in consultation with Gerhard and Sabine Leibholz, Pastors Rieger and Hildebrandt and Bishop Bell organized a memorial service for Dietrich and Klaus Bonhoeffer, which would be held on July 27 at Holy Trinity Brompton Church. Bishop Bell had asked their permission to broadcast it in Germany as well, and they agreed. And this was how Karl and Paula Bonhoeffer heard it in their home and had the news of Dietrich's death confirmed. Bishop Bell wrote Sabine and Gert two days before the service:

> The Palace, Chichester 25th July 1945
> My dear Sabine, (If I may thus call you.) I am deeply grateful for your letter. All you say, so undeserved, is a great comfort to me; and I am very happy to have Dietrich's photograph. You know something, I am sure, of what his friendship and love meant to me. My heart is full of sorrow for you, for alas, it is only too true that the gap he and Klaus leave can never be filled. I pray that God may give peace and strength to your parents, and to all who mourn, and bless them.
> I am greatly looking forward to seeing you both on Friday. I do not know whether your daughters will be there; but my telegram just sent will of course include them. . . .
> Yours very sincerely, George Cicestr

Memorial Service at Holy Trinity Brompton

The memorial service at Holy Trinity Brompton that July 27, to which the Bonhoeffer parents listened in their home at 43 Marienburgerallee, began with the familiar English hymn, "For All the Saints":

> For all the saints who from their labours rest,
> Who thee by faith before the world confest,
> Thy name, O Jesu, be forever blest.
> Alleluya!

The congregation sang the hymn's seven stanzas, and then Bishop Bell prayed the prayer of supplication and the prayer of thanksgiving. Another hymn, "Hark, a Herald Voice Is Calling," was sung in English and in German.

Then the gospel lesson was read. Appropriately enough, it was from the Sermon on the Mount, from Matthew chapters 5, 6, and 7:

> Beware of men: for they will deliver you up to the councils, and they will scourge you in their synagogues; and ye shall be brought before governors and kings for my sake, for a testimony against them and the Gentiles. But when they deliver you up, take no thought how or what ye shall speak: for it shall be given you in that same hour what ye shall speak. For it is not ye that speak, but the Spirit of your Father which speaketh in you. And the brother shall deliver up the brother to death, and the father the child: and the children shall rise up against their parents, and cause them to be put to death. And ye shall be hated of all men for my name's sake: but he that endureth to the end shall be saved. But when they persecute you in this city, flee ye into another: for verily I say unto you, Ye shall not have gone over the cities of Israel, till the Son of man be come. The disciple is not above his master, nor the servant above his lord. It is enough for the disciple that he be as his master, and the servant as his lord. If they have called the master of the house Beelzebub, how much more shall they call them of his household? Fear them not therefore: for there is nothing covered, that shall not be revealed; and hid, that shall not be known. What I tell you in darkness, that speak ye in light: and what ye hear in the ear, that preach ye upon the housetops. And fear not them which kill the body, but are not able to kill the soul: but rather fear him which is able to destroy both soul and body in hell. Are not two sparrows sold for a farthing? and one of them shall not fall on the ground without your Father. But the very hairs of your head are all numbered. Fear ye not therefore, ye are of more value than many sparrows. Whosoever therefore shall confess me before men, him will I confess also before my Father which is in heaven. But whosoever shall deny me before men, him will I also deny before my Father which is in heaven. Think not that I am come to send peace on earth: I came not to send peace, but a sword. For I am come to set a man at variance against his father, and the daughter against her mother, and the daughter in law against her mother in law. And a man's foes shall be they of his own household. He that loveth father or mother more

than me is not worthy of me: and he that loveth son or daughter more than me is not worthy of me. And he that taketh not his cross, and followeth after me, is not worthy of me. He that findeth his life shall lose it: and he that loseth his life for my sake shall find it. He that receiveth you receiveth me, and he that receiveth me receiveth him that sent me. He that receiveth a prophet in the name of a prophet shall receive a prophet's reward; and he that receiveth a righteous man in the name of a righteous man shall receive a righteous man's reward. And whosoever shall give to drink unto one of these little ones a cup of cold water only in the name of a disciple, verily I say unto you, he shall in no wise lose his reward.

In her recollection of the service, Sabine said:

The choir of the community to which Dietrich had formerly ministered gave a particularly beautiful rendering of *Wer nur den lieben Gott lässt walten* (Who makes the will of God his only rule), and later we all sang together the hymn which Dietrich had arranged to be sung the last time he preached in London: *Mir nach, spricht Christus, unser Held* (Follow me, says Christ, our hero).

After that Bishop Bell preached:

He was quite clear in his convictions, and for all that he was so young and unassuming, he saw the truth and spoke it out with absolute freedom and without fear. When he came to me all unexpectedly in 1942 at Stockholm as the emissary of the Resistance to Hitler, he was, as always, absolutely open and quite untroubled about his own person, his safety. Wherever he went and whoever he spoke with—whether young or old—he was fearless, regardless of himself and, with it all, devoted his heart and soul to his parents, his friends, his country as God willed it to be, to his Church and to his Master.

Bell ended his sermon with the words, "The blood of martyrs is the seed of the Church." Julius Rieger and Franz Hildebrandt also spoke. The text of Franz Hildebrandt's sermon follows:

Neither know we what to do; but our eyes are upon Thee.

2 *Chron.* 20.12

In May 1932, a few months before Hitler came to power, Dietrich Bonhoeffer stood in the pulpit of the *Dreifaltigkeitskirche* in Berlin and preached from this text. He was then chaplain to the students of the *Technische Hochschule*, alongside with his *Privatdozentur* in the University. This text was on his mind a long time before and a long time since; today we may use it as a kind of inscription to the life which we remember. To enter into biographical detail on this occasion would be a disservice to our friend and brother; but let personal recollection serve as illustration of the Word that was the centre of his thought and in whose service he was consumed.

He came from an academic home and seemed destined for the academic life. He was unashamed of the scholars' tradition of his ancestors, the culture of his family; he never shared the theological fashion of contempt for the humanities. He knew his classics in art, music, literature before he criticized; he knew how to read and listen before voicing his opinion. And when he voiced it publicly for the first time, in the dissertations on *Sanctorum Communio* and *Act and Being*, he did it with a measure of maturity and a power of concentration which made it almost incredible to think that the author was just 21 or 24 years old. They might well be proud of him in his home in the Wangenheimstrasse, proud of him as of his older brothers, one of whom has shared his lot, one was killed young in the First World War, and only one survives, at this moment still ignorant of Dietrich's fate. . . .

"We know not what to do." The young theologian faced the problem of Christian life and action. He would not be content with provisional and conventional answers. With socratic thoroughness he would go on questioning where others stopped; and his questioning would be taken up by his students. Soon it became clear that he was a born educator. His confirmation class in North Berlin with whom he lived for three months in closest proximity was the prelude to the plans later realized in the seminary of Finkenwalde. The intervening period could have opened for him a brilliant and secure academic career—if he had cared to choose it.

But instead he went to London. This was not his first post abroad; he had been as curate in Barcelona and as exchange student and teacher at Union Seminary in New York. Important ecumenical contacts had been made. But the departure from Berlin in October 1933, had special programmatic significance. It marked his clear break with the church of the Third Reich. When he refused to conceal his stand in his dealings with the London congregation, one of the new Berlin pundits remarked: "What a complicated sort of man you are!" Little did he know Dietrich Bonhoeffer. His complexity was not such as to allow for any doubt between right and wrong. To probe the problem of ethics was not to indulge in the game of "dialectical" theology. The search had to lead to the goal, the quest demanded an answer.

His eighteen months in London finally clarified his course. Others will have to tell of his work as Pastor at St Paul's, Aldgate, and in Sydenham; his parishioners who are amongst us here today all know the impact of his brief ministry upon their own history, and none of us who lived as his guest in Forest Hill can ever forget that time. I vividly remember his sermon on Remembrance Sunday 1933; the text (Wisdom of Solomon 3:4, about the righteous) was "but they are in peace," and he related the story of a patient, given up by the doctors, losing consciousness, hanging between life and death, looking, as it were, across the border and exclaiming: "My God, this is beautiful!" In many conversations of those days he remarked that to reach the age of 36 or 37 was quite enough for a Christian.

Yet he had still ten years left. And still he felt the burden of the word: "we know not what to do." "I shall always remember him" wrote the landlady of the boarding-house next door to his manse, "pacing up and down our lounge, trying to decide whether to remain here or to give up his church here and return to the persecuted church in Germany; longing to visit Gandhi in India and feeling a premonition that unless he seized that moment he would never go. I knew, being himself, how he must eventually decide." The decision repeated itself when shortly before the outbreak of the second war American friends invited him and tried to persuade him to stay. A brief visit ended with his final return to Germany. His place was by the side of his hard-pressed brethren and disciples in the ministry and with his own family which was increasingly drawn into the battle between Christ and Antichrist.

"We know not what to do; but our eyes are upon Thee." The unrest of the quest ends in the discipleship of Christ, the theme of his last book, now carried into practice in his own life. Law and Gospel, command and promise point to the one clear certain way which he had sought: "only the believer is obedient, and only he who obeys believes." From the "life together" of which his brochure treats and which finds expression in the brotherhood of his seminary it becomes clear why the text says in the plural: "we know not . . . our eyes. . . ." For only within the communion of the church can the call of the Lord be heard and followed. But we speak, of course, of the one holy catholic church; and loyalty to his own confession never made Dietrich Bonhoeffer uncritical of the faults even in the Confessional Church, never unmindful of what he had learnt and received from other traditions and witnessed in his writings.

So he remains ecumenical in his attitude and more so, perhaps, than any other German theologian of his generation; so he refuses to enter the Second World War as an active combatant and renews the link with the British brethren, even after the frontiers have been closed, and travels into neutral countries become more dangerous than ever. He sees the growing dilemma of German Christians in their isolation; as in the Samson Story one man's hand threatens to bring down the whole house; and there is, but for the very rarest exceptions, no understanding voice and no helping hand from without. Political action becomes inevitable. "Why," Dietrich said on his last visit here, "should it always have to be the bad people who make the revolutions?"

He risked everything in this battle, as did his brother, his brothers-in-law, his friends. The outcome was at least uncertain, not only for the men, but for the cause. Bishop Bell has spoken of the apocalyptic undertones of his last conversation with him in Stockholm; the impending doom of Germany, even of Europe, appeared to have become certain in his mind. But even now and precisely now the word remained in force: "We know not what to do, but our eyes are upon Thee." Even the last two years in prison with their unexpected pastoral opportunities and the last two months after he and Klaus had been sentenced to death were to him but a new, higher stage of discipleship. He had written of the grace of martyrdom. And the text of his first sermon had been: "Likewise ye, when ye shall have done all those things which are commanded you say, We are unprofitable servants: we have done that which was our duty to do."

It is, perhaps, significant that we have few good pictures of him; he was averse to the photographers; the best shots show him in the family circle, with those to whom he belonged most closely and who escorted him to the end: the parents to the trial, two brothers-in-law to concentration camps and one brother to death. One of the happiest, freest, bravest homes in Germany has been bereft of its children—this is where the real victims of this war are to be found. Speech and hope fail us; we know not what to do. But let us not stop here, but follow the text: our eyes are upon Thee. In this turn from the agonizing quest to the confident discipleship lies the secret of Dietrich Bonhoeffer and his legacy for us. One can study it from the development of his style; from the earliest abstract analyses to the last pages of the *Cost of Discipleship* it grows more and more simple and unburdened. A reviewer of *Creation and Fall* writes: "there is more in these hundred pages than in many a theological tome; every word is weighed and every sentence fits." It was not different with his life. The yoke he took was easy, and the burden of his master light; the vision cleared as he looked to Jesus, away from himself, and what years ago he had written of the Christian's hope, was now fulfilled: "He becomes what he was—or rather, never was—a child."

We know not what to do. After these anxious weeks of uncertainty through which we have lived with you, dear Sabine and Gert, and with your parents, we know less than ever how to carry on without the counsel of our brother on whom we could lean and who was so desperately needed by the Church at this time. Today we understand what Harnack said when Holl had died: "with him a piece of my own life is carried to the grave." Yet: our eyes are upon Thee. We believe in the communion of saints, the forgiveness of sins, the resurrection of the body and the life everlasting. We give thanks to God for the life, the suffering, the witness of our brother whose friends we were privileged to be. We pray God to lead us, too, through his discipleship from this world into His heavenly kingdom; to fulfil in us that other word with which Dietrich concluded his obituary of Harnack: *"non potest non laetari qui sperat in Dominum"*—"while in God confiding I cannot but rejoice."

When the service ended, Karl and Paula Bonhoeffer turned off the radio.

NOTES

CHAPTER 1: FAMILY AND CHILDHOOD

p. 5, **In the winter of 1896**: Eberhard Bethge, *Dietrich Bonhoeffer: A Biography*, rev. ed. (Minneapolis: Augsburg Fortress, 2000), 8.

p. 6, **Both of them**: Bethge, *Dietrich Bonhoeffer: A Biography*, 7.

p. 7, **The Bonhoeffers were among**: Mary Bosanquet, *The Life and Death of Dietrich Bonhoeffer*, (New York: Harper and Row, 1968), 18.

p.7, **Karl Bonhoeffer's father**: Bosanquet, *Life and Death of Bonhoeffer*, 18.

p. 7, **Karl Bonhoeffer's father;"My grandfather and his three brothers"**: Ibid., 19.

p. 8, **All of the Bonhoeffer children**: Bethge, *Dietrich Bonhoeffer: A Biography*, 16.

p. 9, **Despite his busy schedule**: Renate Bethge and Christian Gremmels, ed., *Dietrich Bonhoeffer: A Life in Pictures*, trans. Brian McNeil (Minneapolis: Fortress Press, 2006), 22.

p. 10, **In 1910 the Bonhoeffers**: Bethge and Gremmels, *A Life in Pictures*, 24.

p. 10, **My first memories**: Bosanquet, *Life and Death of Bonhoeffer*, 24.

p. 11, **Dietrich was the only child**: Wolf-Dieter Zimmermann and Ronald G. Smith, eds., *I Knew Dietrich Bonhoeffer*, trans. Käthe Gregor Smith (New York: Harper and Row, 1966), 25.

p. 11, **Dietrich was the only child; "I shall never forget"**: Zimmerman and Smith, *I Knew Dietrich Bonhoeffer*, 27.

p. 11, **His chivalrous bent**: Ibid., 24.

p. 11, **Sabine also remembered**: Bosanquet, *Life and Death of Bonhoeffer*, 24.

p. 11, **When Dietrich and Sabine**: Sabine Leibholz-Bonhoeffer, *The Bonhoeffers: Portrait of a Family*, (New York: St. Martin's Press, 1971), 37.

p. 12, **Paula Bonhoeffer's faith**: Bosanquet, *Life and Death of Bonhoeffer*, 29.

p. 13, **Dietrich was often mischievous**: Ibid., 29.

p. 13, **In 1912**: Bethge, *Dietrich Bonhoeffer: A Biography*, 21.

p. 13, **In intuitive psychology**: Ibid., 22.

p. 14, **There was a strong atmosphere**: Ibid., 17.

p. 14, **Karl Bonhoeffer would not**: Leibholz-Bonhoeffer, *The Bonhoeffers*, 12.

p. 14, **The faith that Paula Bonhoeffer**: Ibid., 7.

p. 14, **The family seemed**: Zimmerman and Smith, *I Knew Dietrich Bonhoeffer*, 37.

p. 15, **great tolerance**: Leibholz-Bonhoeffer, *The Bonhoeffers*, 12.

p. 15, **Professor Scheller**: Ibid., 11.

p. 15, **Professor Scheller; "Of his qualities"**: Bethge, *Dietrich Bonhoeffer: A Biography*, 10.

p. 16, **He feared walking there alone**: Bosanquet, *Life and Death of Bonhoeffer*, 31.

p. 16, **Dietrich did well in school**: Bethge, *Dietrich Bonhoeffer: A Biography*, 24.

p. 17, **The journey**: Leibholz-Bonhoeffer, *The Bonhoeffers*, 7.

p. 17, **The van Horn sisters**: Ibid., 8.

p. 18, **Dietrich was the first to notice**: Ibid., 8–9.

p. 18, **Under the rowan-trees**: Zimmerman and Smith, *I Knew Dietrich Bonhoeffer*, 26.

p. 19, **Sometimes in the evenings**: Ibid.

p. 20, **The village was celebrating**: Leibholz-Bonhoeffer, *The Bonhoeffers*, 4.

p. 21, **The elation of the crowds**: Bosanquet, *Life and Death of Bonhoeffer*, 34.

p. 22, **The Bonhoeffers were sincerely patriotic**: Leibholz-Bonhoeffer, *The Bonhoeffers*, 5.

p. 22, **In time the realities**:

p. 23, **We had supper**: Bethge and Gremmels, *A Life in Pictures*, 28.

p. 23, **While we were playing**: Zimmerman and Smith, *I Knew Dietrich Bonhoeffer*, 24.

p. 25, **On the Sundays of Advent**: Ibid., 27–28.

p. 25, **As the war continued**: Karl Bonhoeffer to Paul Jossmann, 1945.

p. 26, **I can still remember**: Leibholz-Bonhoeffer, *The Bonhoeffers*, 21–22.

p. 27, **My Dears**: Ibid., 22–23.

p. 27, **Later, the family received other letters**: Christoph von Hase interview by Martin Doblmeier, *Bonhoeffer: Pastor, Pacifist, Nazi Resister. A documentary film by Martin Doblmeier*, date of interview, Princeton University. Unused footage quoted here by permission of the director.

p. 29, **Dear Grandmama**: *The Young Bonhoeffer: 1918–1927*, vol. 9, *Dietrich Bonhoeffer Works*, trans. and ed. Hans Pfeifer et al. (New York: Fortress Press, 2002), 19.

p. 29, **On Sunday**: *The Young Bonhoeffer*, 21.

p. 30, **Soon we saw a thick black pillar**: Ibid., 21–22.

p. 31, **I don't know if I already wrote**: Ibid., 23–24.

p. 31, **Yesterday we took my gleanings**: Ibid., 24.

p. 31, **If 1918 can be seen**:

p. 33, **It was a grotesque**: Bethge, *Dietrich Bonhoeffer: A Biography*, 28.

p. 35, **It wasn't too dangerous**: Ibid., 27.

p. 35, **But Dietrich had concerns**: Ibid., 25.

p. 35, **But Dietrich had concerns; "So far mama"**: Ibid., 27.

p. 36, **About eleven o'clock**: Zimmerman and Smith, *I Knew Dietrich Bonhoeffer*, 29.

p. 36, **We had our parties**: Ibid., 35.

p. 37, **To keep a distance**: Ibid., 36.

p. 38, **We liked to ask**: Ibid.

p. 38, **Gerhard von Rad**: Ibid., 177.

p. 39, **Two years later**: Ibid., 31.

p. 39, **The turmoil of the early Weimar Republic**: *The Young Bonhoeffer*, 49.

p. 40, **Peter Olden**: Bethge, *Dietrich Bonhoeffer: A Biography*, 33.

p. 40, **A few weeks later**: *The Young Bonhoeffer*, 50.

CHAPTER 2: TÜBINGEN, 1923

p. 42, **He left at the end of April**: Eberhard Bethge, *Dietrich Bonhoeffer: A Biography*, rev. ed. (Minneapolis: Augsburg Fortress, 2000), 45.

p. 43, **Years later a fellow member**: Bethge, *Dietrich Bonhoeffer: A Biography*, 50.

p. 44, **A new member**: Archilochus, quoted in Isaiah Berlin, *The Hedgehog and the Fox An Essay on Tolstoy's View of History* (London: Weidenfeld & Nicolson, 1953; New York: Simon and Schuster, 1953; New York: New American Library, 1957; New York: Simon and Schuster, 1986).

p. 44, **In Breslau**: *The Young Bonhoeffer: 1918–1927*, vol. 9, *Dietrich Bonhoeffer Works*, trans. and ed. Hans Pfeifer et al. (New York: Fortress Press, 2002), 60.

p. 45, **The sole purpose**: *The Young Bonhoeffer*, 70.

p. 46, **Two days later**: Ibid.

p. 46, **The exercises**: Ibid., 71.

p. 46, **We practiced**: Ibid., 72.

p. 46, **That winter while Dietrich:** Mary Bosanquet, *The Life and Death of Dietrich Bonhoeffer*, (New York: Harper and Row, 1968), 21.

p. 47, **I received all sorts:** *The Young Bonhoeffer*, 78.

CHAPTER 3: ROMAN HOLIDAY, 1924

p. 49, **Like many of their generation:** Eberhard Bethge, *Dietrich Bonhoeffer: A Biography*, rev. ed. (Minneapolis: Augsburg Fortress, 2000), 57.

p. 50, **The eighteen-year-old pilgrim:** *The Young Bonhoeffer: 1918–1927*, vol. 9, *Dietrich Bonhoeffer Works*, trans. and ed. Hans Pfeifer et al. (New York: Fortress Press, 2002), 83.

p. 50, **The answer was not long in coming:** *The Young Bonhoeffer*, 83.

p. 50, **Bonhoeffer spun through Rome:** Ibid., 84.

p. 50, **Bonhoeffer spun through Rome; On the** *Laocoön*: Ibid., 89.

p. 50, **Bonhoeffer spun through Rome; On Trajan's Forum:** Ibid., 86.

p. 50, **Bonhoeffer spun through Rome; On the eunuch:** Ibid., 91.

p. 50, **Bonhoeffer spun through Rome; On Reni and Michelangelo:** Ibid., 101.

p. 51, **I was hardly able to move:** Ibid., 102.

p. 51, **At the moment:** Ibid., 103.

p. 52, **Bonhoeffer's letters home:** Ibid., 94.

p. 52, **Not long after their foul repast:** Ibid.

p. 53, **In his diary:** Ibid., 89.

p. 53, **The occasion for his epiphany:** Ibid., 88.

p. 54, **But another reason:** Ibid., 99–100.

p. 55, **That Palm Sunday:** Ibid., 88–89.

p. 55, **If Protestantism had never:** Ibid., 106–07.

p. 55, **Bonhoeffer typically took complete advantage:** Ibid., 111.

p. 56, **He attended one Armenian-Catholic:** Ibid.

p. 56, **He attended one Armenian-Catholic; "He would really like":** Ibid., 93.

p. 56, **Somehow, before the semester was over:** Ibid., 107.

p. 56, **Before he knew it:** Ibid., 108.

p. 57, **It is hard to overestimate:** Ibid., 528–29.

CHAPTER 4: STUDENT IN BERLIN, 1924–27

p. 58, **Dietrich's decision to study:** Eberhard Bethge, *Dietrich Bonhoeffer: Man of Vision, Man of Courage*, ed. Edwin Robertson (New York: Harper and Row, 1970; Minneapolis: Augsburg Fortress, 2000), 44. Citations are to the Augsburg edition.

p. 59, **What really impressed me:** Bethge, *Man of Vision*, 45.

p. 61, **Bonhoeffer agreed with Barth:** Eberhard Bethge, interview by Martin Doblmeier, *Bonhoeffer: Pastor, Pacifist, Nazi Resister. A documentary film by Martin Doblmeier*, date of interview, Princeton University. Unused footage quoted here by permission of the director.

p. 65, **Many who knew him:** Ruth-Alice von Bismarck, interview with author, Hamburg, Germany, March 2008.

p. 66, **I was once in love:** Ruth-Alice von Bismarck and Ulrich Kabitz, eds. *Love Letters from Cell 92: The Correspondence Between Dietrich Bonhoeffer and Maria Von Wedemeyer, 1943–45*, trans. John Brownjohn (New York: Abingdon Press, 1995), 246.

p. 67, **From this letter:** Dietrich Bonhoeffer, *A Testament to Freedom: The Essential Writings of Dietrich Bonhoeffer*, rev. ed., eds. Geffrey B. Kelly and F. Burton Nelson (New York: Harper One, 1995), 424.

p. 68, **"This offer":** *Barcelona, Berlin, New York: 1928–1931*, vol. 10, *Dietrich Bonhoeffer Works*, ed. Clifford J. Green, trans. Douglas W. Stott (New York: Fortress Press, 2008), 57.

CHAPTER 5: BARCELONA, 1928

p. 70, **I myself find**: *Barcelona, Berlin, New York: 1928–1931*, vol. 10, *Dietrich Bonhoeffer Works*, ed. Clifford J. Green, trans. Douglas W. Stott (New York: Fortress Press, 2008), 58.

p. 70, **I spoke about the man**: *Barcelona, Berlin, New York: 1928–1931*, 58.

p. 71, **On Sunday afternoon**: Ibid., 59.

p. 72, **On Tuesday**: Ibid.

p. 72, **On Tuesday; "The meadows were green"**: Ibid., 59–60.

p. 72, **Bonhoeffer was met at the station**: Ibid., 60.

p. 72, **Bonhoeffer was met at the station; The only place to wash**: Ibid., 62.

p. 73, **In Barcelona**: Ibid., 78.

p. 74, **Recently I saw something**: Ibid., 118.

p. 74, **Bonhoeffer liked Barcelona**: Dietrich Bonhoeffer to Max Diestel, Barcelona, June 18, 1928.

p. 75, **I had already seen one**: *Barcelona, Berlin, New York*, 83.

p. 75, **I have never seen the swing**: Ibid., 89.

p. 76, **But he was not always profound**: Ibid., 147.

p. 76, **Bonhoeffer loved**: Klaus Bonhoeffer to his parents, Tétouan, May 5, 1928.

p. 77, **Before Bonhoeffer's arrival**: Dietrich Bonhoeffer to Paula Bonhoeffer, Barcelona, February 20, 1928.

p. 77, **Although Olbrict**: Dietrich Bonhoeffer to Walter Dress, Barcelona, March 13, 1928.

p. 77, **Although Olbrict; In another letter**: Dietrich Bonhoeffer to Paula Bonhoeffer, Barcelona, February 20, 1928.

p. 78, **This summer**: *Barcelona, Berlin, New York*, 127.

p. 78, **One has to deal**: Ibid., 110.

p. 79, **Every day I am getting to know**: Ibid., 127.

p. 79, **At the end of June**: Ibid., 112.

p. 80, **Still, Bonhoeffer's solo flight**: Ibid., 126.

p. 80, **Bonhoeffer's parents visited**: Ibid., 527–31.

p. 81, **I have long thought**: Ibid., 127.

p. 82, **The second lecture**: Ibid., 343.

p. 83, **We may assume**: Ibid.

p. 84, **With that we have articulated**: Ibid., 354.

p. 84, **In the lectures**: Ibid.

p. 85, **Bonhoeffer's sentences**: Ibid.

p. 85, **Before he was finished**: Ibid., 355.

p. 85, **Humanism and mysticism**: Ibid., 356.

p. 85, **Today I encountered**: Dietrich Bonhoeffer to Walter Dress, Barcelona, September 1, 1928.

CHAPTER 6: BERLIN, 1929

p. 89, **In revelation**: Eberhard Bethge, *Dietrich Bonhoeffer: A Biography*, rev. ed. (Minneapolis: Augsburg Fortress, 2000), 134.

p. 90, **When** *Act and Being*: Bethge, *Dietrich Bonhoeffer: A Biography*, 129.

p. 90, **In the summer**: *Barcelona, Berlin, New York: 1928–1931*, vol. 10, *Dietrich Bonhoeffer Works*, ed. Clifford J. Green, trans. Douglas W. Stott (New York: Fortress Press, 2008), 423–33.

p. 94, **Given all that was about to happen**: Ibid., 138.

p. 95, **It became clear**: Ibid., 139.

p. 97, **My cabin seems not unfavorably located**: *Barcelona, Berlin, New York*, 241.

p. 98, **While he was sailing**: Bethge, *Dietrich Bonhoeffer: A Biography*, 130–31.

CHAPTER 7: BONHOEFFER IN AMERICA, 1930–31

p. 100, **Despite all this activity**: *Barcelona, Berlin, New York: 1928–1931*, vol. 10, *Dietrich Bonhoeffer*

Works, ed. Clifford J. Green, trans. Douglas W. Stott (New York: Fortress Press, 2008), 243.

p. 101, **There is no theology here:** *Barcelona, Berlin, New York: 1928–1931*, 265–66.

p. 103, **Dr. Fosdick proposes:** "Religion: Riverside Church," *Time*, October 6, 1930.

p. 104, **Living together day by day:** *Barcelona, Berlin, New York: 1928–1931*, 306.

p. 104, **Not only quietness is lacking:** Ibid., 306–07.

p. 104, **He believed that students:** Ibid., 308.

p. 105, **Another group was mostly interested:** Ibid., 309–10.

p. 106, **Things are not much different in the church:** Ibid., 266.

p. 106, **The enlightened American:** Ibid., 313.

p. 107, **This is quite characteristic:** Ibid., 313–14.

p. 108, **Powell was the son of slaves:** Adam Clayton Powell Sr., Harlem, New York, November 1927.

p. 109, **Bonhoeffer also read:** Dietrich Bonhoeffer to his parents, Philadelphia, December 1, 1930.

p. 109, **In Washington:** Ibid., 258.

p. 110, **I want to have a look:** Ibid., 293.

p. 110, **His belief that there was no:** Eberhard Bethge, *Dietrich Bonhoeffer: A Biography*, rev. ed. (Minneapolis: Augsburg Fortress, 2000), 151.

p. 111, **Bonhoeffer respected Lasserre:** Mary Bosanquet, *The Life and Death of Dietrich Bonhoeffer*, (New York: Harper and Row, 1968), 89.

p. 113, **Bonhoeffer's voracious appetite:** Dietrich Bonhoeffer to Max Diestel, New York, April 25, 1931.

p. 113, **The sun has always attracted me:** Ruth-Alice von Bismarck and Ulrich Kabitz, eds. *Love Letters from Cell 92: The Correspondence Between Dietrich Bonhoeffer and Maria Von Wedemeyer, 1943–45*, trans. John Brownjohn (New York: Abingdon Press, 1995), 68.

p. 114, **The separation of whites:** *Barcelona, Berlin, New York: 1928–1931*, 269.

p. 114, **It's so unnerving:** Ibid., 270–71.

p. 115, **[Bonhoeffer] was German:** Bosanquet, *Life and Death of Bonhoeffer*, 88.

p. 115, **get entry tickets:** *Barcelona, Berlin, New York: 1928–1931*, 294–95.

p. 116, **Once at night:** Edwin Robertson, *The Shame and the Sacrifice: The Life and Martyrdom of Dietrich Bonhoeffer*, (New York: Macmillan, 1988), 66.

p. 117, **Finally Lasserre and Bonhoeffer:** Paul Lehmann to Jean Lasserre and Dietrich Bonhoeffer, telegram, May 19, 1931.

p. 117, **I just spent a long time:** *Barcelona, Berlin, New York: 1928–1931*, 304.

CHAPTER 8: BERLIN, 1931–32

p. 119, **Bonhoeffer left for Bonn:** Dietrich Bonhoeffer to his parents, Bonn, July 1931.

p. 120, **On July 23:** Dietrich Bonhoeffer, *A Testament to Freedom: The Essential Writings of Dietrich Bonhoeffer*, rev. ed., eds. Geffrey B. Kelly and F. Burton Nelson (New York: Harper One, 1995), 383.

p. 120, **In the next two years:** Eberhard Bethge, *Dietrich Bonhoeffer: A Biography*, rev. ed. (Minneapolis: Augsburg Fortress, 2000), 178.

p. 121, **Bonhoeffer wrote Sutz:** Bonhoeffer, *A Testament to Freedom*, 384.

p. 122, **Bonhoeffer opened with the bad news:** *Berlin 1932–1933*, vol. 12, *Dietrich Bonhoeffer Works*, ed. Larry L. Rasmussen (Minneapolis: Augsburg Fortress, 2009), 439.

p. 123, **I plunged into work:** Bonhoeffer, *A Testament to Freedom*, 424–25.

p. 124, **A young lecturer:** Wolf-Dieter Zimmermann and Ronald G. Smith, eds., *I Knew Dietrich Bonhoeffer*, trans. Käthe Gregor Smith (New York: Harper and Row, 1966), 60.

p. 125, **Talk like this was rare:** Zimmerman and Smith, *I Knew Dietrich Bonhoeffer*, 68.

p. 125, **In my intellectual difficulties:** Ibid., 69.

p. 126, **Whatever he had**: Otto Dudzus, interview by Martin Doblmeier, *Bonhoeffer: Pastor, Pacifist, Nazi Resister. A documentary film by Martin Doblmeier*, date of interview, Princeton University. Unused footage quoted here by permission of the director.

p. 126, **My first impression**: Inge Karding, interview by Martin Doblmeier, *Bonhoeffer: Pastor, Pacifist, Nazi Resister. A documentary film by Martin Doblmeier*, date of interview, Princeton University. Unused footage quoted here by permission of the director.

p. 126, **He was not like**: Albert Schönherr, interview by Martin Doblmeier, *Bonhoeffer: Pastor, Pacifist, Nazi Resister. A documentary film by Martin Doblmeier*, date of interview, Princeton University. Unused footage quoted here by permission of the director.

p. 127, **Nonetheless, a group:**

p. 127, **Student found Bonhoeffer:**

p. 128, **He told us of his colored friend**: Zimmerman and Smith, *I Knew Dietrich Bonhoeffer*, 64–65.

p. 128, **Bonhoeffer was able to get away**: Inge Karding, interview by Martin Doblmeier.

p. 128, **[He said] when you read the Bible**: Ibid.

p, 130, **The old minister**: Dietrich Bonhoeffer to Erwin Sutz, Wedding, November 1931.

p. 131, **The elderly minister**: Bethge, *Dietrich Bonhoeffer: A Biography*, 226.

p. 131, **Bonhoeffer described**: Dietrich Bonhoeffer to Erwin Sutz, Wedding, November 1931.

p. 132, **Years later**: Zimmerman and Smith, *I Knew Dietrich Bonhoeffer*, 57.

p. 132, **I sometimes**: *No Rusty Swords: Letters, Lectures and Notes 1928–1936* , vol. 1, *Collected Works of Dietrich Bonhoeffer*, ed. Edwin H. Robertson, trans. Edwin H. Robertson and John Bowden (New York: Harper and Row, 1965), 151.

p. 133, **The second half of the term**: *No Rusty Swords*, 150.

p. 134, **Dear Confirmation Candidates**: Mary Bosanquet, *The Life and Death of Dietrich Bonhoeffer*, (New York: Harper and Row, 1968), 104.

p. 134, **I am delighted**: Bethge, *Dietrich Bonhoeffer: A Biography*,228–29.

p. 136, **First of all**: Bosanquet, *Life and Death of Bonhoeffer*, 109.

CHAPTER 9: THE FÜHRER PRINCIPLE, 1933

p. 141, **Bonhoeffer stated**: *No Rusty Swords: Letters, Lectures and Notes 1928–1936* , vol. 1, *Collected Works of Dietrich Bonhoeffer*, ed. Edwin H. Robertson, trans. Edwin H. Robertson and John Bowden (New York: Harper and Row, 1965), 195.

p. 141, **If he understands his function**: *No Rusty Swords*, 202.

p. 142, **Only when a man sees**: Ibid., 203–04.

p. 143, **So Hitler gave a speech**: Richard Steigmann-Gall, *The Holy Reich: Nazi Conceptions of Christianity, 1919–1945* (Cambridge: Cambridge University Press, 2003), 115.

p. 143, **So Hitler gave a speech; "May God Almighty take our work"**: Steigmann-Gall, *The Holy Reich*, 116.

p. 143, **From the start**: Eberhard Bethge, *Dietrich Bonhoeffer: A Biography*, rev. ed. (Minneapolis: Augsburg Fortress, 2000), 258.

p. 144, **The church has only *one* altar**: Bethge, *Dietrich Bonhoeffer: A Biography*, 257.

p. 146, **But Goebbels**: Donald Moffitt, letter to the editor, "Tunes With a Past," *Yale Alumni Magazine*, March 2000.

p. 146, **But Goebbels; Shirer described Hanfstaengl**: William L. Shirer, *The Rise and Fall of the Third Reich: A History of Nazi Germany* (New York: Simon and Schuster, 1960), 47.

p. 147, **[Van der Lubbe] was violently ambitious**: Mary Bosanquet, *The Life and Death of Dietrich Bonhoeffer*, (New York: Harper and Row, 1968), 117.

p. 147, **I had the opportunity**: Bethge, *Dietrich Bonhoeffer: A Biography*, 265.

p. 148, **Folding his great arms**: Name, "Germany: Göring Afraid?"*Time*, November 13, 1933, pg.

p. 149, **Restrictions on personal liberty**: Shirer, *The Rise and Fall of the Third Reich*, 194.

CHAPTER 10: THE CHURCH AND THE JEWISH QUESTION

p. 152, **"The fact, unique in history"**: Dietrich Bonhoeffer, "The Church and the Jewish Question," in *No Rusty Swords: Letters, Lectures and Notes 1928-1936* (New York: Harper and Row, 1965), 226.

p. 156, **Bonhoeffer's Jewish brother-in-law**: Sabine Leibholz-Bonhoeffer, *The Bonhoeffers: Portrait of a Family*, (New York: St. Martin's Press, 1971), 83.

p. 159, **I had often heard**: Leibholz-Bonhoeffer, *The Bonhoeffers*, 84.

p. 160, **I am tormented**: Eberhard Bethge, *Dietrich Bonhoeffer: A Biography*, rev. ed. (Minneapolis: Augsburg Fortress, 2000), 275–6.

p. 161, **Young and hitherto**: Bethge, *Dietrich Bonhoeffer: A Biography*, 279.

p. 162, **In Berlin**: Elizabeth Raum, *Dietrich Bonhoeffer: Called by God* (New York: Simon and Schuster, 1960), 80.

p. 163, **Christianity**: Heinrich Heine, *Religion and Philosophy in Germany: A Fragment* (London: Trübner and Co., 1882), 177.

CHAPTER 11: NAZI THEOLOGY

p. 165, **Epigraph**: *Inside the Third Reich: Memoirs by Albert Speer*, trans. Richard Winston and Clara Winston (New York: Macmillan, 1970), 114–15.

p. 166, **The Fuehrer spoke**: *The Goebbels Diaries 1942–1943*, ed. Louis P. Lochner (Garden City, NY: Doubleday, 1948), 375.

p. 167, **Hitler's architect**: *Inside the Third Reich*, 114.

p. 167, **Bormann despised Christians**: Ibid., 147–48.

p. 168, **Nietzsche called Christianity**: *The Complete Works of Friedrich Nietzsche*, ed. Oscar Levy, trans. Thomas Common (New York: Macmillan, 1911).

p. 169, **At the end**: William L. Shirer, *The Rise and Fall of the Third Reich: A History of Nazi Germany* (New York: Simon and Schuster, 1960), 100.

p. 170, **Heydrich**: Hans B. Gisevius, *To the Bitter End: An Insider's Account of the Plot to Kill Hitler 1933–1944*, trans. Richard Winston and Clara Winston (New York: Da Capo Press, 1998), 189.

p. 170, **The SS**: Adolf Hitler quoted in *Inside the Third Reich: Memoirs*, by Albert Speer (New York: Simon and Schuster, 1970), 94.

p. 170, **Rosenberg was one**: Shirer, *The Rise and Fall of the Third Reich*, 240.

p. 171, **13. The National Church**: Ibid.

p. 171, **The most serious Christians**: Karl Barth, "Protestant Churches in Europe," *Foreign Affairs* 21 (1943), 263–65.

p. 172, **For starters**: Georg Schneider, *Our Faith: A Guide for German Christians* (Germany: Institute for Research into and Elimination of Jewish Influence in German Church Life, 1940).

p. 173, **As they bent themselves**: Doris L. Bergen, *Twisted Cross: The German Christian Movement in the Third Reich* (Chapel Hill, NC: University of North Carolina Press, 1996), 47.

p. 173, **But it wasn't merely**: Bergen, *Twisted Cross*, 68.

p. 174, **A people**: Ibid., 158.

p. 174, **How the German Christians**: Ibid., 103.

p. 174, **How the German Christians; Even Luther had questioned**: Ibid., 148.

CHAPTER 12: THE CHURCH STRUGGLE BEGINS

p. 178, **Those who walked out**: Eberhard Bethge, *Dietrich Bonhoeffer: A Biography*, rev. ed. (Minneapolis: Augsburg Fortress, 2000).

p. 180, **Meanwhile, Hitler**: William L. Shirer, *The Rise and Fall of the Third Reich: A History of Nazi Germany* (New York: Simon and Schuster, 1960), 238.

p. 181, **His Holiness**: Adolf Hitler, "Concordant Between the Holy See and the German Reich [With Supplementary Protocol and Secret Supplement],"

July 20, 1933, trans., Muriel Frasier, http://www.concordatwatch.eu/showkb. php?org_id=858&kb_header_id=752&kb_id=1211.

p. 181, **The German Reich:** Adolph Hitler, "Concordant."

p. 182, **Is there theologically:** Bethge, *Dietrich Bonhoeffer: A Biography*, 301.

CHAPTER 13: THE BETHEL CONFESSION

p. 183, **Epithet:** Dietrich Bonhoeffer to Julie Tafel Bonhoeffer, Bethel, August 20, 1933.

p. 183, **He left after the July 23 election:** *No Rusty Swords: Letters, Lectures and Notes 1928–1936*, vol. 1, *Collected Works of Dietrich Bonhoeffer*, ed. Edwin H. Robertson, trans. Edwin H. Robertson and John Bowden (New York: Harper and Row, 1965), 251.

p. 184, **Bonhoeffer attended services:** Dietrich Bonhoeffer to Julie Tafel Bonhoeffer, Bethel, August 20, 1933.

p. 184, **Bonhoeffer attended services; When the war came:** Eberhard Bethge, *Dietrich Bonhoeffer: A Biography*, rev. ed. (Minneapolis: Augsburg Fortress, 2000), 300.

p. 185, **Our work here:** Dietrich Bonhoeffer, *A Testament to Freedom: The Essential Writings of Dietrich Bonhoeffer*, rev. ed., eds. Geffrey B. Kelly and F. Burton Nelson (New York: Harper One, 1995), 419.

p. 187, **He was far ahead of the curve:** Wolf-Dieter Zimmermann and Ronald G. Smith, eds., *I Knew Dietrich Bonhoeffer*, trans. Käthe Gregor Smith (New York: Harper and Row, 1966), 129.

p. 187, **Not even Karl Barth:** Bethge, *Dietrich Bonhoeffer: A Biography*, 308–09.

p. 189, **The only good news:** Ibid., 312.

p. 189, **At the conference:** Ibid., 315.

p. 189, **They also protested:** Ibid., 315.

p. 192, **Bonhoeffer and Hildebrandt:** Ibid., 323.

p. 192, **Even the timing:** William L. Shirer, *The Rise and Fall of the Third Reich: A History of Nazi Germany* (New York: Simon and Schuster, 1960), 211.

p. 193, **In coarse:** Doris L. Bergen, *Twisted Cross: The German Christian Movement in the Third Reich* (Chapel Hill, NC: University of North Carolina Press, 1996), 145.

CHAPTER 14: BONHOEFFER IN LONDON, 1934–35

p. 195, **Although I am working:** Dietrich Bonhoeffer, *A Testament to Freedom: The Essential Writings of Dietrich Bonhoeffer*, rev. ed., eds. Geffrey B. Kelly and F. Burton Nelson (New York: Harper One, 1995), 411.

p. 196, **Simply suffering:** *London: 1933-1935*, vol. 13, *Dietrich Bonhoeffer Works*, ed. Keith Clements, trans. Isabel Best (New York: Fortress Press, 2007), 135.

p. 197, **If one were going to discover:** Ibid., 23.

p. 197, **Dear Colleague:** Ibid., 39–41.

p. 201, **Hildebrandt arrived in London:** Amos Cresswell and Maxwell Tow, *Dr. Franz Hildebrandt: Mr. Valiant for Truth* (Grand Rapids, Smyth and Helwys, 2000), 52–53.

p. 201, **Usually we had a sumptuous breakfast:** Wolf-Dieter Zimmermann and Ronald G. Smith, eds., *I Knew Dietrich Bonhoeffer*, trans. Käthe Gregor Smith (New York: Harper and Row, 1966), 78.

p. 201, **Hildebrandt lived with Bonhoeffer:** Amos Cresswell and Maxwell Tow, *Dr. Franz Hildebrandt: Mr. Valiant for Truth* (Grand Rapids, Smyth and Helwys, 2000), 122.

p. 202, **Also as in Barcelona:** Dietrich Bonhoeffer to Gerhard and Sabine Leibholz, London, November 23, 1933.

CHAPTER 15: THE CHURCH BATTLE HEATS UP

p. 206, **Bonhoeffer knew:** Eberhard Bethge, *Dietrich Bonhoeffer: A Biography*, rev. ed. (Minneapolis: Augsburg Fortress, 2000), 341.

p. 208, **Bonhoeffer followed every detail:** Bethge, *Dietrich Bonhoeffer: A Biography*, 344.

p. 208, **During this tense time of waiting:** *London: 1933-1935*, vol. 13, *Dietrich Bonhoeffer Works,* ed. Keith Clements, trans. Isabel Best (New York: Fortress Press, 2007), 349.

p. 209, **This path will lead:** *London,* 350.

p. 210, **And Jeremiah was just:** Ibid., 351–353.

p. 210, **[Jeremiah] was upbraided:** Ibid.

p. 211, **"I was very frightened":** James Bentley, *Martin Niemöller: 1892-1984* (New York: Free Press, 1984), 86.

p. 211, **Heckel's position:** Theodore Heckel to German Congregations and Pastors Abroad, Berlin-Charlottenburg, January 31, 1934.

p. 212, **Dear Dietrich:** *London,* 97–98.

p. 213, **The day after:** Friedrich Wehrhan, Julius Rieger, Gustav Schönberger, Dietrich Bonhoeffer, Memorandum from the Pastors in London, London, February 5, 1934.

p. 214, **And what of the brazen attempt:** Bethge, *Dietrich Bonhoeffer: A Biography,* 348–50.

p. 217, **My dear Lord Bishop:** *London,* 118–19.

p. 218, **My dear Bonhoeffer:** Ibid., 120.

p. 218, **My dear Henriod:** Ibid., 126–27.

p. 219, **The appointment of Dr. Jäger:** Ibid., 129.

p. 220, **The church regime:** Ibid., 134–35.

p. 220, **All of Bonhoeffer's ecumenical efforts:** Ibid., 144–45.

p. 221, **Just now it is quite lovely:** Ibid., 151–52.

p. 222, **Since it was a watershed:** Barmen Theological Doctrine, May 29–30, 1934.

p. 227, **I have already written Herr Schönfeld:** Ibid., 175.

p. 229, **There is not the claim:** Ibid., 179–80.

p. 229, **The terrible events:** Joachim Fest, *Plotting Hitler's Death: The German Resistance to Hitler, 1933–1945,* trans. Bruce Little (New York: Metropolitan Books, 1996), 26.

p. 231, **If anyone reproaches:** William L. Shirer, *The Rise and Fall of the Third Reich: A History of Nazi Germany* (New York: Simon and Schuster, 1960), 226.

p. 231, **It all had a chilling effect:** Inge Karding, interview by Martin Doblmeier, *Bonhoeffer: Pastor, Pacifist, Nazi Resister. A documentary film by Martin Doblmeier,* date of interview, Princeton University. Unused footage quoted here by permission of the director.

p. 232, **Austria was also:** Alice von Hildebrand, *The Soul of a Lion: Dietrich von Hildebrand: a Biography* (San Francisco: Ignatius Press, 2000), 255.

p. 233, **General Ludwig Beck:** Fest, *Plotting Hitler's Death,* 56.

CHAPTER 16: THE CONFERENCE AT FANØ

p. 236, **Personally, to be quite frank:** *London: 1933-1935,* vol. 13, *Dietrich Bonhoeffer Works,* ed. Keith Clements, trans. Isabel Best (New York: Fortress Press, 2007), 191–92.

p. 236, **The youth conference began:** *Barcelona, Berlin, New York: 1928–1931,* vol. 10, *Dietrich Bonhoeffer Works,* ed. Clifford J. Green, trans. Douglas W. Stott (New York: Fortress Press, 2008), 201.

p. 238, **During the days:** Wolf-Dieter Zimmermann and Ronald G. Smith, eds., *I Knew Dietrich Bonhoeffer,* trans. Käthe Gregor Smith (New York: Harper and Row, 1966), 91.

p. 239, **When I asked:** Zimmerman and Smith, *I Knew Dietrich Bonhoeffer,* 91.

p. 240, **The Countil declares:** Eberhard Bethge, *Dietrich Bonhoeffer: A Biography,* rev. ed. (Minneapolis: Augsburg Fortress, 2000), 479.

p. 241, **There is no way to peace:** *London,* 308–09.

p. 241, **"He was not concerned":** Bethge, *Dietrich Bonhoeffer: A Biography,* 388.

p. 242, **Heckel and other members:** "German Church and State," *London Times,* August 27, 1934.

p. 243, **At the time:** Bethge, *Dietrich Bonhoeffer: A Biography,* 385.

p. 244, **One little friend:** Sabine Leibholz-Bonhoeffer, *The Bonhoeffers: Portrait of a Family,* (New York: St. Martin's Press, 1971), 88.

p. 245, **Next, Bonhoeffer visited Jean Lasserre:** Bethge, *Dietrich Bonhoeffer: A Biography,* 392.

CHAPTER 17: THE ROAD TO ZINGST AND FINKENWALDE

p. 247, **I am hopelessly torn:** London: 1933-1935, vol. 13, Dietrich Bonhoeffer Works, ed. Keith Clements, trans. Isabel Best (New York: Fortress Press, 2007), 217.

p. 248, **In any case:** London, 408.

p. 248, **Before I tie myself down:** London, 152.

p. 249, **From now on:** Ibid., 217–18.

p. 250, **What sort of man:** Ibid., 218.

p. 250, **Bonhoeffer's asking:** Hanna Arendt, Eichmann in Jerusalem: A Report on the Banality of Evil (New York: Viking, 1963).

p. 251, **A wildly enthusiastic crowd:** "Foreign News: Meisser v. Muller," Time, Oct. 22, 1934.

p. 252, **In the meantime:** Eberhard Bethge, Dietrich Bonhoeffer: A Biography, rev. ed. (Minneapolis: Augsburg Fortress, 2000), 394.

p. 252, **Bonhoeffer knew:** Bethge, Dietrich Bonhoeffer: A Biography, 395.

p. 253, **The German Evangelical congregations:** London, 396.

p. 254, **I can well understand:** Ibid., 248–49.

p. 255, **My dear Rössler:** Ibid., 252–53.

p. 255, **This, instead of refusing:** Ibid., 253–54.

p. 256, **Now to a personal question:** Ibid., 254–55.

p. 256, **My dear Bonhoeffer:** Ibid., 266–67.

p. 258, **A friend of mine:** Bethge, Dietrich Bonhoeffer: A Biography, 408.

p. 259, **Dear friend:** London, 229–30.

p. 259, **Perhaps I seem to you:** Ibid., 284.

CHAPTER 18: ZINGST AND FINKENWALDE

p. 264, **Bonhoeffer asked Bethge:** Eberhard Bethge, interview by Martin Doblmeier, Bonhoeffer: Pastor, Pacifist, Nazi Resister. A documentary film by Martin Doblmeier, date of interview, Princeton University. Unused footage quoted here by permission of the director.

p. 266, **The humble accommodations:** Eberhard Bethge, Dietrich Bonhoeffer: A Biography, rev. ed. (Minneapolis: Augsburg Fortress, 2000), 426.

p. 266, **The landed gentry of Pomerania:** Bethge, Dietrich Bonhoeffer: A Biography, 427.

p. 267, **Music formed a huge part:** Eberhard Bethge, interview by Martin Doblmeier, date.

p. 267, **There were two pianos:** Bethge, Dietrich Bonhoeffer: A Biography, 429.

p. 267, **There were two pianos; He loved Beethoven:** Eberhard Bethge, Friendship and Resistance: Essays on Dietrich Bonhoeffer (Grand Rapids: Eerdmans, 1995), 5.

p. 268, **Bonhoeffer requested us:** Albert Schönherr, interview by Martin Doblmeier, Bonhoeffer: Pastor, Pacifist, Nazi Resister. A documentary film by Martin Doblmeier, date of interview, Princeton University. Unused footage quoted here by permission of the director.

p. 268, **We sang a great deal:** Schönherr, interview by Martin Doblmeier, date.

p. 268, **One meditated on the same verse:** Wolf–Dieter Zimmermann and Ronald G. Smith, eds., I Knew Dietrich Bonhoeffer, trans. Käthe Gregor Smith (New York: Harper and Row, 1966), 107.

p. 269, **It wasn't only ordinands:** The Way to Freedom: Letters, Lectures and Notes 1935–1939, vol. 2, Collected Works of Dietrich Bonhoeffer, ed. Edwin H. Robertson, trans. Edwin H. Robertson and John Bowden (New York: Harper and Row, 1966), 121–22.

p. 270, **Whatever they thought** Schönherr, interview by Martin Doblmeier, date.

p. 270, **Whatever they thought; He had always been:** Eberhard Bethge, Friendship and Resistance, 5.

p. 270, **Albert Schönherr remembered:** Schönherr, interview by Martin Doblmeier, date.

p. 270, **Work at the seminary:** Dietrich Bonhoeffer, A Testament to Freedom: The Essential Writings of Dietrich Bonhoeffer, rev. ed., eds. Geffrey B. Kelly and F. Burton Nelson (New York: Harper One, 1995), 431–32.

p. 272, **Yet even when he was not preaching**: Bethge, *Dietrich Bonhoeffer: A Biography*, 443.

p. 272, **In 1932**: Ibid., 234.

p. 272, **In 1932; At Finkenwalde**: Ibid., 442.

p. 273, **Bonhoeffer's teaching**: Zimmerman and Smith, *I Knew Dietrich Bonhoeffer*, 134.

p. 273, **Bonhoeffer felt comfortable**: Ibid., 72.

p. 273, **Bonhoeffer felt comfortable; And it's doubtful**: *Letters and Papers from Prison*, vol. 8, *Dietrich Bonhoeffer Works*, ed. John W. Degruchy (Minneapolis: Augsburg Fortress, 2010), 276.

p. 274, **There was little question**: *Letters and Papers from Prison*, 189.

p. 276, **One day we found ourselves**: Ruth-Alice von Bismarck and Ulrich Kabitz, eds. *Love Letters from Cell 92: The Correspondence Between Dietrich Bonhoeffer and Maria Von Wedemeyer, 1943–45*, trans. John Brownjohn (New York: Abingdon Press, 1995), 306.

p. 277, **Bonhoeffer "always had some distance"**: Ruth-Alice von Bismarck, interview with author, Hamburg, Germany, March 2008.

CHAPTER 19: SCYLLA AND CHARYBDIS, 1935–36

p. 278, **Epigraphy**: Eberhard Bethge, *Dietrich Bonhoeffer: A Biography*, rev. ed. (Minneapolis: Augsburg Fortress, 2000), 607.

p. 278, **The Scriptures said**: Albert Schönherr, interview by Martin Doblmeier, *Bonhoeffer: Pastor, Pacifist, Nazi Resister. A documentary film by Martin Doblmeier*, date of interview, Princeton University. Unused footage quoted here by permission of the director.

p. 279, **Bonhoeffer strove**:

p. 279, **That summer Bonhoeffer**: Bethge, *Dietrich Bonhoeffer: A Biography*, 483.

p. 280, **Entirely convinced**: Germany, *Nuremberg Laws*, September 15, 1935.

p. 282, **During this period**: Sabine Leibholz-Bonhoeffer, *The Bonhoeffers: Portrait of a Family*, (New York: St. Martin's Press, 1971), 90.

p. 282, **Bonhoeffer's grandmother**: Bethge, *Dietrich Bonhoeffer: A Biography*, 490.

p. 283, **A refusal to compromise**: Leibholz-Bonhoeffer, *The Bonhoeffers*, 83.

p. 284, **The trip to Sweden**: Wolf-Dieter Zimmermann and Ronald G. Smith, eds., *I Knew Dietrich Bonhoeffer*, trans. Käthe Gregor Smith (New York: Harper and Row, 1966), 152–53.

p. 284, **He immediately contacted**: Bethge, *Dietrich Bonhoeffer: A Biography*, 510.

p. 285, **I feel impelled**: Ibid., 512.

p. 285, **A corner had been turned**: Ibid.

p. 286, **On April 22**: *The Way to Freedom: Letters, Lectures and Notes 1935–1939*, vol. 2, *Collected Works of Dietrich Bonhoeffer*, ed. Edwin H. Robertson, trans. Edwin H. Robertson and John Bowden (New York: Harper and Row, 1966), 90–91.

p. 287, **The condemnations were thundering**: Bethge, *Dietrich Bonhoeffer: A Biography*, 522–23.

p. 287, **My paper has made me**: *The Way to Freedom*, 110.

p. 288, **The Confessing Church**: Bethge, *Dietrich Bonhoeffer: A Biography*, 536.

p. 289, **The Nazis did their best**: Ibid., 539.

p. 289, **The evangelical American**: Garth Lean, *On the Tail of a Comet: The Life of Frank Buchman, a Small Town American Who Awakened the Conscience of the World* (New York: Concordia House, 2002), 235.

p. 290, **In the fall**: Bethge, *Dietrich Bonhoeffer: A Biography*, 542.

p. 291, **My parish of six hundred**: Ibid., 544.

p. 291, **He said that**: Ibid.

p. 292, **Bonhoeffer visited the village**: Ibid.

p. 292, **1. Christ has given**: *The Way to Freedom*, 149.

p. 292, **3. "Do not give dogs"**: Ibid., 151.

p. 293, **In 1937**: James Bentley, *Martin Niemöller: 1892–1984* (New York: Free Press, 1984), 129.

p. 294, **Even when being brutal**: Bethge, *Dietrich Bonhoeffer: A Biography*, 577.

p. 294, **It is often difficult:** Ibid., 582–23.

p. 294, **He wanted them to know:** Ruth von Kleist-Retzow to Werner Koch, Klein-Krössin, 1937.

p. 295, **Niemöller's ten-year-old:** Amos Cresswell and Maxwell Tow, *Dr. Franz Hildebrandt: Mr. Valiant for Truth* (Grand Rapids, Smyth and Helwys, 2000), 78.

p. 296, **There were always Gestapo:** Cresswell and Tow, *Dr Franz Hildebrandt*, 79.

p. 298, **The superintendent:** Bethge, *Dietrich Bonhoeffer: A Biography*, 591.

p. 299, **Bonhoeffer was an eternal:** Mary Bosanquet, *The Life and Death of Dietrich Bonhoeffer*, (New York: Harper and Row, 1968), 192.

p. 299, **I did not come:** Bosanquet, *Life and Death of Bonhoeffer*, 193–4.

p. 300, **The small house:** Bethge, *Dietrich Bonhoeffer: A Biography*, 591.

p. 300, **We are anxious:** Ibid.

p. 300, **I arrived here yesterday:** Ibid., 591–592.

CHAPTER 20: MARS ASCENDING, 1938

p. 303, **Hitler's troubles:** Hans B. Gisevius, *To the Bitter End: An Insider's Account of the Plot to Kill Hitler 1933–1944*, trans. Richard Winston and Clara Winston (New York: Da Capo Press, 1998), 363.

p. 304, **Hans Gisevius said:** Gisevius, *To the Bitter End*, 283.

p. 304, **Hans Gisevius said; His successor:** Joachim Fest, *Plotting Hitler's Death: The German Resistance to Hitler, 1933–1945*, trans. Bruce Little (New York: Metropolitan Books, 1996), 86.

p. 305, **Göring had known:** William L. Shirer, *The Rise and Fall of the Third Reich: A History of Nazi Germany* (New York: Simon and Schuster, 1960), 314–16.

p. 305, **It must be said:** Lothar Machtan, *The Hidden Hitler*, trans. John Brownjohn and Susanne Ehlert (New York: Basic Books, 2001), pg.

p. 306, **But as we know:** Fest, *Plotting Hitler's Death*, 77.

p. 306, **But as we know; Another German conservative:** Ibid., 26.

p. 306, **Hitler further wiped:** Shirer, *The Rise and Fall of the Third Reich*, 317–19.

p. 307, **Hitler further wiped; Hitler had once told Gobbells:** Fest, *Plotting Hitler's Death*, 62.

p. 307, **Having successfully dealt:** Eberhard Bethge, *Dietrich Bonhoeffer: A Biography*, rev. ed. (Minneapolis: Augsburg Fortress, 2000), 599.

p. 308, **In the recognition:** Bethge, *Dietrich Bonhoeffer: A Biography*, 600.

p. 309, **I am most deeply shocked:** Ibid., 602.

p. 309, **On the bright side:** Ruth-Alice von Bismarck and Ulrich Kabitz, eds. *Love Letters from Cell 92: The Correspondence Between Dietrich Bonhoeffer and Maria Von Wedemeyer, 1943–45*, trans. John Brownjohn (New York: Abingdon Press, 1995), 298.

p. 310, **The sense of imminent war:** Sabine Leibholz-Bonhoeffer, *The Bonhoeffers: Portrait of a Family*, (New York: St. Martin's Press, 1971), 92.

p. 311, **The roof of our car:** Leibholz-Bonhoeffer, *The Bonhoeffers*, 97–100.

p. 312, **During this time:** Bethge, *Dietrich Bonhoeffer: A Biography*, 606.

p. 313, **As things stood:** Shirer, *The Rise and Fall of the Third Reich*, 424–26.

p. 316, **In his Bible:** Eberhard Bethge, interview by Martin Doblmeier, *Bonhoeffer: Pastor, Pacifist, Nazi Resister. A documentary film by Martin Doblmeier*, date of interview, Princeton University. Unused footage quoted here by permission of the director.

p. 316, **In the circular:** Dietrich Bonhoeffer, *A Testament to Freedom: The Essential Writings of Dietrich Bonhoeffer*, rev. ed., eds. Geffrey B. Kelly and F. Burton Nelson (New York: Harper One, 1995), 442.

p. 317, **Hans-Werner Jensen:** Wolf-Dieter Zimmermann and Ronald G. Smith, eds., *I Knew Dietrich Bonhoeffer*, trans. Käthe Gregor Smith (New York: Harper and Row, 1966), 153–54.

p. 317, **I'm not quite sure how:** *The Way to Freedom: Letters, Lectures and Notes 1935–1939*, vol. 2,

Collected Works of Dietrich Bonhoeffer, ed. Edwin H. Robertson, trans. Edwin H. Robertson and John Bowden (New York: Harper and Row, 1966), 199–200.

p. 318, **Bonhoeffer himself encouraged:** Renate Bethge, *Dietrich Bonhoeffer: A Brief Life* (New York: Fortress, 2006), 40.

CHAPTER 21: THE GREAT DECISION, 1939

p. 321, **Epigraph:** Dietrich Bonhoeffer, *A Testament to Freedom: The Essential Writings of Dietrich Bonhoeffer*, rev. ed., eds. Geffrey B. Kelly and F. Burton Nelson (New York: Harper One, 1995), 479–80.

p. 322, **I am thinking:** Bonhoeffer, *A Testament to Freedom*, 468.

p. 324, **The next day:** Eberhard Bethge, *Dietrich Bonhoeffer: A Biography*, rev. ed. (Minneapolis: Augsburg Fortress, 2000), pg.

p. 324, **We had heard:** Bethge, *Dietrich Bonhoeffer: A Biography*, 646.

p. 324, **Bonhoeffer also traveled:** Edwin Robertson, *The Shame and the Sacrifice: The Life and Martyrdom of Dietrich Bonhoeffer*, (New York: Macmillan, 1988), 164.

p. 325, **Two days later:** Bethge, *Dietrich Bonhoeffer: A Biography*, 648.

p. 325, **Even worse:** Ibid.

p. 325, **Bonhoeffer knew:** *The Way to Freedom: Letters, Lectures and Notes 1935–1939*, vol. 2, *Collected Works of Dietrich Bonhoeffer*, ed. Edwin H. Robertson, trans. Edwin H. Robertson and John Bowden (New York: Harper and Row, 1966), 212.

p. 325, **On May 11:** *The Way to Freedom*, 222.

p. 326, **But even as these efforts:** Wolf–Dieter Zimmermann and Ronald G. Smith, eds., *I Knew Dietrich Bonhoeffer*, trans. Käthe Gregor Smith (New York: Harper and Row, 1966), 166.

p. 326, **Before he left for America:** Otto Dudzus, interview by Martin Doblmeier, *Bonhoeffer: Pastor, Pacifist, Nazi Resister. A documentary film by Martin Doblmeier*, date of interview, Princeton University. Unused footage quoted here by permission of the director.

p. 327, **Bonhoeffer kept a journal:** *The Way to Freedom*, 213–216.

p. 328, **If only the doubts:** Ibid., 216–17.

p. 329, **At the dock:** Ibid., 227.

p. 329, **He had not been in New York:** Ibid.

p. 329, **Henry Sloane Coffin:** "Religion: Protagonist," *Time*, November 15, 1926.

p. 330, **13th June, 1939:** Ibid., 228.

p. 330, **14th June, 1939:** Ibid.

p. 330, **15th June, 1939:** Ibid., 228–29.

p. 331, **Torn between his hatred:** Ibid., 229.

p. 331, **That evening they drove:** Ibid.

p. 331, **Alone in his room:** Bonhoeffer, *A Testament to Freedom*, 477–78.

p. 331, **The next morning:** *The Way to Freedom*, 229.

p. 332, **It is almost unbearable:** Ibid., 230.

p. 333, **The whole thing:** Ibid., 230–31.

p. 333, **To find the word of God:** Ibid., 231.

p. 333, **He was again alone:** Ibid.

p. 334, **Now the day:** Ibid.

p. 334, **To have found biblical preaching:** Ibid.

p. 334, **This sermon opened:** Ibid., 231–32.

p. 335, **The news about China:** Ibid., 232.

p. 335, **He had never felt more alone:** Ibid., 233.

p. 336, **On the morning of June 20:** Ibid.

p. 336, **Years later:** Zimmerman and Smith, *I Knew Dietrich Bonhoeffer*, 93.

p. 336, **It is remarkable:** *The Way to Freedom*, 233–34.

p. 337, **He spent the evening:** Ibid., 234.

p. 337, **Of course I still keep having second thoughts:** Ibid., 234–35.

p. 338, **Bewer calms me down:** Ibid., 235.

p. 338, **At lunch with David Roberts:** Ibid., 236.

p. 338, **On the twenty-third:** Ibid.

p. 338, **Finally on Saturday:** Ibid.

p. 338, **I now often wonder:** Ibid.

p. 339, **That evening he wrote:** Ibid., 237.

p. 339, **He jotted a tittle of sarcasm:** Ibid.

p. 339, **Sunday, 25th June 1939:** Ibid.

p. 339, **26th June 1939:** Ibid., 237–38.

p. 340, **27th June 1939:** Ibid., 238.

p. 340, **28th June 1939:** Ibid., 238–39.

p. 340, **You cannot know:** Ibid., 224–25.

p. 341, **Bonhoeffer realized:** Ibid., 226.

p. 341, **29th June 1939:** Ibid., 239.

p. 341, **30th June 1939:** Mary Bosanquet, *The Life and Death of Dietrich Bonhoeffer*, (New York: Harper and Row, 1968), 215–16.

p. 342, **30th June 1939:** *The Way to Freedom*, 239–40.

p. 342, **1st July 1939:** Ibid., 240.

p. 342, **Sunday, 2nd July, 1939:** Ibid., 240–41.

p. 343, **On Monday:** Ibid., 241.

p. 343, **On Monday, Lehmann had received:** Bosanquet, *Life and Death of Bonhoeffer*, 216.

p. 343, **5th July, 1939:** *The Way to Freedom*, 241.

p. 344, **7th July, 1939:** Bosanquet, *Life and Death of Bonhoeffer*, 217–18.

p. 344, **9th July, 1939:** *The Way to Freedom*, 247.

p. 345, **I was happy to know:** Zimmerman and Smith, *I Knew Dietrich Bonhoeffer*, 158–60.

CHAPTER 22: THE END OF GERMANY

p. 347, **Back in March:** Victor, George, *Hitler: The Pathology of Evil* (Dulles, VA: Brassey's, 1998), 184.

p. 347, **The plan was for the SS:** William L. Shirer, *The Rise and Fall of the Third Reich: A History of Nazi Germany* (New York: Simon and Schuster, 1960), 594–95.

p. 348, **But Hitler gave a speech:** Shirer, *The Rise and Fall of the Third Reich*, 596.

p. 349, **I have received the news:** Dietrich Bonhoeffer, *A Testament to Freedom: The Essential Writings of Dietrich Bonhoeffer*, rev. ed., eds. Geffrey B. Kelly and F. Burton Nelson (New York: Harper One, 1995), 445.

p. 350, **Through the Nazi propaganda:** Albert Schönherr, interview by Martin Doblmeier, *Bonhoeffer: Pastor, Pacifist, Nazi Resister. A documentary film by Martin Doblmeier*, date of interview, Princeton University. Unused footage quoted here by permission of the director.

p. 352, **In his diary:** Shirer, *The Rise and Fall of the Third Reich*, 661–662.

p. 352, **There had been warnings:** Joachim Fest, *Plotting Hitler's Death: The German Resistance to Hitler, 1933–1945*, trans. Bruce Little (New York: Metropolitan Books, 1996), 116.

p. 352, **There was something:** Fest, *Plotting Hitler's Death*, 114.

p. 353, **Since the SS perpetrated:** Ibid., 115, 117.

p. 353, **Some generals, however:** Ibid., 118.

p. 354, **It is unlikely:** Victoria Barnett, *For the Soul of the People: Protestant Protest Against Hitler* (New York: Oxford University Press, 1992), 107.

p. 356, **Bust as the military:** Shirer, *The Rise and Fall of the Third Reich*, 641.

p. 356, **It was a performance:** Ibid., 643.

p. 356, **Meanwhile the generals:** Ibid., 347.

CHAPTER 23: FROM CONFESSION TO CONSPIRACY

p. 359, **It must have been**: Emmi Bonhoeffer, interview by Trinity Films, *Dietrich Bonhoeffer: Memories and Perspectives*, distributed by Vision Video.

p. 360, **Bonhoeffer introduced us**: Eberhard Bethge, *Friendship and Resistance: Essays on Dietrich Bonhoeffer* (Grand Rapids: Eerdmans, 1995), 24.

p. 361, **People went wild**: Eberhard Bethge, *Dietrich Bonhoeffer: A Biography*, rev. ed. (Minneapolis: Augsburg Fortress, 2000), 681.

p. 362, **It was then**: Christian Gremmels, interview by Martin Doblmeier, *Bonhoeffer: Pastor, Pacifist, Nazi Resister. A documentary film by Martin Doblmeier*, date of interview, Princeton University. Unused footage quoted here by permission of the director.

p. 363, **In a world**: *Ethics*, vol. 6, *Dietrich Bonhoeffer Works*, ed. Clifford J. Green, trans. Douglas W. Stott (New York: Augsburg Fortress, 2008), 88–89.

p. 364, **Bonhoeffer said that Germany**: Bethge, *Dietrich Bonhoeffer: A Biography*, 682–84.

p. 364, **He had once told a student**: *Conspiracy and Imprisonment: 1940–1945*, vol. 16, *Dietrich Bonhoeffer Works*, ed. Mark S. Brocker, trans. Lisa E. Dahill with Douglas W. Stott (New York: Fortress, 2006), 601.

p. 365, **God's standard of truth**: *Conspiracy and Imprisonment*, 606.

p. 366, **In the essay**: Ibid., 605–06.

p. 366, **It is only the cynic**: *Ethics*, 360–61.

p. 367, **Dohnanyi's boss**: Joachim Fest, *Plotting Hitler's Death: The German Resistance to Hitler, 1933–1945*, trans. Bruce Little (New York: Metropolitan Books, 1996), 138.

p. 367, **Bonhoeffer scholar**: *Life Together; Prayerbook of the Bible*, vol. 5, *Dietrich Bonhoeffer Works*, ed. Geffrey B. Kelly, trans. Daniel W. Bloesch (Minneapolis: Fortress, 2005), 143.

p. 368, **In the book**: *Life Together*, 155–56.

p. 368, **The idea would have seemed**: Ibid.

p. 372, **On November 18**: *Conspiracy and Imprisonment*, 86.

p. 372, **Bonhoeffer enjoyed the routine**: Ibid., 87.

p. 372, **That year Bonhoeffer**: Dietrich Bonhoeffer to Eberhard Bethge, Munich, November 29, 1940.

p. 373, **Just as time-lapse photography**: *Conspiracy and Imprisonment*, 106.

p. 373, **On December 13**: Ibid., 109–10.

p. 374, **On December 13; In a letter to Bethge**: Ibid., 96.

p. 374, **That Christmas Bethge visited**: Ibid., 114.

p. 374, **Bonhoeffer's parents**: Ibid., 113.

p. 374, **He wrote something similar**: Ibid., 115.

p. 375, **While in Munich**: Ibid., 128.

p. 375, **That the two of us**: Ibid., 136.

p. 377, **While in Switzerland**: Bethge, *Dietrich Bonhoeffer: A Biography*, 728.

p. 378, **As he had done when prohibited**: *Conspiracy and Imprisonment*, 190.

p. 378, **In my imagination**: Bethge, *Dietrich Bonhoeffer: A Biography*, 24.

p. 379, **But it was not yet merely a memory**: *Conspiracy and Imprisonment*, 186.

CHAPTER 24: PLOTTING AGAINST HITLER

p. 381, **Some generals were the noble leaders**: "Walther von Brauchitsch," Wikipedia, *http://en.wikipedia.org/wiki/Walther_von_Brauchitsch*.

p. 381, **Murdering all captured**: Joachim Fest, *Plotting Hitler's Death: The German Resistance to Hitler, 1933–1945*, trans. Bruce Little (New York: Metropolitan Books, 1996), 171.

p. 382, **Henning von Tresckow**: Fest, *Plotting Hitler's Death*, 175

p. 382, **The conspiracy leaders bided**: Ibid., 168.

p. 383, **Today I must inform you**: *Conspiracy and Imprisonment: 1940–1945*, vol. 16, *Dietrich Bonhoeffer Works*, ed. Mark S. Brocker, trans. Lisa E. Dahill with Douglas W. Stott (New York: Fortress, 2006), 207–08.

p. 384, **Bonhoeffer corresponded:** Eberhard Bethge, *Dietrich Bonhoeffer: A Biography*, rev. ed. (Minneapolis: Augsburg Fortress, 2000), 703.
p. 384, **His correspondence:** Bethge, *Dietrich Bonhoeffer: A Biography*, 704.
p. 385, **Hearing that his dear friend:** Ibid., 705.
p. 385, **The hope of Protestant Christians:** *Conspiracy and Imprisonment*, 241.
p. 385, **A prominent layman:** Ibid., 244.
p. 386, **The killing of so-called unworthy lives:** Ibid., 245.
p. 386, **In September Bonhoeffer was back:** Wolf-Dieter Zimmermann and Ronald G. Smith, eds., *I Knew Dietrich Bonhoeffer*, trans. Käthe Gregor Smith (New York: Harper and Row, 1966), 167–68.
p. 386, **By the fall of 1941:** Bethge, *Dietrich Bonhoeffer: A Biography*, 738.
p. 387, **Churchill:** Ibid., 740.
p. 387, **Bonhoeffer naively thought:** Mary Bosanquet, *The Life and Death of Dietrich Bonhoeffer*, (New York: Harper and Row, 1968), 229.
p. 387, **As Germany's armies moved:** Fest, *Plotting Hitler's Death*, 179.
p. 387, **As a result of such things:** Ibid., 180.
p. 389, **But the operation:**
p. 389, **The Swiss had their prince:** Eberhard Bethge, *Friendship and Resistance: Essays on Dietrich Bonhoeffer* (Grand Rapids: Eerdmans, 1995), 54.
p. 390, **In November 1941:** William L. Shirer, *The Rise and Fall of the Third Reich: A History of Nazi Germany* (New York: Simon and Schuster, 1960), 861–64.
p. 392, **The conspirators' plans:** Hans B. Gisevius, *To the Bitter End: An Insider's Account of the Plot to Kill Hitler 1933–1944*, trans. Richard Winston and Clara Winston (New York: Da Capo Press, 1998), 435.
p. 393, **Like many in the Kreisau Circle:**

CHAPTER 25: BONHOEFFER SCORES A VICTORY
p. 395, **The next morning:** *Conspiracy and Imprisonment: 1940–1945*, vol. 16, *Dietrich Bonhoeffer Works*, ed. Mark S. Brocker, trans. Lisa E. Dahill with Douglas W. Stott (New York: Fortress, 2006), 267; Helmut von Moltke to his wife, April 15, 1942.
p. 396, **They caught this ferry:** Eberhard Bethge, *Dietrich Bonhoeffer: A Biography*, rev. ed. (Minneapolis: Augsburg Fortress, 2000), 754.
p. 397, **We knew a romantic:** Wolf-Dieter Zimmermann and Ronald G. Smith, eds., *I Knew Dietrich Bonhoeffer*, trans. Käthe Gregor Smith (New York: Harper and Row, 1966), 169–70.
p. 398, **Bell brought Bonhoeffer welcome news:** *Conspiracy and Imprisonment*, 327.
p. 399, **Bonhoeffer observed that despite their differences:** Ibid., 322.
p. 399, **Bonhoeffer and Schönfeld diverged:** Ibid., 300; Bishop Bell, diary notes on the meeting with Bonhoeffer in Sigtuna, date of entry.
p. 400, **Bell minced no words:** Bethge, *Dietrich Bonhoeffer: A Biography*, 761.
p. 400, **June 1, 1942:** *Conspiracy and Imprisonment*, 312–13.
p. 401, **June 1, 1942:** Ibid., 311–12.
p. 401, **Dear Mr. Eden:** Ibid., 318.
p. 402, **Bell met with Eden:** Bethge, *Dietrich Bonhoeffer: A Biography*, 764.
p. 402, **There is no doubt:** Ibid.
p. 402, **I found much evidence:** *Conspiracy and Imprisonment*, 347–48.
p. 403, **Gerhard Leibholz:** Bethge, *Dietrich Bonhoeffer: A Biography*, 763.
p. 403, **Gerhard Leibholz; According to journalist:** Joachim Fest, *Plotting Hitler's Death: The German Resistance to Hitler, 1933–1945*, trans. Bruce Little (New York: Metropolitan Books, 1996), 78–79.
p. 403, **My dear Lord Bishop:** *Conspiracy and Imprisonment*, 349.

CHAPTER 26: BONHOEFFER IN LOVE

p. 405, **Just after his trip:** Ruth-Alice von Bismarck and Ulrich Kabitz, eds. *Love Letters from Cell 92: The Correspondence Between Dietrich Bonhoeffer and Maria Von Wedemeyer, 1943–45*, trans. John Brownjohn (New York: Abingdon Press, 1995), 330.

p. 406, **Hans von Wedemeyer:** Bismarck and Kabitz, *Love Letters from Cell 92*, 291.

p. 406, **In 1936:** Ibid., 291–92.

p. 407, **I would like to tell you:** *Conspiracy and Imprisonment: 1940–1945*, vol. 16, *Dietrich Bonhoeffer Works*, ed. Mark S. Brocker, trans. Lisa E. Dahill with Douglas W. Stott (New York: Fortress, 2006), 328.

p. 408, **Over the years:** *Conspiracy and Imprisonment*, 220–21.

p. 409, **I have not written to Maria:** Ibid., 329–30.

p. 409, **Hans von Wedemeyer:** Bismarck and Kabitz, *Love Letters from Cell 92*, 298.

p. 409, **Dear Max:** *Conspiracy and Imprisonment*, 350–51.

p. 410, **My dear lady:** Ibid., 351–52.

p. 411, **Years later:** Ibid., 331.

p. 411, **Hans-Walter:** Ibid., 365.

p. 412, **I had a very interesting talk:** Bismarck and Kabitz, *Love Letters from Cell 92*, 331–32.

p. 413, **Oct. 16:** Ibid., 332.

p. 413, **Oct. 18th:** Ibid., 332–33.

p. 413, **Dear Miss von Wedemeyer:** *Conspiracy and Imprisonment*, 366–67.

p. 414, **November 13, 1942:** Ibid., 369–70.

p. 415, **But in this letter:** Ibid., 370–71.

p. 416, **What Maria really thought:** Ibid., 373.

p. 416, **Dear Miss von Wedemeyer:** Ibid., 373–74.

p. 417, **Bonhoeffer respected Frau von Wedemeyer:** Ibid., 374–75.

p. 418, **During this very same time:** Ibid., 375.

p. 418, **Nov. 27th:** Bismarck and Kabitz, *Love Letters from Cell 92*, 336.

p. 418, **19 December 1942:** Ibid., 337.

p. 419, **10 Jan 1943:** Ibid.

p. 419, **Dear Pastor Bonhoeffer:** Ibid., 338–39.

p. 420, **Dear Maria:** *Conspiracy and Imprisonment*, 383–84.

p. 422, **When six days passed:** Ibid., 386.

p. 422, **My dear Maria:** Ibid., 387.

p. 422, **You know utterly without saying:** Ibid., 390.

CHAPTER 27: KILLING ADOLF HITLER

p. 423, **Maria's sister:** Ruth-Alice von Bismarck, interview with author, Hamburg, Germany, March 2008.

p. 424, **Bonhoeffer confided to me:** Wolf-Dieter Zimmermann and Ronald G. Smith, eds., *I Knew Dietrich Bonhoeffer*, trans. Käthe Gregor Smith (New York: Harper and Row, 1966), 182.

p. 425, **Werner von Haeften:** Zimmermann and Smith, *I Knew Dietrich Bonhoeffer*, 190–92.

p. 426, **The plan was for:** Gero V. S. Gaevernitz, *They Almost Killed Hitler: Based on the Personal Account of Fabian von Schlabrendorff* (New York: Macmillan, 1947), 54.

p. 427, **On the thirteenth Tresckow:** Gaevernitz, *They Almost Killed Hitler*, 57.

p. 428, **The extent to which Hitler:** Ibid., 56–58.

p. 430, **When Hitler approached him:** Joachim Fest, *Plotting Hitler's Death: The German Resistance to Hitler, 1933–1945*, trans. Bruce Little (New York: Metropolitan Books, 1996), 196.

p. 431, **With exquisite irony:** Eberhard Bethge, *Dietrich Bonhoeffer: A Biography*, rev. ed. (Minneapolis: Augsburg Fortress, 2000), 785.

CHAPTER 28: CELL 92 AT TEGEL PRISON

p. 433, **If you could see me:** Ruth-Alice von Bismarck and Ulrich Kabitz, eds. *Love Letters from Cell 92: The Correspondence Between Dietrich Bonhoeffer and Maria Von Wedemeyer, 1943–45*, trans. John Brownjohn (New York: Abingdon Press, 1995), 342–43.

p. 434, **I can't go on like this:** Bismarck and Kabitz, *Love Letters from Cell 92*, 343.

p. 434, **I've spoken to you:** Ibid., 343–44.

p. 435, **Dear Maria:** Ibid., 344–45.

p. 436, **Two weeks later:** Ibid., 345–346.

p. 436, **Just ten days after this letter:** Ibid., 347.

p. 437, **The formalities of admission:** Mary Bosanquet, *The Life and Death of Dietrich Bonhoeffer*, (New York: Harper and Row, 1968), 247–48.

p. 438, **For the first twelve days:** Eberhard Bethge, *Dietrich Bonhoeffer: Man of Vision, Man of Courage*, ed. Edwin Robertson (New York: Harper and Row, 1970; Minneapolis: Augsburg Fortress, 2000), 734. Citations are to the Augsburg edition.

p. 438, **He was at first:** Wolf-Dieter Zimmermann and Ronald G. Smith, eds., *I Knew Dietrich Bonhoeffer*, trans. Käthe Gregor Smith (New York: Harper and Row, 1966), 222.

p. 439, **He was at first; In the postscript:** *Letters and Papers from Prison*, vol. 8, *Dietrich Bonhoeffer Works*, ed. John W. Degruchy (Minneapolis: Augsburg Fortress, 2010), 21.

p. 439, **Dear Parents:** *Letters and Papers from Prison*, 21–22.

p. 442, **My dear Dietrich:** Eberhard Bethge, *Dietrich Bonhoeffer: A Biography*, rev. ed. (Minneapolis: Augsburg Fortress, 2000), 800–01.

p. 443, **They had also worked:** Bethge, *Man of Vision*, 716.

p. 443, **Renate Bethge recalled:** Renate Bethge , interview by Martin Doblmeier, *Bonhoeffer: Pastor, Pacifist, Nazi Resister. A documentary film by Martin Doblmeier*, date of interview, Princeton University. Unused footage quoted here by permission of the director.

p. 443, **Renate Bethge recalled; Christopher von Dohnanyi:** Christopher von Dohnanyi, interview by Martin Doblmeier, *Bonhoeffer: Pastor, Pacifist, Nazi Resister. A documentary film by Martin Doblmeier*, date of interview, Princeton University. Unused footage quoted here by permission of the director.

p. 444, **Throughout his eighteen months:** Bethge, *Dietrich Bonhoeffer: A Biography*, 813–14.

p. 444, **This had meant a great inner release:** Ibid., 814–15.

p. 445, **I cannot believe:** Bethge, *Man of Vision*, 720.

p. 445, **One may ask:** *Letters and Papers from Prison*, 3–4.

p. 446, **Then he dismissed:** Ibid., 5.

p. 446, **Bonhoeffer talked about:** Ibid., 14

p. 447, **If we want to be Christians:** Ibid.

p. 447, **In recent years:** Ibid., 24.

p. 448, **O God:** Zimmerman and Smith, *I Knew Dietrich Bonhoeffer*, 224–25.

p. 449, **One day he asked me:** Ibid., 223.

p. 449, **When in the summer of 1943:** *Letters and Papers from Prison*, 248.

p. 450, **My dear, dear, Dietrich:** Bismarck and Kabitz, *Love Letters from Cell 92*, 26–27.

p. 451, **June 9, 1943:** Ibid., 33–34.

p. 453, **The visits were always:** Ibid., 27.

p. 453, **I have just come back:** *Letters and Papers from Prison*, 71–72.

p. 454, **Maria's early letters:** Bismarck and Kabitz, *Love Letters from Cell 92*, 40–41, 44, 52.

p. 454, **I was sitting on the red:** Ibid., 55.

p. 455, **After this second visit:** Ibid., 58.

p. 455, **She also continued:** Ibid., 58, 63.

p. 455, **When I consider:** Ibid., 63–64.

p. 456, **We ought not to be in too much:** *Letters and Papers from Prison*, 41–42.

p. 457, **You yourselves know:** Ibid., 42.

p. 458, **As God today adds:** Ibid.

p. 458, **Bonhoeffer was trying**: Ibid., 43.

p. 459, **Und geht es draussen noch so toll**: Ibid., 119.

p. 460, **In a rather haphazard way**: Ibid., 189.

p. 460, **I read some Stifter**: Bismarck and Kabitz, *Love Letters from Cell 92*, 32.

p. 460, **Most people would find**: *Letters and Papers from Prison*, 125.

p. 460, **In my reading**: Ibid., 77–78.

p. 461, **Bonhoeffer's cultural standards**: Bethge, *Dietrich Bonhoeffer: A Biography*, 844.

p. 461, **Bonhoeffer was able**: *Letters and Papers from Prison*, 223.

p. 462, **18 November 1943**: Ibid., 131–32.

p. 463, **Bonhoeffer said the Psalms**: Ibid., 131, 149.

p. 463, **23 January 1944**: Ibid., #.

p. 463, **9 March 1944**: Ibid., 231–32.

p. 464, **11 April 1944**: Ibid., 272.

p. 464, **9 May 1944**: Ibid., 289–90.

p. 465, **A week later**: Ibid., 293.

p. 465, **Bonhoeffer felt free**: Bethge, *Dietrich Bonhoeffer: A Biography*, 861.

p. 466, **The most tortured interpretations**: Bosanquet, *Life and Death of Bonhoeffer*, 279.

p. 466, **What is bothering me**: *Letters and Papers from Prison*, 279.

p. 467, **Bonhoeffer never had time**: Ibid., 279–81.

p. 467, **It always seems**: Ibid., 282.

p. 468, **Bonhoeffer thought of** *Ethics*: Ibid., 163.

p. 469, **In Jesus Christ**: *Ethics*, vol. 6, *Dietrich Bonhoeffer Works*, ed. Clifford J. Green, trans. Douglas W. Stott (New York: Augsburg Fortress, 2008), 54.

p. 469, **As long as Christ and the world**: *Ethics*, 58.

p. 470, **Such people neither steal**: Ibid., 80.

p. 471, **But Bonhoeffer did not take**: Ibid.

p. 471, **Be wise as serpents**: Ibid., 82.

p. 472, **Destruction of the embryo**: Ibid., 206.

p. 472, **A great many different motives**: Ibid., 206–07.

p. 472, **At the heart of Bonhoeffer's theology**: Dietrich Bonhoeffer, *A Testament to Freedom: The Essential Writings of Dietrich Bonhoeffer*, rev. ed., eds. Geffrey B. Kelly and F. Burton Nelson (New York: Harper One, 1995), 448.

p. 473, **It will be with me**: *Letters and Papers from Prison*, 144–45.

p. 473, **The good cheer**: Ibid., 179.

CHAPTER 29: VALKYRIE AND THE STAUFFENBERG PLOT

p. 475, **On June 30, 1944**: *Letters and Papers from Prison*, vol. 8, *Dietrich Bonhoeffer Works*, ed. John W. Degruchy (Minneapolis: Augsburg Fortress, 2010), 340–421

p. 476, **In truth**: Joachim Fest, *Plotting Hitler's Death: The German Resistance to Hitler, 1933–1945*, trans. Bruce Little (New York: Metropolitan Books, 1996), 240–41.

p. 476, **Maria's uncle**: Fest, *Plotting Hitler's Death*, 236.

p. 477, **And so a date was set**: Ibid., 243.

p. 477, **Still, everyone knew**: Dietrich Bonhoeffer to Eberhard Bethge, Tegel, July 16, 1944.

p. 478, **The name Adolf**: Pierre Galante and Eugene Silianoff, *Operation Valkyrie: The German Generals' Plot Against Hitler* (New York: Harper and Row, 1981), 2–3.

p. 478, **At the airport**: Galante, *Operation Valkyrie*, 6.

p. 479, **Their three-hour plane ride**: William L. Shirer, *The Rise and Fall of the Third Reich: A History of Nazi Germany* (New York: Simon and Schuster, 1960), 1048.

p. 480, **The oaken table**: Galante, *Operation Valkyrie*, 15.

p. 481, **"It was Providence"**: Ibid.

p. 481, **If I speak to you**: Shirer, *The Rise and Fall of the Third Reich*, 1069.

p. 482, **Comrades of the** *Luftwaffe*: Hans B. Gisevius, *To the Bitter End: An Insider's Account of the*

Plot to Kill Hitler 1933–1944, trans. Richard Winston and Clara Winston (New York: Da Capo Press, 1998), 574–5.

p. 482, **Men of the Navy:** Gisevius, *To the Bitter End*, 575.

p. 482, **The frightful day:** Eberhard Bethge, *Dietrich Bonhoeffer: Man of Vision, Man of Courage*, ed. Edwin Robertson (New York: Harper and Row, 1970; Minneapolis: Augsburg Fortress, 2000), 730. Citations are to the Augsburg edition.

p. 483, **But another newspaper:** Fest, *Plotting Hitler's Death*, 165.

p. 483, **But another newspaper; But Winston Churchill:** Edwin Robertson, *The Shame and the Sacrifice: The Life and Martyrdom of Dietrich Bonhoeffer*, (New York: Macmillan, 1988), 262.

p. 483, **All I want to do:** *Letters and Papers from Prison*, 369.

p. 484, **During the last year:** Ibid., 369.

p. 484, **I discovered later:** Ibid., 369–70.

p. 485, **Stations on the Road to Freedom:** Ibid., 370–72.

p. 486, **At the end of July:** Ibid., 376.

p. 486, **Two days later:** Fest, *Plotting Hitler's Death*, 278.

p. 487, **The whole world:** Ibid., 289–90.

p. 487, **Everyone remotely involved:** Shirer, *The Rise and Fall of the Third Reich*, 1070, 1023.

p. 487, **But the bravery of men:** Fest, *Plotting Hitler's Death*, 301, 295.

p. 488, **My dearest, most beloved Maria:** Ruth-Alice von Bismarck and Ulrich Kabitz, eds. *Love Letters from Cell 92: The Correspondence Between Dietrich Bonhoeffer and Maria Von Wedemeyer, 1943–45*, trans. John Brownjohn (New York: Abingdon Press, 1995), 254–57.

p. 490, **My dearest Maria:** Bismarck and Kabitz, *Love Letters from Cell 92*, 259–61.

p. 492, **My dearly beloved Maria:** Ibid., 261–62.

p. 492, **Maria visited Bonhoeffer:** *Letters and Papers from Prison*, 393–94.

p. 495, **When Bonhoeffer:** Eberhard Bethge, *Dietrich Bonhoeffer: A Biography*, rev. ed. (Minneapolis: Augsburg Fortress, 2000), 900.

p. 495, **When Bonhoeffer; Nothing leads us:** Bethge, *Man of Vision*, 804–05.

p. 495, **Stifter once said:** Bismarck and Kabitz, *Love Letters from Cell 92*, 118.

p. 496, **19 December 1944:** Ibid., 268–70.

p. 497, **Powers of Good:** *Letters and Papers from Prison*, 400–01.

p. 498, **I must admit:** Wolf-Dieter Zimmermann and Ronald G. Smith, eds., *I Knew Dietrich Bonhoeffer*, trans. Käthe Gregor Smith (New York: Harper and Row, 1966), 226–30.

p. 500, **The first days:** Bethge, *Dietrich Bonhoeffer: A Biography*, 914.

p. 502, **When it was time:** Ibid., 918.

CHAPTER 30: BUCHENWALD

p. 506, **As particularly noticeable:** S. Payne Best, *The Venlo Incident* (Watford, Herts: Hutchinson, 1950), 194.

p. 506, **Best then commented:** Best, *The Venlo Incident*, 194.

p. 506, **Also in this cellar:** Ibid., 181.

p. 507, **According to Best:** Ibid., 180.

p. 507, **Another of the seventeen:** Ibid., 189.

p. 507, **In fairness to Hoepner:** Ibid., 190.

p. 508, **In cell five:** Ibid., 184, 197.

p. 508, **Best described her:** Ibid., 196.

p. 508, **Dr. Hoven stood:** Josef Ackermann, testimony at Nuremberg Military Tribunal, date, *http://www.mazal.org/archive/nmt/02/NMT02-T0003.htm*.

p. 509, **The thirty-six-year-old:** Best, *The Venlo Incident*, 186.

p. 509, **Obviously, he saw:** Ibid.

p. 509, **Esteemed *Reichsführer*:** Sigmund Rascher to Heinrich Himmler, 15 May, 1941, *http://nuremberg.law.harvard.edu/NurTranscript/Archive/full_transcript_6_days.html*.

p. 510, **I have personally seen:** William L. Shirer, *The Rise and Fall of the Third Reich: A History of Nazi Germany* (New York: Simon and Schuster, 1960), 985.

p. 511, **A prisoner was placed:** Shirer, *The Rise and Fall of the Third Reich*, 988.

p. 511, **Rascher hoped to use:** Ibid.

p. 511, **Another method was:** Ibid.

p. 512, **Dear Comrade Milch:** Heinrich Himmler to General Field Marshall Milch, November 13, 1942, *http://www.ess.uwe.ac.uk/genocide/rascher3.htm.*

p. 513, **At Buchenwald:** Eberhard Bethge, *Dietrich Bonhoeffer: A Biography*, rev. ed. (Minneapolis: Augsburg Fortress, 2000), 919.

p. 513, **At first each single person:** Best, *The Venlo Incident*, 176.

p. 514, **He quite obviously saw:** Ibid., 186.

p. 514, **I was not at the time:** Ibid., 187.

p. 514, **It's impossible to think Bonhoeffer:** Ibid., 180.

p. 515, **Best wrote to Sabine:** Mary Bosanquet, *The Life and Death of Dietrich Bonhoeffer*, (New York: Harper and Row, 1968), 271.

p. 515, **Falconer said of Bonhoeffer:** Bethge, *Dietrich Bonhoeffer: A Biography*, 919.

p. 515, **When I first made contact:** Best, *The Venlo Incident*, 179.

p. 515, **Best was sure:** Ibid., 189.

CHAPTER 31: ON THE ROAD TO FREEDOM

p. 517, **The sixteen prisoners:** S. Payne Best, *The Venlo Incident* (Watford, Herts: Hutchinson, 1950), 190.

p. 518, **They had left sometime after ten:** Best, *The Venlo Incident*, 190.

p. 518, **There was no light:** Ibid., 191.

p. 519, **The three guards:** Ibid.

p. 520, **In Weiden:** Ibid., 192.

p. 520, **After leaving Weiden:** Ibid.

p. 521, **The farmer's wife:** Ibid., 192-193.

p. 522, **After dark:** Ibid.

p. 522, **In the morning:** Ibid., 194.

p. 525, **The country seemed to be:** Ibid., 195–96.

p. 526, **Bonhoeffer and his fellow prisoners:** Ibid., 196.

p. 526, **Each person chose his bed:** Ibid., 13.

p. 526, **After their initial settling in:** Ibid., 199.

p. 527, **Of course "Heidl":** Ibid., 198.

p. 527, **[Bonhoeffer] was very happy:** Sabine Leibholz-Bonhoeffer, *The Bonhoeffers: Portrait of a Family*, (New York: St. Martin's Press, 1971), 198–99.

p. 528, **So less than twenty-four hours:** Best, *The Venlo Incident*, 200.

p. 528, **He had hardly finished:** Ibid.

p. 528, **Bonhoeffer also asked Best:** Eberhard Bethge, *Dietrich Bonhoeffer: A Biography*, rev. ed. (Minneapolis: Augsburg Fortress, 2000), 920.

p. 529, **The wheels:**

p. 530, **The summary court:** Bethge, *Dietrich Bonhoeffer: A Biography*, 927.

p. 531, **No one has yet believed:** *London: 1933-1935*, vol. 13, *Dietrich Bonhoeffer Works*, ed. Keith Clements, trans. Isabel Best (New York: Fortress Press, 2007), 331.

p. 532, **On the morning:** Bethge, *Dietrich Bonhoeffer: A Biography*, 927–28.

p. 532, **Pastor [Julius] Rieger:** Leibholz-Bonhoeffer, *The Bonhoeffers*, 184–86.

p. 534, **23rd July 1945:** Ibid., 190.

p. 535, *The Palace, Chichester 25th July 1945:* Ibid., 187–88.

p. 537, **The choir of the community:** Ibid., 188.

p. 537, **He was quite clear:** Ibid., 188–89.

p. 538, **In May 1932:** Amos Cresswell and Maxwell Tow, *Dr. Franz Hildebrandt: Mr. Valiant for Truth* (Grand Rapids, Smyth and Helwys, 2000), 223–27..

BIBLIOGRAPHY

Bailey, J. M., and Douglas Gilbert. *The Steps of Bonhoeffer: A Pictorial Album*. Philadelphia: Pilgrim Press, 1969.

Barnett, Victoria. *For the Soul of the People: Protestant Protest against Hitler*. New York: Oxford University Press, 1992.

Bassett, Richard. *Hitler's Spy Chief: The Wilhelm Canaris Mystery*. London: Cassell, 2005.

Bentley, James. *Martin Niemoller 1892–1984*. New York: Free Press, 1984.

Bergen, Doris L. *Twisted Cross: The German Christian Movement in the Third Reich*. Chapel Hill: University of North Carolina Press, 1996.

Best, S. Payne. *The Venlo Incident*. Watford, Herts: Hutchinson & Co., 1950.

Bethge, Eberhard. *Dietrich Bonhoeffer: A Biography*. Minneapolis: Fortress Press, 1967.

———. *Dietrich Bonhoeffer: Man of Vision, Man of Courage*. Edited by Edwin Robertson. New York: Harper and Row, 1970.

———. *Friendship and Resistance: Essays on Dietrich Bonhoeffer*. Chicago: World Council of Churches, 1995.

———. *Friendship and Resistance: Essays on Dietrich Bonhoeffer*. Grand Rapids: Eerdmans, 1995.

Bethge, Renate, and Christian Gremmels, eds. *Dietrich Bonhoeffer: A Life in Pictures*. Centenary ed. Translated by Brian McNeil. Minneapolis: Fortress Press, 2006.

Bethge, Renate. *Dietrich Bonhoeffer: A Brief Life*. New York: Fortress Press, 2004.

Bird, Eugene K. *Prisoner #7: Rudolf Hess: The Thirty Years in Jail of Hitler's Deputy Fuhrer*. New York: Viking Press, 1974.

Bonhoeffer, Dietrich. *A Testament to Freedom: The Essential Writings of Dietrich Bonhoeffer*. rev. ed. Edited by Geffrey B. Kelly and F. Burton Nelson. New York: Harper One, 1995.

———. *Christ the Center*. Translated by Edwin H. Robertson. New York: Harper San Francisco, 1978.

———. *Collected Works of Dietrich Bonhoeffer*. Edited by Edwin H. Robertson. 3 vols. New York: Harper and Row, 1965–1973.

———. *Creation and Fall: A Theological Exposition of Genesis 1—3*. Edited by John W. De Gruchy. Translated by Douglas S. Bax. New York: Fortress Press, 1997.

———. *Dietrich Bonhoeffer Works Series*. Edited by Victoria J. Barnett and Barbara Wojhoski. 16 vols. Minneapolis: Augsburg Fortress, 1995–2010.

Bosanquet, Mary. *The Life and Death of Dietrich Bonhoeffer*. New York: Harper and Row, 1968.

Cresswell, Amos, and Maxwell Tow. *Dr. Franz Hildebrandt: Mr. Valiant for Truth*. Grand Rapids: Smyth and Helwys, 2000.

De Gruchy, John W. *Daring, Trusting Spirit: Bonhoeffer's Friend Eberhard Bethge*. Minneapolis: Augsburg Fortress, 2005.

De Gruchy, John W., ed. *The Cambridge Companion to Dietrich Bonhoeffer*. New York: Cambridge University Press, 1999.

Fest, Joachim C. *Plotting Hitler's Death: The German Resistance to Hitler, 1933–1945*. Translated by Bruce Little. New York: Metropolitan Books, 1996.

Gaevernitz, Gero V. S., ed. *They Almost Killed Hitler*. New York: Macmillan, 1947.

Galante, Pierre, and Eugene Silianoff. *Operation Valkyrie: The German Generals' Plot against Hitler*. Translated by Mark Howson and Cary Ryan. New York: Harper and Row, 1981.

Gill, Theodore A. *Memo for a Movie: A Short Life of Dietrich Bonhoeffer*. New York: Macmillan, 1971.

Gisevius, Hans B. *To the Bitter End: An Insider's Account of the Plot to Kill Hitler, 1933–1944*. Translated by Richard Winston and Clara Winston. New York: Da Capo Press, 1998.

Goddard, Donald. *The Last Days of Dietrich Bonhoeffer*. New York: Harper and Row, 1976.

Haynes, Stephen R. *The Bonhoeffer Phenomenon: Post-Holocaust Perspectives*. New York: Fortress Press, 2004.

Huntemann, Georg. *The Other Bonhoeffer: An Evangelical Reassessment of Dietrich Bonhoeffer*. Translated by Todd Huizinga. Grand Rapids: Baker, 1993.

Kelly, Geffrey B., F. Burton Nelson, and Renate Bethge. *The Cost of Moral Leadership: The Spirituality of Dietrich Bonhoeffer*. Boston: Eerdmans, 2002.

Kleinhans, Theodore J. *Till the Night Be Past: The Life and Times of Dietrich Bonhoeffer*. New York: Concordia House, 2002.

Kuhns, William. *In Pursuit of Dietrich Bonhoeffer*. Dayton: Pflaum Press, 1967.

Lean, Garth. *On the Tail of a Comet: The Life of Frank Buchman*. New York: Helmers and Howard, 1988.

Leibholz-Bonhoeffer, Sabine. *The Bonhoeffers: Portrait of a Family*. New York: St. Martin's, 1971.

Lochner, Louis P., ed. *The Goebbels Diaries 1942–1943*. Garden City, NY: Doubleday, 1948.

Machtan, Lothar. *Hidden Hitler*. Trans. John Brownjohn and Susanne Ehlert. New York: Basic Books, 2001.

Marty, Martin E., ed. *The Place of Bonhoeffer: Problems and Possibilities in His Thought*. New York: Association Press, 1962.

Patten, Thomas E. *The Twisted Cross and Dietrich Bonhoeffer*. Lima, OH: Fairway Press, 1992.

Rasmussen, Larry L. *Dietrich Bonhoeffer: Reality and Resistance*. Studies in Christian Ethics Series. Nashville: Abingdon Press, 1972.

Raum, Elizabeth. *Dietrich Bonhoeffer: Called by God*. London: Burns and Oates, 2002.

Ritter, Gerhard. *The German Resistance: Carl Goerdeler's Struggle against Tyranny*. Translated by R. T. Clark. New York: Frederick A. Praeger, 1958.

Robertson, Edwin H. *The Shame and the Sacrifice: The Life and Martyrdom of Dietrich Bonhoeffer*. New York: Macmillan, 1988.

Shirer, William L. *The Rise and Fall of the Third Reich: A History of Nazi Germany*. New York: Simon and Schuster, 1960.

Sklar, Dusty. *The Nazis and the Occult*. New York: Dorset Press, 1977.

Slane, Craig J. *Bonhoeffer as Martyr: Social Responsibility and Modern Christian Commitment*. New York: Brazos Press, 2004.

Speer, Albert. *Inside the Third Reich: Memoirs by Albert Speer*. Translated by Richard Winston and Clara Winston. New York: Macmillan, 1970.

Steigmann-Gall, Richard. *The Holy Reich: Nazi Conceptions of Christianity, 1919–1945*. Cambridge: Cambridge University Press, 2003.

Von Bismarck, Ruth-Alice, and Ulrich Kabitz, eds. *Love Letters from Cell 92: The Correspondence Between Dietrich Bonhoeffer and Maria Von Wedemeyer, 1943–45*. Translated by John Brownjohn. New York: Abingdon Press, 1995.

Wind, Renate. *Dietrich Bonhoeffer: A Spoke in the Wheel*. Translated by John Bowden. Grand Rapids: Eerdmans, 2002.

Wustenberg, Ralf K. *A Theology of Life: Dietrich Bonhoeffer's Religionless Christianity*. Translated by Douglas Stott. Grand Rapids: Eerdmans, 1998.

Zimmermann, Wolf-Dieter, and Ronald G. Smith, eds. *I Knew Dietrich Bonhoeffer*. Translated by Käthe G. Smith. New York: Harper and Row, 1966.

EPILOGUE AND ERRATA

The hustle and bustle of getting this book into print in April 2010—to coincide with the sixty-fifth anniversary of Bonhoeffer's death on April 9, 1945—resulted in a number of typographical and other small errors in that first edition, which we are pleased to correct in this new edition. Gone forever are all unintentionally funny errors, such as inanely saying "Alfred Einstein" when we obviously meant "Albert Einstein." Gone, too, are the less funny errors, as when a heroic Sasse was somehow conflated with a villainous Sasse. The erroneous spellings of many German words have also been corrected, and we are grateful to the many careful and conscientious readers who helped us put these things in order.

But for every communication we received about such errors, we received ten communications about something that is less an unintentional error than an unintentional ellipsis. We had always meant to include a brief word on the fate of Maria von Wedemeyer. For punishment we were reminded of this constantly, both verbally in the question-and-answer portions of speaking engagements, or in the form of emails. "Whatever happened to Maria von Wedemeyer?" we were asked repeatedly. "Can you tell us what happened to Maria?"

What happened to Maria after Dietrich's death bears fuller explanation than what we provide here. But the short answer to the question is that after she learned of her beloved Dietrich's fate in the summer of 1945, Maria von Wedemeyer was understandably heartbroken. Not long afterward she left Germany for the United States, enrolling as a student at Bryn Mawr. There, far from the horrors of her recent past, she studied mathematics, as she had always planned to do, and she eventually took a position with Honeywell in Massachusetts, rising to become the head of a department there, no small accomplishment for a woman at that time. Maria's personal life was less happy. She married twice and divorced twice, and in 1977, at the age of fifty-two, she died of cancer. She was survived by two sons.

For many years following Bonhoeffer's death, Bonhoeffer devotees and scholars had wanted to know more about the woman to whom Bonhoeffer had been engaged. But perhaps because she was married and had a new life, Maria wasn't so keen on revisiting her relationship with Dietrich Bonhoeffer publicly. Just a few years before her death, however, Maria thought the time had come to reveal this part of her life to the world. So she gave her eldest sister, Ruth-Alice, permission to publish the many letters between her and Dietrich Bonhoeffer. They were published in 1992 in a volume titled *Love Letters From Cell 92*, from which I quote copiously in this book, and which I heartily recommend to anyone wishing to know more about the life of this extraordinary woman.

ABOUT THE AUTHOR

Eric Metaxas was born in New York City in 1963, on his father's 36th birthday. He grew up in Danbury, Connecticut, attending the public schools there, and graduated from Yale University. At Yale he made a literary splash as editor of the *Yale Record*, the nation's oldest college humor magazine, and a subsequent *literal* splash when, following the 99th Yale-Harvard Game, he commandeered a successful effort to throw Harvard's goalpost into the Charles. At graduation Eric was awarded two senior prizes for his undergraduate fiction. He was also "Class Day Speaker," co-writing and -delivering "The Class History," a satirical address that is a Yale commencement tradition, in the process upstaging Dick Cavett, the next speaker. They would not speak for nearly two decades.

Metaxas' humor writing was first published in the *Atlantic Monthly*, and has appeared in *The New York Times*. Woody Allen has called these pieces "quite funny." Eric's book and movie reviews, essays, and poetry have appeared in *The New York Times*, *The Washington Post*, *Christianity Today*, *National Review Online*, *Beliefnet*, and *First Things*. He has been awarded fellowships to Yaddo and the MacDowell Colony for his short stories. The cult-classic *Don't You Believe It!*—his book-length parody of the Ripley's "Believe It Or Not!" books—led novelist Mark Helprin to dub Metaxas "the true heir to the *Far Side's* Gary Larson."

From 1988–1992, Metaxas was editorial director and head writer for Rabbit Ears Productions, writing over 20 children's videos and books narrated by such actors as Mel Gibson, Robin Williams, Sir John Gielgud, Danny Glover, Sigourney Weaver, John Candy, Michael Caine, Michael Keaton, Geena Davis, Jodie Foster, Emma Thompson, and Raul Julia. His Rabbit

Ears videos have won numerous Parent's Choice Awards and three Grammy nominations for Best Children's Recording; they all aired on *Showtime* and as popular audio programs on NPR's *Rabbit Ears Radio*, hosted by Mel Gibson and Meg Ryan, whose radio scripts Eric has also written. *Parenting* magazine and others have called Metaxas "the unsung hero" of Rabbit Ears and a "children's author nonpareil."

Mr. Metaxas' *The Birthday ABC* was chosen as a 1995 "Pick of the List" by the American Bookseller's Association. Reviewers said the book's light verse "sparkled" and "sizzled," comparing it with Odgen Nash, Edward Lear, and Lewis Carroll.

Eric's many other children's books include the Angel Award-winning *Prince of Egypt A to Z*, a tie-in to the Dreamworks film; and the acclaimed *Uncle Mugsy & the Terrible Twins of Christmas*. His book *Squanto and the Miracle of Thanksgiving* was awarded an Amazon.com "Number One Bestseller" Award in 1999.

Eric's children's book, *It's Time to Sleep, My Love*, illustrated by Nancy Tillman, had a first printing of 175,000 and debuted in Barnes&Noble.com's Top 100 books in October 2008, where it was hailed as a "*Goodnight Moon* for the 21st century." Sally Taylor, the daughter of James Taylor and Carly Simon, wrote a lullabye song to Eric's words, and sings it on the book's audio CD.

Metaxas was for two years a writer and editor for Chuck Colson's *Breakpoint*, a nationally syndicated daily radio program with over 400 stations and a weekly audience of five million. He then worked as a writer for VeggieTales, where he co-wrote *Lyle the Kindly Viking*, and provided the voice of the narrator on *Esther*. In *3-2-1 Penguins!* he provided the voice for "President Wait-Your-Turn" and "Vacuum #10 . Eric's children's books for VeggieTales include the #1 bestseller *God Made You Special!* (over 600,000 copies in print), as well as *Even Fish Slappers Deserve a Second-Chance* and *The Pirates Who (Usually) Don't Do Anything*, both also bestsellers.

Metaxas has been frequently featured as a cultural commentator on *CNN* and the *Fox News Channel*; and has appeared on *C-Span's Book TV* and *Hannity & Colmes*. He has been featured on many radio programs, including NPR's *Morning Edition* and *Talk of the Nation*, *Hugh Hewitt*, *Monica Crowley*, and *The Alan Colmes Show*.

He is the founder and host of *Socrates in the City: Conversations on the Examined Life*, a monthly event of entertaining and thought-provoking discussions on "life, God, and other small topics" that features such speakers as Dr. Francis

Collins, Sir John Polkinghorne, Baroness Caroline Cox, Rabbi Sir Jonathan Sacks, and Os Guinness.

Eric has debated at the Oxford Union, the world's oldest debating society, and speaks widely on a variety of topics. His no-holds-barred introductions of such figures as U. S. Senator Joseph Lieberman, former Attorney General John Ashcroft, and Rick Warren have made him much sought after as an emcee and moderator. He has moderated debates with Bishop Spong and President Obama's former pastor, the Rev. Jeremiah Wright, and has spoken at the White House, on Capitol Hill, at West Point, Yale, Cornell, Princeton, and many other venues, and was the featured speaker at the Lousiana Governor's Prayer Breakfast in Baton Rouge. In 2007 he was made an Honorary Fellow of the prestigious British-American Project, the only person ever to have been afforded this privilege.

Eric's acclaimed biography, *Amazing Grace: William Wilberforce and the Heroic Campaign to End Slavery* was published by HarperSanFrancisco, and is the "official companion book" to the feature film, also titled *Amazing Grace*. The book was #23 on the *New York Times* Bestseller list, and has been lauded by Stanley Crouch ("...a superb history of the British fight against slavery"); Former NYC Congressman Floyd Flake ("magnificent . . . will stand as a living landmark..."); John Wilson ("a crackling bonfire of clarity and truth"); Rudy Giuliani ("better than the movie!"), and many others.

Eric's *Everything You Always Wanted to Know About God (but were afraid to ask)*, came out in 2005, and was praised by Ann B. Davis, Alice on *The Brady Bunch* ("I am absolutely smitten with this book!"), Tim Keller of Redeemer Presbyterian Church ("The difficulty is not to gush."). The sequel, titled *Everything ELSE You Always Wanted to Know About God (but were afraid to ask)* was published in 2007. The final book of the trilogy—titled *Everything You Always Wanted to Know About God (The Jesus Edition)*—was published by Regal in January 2010.

Eric attends Calvary/St. George's Episcopal Church, and lives in Manhattan, New York, with his wife and daughter.

For more information, or to contact Eric Metaxas,
visit www.ericmetaxas.com

ACKNOWLEDGMENTS

I t was in the summer of 1988—that glorious season of my spiritual nativity—that I first heard of Dietrich Bonhoeffer. For this I am indebted to my dear friend Ed Tuttle, who himself attended the Great Physician at my happy renaissance, not least by giving me a copy of *The Cost of Discipleship* and sharing with me the fascinating story of the man who because of his Christian faith stood up to the Nazis and ultimately gave his life. As the son and grandson of Germans who had suffered through the period I was profoundly moved and thrilled and proud to hear it and immediately began telling the story to others. Among them was another dear friend, Gilbert von der Schulenberg Ahrens, who like me had lost a grandfather in the war, and who told me that his own grandfather and uncle were among those noble Germans who gave their lives in the plot to assassinate Hitler. I am indebted to Gil for over the years helping keep alive my hope of telling Bonhoeffer's story to a wider audience and to Mickey Maudlin, my editor at HarperOne, for making this possible by first suggesting I might write biographies by inviting me to write one about William Wilberforce.

I am especially indebted to my great friend, Joel Tucciarone who, Isaac Milner-like, spied me in a slough of despond and pluckily plucked me therefrom, squiring me to a Brooklyn diner to meet his friend Arthur Samuelson, who presciently thought that Thomas Nelson might be the right publisher and who there in the booth dialed David Moberg, who contacted my editor Joel Miller, and to all three of whom I am also greatly indebted. *To logariazmo, se parakalo!*

I am also deeply indebted to Martin Doblmeier, director of the spectacular

Bonhoeffer documentary film, for generously making available to me interview footage that did not make it into the final cut of the film, as well as for helping me to make contact with two of those interviewees, Ruth-Alice von Bismarck, the elder sister of Bonhoeffer's fiancee, and Renate Bethge, the widow of Eberhard Bethge and the niece of Dietrich Bonhoeffer. I am in turn grateful to each of these delightful saints of God for welcoming my wife and me into their homes in Hamburg and Villiprot respectively on consecutive afternoons in the early spring of 2008, and for treating us to German hospitality by regaling us with *Kaffee und Kuchen* and thrilling us with stories from their living memories of Dietrich Bonhoeffer in the Thirties and Forties. To have broken bread with those who broke bread with the subject of this book was an unmerited honor I will treasure all my life.

Lastly, I am indebted to all the writers and publishers of previous books on Dietrich Bonhoeffer, upon whose shoulders I and this book gratefully stand. To the editors and publishers of Dietrich Bonhoeffer Works at Augsburg Fortress I and all students of Bonhoeffer are particularly indebted, as well as to Ruth-Alice von Bismarck, who edited *Love Letters from Cell 92*, the book of her sister's correspondence with Bonhoeffer. Finally and most profoundly, I am indebted to Eberhard Bethge, whose entire life and whose monumental biography form the great foundation upon which every syllable thenceforth written or spoken about his best friend Dietrich Bonhoeffer gratefully rest.

Lobet den Herrn!

Eric Metaxas
New York City
February 2010

INDEX

A

abortion: Bonhoeffer's views on, 472
abortions (forced), 250
Abwehr (German military intelligence),
      307, 319, 348, 359, 365, 369–71,
      376, 377, 383, 386, 388, 389,
      392–94, 396–97, 409, 423, 424, 427,
      436–37, 441, 443, 444, 447, 474,
      502: Bonhoeffer's involvement with,
      369–71, 376, 377, 386, 388, 392, 394,
      396, 409, 423, 444
Abyssinian Baptist Church (New York
      City), 39, 107–9
Abyssinian crisis, 237
Act and Being (Bonhoeffer), 53, 80, 89–90,
      96, 538
Adler, Alfred, 13
"After Ten Years: A Reckoning Made at
      New Year 1943" (Bonhoeffer essay),
      445–47
Ahrens, Gilbert von der Schulenberg, 573
Alexanderplatz (Berlin), 127, 296, 297, 302
Allied Control Commission (Allied
      Commission), 45
Allies, 1, 34, 45, 96, 192, 295, 355–56,
      476, 493, 504, 515, 516, 525, 532,
      534: declare victory, 1
All Quiet on the Western Front (Remarque), 111
All Quiet on the Western Front (film), 111–13
American Jewish Committee, 158
American South, 110, 114, 152, 343
Ammundsen, Valdemar, 189, 215, 227,
      229, 235–36, 238–39
Anglicans, 199
Anschluss, 307–9, 312
anti-Semitism: Lutheran, 91–94; of the
      German Christians, 222, 398

Arendt, Hannah, 250
"Aryan Clause in the Church, The,"
      (Bonhoeffer pamphlet), 186
Aryan paragraph, 48, 150, 152, 154, 179,
      186–88, 190, 193, 197, 200, 206,
      213–15, 323
Aryan race: Hitler's perception of, 168
"Ascension Day Message" (Bell), 220–21,
      235, 239, 240
atonement, 102
Augsburg Confession, 190, 339
Augustine, 77
Auschwitz (concentration camp), 511
Austro-Prussian war, 393

B

Bach, Johann Sebastian, 138, 267
Baillie, John (prof.), 106, 261
Barcelona: Bonhoeffer in, 64, 65, 67–91,
      94, 202, 363, 539
Barmen Declaration, 61, 220–22, 226, 228,
      287
Barnett, Victoria, 354
Barth, Karl, 60–62, 81, 83, 84, 89, 106,
      119–20, 155, 157, 171, 173, 174, 184,
      187–88, 194, 197–98, 222, 248, 249,
      269, 270, 309, 312, 324, 326, 329,
      366, 368, 376, 377, 389, 469, 473
Basilica of St. John Lateran (Papal
      Archbasilica of St. John Lateran), 56
Bauer, Walter, 160
BBC (British Broadcasting Company), 3,
      4, 115
Beck, Ludwig (general), 233, 275, 303–4,
      306, 355, 381, 392, 505
Becket, Thomas à, 199
Beer Hall *Putsch*, 44, 45, 143

Bekennendekirche, 222
Bell, George (bishop of Chichester), 3,
    158, 182, 188, 189, 197, 198–200,
    204, 208, 215, 217–21, 226, 227, 229,
    235, 239, 240, 252, 258, 275, 297,
    314, 322–24, 344, 357, 377, 380, 386,
    394, 397–404, 528, 535, 537, 540
Bergen, Doris, 172
Berggrav, Eivind (bishop), 395, 396
Berlin Cathedral, 207, 251, 255
Berlin University, 42, 58–60, 66, 67, 89,
    90, 101, 120, 124, 128, 161, 162, 178,
    286, 329, 505
Berneuchen movement, 407
Bernard of Saxe-Weimar (duke), 6
Best, Payne, 503, 504–9, 513–16, 517–21,
    523, 524, 525, 526, 527, 528
Bethel Confession, 182–94, 287: failure of,
    185–86
Bethel community (Biesenthal), 177, 184,
    185, 250, 269, 504
Bethge, Eberhard, 5, 7, 10, 13, 14, 42, 54,
    58, 59, 84, 89, 94, 95, 98, 131, 241,
    243, 263–64, 267, 269, 270, 272–75,
    285, 290, 294, 295, 297–300, 310–
    13, 317, 322, 326–27, 358, 360–62,
    369, 370, 372–75, 392, 400, 402,
    408, 409, 412, 414, 417, 418, 423,
    427, 431, 436, 438, 439, 445, 446,
    456, 459, 461–63, 465–66, 468, 473,
    475, 477, 483, 486, 492, 495, 501,
    520, 530
Bethge, Renate. *See* Schleicher, Renate
Bewer, J. W., 337–39
Bierhall Putsch. See Beer Hall *Putsch,*
Björquist (bishop, head of the Nordic
    Ecumenical Institute), 400
Blackman, E. C., 237
Black Reichswehr, 45
Blaskowitz, Johannes (general), 353
Block, Eduard, 299, 371
Blomberg-Fritsch Affair. *See* Fritsch Affair
Bodelschwingh, Friedrich von, 177–79,
    182–84, 188, 207, 219, 229, 234, 235,
    250, 504
Boenhoff (Bonhöffer), Caspar van den, 7
Boericke, Harold and Irma, 100, 377
Boericke, Ray, Betty, and Binkie, 100
Bojack, Konrad, 383
Bolshevism, 32, 151
Bonhöffer, Sophonias, 7
Bonhoeffer, Christine (Christel). *See*
    Dohnanyi, Christel (Christine) von
Bonhoeffer, Dietrich : and confirmation

class (Wedding), 130–35; arrest in
    Dahlem, 302; as monastic leader,
    246–77; 261–77; association with
    the Abwehr, 369–71, 376, 377, 386,
    388, 392, 394, 396, 409, 423, 444; as
    university student in Berlin, 58–68; at
    Buchenwald, 504–16; at Ettal, 371–75;
    at Flossenbürg, 530–32; at Gestapo
    prison, 494–500; at Tegel prison, 432–
    74; battle with the Reich Board for
    the Regulation of Literature, 367–68;
    birth, 8; chaplaincy at Charlottenberg
    Technical College, 130; childhood,
    8–30, 35–36; conscription to Black
    Reichswehr, 45; decision to return to
    Germany (1939), 333–44; decision
    to study theology, 37; depression
    of, 273–74; early lectures of, 82–85;
    education (childhood), 16–17, 36;
    engagement of, 419–21, 433–36;
    execution, 531–32; family, 5–8;
    habilitation in Berlin, 88–98 ; holiday
    in Rome, 49–57; in America (1931),
    99–118; in the American South, 114;
    in Barcelona (1928), 64, 65, 67–91,
    94, 202, 363, 539; in Berlin (1931–
    32), 119–37; in London (1934–35),
    195–203; in love, 105–22; innermost
    thoughts of, 461–65; last day of,
    527–32; memorial service, 3, 535–42;
    memo to Hitler, 287–89; move
    to Berlin (childhood), 15; musical
    background, 22–24; on abortion,
    472; on death, 447; on preaching the
    Word, 272–73; on telling the truth,
    365–66; ordination of, 130; "Peace
    Speech" of, 240–41; proposal to
    Maria von Wedemeyer, 417–19; radio
    address at Potsdammerstrasse, 139–
    40; return to America (1939), 332–44;
    road trip to Mexico, 116–18; speech
    at the College of Political Science in
    Berlin, 140–42; trip to Cuba, 113–14;
    role in plot against Hitler, 4, 60, 304,
    318–20, 350, 358–59, 362, 369–71,
    374–77, 383, 386–87, 388, 389, 392,
    394, 396, 397, 399, 412, 441, 458,
    529; role in Resistance, 113, 360, 362,
    364, 372; trip to Geneva (first), 36–
    79, (second), 386–88, (third), 396–97;
    trips to Sweden, 283–86, 397–402;
    views on the Bible as answer to all
    questions, 136–37; visits to Christian
    communities, 261

Bonhoeffer, Emmi (Delbrück), 15, 23, 36, 37, 90, 96, 359, 493, 504

Bonhoeffer, Friedrich Ernst Philipp Tobias, 7

Bonhoeffer, Julie (neé Tafel, grandmother to Dietrich), 7, 23, 30, 35, 38, 42, 46, 63, 71, 73, 76, 97, 115, 135, 156–57, 184, 185, 221, 248, 282, 283

Bonhoeffer, Karl, 5, 7–10, 13–15, 21, 24, 26, 29, 41, 43, 44, 60, 62, 95, 139, 146, 147, 161, 184, 283, 303, 313, 319, 427, 430, 431, 494

Bonhoeffer, Karl-Friedrich, 8, 23, 25, 26, 28, 29, 31, 33, 36, 38, 41, 42, 59, 63, 72, 78, 80, 90, 94, 100, 109, 110, 127, 259, 342–44, 348: conscription to the army, 25

Bonhoeffer, Klaus, 4, 8, 11, 15, 23, 26, 29, 33, 36, 38, 41, 42, 48, 49, 52, 75, 76, 90, 96, 127, 158, 238, 319, 320, 358, 359, 374, 389, 392, 399, 480, 493–95, 501, 533, 534, 535, 540

Bonhoeffer, Paula (von Hase), 6, 8–10, 12–15, 17, 22–28, 30, 35, 36, 39, 44, 63, 90, 126, 136, 156, 175, 200, 208, 212, 295, 270, 295, 298, 299, 319, 321, 349, 451, 458, 473, 491, 494, 534, 535, 542

Bonhoeffer, Sabine. *See* Leibholz, Sabine (Bonhoeffer),

Bonhoeffer, Susanne (Susi). *See* Dress, Susanne (Bonhoeffer)

Bonhoeffer, Ursula. *See* Schleicher, Ursula (Bonhoeffer)

Bonhoeffer, Walter, 8, 23, 25–31, 33, 35, 39, 90: conscription to the army, 25–26; death, 26–28, 29, 31, 33, 35, 90, 175, 374, 378, 441

book burning, 161–64

Booth, Bramwell, 39

Bormann, Martin, 166–67, 169, 392

Bornkamm, Günther, 67

boycott (Hitler's), 156–57, 158, 159

Brandt, Heinz (Lt. col.), 428–29

Brandt, Karl, 250, 355

Brauchitsch, Walther von (general), 353, 360, 381, 382, 390, 391

Braun, Eva, 481

Breslau (Poland), 5, 8, 9, 10, 16, 30, 31, 44, 58

Broadway Presbyterian Church (New York City), 101, 334

Brown House (national headquarters of the Nazi Party), 251

Brownshirts (SA), 146

Brown Synod, 187–91

B-17 Flying Fortress bombers, 501

Buchanan, Walter Duncan, 101

Buchenwald concentration camp, 344, 500, 502, 503, 504–16, 520, 521, 523, 524, 527, 530, 534

Buchman, Frank, 199, 250, 289–91

C

Calvary Church (New York),

Canaris, Wilhelm, 319–20, 348, 351–52, 367, 370, 381, 382, 388, 389, 392, 393, 397, 437, 447–48, 458, 474, 486, 495, 502, 507, 529–30, 532

Carter, James Earl, Jr., 391

Catholicism, 20, 53, 55–57, 263, 372

Central Bureau of Interchurch Aid, 326

Chalcedon, 179

Chamberlain, Houston Stewart, 169

Chamberlain, Neville (Brit. prime minister), 314, 319, 322, 347, 348, 356

Charlottenburg district (Berlin), 3, 42, 161, 283

Charlottenberg Technical College, 130

Chartres Cathedral, 102

"cheap grace," xi, xii, 14, 240, 263, 279, 292, 314, 360

Christ Church Cathedral, Oxford, 198, 252

Chronicle of Shame (file), 320, 355, 487

church and the Jewish question, 150–64

"Church and the Jewish Question, The," (Bonhoeffer), 151, 156, 186

Church Dogmatics (Barth), 120, 312

church elections, 180–82

Churchill, Winston, 2, 310, 314, 319, 377, 386–87, 396–98, 400–2, 476, 483, 534

church music (German Christian), 173

church struggle, 91, 121, 161, 171, 173, 176–82, 186, 191, 195, 196, 200, 201, 206, 212, 217, 220–22, 247, 251–54, 256–58, 264–65, 341, 396

Cicestr, George, *See* Bell, George

Clement III (pope), 92–93

Coffin, Henry Sloane, 325, 329, 343

collective pastorates, 298–302, 346, 349, 350, 477

Columbus (German ship), 96–97

Commissar Order, 381–82

communal living, 104. *See also* Zingst and
    Finkenwalde
concentration camps, 3, 65, 149, 158,
    181, 192, 231, 250, 282, 288, 294,
    295, 305, 329, 347, 381, 438, 471,
    482, 487, 500, 502, 506–9, 511,
    512, 515, 516, 518, 520, 523, 526,
    533, 534, 541. *See also* Auschwitz;
    Buckenwalkde; Dachai; Flossenbürg;
    Sachsenhausen.
Confessing Church, 55, 61, 67, 129, 154,
    171, 173, 182, 188, 202, 205, 207,
    208, 211, 218, 222–29, 235–37, 243,
    244, 246–49, 252–54, 257–58, 261–
    63, 265, 266, 278–82, 286–98, 308–9,
    312, 317–18, 322–24, 326, 334, 341,
    344, 345, 349, 358, 361, 364, 367,
    370–71, 375–77, 383, 385, 377, 398,
    426, 438, 441, 499
"Confessing Church and the Ecumenical
    Movement, The" (Bonhoeffer), 279
Confessional Movement (Confessing
    Movement), 55, 222, 287
Confessional Synod of the German
    Evangelical Church, 222–23, 243,
    252
Confessing Synod, 227, 228, 234, 243,
    253, 281, 321
Cost of Discipleship, The (Bonhoeffer:
    originally titled *Discipleship*), xi, 113,
    142, 240, 263, 275, 279, 468, 484,
    533, 541, 573
Courvoisier, Jacques, 377
Cripps, Stafford (Sir), 396, 402
Czech resistance to Nazi occupation, 404
Czeppan, Maria, 431
Czeppan, Richard, 41, 49

D

Dachau concentration camp, 295, 509
Dahlemites, 263
Dahlem Resolution, 252
Darwinism, 351–52
Das Gebetbook der Bibel (*The Prayerbook of the
    Bible*) (Bonhoeffer), 367
Davidson, Randall (archbishop), 198–99
Decree for the Restoration of Orderly
    Conditions in the German
    Evangelical Church, 206. *See also*
    "muzzle decree"
Deissman, Adolf, 60
Delbrück , Emmi. *See* Bonhoeffer, Emmi
    (Delbrück)
Delbrück, Justus, 90

Delbrück, Max, 90
des Prez, Josquin, 267
Deutsche Hilfsverein, 78–79
"Deutsche Gottesworte" ("German Words
    of God") (Müller), 290–91
Deutsche Volk, 20
Dibelius, Otto, 130
Diestel, Max, 74, 94, 101, 113
disabled: Bethel community for, 183–84,
    250, 504; Hitler's view toward, 184;
    murder of, 250, 354, 504, 518
Dimitroff (Communist Party leader), 147–48
Dilthey, Wilhelm, 6, 460
discipleship, 142, 196, 246, 260, 540–41
Discipleship (Bonhoeffer). *See Cost of
    Discipleship, The*
Distler, Hugo, 416
Dittman (guard at Buchenwald), 515, 516
dogmatics, 56, 62, 63, 101
Dohnanyi, Barbara, 374
Dohnanyi, Christel (Christine) von, 8, 42,
    90, 135, 150, 202, 282, 374, 430, 437,
    495, 442
Dohnanyi, Christoph von, 135, 374
Dohnanyi, Hans von, 90, 135, 146, 150,
    202, 229, 231, 252, 280, 297, 298,
    303–6, 310, 313, 319–20, 350–51,
    355, 359, 367, 369–71, 374, 375,
    380–83, 387–89, 392, 395–97, 409,
    424, 426, 427, 429, 430, 432–33,
    441–47, 458, 487, 495, 499, 504, 529
Dohnanyi, Grete von, 90
Dolchstoss (stab-in-the-back), 32, 255, 355
Dollfuss, Engelbert, 231–32, 235, 237
Dönitz, Karl, 430, 482
Don Quixote, 471
Dress, Ilse, 63
Dress, Susanne (Bonhoeffer), 10, 23, 29,
    36, 11, 18, 63, 64, 90, 202
Dress, Walter, 48, 63, 67, 85–86, 90, 202,
    254
Dudzus, Otto, 125–26, 128, 238, 240–41,
    326
Dulles, John Foster, 102
dualism, 54, 80, 85

E

Ebeling, Gerhard, 326
Ecumenical Federation, 229
ecumenical movement, 53, 60, 67, 111,
    113, 152, 182, 189, 190, 199, 217–20,
    227, 236, 237, 243, 279, 289, 292,
    322–24, 397
Eden, Anthony, 377, 387, 394, 401–4

"Eight Articles of Evangelical Doctrine,"
(Vogel), 161
Eighth Air Force (U.S.), 501
Einsatzgruppen (SS paramilitary), 320–21, 381
Einstein, Albert, 59, 135, 162
elections: of 1928, 89; of 1932, 134, 139;
1933, 144
Eliot, T. S., 199
Elmhurst College (Ill.), 325
Enabling Act, 149, 156
Enlightenment, 83
Epistle to the Romans, The (Barth), 60
Ern, Mrs., Richard (Bonhoeffer's fellow
passengers on the *Columbus*), 97, 113,
116
Ern, Richard, 97, 113, 116, 117
Ethics (Bonhoeffer), 275, 363, 366, 371,
372, 375, 378, 379, 383, 395, 424,
468, 471, 472
Ettal Abbey (Benedictine monastery), 297,
359, 371–75, 424, 439, 468
Euthanasia Program. *See* T4 euthanasia
program
Evangelical Youth, 206
Evangelische Theologie, 287

F
Falconer, Hugh, 505, 508, 515, 517, 519,
521, 524, 527
Fanø (Denmark): conference at, 227, 229,
234–45, 248, 325, 398, 425
Federal Council of Churches, 329
Federation of Swiss Churches, 389
Fellgiebel, Erich, 477, 479
Fezer, Karl, 199, 216
Finkenwalde (Zdroje, Szczecin):
community/seminary at, 56, 61, 65,
67, 76, 104, 109, 128, 129, 266–70,
272–74, 275–79, 281, 283, 284, 294,
299, 326, 328, 349, 361, 368, 372,
373, 438, 462, 538; correspondence
to the brethren and families of, 316;
318, 407, 410, 468; daily routine
at, 267–69, end of (community),
297–98
First Presbyterian Church (New York), 102
First War, 3, 141, 177, 180, 199, 275, 363,
378, 502, 507, 508
Fischer-Hüllstrung, H. (camp doctor at
Flossenbürg), 531
Fisher, Albert Franklin "Frank," 107, 109, 235
Fjellbu, Arne, 394
Flossenbürg concentration camp, 3, 237,
502, 507, 519–21, 529–32, 534

forced labor, 93, 351, 5004
Ford, Henry, 399
Fosdick, Harry Emerson, 101–3, 106, 332,
334
France: Battle of, 478; defeat of, in the
Franco-Prussian war, 42, 162; Hitler's
attack on, 361; Hitler's plan to attack,
355; surrender/fall of, to Hitler, 361,
364, 380; Walter Bonhoeffer's death
in, 26
Franco-Prussian War, 42, 162, 393
Frederick III (German emperor), 6
Free Church, 187, 217, 228, 229, 254
Freisler, Roland, 487, 501
Freud, Sigmund, 13, 162
Freudenberg, Adolf, 326, 377, 397
Frick, Wilhelm (interior minister), 235
Friedrichsbrunn (Germany), 17–20, 22, 63,
119, 134, 135, 186, 254, 331, 378,
468
Fritsch, Wilhelm von, 305–6
Fritsch Affair, 304–7
Fry, Christopher, 199
Führer principle, 138–49, 151, 157, 211
fundamentalism, 102
fundamentalists, 101–3, 105, 257, 270,
334: battle between liberals and,
101–3, 105, 334

G
Gandhi, Mahatma (Mohandas), 46–47, 76,
115, 199, 247, 248, 258–59, 261, 539
Gaupp, Robert, 13
Geneva (Switzerland), 192, 227, 229, 374,
377–77, 387, 396–97
Geneva Convention, 393
Gerhardt, Paul, 36, 178, 440, 463, 483
German Christians, 151, 157–58, 160–61,
171–76, 177–79, 180–82, 185, 186–
88, 191, 191, 193–94, 199–200, 205,
212, 213, 222, 224, 227, 235, 236,
243, 247, 263, 265, 286, 289, 291,
345, 540: and church music, 173;
and Communion, 173; anti-Semitism
of, 222; attach on Reich Bishop
Bodelschwingh, 177–78; conference
in Berlin, 157–58, 161; "orders of
creation" theology of, 186; overreach
of, 193–94
German church, xi, xii, 61, 91, 103, 122,
151–52, 154, 157, 173, 176, 178, 182,
186–89, 193, 200, 201, 204, 206,
215, 217–22, 226, 228–29, 240, 243,
251–54, 286, 317, 396

German mark, 43–44
German Empire, 42, 393
German Evangelical Church (aka Protestant Reich Church), 206, 211, 222–24, 228, 243, 251–54
German Lutheran Church (United Evangelical Lutheran Church of Germany), 55
German Lutherans, 54–56
German Resistance, 3, 113
Germanness, 171, 172
German Students Association, 162
German *Weltanschauung* (worldview), 173
German Youth Movement, 73, 139
Gersdorf, Rudolf Christoph Freiherr von (general), 382, 429–31
Gestapo, 175, 177, 180–81, 288, 290, 295–97, 302–3, 306, 315, 360, 369–70, 380, 385, 386, 392, 421, 423–24, 426, 430–33, 436–37, 441–42, 444, 447–48, 474, 494, 498–502, 507, 508, 511, 515, 526, 534
Gestapo prison, 274, 424, 465, 494–501, 503, 523, 528
Gifford Lectures, 322
Gilbert, Felix, 339
Gisevius, Hans, 170, 304, 348, 370, 389, 392
Gleischaltung (synchronization), 150, 161, 176
Godesberg Declaration, 324
Goebbels, Joseph, 93, 112, 145–46, 156, 162, 163, 166, 167, 289, 307, 460, 480
Goerdeler, Carl, 307, 314, 319, 374, 381, 477, 495, 499, 505, 523, 528–29
Goes, Helmuth, 59
Goethe, Johann Wolfgang von, 6, 65, 138, 473: book in Bonhoeffer's possession at prison, 526, 529, 532
Goethe Medal, 431
Göring, Hermann, 146–48, 157, 161, 67, 208, 211, 231, 305, 307, 347, 429, 430, 482, 511, 523
Gorkmann, Rev. (radio preacher), 342
Göttingen (Germany), 60, 156, 159, 160, 162, 221, 244–45, 297, 310, 312, 313
Great Britain: declaration of war on Germany, 348
Greek Orthodox Church, 286
Grosch, Goetz, 65
Gross, Wilhelm, 266
Gross-Schlönwitz (underground seminary), 284, 299, 300, 312, 315, 374

Grünewald, Matthias, 68
Grunewald district, 24–25, 33, 36, 44, 59, 61, 63, 65, 70, 78, 90, 91, 95, 110, 135, 264, 274, 283, 391, 406: church, 38, 64, 70, 95, 125, 425
Grunewald Gymnasium, 36, 41, 49
Guderian, Heinz (general), 390, 391
Gumpelzhaimer, Adam, 267
Gürtner, Franz, 319, 374–75

H
Haack, Herr (businessman), 72
Halder, Franz, 304,
Halder, Fritz, 356, 502, 523
Halensee (Berlin, train station), 35, 59
Hall of Mirrors (Palace of Versailles), 34
Hammelsbeck, Oskar, 424
Hanfstaengl, Ernst (Putzi), 146
Harnack, Adolf von, 59–62, 90, 94–95, 101, 103, 128, 135, 174, 345, 541–42
Hase. *See* von Hase
Headlam, Arthur Cayley, 199
Heberlein, Erich, 506, 526
Heberlein, Margot, 506, 518, 521, 526, 527
Heckel, Theodor, 183, 186, 188–90, 195, 196, 204, 206, 208, 211, 212, 213–16, 217, 218, 220, 228, 229, 234, 239, 242–43, 253, 255, 256, 257, 279, 284, 285, 398, 400
Hegel, Georg Wilhelm Friedrich, 77, 178
Heidegger, Martin, 6
Heidl (Bonhoeffer's fellow prisoner), 508, 518, 521, 526, 527
"Heil," 128, 178, 210, 251, 362, 371, 510, 513
Heim, Karl, 125
Heine, Heinrich, 150, 162, 163
Henriod, Henry Louis, 217–18, 228, 229, 239
Henry VIII (king), 92
Heroes of Everyday, 19
Herrnhut (Germany), 11, 12
Herrnhüter (Moravian Church), 12, 248
Hess, Rudolf, 258
Heydrich, Reinhard, 165, 169, 170, 306, 315, 370, 382, 389, 392, 404, 487
Hildebrandt, Franz, 91, 94, 151, 177–78, 179, 183, 186, 187, 188, 190–92, 196, 198, 200, 201–2, 205, 212, 221, 234, 235, 246, 251, 261, 272, 275, 281, 288, 295–97, 314, 323, 344, 391, 397, 535, 537

Himmler, Heinrich, 166–67, 169, 170,
    231, 232, 290, 291, 305, 306, 317,
    370, 385, 388, 389, 429, 430, 448,
    477, 480, 495, 509, 511–13
Hindenburg, Paul von, 33, 121, 148–49,
    179, 207, 208, 211, 229–35, 275, 431
historical-critical liberals, 61
historical-critical method (aka "higher
    criticism"), 59, 60
Hitler, Adolf: announcement of intent
    to attack Belgium, Holland, France,
    England, Norway, Denmark, 355;
    announcement of Germany's pullout
    from the League of Nations, 191,
    192; assassination attempts on, 180,
    426–28, 429–31, 453, 455, 477–80,
    483, 488; attack on Holland, 361;
    attack on Poland, 347–48; attack
    on Russia, 390; attitude toward
    Christianity, 166; attitude toward
    the disabled, 184; Bierhall Putsch of,
    44; campaign to undo the Versailles
    Treaty, 258; Bonhoeffer's memo to,
    287–88; capitulation of the German
    church to, xi; conspiracy against,
    4, 6, 60, 170, 233, 274, 304, 313,
    318–20, 350, 354–55, 359–60,
    380–393, 398, 399, 407, 421, 424–31,
    458, 474, 476–80; election of (as
    Reich chancellor), 120, 138–40, 142,
    143–44; ineligibility for office, 134;
    fiftieth birthday of, 325; march on
    Prague, 347; oath of obedience to (for
    German pastors), 308; on Jesus, 168,
    172; plans for the church, 180; plans
    to attack Austria and Czechoslovakia,
    303, 309; plausible connection with
    homosexual activity, 305; proposal
    of the office of Reich bishop, 157;
    resistance against, 158, 386, 424, 537;
    suicide of, 1, 529, 532; takeover of
    the German military, 306; thoughts
    on the Aryan race, 168
Hitlerjugend (Hitler Youth), 112, 206, 214,
    395
Hoepner, Dr. (brother of Erich Hoepner,
    and Bonhoeffer's fellow prisoner),
    507, 521, 522
Hoepner, Erich, 391, 507
Hoffer, Margarete, 236
Hohenasperg fortress (Germany), 8
Hohenzollern dynasty (House of
    Hohenzollern), 42, 230, 231, 399
Höhle, Herr (Gestapo official), 295

Holl, Karl, 60, 63, 541
Holland: Hitler's attack on, 361
Holy Trinity Brompton Church (London),
    2, 535
Horn, Käthe van, 11, 12–13, 17, 29, 113
Horn, Maria van, 11, 12, 17–18, 23, 29, 41
"Horst Wessel Song" (Nazis' official
    anthem), 178, 362
Hossenfelder, Joachim, 199, 216
humanism, 85
Huppenkothen, Walter, 530

I
Igel fraternity, 41–43, 45, 48, 63, 238
I Knew Dietrich Bonhoeffer (Schlabrendorff),
    498–500
Institute for Research and the Elimination
    of Jewish influence on German
    Church Life (aka Institute for the
    Study and Elimination of Jewish
    Influence on German Church Life),
    172
intellectual assent, 12
intercourse between Jews and Germans,
    280
Iron Cross, 177
Islam, 65

J
Jacobi, Gerhard, 121, 151, 161, 180, 181,
    187, 196, 200, 216, 246, 273, 289
Jäger, August, 219, 242, 251–52, 279
James, William, 333
Japan: attack on Pearl Harbor, 390; U.S.
    declaration of war on, 391
Jehle, Herbert, 128
Jensen, Hans-Werner, 284, 312, 317
Jews: abductions of, 310; academia
    closed to, 286; banned from cultural
    and entertainment activities, 160;
    beginning of Hitler's persecution
    of, 315; "curse" upon, 315–16;
    deadly beatings of (Lithuania), 387;
    deportations of, 391, 393; expelled
    from the world of journalism, 160;
    forbidden to display the Reich,
    national flag, national colors, 280;
    forbidden to employee female
    Germans ages 45 or less, 280;
    forbidden to marry Germans, 280;
    Hitler's boycott of businesses owned
    by, 156–58; in the concentration
    camps, 471; law prohibiting
    extramarital intercourse with

Germans, 280; Luther and, 91–94; numbers limited in public schools, 160; Nuremburg Laws, 279–80; officially barred from the church, 189; prohibited from serving as patent lawyers or as doctors, dentists, or dental technicians in institutions with state-run insurance, 160; prohibitions expanded to include spouses of, 160; requirement to wear the yellow star, 368

John, Otto, 392
Juarez (film), 331
Judaism, 172, 193, 324
Jung, Carl, 13
Junge, Gertraud, 481
Junge Kirche, 325
Junkers, 274

K

Kaiser Wilhelm Institute (Kaiser-Wilhelm-Institut, aka Kaiser Wilhelm Society), 41
Kaiser Wilhelm Memorial Church, 121, 151
Kaiser Wilhelm Society. *See* Kaiser Wilhelm Institute
Kalkreuth, Leopold (Count), 6
Kalkreuth, Stanislaus (Count), 6, 24
Kalckreuth, Countess, 371
Kamnitz, Joachim, 267
Kanitz, Joachim, 128, 129
Kant, Immanuel, 77, 83
Karding, Inge, 119, 126, 128–29, 231
Karlström, Nils, 284
Kaufhaus des Westens (department store), 156, 172
Keitel, Wilhelm, 307, 351, 352, 391, 393, 430, 479–480
Keller, Helen, 162
Kelly, Geffrey, 367
Kierkegaard, Søren Aabye, 15
King James Bible, 20
Kirchenkampf (church struggle), 167, 171, 212. *See also* church struggle
Klapproth, Erich, 385
Klein-Krössin (Krosinko, Poland), 275, 294, 371, 395, 401, 405–7, 409, 411, 416, 418, 451, 468
Kleist, Hans-Friedrich, 276
Kleist-Schmenzin, Ewald von, 266, 274–75, 310, 319, 487–88
Knoblauch (corporal, at Tegel), 448, 493, 494
Koch, Ilse, 508

Koch, Karl, 227, 229, 234, 235, 243, 247, 253
Koch, Werner, 288, 294
Koenigsplatz (Königsplatz, Munich), 33, 232
Kokorin, Vassily, 505, 508, 521, 526, 527, 528
Köslin (Koszalin, Middle Pomerania, Poland), 298–99, 315, 346, 349
Krause, Reinhold, 174, 193–94
Kreisau Circle, 364, 392–93, 395, 396, 399, 425
Kreutzer, Leonid, 39
Kreuzzeitung (newspaper), 140
Kristallnacht (Night of Broken Glass), 314–17, 522
Kube, Wilhelm, 387
Kulturkampf (culture wars), 96

L

Laocoön and His Sons (sculpture), 50, 54
Lansberg am Lech (Germany), 44
Lasserre, Jean, 107, 111–13, 116–18, 235, 245
League of Nations, 191–92
Legal Gazette, 308
legalism, xi, xii, 270, 271, 365, 366
Lehmann, Paul, 107, 115, 116, 117, 124, 157–58, 235, 325, 326, 335, 340, 341, 343, 344
Lehmann, Marion, 115, 116, 124, 157–58, 235
Leibholz, Christiane, 244, 311, 344
Leibholz, Gerhard (Gert), 58, 156, 159–60, 162, 203, 205, 244, 282, 286, 310, 311, 312, 313, 314, 322, 323, 344, 377, 386, 398, 400, 403, 431, 517, 527, 532–33, 534–35, 541
Leibholz, Marianne, 244, 310–11, 344
Leibholz, Sabine (Bonhoeffer), 8, 10, 11, 14, 15, 16, 17, 18, 19, 20–21, 22, 23, 25, 26, 27, 28, 29, 31, 36, 38, 39, 42, 46, 47, 58, 64, , 66, 73, 75, 91, 114, 115, 156, 159–60, 202, 205, 221, 244, 282, 297, 310, 311, 312, 313, 314, 322, 323, 338, 344, 377, 386, 391, 398, 400, 431, 504, 514, 532–33, 534, 535, 537, 541
Leiper, Henry Smith, 239, 240, 325–27, 329, 331, 335, 336
Leipzig (Germany), 147, 148, 307, 319, 374
Lemelsen, Joachim (general), 353
Lenchen (Fräulein: governess to Bonhoeffer children), 16, 17, 18, 22

Leo X (pope), 308
Letters and Papers from Prison (Bethge, ed.), 439
Lewis, C. S., 82, 314
Liebknecht, Karl, 33, 34
Liedig, Franz, 502, 520, 530
Life and Work (ecumenical organization), 188, 220, 290
Life Together (Bonhoeffer), xi, 312, 372, 468
Liszt, Franz, 6
"living faith," 12, 384
Loccum (Germany), 176
London, Jack, 162
Losungen ("watch words"): publication of the Moravian Church), 12, 333, 483
Louis Ferdinand (prince of Prussia), 392, 399
Love Letters from Cell 92, 66, 438, 574
Lucas, Edmund De Long, 97, 115
Lufthansa (Deutsche), 318, 319, 392
Luftwaffe (air force), 305, 347, 482, 511, 512
Luther, Martin, xi–xii, 19–20, 65, 88, 91–94, 105, 120, 121, 122, 153, 155, 173, 174, 190, 207, 212, 251, 254, 263, 267, 273, 281, 287, 308, 318, 324, 329, 370
Lutheran Christians, 174, 263
Lutheranism, 12, 54
Luther Bible, 20
Luxemburg, Rosa, 32, 33, 34
Lyman, Dr. (Union prof.), 105

M

Maass, Theodor, 349
Macy (Rev.), 329
Madison Avenue Church, 329
Maechler, Winfried, 128, 266, 326, 465
Magdeburg Cathedral, 190
manifesto: Hitler's (*Mein Kampf*, 44; of George Schultz (Sydow brotherhood), 161; of the Meisserites, 252–53; of the Pastors' Emergency League, 190; of the Provisional Committee of the World Council of Churches, 324
Mann, Thomas, 162
mark (German monetary unit). *See* German mark
marriages between Jews and Germans, 280
McComb, Dr. (Broadway Presbyterian Church), 334
medical experiments (on concentration camp inmates), 250, 504, 509, 510–13
Mein Kampf (Hitler), 44, 168, 171, 352

Mendelssohn, Felix: removal of statue of, 307
"mercy killings," 184
Meumann, Karl (Rev.), 64
Meyer, Oscar (physicist), 5
Michaelskirche (St. Michael's Church), 7
Milch, Erhard, 511–12
miracles, 59, 102
Moltke, Helmuth von (count), 389, 392–94, 395–96
monarchy, 33
Moravian Brethren, 12
Morgenstern, Christian, 238
Morning Post (London), 288
Morrell, Theodor, 428
Müller, Johann Heinrich Ludwig, 157, 173–74, 176–79, 182, 185, 188, 189, 190–91, 194, 196, 199, 204–8, 210, 211, 213, 214, 219, 220, 222, 227, 235, 239, 240, 242, 244, 251–52, 253, 255, 257, 263, 264, 279, 290–91
Müller, Joseph, 359, 371–72, 374–75, 376, 424, 437, 495, 502–3, 507, 508, 516, 520, 530
Müller, Rev. (superintendent at Zionskirche), 130
Mussolini, Benito, 232, 237, 312, 479
"muzzle decree," (Decree for the Restoration of Orderly Conditions in the German Evangelical Church), 206, 235
mysticism, 85

N

Nacht der Langen Messer, 230. *See also* Night of the Long Knives
Nachfolge (*Discipleship*), xi, 113, 275, 297. *See also Cost of Discipleship, The*
National Reich Church, 170–71
National Socialists (Nazi Party), 32, 54, 112, 136, 150, 151, 159, 165, 166, 193, 194, 263, 282, 326, 368, 481: orthodoxy of, 3
national synod, 182, 186, 187, 188, 190. *See also* Brown Synod
Nazi: official anthem, 178; theology, 165–75; worldview at home, 354–55
Nazi storm troopers, 146, 149. *See also* Brownshirts (SA)
Neckar (river), 42, 47
neo-orthodoxy, 60
neo-Protestantism, 257
Neurath, Konstantin von (baron, Reich minister of foreign affairs), 303

New Testament: German Christians'
distortion of, 172
New York City, 39, 94, 99–100, 106, 108,
112, 334, 335
New York Times, 483
New York World-Telegram, 290
Nicea, 179
Niebuhr, Reinhold, 111, 321, 322, 323–24,
325–26, 329, 337, 338, 343
Niemöller, Martin, 170, 171, 177, 182,
186, 187, 188, 191–92, 196, 200, 207,
208, 211, 212, 215, 216, 220, 227,
247, 258, 262, 288, 289, 293, 294,
295–96, 297, 333, 352, 381, 425, 465
Nietzsche, Friedrich Wilhelm, 168–69
Nietzscheanism, 173, 184
Night of the Long Knives, 229–33, 406
Nikolaikirche (Church of St. Nicholas,
Berlin), 178
Nithack, Ulrich, 383
Nordic Ecumenical Institute, 398, 400
Novi Sad (Serbia), 186, 188, 189
Nuremberg Laws, 279–82
Nuremberg trials, 258, 508–9, 511
Nymwegen (Nijmegen, Netherlands), 7

O
Oberkommando der Wehrmacht (OKW), 306–7.
See OKW
Oetinger, Friedrich Christoph, 66
OKW, 306–7, 348, 351, 479
Olbricht, Friedrich, 72–73, 77–78, 79, 80,
82, 83, 426
Olden, Peter, 40, 71
Old Testament: German church view on, 172
Olympic Games, 288–90
On the Jews and Their Lies (Luther), 93
Onnasch, Fritz, 298–99, 302, 318
Operation Barbarossa, 381, 382
Operation Flash,
Operation Hummingbird. See Night of the
Long Knives
Operation 7, 388–89, 423, 441
Opernplatz, 162–63
Order of Olga, 47
Oster, Hans, 307, 319, 367, 370, 380–83,
389, 392, 397, 399, 424, 429, 437, 443,
445, 446, 495, 502, 507, 529–30, 532
overcoat bombs, 429–31
Oxford Movement, 199, 249, 289–90

P
Panzer divisions, 348
Park Avenue Baptist Church, 102

Parsifal (Wagner), 65
Pastors' Emergency League, 188, 190, 191,
192, 207, 216, 222, 281, 295
People's Court, 487, 494, 501
Perels, Justus, 375, 385, 389, 499
Petition to the Armed Forces (Perels and
Bonhoeffer), 385
Petzel, Walter, (general), 353
"Pfaffen," 213
Pfarrernotbund. See Pastors' Emergency League
Philadelphia, 100, 113, 337
Philip of Hesse (prince), 532
Picasso, Pablo, 76
pietism, 12, 135, 248, 270
Pinocchio (The Adventures of Pinocchio
[Collodi]), 18
Pius XI (pope), 181
Pius XII (pope), 375
Planck, Max, 59, 135
Plato, 77, 83
Plutarch's Lives, 19, 526
Poelchau, Harald, 448–49
Poland: Hitler's attack on, 314, 319,
347–48; end of fighting in, 350;
mass executions in, 352, 364; SS
atrocities in, 351, 355; surrender of
(in Warsaw), 355
Poles: treatment after Germany's defeat of,
351–53, 364
Pomerania, 41, 266, 274–75, 298, 300,
303, 315, 346, 350, 370, 371, 401,
414: aristocratic class in, 406
Pomeranian Council of Brethren, 276
"positive Christianity," 151, 174, 213, 287
Powell, Adam Clayton, Sr., 108
"Powers of Good" (Bonhoeffer poem),
497–98
Prayerbook of the Bible, The (Bonhoeffer),
367–69
Prenzlauer Berg (Berlin), 130
Preuß, F. A., 383
Priebe, Hermann (pastor), 38
Prohibition (of alcohol), 114
Protestantism, 19, 54–56, 174, 254, 287
Provisional Committee of the World
Council of Churches, 324
Pünder, Hermann, 502, 505, 521, 522, 526,
527–28

Q
"Question of the Boundaries of the Church
and Church Union, The," (Bonhoeffer
lecture), 286–87
Quisling, Vidkun, 394–95

R

RAF (Royal Air Force, Great Brit.), 121
racism (in American South), 109–10, 114,
    152, 338
Rascher, Sigmund, 508–15, 518, 520, 521,
    526
Rathenau, Walther, 39–40
reason (e.g., rationality, logic), 14, 93
Reformation (Protestant), 55, 121, 153,
    182, 190, 223, 224, 228
Red Cross, 420, 434, 491, 492
Reich church (*Reichskirche*), 151, 170, 176,
    190, 197, 204, 205–7, 213–17, 220,
    224, 226–28, 235, 236, 242, 243,
    246–48, 252, 279, 289, 292, 308, 324,
    325, 334, 375, 398, 400
Reichsbank, 229, 306, 502
Reichssicherheitshauptamt (Reich Main
    Security Office). *See* RSHA
Reichstag (institution), 33, 100, 145, 149,
    176, 231, 280, 348, 356: abolition
    of, 149,
Reichstag building, 34, 35, 39: burning of,
    145–49, 315, 487
Reichstag Fire Edict, 148–49, 158
Reichstag fire trial, 487
Reich Writers' Guild, 377
Religion and Philosophy in Germany (Heine),
    163–64
"religionless Christianity," 84, 465–69, 472
Remarque, Erich Maria, 111, 112, 162
Rembrandt, 65
Resistance (against Germany). *See* German
    Resistance
Rhineland Bible School, 262
Riefenstahl, Leni, 289
Rieger, Julius, 205, 221, 235, 243, 252,
    258, 297, 314, 323, 344, 397, 532,
    533, 535, 537
Rise and Fall of the Third Reich (Shirer), 145
Riverside Church, 101, 332, 334
Roberts, David, 338
Rockefeller Foundation, 102
Rockefeller, John D., 101, 102
Roeder, Manfred, 433, 441–44, 450, 451,
    453, 454, 473
Röhm, Ernst, 230–32, 305
Roman Catholic Church, 54, 263, 286
Rommel, General, 380
Roosevelt, Franklin D., 158, 399, 403
Rosenberg, Alfred, 39, 169, 170–71, 505
Rössler, Helmut, 67, 78, 79, 81, 253–57
Rott, Wilhelm, 262, 273, 285, 389
RSHA, 370–71, 474

Ruhr region, 44
Rulamann, 18
Russia: Germany's declaration of war on,
    20; Germany's defeat of Russia, 35;
    Germany's retreat from, 390; shell
    attack by, 409

S

SA Brownshirts, 146
Sachsenhausen concentration camp, 288,
    487, 506, 508, 515, 523
Sack, Karl (judge), 319, 458, 495, 502,
    507, 529–30, 532
Salvation Army, 39, 347, 352
Sammelvikariat. See collective pastorates
Sanctorum Communio (Bonhoeffer, doctoral
    dissertation), 53, 63, 79, 89, 98, 538
Sanderhoff, Herr and Frau, 17
Sasse, Hermann, 182, 185, 287
Saüberung (cleansing), 162
Sauerbruch, Ferdinand, 319
Sayers, Dorothy, 199
Schacht, Hjalmar, 229, 302, 303, 306,
    502
Scheidemann, Philipp, 33–35
Scheidt, Samuel, 267
Schein, Johann, 267
Schiller, Friedrich von, 37, 65, 138, 375
Schlabrendorff, Fabian von, 274, 389, 399,
    407, 413, 426–30, 486, 495, 498–501,
    530, 532
Schlatter, Adolf, 55
Schlawe (Sławno, Middle Pomerania,
    Poland), 299–300, 349, 370, 371, 438
Schleicher, Hans-Walter, 411
Schleicher, Renate, 418, 427, 436, 456,
    464, 465, 493, 574
Schleicher, Rolf, 501–2
Schleicher, Rüdiger, 41, 76, 136, 230, 298,
    319, 320, 389, 430, 433, 456, 494,
    501, 502, 534
Schleicher, Ursula (Bonhoeffer), 8, 17, 29,
    41, 42, 76, 298, 411, 418, 430, 432,
    456, 493, 494
Schleiermacher, Friedrich Daniel Ernst, 59,
    60, 120, 128, 174
Schlönwitz (underground seminary). *See*
    Gross-Schlönwitz
Schmidhuber, Wilhelm, 424
Schneider, Georg, 172
Schneider, Paul, 344
Schönes (neighbors of the Bonhoeffers),
    29, 36, 90
Schönfeld, Hans, 227, 398–99, 402

Schönherr, Albrecht, 126, 128, 268, 270, 326, 349, 465
Schroeder, Baron, 206
Schulz, George, 161
Schulze, Bertha, 212
Schulze, Gerhard, 383
Schumann, Clara, 6
Schutz, Erwin, 374
Schutz, Heinrich, 267
Schutzstaffel. See SS
Schwäbisch Hall (German city), 7
Scottsboro, Alabama, rape case, 110
SD, 524–25
Seeburg, Reinhold, 60, 62–63, 91
Sennacherib, 220, 249, 250
"separate, but equal," 152
separation of church and state (American), 130, 341
Seydel, Gustav, 407, 408, 424
"Shall the Fundamentalists Win?" (Fosdick), 102
Shirer, William, 145, 146, 168, 169, 487
Sigtuna (Sweden), 398, 399, 401
Sigurdshof, 300, 337, 338, 344, 346, 349, 350, 359, 360, 438
Sippach (chief guard at Buchenwald), 515, 516
Sloane Fellowship, 94
social Darwinism, 173
Social Democrats, 33
Sofia (Bulgaria), 186, 188, 189
Spa (Belgium), 33
Spartacists, 33
Speer, Albert, 167, 170
Sportpalast, 173, 193, 205
SS, 112, 167, 170, 232, 306, 315, 319–20, 347, 351, 352, 353, 355, 381, 387, 390, 477, 479, 495, 504, 505, 511, 512, 513, 520, 524, 529, 530: clergy barred from serving in, 170; identification of, 112; members forbidden to attend church, 170; members required to resign from leadership in religious organizations, 170; murders by: in Lithuania, 387; in Poland), 351; prison, 534; rituals of, 170
"Statements About the Power of the Keys and Church Discipline in the New Testament" (Bonhoeffer), 292–93
St. George's Church (London), 205
St. Peter's Basilica, 50, 53, 54, 56, 207
Stab-in-the-Back Legend, 32, 255, 355, 381

Staewen, Gertrud, 190
"Stations on the Road to Freedom" (Bonhoeffer poem), 485–86, 531
status confessionis (state of confession), 154, 187, 197, 207, 217
Stauffenberg, Claus Schenk Graf, 6, 387–88, 393, 425, 426, 474, 475–82, 486
Stauffenberg, Nina von, 522
Stauffenberg plot, 180, 388, 393, 426, 441, 475–82, 502, 507, 522
stock market crash, 100
Stoltenhoff, Ernst, 287
Strauss, Richard, 157
Streicher, Julius, 94
Strünck, Theodor, 502, 530
Sturmabteilung (SA: "Storm troopers"), 146
Sudeten Crisis, 312, 319, 348
Sutz, Erwin, 107, 113, 116, 119, 120, 121, 131, 132, 133, 195, 220, 247, 249, 250, 287, 355, 377, 397, 403, 408, 424, 431
swastika, 171, 251, 307, 308

T
Tafel, Gottlob, 8
Tegel military prison: Bonhoeffer's first days at, 436–42; Bonhoeffer's plan for escape from, 493–94; Bonhoeffer's reading at, 458–61; Bonhoeffer's strategy while at, 442–45; life at, 447–50, visits by Maria at, 453, 474, 492
T-4 euthanasia program (Action T4), 250, 354, 355, 377, 386, 518
Thale (Germany), 17
They Almost Killed Hitler (Schlabrendorff), 495
Thierack, Otto, 501–2
Third Reich: beginning of, 138; "church" newspaper of the, 482; Jews becoming subjects of the, 280; two of the most evil characters in the, 508
Tholuck, Friedrich, 271
Thomas (General, Bonhoeffer's fellow prisoner), 502, 532
Thumm, Hermann, 72, 74, 75, 77, 94
Thuringian Evangelical Church, 307
Thursday Circle, 56, 64, 65, 70, 82, 125, 127
Thyssen, Fritz, 522
Time magazine, 102, 148
Times (London), 200, 201, 219, 221, 226, 242
Traub, Helmutt, 127, 337, 344–45
Treaty of Versailles, 34, 35, 40, 43, 45, 151,

191, 235, 258, 265, 307, 363, 381
Tresckow, Gerhard, 455
Tresckow, Henning von, 380, 382, 389,
    412–13, 426, 427, 428–29, 455, 476,
    486, 487
Trinity Church (Berlin), 144
Tübingen (Germany), 5, 7, 38, 40, 41–48,
    58, 63, 162
Tübingen (university). *See* University of
    Tübingen
20 July plot (1944). *See* Valkyrie
    conspiracy; Stauffenberg plot

U

Ulex, Wilhelm (general), 353
Ulm (Germany), 7, 45
Uncle Tom's Cabin (Stowe), 19
Union Theological Seminary, 30, 94,
    101–8, 111, 116, 124, 132, 155, 157,
    235, 239, 261, 270, 322, 324, 325–26,
    327, 329, 332, 333, 334, 335, 337,
    338, 340–41, 539
United States: declaration of war against
    Japan and Germany, 391
University of Tübingen (aka Eberhard
    Karls University, Tübingen), 41, 42,
    45, 55
Uppsala (Sweden), 284, 285
U7 *Unternehmen 7. See* Operation 7

V

Valkyrie conspiracy, 319, 393, 476, 479
van der Lubbe, Marinus, 146
Vatican, 51, 54, 181, 359, 375, 376
Vermehren, Erich, 523
Vermehren, Isa, 508, 523
Vibrans, Gerhard, 290, 291–92, 385
Victor, Wilhelm. *See* Wied, Prince Victor zu
Victoria (Princess Royal), 6
virgin birth, 102, 106
Visser 't Hooft, Willem A., 324, 377, 386,
    387, 396, 401, 402
Visser 't Hooft, Frau, 397
Vogel, Heinrich, 161, 198
Volksgerichtshof. See People's Court
vom Rath, Ernst, 315
von Alvensleben, Werner, 502, 507, 521
von Bismarck, Gottfried, 502
von Bismarck, Hans-Otto, 276
von Bismarck, Klaus, 436, 438
von Bismarck, Luitgard, 426
von Bismarck, Otto 42, 43, 253, 274, 502
von Bismarck, Spes 277, 309
von Bismarck, Ruth-Alice (von

Wedemeyer), 276–77, 423, 438, 488,
    574
von Blomberg, Werner (field marshal), 305
von Cramon, Moni, 290
von dem Bussche, Axel, 477
von der Goltz, Rüdiger Graf (general), 208
von der Schulenburg, Fritz-Dietlof, 363–64
von Dohnanyi. *See* Dohnanyi (*individual
    family members*)
von Falkenhausen Alexander, 502, 508,
    515, 522, 523
von Gersdorff, Rudolf-Christoph, 429–31
von Haeften, Hans-Bernd, 425, 488
von Haeften, Werner, 423, 425–26, 478,
    480, 486
von Hase, Clara (née Countess Kalkreuth),
    6
von Hase, Hans, 28, 30
von Hase, Hans-Christoph, 18, 28
von Hase, Elizabeth, 10
von Hase, Karl Alfred, 6, 8, 9
von Hase, Karl August, 6, 8, 25–26, 49,
    135, 267, 474
von Hase, Paul, 319, 349, 448, 450, 475,
    476, 477, 487, 494
von Hassell, Ulrich, 523
von Kleist-Retzow, Hans Jürgen, 275, 419
von Kleist-Retzow, Hans-Friedrich, 276,
    277, 309
von Kleist-Retzow, Ruth, 275–77, 294,
    303, 309, 401, 405, 409, 411, 413,
    414, 422, 436
von Küchler, Georg, 353
von Papen, Franz, 406, 523
von Petersdorff (Bonhoeffer's fellow
    prisoner), 507, 516, 521, 523
von Rad, Gerhard, 38
von Rundstedt, Gerd (field marshal), 390
von Schlabrendorff, Fabian, 274, 389, 399,
    407, 413, 426–30, 486–87, 495, 498,
    501, 530, 532
von Schuschnigg, Kurt, 502, 508
von Wedemeyer, Hans, 274, 406–7, 409,
    411
von Wedemeyer, Hans-Werner, 436
von Wedemeyer, Maria, 66, 274, 276,
    277, 405, 407, 408–9, 411, 412–23,
    426, 432, 433–36, 438, 439, 450–55,
    456–57, 458, 459, 473, 474, 475, 476,
    488–92, 494, 495–98, 523, 432, 534
von Wedemeyer, Max, 274, 276, 277, 309,
    406, 409–10, 413–14, 491
von Wedemeyer, Ruth, 274, 405, 406, 407,
    409, 410, 414, 416–19, 423, 436, 450

von Wedemeyer, Ruth-Alice. *See* von Bismarck, Ruth-Alice
von Welczeck, Johannes, 315
von Zedlitz-Trützschler, Count and Countess, 275

W–Y

Wagner, Cosima, 478
Wagner, Richard, 478
Waldau (Germany), 30
Wangenheimstrasse, Bonhoeffer family home at 14, 24, 29, 41, 58, 59, 63, 90, 158, 190, 212, 283, 538
War Ministry: abolition of, 306
Wartburg castle (Thuringia, Germany), 308
"weaker brethren" argument, 179, 186
Wedding (Berlin): confirmation class at, 130–35, 157
Wehrle (Fr.), 478
Weimar Republic, 33, 39, 88, 176, 265
Weltanschauung (worldview). *See* German *Weltanschauung*
Wells, H. G., 162
Werner, Friedrich, 308–9, 324, 325
Wernicke, Karl, 5, 13
Wesley, John, 12
Wessel, Horst, 178
Wessel, Wilhelm, 178
"What Does It Mean to Tell the Truth? (Bonhoeffer essay), 365–66
"What is the church?" (question pondered by Bonhoeffer), 52–54, 63, 89, 152, 286
Wied, Victor zu (Wilhelm Friedrich Adolph Hermann Victor, prince to Wied). 285
Wilhelm I (German emperor), 42
Wilhelm II (German emperor), 6, 207, 392
Wilhelmstrasse (Berlin street), 40
Will to Power, The (Nietzsche), 168

Winant, John Gilbert, 403
Winterhager, Jürgen, 128, 235
Wise, Stephen (rabbi), 115, 158
Wittenberg: national synod at, 188, 190
Wittenberg castle church, 190
Wobbermin, Georg, 120
Wolfesgründ, 10, 17
Wolfsschanze (Wolf's Lair), 390, 391, 477, 478, 479
World Alliance, 188, 217, 236, 243
World Council of Churches, 324
World War I. *See* First War
World War II: beginning of, 348; end of, 532
Württemberg (Germany), 6, 7, 8, 47, 251
Wycliffe Hall, Oxford (Low Church Anglican community), 261
Yorck von Wartenburg, Hans Ludwig (Count), 6
Yorck von Wartenburg, Peter, 6, 387–88, 393
Young Reformation movement, 161, 180, 181, 182

Z

Zdroje (Poland). *See* Finkenwalde
Zimmermann, Wolf-Dieter, 124–25, 127–28, 139, 201–2, 268–69, 425, 465
Zingst, 262–65: end of golden era at, 360. *See also* Zingst and Finkenwalde
Zingst and Finkenwalde: daily routine at, 267–71; illegal seminaries of: 56, 61, 104, 109, 128, 246–77; role of music at, 267
Zinn, Elizabeth, 66–67, 90, 123, 202, 212, 407, 489
Zinzendorf und Pottendorf, Nikolaus Ludwig von (Count), 11–12
Zionskirche, 130
Zossen files, 320, 487, 529
Zweig, Stefan, 157

READING GROUP GUIDE

Prologue

1. In the prologue, the author wrote that "Winston Churchill fused the Germans and the Nazis into a single hated enemy, the better to defeat it swiftly." Who is our nation's "enemy"? In our own society, are we, like Churchill, ever prone to fusing *another* group of individuals with this enemy, thus creating a "single hated enemy"? Who might that be? Are our feelings justified? On a person-to-person basis, are there people in your life or neighborhood or place of work who qualify as "single hated enemies"? How would Bonhoeffer have counseled you in dealing with that person?

Chapters 1–3

1. In chapter 1 we learned that during Dietrich's childhood, the Bonhoeffers rarely went to church. Their faith was "mostly of a homegrown variety." Is God satisfied with a homegrown-variety faith, or are Christians meant to attend church, living out their faith *together*? What Scriptures support your view? Can a person still be influential for good while practicing "homegrown" faith? How?

2. As a young man, Bonhoeffer was encouraged to "make the church live out what it claimed to believe by speaking publicly against Hitler and the Nazis, and taking actions against them." Many

Christians today also believe that the church is called to speak out against government when its actions are questionable, and to have an active role in politics. Others believe the church has no place in politics and the shaping of public policy. Instead, they say, we should simply pray for our leaders while "suffering in silence." Whose opinion do you embrace? Why?

3. Death tends to change people's focus and priorities—at least for a time. After the war deaths of several Bonhoeffer cousins, the younger members of the family would often lie in bed at night and talk about death and eternity. Do you spend much time thinking about eternity? Should a person concentrate on life after death, or is it better to keep one's focus solely on this life and what can be accomplished now?

4. Two weeks after being called to serve in the war, Walter died of a shrapnel wound. Meanwhile, Karl-Friedrich was still in the infantry, and soon, seventeen-year-old Klaus was also called to serve. "It was too much," we read. Their mother collapsed and stayed in bed for weeks.

Currently, America has soldiers fighting in Afghanistan, and lives are lost almost daily. Put yourself in Mrs. Bonhoeffer's place: You have already lost one child to war; now you have two more involved in it. How will you deal with it? Where will you turn for support? Or perhaps you have relatives in the military. If so, do you spend much time praying for these servicemen and -women? If not, do you know someone whose adult child, or children, are involved in the fighting? What can you do to help ease that mother's or father's burden?

Do you think that if there were a stronger faith commitment Mrs. Bonhoeffer might have been able to handle the tragedy of loss more effectively? Why or why not? How have you or your family and friends handled tragic situations? Have you "folded" as Mrs. Bonhoeffer did for a while? What lesson(s) did you learn from the situation that helped to strengthen your faith? If your faith was not strengthened, why do you think that was the case?

5. In 1919, following the German Revolution, the Allies demanded

that Germany give up many of its territories. What's more, the Germans were ordered to eviscerate their military.

Imagine that your country is in the Germans' position, and another power is making similar demands: "Give up your lands, and decimate your military." Could that ever become a reality? If so, how would you expect your government to react? Would you get involved against such an assault? What role would you want to play?

6. In 1920, Bonhoeffer announced that he had chosen theology over music as his life's pursuit—against the wishes and expectations of family and friends. Not everyone reacted to his choice with grace. Among the academic elite (of which he was a part), "the study of theology, and the profession of theologian, were not highly respected."

When have you made a big decision that was at variance with everyone's expectations for you? What reactions did you face from friends and relatives? Did this weaken your resolve, or were you more determined than ever to "stick to your guns"? How would you advise someone else who has made a pivotal choice that goes against the expectations of his or her "circles"?

Chapters 4–6

1. While traveling in Italy, young Bonhoeffer wrote in his diary that he was suddenly beginning "to understand the concept 'church.'" Having seen for the first time "a vivid illustration of the church's transcendence of race and national identity," he began to view the church as something universal, leading him into the ecumenical movement in Europe.

What is your conception of "the church"? When you think *church*, do you envision a body made up of a certain kind (or color) of people who embrace a particular set of beliefs? Or do you picture a worldwide body, with varied convictions, multiple languages and ethnicities, and wide-ranging worship styles? What about your church? Is it all white? all black? all

Hispanic, Asian, etc.? Are you okay with that, or does it bother you? Does it bother God? What do you think you could or should do about it?

2. After visiting a church in Paris, where Bonhoeffer witnessed both prostitutes and their customers attending mass, he wrote, "It's much easier for me to imagine a praying murderer, a praying prostitute, than a vain person praying. Nothing is so at odds with prayer as vanity." Do you agree with this statement? Why or why not?

3. "[The church] must completely separate herself from the state," wrote Bonhoeffer. Interestingly, this is precisely the stand that groups such as the ACLU take as they endeavor to remove God and anything that points to religion from the classroom, the courthouse, and any other public place. Do you think this is what Bonhoeffer had in mind when he wrote these words, or did he mean something else? What is your understanding of "separation of church and state"?

4. In one essay, Bonhoeffer "expressed the Barthian idea that in order to know anything at all about God, one had to rely on revelation *from* God. In other words, God could speak into this world . . ." There are many today who believe that God no longer reveals Himself in any way except through the Bible. Others believe that, while He does, in fact, speak through His Word, He also speaks in other ways. Do you believe that God speaks to individuals today, or do you think any form of personal revelation ended with the Bible days?

5. Bonhoeffer was violently opposed to the notion of "religion," stating that the real message of Christ "is basically amoral and irreligious, paradoxical as that may sound." What did he mean by that? Do you agree with this statement? In what way is the Christian message "basically amoral and irreligious"? What examples would support this?

6. In Bonhoeffer's Thursday Circle, he often asked his young attendees difficult questions. One such question was, "Is there such a thing as a necessary lie?" How would you answer this question?

Can you think of an example of a lie that would be "necessary"? Would God condone it? Why or why not? Support your answer with Scripture.

7. Bonhoeffer was taken aback by the "languorous" climate of Barcelona and was amazed "at how people of all ages seemed to while away the hours sitting at cafés in the middle of the day, chattering about little of any real substance." Still, rather than speak out against what he considered an indolent lifestyle, he adapted to it, entering "the lives and, to some extent, the life-styles of the people he was charged with serving" as a pastor. Do you believe it is necessary for a minister to embrace the lifestyle of the people he or she serves in order to be effective? To what degree? Where should a servant of Christ draw the line in adapting to his/her surrounding culture? Can you think of examples, both modern and from the Bible?

8. In 1929, for a time, Bonhoeffer was in a position that was well beneath his qualifications, yet he performed his duties with enthusiasm and purpose. Have you ever had to take work that was "beneath" you? How did you perform? How are we supposed to perform, according to the Bible, regardless of our rank and responsibilities? (Hint: Read the parables in Matthew 25:14–30 and Luke 19:12–27; as well as Colossians 3:22–24.)

Chapters 7–9

1. "Things are not much different in the church," Bonhoeffer lamented. "The sermon has been reduced to parenthetical church remarks about newspaper events." How do you feel about sermons that weave current events in with Scripture? About preachers who bring the politics of the day into the pulpit? About those who tie world news in with ancient prophecy? Is the pulpit a place for "the Word only," or should ministers be able to use the happenings in the world for "practical application" of Scripture?

2. Deeply dissatisfied with the "skim milk" he encountered in most churches, Bonhoeffer was, conversely, fascinated with the "negro

churches," in particular, their music. So transfixed was he with the "negro spirituals" he heard at Abyssinian Baptist Church (a congregation started by black merchants) that he searched record shops all over Harlem to find recordings of these songs to take back to Germany. "The joyous and transformative power of this music solidified his thinking on the importance of music to worship." How important is music to worship? Does it really have "transformative power"? Has music ever moved you to change? If so, was the change permanent or short-lived?

3. Bonhoeffer found the racism in America troubling. So did his brother Karl-Friedrich. In fact, it had even caused him to decline a position at Harvard: he feared that the prejudice might, in time, "taint him and his future children as part of 'that legacy.'" Doubtless, he gave up a prestigious and high-paying career because of a deep conviction. How deep do you believe was his inner turmoil before reaching his decision? Do you believe he wrestled with it, or do you think his was an immediate conclusion? Have you ever been in a similar situation? Can you think of any biblical parallels?

4. When Bonhoeffer began to teach, he taught his students to investigate biblical, ethical, and theological questions with the same rigorousness that one would examine questions of science or law. Further, one should "arrive at answers that could stand up to every scrutiny because one would have to live out those conclusions." Each of us has a set of particular convictions, some of them very strong. What are your strongest beliefs? Think of your two or three most deeply held beliefs/convictions. Can you defend these convictions? How can you support—logically, biblically, or both—what you believe?

5. In Bonhoeffer's radio speech given two days after Hitler's election as chancellor, he made the following statement: "We forget that man stands alone before the ultimate authority and that anyone who lays violent hands on man here is infringing eternal laws and taking upon himself superhuman authority which will eventually crush him." Remember that this same man was himself

later involved in the plot to kill Hitler. Do you think this was a contradiction? A self-fulfilling prophecy? How so?

6. "After the war," the author wrote, "many were happy to wipe away the old order and rid themselves of the kaiser (emperor). But when the old monarch at last left the palace, the people who had clamored for his exit were suddenly lost. . . . The country broke apart into a riot of factions . . . Under the kaiser there had been law and order and structure; now there was chaos."

Recently, several countries in the Middle East have overthrown or are attempting to overthrow their current government. What could happen if these countries don't have a solid plan of action regarding future government? Can you see any imminent dangers already?

7. The day after the Reichstag fire, the Reichstag Fire Edict officially suspended the parts of the German constitution that guaranteed personal liberties, turning the once democratic republic into a dictatorship. The decree placed, among other things, "restrictions on . . . the right of free expression of opinion, including freedom of the press; on the rights of assembly and association; and violations of the privacy of postal, telegraphic and telephonic communications"—and it was made law before citizens even had time to think of it!

Picture this same scenario taking place in twenty-first century America. Would the perpetrators get away with it? Would anyone immediately come to the fore to oppose the proclamation? Who? Would you join the effort? How far would you be willing to go, and how hard would you fight, to regain the liberty guaranteed in the U. S. Constitution?

Chapters 10–15

1. Soon after Hitler came to power, the "Aryan paragraph" took effect, resulting in the expulsion of all Jewish-descent people from civil service. Eventually it would lead to their exclusion from the church and, ultimately, to their mass murders.

Choose an ethnicity other than your own. Now imagine that suddenly, your government targeted this group for discrimination of the type announced as Hitler's "Restoration of Civil Service." How would you respond? Would you oppose these laws? What type of action, if any, would you take? If you did choose to join in efforts to repeal such discriminatory laws, would you fight as hard for this ethnic group as you would if the laws had targeted your own race/ethnicity?

2. "One week after passage of the Enabling Act, Hitler declared a boycott of Jewish stores across Germany." It is easy for people to say what they would have done in a given situation—"Well, if *I* had been there . . ."—but say this act were instituted today, where you live. You were forbidden, by government, to shop at any market or department store owned by members of a specific people group. Would you, like Dietrich's grandmother, defy the legislation and shop there anyway? Would you try to get others to join in the rebellion with you, or out of fear, would you meekly submit to the new statute?

3. What if, today, in your country, there was a book burning similar to that instigated by Hitler, but all of the works burned were those written by, say, Christian authors? Would that have an impact on education? philosophy? religion? What would your society lose? Would it be a great loss? Would illegalization of Christian-authored books directly affect you?

4. At one point, "Bonhoeffer began to see that the opposition to Hitler . . . was weak and divided, and he was gradually losing hope that anything positive could be done." No doubt, countless others—both German and Jew—saw the same thing. One could wonder why more people of both descents didn't just leave the country while they still could. What are some of the possible reasons that so many didn't? Discounting your present knowledge of the outcome of Hitler's fanaticism, had you been living in Germany in the 1930s as a German, would you have considered leaving the country? If not, what would have prevented you? What if you had been a Jew?

5. By 1933, Hitler was moving swiftly toward the legalized murder of the disabled, including those who suffer from epilepsy, considering them, like the Jews, to be "a drain on Germany." Their exterminations would begin in earnest by the end of the decade.

   Do you think this scenario could ever repeat itself in Europe? Could it happen in North America? South America? Have you heard or read of any steps in this direction in any of these places, or elsewhere? Where? What signs can you see, if any, that such "genocide" (masquerading as "mercy killings") could become a reality where you live?

6. There were some who wondered why Bonhoeffer didn't "join the German Christians in order to work against them from within." He refused, saying, "If you board the wrong train, it is no use running along the corridor in the opposite direction." Do you agree, or do you think it could have been advantageous to join with the enemy and seek to destroy them from within? How could he have done this, had he chosen to? Had you been in his place, what would you have done? If you had chosen to join the opposition, what kinds of actions would you have taken to undermine the German church?

7. Nietzsche called Christianity "the one great curse, the one enormous and innermost perversion . . . the one immortal blemish of mankind." Through history, what other prominent leaders or writers have shared this point of view? What were the results? Why would these people have such a terrible attitude toward Christianity? What could Christians do to help alter such a view?

8. After three weeks of work on the Bethel Confession, Bonhoeffer sent it to twenty theologians, for their review and comments. "By the time they were through, every bright line was blurred; every sharp edge of difference filed down; and every point blunted." The author tells us that Bonhoeffer was horrified at his fellow Christians' unwillingness to take a definite stand. They had, effectively, watered down the confession.

   Do you see this tendency today? Can you think of preachers whose message is "soft on sin" and in direct conflict with the "hard sayings" of Jesus? Can you see this "watering down" in any popular Bible translations today? Do you know of churches that have blurred their once-clear lines on certain issues, perhaps for political correctness' sake? Could political correctness itself be an example of the blurring of bright lines and the filing down of sharp edges?

9. Read Niemoller's prison poem on page 192. Can you think of other people who could have spoken out against wrongs that were being done—but didn't? What were the outcomes? Could they have been prevented? Here's one to consider: What if Americans had gone to bat against Madalyn Murray O'Hare when she first began her campaign to remove prayer and Bible reading from public schools. Could the 1962 and 1963 Supreme Court decisions have been nipped in the bud? Could her attempts have been thwarted far in advance of their reaching the Supreme Court? What other rights—religious or otherwise—have been lost to citizens' unwillingness to get involved?

Chapters 16–22

1. Soon after Hindenberg's death, the Reichskirche held a synod in which it was decreed that all new pastors must swear upon ordination "I swear before God . . . that I . . . will be true and obedient to the *Führer* of the German people and state, Adolf Hitler." To do so, in effect, barred them from preaching the real Jesus and the gospel as He taught it. Can you think of stories in the New Testament where individuals were forbidden to preach the gospel message? How did they respond? Are there efforts today to silence those who would preach the full gospel? Where? What attempts are being made to stifle Bible truth?

2. Most of us today have never faced fundamental racial prejudice of the kind that Sabine's daughters encountered. For example, "One little friend actually called out to [Christiane] over the fence, 'Your father is a Jew.' One day a notice-board was fixed to one of the trees in front of the school on which was written 'The

Father of the Jew is the Devil.'" According to this account, these kinds of events took place *every day*. Imagine that you or your children were subjected to this type of bigotry and persecution on a daily basis. How long would you tolerate it? Would you fight back (or encourage your children to)? Or would you hold your tongue? As a parent, would you take your kids out of the school? the country?

3. Bonhoeffer was impressed with Gandhi's methods of social resistance, so much so that he wondered if the church ought to emulate them. This leads us to the topic of civil disobedience. What do you think of Christians disobeying their leaders? Does a Christian's refusal to submit to a wicked government or an immoral law contradict Hebrews 13:17 and Romans 13:1–5? Are there other verses from Scripture that seem to conflict with these verses? Can you think of biblical characters, Old or New Testament, whose actions or inactions were in direct opposition to those in authority and thus a violation of Hebrews 13:17? If you were one of these characters today, what Bible verses, if any, could you uses to defend your actions? What reasoning did they use?

4. When Bonhoeffer began his monastic community at Zingst, he asked that the ordinands not call him *Herr Direktor*, but *Bruder* (Brother) Bonhoeffer instead. Why do you think he did that? Would there have been any harm in allowing the ordinands to call him *Herr Direktor*? He was, after all, the director. How important, then, was his title to him? How important are titles to you? Can you think of any Bible stories where a character purposely sought a lower position, either real or perceived, than that in which people sought to place him?

5. In his sermon "The Question of the Boundaries of the Church and Church Union," Bonhoeffer made the controversial statement "Whoever knowingly separates himself from the Confessing Church in Germany separates himself from salvation." Though he doubtless didn't mean it quite the way it was taken by his critics, it nonetheless immediately created a firestorm of debate.

　　Suppose your church/denomination issued a similar statement, in essence saying that anyone who left the church forfeited heaven. (There are denominations that teach this.) How would you react? Are you acquainted with Christian individuals who believe that theirs is the "only way"? Do you believe that too? How did the apostle Paul speak to this kind of thinking? (Hint: See 1 Corinthians 1:10–17; 3:3–11.)

6. Hitler's ultimate goal was to take over Europe. Are there any individuals or groups today whose goal is the same? Who? Could they succeed? If so, what sequence of events could aid in their success?

7. In 1939, all men born in 1906 and 1907 were ordered to register for the military. This presented a conundrum for Bonhoeffer. He couldn't declare himself a conscientious objector. To do so would be risking his life. Further, he mused, it would give Germans the impression that the entire Confessing Church agreed with that stance, and would give Confessing pastors the impression that they, too, should refuse to take up arms. On the other hand, fighting for Hitler's Germany seemed unconscionable. We know what he finally decided, but this brings up the problem of war in present times. Is it wrong to fight in war? Does the command "Thou shalt not kill" apply to wartime? to self-defense? If not, should everyone be made to participate, if called upon? What about the conscientious objector? Should his or her participation be mandatory if that individual is going to live in the nation at war?

8. World War II involved many nations, on almost every continent, beginning with Germany's invasion of Poland in 1939. Two days later, Britain and France declared war on Germany. Other nations soon joined in the fray.

Currently, the United States is at war in Afghanistan over the Taliban's atrocities against Afghan people. In recent years, Western powers have also come to the aid of the Iraqis, the Libyans, and others being oppressed by those in power. People globally are sharply divided on this issue. On one hand are those who believe that stronger nations should go help to defend those who can't defend themselves. Others say it is no one else's business what goes on inside a country. Its people should take care of themselves, they contend, and if the citizens don't like the current administration, they should take responsibility for its overthrow themselves. Where do you stand? Did the U. S. have any right to invade and bomb Afghanistan? Does the UN have any business getting involved in Libya's internal turmoil? When a country's citizens are being subjugated and abused, should stronger powers take up arms in their defense or mind their own business?

Chapters 23–27

1. Read the section titled "From Confession to Resistance" in chapter 23, in particular, the Bethge quote on pages 360–61. Then read James 4:17 in the New American Standard Bible or the New Living Translation. Do you see a connection? What other Bible verses may have convicted those who wrestled with their involvement in the assassination plot? Do you agree with Bethge that Bonhoeffer's steps toward political resistance should be "a natural and inevitable outworking" of his recognition that Hitler was evil and should be taken down?

2. When France surrendered to Germany, Bonhoeffer and Bethge witnessed people throwing out their arms in the Nazi salute and bursting into patriotic song. To Bethge's dismay, Bonhoeffer joined right in with them. "As Bethge stood there gawking, Bonhoeffer whispered to him: 'Are you crazy? Raise your arm! We'll have to run risks for many different things, but this silly salute is not one of them!' . . . It was then, Bethge realized, that Bonhoeffer crossed a line."

   In the Bible, three men were put in a similar position. But while everyone else fell down in worship before an image of gold, these three remained standing. They were sentenced to death. We know how the story ends (see Daniel 3), but Bonhoeffer's actions beg the question: Is pretense ever acceptable, even called for? What harm would it have done for the three Hebrew children to at least *pretend* to worship the golden statue? Though conspiracy wasn't part of their agenda, they could have followed the crowd, at least physically, just to save their lives. Only they would have known their hearts weren't in it. Were they wrong to risk their lives? On the other hand, instead of engaging in pretense, should Bonhoeffer have just openly opposed Hitler? Or are these situations totally different? Why or why not?

3. The author tells us that Bonhoeffer believed "we cannot reach God with our own prayers, but by praying 'his' prayers—the Psalms of the Old Testament, which Jesus prayed—we effectively piggyback on them all the way to heaven." Do you agree with this? There have been many books and sermons in recent years about "praying the psalms." Do you believe these are the only prayers God will hear and accept? If not, can you think of other examples of prayers that were heard and answered, but were not prayed from the book of Psalms?

Chapters 28–31

1. After Bonhoeffer's engagement to Maria, his fiancée asked that they not write each other for six months. If you were in Bonhoeffer's shoes, how would you react to that request? What would it do, if anything, to your relationship? Could you be as patient as he, or would you consider "moving on"?

2. So many people—millions—died at Hitler's hands, and many of them were Christian. Some Christians seem to believe that God will save His people from martyrdom, even that He is *obligated* to, and that they should "claim" this promise for themselves. (Some use Psalm 91, among other passages, to substantiate this belief.) Do the promises we read in the Bible obligate God to come to our rescue every time? anytime? Think of examples from the Bible where He did. Now list times when He didn't. What did Jesus say about this? (For help with this question, see Revelation 6:9; Matthew 24:9; John 16:1–4; Acts 6:8–8:1, for starters.)

3. During Bonhoeffer's first days in prison, the author tells us, he read "the wry graffito of a previous occupant: 'In a hundred years

it'll all be over.'" This sounds a great deal like the oft-used cliché "This, too, shall pass." Though the onetime prisoner may have written his statement with a note of bitterness, rather than optimism, the fact remains: all of the storms of life eventually pass, one way or another. How much better would people be able to handle their present struggles if they would adopt the attitude displayed on that cell wall? Is it even possible to think this way? In the midst of your trials, is there comfort in knowing that in even *five* years, your immediate concern will be forgotten?

4. While imprisoned in cell 92, Bonhoeffer was determined to not wallow in self-pity. If you had been the one in that cell, would your resolve have been so strong? At this point, do you think he had any suspicions that he might not ever get out of prison (even though it was not for his involvement in the assassination plot that he was arrested)? If not, how do you think he managed to remain cheerful and turn his attention toward the well-being of his fellow prisoners, rather than himself?

5. While at Tegel, Bonhoeffer was often given preferential treatment because of who he was related to. He despised it. He was offered a cooler cell, and he refused it. He was offered bigger food portions, and he turned those down too. With an honest heart, ask yourself if you would do as Bonhoeffer did. Knowing that bigger plates for you would mean smaller plates for others, could you refuse the larger portions, or would you be tempted to take them and just keep quiet about it? Would you gratefully move into a better cell, knowing that someone else would soon be occupying the hot, stuffy one?

6. According to the author, Bonhoeffer's "very engagement was his way of living out what he believed. He did everything, including become engaged to Maria, 'unto God.'" Imagine if, in our relationships, we did everything "unto God," or, put another way "as unto the Lord." If teenagers remembered to conduct themselves on dates as "unto God," what evils could be avoided? If men and women made their choice of a future spouse "unto God," and later treated each other in marriage with this thought in mind

(see Colossians 3:17 NLT), what effect would that have on divorce statistics in our nation? Think about other areas of life that would be greatly affected if all our actions were "unto God." What scenarios can you envision if we worked, played, and loved really "living out" what we believe?

7. The camp doctor at Flossenbürg, H. Fischer-Hüllstrung, wrote of Bonhoeffer's execution, "He . . . said a short prayer and then climbed the steps to the gallows, brave and composed. His death ensued after a few seconds. In the almost fifty years that I worked as a doctor, I have hardly ever seen a man die so entirely submissive to the will of God."

Execution is a horrible thing to think about, but many throughout history have faced it. If you had been in Bonhoeffer's place, how do you think someone writing after your death would have described it? Would they say that you remained calm, or that you resisted? That you kept your composure and "died well," or that you struggled and fought death? Think about others who have been martyred in the past. Who "died well"?